Inventing a Voice

Communication, Media, and Politics

Series Editor
Robert E. Denton, Jr., Virginia Tech

This series features a broad range of work dealing with the role and function of communication in the realm of politics, broadly defined. Including general academic books, monographs, and texts for use in graduate and advanced undergraduate courses, the series will encompass humanistic, critical, historical, and empirical studies in political communication in the United States. Primary subject areas include campaigns and elections, media, and political institutions. *Communication, Media, and Politics* books will be of interest to students, teachers, and scholars of political communication from the disciplines of communication, rhetorical studies, political science, journalism, and political sociology.

Titles in the Series

The Millennium Election: Communication in the 2000 Campaign
Edited by Lynda Lee Kaid, John C. Tedesco, Dianne G. Bystrom, and Mitchell McKinney

Strategic Political Communication: Rethinking Social Influence, Persuasion, and Propaganda
Karen S. Johnson-Cartee and Gary A. Copeland

Campaign 2000: A Functional Analysis of Presidential Campaign Discourse
William L. Benoit, John P. McHale, Glenn J. Hansen, P. M. Pier, and John P. McGuire

Inventing a Voice: The Rhetoric of American First Ladies of the Twentieth Century
Edited by Molly Meijer Wertheimer

Communicating for Change: Strategies of Social and Political Advocates
John P. McHale

Political Campaign Communication: Principles and Practices, Fifth Edition
Judith S. Trent and Robert V. Friedenberg

Forthcoming

Reelpolitik II: Political Ideologies in '50s and '60s Films
Beverly Merrill Kelley

New Frontiers in International Communication Theory
Edited by Mehdi Semati

The Rhetoric of Redemption
David A. Bobbitt

Women's Political Discourse
Molly A. Mayhead and Brenda DeVore Marshall

Politeness and Political Debate
Edward A. Hinck, Shelly S. Hinck, and William O. Dailey

Inventing a Voice

The Rhetoric of American First Ladies of the Twentieth Century

EDITED BY MOLLY MEIJER WERTHEIMER

ROWMAN & LITTLEFIELD PUBLISHERS, INC.
Lanham • Boulder • New York • Toronto • Oxford

ROWMAN & LITTLEFIELD PUBLISHERS, INC.

Published in the United States of America
by Rowman & Littlefield Publishers, Inc.
A wholly owned subsidary of The Rowman & Littlefield Publishing Group, Inc.
4501 Forbes Boulevard, Suite 200, Lanham, MD 20706
www.rowmanlittlefield.com

P.O. Box 317, Oxford OX2 9RU, UK

Copyright © 2004 by Rowman & Littlefield Publishers, Inc.
First paperback edition 2004

British Library Cataloguing in Publication Information Available
The hardback edition of this book was catalogued by the Library of Congress as follows:

Inventing a voice : the rhetoric of American first ladies of the twentieth century / edited by Molly Meijer Wertheimer.
    p. cm. — (Communication, media, and politics)
  Includes bibliographical references and index.
    1. Presidents' spouses—United States—History—20th century. 2. Presidents' spouses—United States—Biography. 3. Presidents' spouses—United States— Language—History—20th century. 4. Rhetoric—Political aspects—United States— History—20th century. 5. Communication in politics—United States—History—20th century. 6. Women in politics—United States—History—20th century. 7. United States—Politics and government—20th century. I. Wertheimer, Molly Meijer. II. Series.

E176.2.I57   2004
973.91'092'2—dc22
                                                                    2003018365
ISBN 0-7425-2970-3 (cloth : alk. paper)
ISBN 0-7425-2971-1 (paper : alk. paper)

Printed in the United States of America

♾™ The paper used in this publication meets the minimum requirements of American National Standard for Information Sciences—Permanence of Paper for Printed Library Materials, ANSI/NISO Z39.48-1992.

To our first ladies past and present, who did not always choose their roles, and to their successors who "will preside over the White House as the President's spouse." As Barbara Bush once put it, we "wish him [or her] well."

Contents

Acknowledgments

Serendipity probably plays a larger role in instigating scholarship than any of us would care to admit. That is certainly true in the case of this work, which sprang from a chain of events beginning with an assignment given to my son when he was in third grade. As an antidote for the late-January blahs, his class was asked to read a book, and then come to class as one of the characters. Since he had a Ninja warrior costume which he insisted on wearing, we had to find a book to justify his outfit. A trip to the library produced *The Magic Fan*—all we needed was a fan to use as a prop. Our local Dollar Store didn't have a fan, but it did have remaindered copies of Barbara Bush's *A Memoir*. Blessed with snow the next day, I curled up in front of the fireplace to read about Mrs. Bush's experiences. Another coincidence set the stage for this book. Nola Heidelbaugh phoned to invite me to participate on an ECA roundtable panel on the rhetorical uses of motherhood. Inspired by Mrs. Bush's *A Memoir,* I proposed a paper exploring her uses of motherhood. At the conference, all of the panelists agreed on the need for a book examining the rhetoric of first ladies. Through a call placed on CRTNET and in other ways, we located chapter authors.

Although this book began amidst a great deal of fluidity and coincidence, finishing it was a different story, involving a great deal of deliberate and painstaking work—by the authors of these chapters, the archivists at many of the presidential libraries who helped us locate materials, and by colleagues at our institutions who helped us find funds for travel and released time.

In the chapters to follow, the authors acknowledge the help they received in the "notes" sections of their chapters. As editor of this volume, I would like to offer my heartfelt appreciation to several individuals here. Nichola Gutgold was an enthusiastic supporter of the project from the moment she first heard about the idea; she encouraged me to take on the project and helped me identify scholars who were willing to write the chapters. Robert Denton was another early supporter, who waited patiently for us to finish the manuscript, then recommended it to Brenda Hadenfeldt, Acquisitions Editor in Communication and Journalism at Roman and Littlefield Publishers. Much appreciation goes to her as well, for helping us move this project to completion.

I would also like to acknowledge the support of three colleagues from the Pennsylvania State University's Commonwealth College: Dr. Monica E. Gregory, Associate Professor of Psychology and Director of Academic Affairs at the Hazleton Campus; Dr. Priscilla F. Clement, Professor of History and head of the Arts and Humanities Division at the Delaware County Campus; and Dr. Sandy E. Gleason, Professor of Economics and Associate Dean of Faculty and Research at the University Park Campus. They approved released time from teaching, including a sabbatical leave in spring 2001. Their willingness to read material not in their own fields and to offer encouragement has made the work more appealing to a wider audience and, for me, more pleasant because shared.

Special gratitude goes to my son Aaron who, during the completion of this manuscript, has grown from being a little Ninja warrior to a card-carrying member of a local dojo. His sunny temperament and antics have kept me lighthearted even when standardizing the endnotes and bibliographies across twenty-two chapters! Thanks, as well to Frits Meijer for insisting on backing up my files (I could be cool when the hard drive crashed) and for helping me assemble them into one consistent document. He also took on the daunting task of preparing the camera ready copy.

Molly Meijer Wertheimer
Hazleton, PA

Editor's Introduction

First Ladies' Fundamental Rhetorical Choices
When to Speak? What to Say? When to Remain Silent?

Molly Meijer Wertheimer

> I have been so used to freedom of sentiment that I know not how to place so
> many guards about me, as will be indispensable, to look at every word before I
> utter it, and to impose a silence upon myself, when I talk.
>
> —Abigail Adams

Used to the freedom of speech afforded by private life, Abigail Adams agreed
with a friend who called the "ladyship" a "splendid misery." When to speak,
what to say, when to remain silent—all must be newly considered. The construction of a public persona must have been difficult for Mrs. Adams because the
Constitution was silent about the duties of the president's wife, and Abigail had
only one role model upon which to base her actions—Martha Custis Washington, a woman of decidedly different temperament and personality. As different
as they were as individuals, however, they shared a common feeling; Mrs.
Washington felt just as "fettered by political considerations" as did Mrs. Adams
(Brady 2001, 13). Writing to Fannie Bassett Washington, one of her friends,
Martha Washington lamented the set "boundaries . . . I must not depart from"
(Anthony 1990, 42). Years later, Grace Coolidge expressed similar sentiments
when she wrote in her memoirs after leaving office: "this was I and yet not I,
this was the wife of the President of the United States and she took precedence
over me" (Coolidge 1992, 62).

Other twentieth-century first ladies have felt every bit as constrained; for
example, Pat Nixon, described as "privately spontaneous and lively," controlled

her public image so much that she came across as "stiff and wooden" (Mayo 1996, 240). Recently, Sheila Tate, George Bush's press secretary, described Barbara Bush as "irrepressible," but Barbara admitted to "muzzling" herself "ever since her husband was first elected to public office" (Grimes 1990, 296). Before that, when Nancy Reagan's promptings of her husband were caught on camera, they sparked negative commentary, showing how vigilant the press and public are to any lapses.

The difficulty of learning how to funnel one's spontaneous verbalizations and visible actions into a form appropriate to the public role is illustrated well by the candidates' wives during Campaign 2000 for the presidency. Although first-ladies-to-be serve sometimes long political apprenticeships as their husbands move up the ladder of public service, often they have not practiced enough to cope with the demands placed upon them as public communicators. For example, the demand to remain silent and in rapt attention requires much concentration. Realizing how uncomfortable Laura Bush must have become as her husband answered several questions, interviewer Judy Woodruff apologized to Mrs. Bush for putting her in such an awkward position. Mrs. Bush was gracious as she listened to her husband's answers, all of which she must have heard countless times before. She was far more controlled than Ernestine Bradley, who goofed while on stage. As her husband conceded to Al Gore in the Democratic primaries, Ernestine wiggled in her chair, rubbed her eyes, looked up at the ceiling and down at the floor; she blurted out an answer to a question that was asked of her husband. When she realized what she had done—spoken at a time when she should have remained silent—she became embarrassed. In contrast, when John McCain conceded to George W. Bush, Cindy McCain stood absolutely motionless, a serene smile on her face (Auster 2000, 3G).

Silence and measured speech are requirements of being a first lady; some first ladies err because they speak "too much" or not in the right way, while others err because they speak "too little." In fact, the rhetorical demands of the position can be so tricky to enact, as I will discuss below, that no first lady has ever received unanimous acclaim for her performance as a first lady. On the whole, however, first ladies have helped their husbands win public support, which is their fundamental rhetorical exigency. They have also accomplished much more, even becoming a critical part of the United States presidency. As first lady scholar Robert P. Watson writes, "It is no longer a bold statement to suggest that the office of the first lady has shaped the course of U.S. history. . . . [A] new view of the first lady as an activist political partner is beginning to emerge as we recognize the power that has been operating behind the throne" (2000, 205). First ladies exercise considerable power, and they do so both in private and in public through the effective use of rhetorical communication.

First Ladyship: A Position of Constraints and Opportunities

In many ways, the position of first lady is more difficult to perform than the position of United States president. Like Ginger Rogers dancing with Fred

Astaire, she must follow his lead, doing whatever he does only backwards and in high heels. While the president is elected and his duties are spelled out in the Constitution, the first lady is neither elected nor given any constitutional or legal guidelines to follow.[1] For better or worse, the basis of her service is her marriage, although she may turn to the precedents established by her predecessors for guidance. Calling the role "undefined," Margaret Truman, daughter of First Lady Bess Truman, stresses the unique obligation that each first lady has to invent the role for herself (Truman 1995, 4–5); the same point is made in a different way by Mary Hoyt: each first lady is "given 'a magic wand' . . . with no instructions on its use—each woman . . . [must] figure that out for herself" (quoted in Caroli 1995, xxii). The difficult part is that she must invent a public persona while onstage, amid much public scrutiny and criticism. No matter how much experience she has had with audiences and the media, this cannot be an easy task.

The public has always been interested in the wife of the president, beginning with Mrs. Washington. In her biography, *Martha Washington: First Lady of Liberty*, Helen Bryan writes that from the time of Martha's arrival in New York (then the nation's capital), she "remained under constant public scrutiny." Although she was treated well by the press, "had Martha put a foot wrong, George's critics and political opponents would surely have pounced on her" (2002, 294). Her successors have experienced the same degree of evaluative attention, leading first lady scholar Robert P. Watson to claim that a first lady is the "most scrutinized lady in the world and must watch her every step" (2000, 39).

Since Martha Washington's day, newspaper coverage has expanded to include magazine, radio, television, and now electronic commentary. Life under such scrutiny has prompted Margaret Truman to say that the American people tend to treat the first family like "public property, like the White House itself" (1995, 8). With the public's sense of ownership have inevitably come expectations of what a first lady can and cannot say and do (10–11). These expectations transcend the individuals who hold the office, that is, the office itself carries a heavy symbolic burden.

Every first lady faces the same dilemma. She is an individual, but she becomes more than that when she assumes the office of first lady. As we have seen, Grace Coolidge early acknowledged the public's demand on her identity when she wrote, "this was the wife of the President of the United States and she took precedence over me; my personal likes and dislikes must be subordinated to the consideration of those things which were required of her." Like Mrs. Coolidge, all first ladies become symbols of American womanhood and as such they are expected to conform to the public's image of "the ideal woman" of their times. The problem is that those "constantly change as the public's view of women evolves and develops" (Gould 1996, xv). Karlyn Kohrs Campbell puts the problem this way, "presidential wives face insuperable obstacles arising out of expectations that they are to represent what we pretend is a single, universally accepted ideal for U.S. womanhood" (1996, 191). In reality, no single standard does, nor ever will, exist.

Although the American public cannot articulate with one voice what they want from a first lady, many are quick to point out what they as individuals do not want once she performs that action. Of course, the public learns about her actions and words through the filter of press coverage, which is governed by cultural "news norms." According to Campbell, "news norms" "affect the kind of coverage the First Lady receives." Today's journalists, she contends, focus especially on whatever is "deviant, dramatic, and controversial" (1996, 190–91). They tend to ignore conservative words and actions, witness the dearth of press coverage of Laura Bush in her first six months as first lady. By exaggerating the unusual and discounting the ordinary, they set the stage for much criticism; "the variety and scope" of which, writes Watson, "seems endless" (2000, 35). Betty Boyd Caroli makes a similar point when she writes:

> First Ladies [have] never lacked detractors . . . [who] pointed to their extrava-
> gance (Mary Lincoln), coarseness (Margaret Taylor), casual entertaining (Dol-
> ley Madison), elitism (Elizabeth Monroe), prudishness (Lucy Hayes), gaiety
> (Harriet Lane), excessive grief (Jane Pierce), advanced age (Martha Washing-
> ton), and youth (Julia Taylor). (Caroli 1995, xxi)

The public has been especially critical of first ladies who have seemed to exert power over their husbands' decisions. The offenders have been "charged with exercising 'petticoat government' (Edith Wilson), running their husbands' careers (Florence Harding), putting words into the president's mouth (Eleanor Roosevelt), 'getting people fired' (Nancy Reagan), and making her husband look like a wimp (Hillary Rodham Clinton)" (Caroli 1995, xxi). These kinds of comments made in the media, according to Campbell, "make it far more difficult for a presidential wife to modify or enlarge her role" (1996, 190–91).

Although press coverage and public criticism challenge the first lady, at the same time they propel her to a position of great visibility on the national and international stages, thereby providing her with an opportunity to exert enormous influence. Edith P. Mayo writes, "even though the first ladies of the twentieth century have felt the burden of intense media coverage, many have used the power of the media to their advantage" (1996, 155) Edith Roosevelt, for example, took control of the first family's image by screening photographers and choosing the journals in which she would place the photographs. She even "selected the authors she thought would place her husband and family in the best light" (Mayo 2001, 34). Lou Hoover delivered radio addresses to further her own agenda, while Jackie Kennedy used the medium of television to present a tour of the White House to the American people. Both Hillary Clinton and Laura Bush have made effective use of the White House website to carry texts of their speeches and official press releases. Indeed, today's "First Lady of the United States," writes Myra Gutin, "has one of the most influential podiums in the world at her disposal" (2001, 57–58). The public has grown so eager for news about the first family and expects some degree of public activism from her that it is "virtually impossible for a first lady to remain incommunicado in the White House" (1989, 177). Besides, a first lady has little choice but to use her rhetorical platform since, as we have seen, with no mandate from the Constitution, the legal statutes, or the public via election to office, the first lady "is required to rely almost exclusively on her ability as a public communicator" (Watson 2000, 126).

Rhetoric and the Performance of Her Political Role

Ever since first ladies have become aware of their power to influence, increasingly have they used that power rhetorically to advance their husbands' and their own agendas. This conclusion is obvious to anyone who has visited the first lady exhibit, "Political Role and Public Image," at the Smithsonian Institute's National Museum of American History. The duties curators use to organize the exhibit's texts and artifacts are: "The Nation's Hostess," "Advocate for Social Causes," "The President's Political Partner," "Political Campaigner," and "Widowhood and National Mourning." As I walked through the exhibit the first time and read through the accompanying book afterwards (Mayo and Meringolo 1994), it occurred to me that all of the duties identified as part of the first lady's "political role," at the same time identified "rhetorical processes." All required the use of rhetorical discourse or communication as the means by which they could be achieved. Robert Denton Jr., has argued this point about presidential communication in many forums: "that the essence of politics is 'talk' or human interaction" (1996, xi).[2] There is no reason why the claim would not be just as true when applied to the political role played by first ladies.

In *The Presidents' Wives: Reassessing the Office of First Lady*, Watson expands the number of duties first ladies perform to eleven,[3] including wife and mother, public figure and celebrity, nation's social hostess, symbol of American womanhood, White House manager and preservationist, campaigner, social advocate and champion of social causes, presidential spokesperson, presidential and political party booster, diplomat, and political/presidential partner (2000, 71–93). These duties, he argues, are "functions of the office" that have developed through custom or necessity rather than being just the "preferences . . . of individual first ladies per se" (2000, 71). Indeed, a major contribution of Lewis L. Gould's work *American First Ladies: Their Lives and Legacy* (1996) is his focus on the institution of first lady. After two hundred years, the office has developed a "true institutional apparatus," as first ladies introduced innovations and used each others' achievements as precedents (xiii–xix). Still, not every first lady will perform all of the duties available to her. External factors such as a war or the economy as well as internal factors such as her personality or interests may constrain her. Myra Gutin points to other factors that may modify whether and how actively a first lady performs these duties, including her health, world view, experience, and social considerations such as her relationship with her husband, how they view women, and whether she has access to presidential decision-making (1989, 175–78). First ladies also prioritize the duties they perform, devoting more time to those most meaningful to them. The hierarchy of duties and the pattern of choices a first lady makes cannot be reduced to formula or stereotype. One mistake made in the "media, public, and scholarly literature," writes Watson, "is to see the first lady as either traditional or modern. The office is much more complex and multidimensional" (2000, 24–25).

Regardless of the subset of duties a first lady performs, she must invariably use strategic communication—that is rhetorical communication—to perform them. Her communication activities may vary in that some are "formal or informal, verbal or nonverbal, public or private" (Denton 1996, xi); the kinds of media used may vary as well. In the chapters to follow, authors present an abundance of examples to demonstrate how first ladies have used rhetorical communication or discourse to perform their "political role." Many of them have practiced a rhetoric of actions more than a rhetoric of words.

With regard to the duty of "hostess," for example, Edith Mayo contends that the social role the first lady plays is "far from being mere 'cultural fluff.'" "A woman who is socially adept and politically savvy," she writes, "can promote her husband's political agenda, and structure the style and image of her husband's presidential administration" (2001, 31–32). On social occasions, first ladies use what Allgor calls "unofficial space" to achieve political goals. These sorts of situations are flexible enough to allow the successful transaction of business; good food, drink, and other distractions provide "an atmosphere of sociability to propose, to probe, to negotiate, and to compromise," as well as to change the subject or to "withdraw if the situation warrants it" (2001, 22). For example, many first ladies have expended great efforts on orchestrating state dinners to stimulate productive conversations among their guests. Lou Hoover employed an elaborate set of hand gestures to coordinate the pace of courses served during dinners, while Jackie Kennedy planned seating arrangements by literally spreading out charts on the floor. In the chapters to follow, authors suggest or detail many of the ways in which the first ladies have helped their husbands achieve political goals by demonstrating brilliant rhetorical invention on an interpersonal level and by practicing a "sociable" rhetoric—what Kari Anderson, adapting Robert Hariman's work,[4] identifies as a "social style."

The political duty of "campaigner" also requires significant rhetorical activity for its performance. At the end of the nineteenth and continuing throughout the twentieth centuries, first ladies have helped their husbands campaign for political office (Mayo 1996, 237–39). Even Ida McKinley, an invalid, helped her husband during his 1896 bid against William Jennings Bryan, with whose wife, Mary, a lawyer, she was often compared. She was made the subject of a campaign brochure, and her husband's managers used her image as a campaign symbol; she developed a following of her own (Mayo 1996, 145; Mayo and Meringolo, 38). Other early-twentieth-century political wives have helped their husbands via front porch campaigns, which are interesting because the front porch marks a bridge between the private life inside the home and the public life in the streets. Florence Harding, for example, organized "photo opportunities" during her husband's front porch campaign, which were viewed with interest by the public, including women, who had just gotten the vote. Others candidates' wives have joined their husbands' whistle-stop campaigns, such as Bess Truman and Mamie Eisenhower. Their participation was "visual"; mostly they smiled and waved, giving rise to Bess Truman's quip: "A woman's place in public is to sit beside her husband, be silent, and be sure her hat is on straight" (1986, 132).

During the 1950s, when women began to vote in equal numbers with men, the political parties used the wives of candidates as a way to appeal to women voters. Artifacts, such as pink nylon stockings embroidered with "I like Ike," were worn by female campaign workers. Lady Bird Johnson went further than her predecessors, when she traveled solo on her own whistle-stop train across the South (Mayo 1996, 239). Of course, she was preceded by Eleanor Roosevelt, who had already presented campaign speeches for her husband, including one at the 1940 Democratic National Convention (Blair 2000). Today, writes Mayo, campaigning is "an integral part of every modern race for the White House." The first lady "must be able to speak well and be persuasive and informed on the issues" (1996, 239).

Maintaining a working relationship with members of the press, another duty of the first lady's political role, requires a great deal of rhetorical acumen. Although press relations have been challenging since the inception of the office (Brady 2001, 11), the challenges have increased with the growth and development of the media. As we have seen, media scrutiny has been pervasive, and news norms have changed over time. The press, for example, was relatively silent about the nature of Ida McKinley's illness, but went into elaborate detail when Betty Ford was diagnosed with breast cancer. Many first lady scholars detail the historical relationship between the first lady and the press, tracing the development of different forms of media used to cover the first lady as well as the kinds of stories covered.[5] One generalization stands out—as the media grew in popularity, so did the public's interest in stories about the first lady. In fact, the public became interested in the entire first family, including the presidents' parents, siblings, children, and even their pets.[6] Today, writes Myra Gutin, "the press plays a critical role in transmitting both the image and the substance of a First Lady" (1989, 176), so much so that the first lady's office now has a specialized staff to handle press relations, including "a press office, press secretary, pollsters, speech writers, communications directors, and media advisors whose job it is to ensure favorable coverage of the president and first lady" (Watson 2000, 151). Her office also "actively attempts to guide or manipulate public opinion . . . by controlling media coverage, seeking favorable coverage, staging and timing public appearances, and the like" (151).

Interestingly, journalism professor Betty H. Winfield, University of Missouri, advises First Lady Laura Bush to become proactive when it comes to press relations. Although a first lady has a great deal of potential influence, Winfield contends, she can only wield it if she can control her image, including her photographic and video images, as well as written and electronic statements. Winfield advises the first lady to select a top-notch staff, plan a coherent strategy concerning the image she wants to project as she performs her many duties—as wife, mother, advocate, and so on—and stick with it by reinforcing aspects of it on a daily basis (2001, 45–51). Years before this advice was written, Eleanor Roosevelt held press conferences with women journalists that became productive, collaborative strategy sessions. The importance of the staff in the first lady's office is further underscored when archivist Nancy Kegan Smith offers Mrs. Bush advice on how to maintain office records and personal papers. She provides a fascinating discussion of the history and usefulness of first lady papers to scholars (2001).

I have touched only briefly on three of the eleven duties Robert Watson presents in *The Presidents' Wives*. From what I have suggested, it must be obvious how much first ladies rely on rhetorical communication to perform those roles. Yet, as important as rhetorical communication is and has been especially to modern American first ladies, unfortunately, they have not been much studied from that perspective. In fact, study of the first lady is a relatively new area of research.

Scholarly Literature on the First Lady

"The first lady remains one of the most fascinating and unexplored facets of the American presidency and the history of women in the United States" (1989, viii), writes Don W. Wilson, former national archivist. He credits the growth of the presidential library system in the 1970s and 1980s with stimulating research on this neglected area of scholarship. Like a treasure trove, presidential libraries from Herbert Hoover through George Bush contain the Social Files of First Ladies, which he says include "thousands of boxes of documents and letters" (vii).[7] Cataloguing these materials is a painstaking, time-consuming process by libraries that are largely understaffed. Increasingly, however, more material is becoming available; some libraries are putting their finding guides online. The papers of first ladies before Lou Hoover are much more difficult to access. What exists is mostly in private hands. Scattered documentation of twentieth-century first ladies from McKinley to Coolidge may be found in the Library of Congress.[8] A resource that continues to increase in usefulness since its incorporation in 1997, is the National First Ladies' Library in Canton, Ohio, which is committed to becoming "a research facility and educational center for scholars of all ages" (Krider 2001, 93). One of their primary goals is: "To update each year a complete, annotated bibliography developed on First Ladies from Martha Custis Washington to Hillary Rodham Clinton" and beyond (94).[9]

With increased availability of first lady material comes increased scholarly output in the forms of conference sessions, journal articles, and published books.[10] In the late 1980s, works such as Betty Boyd Caroli's *First Ladies* (1987) and Myra Gutin's *The President's Partner: The First Lady in the Twentieth Century* (1989) appeared. More popular treatments—anecdotal in nature— appeared as well, such as James. S. Rosebush's *First Lady, Public Wife: A Behind-the-Scenes History of the Evolving Role of the First Ladies in American Political Life* (1987) and Paul F. Boller Jr.'s *Presidential Wives: An Anecdotal History* (1988). In the 1990s, other significant scholarly works appeared, such as Carl S. Anthony's *First Ladies: The Saga of the Presidents' Wives and Their Power* (1990–1991) and Lewis L. Gould's *American First Ladies: Their Lives and Their Legacy* (1996). Important books of a less scholarly nature were published, such as Margaret Truman's *First Ladies: An Intimate Group Portrait of*

White House Wives (1996) and Gil Troy's *Affairs of State: The Rise and Rejection of the Presidential Couple since World War II* (1997). Recent scholarship—directed to both the academic and popular communities—stresses the presidential partnership, such as Robert P. Watson's *The Presidents' Wives: Reassessing the Office of the First Lady* (2000) and Kati Marton's *Hidden Power: Presidential Marriages That Shaped Our Recent History* (2001). *Laura Bush: The Report to the First Lady* (Watson 2001) is an essay collection written by first lady scholars from several disciplines; it was prepared for Laura Bush when she began her tenure as first lady.

Research on first ladies in the disciplines of rhetoric and communication has been limited, but is increasing. To date, the only book-length treatment of first ladies written from the perspective of communication is Myra Gutin's groundbreaking study: *The President's Partner: The First Lady in the Twentieth Century* (1989).[11] Based on her dissertation, Gutin's argument is that by studying "the speeches, radio and television broadcasts, interviews, press conferences, and magazine and newspaper articles written by the First Lady . . . one is best able to understand and appreciate the changes [in the office] that have taken place over sixty years," the time frame of her study, 1920–1988 (2). Gutin places each of the first ladies from Harding through Carter in one of the following categories: "White Housekeepers: Social Hostesses and Ceremonial Presences" (Harding, Coolidge, Truman, and Eisenhower), "Emerging Spokeswomen" (Hoover, Kennedy, and Nixon), and "Political Surrogates and Independent Advocates" (Roosevelt, Johnson, Ford, and Carter). Her study ends with Nancy Reagan, who, Gutin admits, "defies pigeonholing," shuffling instead between "these classifications as her role has evolved during the Reagan administration" (165).[12] Within each chapter, Gutin traces the forms of communication each first lady uses as well as some of the factors that constrain her, including the quality of the marital relationship and the president's view of what his wife should do as a first lady.

Two significant studies of first ladies from a rhetorical perspective are by Karlyn Kohrs Campbell: "The Rhetorical Presidency: A Two Person Career" (1996) and "The Discursive Performance of Femininity: Hating Hillary" (1998). Both studies provide a framework for understanding why the office of the first lady is "a vital part of the presidency" as well as a difficult ("impossible")—damned if you do, damned if you don't—rhetorical role to play. In the earlier article, Campbell inserts the first lady into the "presidential corporation" of cabinet members, advisors, speechwriters and others. She identifies the blurring of public and private aspects of her office as one of the factors that contributes to the difficulty of its performance as well as a source of public criticism. Summarizing the "factors that make the role so difficult" from a slightly different perspective taken in her later article, Campbell highlights "the ill-defined character of an ambiguous role," the public expectation that she "personify an idealized vision of women when one no longer exists," her function as a "lightning rod for hostile feelings about her husband," and the public demand that women who perform professional roles in public "discursively enact their femininity" (1998, 15). Although these are general problems of the office of first lady,

Campbell contends, in the case of Hillary Rodham Clinton they are "writ large." Mrs. Clinton's inability to "feminize her rhetorical style, to perform a culturally defined feminine role publicly" made it difficult for her to achieve her rhetorical goals. Campbell laments the public's "failure to appreciate" the argumentative skills of talented women like Mrs. Clinton and, more broadly, the rejection of educated, potentially contributive women like her: "If we reject all those who lack the feminizing skills of an Elizabeth Hanford Dole, we shall deprive ourselves of a vast array of talent" (15).

The conclusions reached by Shawn J. Parry-Giles and Diane M. Blair are consistent with Campbell's.[13] In "The Rise of the Rhetorical First Lady: Politics, Gender Ideology, and Women's Voice, 1789–2002," they trace "the rise of the *rhetorical first lady* from Martha Washington through Laura Bush." The first lady, they argue, occupies a "contested space" because she functions both as a site "for the performance of archetypal femininity that privileges the ideal republican mother" and also as a site of "feminist advancement that challenges gender stereotypes, expanding women's political space." Their argument, though developed differently, reaches conclusions similar to those put forward by Karrin Vasby Anderson's "The First Lady as a Site of 'American Womanhood,'" which is included in this volume. Anderson further argues for viewing each first lady as a site of heterogeneity and paradox; she stresses the multifaceted nature of identity and advises scholars not to reduce the complexity of first ladies by using a dichotomous logic.

Some other published works that focus in whole or in part on a particular first lady include Barbara C. Burrell's *Public Opinion, the First Ladyship, and Hillary Rodham Clinton* (2001), Diane M. Blair's, "No Ordinary Time: Eleanor Roosevelt's Address to the 1940 Democratic National Convention" (2000), and Karrin Vasby Anderson's, "From Spouses to Candidates: Hillary Rodham Clinton, Elizabeth Dole, and the Gendered Office of U.S. President" (2002). Fortunately, at the time of this writing, faculty and graduate students in rhetoric and communication continue to present conference papers, complete dissertations, and prepare master's theses.[14] Many faculty members are also designing courses on the rhetoric of first ladies, and others are including units on first ladies in their political and/or presidential rhetoric and communication courses.[15] Materials to teach these courses are also forthcoming.[16] All indicate continued and increasing interest in studying the president's spouse from a rhetorical perspective.

Contribution to the Growing Literature

The authors of the chapters in this volume write with a single purpose: to make a contribution to the growing literature on first ladies, revealing especially how each used rhetorical communication to carry out her duties. For readers unfamiliar with "rhetoric" as an area of scholarship, Aristotle's definition of rhetoric as "the faculty of discovering in any given case all of the available means of persuasion" (Cooper 1932) is foundational, although there are countless other definitions from the history of rhetoric, including contemporary rhetorical theory, readily available.[17] Scholars of rhetoric and communication focus on different kinds of situations, among them dyads, small groups, public speaking events; they examine oral, written, mass mediated, and electronic forms of communication, including verbal and nonverbal (pictorial) symbols. Combining the variability of definition with the alternatives of focus produces a veritable kaleidoscope of potential perspectives from which scholars may select and interpret material. As editor of this work, I welcomed the differences, encouraging each author to choose the most striking ideas about her first lady from the material available, which, in some cases, was thin, revealing how little attention has been paid to the preservation of early first lady artifacts. In addition, some material has been destroyed, either intentionally or by accident. For example, most of the letters of Ida McKinley were lost in a warehouse fire, while Bess Truman burned her own letters herself. For other first ladies, the material is more plentiful, with archivists struggling to make it available to scholars.

The essays in this work focus on United States first ladies of the twentieth century, including Ida McKinley through Hillary Clinton. We also include a chapter on the first twenty-first-century first lady, Laura Bush, who was in that position for only eighteen months when that essay was written. To a certain extent, the choice to begin the study at 1900 is arbitrary; on the other hand, as Watson advises: "it has only been in the twentieth century that the office [of first lady] has become a highly visible and overtly public institution" (2000, 150). With the exception of chapter one, all of the authors use the same general headings: Biography, Rhetorical Activities as First Lady, and Legacy. What material to include under each heading and how to organize it were the choices of each author. Consequently, this book is systematic, but only to a certain extent. The headings provide the only preconceived set of topics used; definitions of rhetoric, rhetorical perspectives, the interests, training, and personality of the authors all intersected to determine the content selected. The first ladies themselves also "contributed" to what was written about them. For example, as the author of two of the chapters, I was not always able to write about the same activities largely because these two first ladies are so different and the materials available about them differ widely.

The time for constructing a definitive set of *topoi* for analyzing the rhetorical activities of first ladies is not yet here. Campbell's framework, stressing both the importance of the first lady to the presidential corporation as well as the difficulties involved in performing her ambiguous position, maps out the general terrain, while the duties identified by Watson add the key landmarks. Neither scholar, however, identifies the rhetorical processes in operation. Gutin identifies some of these processes, but the chief strength of her work—her systematic method of analysis—gives rise to its chief weakness—the rhetorical activities and processes that did not fit easily into her categories largely slipped through her analytical net. As editor of this work, my hope is that the freedom of method afforded the authors—their use of conceptual nets that made sense to them— will generate new insights and stimulate future research.

One central theme does emerge from the crisscrossing mesh of our research and that is the theme suggested at the beginning of this introduction by the quotation from Abigail Adams: her realization that her conversation as a first lady could no longer be spontaneous but had to be constrained. For better or worse, a first lady cannot *not* communicate. Whatever she says or does not say and whatever she does or does not do reflect upon her husband and herself. It is the ethos of the presidential couple in the public mind that defines the president's administration. We hope our essays contribute to an awareness of the central part the first lady plays in the American presidency. She is a key player in the presidential administration who must use rhetorical discourse to help advance her own and her husband's agendas.

Notes

1. That she can't be appointed to any official position seems covered under the "Bobby Kennedy rule," which states that "immediate members of the president's family can no longer be appointed to positions in the federal government" (Watson 2000, 69).

2. Robert Denton Jr., *The Symbolic Dimensions of the American Presidency*; Robert Denton Jr. and Gary Woodward, *Political Communication in America*; Robert Denton Jr. and Dan Hahn, *Presidential Communication*; and Robert Denton Jr., *The Primetime Presidency of Ronald Reagan*.

3. To arrive at his list, Watson summarized the attempts of other first lady scholars to categorize these duties.

4. Robert Hariman, *Political Style: The Artistry of Power* (1995).

5. For example, see Gutin (1989, 3–4) and Watson (2000, 150–51).

6. For example, see Bonnie Angelo, *First Mothers: The Women Who Shaped the Presidents* (2000); Harold I. Gullen, *Faith of Our Mothers: The Stories of Presidential Mothers from Mary Washington to Barbara Bush* (2001); Roy Rowan and Brooke Janis, *First Dogs: American Presidents and Their Best Friends* (1997); and Margaret Truman, *White House Pets* (1969).

7. Temporarily, the Clintons' papers are housed in a presidential "Project" and will be turned over to the United States Archivist once the Clinton Library is constructed (Smith 2001, 80).

8. A succinct overview of the way first lady papers have been handled historically is Nancy Kegan Smith's "Advice to the Incoming First Lady on Her Records and Establishing Files That Successfully Reflect Her Role" (2001, 79–83). Myra Gutin's "Biographical Notes" provides a starting point for using primary material on the first ladies she studied (1989, 179–184). Another work worth consulting is Nancy Kegan Smith and Mary C. Ryan's (1989) *Modern First Ladies: Their Documentary Legacy*. A bibliography of resources on first ladies, including guides to locate their papers may be found in Elizabeth Lorelei Thacker-Estrada's "Presidential Wives, the White House, and Washington, D.C.: Recommended Readings and Resources for the First Lady" (2001, 92).

9. This material may be accessed at www.firstladies.org.

10. A good review of the literature on first ladies (biographical, anecdotal, and scholarly) may be found in Elizabeth Lorelei Thacker-Estrada's "Presidential Wives, the White House, and Washington, D.C.: Recommended Readings and Resources for the First Lady" (2001, 85–92). My summary of the literature here follows Robert Watson's work (2000).

11. Burrell's *Public Opinion, the First Ladyship, and Hilary Rodham Clinton* (2001) is on a particular first lady from a mass communication perspective.

12. In all fairness, Gutin had little access to primary materials on Nancy Reagan who was just finishing her term as first lady when Gutin was preparing her manuscript (1989, 165).

13. See also: Janis L. Edwards and Huey Rong Chen. "The First Lady/First Wife in Editorial Cartoons: Rhetorical Visions through Gendered Lenses" in *Women's Studies in Communication*.

14. On August 19, 2002, I placed a request on CRTNET, a widely circulated listserv sponsored by the National Communication Association, to hear from scholars who are presently engaged in research on first ladies. Several scholars e-mailed me, sending the titles of papers which they have presented or are scheduled for presentation at national and regional conferences. In addition, two graduate students e-mailed me the titles and brief descriptions of their dissertations: Lisa M. Burns, University of Maryland, "Presidential Wives and the Press: News Framing and the Construction of the First Lady Institution in the Twentieth Century"; and Misty L. Knight, University of Southern Mississippi, "In Defense of First Ladies Rhetoric: A Case for a Critical Genre." Other graduate students informed me of their completed research and interest in writing their master's theses on first ladies. Although information to include in this note and the next was not collected systematically, for my purposes, it is sufficient to indicate the interest of scholars in the fields of rhetoric and communication on first ladies.

15. Several authors of chapters in this collection teach courses on the rhetoric of American first ladies including: Beth M. Waggenspack (Virginia Polytechnic Institute and State University) and Linda Hobgood (University of Richmond). Other faculty members teach courses devoted in part to first ladies such as Diana B. Carlin (University of Kansas), Janis L. Edwards (University of Alabama), and Shawn J. Parry-Giles (University of Maryland). Faculty members other than authors of chapters in this book also offer similar courses such as Myra Gutin (Rider University) and Barbara Garvey (Hanover College in Indiana). Doubtless, this list just scratches the surface of the graduate and undergraduate courses in the United States that devote a substantial amount of class time to first ladies as rhetoricians.

16. Paula Wilson Youra sent me an e-mail message to announce the release of a videotape produced by the Educational Video Group/Alistair Press, Greenwood, Indiana. The videotape contains speeches by Barbara Bush, Hillary Clinton, Elizabeth Dole, Tipper Gore, Hadassah Lieberman, and Laura Bush. They were given at different Democratic and Republican national conventions and they are all speeches of nomination.

17. For definitions drawn from the history of rhetoric, see for example: www.stanford .edu/dept/english/courses/sites/lunsford/pages/defs.htm; www.hf.ntnu.no/engelsk/shake speare/defs.htm; www.missouri.edu/~engjnc/rhetoric/defining_main.html. In addition, there are rhetorical scholars who argue against defining rhetoric and those who object to the idea of needing a foundation for rhetoric (Scott 1973). For a summary of the variety of scholarship produced by those who "profess rhetoric at the end of the twentieth century," see Antczak, Coggins, and Klinger (2002, ix).

References

Allgor, Catherine. 2000. *Parlor Politics: In Which the Ladies of Washington Help Build a City and a Government*. Charlottesville, Va.: University of Virginia Press.

Anderson, Karrin Vasby. 2002. From Spouses to Candidates: Hillary Rodham Clinton, Elizabeth Dole, and the Gendered Office of U.S. President. *Rhetoric and Public Affairs*, 5:1, 105–32.

Angelo, Bonnie. 2000. *First Mothers: The Women Who Shaped the Presidents.* New York: HarperCollins.

Antczak, Frederick J., Vinda Coggins, and Geoffrey D. Klinger. 2002. *Professing Rhetoric: Selected Papers from the 2000 Rhetoric Society of America Conference.* Mahwah, N.J.: Lawrence Erlbaum Associates.

Anthony, Carl Sferrazza. 1990. *First Ladies: The Saga of the Presidents' Wives and Their Power 1789–1961,* Vol. 1. New York: William Morrow.

Auster, Elizabeth. 2000. Political Wives, Smiling, Stoic, Silent Partners. *Plain Dealer* (Cleveland), 12 March, 3G.

Blair, Diane. 2000. No Ordinary Time: Eleanor Roosevelt's Address to the 1940 Democratic National Convention. *Rhetoric and Public Affairs,* 4:2, 203–22.

Brady, Patricia. 2001. Martha Washington: The Lady Who First Created the Role. In *Laura Bush: The Report to the First Lady,* ed. Robert P. Watson, 11–15. Huntington, N.Y.: Nova History Publications.

Bryan, Helen. 2002. *Martha Washington: First Lady of Liberty.* New York: John Wiley & Sons.

Burrell, Barbara C. 2001. *Public Opinion, the First Ladyship, and Hillary Rodham Clinton,* rev. ed. New York: Garland.

Campbell, Karlyn Kohrs. 1996. The Rhetorical Presidency: A Two Person Career. In *Beyond the Rhetorical Presidency,* ed. Martin J. Medhurst, 179–95. College Station, Tex.: Texas A & M University Press.

———. 1998. The Discursive Performance of Femininity: Hating Hillary. *Rhetoric and Public Affairs,* 5:1, 1–19.

Caroli, Betty Boyd. 1995. *First Ladies,* expanded edition. New York: Oxford University Press.

Coolidge, Grace Goodhue. 1992. *Grace Coolidge: An Autobiography.* Ed. Lawrence E. Wikander and Robert H. Ferrell. Worland, Wyo.: High Plains Publishing Company, Inc.

Cooper, Lane, trans. 1932. *The Rhetoric of Aristotle.* New York: Appleton Century Crofts.

Denton, Robert E., Jr. 1982. *The Symbolic Dimensions of the American Presidency.* Prospect Heights, Ill.: Waveland.

———. 1988. *The Primetime Presidency of Ronald Reagan.* New York: Praeger.

———. 1996. Series Introduction to *From the Margins to the Center: Contemporary Women and Political Communication,* ed. Patricia A. Sullivan and Lynn H. Turner, xi–xiii. Westport, Conn.: Praeger.

Denton, Robert E., Jr., and Dan Hahn. 1986. *Presidential Communication.* New York: Praeger.

Denton, Robert E., Jr., and Gary Woodward. 1990. *Political Communication in America,* 2nd ed. New York: Praeger.

Edwards, Janis L., and Huey Rong Chen. 2000. The First Lady/First Wife in Editorial Cartoons: Rhetorical Visions through Gendered Lenses. *Women's Studies in Communication,* 23:3, 367–91.

Gould, Lewis. 1996. The First Lady as Symbol and Institution. In *American First Ladies,* ed. Lewis L. Gould, xiii–xx. New York: Garland.

Grimes, Ann. 1990. *Running Mates: The Making of a First Lady.* New York: William Marrow & Co.

Gullen, Harold I. 2001. *Faith of Our Mothers: The Stories of Presidential Mothers from Mary Washington to Barbara Bush.* Grand Rapids, Mich.: William B. Eerdmans.

Gutin, Myra. 1989. *The President's Partner: The First Lady in the Twentieth Century.* New York: Greenwood.

———. 2001. Public Discourse and the American First Lady in the 20th Century. In *Laura Bush: The Report to the First Lady*, ed. Robert P. Watson, 53–63. Huntington, N.Y.: Nova History Publications.

Hariman, Robert. 1995. *Political Style: The Artistry of Power.* Chicago: University of Chicago Press.

Krider, Pat. 2001. National First Ladies' Library. In Laura Bush: The Report to the First Lady, ed. Robert P. Watson, 93–96. Huntington, N.Y.: Nova History Publications.

Mayo, Edith P., ed. 1996. *Smithsonian Book of the First Ladies: Their Lives, Times, and Issues.* New York: Henry Holt and Co.

Mayo, Edith P. 2001. "Party Politics": The Social Role of the First Lady and its Political Influence. In *Laura Bush: The Report to the First Lady*, ed. Robert P. Watson, 31–35. Huntington, New York: Nova History Publications.

Mayo, Edith P., and Denise D. Meringolo. 1994. *First Ladies: Political Role and Public Image.* Washington, D.C.: Smithsonian Institution.

Parry-Giles, Shawn J., and Diane M. Blair. 2002. The Rise of the Rhetorical First Lady: Politics, Gender Ideology, and Women's Voice, 1789–2002. *Rhetoric and Public Affairs,* 6:5, 565–600.

Rowan, Roy, and Janis Brooke. 1997. *First Dogs: American Presidents and Their Best Friends.* Chapel Hill, N.C.: Algonquin Books.

Scott, Robert. 1973. On *Not* Defining "Rhetoric." *Philosophy and Rhetoric,* 6:2, 81–96.

Smith, Nancy Kegan. 2001. Advice to the Incoming First Lady on Her Records and Establishing Files That Successfully Reflect Her New Role. In *Laura Bush: The Report to the First Lady*, ed. Robert P. Watson, 79–83. Huntington, N.Y.: Nova History Publications.

Smith, Nancy Kegan, and Mary C. Ryan. 1989. *Modern First Ladies: Their Documentary Legacy.* Washington, D.C.: National Archives and Records Administration.

Thacker-Estrada, Elizabeth Lorelei. 2001. Presidential Wives, the White House, and Washington, D.C.: Recommended Readings and Resources for the First Lady. In *Laura Bush: The Report to the First Lady*, ed. Robert P. Watson, 85–92. Huntington, N.Y.: Nova History Publications.

Troy, Gil. 1997. *Affairs of State: The Rise and Rejection of the Presidential Couple since World War II.* New York: The Free Press.

Truman, Margaret. 1969. *White House Pets.* New York: David McKay Company.

———. 1986. *Bess W. Truman.* New York: Macmillan.

———. 1995. *First Ladies: An Intimate Group Portrait of White House Wives.* New York: Fawcett Columbine.

Watson, Robert P. 2000. *The Presidents' Wives: Reassessing the Office of First Lady.* Boulder, Colo.: Lynne Reinner Publishers.

———, ed. 2001. *Laura Bush: The Report to the First Lady.* Huntington, N.Y.: Nova History Publications.

Wilson, Donald W. 1989. Foreword to *Modern First Ladies: Their Documentary Legacy,* ed. Nancy Kegan Smith, vii–viii. Washington, D.C.: National Archives and Records Administration.

Winfield, Betty H. 2001. The First Lady's Relations with the Mass Media. In *Laura Bush: The Report to the First Lady*, ed. Robert P. Watson, 45–51. Huntington, N.Y.: Nova History Publications.

Chapter 1

The First Lady
A Site of "American Womanhood"

Karrin Vasby Anderson

> The way that she fulfills her role as First Lady marks a real "departure." Her husband consults her on political policy and trusts her as his closest adviser. An unelected force in the White House, she is highly controversial. She may even draft legislation. Hillary Rodham Clinton? No. "She" is Nellie Taft, Florence Harding, Edith Bolling Wilson, Eleanor Roosevelt and Rosalynn Carter.
> —Edith P. Mayo

During the 1992 presidential campaign, Hillary Rodham Clinton was asked about a potential conflict of interest between her duties as a lawyer and her status as the wife of the governor of Arkansas. Her reply revealed an attempt to balance career and family obligations in an effort "to have an independent life and to make a difference." At the conclusion of her explanation she quipped, "I suppose I could have stayed home and baked cookies and had teas but what I decided to do was fulfill my profession which I entered before my husband was in public life" (Jamieson 1995, 27). That offhand remark came to be known as "one of [Rodham Clinton's] most serious gaffes in primary season," (Sullivan and Levin 1995, 277) and it sparked commentary both in scholarly and popular circles (Barone 1992, Caroli 1995, Jamieson 1995, Sullivan and Levin 1995). Rodham Clinton's remark was cited as an indication of her choice to depart from the traditional roles played by United States first ladies, in favor of more activist roles. Rather than being the product of twentieth-century feminism, however, her remark echoed sentiments uttered nearly 150 years earlier by one

17

of her predecessors, Sarah Polk. When the wife of Henry Clay, James Polk's opponent in the 1844 presidential election, was heralded for her domesticity, she countered, "If I get to the White House, I expect to live on $25,000 a year and I will neither keep house nor make butter" (Caroli 1995, 62). As Polk's retort suggests, first ladies have been challenging norms and churning up controversy ever since the inception of the role.

Historically, first ladies have functioned as "symbols" of traditional white middle- to upper-class femininity in America, a condition that has both constrained and empowered them (Mayo and Meringolo 1994). Critics who have reflected on how first ladies have performed their roles often comment on the nature and extent of their power within presidential administrations. While that is a significant question, it is not the only one to study. My argument in this chapter is that first ladies also influence conceptions of "American womanhood," and how they do that has broad implications for all women. Indeed, by virtue of their husbands' elections, first ladies become "sites" for the symbolic negotiation of female identity. Discourses by and about first ladies function culturally to shape notions of femininity and so both foster and constrain women's agency. Thus, the study of first ladies is important not only for a historical appreciation of some of the "great women" who have contributed to that institution, but also as a critique of how "American womanhood" has been and continues to be inscribed, negotiated, and contested in the United States. On the one hand, first ladies are viewed as reflections of traditional femininity, notions of which have been disciplined by long-standing cultural metaphors—such as the metaphor of containment. Yet, even corralled within this cultural milieu, first ladies have also been able to develop "social styles" that are rhetorically responsive to the political situations they (and their husbands) face. Moreover, many have been able to confound the ambiguities latent in gender dichotomies by deploying paradox in ways that deconstruct female identity and open possibilities for political agency, thereby proving liberating for women. Before this more progressive view of the U.S. first ladyship can be explored, however, one must examine how the role developed within the cultural milieu of containment.

Containment and U.S. Identity

First ladies became icons of American femininity partly because their role was undefined and partly because their role was constructed within the larger culture of "containment," a metaphor that has influenced American culture, identity, and practice since colonial times.[1] David Campbell explains that America, as an imagined community, used the dichotomy between "civilized" and "barbarian" to justify its colonization of the New World (1992, 116). The impulse to colonize was further legitimated by the myth of American exceptionalism, which originated with the Puritans and suggested that the "American self was the product of divine intent" (121). These two discourses combined to foster a culture that strove to contain "barbarism" wherever it was found (127). Campbell explicates the ways in which containment metaphors surfaced in Puritan doctrines of civility (the need to contain the internal barbarian), in frontier structures designed to keep Native Americans out of settled areas (the need to contain the pagan barbarian), and in colonial slave codes (the need to contain the racialized barbarian). He argues that fear of the Other is inscribed into U.S. identity, and the strategy of containment historically has been the mode of operation for combating that fear.

Like other containment rhetorics, sexual containment has roots in early American discourse. Most notably, containment metaphors emerged in the debates over women's suffrage, with opponents of suffrage arguing that women should remain cloistered in the private sphere (Campbell 1989, Zaeske 1995). Not only did they object to women voting, they deemed any woman who spoke to "promiscuous" audiences composed of women and men to be "masculine, unwomanly, aggressive, and cold" (Campbell 1989, 12). Sexual containment, therefore, was enacted through nineteenth-century attempts to label women's power as unnatural, desexed, and threatening.

Sexual containment strategies did not disappear after U.S. women won the vote in 1920. The fear of outspoken, politically active women has informed much of popular culture and political discourse throughout the twentieth century. In fact, the discursive strategies of nineteenth-century antisuffragists reemerged during the debate over women's liberation and the Equal Rights Amendment (ERA) in the 1970s. Susan Douglas notes the ways in which "radical feminists" at this time were castigated in the media as "ugly, humorless, disorderly man-haters in desperate need of some Nair" (1994, 189). The image of the desexed woman's rights advocate was subsumed into popular culture and political discourse almost as easily in the late twentieth century as it had been one hundred years earlier.

Like other women, U.S first ladies have felt the impact of containment rhetoric. In fact, they have developed as symbols of "American womanhood" within this long-standing containment milieu. For example, Mamie Eisenhower's preoccupation with pink and her prowess as a presidential hostess exemplified the domestic ideal that governed the Cold War era.[2] Yet first ladies have been held up as icons of traditional femininity long before the Eisenhowers' tenure in the White House, and contemporary first ladies like Hillary Rodham Clinton are castigated for supposed breaches of tradition. Today, the tension between the traditional role of first ladies and the modern roles they can play remains.

The First Lady: A Site of Traditional Femininity

The term "first lady" appeared in journalistic references to the president's wife as early as 1870, although its use hearkened back to 1789 when "crowds accustomed to the pomp of royal persons heralded the wife of their new president as 'Lady Washington'" (Caroli 1995, xv). During the nineteenth century, it was assumed that the first lady would occupy a position "at the head of the female society of the United States" (Caroli 1995, 38). Today, although phrases like "female society" sound arcane, the first lady continues to stand as a symbol of American womanhood, reflecting, as Betty Boyd Caroli states, "the status of American women of their time while helping shape expectations of what women can properly do" (1995, xxi).

The United States historically has "expected first ladies to reflect ideals of home, family and womanhood," with the term "lady" connoting "middle-and upper-class respectability and suggest[ing] a certain kind of demeanor" (Mayo and Meringolo 1994, 8). Margaret Carlson calls the first ladyship "the most tradition-bound and antiquated model of American womanhood" (1992, 28), while Germaine Greer concurs, quipping that the first lady "is the archetypal lipstick-skirt-high-heels beside the archetypal suit" (1995, 20). Caroli explains that norms of femininity were inscribed into the role of first lady in the eighteenth century, since the majority of early first ladies "acquiesced in limiting themselves to a supportive role reflecting the predominant attitude about femininity" (1995, 32). This standard continued through the mid-nineteenth century, when "[y]outhful surrogates [as first ladies] became a tradition because they evidently fit in with prevailing ideas about femininity—womanliness could be exemplified in obsequious, smiling mannequins who showed little evidence of thinking for themselves" (Caroli 1995, 57).

Certainly, not every early first lady reacted to cultural norms of femininity by declining to think for herself. Abigail Adams, Sarah Polk, and Mary Lincoln each were vocal, independent presidential spouses. Mayo notes, however, that "virtually every First Lady who has used her influence has been either ridiculed or vilified as deviating from women's proper role or has been feared as emasculating" (1993, A52). Historian Simon Schama attributes America's resistance to assertiveness in the first lady, in part, to cultural *mythos*, stating:

> Haunting the West is the ancient myth of women as swallowers of virile men. In the White House, the choice is to be a dutiful reflection of the husband's virtue or to devour the husband's strength. And this Delilah image is so deeply rooted that it's incredibly difficult to transcend. (Kornbluth 1995, 34)

This cultural fear of feminine strength is complicated by the expectations of masculinity tied to the presidency (Daughton 1994; Kimmel 1996, 36–38). Assertive presidential wives may fare better if their husbands are viewed as strong and effective (i.e., as the "man in charge"), whereas presidents lacking overtones of masculinity and strength can be perceived as too easily swayed by the opinions of politically involved wives. Caroli asks, for example, "[c]ould Eleanor Roosevelt have broken so many precedents if Franklin had accomplished less? Did Rosalynn Carter's determination make Jimmy look less decisive?" (1995, 65). Even in the face of FDR's popularity, many contemporary journalists derided Eleanor Roosevelt's political activism. After criticizing her propensity for travel, which resulted from her taking on the role of FDR's "eyes and ears," journalist Malcolm Bingay advised the first lady to "light somewhere and keep quiet" (quoted in Beasley 1987, 103). Former President Richard Nixon echoed Bingay's admonition, warning: "[i]f the wife comes through as being too strong and too intelligent it makes the husband look like a wimp" (Steele 1992, 43).

Journalist Michael Barone charged that Hillary Rodham Clinton "makes [President Bill Clinton] appear weak" (1994, 32), and his observation was borne out by several cultural examples. *Time* magazine described the caption under a photo of Rodham Clinton, which hung in a Pentagon briefing room as "the Commander in Chief" (Farley 1993, 7). A caption in the same article underscored this perspective by stating, "Five-star first lady: Ms. Rodham Clinton's real boss, according to Pentagon wags" (Farley 1993, 7). This same perception was fostered during the health-care reform campaign, at which time, "[a]fter Clinton signaled a willingness to compromise on health care, a highly placed Democrat reports, one senator said, 'Wait, he hasn't checked with Mama yet'" (Barone 1994, 32).

This cultural prohibition against assertive and independent first ladies has influenced many of them to play up their own femininity. For example, Mamie Eisenhower "exemplified the supportive wife who immersed herself in her husband's life and career—an ideal of femininity strongly promoted in the 1950s" (Mayo and Meringolo 1994, 22). Pat Nixon emphasized "her domesticity" and once confided to reporters that whenever she had a free evening, she took down her husband's suits and pressed them. Rather than talking about what she read or her views on national issues, she shared her thoughts on sewing dresses for her daughters and stitching up draperies on her home machine. Her husband emphasized the same helpmate quality in Pat when in the famous "Checkers" speech, he referred to her as a "wonderful stenographer" (Caroli 1995, 247). Richard Nixon's later statement about the proper comportment for a political wife suggests that Pat Nixon's domestic persona was a strategic rhetorical move designed to facilitate a political goal. Barbara Bush, similarly, cast herself in "the role of national grandmother," a persona that garnered her consistently favorable approval ratings (Walsh 1992, 36; Truman 1995, 313–19).

This preference for domestic first ladies stems, in part, from cultural interpretations of women's roles. Although "for the past 20 years more wives have worked [outside the home] than have not," "[t]hree-quarters of married couples say that mothers should make a full-time job of bringing up their children, if money allows it" ("Merry Wives" 1992, 26). Cultural attitudes toward working women in the public and private spheres suggest that "Ozzie and Harriett, the mythical television couple of the 1950s, are still alive in spirit, if not always in fact" ("Merry Wives" 1992, 26). Many critics agree that the angst over the first lady goes beyond expectations for domesticity inscribed into this traditionally feminine role. The controversies that run "throughout our history" also are about "America's continuing, deep-seated ambivalence, even hostility, toward power in the hands of women" (Mayo 1993, A52). Journalist Susan Riley asks:

Why does society insist on an archetypal wife, an Everywife, a figurehead with no political power but potent symbolic performance? What is the political wife saying about women, about marriage, about the way power is distributed in our society? It sounds as if she is saying that women are status symbols, possessions, and mirrors for the men they live with. But aren't those days gone? (1987, 3–4)

In response to Riley's question, Ann Grimes concludes, "[e]vidently not. The public behavior of political wives—and of the first lady—and the public acceptance and expectations of their largely ceremonial, symbolic role say a lot" (1990, 318).

Since the inception of the role of first lady, it has come to signify traditional femininity and domesticity, operating to constrain the actions and speech of the women who occupy that role. The implications of this culture, however, reach beyond the office of the first lady. Since first ladies are taken as signifiers of American womanhood, the constraints that affect them will, in turn, impact all women to some extent. To view the role as only a reification of traditional femininity, however, is to oversimplify the rhetoric of the first ladyship. In the next section of this essay, I explore the ways in which United States first ladies have achieved political agency within presidential administrations and have fostered that agency on a broader scale through the development of a strategic social style. Some used social style to promote their husbands' political agendas, while others used it to promote their own political and personal goals.

The First Lady: A Site of Women's Agency

Although the duties and responsibilities of the first lady are not prescribed in the Constitution, presidents' wives have always had to assume a visible position in American politics, due, in part, to the unique nature of the American presidency. Caroli points out that the office of the president combines two jobs which typically are distinct in other governmental systems: "a head of state who presides over ceremonial functions, and a head of government who makes major appointments and takes a decisive role in legislation" (1995, xviii). Because the president is occupied with responsibilities as the head of government, presidential spouses often have assumed many of the ceremonial functions performed by the head of state, placing them in the limelight on the national and international stage. Furthermore, Caroli notes the ways in which the president's "living arrangements" foster the involvement of first ladies in national governance, since private and public spaces coalesce in the White House (1995, xviii).[3] Finally, Caroli highlights the fact that the election process, particularly the heightened involvement of candidates' wives in political campaigns during the twentieth century, expands the role and significance of political spouses (1995, xix).

Even without "a constitutional directive or formal portfolio," the majority of first ladies have "exercised authority . . . by virtue of marriage," insofar as most have "support[ed] a two-person/one career White House" (Winfield 1994, 59, 61). Some first ladies have achieved political agency without violating norms of femininity by cultivating what I term a "social" political style. Since the inception of the role, first ladies have been expected to perform social and ceremonial functions. The political power that inhered in this social role historically has been occluded, but even a brief examination of the actions of first ladies reveals the impact of social style. The exemplar for first ladies' social style is Dolley Madison, a presidential spouse typically remembered for "throwing great parties" (and wrongly credited with introducing the United States to ice cream). Madison's "parties," however, were strategically orchestrated political events designed to facilitate the political aims that she shared with her husband, James Madison. Mayo and Meringolo cite one example of her social style as follows:

> She invited James Madison's enemies in Congress to dinner, and with her warmth and gregariousness won support for him before the 1812 election. So charming and hospitable was she at these gatherings that Congressman Jonathan Roberts observed, "You cannot discover who [are] her husband's friends or foes." Her sixteen years as a leader of Washington society established Dolley Madison as the most dominant force in the social life of the early republic. (1994, 16–17)

Not only did Madison's social prowess earn her the reputation as a "dominant force in the social life of the early republic," it also promoted her and her husband politically. Caroli observes that Madison's dinner for members of Congress during the 1812 campaign led politician James Blaine to "credi[t] Dolley with a large share in her husband's 1812 victory" (1995, 15).

This version of social style is based upon Robert Hariman's (1995) theory of political style, which posits that style is connected to power in intimate and fundamental ways. He defines political style as "a coherent repertoire of rhetorical conventions depending on aesthetic reactions for political effect," and identifies four styles prominent in male-dominated political spheres: realist, republican, courtly, and bureaucratic (13). According to Hariman, political style operates through rules for speech, interaction, and performance. It functions to shape identity, generate consensus, and distribute power. For example, the realist style is exemplified in Machiavelli and instantiates the political actor as strategist. Speech is devalued in the realist style, artlessness is professed, and text is sublimated for a focus on "unencumbered experience" (13–49). Conversely, the republican style, which is premised on the Ciceronian citizen-orator, privileges rhetoric, operates from consensus, and draws power from heroic *mythos* (95–140). In the courtly style, roles of decorum are sovereign, attention is focused on the body, and speech is suppressed (51–94). The bureaucratic style, drawing on the work of Franz Kafka, catalogues the "set of communicative conventions uniquely constitutive of office culture" (142) and examines the power of assimilation (141–76).

Hariman presents his four political styles as androgynous, equally employable by women and men. Yet, the archetypes used to generate each style (Machiavelli, Kapuscinski, Kafka) are male and the gendered nature of political power is not a question tackled by Hariman. He does suggest, however, that his typology is just a beginning, and he urges other scholars to explore additional versions of political style. The analyses in this book respond in part to that call by suggesting a social style derived from the first lady's role as hostess and social partner of her husband.

Dolley Madison was not the first presidential spouse to enact the social style. Social obligations of first ladies began to be defined earlier at the turn of the nineteenth century, when Louisa Adams "traveled around Washington, calling on as many as twenty-five women in a single day from a list her husband drew up for her" (Mayo and Meringolo 1994, 18). The fact that John Quincy Adams took the time to prescribe an itinerary for his wife testifies to the political import of social interactions.

The political nature of private sphere activities routinely is downplayed, particularly in reference to the activities of political wives. For example, when First Lady Edith Roosevelt held weekly meetings with wives of cabinet members, presidential aide Archibald Butt assumed that the women did little more than "take tea and compare crochet patterns." Helen Taft, wife of the secretary of war, also referred to these gatherings as social affairs, and her assertion shows an understanding of "social affairs" as innocuous and apolitical (Caroli 1995, 121–22). From another perspective, however, Roosevelt's gatherings were every bit as much an enactment of a social style that fostered the accomplishment of political goals.

Grace Coolidge facilitated her husband's political achievements by using social style to temper Calvin Coolidge's interpersonal uneasiness. Caroli notes that "[a]t official receptions, the president curtly nodded to the people and quickly passed from one obligatory handshake to the next while Grace's exceptional memory for names and her genuine concern for guests' comfort made them feel at ease" (1995, 168). Mamie Eisenhower also achieved political advancement for Ike by embodying hospitality. Mayo and Meringolo explain that "[t]hroughout the nation's history, advancing a husband's career through social entertainment has been a traditional female role, and Mamie saw her primary duty as first lady as that of a successful White House hostess" (1994, 21). Similarly, Lady Bird Johnson fulfilled the "responsibilities" of a "political wife" early in her marriage to Lyndon Johnson by accommodating "any of Lyndon's political friends," as well as "those he hoped to bring into that category," whom he frequently brought home unannounced (Caroli 1995, 232–33). Barbara Bush testifies in her autobiography about George Bush's propensity to bring home guests with virtually no notice, both before and after their arrival in the White House (1994).

These examples illustrate how the social style of first ladies functions to support the political achievements of United States presidents, deflating the myth that politics historically has been transacted only by men in the public sphere. As early as the eighteenth century, women participated in politics through their social interactions. One assumption underlying this social style is that political power is rooted not just in the public sphere but also in private interactions. Consequently, one implication of defining political power in this manner is the collapse (or, at least, intermingling) of public and private spheres.

Abigail McCarthy notes that political wives contribute to their husbands' careers by providing "status maintenance, intellectual contributions, and public performance" (1984, 215). Social style, however, has not been used exclusively to further the political agendas of male politicians. Some first ladies have also employed the social style in service of their own political or personal goals. Florence Harding garnered favorable journalistic coverage by "invit[ing] newspaperwomen to cruise down the Potomac with her on the presidential yacht"

(Caroli 1995, 162). Eleanor Roosevelt invited young African American women from the National Training School for Girls to a White House garden party, using a feminine medium of entertaining to make a progressive statement about race (Beasley 1987, 101–2). Mayo and Meringolo note that many first ladies extended their role as the "nation's hostess" in order to act "as diplomats," identifying Eleanor Roosevelt, Jacqueline Kennedy, Pat Nixon, and Nancy Reagan as examples of first ladies who used the social style in this manner (1994, 23).

Each of these anecdotes begins to suggest a typology for social style. First, social style is gendered feminine and power resides in the ceremonial presence. As such, it challenges the masculinized forms of public, political power that dominate most critical discussions. Second, the social style brings together components of Hariman's (1995) courtly and republican styles. From the courtly style it draws a focus on decorum, minimization of speech, and attention to the body. Since first ladies have always been quasi royalty in America, their style is likely to dovetail in some respects with the courtly style (Campbell 1996, 188). From the republican style the social style garners an emphasis on consensus, efforts to foster a constituent base, and the standard of civic virtue. Although first ladies have been America's royals, they also are expected to be "regular citizens." First ladies like Nancy Reagan who have embraced the royal air too enthusiastically are harshly criticized. Like their presidential counterparts, republican first ladies must exude the air of civic virtue and embody American patriotism and spirit, an aspect of social style at which Barbara Bush was especially adept.

The social style has developed, in part, as a response to the double bind that casts first ladies as simultaneously courtly and republican. They are caught between styles that sublimate and privilege speech, and attend (alternately) to the body and the mind. Consequently, a third component of the social style is that it enacts political power while disguising its nature as political. In this way, the social style invokes the realist style's artistry disguised by professed artlessness. First ladies have been forced to disguise their political power by professing apoliticism. Some of the most political first ladies such as Barbara Bush have been the most insistent about their disconnection from political matters (Sullivan 1992, 42). Finally, the social style is defined by the constraint of conforming to norms of femininity while, at the same time, developing a tacit ability to employ femininity in order to achieve political agency.

First ladies have generated limited political agency by strategically employing social style and outwardly conforming to norms of traditional femininity. Yet, the first ladyship remains a controversial role because so many first ladies transgressed expectations that they would "stay out" of politics, involving themselves explicitly in national governance. Some first ladies acted as gatekeepers, influencing governance by monitoring communication exchanges. Abigail Adams "kept [John Adams] informed of political sentiment" in Massachusetts while he was away (Caroli 1995, 11). Eleanor Roosevelt left notes for FDR beside his bedside at night so he would attend to matters she deemed important, and she "brought individuals to meet the president and steered the conversations into fields of her own interest (Beasley 1987, 103).[4] After Woodrow Wilson had his stroke in 1919, Edith Wilson began to monitor correspondence so that "[a]ny communication that reached the president went first to the president's wife" (Caroli 1995, 149). Caroli reports that "[r]equests to the president frequently began 'Dear Mrs. Wilson,' indicating that the writers recognized her as controlling access to the president." Some first ladies downplayed the significance of their influence by tying their actions to their "wifely" duty to care for their husbands. Roosevelt garnered the reputation as FDR's "eyes and ears," promoting her activist outings as actions of a devoted wife (Beasley 1987, 104). Sarah Polk justified her involvement in James Polk's political activities by claiming that she was "assisting her husband in order to protect his health" (Caroli 1995, 63). After James Polk became fatigued due to the late hours he kept reading papers, Sarah Polk began to read them for him, marking "those portions she thought deserving of his attention" (Caroli 1995, 63).

In addition to garnering political agency by serving as gatekeepers for their spouses, many first ladies have participated explicitly in political decision-making. Caroli explains that while "an NBC special on [First Lady Nancy Reagan], broadcast in June 1985, showed her laughingly dismissing accounts of her political expertise and interest," only "the naive believed," since "high White House sources . . . described her as 'indispensable,' 'a savvy adviser,' and important on political matters, such as 'getting the Russians to a summit,' personnel decisions, such as removing Alexander Haig from the cabinet, and procedures, such as preparing her husband for debates against Walter Mondale during the 1984 campaign" (1995, 277). Sarah Polk, one of Reagan's nineteenth-century predecessors, achieved political agency by developing "her own supporters—people who valued her abilities and judgment apart from her husband's. In that respect, she foreshadows a later development that saw its culmination in the campaign buttons, 'Betty's husband for President'" (Caroli 1995, 62).

This history of involvement by first ladies in presidential administrations has resulted in widespread recognition of the influence of first ladies in American politics. Caroli notes that "[b]oth outspoken Eleanor Roosevelt and reticent Bess Truman were named during their husbands' administrations as among the 'most powerful people in Washington,' while the vice-presidents were conspicuously absent from such lists" (1995, xvii). Of course, such influence is not always well received. Opponents of first ladies' power have disparagingly used such terms as "Madame President" for Abigail Adams (Winfield 1994, 61), "petticoat government," referring to the Wilson administration (Caroli 1995, 149), and "Lady Macbeth in a headband" in reference to Hillary Rodham Clinton (Miller 1992, 280; Sullivan and Levin 1995, 279). But scholars of the first ladyship agree that while derogatory labels are often applied to so-called "exceptional" first ladies such as Adams, Roosevelt, and Rodham Clinton, the vast majority of first ladies have used their position to enact political power. Caroli and Winfield (1994, 66) note that Rodham Clinton received unusual attention because she was particularly candid about her involvement in administration activities; Caroli underscores that "[t]he candor—not the power—was new" (1995, 307).

In order to further women's agency in the political sphere, the "overt, not covert, power" of first ladies must be recognized (Grimes 1990, 328). Although the "private influence" of first ladies through the employment of "pillow talk" is widely acknowledged and accepted, their public participation in administration business is deemed improper. Pierre Saint-Amand explains the ramifications of that bias for women, claiming:

> Influence is perceived as a form of hysterical persuasion, the incessant effort on the part of the woman to meddle in male discourse or performance. But at the same time influence condemns the woman to illegitimacy; it is a sort of enunciator who is revealed only in the utterance of the other, the one vested with authority of discourse and action. Influence, in the end, always exposes a woman in her impotence. (1994, 385)

Thus, although first ladies may achieve legitimate political agency through private influence, if that is the only type of agency sanctioned by the culture, political discourse and action are reified as male activity. Some locate concern over the first lady's power in her status as a "behind the scenes" operator or as an unelected official, but both of those concerns prove to be disingenuous. First, if critics truly were more concerned about covert influence, they would have been more deeply troubled by, for example, Barbara Bush or Nancy Reagan than Hillary Rodham Clinton. The outcry over Rodham Clinton's appointment to head the task force on health-care reform demonstrated that the public experienced greater consternation over a first lady who exercised her power in public, perhaps because in order to assess Rodham Clinton's use of political power, everyone had to acknowledge it. That acknowledgment countered the cultural narrative that casts the first lady as an embodiment of domestic femininity, and undermines the ways in which American womanhood has been defined. With reference to the second charge, that first ladies' political power is improper because they are not elected, Katha Pollitt rightly points out that "no one who serves in a presidential administration is elected except the Vice President" (1993, 657). Moreover, those who impugn the political involvement of first ladies in their husbands' administrations routinely trade on sexist stereotypes, illustrating the misogynistic assumptions that guide the ways in which first ladies often are perceived. Uncovering sexist assumptions in the discourses surrounding the first ladyship facilitates a broader recognition of the ways in which stereotypes constrain all women in the public sphere and operate as rhetorics of containment.

The first ladyship in the United States can be conceived of as a site of women's agency because of the pragmatic and creative strategies employed by first ladies who found themselves situated within cultural narratives of containment and expected to fulfill norms of traditional femininity. Historically, first ladies have balanced personal desires to facilitate the political goals of the presidential administrations they supported with impulses to achieve political agency for themselves. Although presidential spouses exhibit a variety of responses to the rhetorical situations they face, many have helped create a political style premised on the power of ceremonial, social, and private exchanges. In so doing, first ladies challenge the legitimacy of drawing distinctions between social and political spheres. An even more important contribution of U.S. first ladies to the project of promoting women's political agency, however, is the implicit challenge many have posed to understanding identity as discrete and uniform. Insofar as the rhetoric of the first ladyship exhibits paradox and heterogeneity, it offers potential correctives to the double binds faced by all women. In the concluding section of this essay, I argue that by enacting rhetorical strategies that employ paradox, U.S. first ladies have challenged the double bind and modeled the ways in which political women can develop more complex public personae.

The First Lady: A Site of Heterogeneity and Paradox

One characteristic of the public personae of many first ladies is heterogeneity, and this characteristic, perhaps above all others, has the potential to liberate women insofar as it helps to confound the double binds that constrain women. Diane Shoos theorized the "heterogeneity of the individual female subject," underscoring the complex, multifaceted nature of identity and challenging the dichotomous logic that curtails women's agency (1992, 225). For example, Abigail Adams's heterogeneity is illustrated in a description provided by her grandson, Charles Francis Adams, who wrote that she was "a farmer cultivating the land and discussing the weather and the crops; a merchant reporting prices current and the rates of exchange and directing the making up of invoices; a politician speculating upon the probabilities of war, and a mother . . . and in all she appears equally well" (Caroli 1995, 27).

The potential of heterogeneous individual identities to liberate women lies not in the mere recognition of the multiple roles played by each person, but rather is located in the notion that identity is complex. Tamara K. Hareven observes that "between the two extreme images of Eleanor Roosevelt—that of the shallow busybody first lady and that of the humanitarian reformer and consummate politician—stands a complex figure full of contradictions and paradoxes, a social reformer who could not be easily stereotyped" (1984, 201). Many, in particular the mass media, reinforce dichotomous thinking because it helps to order complicated social narratives and makes political actors more easily identifiable as "heroes" or "villains." The January 15, 1996, cover of *Newsweek* magazine that labeled Hillary Rodham Clinton "Saint or Sinner?" oversimplified a complex public persona, fostered vilification and scapegoating, and ignored the evolutionary nature of human identity. Identity is best conceived of as a process characterized by contradiction and paradox. Mayo and Meringolo observe that Mamie Eisenhower was noted both for her traditional femininity and for a "spine of steel" that made it appear "as if it were she who had been a five-star general" (1994, 22). Similarly, Caroli notes that Caroline Harrison is remembered for two very "different achievements—starting the White House china collection and helping make one of the country's major medical schools [Johns Hopkins] coeducational" (1995, 108). As these examples suggest, to label any first lady "feminine" or "feminist," "activist" or "reticent," "influential" or "marginal," ignores the nuances of first ladies' political identities.

This book examines modern U.S. first ladies from a rhetorical perspective. Each chapter augments the standard portraits with an appreciation of the symbolic—the persuasive power of the words and visual images of first ladies, the rhetorical use of first ladies as symbols, and the complexity of identity as it is constructed symbolically.

Notes

1. My analysis regarding containment and U.S. culture first appeared in Karrin Vasby Anderson, "'Rhymes with Rich': 'Bitch' as a Tool of Containment in Contemporary American Politics" (1999, 599–623).

2. For elaboration of the argument that domesticity was a governing ideology of the Cold War era see, for example, Kozol (1996, 231–50).

3. For an excellent illustration of the ways in which public business gets transacted in the private spaces of the White House, see Doris Kearns Goodwin (1994).

4. Also see Goodwin (1994, 15) for references to "the Eleanor basket—in which the first lady regularly left memoranda, communications, and reports for the president to read."

References

Anderson, Karrin Vasby. 1999. "Rhymes with Rich": "Bitch" as a Tool of Containment in Contemporary American Politics. *Rhetoric & Public Affairs*, 2, 599–623.

Barone, Michael. 1992. Entering the Combat Zone. *U.S. News & World Report*, 30 March, 39. [Online] *Expanded Academic ASAP*, accessed 29 March 1995.

———. 1994. Bad News for Boomer Liberals. *U.S. News & World Report*, 29 August, 32. [Online] *Expanded Academic ASAP*, accessed 27 October 1995.

Beasley, Maurine H. 1987. *Eleanor Roosevelt and the Media: A Public Quest for Self-Fulfillment*. Urbana, Ill.: University of Illinois Press.

Bush, Barbara. 1994. *A Memoir*. New York: St. Martin's Press.

Campbell, David. 1992. *Writing Security: United States Foreign Policy and the Politics of Identity*. Minneapolis, Minn.: University of Minnesota Press.

Campbell, Karlyn Kohrs. 1989. *Man Cannot Speak for Her*, Vol. 1. New York: Greenwood.

———. 1996. The Rhetorical Presidency: A Two-Person Career. In *Beyond the Rhetorical Presidency*, ed. Martin J. Medhurst, 179–95. College Station, Tex.: A & M University Press.

Carlson, Margaret. 1992. All Eyes on Hillary. *Time*, 14 September, 28. [Online] *Expanded Academic ASAP*, accessed 27 October 1995.

Caroli, Betty Boyd. 1995. *First Ladies*, expanded edition. New York: Oxford University Press.

Daughton, Suzanne M. 1994. Women's Issues, Women's Place: Gender-Related Problems in Presidential Campaigns. *Communication Quarterly*, 42, 106–19.

Douglass, Susan J. 1994. *Where the Girls Are: Growing Up Female with the Mass Media*. New York: Random House.

Farley, Christopher John. 1993. Commander Hillary. *Time*, 26 April, 7, [Online] *Expanded Academic ASAP*, accessed 27 October 1995.

Goodwin, Doris Kearns. 1994. *No Ordinary Time: Franklin and Eleanor Roosevelt: The Home Front in World War II*. New York: Simon & Schuster.

Greer, Germaine. 1995. Abolish Her: The Feminist Case against First Ladies. *New Republic*, 26 June, 20–26, [Online] *Expanded Academic ASAP*, accessed 27 October 1995.

Grimes, Ann. 1990. *Running Mates: The Making of a First Lady*. New York: William Morrow.

Hareven, Tamara K. 1984. ER and Reform. In *Without Precedent: The Life and Career of Eleanor Roosevelt*, ed. Joan Hoff-Wilson and Marjorie Lightman, 201–13. Bloomington, Ind.: Indiana University Press.

Hariman, Robert. 1995. *Political Style: The Artistry of Power*. Chicago: University of Chicago Press.

Jamieson, Kathleen Hall. 1995. *Beyond the Double Bind: Women and Leadership*. New York: Oxford University Press.

Kimmel, Michael. 1996. *Manhood in America: A Cultural History*. New York: Free Press.

Kornbluth, Jesse. 1995. Free Advice: Five Historians Comment on Hillary's Dilemma. *New Yorker*, 30 January, 34.

Kozol, Wendy. 1996. Good Americans. In *Bonds of Affection*, ed. John Bodnar, 231–50. Princeton, N.J.: Princeton University Press.

May, Elaine Tyler. 1988. *Homeward Bound: American Families in the Cold War Era*. New York: Basic Books.

Mayo, Edith P. 1993. The Influence and Power of First Ladies. *Chronicle of Higher Education*, 15, A52.

Mayo, Edith P., and Denise D. Meringolo. 1994. *First Ladies: Political Role and Public Image*. Washington, D.C.: Smithsonian Institution.

McCarthy, Abigail Q. 1984. ER as First Lady. In *Without Precedent: The Life and Career of Eleanor Roosevelt*, ed. Joan Hoff-Wilson and Marjorie Lightman, 214–25. Bloomington, Ind.: Indiana University Press.

The Merry Wives of Washington. 1992. *Economist*, 8 August, 26.

Miller, Judith. 1992. The Cookie-Cutter Wives of Politics. *Vogue*, November, 280–83.

Pollitt, Katha. 1993. The Male Media's Hillary Problem: First Lady Bashing. *The Nation*, 17 May, 657. [Online] *Expanded Academic ASAP*, accessed 27 October 1995.

Riley, Susan. 1987. *Political Wives: The Lives of the Saints*. Toronto: Deneau.

Saint-Amand, Pierre. 1994. Terrorizing Marie Antoinette. *Critical Inquiry*, 20, 379–400.

Shoos, Diane. 1992. The Female Subject of Popular Culture. *Hypatia*, 7, 215–26.

Steele, Scott. 1992. A Man of Hope (Ark.). *Maclean's*, 16 November, 43.

Sullivan, Andrew. 1992. Sacred Cow. *New Republic*, 22 June, 42.

Sullivan, Patricia A., and Carole Levin. 1995. Women and Political Communication: From the Margins to the Center. In *Political Rhetoric, Power, and Renaissance Women*, ed. Carole Levin and Patricia A. Sullivan, 275–82. New York: State University of New York Press.

Truman, Margaret. 1995. *First Ladies: An Intimate Group Portrait of White House Wives*. New York: Fawcett Columbine.

Walsh, Kenneth T. 1992. Barbara Bush's Subtle and Significant Campaign Role. *U.S. News & World Report*, 27 April, 36.

Winfield, Betty Houchin. 1994. "Madame President": Understanding a New Kind of First Lady. *Media Studies Journal*, 8, 59–71.

Zaeske, Susan. 1995. The "Promiscuous Audience" Controversy and the Emergence of the Early Woman's Rights Movements. *Quarterly Journal of Speech*, 81, 191–207.

Chapter 2

Ida Saxton McKinley
Indomitable Spirit or Autocrat of the Sick Bed

Nancy L. Herron

> The country saw Mrs. McKinley just as she liked to see herself—a frail and gentle lady, martyred by the demands of her position, but sweetly resigned to meeting them because of her love for her husband.
>
> —Margaret Leech

Ida Saxton McKinley was born too soon. An intelligent, vivacious, and well-educated young woman, her bright mind was shattered by deaths she could not understand, including the loss of her two young daughters. Her world was dimmed by bromides, a medicine prescribed to prevent the dreaded grand mal seizures, whose side effects left her with dulled wits, skin rashes, headaches and the ever-ready petit mal seizures, which her husband deftly finessed with his handkerchief. This first lady functioned as the distaff side of a political dyad in a world only beginning to recognize the rhetorical potential of a woman in the White House. At the turn of the century, media coverage of presidential affairs was just beginning to include the activities of first ladies; a national audience with an appetite to know about the president's wife and family had just begun to emerge (Caroli 1995, 108–9).

Despite Mrs. McKinley's neurological challenges, her life as first lady covered two presidential terms and spanned two centuries. Her American biographers view her as "an obscure first lady," and her paradoxical story raises many questions. On the one hand, she was a well-to-do, beautiful, educated young woman who married for love a man of poorer and humbler background. As a

31

young girl, she was healthy, even vigorous, and could walk ten miles a day as a
tourist, climbing mountains in Switzerland and riding mules in an Alpine
meadow. But this same young woman, after two consecutive pregnancies, became sick with phlebitis, possibly suffered irretrievable brain damage, and was
diagnosed with epilepsy. Her life was transformed by fate and circumstance
from that of a young career woman to "a revelation of the glory of the woman at
Home" ("Mrs. McKinley and Mrs. Bryan" 1900, 955). Interestingly, as her health
declined her husband's career advanced; he won the presidency in the election
of 1896.

This chapter is a commentary on the life of a potentially powerful first lady
who was robbed of her strengths by disability and possibly over-medication. So
severe were her infirmities that she was frequently propped up at state dinners
so, when convulsing, her presidential husband could toss a handkerchief over
her face until she composed. Most remarkable was her unwavering determination to assume her role as First Lady of the Land and to stay close to her husband no matter what the cost. So little was expected of a first lady at this time
that the public could easily accept "a doll-like figure propped up against some
cushions" (Caroli 1995, 112).

Biography

Ida Saxton McKinley was born in Canton, Ohio, on June 8, 1847. The National
First Ladies Library website (www.firstladies.org) describes her as the elder
daughter of a socially prominent family. She came from strong stock. Her paternal grandfather established his own newspaper, *The Ohio Repository*, in 1815
and continued to manage and edit it for the next fifty years. In addition to his job
as the town of Canton's printer, Saxton also became a land agent and took on the
civic offices of county commissioner, county auditor, and postmaster. He died in
1871 at the age of 79. His son James A. Saxton, Ida's father, was president of
the Stark County Bank and one of the most influential and prominent citizens
during his active life. He was an accomplished businessman, who was known to
be indulgent to his two daughters, Ida and Mary. He educated them well in local
schools, and they attended a fashionable finishing school for young women; he
also sent them to Europe on the "Grand Tour." In the letters Ida sent home to her
parents, she showed a sincere fondness for her family and demonstrated a high
level of intelligence, an intellectual curiosity, and an ability to communicate
clearly in writing. Traveling with an older woman chaperone, a demand of the
mores of the time, Ida often handled the finances and made the travel arrangements. She demonstrated shrewdness for organization and because the chaperone showed no talent for adequately leading the group, Ida often had the final
word.

Ida's biographers indicate that being pretty, fashionable, and a leader of the
younger set in Canton did not satisfy her. She was interested in a career and
became a cashier in her father's bank. She learned to perform her duties so well
that she would at times take over for her father when he was out of town (Olcott

1916, vol. 1, 68). She caught the attention of Major William McKinley, a Civil War hero, who had come to Canton in 1867 to establish a law practice. They fell deeply in love. According to historians, McKinley met his future wife at a church picnic and visited her regularly on Sunday mornings when they were both on their way to church. McKinley attended the Methodist church and Ida taught Sunday school at the Presbyterian church in Canton (Heckler-Feltz 1995, 7E). The two were married on January 25, 1870, in Christ Presbyterian Church; the wedding reception was held in the bride's home on South Market Avenue. While McKinley advanced in his profession, his young wife devoted her time to home and family. A daughter Katherine was born on Christmas Day, 1871; a second daughter Ida was born in April 1873. Tragically, Ida Saxton McKinley and her second infant fell seriously ill and the frail baby died in August 1874. Ida McKinley's health shattered; she became a confirmed invalid even before her elder child Katie died two years later.

After an early life of comfort and privilege, her married life while blissful in the early days was fraught with other great sorrows. In 1873, a series of deaths in the family almost unhinged Ida McKinley; her grandfather Saxton passed away, then her mother Katherine Dewalt Saxton died unexpectedly. Ida developed phlebitis, which left her partly crippled. She also suffered brain damage, severe headaches, and epileptic seizures both mild and major. In 1876, the year her husband was elected to Congress, four-year-old Katie died of typhoid fever. These losses, coupled with her weakened physical and mental state, greatly debilitated this once attractive banker's daughter with the "languorous eyes" and turned her into a sickly, self-centered, and at times querulous semi-invalid who was totally dependent on her husband for getting around in the world (Beer 1929, 102–3). On October 7, 1898, during the first presidential term, more family tragedy unfolded with the murder of her only brother George, an alcoholic, who was shot dead by his mistress. This event created the most sensational murder case of the time and made headlines in newspapers across the country.

While tragedy plagued her personal life, success followed her husband's professional life. He was awarded a law degree in 1871, and his fledgling law practice prospered. With his warm and outgoing personality, his legendary war record, and his reputation for integrity and fair play, he became a successful candidate for Congress in 1876. He was elected governor of Ohio in 1892. Biographers note that as governor, he stopped business every day at 3:00 p.m. to wave a handkerchief to his ailing wife who lived across the street in a hotel. McKinley won the election for president of the United States in 1896, defeating the popular Nebraska orator William Jennings Bryan.

During the much-publicized campaign of 1896 and after that as well, much was made of the differences between Mrs. McKinley and Mrs. Bryan. Mrs. McKinley was presented to the American public as a helpmate, although often sickly. When she felt well enough, she campaigned with her husband from their front porch in Canton. When she could not be present because of her illness, her absence still helped McKinley's public image. Women were attracted to his compassion for his wife, and they would bring their husbands to meet him. His devotion to Ida became part of his appeal as a candidate. Sometimes she looked so terrible that rumors began to fly about the causes. To set the record straight, a special campaign biography was circulated. According to Anthony, this was "the first of its kind for a candidate's wife" (1990, 283).

Mrs. Bryan projected a much different image in the newly emerging mass media. A lawyer by training, she functioned more as her husband's political partner, researching and editing his speeches. The two women were seen as coming from contrasting schools of culture. In a popular magazine article written during the reelection campaign of 1900, the public portrayal of Ida Saxton McKinley was:

> An invalid for very many years past, Mrs. McKinley's faithful presence beside her husband at state functions, her frail form clad in the rich, ceremonious dress proper to the occasion, describes a gentle martyrdom, the indescribable pathos of which is written in the expression of her sweet pale face. Her meager physical ability may accomplish no marvelous intellectual or social feats. When she has not appeared as First Lady of the Land, seated, for want of strength to stand, beside her husband discharging the social duties of his illustrious office, she has done her utmost, and doing this, she becomes an inspiration to all women who for one reason or another are hindered from playing a brilliant individual role in life. She is a revelation of the glory of the woman at home. Mrs. McKinley's want of strength is the obverse of her husband's highest power. It is the occasion of his supreme devotion, the chief source of the great moral force emanating from self-forgetful concern for the weak ones of earth. President McKinley's never-failing thought of his invalid wife is a matter of history. His re-election would provide the American people a First Lady who exalts mere womanliness above anything that women dare to do. ("Mrs. McKinley and Mrs. Bryan" 1900, 955)

In contrast, Mrs. Bryan was described in the same article as follows:

> Mrs. Bryan is a woman of action—a successful woman. She has been admitted to the bar—a full-fledged lawyer. She is interested in the reforms in which her sex takes today the initiative; she is a club woman; she is a student, whose mind is a storehouse of information on all subjects that pertain to her husband's duties and ambitions. It was said that the speech in Congress which first brought Mr. Bryan into national prominence was written by his wife. She is eminently able to have done this and the rumor doubtless arose from the well-known fact that she does assist her husband in his work. . . . Mrs. Bryan's influence as wife of the President of the United States would compel women to know and to think about the questions of the day. She would be a needed stimulant to the woman who aims at nothing at all. Mrs. McKinley—a vivid antithesis—is always a needed gentle sedative to the typical woman of today who aims to do too much. ("Mrs. McKinley and Mrs. Bryan" 1900, 956)

This type of journalism was a landmark approach to examining first ladies and the roles they played in the advancement of their husbands' careers. As the century turned, newspapers and magazines began to compare not only the political contenders but their spouses as well. A national audience began to emerge with an appetite for news about the president, his wife, and family (Caroli 1995, 108). In the case of Ida McKinley, biographers indicate that newspapers and magazines were silent about her illness and medication. When William McKinley stepped onto the national stage as a political figure, his wife was already taking large quantities of bromides to control her seizures. Bromide salts, used as early as 1857, were the first of the depressant drugs prescribed for the treatment and control of epilepsy. How this medication affected Ida McKinley is a matter of conjecture because bromides were a valuable sedative when properly employed, but when used in excess, they often produced harmful results. How her use of the medication affected her public image is also a matter of conjecture. It is difficult to tell how much the press actually knew. Even if they were aware of her medical problems and treatment, they would have thrown a veil of silence over matters this personal. For the most part, the press presented her in formal pose—maintaining a distance, so she seems "obscure" from a contemporary perspective, as will be discussed further below.

Despite her neurological problems, biographers like Lewis L. Gould repeatedly mention that Ida McKinley was at the center of William's emotional life in the White House. She insisted on being his hostess despite her frequent fits and fainting spells, and he bore with her determination. Her physical resources were too limited to meet the demands of so public a life and, during the years of his first term as president, there was a round of near embarrassments, periodic relapses, and incessant demands on his time. Through it all, McKinley remembered his wife as he first knew her: "Ida was the most beautiful girl you ever saw," he said, "She is beautiful to me now" (Gould 1980, 5). Nothing gave him more pleasure than, in 1899, acquiring their old house in Canton and discussing with his wife how they would renovate and restore it. Biographers agree that McKinley loved her as he did no one else, and he never chafed under the weight of her invalidism and selfishness. Often, when her headaches required it, they sat together in the dark. To her he was, until he died, "Your faithful husband and always your lover" (Gould 1980, 242).

The final and tragic blow in her life came on September 6, 1901, at the Pan-American Exposition in Buffalo, when Ida Saxton McKinley's husband was shot by Leon Czolgosz, a paranoid whose fantasies had been excited by revolutionist propaganda and the recent assassination of the king of Italy. Before taking on his presidential duties that day and always thinking about what was best for his wife, the president had taken Ida for a carriage ride to see a scenic gorge outside the city. Returning within the hour to deliver an important speech, McKinley, accompanied by three secret service men and his entourage, entered the Temple of Music to receive guests. Czolgosz was among those waiting to welcome the president; unbeknownst to anyone, he had camouflaged a small caliber pistol with a handkerchief. As the president extended his hand, Czolgosz fired the gun at point-blank range, wounding McKinley in the chest. Moments after being struck by the bullet that finally killed him, his thoughts were for his wife who was resting nearby at a private residence. Fearing the shock of the incident might imperil her delicate health, he turned to his secretary, George B. Cortelyou, and said: "My wife, be careful how you tell her—oh, be careful." At the time, his doctors thought the president's life would be saved, but unfortunately, they could not find the bullet that had lodged in his pancreas. Eventually, gangrene set in and on September 13 his condition worsened. Putting his arm around his wife he began to whisper the words of the hymn, "Nearer, my God to Thee, nearer to Thee." He died at 2:15 a.m. on September 14 with Ida beside him.

After her husband's death, Ida returned to Canton where she lived for the six remaining years of her life. Murat Halstead, interviewing her for an article that appeared in *The Saturday Evening Post* of September 6, 1902, described her appearance as follows:

> She has aged since that sad, dread September, as if many bitter years had passed. There is a depth of grief newly written in her face, leaving the beauty of feature, but there is a haunting, tremulous, wistful expression there, even keener than her words: "There is now nothing for me but to wait, and I want to go." (6–7)

Interestingly enough, after William McKinley's untimely death, Ida never again suffered the epileptic seizures that ravaged her throughout her married life. She died at her home in Canton in 1907.

From the perspective of history, in those very early years Ida had been a visionary. She emerges from a web of secondary sources including statements of friends, notes of political colleagues of her husband, and biographers, as the only one who saw in her young Civil War hero husband a caliber of individual equal to the task of leading others. This perception came at a time when many political contemporaries deemed him as "not good enough." From a rhetorical perspective and because of the absence of formal statements that could be attributed to her, Mrs. McKinley's life as a public figure must be defined in terms of her actions rather than by her words. In her personal life and in the political life she shared with her husband, there can be seen a "rhetoric without words" just as Andre Malraux, late minister of culture of France in the 1960s, spoke of "museums without walls." It is through her controlled and her controlling actions that the power of this first lady can be examined and analyzed.

Rhetorical Activities as First Lady

Mrs. McKinley was viewed in her time as a traditional wife; her husband's career was at the center of her life, especially after she lost her children. When the McKinley's entered the White House in 1897, Ida wanted to play an active role in all of the presidential events, but what she could do was limited by her illness. Nonetheless, she insisted on attending dinners, meeting with visiting dignitaries, and even accompanying the president on trips outside the White House, including travel by train across the country. Her husband was always attentive, even when she would lapse into seizures or exhibit other inappropriate behaviors such as outbursts of temper. His devotion to her was reported to the public and it enhanced his reputation. As we have seen, it may even have secured him votes. Though there is little evidence of any written or oral communication by the first lady to the public, she seems to have influenced her husband on some public policies through their private conversations, and she also helped him financially. In the press, her image was positive; she appeared a devoted wife, realizing her own ambitions through her husband's successes.

When Mrs. McKinley entered the White House, she "insisted on going everywhere with him," says biographer Kohlsaat, "with a persistence that was part of her disease" (1923, 156). From the beginning, she participated in inaugural events, and even attended both of the inaugural balls. Wearing a white satin dress and diamonds in 1897, as the McKinleys made their way to join the procession, Ida fainted and her husband picked her up and took her home. During the second inaugural ball, she was very sedated and sat propped up in an armchair overlooking the crowd (Anthony 1990, 282, 291). These public appearances continued throughout the years they were in the White House.

Mrs. McKinley wanted to play the social role of first lady, accompanying her husband on all of his official duties. She insisted on meeting important statesmen who visited the White House and to be part of formal receiving lines. She would sit enthroned in a blue velvet chair among pillows that propped her up, holding a bouquet of flowers. This strategy enabled her to avoid shaking hands with anyone; she was probably too weak to do so (Anthony 1990, 285–87). She attended state dinners, altering protocol so that she could sit with her husband, always on his left according to Kohlsaat, who describes one of her fainting spells:

> Frequently, the excitement was too much for her and she fainted. She did not fall out of her chair, but became rigid. The president would throw a handkerchief or napkin over her face and proceed with the conversation as though nothing had happened. The guests would look away and pay no attention to the invalid. When the spasm passed she would be taken to her room by her maid and the White House physician. (1923, 156)

She also insisted on accompanying her husband when he traveled in Washington. His staff had to mark out a special route so that she could be taken home, if she began to have a seizure. On train trips, Mrs. McKinley insisted that she appear on the platform with her husband; she would be pushed out and seated by his side.

How citizens of that day dealt with Mrs. McKinley's illness has interesting rhetorical dimensions. She and some members of the press did form a relationship; she granted interviews and was gracious to reporters. Mostly, the press wrote about her beautiful gowns, sometimes mentioning how much she had spent on them. Mrs. McKinley could afford her luxurious wardrobe because she had a large independent inheritance from her father. However, the press did not write about her infirmities. Margaret Leech says that the unpleasant clinical details were viewed as inappropriate to the sentimental gratification the marriage of the McKinley's afforded the country (1959). Reporters who covered the White House tended to praise Mrs. McKinley's characteristics of sweetness and docility (Caroli 1995, 111–12), while William was viewed very much as a saint, as a model of "presidential compassion" (Anthony 1990, 283). No reporters used the words "epilepsy" or "fits." According to Margaret Leech,

The press . . . could not touch the subject. Opposition newspapers, when not restrained by taste, were muzzled by expediency. Any crude exposure of the facts
would have outraged propriety and induced an outpouring of sympathy for the
President. Besides, there was very little curiosity about the facts. That Mrs.
McKinley was "delicate" was explanation enough. (1959, 433)

Ill health had not yet lost its romantic nineteenth-century aura.

Mrs. McKinley often appeared in magazine photographs throughout the
1890s. She sat in posed position, wearing her beautiful lacey gowns and expensive jewelry. She appeared quite doll-like. Newspapers of the day also pictured
her as a delicate, beautiful invalid. The world came to know her as the lily-like-
lady of the White House, drooping and desolate, but dutiful (Halstead 1901, 6)
Says Margaret Leech:

Many photographs had acquainted the public with her beautiful brow and
dreamy unfocused eyes. An impression of charming fragility was enhanced by
the grace with which she posed, drooping in velvet in the Green Room with a
fan, or languishing in lace in the conservatory. The country saw Mrs. McKinley
just as she liked to see herself—a frail and gentle lady, martyred by the demands of her position, but sweetly resigned to meeting them because of her
love for her husband. (1959, 433)

The public also saw images of Mrs. McKinley projected on the movie screen;
she and her husband being the first presidential couple to be so immortalized.
Always beautifully dressed, coifed, and bejeweled, she was seen on the screen
as small, thin, and frail, walking or sitting beside the robust William McKinley
who had grown portly in middle age.

According to biographers and historians, William McKinley dealt well with
his infirm wife. He projected an image of matrimonial sanctity to the public and
White House staff. Brogan and Mosley tell us that he paid for the few years of
private happiness with the young and beautiful Ida by devoting the rest of his
life to her. He became her psychiatric nurse, and her condition was not always
easy to deal with. There was a fine line between her personality and real illness.
She was often possessive and clinging in a way that might be forgiven in an
invalid, still her actions were often infantile and demanding. Says Carl Anthony:
she was "unpredictable, irrational, and jealous of any woman who neared the
president. . . . Her epilepsy may have been used as an excuse to restrain her, for
when she was either in physical pain or throwing a tantrum, the First Lady was
dosed by the doctors with barbiturates, bromide sedatives, lithium and other
powerful narcotics" (Anthony 1990, 284). When she was sedated, she became
milder, but her mind was duller. Apparently, she had to be sedated because of
how much she insisted on appearing in public and how unsure they were of her
behavior. William was always ready to deal with any signs of seizure, carrying
off what was then perceived to be the "embarrassments of epilepsy" with amazing tact. His essential strength and goodness were shown in the perfect way he
performed his role.

Mrs. McKinley spent most of her time in her room engaged in needlework,
scrubbing her jewelry, and playing cards. She raised a considerable amount of

money for charity through her crocheting. She made 3500 pairs of bedroom slippers and gave them to different charities to raise money (Anthony 1990, 291). She often had her husband called to her side, and they spent much time in discussions. Well-educated, Mrs. McKinley provided the president a dimension of culture and filled in some of the gaps left by his scanty education (Brogan and Mosley 1993, 537). In this way, she was able to play a small part in his life by broadening his horizons and diversifying his social rounds, which would otherwise have been passed exclusively in smoke-filled offices with other politicians. According to Anthony at least some of their discussions touched on matters of public policy. She is said to have influenced his stance at least on the issue of temperance. William McKinley was also president when the *Maine* was sunk in 1898, and subsequently when war was declared on Spain. Ida seems to have influenced her husband to retain the Philippines, once Admiral Dewey had won at Manila Bay. She had been in contact with members of the Presbyterian Church who wanted to convert some of the islanders to Christianity. Her husband decided that he could not leave them to govern themselves; he would have to make sure they were educated and christianized (Anthony 1990, 289–90).

With him she was also generous. In 1893, when he was having financial difficulties, she offered to give him all of the money she had inherited from her father. Her attorneys advised against it, but she told them: "My husband had done everything for me all of my life. Do you mean to deny me the privilege of doing as I please with my own property to help him now?" (Olcott 1916, vol. 1, 291).

There is no evidence of speeches or agendas attributed to Mrs. McKinley or honorary engagements she attended without the involvement of her presidential husband. And little formal evidence exists of written communication when she was first lady. For the most part, her correspondence was social and was frequently written for her by a secretary or by her husband. But sometimes in a demonstration of the independence shown in her youth, Ida would take the completed correspondence and add, in her own clear and firm hand, a short postscript. Unfortunately, much of the early personal correspondence between Ida and William, including love letters, were burned in a warehouse fire in Philadelphia where they had been stored for safekeeping. Surviving only are some early letters sent by Ida from Europe to her parents. Two of her original letters in a firm and beautiful hand presently lay on the desk in the main parlor of her restored childhood home. Also, because President and Mrs. McKinley made extensive use of the telephone, there are few evidences of letters written between them in their later years.

After her husband's death, Ida McKinley returned to Canton where her younger sister cared for her. Once again, she projected the image of dutiful sorrow to those who saw her:

> The most pathetic figure in the world is the widow of President McKinley. Her slender form in black and pale face may be seen nearly every day, and sometimes twice a day, in a heavy dark carriage drawn by a pair of black horses, an equipage of dignity and comfort without display going to and from the McKinley home to the receiving sepulcher where the casket that contains the

remains of her husband is guarded under the flag and palms, and flowers. (Halstead 1901, 6)

Mrs. McKinley died in 1907 and lies entombed beside the president and near their two daughters in Canton's McKinley National Memorial Mausoleum in West Lawn Cemetery. Adjoining the memorial is the McKinley Museum that houses a library and a gallery where animatronics of President and Mrs. McKinley interpret history in their Canton parlor. The gallery contains the world's largest collection of McKinley memorabilia.

Legacy

In spite of her physical limitations, Ida McKinley provided the twentieth century some major characteristics that later first ladies would share throughout the next one hundred years. These characteristics are her legacy. First and foremost, she brought to the position intelligence and education, critical attributes necessary for her to function well as a presidential spouse. She provided, as a matter of course, training in social skills and culture to a less educated husband. As we have seen, Ida Saxton McKinley was world traveled in her early years; she possessed an international perspective and appreciated the culture and arts of other countries. Her background must have been useful during discussions with her husband, as he wrestled with thorny international issues.

As a single young woman, Ida displayed a marked resolve that lasted throughout her life. She first demonstrated the power of her will when she convinced her father that she should have a professional career working outside the home, an unusual choice for a young woman of her day. Employed in her father's bank in Canton, Ohio, she demonstrated facility with accounting and financial enterprise, skills that later helped save her husband's career at a time when financial challenges overwhelmed him. Through her experience and expertise, as well as her inherited income and family connections, she was able to provide financial stability and support for her husband's political aspirations.

In later years, because of her limited physical strength, she practiced a "rhetoric without words" in carrying out her duties as first lady. While often autocratic and jealous in private, she provided the public a picture of culture, grace, and taste that dignified the office. She projected a traditional model of matrimonial expectations that stereotyped women of the day. She was "seen but not heard," was "perfectly groomed," and was "tremendously fond of children." But she also by her visibility as first lady legitimized physical disabilities and forced public acceptance of them in a well-known public figure. She provided a new view of women in the spotlight dealing with family tragedies including death of children and infidelity and alcoholism of a sibling. Her noble way of dealing with the deaths of her daughters, her parents, her brother, and the assassination of her husband showed others how to cope with unbearable sorrow. The way in which she handled adversity demonstrated to the world her iron will and her great courage. The determination to be an exemplary partner for William

McKinley was at the heart of her life. Ida McKinley always assumed her rightful place beside her presidential husband, regardless of the circumstances of her health. Through force of personality and will she provided the emotional stability he needed from the marriage to support a man immersed in the turmoil of the political arena during a turbulent time in American politics.

Regardless of her limitations, Ida McKinley did provide a certain rhetorical perspective on the nature of first ladies as the United States moved into the twentieth century. It is the continuation of the paradox that was her life that the Saxton-McKinley family home, in June 1998, was christened the First Ladies' Library. The restored Victorian house in Canton, Ohio, built in the mid-1800s, was the home of President and Mrs. McKinley during his fourteen years in the U.S. Senate. Located in the historically documented Saxton-McKinley home in downtown Canton, the National First Ladies' Library houses books, newspapers, and other printed materials related to the lives of first ladies as well as the social movements and political policies they influenced. Visitors not only have access to the library's educational materials, they also get a glimpse of a bygone era as they tour the childhood home of America's twenty-fifth first lady.

Distressed that for decades the Smithsonian Museum's only tribute to first ladies was a collection of inaugural gowns and unable to find a reading list for a talk she was to give on Mary Todd Lincoln, Mary Regula, wife of Ohio congressman Ralph Regula, decided that there must be a complete bibliography on all the women who have served in the White House. She assembled a group of thirteen influential women from north-central Ohio and pitched the idea for the library. Together they raised the $100,000 needed to hire noted historian Carl Sferrazza Anthony to assemble the only complete bibliography of all the books, writings, articles, and manuscripts written by and about America's first ladies. That bibliography is the heart of the project. "We will never be about gowns and gloves," Regula says. "We are an educational and resource facility" (quoted in "Historic House Now First Lady Museum" 1999, 10).

After McKinley's assassination his secretary George B. Cortelyou packed up and shipped their personal belongings to Canton, including a closet full of costly dresses, presents, souvenirs and photographs, an oil painting of little Katie, and two small rocking chairs. In contrast to what departed, what arrived for the new presidential family spoke volumes about the changes that were imminent at the White House.

> Delivery wagons rattled up to the Executive Mansion with loads of rugs and furniture, with crates of toys and cases of books, with saddles, stilts, and bicycles. Dogs arrived and guinea pigs. Hunters and hacks pranced in the driveway. Shrieking children rode ponies on the lawn. And a large blue macaw came to live in the conservatory where Mrs. McKinley had lingered, holding a single rose. (Leech 1959, 605)

A new and exciting era in American presidential history had begun with the move of Theodore Roosevelt, his wife Edith, and their family into the executive mansion.

References

Anthony, Carl Sferrazza. 1990. *First Ladies: The Saga of the Presidents' Wives and Their Power, 1789–1990*, Vol. 1. New York: William Morrow.

———. 1992. The First Ladies: They've Come a Long Way, Martha. *Smithsonian*, October, 135–59.

Bassett, Margaret Byrd. 1969. *Profiles and Portraits of American Presidents and Their Wives*. Freeport, Maine: Wheelwright Company.

Beer, Thomas. 1929. *Hanna*. New York: Alfred Knopf.

Belden, Henry S., III, comp. and ed. 1985. *Grand Tour of Ida Saxton McKinley and Sister Mary Saxton Barber, 1869*. Canton, Ohio: Reserve Printing.

Boller, Paul F., Jr. 1988. *Presidential Wives*. New York: Oxford University Press.

Brogan, Hugh, and Charles Mosley. 1993. *American Presidential Families*. New York: Macmillan.

Caroli, Betty Boyd. 1987. *First Ladies*. New York: Oxford University Press.

———. 1995. *First Ladies*, expanded edition. New York: Oxford University Press.

Colman, Edna M. 1927. *White House Gossip: From Andrew Jackson to Calvin Coolidge*. Garden City, N.Y.: Doubleday, Page & Co.

Cortelyou, George Bruce Papers. 1903–1907. Ida McKinley Letters, Cards, and Telegrams. Containers 6, 11, and 40. Washington D.C.: Library of Congress, Manuscript Division.

Diller, Daniel C., and Stephen L. Robertson. 1997. *The Presidents, First Ladies, and Vice Presidents: White House Biographies 1789–1989*. Washington, D.C.: *Congressional Quarterly*.

Evans, Harold. 1998. *The American Century*. New York: Alfred A. Knopf.

Foraker, Julia B. 1932. *I Would Live It Again*. New York: Harper & Brothers.

Frolik, Joe. 1896. The Election of 1896, Much of What We Will See and Hear during This Year's Presidential Campaign Originated at a Time When Many Wondered If the Nation Would Survive. *Plain Dealer* (Cleveland), 19 May, 8.

Furman, Bess. 1951. *White House Profile: A Social History of the White House, Its Occupants, and Its Festivities*. Indianapolis, Ind.: Bobbs-Merrill.

Garfield, Lucretia Papers. 1896–1897. Invitation Card to the McKinley Home and Letter from Mrs. Garfield to William McKinley. Container 59. Washington, D.C.: Library of Congress, Manuscript Division.

Goodman, Louis S., and Alfred Gilman. 1958. *The Pharmacological Basis of Therapeutics*, 2nd ed. New York: Macmillan.

Gould, Lewis. 1980. *The Presidency of William McKinley*. Lawrence, Kans.: The Regents Press of Kansas.

———, ed. 1996. *American First Ladies*. New York: Garland.

Halstead, Murat. 1901. *The Illustrious Life of William McKinley, Our Martyred President*. Chicago: n. pub.

———. 1902. Mrs. McKinley. *Saturday Evening Post*, 6 September, 6–7.

Hartzell, Josiah. 1896. *Sketch of the Life of Mrs. William McKinley*. Washington, D.C.: The Home Magazine Press.

Hay, Peter. 1988. *All the Presidents' Ladies: Anecdotes of the Women behind the Men in the White House*. New York: Viking.

Healy, Diana Dixon. 1988. *America's First Ladies: Private Lives of the Presidential Wives, 1789–1989*. New York: Athenaeum.

Heckler-Feltz, Cheryl. 1995. Presidents' Wives Served with Grace and Resolve. *Plain Dealer* (Cleveland), 17 October, 7E.

Herrick, Myron Timothy Papers. 1889–1906. Correspondence from Ida and William McKinley. *Western Reserve Historical Society Collections.*

Historic House Now First Ladies' Museum. 1999. *Daily News* (McKeesport, Pa.), 24 March, 10.

Historic Walking Tour of West Lawn Cemetery. The McKinley Museum, Canton, Ohio.

Hoover, Irwin A. 1943. *Forty-Two Years in the White House.* Boston: Houghton Mifflin Co.

Johnson, Marilyn. 1992. Ladies of the House. *Life,* 30 October, 80–81.

Kohlsaat, H. H. 1923. *From McKinley to Harding.* New York: Charles Scribner's Sons.

Ladies and Their Gowns. 1897. *Washington Post,* 5 March, n.p.

Leech, Margaret. 1959. *In the Days of McKinley.* New York: Harper & Row.

Logan, Mrs. John A. 1901. *Thirty Years In Washington.* Hartford, Conn.: A. D. Worthington & Co.

McKinley, William Papers. 1895–1901. Correspondence. Series E. Washington, D.C.: Library of Congress, Manuscript Division.

Mayo, Edith, ed. 1996. *The Smithsonian Book of First Ladies.* Washington, D.C.: Smithsonian Press.

Melick, Arden Davis. 1972. *Wives of the Presidents.* Maplewood, N.J.: Hammond.

Morgan, Wayne C. 1963. *William McKinley and His America.* Syracuse, N.Y.: Syracuse University Press.

Mrs. M'Kinley Coming. 1897. *Chicago Times-Herald,* 26 January, n.p.

Mrs. McKinley and Mrs. Bryan: A Comparison. 1900. *Harper's Bazaar,* 11 August, 954–56.

Mrs. McKinley's Child Friends. 1897. *Washington Post,* 5 March, n.p.

National First Ladies Library. The Ida Saxton McKinley House, 331 South Market Avenue, Canton, Ohio 44702. www.firstladies.org.

Nation's First Lady. 1897. *Washington Post,* 5 March, n.p.

Notes on the Presidential Family. 1897. *Washington Post,* 5 March, n.p.

Olcott, Charles S. 1916. *The Life of William McKinley,* Vols. 1 and 2. Boston: Houghton Mifflin.

Porter, Robert P., and James Boyle. 1897. *Life of William McKinley.* Cleveland: N. G. Hamilton Publishing Co.

President and Mrs. McKinley in the Costumes They Will Wear on Inauguration Day. 1897. *Chicago Tribune,* 26 January, n.p.

Prindiville, Kathleen. 1954. *First Ladies.* New York: Macmillan.

Singleton, Esther. 1907. *The Story of the White House,* Vol. 1. New York: McClure and Co.

Slayden, Ellen Maury. 1963. *Washington Wife.* New York: Harper and Row.

Walk with the President. A Permanent Historic Walk by the McKinley Museum. 800 McKinley Monument Drive NW., Canton, Ohio 44708. (330)-455-7043.

Chapter 3

Edith Kermit Roosevelt
First Lady, First Mommy

Catherine M. Hastings

> Maternity was Edith's stock-in-trade. She not only liked it, she made it the symbol of the Roosevelt White House, with spectacularly popular results.
> —Margaret Truman

Edith Kermit Roosevelt gave few public speeches in her lifetime. On the occasion that she spoke to her largest audience, a rally for Republican presidential candidate Herbert Hoover in 1932, her words were not even preserved. Instead, her rhetorical legacy must be read in her more traditional activities, such as hosting an array of White House events and assisting her husband with his mail and his speech writing. A private and somewhat controlling woman, Roosevelt was so protective of her family's image that she tried to manipulate press coverage of her brood by releasing carefully posed photographs of herself and her children to the media at regular intervals. Coming at a time when childhood was being transformed by social changes anyway, she became defined by her role as mother and can be seen to be representative of the new paradigm of parenting. Her achievements as first lady—the establishment of a first lady staff, the renovation of the White House, the china collection, and the first lady portrait collection—are largely forgotten. This essay provides a capsule view of Roosevelt's life and times and an analysis of her rhetorical activities, positing that her rhetorical positioning of herself as "First Mommy" has superseded her other activities as first lady in the public's memory of her.

Biography

Edith Kermit Carow was born in Norwich, Connecticut, on August 6, 1861, the second child of Charles and Gertrude (Tyler) Carow. Both the Carows and Tylers were distinguished families; Charles Carow of Huguenot extraction made his living as a shipping executive in New York, and the Tylers were American aristocracy, settling in Rhode Island in 1638 and claiming descendancy from Jonathan Edwards. Two years after Edith's birth, another girl, Emily, completed the family. As Charles Carow was a lifelong friend of Theodore Roosevelt, father of the future president (McCullough 1981, 37), and the two families lived close by one another (Pringle 1956, 75), Edith and Emily grew up in close contact with the four Roosevelt children. Edith was the same age as Corinne Roosevelt, and they were close friends (Morris 1980, 23). When the Roosevelts took a family trip to Europe in 1869–1870, Edith and Corinne corresponded, as did Edith and Teedie, as Corinne's oldest brother Theodore was known to the family. In fact, when the twelve-year-old Teedie was shown a photograph of Edith during this European trip, he became horribly homesick (McCullough 1981, 105). For a time, the Carow girls were educated at the Roosevelt home by "Aunt Anna" Bulloch Gracie (Morris 1980, 17).

As Edith grew up, her father's fortunes dwindled. Most biographers agree that her childhood was at best insecure (Morris 1980, 15). Her father's business often took him on sea voyages that kept him away from home for months. He may have been an alcoholic (Morris 1980, 15); at best, he was extremely unlucky in business. While her family kept up appearances as long as they could, in later life Edith recalled being embarrassed when the Roosevelt children came to play at her house because her toys were so worn. From Edith's remembrances, Gertrude Carow did not shield her daughters from the realities of the family's gradually diminishing security (20).

In the meantime, by their midteens, Teedie Roosevelt had become Edith's frequent companion. Her friendship with his sister and the closeness of the families made it acceptable for the two to spend time together almost as brother and sister, boating, riding, walking, and debating issues of the day. The elder Roosevelts, understanding Charles Carow's "temporary reverses," invited Edith to accompany them on extended holidays to their summer cottage at Oyster Bay, New York, then a rural garden spot on Long Island's North Shore (McCullough 1981, 143). Teedie and Edith virtually grew up together, which freed them from the exhaustingly elaborate rites of courtship of their class and day as depicted by their friend (and Edith's distant cousin) Edith Wharton in the *Age of Innocence*. In 1876, having named his rowboat after Edith, Teedie left for Harvard (McCullough 1981, 64). He and Edith corresponded, and she visited the college with his family (75).

Edith's education, which had begun with the Roosevelt children under their aunt's tutelage, was completed at the Miss Comstock's School in New York (Caroli 1995, 123), where she was enrolled from 1871 to 1879. Her husband, himself an avid reader, apparently believed that she was better read in literature than he (123), and during his presidency, Edith was known to read several newspapers daily and mark articles for his attention (Truman 1995, 309).

Teedie Roosevelt began his transformation into Theodore Roosevelt (no one close to him called him Teddy) with the death of his father on February 9, 1878. The elder Theodore was forty-six years old and a vigorous New York businessman and philanthropist when he was felled by stomach cancer in just a few months. Later, Theodore called his father "the best man I ever knew" (Brands 1997, 82). He made it through the spring of his sophomore year in shock.

In the summer of 1878, when Theodore was almost twenty and Edith Carow almost seventeen, everything changed. Edith was visiting the Roosevelts at Oyster Bay, and she and Theodore took a walk together and quarreled (McCullough 1981, 190). While the substance of the quarrel has never been explained by either party, both marked it as a turning point in later years (Morris 1980, 58). At the end of the day, Theodore and Edith were barely speaking. Theodore went back to college for his junior year, and while they maintained a civil friendship, they were no longer as close as they had been.

While at Harvard, Theodore had no trouble attracting female companions for chaste activities like sleighing, skating, walking, riding, and conversation. In the early fall of 1878, Theodore met Alice Hathaway Lee, a beautiful and vivacious girl Edith's age who lived in the Boston area, and fell in love. From all accounts, Alice Lee and Edith Carow were very different young women. Alice was sunny, pretty, blonde, outgoing, charming, warm, sweet, and flirtatious. Edith was moody (McCullough 1981, 221; Teichmann 1979, 15), handsome instead of pretty, a brunette, strong-willed (Caroli 1998, 85), serious, more intellectual, and somewhat reserved (McCullough 1981, 358). Following his Harvard graduation, Theodore and Alice were married on October 27, 1880, with Edith sitting in the family pew at the wedding. She remained a family friend, giving a party in honor of the newlyweds the next year (McCullough 1981, 230). Edith filled her days with reading, going to museums, doing needlework, attending the opera and theater, socializing within a set of established New York families, and caring for her unwell parents (Cordery 1996, 297).

Theodore, with Alice at his side, left law school and entered local politics in New York City (Morris 1980, 69). By the time Alice was to have his child, in February 1884, he was serving as a representative in the New York State Assembly. But two days after the arrival of baby Alice Lee Roosevelt in the Roosevelt family brownstone in New York, both Theodore's mother and wife died, the former of typhoid fever and the latter of what was called Bright's disease, a kidney ailment now known as chronic nephritis. Theodore, devastated, turned his daughter over to the care of his eldest sister, Anna, and moved out west, pouring his inheritance into a cattle ranching enterprise.

Edith attended the double funeral of the Roosevelt women and was on the fringes of the family during the crisis. However, her family's fortunes had become dire. Her father had died on March 17, 1883, at age fifty-eight of alcoholism (Morris 1980, 72), leaving Edith, her mother, and sister with debts and little income. They struggled to maintain a genteel lifestyle, probably in part because twenty-one-year-old Edith and nineteen-year-old Emily would need the proper connections to make good matrimonial matches. The three Carow women determined that they could live far more cheaply in Italy, which would also re-move them from the prying and judging of New York society. By 1885, they had resolved to tie up their loose ends in New York and prepare for the move to Europe (Morris 1980, 79).

But in the fall 1885, Theodore, visiting from the West, happened to meet Edith at his sister Anna's house. There is no record in their diaries or letters of a courtship that fall, especially because Theodore thought it unseemly while he was still in mourning eighteen months after Alice's death (Brands 1997, 201). Although Theodore and Edith were seen together that fall at public events, ap-parently no one suspected that they were companions for reasons of anything but convenience. In fact, the couple became secretly engaged on November 17, 1885. The Carow women moved to Europe in the spring of 1886 as planned. From Europe, Edith wrote long letters to Theodore detailing her social life, musicales she had attended, and books she had read (Morris 1980, 84–88). The secret was revealed in August 1886, and the two were married quietly in London on December 2, 1886. Edith decided not to use her maiden name as her middle name in marriage, and thus she became Edith Kermit Roosevelt.

Following a European honeymoon, the Roosevelts set up housekeeping in Oyster Bay, and Theodore Jr. was born on September 13, 1887. It was a produc-tive marriage. In 1888, Edith suffered a miscarriage, but in October 1889, Kermit Roosevelt joined the family. He was followed by Ethel Carow Roosevelt in August 1891; Archibald Bulloch Roosevelt in April 1894; and Quentin Roose-velt in November 1897.

To support this brood, Theodore had accepted a job on the Civil Service Commission in 1889, which moved the family to Washington, D.C. With the help of Theodore's eldest sister, Anna, who had settled in Washington a few years before, Edith quickly found a social set and the couple entertained three or four nights a week (Morris 1980, 148). She counted among her friends the Bos-ton blueblood Henry Cabot Lodge, the writer Henry Adams, and the sculptor Augustus St. Gaudens. The Roosevelts also dined with the Clevelands at the White House. Edith enjoyed the stability of her husband's job in Washington and dissuaded him from accepting the Republican nomination for mayor of New York in 1894. However, he became New York City's police commissioner in 1895, with the family moving back to Oyster Bay. Two years later, Theodore was appointed assistant secretary of the navy, and the family moved again to Washington. During all of these moves, Edith was responsible for all of the packing with no help from Theodore (Cordery 1996, 301). It was his proximity to President William McKinley and other armed forces officers that led to his leadership role at the outset of the Spanish-American War in 1898. Once more, the Roosevelts moved to Oyster Bay. Theodore distinguished himself in combat leading the Rough Riders at the Battle of San Juan Hill, which earned him na-tional recognition in the U.S. press. In a controversial decision, he was added to the Republican ticket as McKinley's vice president in the 1900 election. The family moved to Washington yet again in 1901 when McKinley won.

McKinley died on September 14, 1901, after being shot in Buffalo, New York, and Theodore Roosevelt became the country's twenty-sixth president.

Edith Roosevelt, who feared and detested public scrutiny, became the most well-known wife and mother in the United States. She had more children than any other first lady, and miscarriages prevented the addition of two more children during her White House occupancy (Anthony 1990, 307). In 1901, when the Roosevelts became the first family, Alice was 17 and even prettier than her late mother; Ted Jr. was just 14; Kermit was almost 12; Ethel was 10; Archie was 7; and Quentin was almost 4. At 40 years old, Edith Roosevelt was at the time the third youngest woman to become first lady (Frances Cleveland had been 21 when she married President Grover Cleveland, and Julia Tyler was 24 and 30 years her husband's junior when John Tyler became president).

After Theodore's presidency ended in 1909, the couple made Oyster Bay their home base for extensive travel. Theodore was badly defeated in the 1912 presidential election. That decade saw the Roosevelt children marry and start families, except for Alice, who married in 1906 and had her only child in 1925, and Quentin, who was killed in 1918 in France during a World War I skirmish. On January 6, 1919, Theodore Roosevelt died in his sleep at their home in Oyster Bay. Edith traveled the world, took figurehead leadership roles in Republican women's organizations and in the Needlework Guild of which she was a long-time member (Riis 1904, 327–30), gave a few brief speeches that no one thought to record, and died on September 30, 1948, in Oyster Bay, age 87.

By the time of her death, the world in which Edith Kermit Roosevelt had grown up and presided over was gone. Immigration, two world wars, labor laws, women's suffrage, the Depression, income taxes, and Franklin Delano Roosevelt's social programs had contributed to dramatic social changes. Theodore's niece Eleanor Roosevelt had been a very different kind of first lady from 1933 to 1945. Edith's maiden sister Emily had died in Italy in 1939, and Theodore's siblings, including Corinne, were all gone by 1948. Her son Kermit had killed himself in 1943, and Ted Jr., had died of a heart attack in France immediately after leading the Normandy Invasion. Alice, Ethel, and Archie all outlived Edith, Alice dying in 1980 at age 96, Ethel dying in 1977 at age 81, and Archie dying in 1979 at age 85.

Rhetorical Activities as First Lady

The singular greatest obstacle to scholarly chronicles of Edith Kermit Roosevelt's life has been Edith's desire to protect her family's privacy. She asked Theodore to destroy the letters she wrote him upon receipt (Morris 1980, 323), and she destroyed other documents herself (457). There is no repository of her papers *per se*, although letters that she sent to others, such as Edith Wharton, other family friends, and some relatives, were preserved. Upon the death of Ethel Roosevelt Derby, papers and letters that Ethel had collected were added to the Theodore Roosevelt Collection at Harvard. A solid biography of Edith Roosevelt was written by Sylvia Jukes Morris in 1980 with the aid of the family, and David McCullough's 1981 portrait of Theodore Roosevelt's parents, siblings, and childhood, *Mornings on Horseback*, also received support from the family.

Betty Boyd Caroli in 1998 wrote a part of a chapter about Edith in her *Roosevelt Women*. And because Myra G. Gutin's book on the rhetorical activities of first ladies took 1920 as its starting point, Edith Roosevelt has not been the focus of any rhetorical scholarship. In this section, the backdrop for Edith's rhetorical activities and effects are painted, her tangible accomplishments as first lady are described, and it is argued that her more lasting message was tied up in her maternal image.

Edith Roosevelt was born at the beginning of the era that Neil Postman described as "the high-water mark of childhood" (Postman 1982, 67). In the understanding of childhood as a golden, carefree, innocent age, one job of the parent was to provide a standard of living that preserves the myth of the perfectly ordered society. For people of the Roosevelts' and Carows' social class, this was accomplished in part by strict control over the children's education, one that did not involve leaving the house or neighborhood. As the middle class grew between 1870 and 1920, this concept of childhood was more broadly assimilated.

Not only was childhood and thus parenthood evolving, but Edith entered a White House that only recently had starred young children. Grover and Frances Cleveland were married during the former's first term as president (1884–1888). The first child to be born to a sitting president, Esther Cleveland, came during her father's second term of office (1892–1896). Esther was followed by another baby girl. Because the technology for the reproduction of photographs had improved by this time, the public developed a hunger for pictures of the Cleveland children. The Clevelands responded by withdrawing and trying to shield the children from public scrutiny, which only resulted in more prying by the press. The McKinleys had no children, and Ida's illness limited what could be written about her.

By the time of the Roosevelt presidency, the public was hungrier for information about the president's family than ever before. As Watson put it, "Theodore Roosevelt's presidency was one of the first to receive daily, personal press coverage, owing in part to the president's charisma, his attractive, young family, and a changing style of journalism developing around the time of his presidency" (2000, 110). Through her actions as first lady, Edith Roosevelt gave the press something to write about—the tangible contributions she made to the office of first lady as well as the images she released of her family that make up her larger rhetorical legacy.

Edith was as surprised as anyone else to inherit the mantle of first lady in September 1901, after her husband had been vice president for only six months. She is most widely credited with four accomplishments: hiring the first secretary to serve the first lady, presiding over extensive renovations to the White House that created more private living quarters, formalizing the china collection begun by Caroline Harrison, and establishing the first lady portrait gallery.

Edith's motivation for hiring a social secretary has not been established, but Anthony attributed the action to her need for help with Alice's 1902 debutante ball (1990, 298). Isabelle "Belle" Hagner was hired at a salary of $1,400 per year to handle the details of correspondence, bill paying, and entertaining. She also was the press liaison for Edith (Watson 2000, 110; Caroli 1995, 121). Edith also created the position of chief usher, essentially the foreman of the household staff (Anthony 1990, 298), which allowed her to delegate the more repetitive household duties. Every first lady since Edith's time has had a personal staff, which in recent years has fluctuated between twelve and twenty-four members (Watson 2000, 112–13). Margaret Truman wrote, "Edith reorganized the White House in a style that made her a truly pivotal First Lady" (1995, 306).

A significant symbol of Edith's desire to keep her family life shielded from the public was her involvement in extensive renovations to the White House. Margaret Truman wrote, "With six children and at least two maids living on the second floor, not to mention herself and her husband, Edith put herself vigorously on record in favor of an expanded White House" (1995, 307). For instance, when the Roosevelts first took up residency, daughter Alice shared a bathroom with the Cabinet Room. The same month that Edith moved into the White House, she wrote a letter that contained a sketch of how she would like to redesign the second floor.

With an emergency appropriation of over half a million dollars from Congress, Edith hired the preeminent New York architectural firm of McKim, Mead, and White. Records indicate that she served almost as general contractor, overseeing all phases of design and construction, in an enormous rebuilding project (Morris 2001). The state dining room was almost doubled, so it could host as many as 107 guests for dinner or a smaller group for the weekly musicales, which boasted soloists such as Ignace Paderewski and Pablo Casals. The other public rooms were stripped of their heavy Victorian ornamentation and transformed into highly formal receiving rooms for small group gatherings. For example, Edith hosted a weekly tea with the wives of the cabinet members at which they plotted Washington's social calendar months in advance. The president's office and Cabinet Room were moved to a newly constructed West Wing, where Edith created an office for herself and her staff. Here she handled correspondence of her own and some of her husband's until he found an appropriate assistant. Now that the second floor was used solely as the family quarters, the staircase was moved and diminished in emphasis to discourage the public from violating the private areas. As these improvements were made at the public's expense, they were covered in the press, although Edith's role was seldom mentioned.

Edith is also remembered for making the china collection a more permanent aspect of the White House and for establishing the first lady portrait collection (Morris 1980, 254). When Edith came to the White House, she found the beginnings of a china collection started by Caroline Harrison. Edith enlarged the collection and drew attention to it. The portrait gallery was a second project that showed Edith's understanding of the White House as a museum of the American presidency. During the renovation, she had a gallery built on the ground floor of the White House near the south entrance. Portraits of first ladies were hung here, attracting some displeasure that they had been relegated to the basement (Truman 1995, 310). However, the portraits now hang in the East Wing in a more public lobby.

These accomplishments in hiring staff, renovating the White House, and collecting china and portraits were eclipsed in the public consciousness by her rhetorical strategies of protecting her family by controlling how they were covered in the press, thus creating a public image of herself as "First Mommy" as well as first lady. To a public eager to see and know the first family, maintaining a private family life was a significant achievement, especially with an uncontrollable stepdaughter like Alice.

Edith had married Theodore when Alice was two, and soon after the couple had settled down together, Alice came to live with them. Although of different temperaments, Edith was as close to Alice as anyone was, which Alice demonstrated at her wedding (Morris 1980, 305). Alice Lee Roosevelt was smart, spottily educated thanks in part to her family's constant moves (Howard 1902, 6), rebellious, and by all accounts spoiled (Teichmann 1979, 73). She was beautiful but so headstrong that Theodore once told a visitor that he could run the country or manage Alice but not both (Howard 1902, 6). The public was smitten with the pretty blonde who entered the White House at age seventeen, and she was called by the press "Princess Alice." According to biographer Howard Teichmann, Alice Lee Roosevelt was the most photographed person in the world by 1906 (1979, 35). She inspired songs like "Alice Blue Gown," a brand of gloves was named for her, and even wallpaper was named for her. Alice became a popular name for girls during the time period (37). She called attention to herself by holding her debut in the White House on January 3, 1902, and by being married there in 1906.

Alice's wedding was handled much the same way Edith handled publicity in general. Edith had discovered that she could prevent the press from ambushing her and her children by having portraits taken of them frequently and having the pictures released regularly (Truman 1995, 307). According to Caroli, "When the time came for Alice Roosevelt's wedding to Nicholas Longworth and for Edith's daughter's debut, photographers and reporters were included in the preparations so that the uncontrolled snooping that had marred the Cleveland wedding would not be repeated" (1995, 121).

Using her stepdaughter's beauty, outgoing personality, and antics, Edith was able to divert attention from the younger, more vulnerable children. At the same time, she used the medium of photography to promote an image of her family that she could control. Edith retained several photographers to produce family pictures for public consumption, most notably Frances Benjamin Johnston. The photographs that were released were posed but appeared candid. The children were generally shown with props such as pets and bicycles. The photographs of Edith that were released usually showed her surrounded by the children. Edith almost never faced the camera but modestly looked down or away, a serene counterweight to her husband.

A popular women's magazine of the day, *The Ladies' Home Journal*, demonstrates the public face of the Roosevelts. In 1902, the magazine's contents ranged from fiction by Rudyard Kipling and nonfiction by Helen Keller to practical articles on gardening, bird-watching, child rearing, cooking, needlework, fashion, entertaining, and church socials. Women's education was emphasized, as was saving for a home, and house plans. The advertisements featured pianos, corsets, silverware, Ping-Pong tables, soap and detergent, doilies, hats, sewing machines, flour, grandfather clocks, skates, and cereal.

The first article featuring the new president's family was "The President's Daughter," in April 1902. The feature story about Alice is the lead article and includes four photographs: Alice as a child, Alice in a velvet dress, Alice in her coming-out gown, and the East Room of the White House "as it appeared when Miss Roosevelt made her debut" (Howard 1902, 5). Edith is called "the present gracious mistress of the White House," and is defined by her maternal relationship to Alice: "She is the only mother Alice has ever known, and it was under her loving care that Alice grew to girlhood and received her early training" (5).

The next month, May 1902, the same magazine featured an article about the new president called "The Outdoor President" (Denison 1902, 11–12). Theodore is pictured chopping wood, posed on horseback, riding horseback at Oyster Bay, on his daily walk, and with Edith. The latter photograph is so small and dark that Edith's features cannot be made out under her large hat. The two-page article describes Theodore's physical stamina and abilities, but if not for the references to his sons and the photograph, the reader would not know he was married. Edith is not mentioned. However, at the bottom of the second page of the article, appears a teaser under the headline "The President's Mother, His Wife and His Children," which reads:

> The families of few Presidents have awakened so much interest as the American people feel about the wife and the interesting group of children now in the White House. And in authoritative articles The Journal will tell what is most interesting about the Roosevelt family, which is now attracting the world's attention. In the next (the June) issue, The Journal will contain an article about the President's mother; and then, in a later issue, another article on Mrs. Roosevelt and the children. ("President's Mother" 1902, 12)

As promised, in June 1902, *The Journal*'s lead article was on Theodore's mother, Martha Bulloch Roosevelt. Accompanied by photographs of Mr. and Mrs. Roosevelt and of her ancestral home in Georgia, the short article primarily recounts the gentility of her family and upbringing, her beauty, and details of her wedding to the elder Theodore Roosevelt. There is a brief mention that she considered her household duties and child rearing to be among her most important activities (Bulloch 1902, 5).

A reproduction of a painting of Edith graced the cover of the August 1902, issue of *Ladies' Home Journal*. The oval painting by Theobald Chartran shows Edith on a white wooden bench outside the White House. She is wearing a large, dark hat, a dark coat trimmed with lace, and a light dress with a high neck and ruffled front. In her right hand, she holds her white gloves, and in her left hand, she holds a folded parasol. She is looking off to the viewer's right. Inside the magazine, readers are offered a print of the cover for 10 cents. According to the offer, it is the first reproduction to be made of the painting that had been completed in March.

The lead article, "Mrs. Roosevelt and Her Children," was written by Jacob

Riis, a journalist friend of Theodore's since the latter's New York police commissioner days. There is one cameo photograph of Edith, which shows her in profile and looking down with her eyes almost closed. There are individual portraits of Theodore Jr., Kermit, Ethel, and Archibald as well as three small snapshots of Quentin, two of which show him playing with Roswell Pinckney, the son of a White House steward. Pinckney, about the same age as four-year-old Quentin, is African American.

The article first mentions Edith as "Quentin's mother," immediately casting her in maternal terms (Riis 1902, 5). She is compared to Frances Cleveland, and they are called "types of perfect American womanhood, adorning their high station with every grace of the wife and mother that appeals to all that is best in man." Riis describes Edith as gentle, high-bred, tactful, mindful of her duties, and charming. "A mistress of the White House, Mrs. Roosevelt has won the hearts of everybody," Riis writes (5). He sketches a typical day at the White House and highlights Edith's relationship to the children as one of love, obedience, and trust. She makes time twice a day for "mothering," and her room is called the children's lodestone (6). There are two mentions of the fact that she practices economy in her housekeeping, a vignette of her crocheting while she discusses the day's events with Theodore, and a mention of her skill in growing flowers for cutting (6). The rest of the article is about the children, although Alice and the boys receive more attention than Ethel, who is depicted only as "the dear little haus-frau of the family. She has the mother-heart, and there is nothing better in all the world" (6).

Also in the magazine are two pages of photographs of the family taken by Frances Benjamin Johnston. The photos show Alice holding a small dog, Archie on a bicycle, Ted with his macaw, Archie and Quentin playing with a camera, Kermit and his dog, Archie and Quentin with the White House police, Ethel holding a hat, Archie with a policeman, Quentin on his pony, and Quentin in a tree. Thus, the only depictions of Edith in the magazine are the cover and the small cameo. There are no biographical details about her, such as her maiden name, place of birth, age, or education. There is not a single quotation from Edith in the story.

Not until 1904, when Theodore was nominated by the Republican Party as its presidential candidate, was the family given great publicity again. *The American Monthly Review of Reviews* published several articles about him following the nomination in its July 1904 issue. There were two full-page photographs of Theodore and one of Edith—she is seated sideways in a chair with her left arm propped on the chair back and she is seen in profile facing to the reader's right. There is also a family portrait of Theodore, Edith, and the three youngest boys on horseback at Oyster Bay, with Edith's eyes hidden by her hat. The accompanying article, "Theodore Roosevelt as a Presidential Candidate," makes no mention of the family whatever.

The president and his family are depicted in full-page portraits in the July 1905 issue of *McClure's Magazine*. The photos have no accompanying text and appear in chronological order. The photograph of Edith, showing her 1905 inaugural gown, is unusual in that she is seated and looking directly at the camera with a small smile, although the light is coming from the reader's left, illuminating only one side of her face. The portraits of Alice, Ted, and Kermit are quite formal, while Ethel is wearing a sailor dress, and Archie appears to be wearing his father's Rough Riders hat tipped back on his head, an oversized shirt, and a loosely tied tie, rather like a child dressing up in his father's clothes. Quentin is dressed in a child's blouse that has buttons on the shoulder seams and down one side of the front. The effect *in toto* is charming.

An article by Charles Wagner in the October 1905 *McClure's Magazine* depicts "A Visit at the White House." The first-person account of being invited to dinner at the White House includes the detail that Wagner, an Alsatian, discoursed at length with Edith in French, which he said she spoke "with perfect ease" (Wagner 1905, 644). This is a rare disclosure of Edith's education. However, his other mentions of her are more traditional, such as his admiration of her rosebushes. The article is accompanied by photographs of Wagner, of Theodore with Archie and Quentin, and a rather poor composition of the same subject from the *Review of Reviews* article: members of the family on horseback at Oyster Bay. In this shot, Edith's horse has turned and she is seen from the left back, while everyone else faces the camera.

Legacy

Edith Roosevelt was firmly in control—of a household staff, the press, and the public's image of her as a mother, in an era in which parenthood was evolving. Long after Theodore's death, she emerged from her private sphere to support Herbert Hoover's campaign against Democrat Franklin Delano Roosevelt, her husband's distant cousin who was married to her husband's niece. However, she told reporters who asked for a statement in August 1932, "I haven't talked to the press in 71 years, and it's too late to begin now" (Morris 1980, 477). Her first notable public appearance was at a Hoover rally at Madison Square Garden on October 31, 1932. The building was jammed with 22,000 spectators and left 30,000 people milling outside the Garden. *The New York Times* of the next day noted only that the Hoovers were "greeted by Mrs. Theodore Roosevelt" and that Mrs. Hoover wore brown ("Hoover Charges Roosevelt" 1932, 1, 13). Ironically, a thirty-one-word statement made by Alice Roosevelt Longworth to the press on November 1 merited a small article in the November 2 *New York Times* ("Makes 31-Word Speech" 1932, 13).

Another speech by Edith, to 300 women at the Women's National Republican Club in New York, was reported on in somewhat more detail. It is, in fact, the only speech she ever gave that quotes her; her speeches as president of the Long Island Needlework Guild have not survived. Her five-paragraph speech started with a quotation from George Washington about the sanctity of the Constitution and called for loyalty to the Constitution. She concluded:

> To them in this crisis we dedicate our lives, never to falter in our high devotion;
> never to fall back in our purpose to leave to our children and to our children's

children the freedom of life and thought that has been ours. For if we fall we fall like Lucifer, never to hope again. ("Women Open Drive" 1935, 18)

Edith's influence on women in her day can not be measured by modern polling, although in a 1980 study conducted by *Good Housekeeping*, she earned perfect scores in the categories of "traditionalist" and "inspiration to women" (Watson 2000, 182). Margaret Truman observed that "maternity was Edith's stock-in-trade. She not only liked it, she made it the symbol of the Roosevelt White House, with spectacularly popular results" (Truman 1995, 306). Truman continued, "Edith Roosevelt left the White House in 1909 arguably the most esteemed, beloved First Lady since Martha Washington" (313). To give Margaret Truman, a one-time resident of the White House, the final word, "Edith Roosevelt conquered the White House as everybody's mother" (314).

References

Anthony, Carl Sferrazza. 1990. *First Ladies: The Saga of the Presidents' Wives and Their Power 1789–1961*, Vol. 1. New York: Quill.

Brands, H. W. 1997. *T. R.: The Last Romantic*. New York: Basic.

Bulloch, Emma Hamilton. 1902. The President's Mother. *Ladies' Home Journal*, 5 June.

Caroli, Betty Boyd. 1995. *First Ladies*, expanded edition. New York: Oxford University Press.

———. 1998. *The Roosevelt Women*. New York: Basic Books.

Cordery, Stacy A. 1996. Edith Kermit Roosevelt. In *American First Ladies*, ed. Lewis L. Gould, 294–320. New York: Garland.

Denison, Lindsay. 1902. The Outdoor President. *Ladies' Home Journal*, May, 11–12.

Gutin, Myra G. 1989. *The President's Partner: The First Lady in the Twentieth Century*. New York: Greenwood.

Hoover Charges Roosevelt "New Deal" Would Destroy Foundation of Nation. 1932. *New York Times*, 1 November, 13.

Howard, Clifford. 1902. The President's Daughter. *Ladies' Home Journal*, April, 5–6.

Makes 31-Word Speech. 1932. *New York Times*, 2 November, 13.

McCullough, David. 1981. *Mornings on Horseback*. New York: Touchstone Press.

Morris, Edmund. 2001. *Theodore Rex*. New York: Random House.

Morris, Sylvia Jukes. 1980. *Edith Kermit Roosevelt: Portrait of a First Lady*. New York: Coward.

Postman, Neil. 1982. *The Disappearance of Childhood*. New York: Laurel.

President Roosevelt's Children. 1902. *Ladies' Home Journal*, August, 18–19.

The President's Family. 1905. *McClure's Magazine*, July, 284–92.

The President's Mother, His Wife and His Children. 1902. *Ladies' Home Journal*, May, 12.

Pringle, Henry. 1956. *Theodore Roosevelt: A Biography*. New York: Harvest.

Riis, Jacob A. 1902. Mrs. Roosevelt and Her Children. *Ladies' Home Journal*, August, 5–6.

———. 1904. *Theodore Roosevelt the Citizen*. New York: Outlook.

Schlereth, Thomas J. 1991. *Victorian America: Transformations in Everyday Life 1876–1915*. New York: Harper.

Teichmann, Howard. 1979. *Alice: The Life and Times of Alice Roosevelt Longworth*. Englewood Cliffs, N.J.: Prentice Hall.

Theodore Roosevelt as a Presidential Candidate. 1904. *American Monthly Review of Reviews*, July, 34–42.

Truman, Margaret. 1995. *First Ladies: An Intimate Group Portrait of White House Wives*. New York: Fawcett Columbine.

Wagner, Charles. 1905. A Visit at the White House. *McClure's Magazine*, October, 641–48.

Watson, Robert P. 2000. *The Presidents' Wives: Reassessing the Office of First Lady*. Boulder, Colo.: Lynne Reinner.

Wilson, Dorothy Clarke. 1989. *Alice and Edith*. New York: Doubleday.

Women Open Drive to Rout New Deal. 1935. *New York Times*. 17 September, 18.

Chapter 4

Helen Herron Taft
Opportunity and Ambition

Beth M. Waggenspack

It always has been my ambition to see Mr. Taft President of the United States.
—Nellie Taft

The generation of women who came of age in the late 1800s arrived at a juncture of change. Women had begun to redefine their lives to reach beyond their own families through the establishment of female-run organizations formed after the Civil War. The entry of more women into colleges and universities, the fight for women's suffrage (women could vote in only four states in 1900), and the admission of women to practice law before the U.S. Supreme Court all added to these modifications. Yet fundamental societal ideas about femininity had not altered. Wives who took an activist role in the world outside their families were criticized for attempting too much. A young woman might attend college, but her studies were in the typical women's domains of teaching, literature, or nursing. While she might present a serious, mature image, she was not a totally liberated woman as we might picture her today.

Prior to 1920, most first ladies did not vigorously become involved in their husbands' political lives. Direct participation in the political sphere was taboo, and many women felt uncomfortable treading in a domain for which they were unprepared and unwelcome. The public simply was unwilling to grant acceptance for a first lady taking on a political or policy maker role. The nation expected its first lady to "reflect ideals of home, family and womanhood" (Mayo and Meringolo 1994, 8). Gradually, presidents' wives in the early twentieth century began to hire separate staffs of their own, take more public roles in policy and personnel decisions, and lead important reforms. Helen ("Nellie") Herron Taft was at the inception of this shift, and although she is not as preeminent in the public mind as later first ladies, she left a mark to guarantee that her successors would not find the White House a place to retreat from an active public role.

Nellie Taft, wife of the twenty-seventh president, William Howard Taft, was one of the early-twentieth-century first ladies whose relentless drive and political acumen began the transformation of the acceptable role of a first lady. They formed a partnership and through it she was able to exercise a great deal of influence on her husband, not only politically, but also in cultural, social, and aesthetic decisions made about Washington and elsewhere. She brought to the White House a cosmopolitan and international bent born of her own extensive travels in Europe and Asia. In the Taft administration, Nellie Taft played a prominent part. Her primary interest was her husband's career; entertaining and civic improvements were always secondary. She rarely gave interviews or speeches but occasionally handed out a statement on some formal function. *Recollections of Full Years,* her memoirs, was written twenty-nine years before her death, leaving much of her personal rhetoric to be gleaned from letters and her actions, as well as the interpretations of those around her. It was the first published memoirs of a first lady, but the work provided only a vague, abstract view of her political role. Margaret Truman later said, "Helen Herron Taft is one of the few first ladies who wanted the job; in fact, it has been said that she wanted it far more than her husband," whose ambition was to become a Supreme Court justice (Truman 1995, 102). It has been said that Nellie's ambition never slept.

Biography

Born September 2, 1861, in Cincinnati, Ohio, Nellie Herron was one of eleven children of John Williamson Herron, a prominent Cincinnati lawyer and influential Republican former state senator, and Harriet Collins, daughter of New York congressman Eli Collins. Nellie acquired a passion for politics from her father and grandfather. She also had early ties with the White House: her father attended Miami University with twenty-third president, Benjamin Harrison, and was a law partner of nineteenth president, Rutherford B. Hayes. Members of the Herron family were often guests at the Hayes' White House. Because Nellie was not yet "out" as a debutante, she later lamented to a *New York Times* reporter that she could not spend her time "in the White House as I would have liked, in going to brilliant parties and meeting all manner of charming people." Nevertheless, her visits were momentous, for they gave birth to her fantasy of becoming a first lady herself (Anderson 1981, 49).

Nellie Herron was a young lady of unusual intelligence and was reported to have been an exceptional student at Miss Nourse's School (Pringle 1939, vol. 1,

70). Upon graduation, she attended Miami University in Oxford, Ohio, where she studied German, literature, history, and sciences. She also spent long afternoons in her father's law office, familiarizing herself with the law by reading books and helping him with his work. She began to appreciate politics and jurisprudence. She believed that the only way she could retain her individuality was to rely on her intellectual strengths, which she could enhance through teaching, traveling, and writing books (Anderson 1981, 52).

With the purposefulness and ambition that marked her adult life, Nellie enlisted the help of two of her friends to start a Sunday afternoon salon, where young people could be invited to argue pressing questions and "engage in what we consider brilliant discussion of topics intellectual and economic" (Taft 1914, 10). The salon provided her with mental exercise and a convenient forum in which to demonstrate her skills, and it was to this salon that she invited the Taft brothers, William and Horace. She noted, "We were simply bent on improving our minds in the most congenial atmosphere we could create" (Taft 1914, 10).

William Howard Taft was the second son of Louisa Torrey and Alphonso Taft, prominent and well-regarded Cincinnati residents. Alphonso Taft had a promising judicial and potentially promising political career in Ohio, and he served as both secretary of war and attorney general in Grant's cabinet. Louisa Torrey Taft maintained a very intense relationship with Will, and until her death on the eve of his nomination as a presidential candidate, she advised and criticized every step of his career.

Nellie Herron's personality was very much akin to Louisa Torrey Taft's: she advised and criticized Will. He valued this critical quality in her and in 1897 wrote: "The thought of you has so much intellectual flavor, and sweet sentiment too. I am so glad that you don't flatter me and sit at my feet with honey. You are my dearest and best critic and are worth so much to me in stirring me up to best endeavor" (Ross 1964, 121). Biographer Judith Anderson concludes that William Howard Taft sought Nellie's approval in the same way he sought it from his parents (1981, 47).

Their courtship was not an easy one. They met at a sledding party when she was eighteen and kept company for the next six years. Her memoirs describe amateur theatricals, parties in the country, and vaudeville and charade parties. She duly noted: "In spite of this gaiety, Mr. Taft was making very satisfactory progress in his career" (Taft 1914, 9). In one love letter to her, Will Taft pleaded: "Oh Nellie, do say that you will try to love me. Oh, how I will work and strive to be better and do better, how I will labor for our joint advancement if you will only let me" (Pringle 1939, vol. 1, 69). Following the custom of well-bred young women, Nellie rebuffed Will's marriage proposals twice, until he again proposed on May 1, 1885, and she responded affirmatively a month later. Anderson suggests that in Nellie, Taft got what he felt he needed in his life: a whip that would drive him to achieve. For Nellie, marrying Will Taft was the best alternative available to her having a career: "He gave her a mandate to make of him what she could" (Anderson 1981, 53). Will Taft told her that once they married, she would be his senior partner for life.

Will and Nellie Taft were married on June 19, 1886, in the parlor of the

Herron home. In her *Recollections*, Nellie devotes one line to her engagement and marriage: "Mr. Taft and I were engaged in May, 1885, and were married in June of the following year" (1914, 14). Interestingly, this brief description follows six pages detailing a court case Taft argued, which resulted in him becoming the assistant county solicitor. They took a one-hundred-day honeymoon to Europe, visiting Great Britain, Scotland, France, and Holland. She recalled that the wedding trip afforded her the "first taste of the foreign travel of which I had always dreamed" (Taft 1914, 16).

They set up house in Cincinnati, where Will practiced law and served as an assistant to the prosecuting attorney of Hamilton County. Less than a year after the wedding, Taft was named to fill a vacancy as a judge for the state superior court at age twenty-nine, and in the next election, he won the post outright. While Nellie was pleased, she also was unsure about the offer, fearing "the narrowing effects of the Bench" (Taft 1914, 22).

Will's appointment by President Harrison in 1890 as solicitor general of the United States was more to Nellie's liking; the position took them to Washington, which she soon came to love. Taft would represent the federal government in cases heard before the Supreme Court. Nellie was pleased with the move, noting that she was glad "because it gave Mr. Taft an opportunity for exactly the kind of work I wished him to do" (Taft 1914, 25).

Taft's return to Cincinnati in 1892 as a member of the Sixth Federal Circuit Court of Appeals dismayed Nellie, who feared he would be fixed in a groove for the rest of his life (Taft 1914, 30). But his appointment to the circuit court (the highest federal bench except for the Supreme Court) provided him with the legal profile he desired: he heard motions, wrote decisions, and presided at civil and criminal trials, holding court in Cincinnati, Cleveland, Toledo, Detroit, and Nashville. He saw the position on the circuit court as leading to the Supreme Court, which was his ultimate goal. Nellie Taft apparently felt forced to struggle against her husband's judicial tastes. She wrote, "If you get your heart's desire, my darling, it will put an end to all the opportunities you now have of being thrown with the bigwigs" (quoted in Pringle 1939, vol. 1, 109). Taft could never regard the bigwigs with quite the pleasure they provided his wife.

Nellie busied herself with the children and cultural activities. Unable to attend House and Senate debates as she had done in Washington, she turned to community activities to relieve the monotony, attending art classes, joining a book club, and playing a leading role in the formation of the Cincinnati Symphony Orchestra. She assisted in voluntary administrative work at the city hospital and museum, attended university classes in current events and art, and read extensively, especially in history. She was also active in the kindergarten movement. Son Charlie was born in 1897. She recalled this time as tranquil and "quite too settled" (Taft 1914, 31).

As Taft's reputation grew, he began to address legal groups and civic assemblies, where he would read from prepared texts. He admitted that he had trouble holding the attention of others and that speaking was not his forte. Nellie took on the role of coach, saying: "I know how uncomfortable you felt at having to speak without more preparation when you always give so much to anything you do" (Ross 1964, 59). She cautioned him not to cite too many precedents or talk too long. His style was thorough and ponderous, going through ideas point-by-point, and although her goal of molding him into a compelling orator was never realized, he did become a competent speaker. When asked to speak before the American Bar Association in 1895, he anticipated the event with anxiety. With Nellie and the children off vacationing, he was unable to compose the speech. He wrote to her, "If you have any fitting ideas, write them down for me" (Ross 1964, 64). She also encouraged him to become immune to the inevitable criticism that a public figure would engender. She wrote him, "You have been remarkably free from attacks of that kind and of course you must expect your share" (Ross 1964, 64).

In January 1900, Taft met with President McKinley, who invited him to head a commission to establish a civil government in the Philippines. America had recently assumed control of the islands as part of the Spanish-American War settlement. Although General Arthur MacArthur was currently in charge of the military government in control, McKinley wanted a civilian government in place. Although Taft did not consider himself qualified to cope with a colonial administration, Nellie cast her vote at once in favor of acceptance. She had always been keen on travel and adventures, and the position was a sound political appointment, good for her husband's career.

From 1900–1904, Nellie was a well-publicized success as a figurative first lady in Manila, Philippines. In her memoirs, she pronounced her years there among the happiest of her life. In fact, 196 pages out of 395 are devoted to the Philippines experience (her *Recollections* ends twenty-seven years before her death). She quickly learned Philippine protocol and became a valuable assistant to Taft. Tactful and diplomatic, she gave garden parties at the Malacanan Palace, held afternoon receptions and elaborate buffets.

As early as 1901, press clippings and correspondence suggested Republican interest in the possibility of Will running for the presidency. Taft scoffed at the notion, admitting that a presidential campaign held nothing but horrors and the office held no attraction for him. President McKinley's assassination in September 1901 came as a stunning blow to Taft, but eventually he and the new president, Theodore Roosevelt settled into a working relationship where Taft would be sent as a presidential envoy or troubleshooter whenever the United States was in a crisis in a foreign country.

A few days after the president was assassinated, an insurrection in the Philippines brought its own crisis, which took many months to resolve. At the same time, Nellie's mother became ill, and Nellie admits that she needed "to get out of the Philippine Islands or suffer a nervous breakdown" (Taft 1914, 226). This was one of her passing references to her fragile psychological state that would later dominate depictions of Nellie Taft as first lady. For respite, she traveled to China and wrote with great detail of her varied experiences with the novel culture.

During the winter of 1902 the Tafts traveled back to Cincinnati for a period of bereavement, grief, and worry. William was recovering from dengue fever and an abscess, and before Nellie was able to reach home, her mother died.

Nellie suffered what she termed "an inevitable collapse" from which it took her two months to recover (Taft 1914, 234). That year Will traveled to Washington, where President Roosevelt dispatched him to Rome to negotiate with the Catholic Church over the Philippine lands. Nellie accompanied him throughout Europe.

In January 1903, Theodore Roosevelt offered Will an appointment to the Supreme Court. Taft turned it down, saying he had too much to do in the Philippines. Nellie was uninterested in returning to the sedate stateside life of a judge's wife and was enjoying the position she held in the islands. Two months later, Roosevelt asked Taft to join his cabinet as secretary of war, and since the position permitted him to continue dealing with the Philippines, he accepted. Taft was somewhat reluctant because the appointment was likely to involve him in the 1904 presidential campaign. Politics were more to Nellie's taste; she said, "This was much more pleasing to me than the offer of the Supreme Court appointment, because it was in line with the kind of career I wanted for him and expected him to have" (Taft 1914, 269).

Taft's Philippine years were a significant period in his personal and political history. He had set up a government, become internationally known, and had unconsciously paved the way for his own ascent to the presidency. As early as 1903, Taft was telling friends, "Don't sit up nights thinking about making me President. I have no ambition in that direction. Any party which would nominate me would make a great mistake" (Truman 1995, 104). However, his wife's view of their future was different. The Philippines experience accustomed Nellie to the high life, and after living at the palace, nothing less than the White House apparently could hold a similar attraction for her.

Taft and Theodore Roosevelt grew increasingly friendly in 1905 when Taft served as secretary of state during John Hay's absence. Taft continued to act as Roosevelt's special troubleshooter, and as a result Taft was absent from Washington more than any other member of the cabinet. Their partnership evolved to the point where in many cases, Roosevelt initiated ideas and Taft managed them. Roosevelt eventually appointed Taft his attorney general, and Taft agreed that the Department of Justice would be much more to his liking than the War Department. During these years, Taft made three trips to Panama, where the United States was building the canal. Nellie admitted, "Fortunately for me my husband was, from the very beginning, a traveling Secretary" (Taft 1914, 297).

In the winter of 1905, the Tafts were dining at the Roosevelt White House. A front-page story in the morning's *Washington Post* had mentioned Taft as a leading possibility for the Republican presidential nomination in 1908, since Roosevelt had already announced that he would not try for a third term. After dinner, Roosevelt led his old friends into the library, and according to several accounts, he said, "this is my crystal ball" and intoned with a deep faraway voice: "I am the seventh son of a seventh daughter, and I have clairvoyant powers. I see a man weighing three hundred and fifty pounds. There is something hanging over his head . . . I cannot make out what it is. . . . At one time it looks like the presidency. Then again it looks like the chief justiceship?" "Make it the chief justiceship," said Taft. "Make it the presidency," said Nellie (Hay 1988, 182).

Nellie did all she could to help her husband win the nomination and the election, including lavish entertaining of Republican bigwigs. Taft easily beat his opponent William Jennings Bryan to become the twenty-seventh president of the United States. Upon hearing the election results, Taft said to a friend: "I feel just a bit like a fish out of water. However, as my wife is the politician and she will be able to meet all these issues, perhaps we can keep a stiff upper lip and overcome the obstacles that just at present seem formidable" (Ross 1964, 203).

Nellie Taft became first lady under terrific personal and physical stress, much brought on by her own personality which placed harsh demands on herself and those around her. Unfortunately for her, her activist reign was short lived. In May 1909, two months after her husband's inauguration, the Tafts and a party of friends boarded the presidential yacht for some relaxation. Nellie was pale and drawn from watching her son Charles having his adenoids removed that morning. In those days, any kind of surgery was life threatening, and Nellie's tense nerves and vivid imagination played on her anxiety. As they sailed toward Mount Vernon, the attorney general sat in a deck chair next to Nellie, conversing, when her eyes became glazed and she lost consciousness. She was rushed back to the White House, unable to speak, her right side paralyzed by a stroke.

The distraught president spent hours each day in her bedroom, helping her regain her speech. He barred all mention of politics from the second floor of the White House, fearing it would trigger another, possibly fatal episode. "The President looked like a great stricken animal. I have never seen greater suffering or pain on a man's face," said aide Archie Butt (1930, vol. 1, 88). Nellie eventually recovered, but her health remained fragile.

In 1912, Roosevelt announced that he was unhappy with Taft's conduct in office and that he would contest Taft's nomination for reelection and run on an independent ticket of his own. Taft seemed surprised, but Nellie wasn't. "I told you so four years ago but you would not believe me," she reportedly said (Pringle 1939, vol. 2, 769). Rather than split their Grand Old Party, Taft was inclined to let him have the Republican nomination, but Nellie talked against quitting.

Nellie's written statements of this time in her *Recollections* are brief and bittersweet (four pages, which constitute the end of her memoirs). She stopped reading the accounts of the political contest and began to make plans for the future "in which the White House played no part" (Taft 1914, 392). She acknowledged her desire to remain the first lady but "never entertained the slightest expectation of it and only longed for the end of the turmoil when he [her husband] could rest his weary mind and get back into association with the pleasant things of life" (Taft 1914, 393).

As the incumbent, Taft controlled enough party machinery to win the Republican nomination, but he had lost the confidence of the electorate. Roosevelt stunned the country by organizing the Bull Moose Party, whose platform encompassed direct primaries, women's suffrage, and various reforms. Woodrow Wilson entered as the Democratic candidate and became a formidable opponent with two positive points on his side: he was both eloquent and he faced a divided party. The 1912 campaign was one long humiliation, and Taft ended up carrying only Utah and Vermont, winning enough votes to keep Roosevelt out of the White House. Democrat Woodrow Wilson, who tallied nearly 1.5 million votes less than the combined Taft–Roosevelt tickets, was elected. Taft's defeat was the worst in presidential history and certainly one of the worst beatings ever inflicted on a sitting president.

Nellie was reportedly miserable on Inauguration Day—she stayed upstairs packing while Taft lunched with the Wilsons after the inaugural ceremony. She left the White House without saying good-bye to the staff. Later, when a reporter asked her daughter Helen whether her mother was relieved to be free of White House responsibilities, the latter said frankly: "Mother was never much for relief. She always wanted something to be happening" (Means 1963, 134).

The post–White House years led the Tafts back to the public legal arena. In 1913, Taft accepted the position of Kent Professor of Law at Yale, with a salary of $5,000 per year which he could augment with lectures and magazine articles. He then accepted appointment as chief justice of the Supreme Court in 1921. Taft was very happy and Nellie discovered that she didn't miss politics or being in the public eye the way she thought she would. She played golf, read widely, attended plays and concerts, and entertained two or three nights a week.

Mrs. Taft had been ill for a year before she died at home in Washington, D.C., on May 22, 1943, at the age of 83. She was the first first lady to be buried in Arlington National Cemetery. Margaret Truman says of Nellie:

> Although I admire Helen's determination to make her woman's voice heard in an era when this was anything but fashionable, objectivity forces me to conclude she was a disaster as a political partner, by almost any standard. Part of this failure must be attributed to bad luck. She had more than her share of strength and courage, two of the three gifts Grace Coolidge said that all First Ladies need. But Nellie fatally lacked the third, health. (Truman 1995, 115)

Rhetorical Activities as First Lady

Nellie Taft's rhetorical activities as first lady don't fall easily into the categories of speeches, letters, and positions on issues. She rarely gave interviews or speeches, so those are not available to the researcher. *Recollections* was written twenty-nine years before her death, and together with her letters, they provide a guide to her understanding of the roles she played, rhetorical and otherwise. As first lady, she served primarily as homemaker and hostess, but she continued to function as her husband's political partner. She advised him on personnel matters, participated in political discussions, strategized for his reelection, and assisted him on speeches. Her stroke hampered her, but did not prevent her from playing these roles.

Her extensive travels, both with her husband and on her own were a precursor to contemporary sociopolitical trips taken by presidential families. Nellie's adventurous spirit and journalist's eye provided narratives of extraordinary travels in which she represented the United States government to far-flung powers. Her *Recollections* demonstrates her love of drama, beauty, and power. Yet she refused to credit herself with the importance of this "ambassadorial" role, as midway through her *Recollections* she pauses and addresses the reader directly:

> I should like to say here, by way of explanation, which may or may not be necessary, that I am not trying in this narrative to pose as a woman endowed with a special comprehension of such problems of state as men alone have been trained to deal with. I confess only to a lively interest in my husband's work which I experienced from the beginning of our association and which nothing in our long life together, neither monotony, nor illness, nor misfortune, has served to lessen. (1914, 182)

When Nellie Taft became first lady, the role as developed by her predecessors focused almost exclusively on the duties of the homemaker. Given her lifelong ambition to achieve the White House, Nellie wasted no time in making this house her own. She maintained, "I made very few changes, really," (Taft 1914, 347) and then described the "minor matters" that she wanted to alter. Her descriptions of the inaugural and first impressions of the White House consume twenty-two pages of her *Recollections*, a fairly extensive account. Following the swearing-in, Nellie changed history by riding with her husband from the Capitol to the White House. Taft historian Pringle says that Roosevelt had decided two years before, at a time when he didn't know who would be his successor that he would not ride back from the inaugural with the new president (1939, vol. 1, 396). It had been customary for the outgoing president to accompany the new president to the White House. When Nellie learned that Theodore Roosevelt planned to head for the railroad station instead, she decided on an innovation:

> Since the ex-President was not going to ride back to the White House with his successor, I decided that I would. No President's wife had ever done it before, but as long as precedents were being disregarded I thought it might be not too great a risk for me to disregard this one. Of course there was objection, but I had my way and in spite of protests took my place at my husband's side. (Taft 1914, 331)

She described the ride as one of "secret elation" because she was doing something no woman had ever done before. "For me that drive was the proudest and happiest event of Inauguration Day," she wrote (Taft 1914, 332).

Nellie tried hard to take charge of everything in the White House, but soon she discovered that this was a very big job. She converted some of the public rooms into private ones for use of her family. The soft ground-glass globes of electric lights on the terraces were changed to flaring red-covered shades. She brought in Oriental furniture and tapestries and floor mats called "petates." Huge Oriental screens stood in strategic places, and the maids were kept busy polishing teakwood. She kept the White House overflowing with greenery: plants, ferns, and exotic flowers on every ledge and surface. No first lady took more pleasure than Mrs. Taft in the abundance of flowers she could command from the greenhouses and nurseries, and as Parks noted, no one around the White House was more important than the horticulturist in those days (1961, 111). In the end it was all a complete failure: "There was no comparison between the bugs and dampness of the terraces and the quiet comfort of the grand old rooms inside . . . conditions, precedent, everything favored the old way" (Parks 1961, 43).

She dismissed most of the ushers and replaced them with black footmen in blue livery who were to stand at the White House entrance to receive visitors and give instructions to sightseers. Her explanation was that prior to the liveried footmen, visitors were unaware as to whom one should approach with a question or to leave a card, and she believed that "many a timid visitor has had reason to be thankful for the change" (Taft 1914, 348). Nellie reacted to the criticism of her innovation by saying that the footmen served to direct the public to the right place, and they lent "a certain air of formal dignity to the entrance which, in my opinion, it had always lacked" (Taft 1914, 348). With this alteration and others, she attempted to change the image projected by the building—making it more regal.

While Edith Roosevelt had preceded Nellie for eight years as a confident administrator, keeping herself aloof from the details of White House management, Nellie was a micromanager. She appeared aware of her own perfectionist shortcomings:

> The members of my family . . . like to make the most of my serious attitude toward my domestic responsibilities, saying that I make them three times as difficult as they need be by a too positive insistence on my own methods. (Taft 1914, 347)

Nellie found that Edith Roosevelt had left her with a depleted linen supply, inadequate table service, and other areas needing refurbishing. She was satisfied with Edith's choice of china but increased the holdings in order to build one hundred place settings. She also found that the fine silver, much of it having historic value, was haphazardly kept in chests or boxes in the storeroom. She remedied this by requesting that a silver closet be built, with regular vault doors and locks, special compartments and receptacles, and velvet-lined trays (Taft 1914, 358).

The Tafts were the first to employ personal aides, and the president often teased Nellie about her liking for fuss and feathers. She replaced the White House steward who had been responsible for meals and general housekeeping and hired the first of the housekeepers, Elizabeth Jaffray, whom she expected to relieve her of "the supervision of such details as no man, expert steward though he be, would ever recognize" (Taft 1914, 349) such as keeping the rooms spotlessly clean. Nellie checked up on everybody, ran her fingers along things to find dust (Parks 1961, 118). Symbolically, then, we might conclude that Nellie Taft took on the role as the nation's "first housewife" with her customary zeal.

Nellie's household innovations produced considerable criticism. Edith Roosevelt's admirers thought the changes were an insult, and others thought Taft was substituting regality for democratic simplicity. Amusing stories about Mrs. Taft's dealings with the servants abounded. She decreed that all waiters at the White House must have hair, that no bald-headed butlers would be permitted in the dining room, and that all White House employees must be clean shaven. She was one of the few first ladies who ever came into the kitchen (Parks 1961, 108). Captain Archie Butt, senior White House aide, saw Nellie as an intellectual type with considerable executive ability. He also found her tactless in pushing through changes in staff before the inauguration and having them in operation the moment she stepped into the White House. There was certainly no hesitancy in the way she had taken hold. After a month's scrutiny of the president, Butt decided that Will Taft was "easily influenced to do what he wants to do." However, Butt conceded that Nellie was "without vanity" (Butt 1924, 600).

Ike Hoover was retained as chief usher, and no one would write more scathingly of the Taft administration than he. As chief usher he was the executive head of the household, in charge of all social affairs and entrusted with confidential matters. He portrayed Mrs. Taft as continually projecting herself into official discussions and joining her husband when she saw him deep in conversation with important politicians. Calling his years with the Tafts "Four Years of Strife," Hoover characterized Nellie's activities as an attempt to revolutionize the White House as a "disposition to change things for the sake of changing, as if there were no possibility that anything had been conducted properly before this time" (Hoover 1934, 41). He added, "Fortunately, circumstances stepped in to prevent many of the plans [from] becoming actualities, and others failed of their own weight. Few of Nellie Taft's changes survived the coming of other families" (Hoover 1934, 41).

True to her lifelong frugal ways, Nellie insisted that her vigilance could save money. Since the chief executive's salary had just been increased from $50,000 to $75,000, Nellie resolved to budget carefully so that $25,000 could go into the family's personal bank account. Like most objectives, she succeeded in this one and accumulated $100,000 during the four-year term. Her zeal during the first two years alone resulted in an $80,000 nest egg, which the president bragged to his aide, was a "pretty good sum" (Butt 1924, 623). Nellie ordered all foods bought in wholesale lots through comparison shopping and disallowed out-of-season food to be served at the White House. The first lady as a good money manager was an image appreciated by the public.

Nellie also embarked on a campaign to get the first family out of the horse-and-buggy era. She extracted a $12,000 appropriation from Congress for motorcars, and when she found the prices of the best cars too high, she struck a deal with their manufacturers for a discount, giving them the privilege of advertising their brand as the choice of the White House (Ostromecki 1995). Making the car deal even more unpalatable for many was the fact that the Tafts could easily have afforded to pay a little extra for the models Nellie wanted. Although the chief executive had a $25,000 allowance for travel, Nellie resolved to save from this bonanza. One way she did this was by keeping a cow on the White House grounds. Of course, everyone was shocked. They called the cow "Mooly Wooly" (Parks 1961, 119).

Nellie Taft also reveled in her role as a governmental hostess and cultural stylist, both in the Philippines and at the White House. Her social dinners were thought by the discriminating to have considerable charm. In Manila, she presided over a large estate (thirty-five rooms) with a multitude of servants, where she entertained a stream of visiting congressmen, generals, and other VIPs. This experience greatly influenced her role as America's first hostess. At the White House, she changed the dinner hour from eight to half past seven because of her devotion to the theatre. The musicales she gave there were sophisticated. As soon as the weather permitted, rugs were spread on the White House South Portico and the Tafts spent the evening outdoors with end terraces transformed with flowers, shrubs, and tables.

The Taft's silver wedding anniversary on June 19, 1911, was their last major White House social event. Major Archie Butt considered the silver wedding ceremony the most brilliant function in White House history, and it certainly was unique in the display of gifts and its 3,400 guests. Reminiscent of the Venetian ball she had thrown in Manila, the White House was outlined by thousands of multicolored lights; every tree and shrub on the grounds twinkled. Searchlights illuminated the American flag waiving above, paper lanterns hung from the trees. An arch inscribed with the wedding dates was overhead. Nellie wore a diamond tiara that Will had given her for the anniversary; her gown was white satin, with silver brocaded flowers and point lace, and she carried pink roses. The anniversary cake had twenty-five crystal hearts embedded in scrolls, replete with twenty-five silk Stars and Stripes and the president's flag. The event aroused a groundswell of criticism over the carloads of presents and the circus-like atmosphere. Although some of her friends thought gifts were inappropriate, Nellie saw no reason to discourage generosity. The president attempted to head off criticism by ordering that none of the gifts go on display, but Nellie showed much less embarrassment. She said "I have a right to be enthusiastic in my memory of that party, because without enthusiasm it could not have been given at all. And why should not one be frankly grateful for success?" (Taft 1914, 392).

Nellie Taft's cultural and aesthetic influences expanded into Washington, D.C., and she played a major role in some grand changes in the city. She sponsored musicales in the White House and Shakespeare performances on the lawn. During her Manila days she had been impressed by the throngs that gathered each evening in the city's waterside park, the Luneta, and she was determined to duplicate that in the city. With some help from the army officer in charge of public grounds, Nellie chose a road along the Potomac River, renaming it Potomac Drive. On April 17, 1909, she and Will drove in one of the new White House cars down Potomac Drive when it was formally opened for afternoon concerts. She converted the drive into a promenade, with bandstands at each end, where people could walk or ride and listen to band music in the late afternoon two or three times a week. The first concert featured Sousa marches. Her music was just as apt to be by Verdi, Strauss, Gounod, Bizet, or Mascagni. Parks noted that Mrs. Taft loved pageantry, and her concerts continued to be held on Wednesdays and Saturdays, from 5 to 7, for many years.

The swampy, mosquito-infested landscape along Potomac Drive left much to be desired, and Nellie solved that problem with another inspiration from her years in the Far East—the beautiful Yoshino (single white flower) cherry trees of Tokyo. She had experienced the Cherry Blossom Festival which opened the

Tokyo social season, and she believed that the soil and climate in Potomac Park encouraged a similar endeavor. She sent out a rush order to all the nurseries in America to ship their Japanese cherry trees to Washington; when only a hundred showed up, the mayor of Tokyo, Ukio Ozaki, offered another two thousand. The first shipment died, but subsequent deliveries made this project of Nellie Taft's one of the nation's most popular springtime tourist attractions. Unfortunately, she suffered a stroke less than a month after the opening of West Potomac Park, but the legacy she planted remains.

Although Nellie Taft displayed much skill at creating aesthetically pleasing environments and in efficient household management, one of her most signifi-cant, yet unseen, efforts was in the area of altering sociopolitical dimensions of public consciousness. This expansion of the first lady role into new territory would be continued by later first ladies. Specifically, Mrs. Taft was very much interested in racial reform, and she may be considered one of the earlier reform-ers on the issue of race. One of the first discoveries Taft made in the Philippines was that the army had drawn a color line, alienating the more friendly Filipinos in Manila. When Nellie arrived, she led the efforts to break down this barrier, saying: "We insisted upon complete racial equality for the Filipinos, and from the beginning there were a great many of them among our callers and guests" (Taft 1914, 125). Nellie made intensive efforts to show the Filipinos that they were their friends. She held "at home" receptions each week at the Malacanan palace for all to attend and employed local musicians. Mrs. Taft demonstrated a cosmopolitan tolerance of religion in her written depictions of the role of the Catholic Church in the Philippines. She described with insight the competing issues and conflicting personalities through a complex interweaving of religious and political observations. Even after her stroke, she made a rare appearance at a conference on American Jewry to which Will Taft was speaking. Taft said that he had come to know Jewish families through his wife, who had worked with Jews in forming the Cincinnati Orchestra and through its fund-raising efforts. As first lady, Nellie Taft also displayed genuine sympathy for immigrants, continu-ing the openness she had demonstrated in the Philippines with the natives. She interceded when an immigrant child was prohibited from entering the country, as he had been deemed "undesirable." When Nellie Taft discovered this was because the child had a speech defect, the ruling was overturned at her behest. During the Lawrence, Massachusetts, textile worker's strike, Nellie Taft ap-peared in the audience as the House Rules Committee heard the grisly tales. The press reports of her conspicuous presence have been credited with pushing the investigations of working conditions along (Anthony 1990, 321).

Nellie and Will didn't always agree on social issues: he supported prohibi-tion, while she opposed it. He favored full women's suffrage: she affirmed it in a more limited fashion. Nellie favored giving women every civic right—including the vote—but she wanted a prohibition on their running for office because that would upset the natural scheme of the home (Anthony 1990, 321). Nellie Taft supported higher education for women, believing that it could help women gain careers when necessary: "Education for women, as much as is obtainable, pos-sesses to my mind, far greater advantages than the commercial one of providing means for making a livelihood. This is a very great benefit, when necessary" (quoted in Colman 1926, 324). She also said, "My idea about higher culture for women is that it makes them great in intellect and soul, develops the lofty conception of womanhood; not that it makes them a poor imitation of man . . . woman is the complement of man. No fundamental superiority lies in the way in which the responsibilities of life are discharged" (quoted in Colman 1926, 324). But she was clearly conflicted, because Nellie was very concerned when her daughter Helen, dean at Bryn Mawr, became a nationally known speaker on issues of suffrage and world peace.

Nellie Taft's rhetorical activities were primarily focused on promoting her husband's career. Without her political influence and prodding, Taft might never have become president; his interest was for the judicial bench and not for political office. Her memoirs are extremely guarded in detailing her role in his campaign, and she describes her role as a "mere onlooker" whose political enthusiasm would "wane slightly, though temporarily" as she watched her husband grow hoarse from campaign speeches. In fact, she advised him on content, criticized him for dull speeches, read his manuscripts, and rebuked him for messages that sounded like judicial opinions. In her letters, Nellie prodded him: "Never mind if you cannot get off fireworks. It must be known by this time that is not your style and there is no use trying to force it" (Ross 1964, 95). She encouraged him and lent her critical eye and ear to help sustain his lackluster campaign. At no time in his life did he build up any faith in his own oratory, and his dislike for it caused him to procrastinate so that he would leave preparation of addresses until the last minute. Subject to heavy colds, he was often hoarse and particularly disliked speaking outdoors. As a campaigner, even with all of her help Taft was at best merely adequate.

The 1908 election illustrates only one of many occasions on which Nellie swayed Will's political decisions and future. Theodore Roosevelt was never in any doubt about Mrs. Taft's political ambition; in fact, she was so intense by nature that she made no secret of her aims. Later, she wrote with apparent humility in her *Recollections* that she possessed no special knowledge of the issues on which only men are trained and that her interest in the election was purely to help her husband (Taft 1914, 321). Her modest tone, however, was contradicted by others' reports of her importance in Will Taft's eventual election and political career. Of Taft's second campaign for the presidential nomination, Nellie's memoirs provide one line: "I cannot go into the details of the preliminary convention fight" (Taft 1914, 322). Unfortunately, the extent of her role in his campaign and her views of events during the months leading to the actual convention are not documented, but it would seem apparent that she played a strong role as a behind-the-scenes political advisor and strategist. Observers sometimes thought she seemed invincible in her determination to see him go higher. She had a relentless drive, yet she was only grudgingly respected.

Taft was more realistic; he described Nellie as the family politician who could meet all issues. She could be sharp with him in giving advice and snap at him in public. She had the Herron candor but functioned with quiet dignity as a Washington hostess. Her burning ambition was never far from the surface, and time and again she had urged Will to hold out for the greater prize. She believed Will did not fully understand his potential. She also supplied him with a touch of skepticism that Taft lacked. Even when she nagged and criticized him, he listened without resentment and gave thought to what she had to say.

She had frequently complained that on campaign trips her husband was "taken in charge and escorted everywhere with honor while I am usually sent with a lot of uninteresting women through some side street to wait for him at some tea or luncheon" (Butt 1924, 362). Unlike her predecessor, Edith Roosevelt, Nellie Taft didn't care for women's company and dispensed with the meetings of cabinet wives, an "approved" political role for the first lady. Nellie described her life as a "Cabinet Lady" as one of rather monotonous stress, where one had to manage the irksome duty of calling on nearly everybody, from other cabinet wives to congressional wives to Supreme Court wives to army wives. As first lady, she was "at home" informally at the White House about three afternoons a week, always receiving in the Red Room. But if given the choice (and as first lady she was given the choice) she preferred staying close to the center of power rather than being shunted off on a peripheral social mission.

Mrs. Taft maintained a major political presence in her husband's early White House tenure, and entertaining and civic improvements were always secondary to Nellie's involvement in her husband's career. She kept track of official appointments for Taft and discussed issues with him; she sat in on important White House conferences, afterward talking over the agenda with him. Nellie insisted on joining conferences in the president's office on every subject, claiming she was needed to make sure her husband did not fall asleep. At receptions, the sight of a politician in a private tête-à-tête with her husband brought the first lady rushing over to make sure Will was not being led to a policy she disapproved. It was apparent at once to observers that Nellie understood statecraft and that she shared in official discussions. Her husband relied on her memory for names and statistics. She listened to Senate and House debates. At the swearing-in of new Supreme Court justices, she requested a seat within the bar of the Court and was the first woman ever to sit there. She defended herself, saying,

> I do not believe in a woman meddling in politics or asserting herself along those lines, but I think any woman can discuss with her husband topics of national interest and, in many instances, she might give her opinion of questions with which, through study and contact, she has become familiar . . . Mr. Taft always held his conferences at our home, and, naturally, I heard these matters discussed more freely. (quoted in Anthony 1990, 321)

Nellie seemed to feel responsible for everything—her household and her husband's success. Their intense involvement with each other and Nellie's jealousy of potential rivals for the presidency had left them with few close friends to act as advisors. Instead of charming powerful congressmen and Washington insiders, she kept them at arm's length.

Her stroke, described by newspapers as "a nervous breakdown" (Anderson 1981, 58), kept her away from the White House until October 1909. She made only token appearances that didn't require her to speak, and her illness necessitated her absence from important decisions of the administration. Slowly over a year, Nellie began to reassert her authority, and her speech gradually improved while her health remained fragile. As late as January 1911, nineteen months after her stroke, Ellen Slayden noted in her journal, "Poor Mrs. Taft is still too ill to take part in anything" (Truman 1995, 111). Missing politics, she ate her meals behind a screen outside of the State Dining Room, listening quietly and closely. After about a year, Taft reported to his brother Horace, "She is quite disposed to sit as a pope and direct me as of yore which is an indication of the restoration of normal conditions" (Pringle 1939, vol. 2, 70).

People were soon murmuring about the president's indecision as he took months to name a cabinet, partly attributed to Nellie's involvement. Personnel decisions interested Nellie particularly, and she frequently based her judgments on subjective or irrelevant considerations. Truman (1995) says that almost certainly the stroke affected Nellie's political judgment. Her distrust of Teddy Roosevelt made her an easy target for the schemes of Taft's secretary, Charles Norton, who saw himself as a Machiavellian destined to reshape the Republican Party. Together, he and Nellie relentlessly persuaded Taft to remove more of Roosevelt's appointees. The split between Taft and Roosevelt began (according to Margaret Truman) over the firing of Henry White, whom Roosevelt had appointed as the ambassador to France. Twenty years before, on her European honeymoon, Nellie had asked White, at the time a minor diplomat in the American embassy in London, for tickets to Parliament. Instead, the Tafts got tickets to the Royal Mews, and she had never forgiven White. When she became first lady, firing White became a top priority for the Taft administration. While Taft would have forgotten the matter, Nellie Taft was less forgiving. Soon after the election, Washington was buzzing with this tale and the report that Taft intended to ask for White's resignation in revenge for the slight. When confronted by Alice Roosevelt Longworth, Taft reproached her, saying that she ought to know that he was "big enough to forget that sort of thing" (Longworth 1933, 158). However, very shortly after the inauguration, White's resignation was accepted, and this seemed to the Roosevelts like another betrayal. The rift between Taft and Roosevelt would eventually wreck the Republican Party. The split was widened when Nellie vetoed the appointment of Alice Roosevelt's husband, Nicholas Longworth (an Ohio congressman) as ambassador to China.

Taft's reliance on his wife was not unknown. National magazines spoke openly of her influence. In March 1909, the *Ladies' Home Journal* informed its readers that the new first lady had a touch of domesticity and a healthy respect for the arts but was most remarkable because of the mentor role she played for her husband. Her "intense ambition" had helped propel him into the job and she remained his close confidante. "Had it not been for his wife," the *Journal* noted, "Mr. Taft would never have entered the Presidential race" (Hill 1909, 6). One acquaintance characterized their relationship as resembling that of "two men who are intimate chums." She admitted, "I had always had the satisfaction of knowing almost as much as he (Taft) about the politics and intricacies of any situation in which he found himself, and my life was filled with interests of a most unusual kind" (quoted in Anthony 1990, 318). Nellie's demurral that her "active participation in (her) husband's career came to an end when he became President" rings false in light of so many descriptions to the contrary (Taft 1914, 365).

Nellie Taft fulfilled her expected role as the social hostess of the land. At the same time, she was criticized for her active role in advising her husband on issues ranging from cabinet appointments to world affairs. Again, it is difficult to assess the impact of those roles because of Nellie's illness during the first few months of her White House tenure. Some depictions vilify her influence, but they are few. Her determination and ambition were recognized, but many also acknowledged those qualities as essential to Taft's presidency. Nellie Taft's varied rhetorical activities as first lady might be termed more conventional now.

Legacy

Symbolically, Nellie Taft's rhetoric as first lady was both a product of her times and a foreshadowing of changes to come to the role. As the nation shifted from the image of women's main role as purely social, Nellie Taft was an ambitious, strong-willed, acute woman who was offered the opportunity to alter the image of first lady as the nation's first wife, head hostess, and leading homemaker. She set a formal White House tone that was often labeled more royal than democratic. She insisted on liveried footmen, a lavishly redecorated White House, greenhouses, and formal "at home" events for callers three times a week in the Red Room. A generous hostess who worried about money but didn't stint on entertainment, Nellie Taft initiated the practice of following state dinners with musical or theatrical performances. She created the stately outdoor garden parties on the White House lawn. An avid supporter of the arts in Washington, she habitually attended the theater, the symphony, and the opera. Perhaps her most lasting legacy was the planting of the first cherry trees on the Potomac, giving rise to the annual Cherry Blossom Festival which draws thousands of visitors to Washington each year.

Nellie played a leading role in Taft's political ascendancy. On political questions, she was essentially conservative. She considered it imprudent to rock the boat, and she was slow to respond to evolving social changes. Although a rebel in her adolescent days, eager to carve a career for herself, in her mature life she never seemed to doubt that a woman's place was in the home. Yet she displayed a backroom political acumen that resulted in her husband's election to the highest position in the nation. She issued disclaimers about her influence over Will, but her actions spoke louder than her words. On March 4, 1909, Inauguration Day, the *Washington Post* commented: "There is every reason why she (Mrs. Taft) should feel satisfaction in her husband's success, for had it not been for her determination to keep him from becoming a Supreme Court Justice he would not have been able to accept the nomination. . . . 'I want you to be in line for the presidential nomination' she told him, and he followed what turned out to be excellent and timely advice" (Hay 1988, 182). She was quoted that day as saying, "It always has been my ambition to see Mr. Taft President of the United States, and naturally when the ceremonies of the inauguration were in progress I was inexpressibly happy" (Hay 1988, 182).

Nellie Taft had a deep understanding of her husband's noble qualities as well as his weaknesses and indecision. Of his varied achievements, she regarded his Philippines work as his most enduring monument. Will found consolation and deep reserves in her; his open and generous nature shows itself clearly in the continuous stream of letters he sent to Nellie over the years. Will wrote to her on August 5, 1902, as he traveled back to the Philippines: "I measure every woman I meet with you and they are all found wanting" (Ross 1964, 147). Few first ladies can have had such constant reminders of their husband's devotion as Will lavished on Nellie.

Her own collapse so soon after Taft became president was the great tragedy of her life, as biographer Ross says, "No First Lady ever harbored more ambition for this role, or worked more persistently to achieve it" (1964, 393). Although she lacked Will's magnetic and popular touch, she was a respected public figure. She was resourceful and self-contained, and her common sense and good management were proverbial. William Howard Taft never underestimated the role his wife played in his life.

Nellie Taft's decision to seek status and power through her husband's career was a mark of her ambition; she chose the traditional route to the top, through her husband, rather than taking the unconventional route of women who were avoiding marriage and seeking social change. She was a first lady of many firsts: first to publish her memoirs, first to ride in the inaugural parade, first to be buried in Arlington National Cemetery. In a sense, her ambitions were fulfilled in a vicarious vocation through the opportunities provided by her husband's career. She outdistanced many of her predecessors in her ambition and effort, as well as her desire for adventure and search for impossible perfection.

References

Anderson, Judith Icke. 1981. *William Howard Taft: An Intimate History*. New York: Norton.

Anthony, Carl Sferranza. 1990. First Ladies: The Saga of the Presidents' Wives and Their Power 1789–1961, Vol. 1. New York: Quill William Morrow.

Barker, Charles E. 1947. *With President Taft in the White House*. Chicago: A. Kroch & Son.

Barzman, Sol. 1970. *The First Ladies*. New York: Cowles.

Boller, Paul F., Jr. 1988. *Presidential Wives: An Anecdotal History*. New York: Oxford University Press.

Busbey, Katherine Graves. 1911. Mrs. Taft's Home-Making. *Good Housekeeping*, September, n.p.

Butt, Archie. 1924. *Taft and Roosevelt: The Intimate Letters of Archie Butt*. 2 Vols. Garden City, N.Y.: Doubleday.

Caroli, Betty Boyd. 1995. *First Ladies*, expanded edition. New York: Oxford University Press.

Colman, Edna M. 1926. White House Gossip: From Andrew Jackson to Calvin Coolidge. New York: Doubleday.

Coletta, Paola. 1973. *The Presidency of William Howard Taft.* Lawrence, Kans.: University of Kansas Press.

Cordery, Stacy A. 1996. Helen Herron Taft. In *American First Ladies: Their Lives and Their Legacy*, ed. Lewis L. Gould, 321–39. New York: Garland.

Duffy, Herbert S. 1930. *William Howard Taft.* New York: Minton, Balch and Company.

First in the President's Heart—His Home. 1912. *Home Life*, April, n.p.

Furman, Bess. 1951. *White House Profile.* Indianapolis, Ind.: Bobbs-Merrill Co.

Gutin, Myra G. 1989. The President's Partner: the First Lady in the Twentieth Century. New York: Greenwood.

Hay, Peter. 1988. *All the Presidents' Ladies.* New York: Viking.

Hill, George G. 1909. The Wife of the New President. *Ladies' Home Journal*, March, n.p.

Jaffray, Elizabeth. 1927. *Secrets of the White House.* New York: Cosmopolitan Book Co.

Jensen, Amy LaFollette. 1958. *The White House and Its Thirty-Three Families.* New York: McGraw-Hill.

Johnson, Martha Waller Papers. 1864–1926. Correspondence of Frances Cleveland, Florence Harding, Harriet Lane, Edith Roosevelt, and Helen Taft. Richmond, Va.: Virginia Historical Society Collections.

Kutler, Stanley. 1971. Helen Herron Taft. In *Notable American Women*, Vol. 3, ed. Edward T. James. Cambridge, Mass.: Belknap.

Longworth, Alice Roosevelt. 1933. *Crowded Hours: Reminiscences of Alice Roosevelt Longworth.* New York: Charles Scribner's Sons.

Manners, William. 1969. *TR and Will: A Friendship That Split the Republican Party.* New York: Harcourt Brace Jovanovich.

Mayo, Edith P., and Denise D. Meringolo. 1994. *First Ladies: Political Role and Public Image.* Washington, D.C.: Smithsonian Institution.

Means, Marianne. 1963. *The Woman in the White House.* New York: Random House.

Morris, Sylvia Jukes. 1980. *Edith Kermit Roosevelt, Portrait of a First Lady.* New York: Coward, McCann & Geoghegan, Inc.

Noted Women Collection. Correspondence of Helen Taft, Grace Coolidge, Lou Hoover, Alice Roosevelt Longworth, and Eleanor Roosevelt. Stanford, Calif.: Stanford University Libraries, Manuscripts Division.

Ostromecki, Walter J. 1995. Helen Herron Taft: Influence and Automobiles. *Manuscripts*, 45:3, 216–24.

Paletta, Lu Ann. 1990. *The World Almanac of First Ladies.* New York: World Almanac.

Hoover, Irwin Hood. 1934. *Forty-Two Years in the White House.* Boston: Houghton Mifflin.

Parks, Lillian Rogers. 1961. *My Thirty Years Backstairs at the White House.* New York: Fleet Publishing Co.

Pringle, Henry F. 1939. *The Life and Times of William Howard Taft.* 2 vols. New York: Farrar and Rinehart, Inc.

Ross, Ishbel. 1964. *An American Family: The Tafts 1678 to 1964.* New York: Greenwood.

Slayden, Ellen Maury. 1963. *Washington Wife.* New York: Harper & Row.

Stoddard, Henry L. 1927. As I Knew Them: Presidents and Politics from Grant to Coolidge. New York: Harper & Brothers.

Taft, Mrs. Willam Howard (Helen Herron). Nd. Diary of Helen Herron. In the Papers of William Howard Taft. Series II. Washington, D.C.: Library of Congress, Manuscript Division.

———. 1914. *Recollections of Full Years.* New York: Dodd, Mean, & Company.

Taft, Helen Herron Papers. 1908–56. Correspondence and Papers. Washington, D.C.: Library of Congress, Manuscript Division.

Taft, Robert Alphonso Papers. 1885–1962. Correspondence. Washington, D.C.: Library of Congress, Manuscript Division.

Taft, William Howard Papers. Correspondence between William and Helen Taft. Diaries of Helen Herron Taft. Washington, D.C.: Library of Congress, Manuscript Division.

Truman, Margaret. 1995. *First Ladies*. New York: Random House.

Willets, Gilson. 1908. *Inside History of the White House*. New York: The Christian Herald.

Wolford, Jane Collins. 1982. Helen Herron Taft. Unpublished MA thesis. San Francisco State University.

Chapter 5

Ellen Axson Wilson
A Rhetorical Reassessment of a Forgotten First Lady

Lisa M. Burns

> I wonder how anyone who reaches middle age can bear it if she cannot feel on looking back that, whatever mistakes she may have made, she has on the whole lived for others and not for herself.
>
> —Ellen Axson Wilson

Every year, thousands of museum-goers tour the popular first ladies exhibit at the Smithsonian Museum of American History. Aptly titled "First Ladies: Political Role and Public Image," the exhibit's introduction presents first ladies as "a focus of the public's preoccupation with fame, status, and social position. They are America's democratic version of royalty." The introduction notes that some first ladies chose to remain within the boundaries of what was considered a proper role for women in their day, while others challenged and extended these boundaries "depending on the personality and interests of the woman and the social climate of the times." The exhibit, filled with photographs and artifacts, touches on every first lady; the restrictions of exhibition space, unfortunately, limit the material covered, which produces problematic consequences for our collective memory of individual first ladies. Particularly troubling are the omissions in regards to Ellen Axson Wilson, the first wife of Woodrow Wilson.

The Smithsonian exhibit does not adequately represent Ellen Wilson's accomplishments during her brief tenure as first lady. The exhibit's text erroneously states that Wilson "gave up a promising career as an artist when she married." However, she actually continued to create, exhibit, and sell her paintings during her time in the White House, making her the only first lady to hold on to her career while in that position. The Smithsonian exhibit also critiques her work on the Slum Clearance Act as "misguided charity" without recognizing the fact that she was the first presidential spouse to attach her name to a legislative bill. The text notes her failure to achieve the building of new housing for those living in the unsanitary slums of Washington, D.C., totally ignoring both the nature of the original proposal and her unprecedented involvement in drafting and lobbying for the legislative measure.[1]

Although Ellen Wilson was first lady for only seventeen months, she epitomized the modern first lady—a woman who performs multiple roles. Her accomplishments rivaled those of successors Lady Bird Johnson, Betty Ford, Rosalynn Carter, and Hillary Rodham Clinton. She even served as a role model for Eleanor Roosevelt, who is considered by many scholars such as Myra Gutin to be "the most committed and respected first lady in history" (1989, 81). Ellen Wilson worked as an advocate for the controversial Slum Clearance Act, much as Lady Bird Johnson and Betty Ford would do half a century later for other legislation. Her marriage to Woodrow Wilson was a political partnership on par with couples like the Carters and Clintons. And she was the only first lady to carry on a career independent of her institutional role while in the White House. Yet not only is Ellen Wilson misrepresented in the first ladies exhibit, she has all but faded from our collective memory despite these accomplishments. This is due in part to limited texts remaining from her first lady years[2] and the fact that the study of women, particularly first ladies, is a more contemporary phenomenon.

But it is precisely for these reasons that Ellen Wilson warrants attention. Part of the work of first lady scholars is to recover voices that have been neglected. These voices function as "mirrors of history," informing our understanding of both the first ladies studied and the eras in which they lived. Recovering Ellen Wilson's discourse, for example, shows her to be an exemplar of progressive ideals and a groundbreaking first lady. Studying her discourse in its historical context makes evident constraints upon all women at the time when prevailing notions of gender severely restricted women's participation in the public sphere, constraining the forms of discourse they could use. Although public advocacy was largely off limits for women, other avenues were open to those who wished to engage in political action, such as letter writing, club activity, and volunteering.[3] Scholars need to study these kinds of sources, but much of this material has not been preserved. Additionally, scholars must also study women's "actions as discourse" for often their actions spoke eloquently in that they were noticed and proved influential. A first lady such as Ellen Wilson used letters, private conversation, and actions in her performance of the position. If this discourse is overlooked, we will not understand her true contribution to the first lady institution and how it evolves through social construction.

Therefore, this essay seeks to reexamine Ellen Axson Wilson's performance as first lady by looking at the discourse available from a rhetorical perspective. By combining a feminist critical stance that seeks to recover lost voices with a historical interest in understanding the context of the discourse, this essay seeks to reclaim Wilson's place in the first lady lineage and in the history of women's discourse. Furthermore, as Kathleen J. Turner argues, "the melding of historical and rhetorical methodologies can contribute to an understanding of the complex latitudinal and longitudinal processes of social influence" (1998, 4). Such an examination reveals that Ellen Wilson exemplifies progressive ideals and the "new woman ideology." Even though she is often excluded from the modern era, this study suggests that she is actually a precursor to those who followed in her footsteps, including Eleanor Roosevelt, Lady Bird Johnson, Betty Ford, Rosalynn Carter, and Hillary Rodham Clinton. Although Wilson was precluded from speaking publicly by cultural restrictions, her private letters, conversations, and public actions nevertheless position her rhetorically in the modern era. Her discourse offers great insight into her performance of the first lady position.

Ellen Wilson was a by-product of the progressive era, and the era influenced her performance as first lady. Her religious background, which stressed charity and service to others, as well as her headstrong and independent nature allowed her to embrace the spirit of progressivism and embody the ideals of the "New Woman." The values she gained as a young woman foreshadowed the first lady she would later become.

Biography

Ellen Louise Axson was born in Rome, Georgia, in 1860.[4] The daughter of a Presbyterian minister and a book-loving mother, she showed an interest in intellectual pursuits at an early age and excelled in her studies at the Rome Female College (which offered schooling for girls of all ages), particularly French, English literature, and composition. Ellen was an eager pupil. After taking geometry, she taught herself trigonometry the next summer. Following her graduation in 1876, Ellen planned to enter the Normal Department of Nashville University, which required applicants to pass proficiency examinations. She passed the exams with very high marks, but her father could not afford to send her away to college. So she instead enrolled as a postgraduate at Rome Female College, taking advanced classes in French and German, skills that would later be put to use as she translated German manuscripts for her scholar husband, Woodrow Wilson.

But art was always Ellen's first love. Along with her foreign language courses, she also continued her drawing lessons with instructor Helen Fairchild, who had spent several years studying at the prestigious National Academy of Design in New York City. While under the tutelage of Fairchild, Ellen won her first award as an artist, a bronze medal for excellence in freehand drawing from the Paris International Exposition. By the age of eighteen, Ellen began charging a small fee for portraits she drew from photographs, and in a short time she was earning enough money to support herself, which she recognized as a key to independence for women. She also started to talk about going to New York City to study art.

Ellen possessed the same love of literature as her mother, and throughout her life she was a voracious reader. In her early years, she read the classics of Shakespeare, Scott, Dickens, Ruskin, and Emerson interspersed with the contemporary works of George Eliot, Thomas Hardy, and Benjamin Disraeli. She was particularly fond of romantic and Victorian era poets such as Wordsworth, Browning, and Elizabeth Barrett Browning. She shared this fascination with literature with her future husband. However, her intellectual and financial independence did not please Reverend Edward Axson, her father, who thought his daughter "obstreperous" and "entirely too much inclined to have her own opinions" (Elliot 1944, 8; Saunders 1985, 18). She planned on making a career for herself as an artist, but her plans were put on hold when her mother died in 1881, leaving her to care for her father and brothers at the age of twenty-one.

On April 8, 1883, two years following her mother's death, Ellen attended her father's weekly church service as usual. Seated behind her was a young Atlanta lawyer, who was distracted by the minister's young daughter sitting in the pew before him. Twenty-seven-year-old Woodrow Wilson, whose father was also a Presbyterian minister, was in Rome on business and staying with relatives who attended Reverend Axson's church. When he called on Reverend Axson that afternoon, Woodrow was formally introduced to Ellen. When he returned to Rome the following month, Woodrow began to court Ellen, who had previously discouraged a string of would-be suitors, earning the nickname "Ellie, the Man Hater." They went on their first date on May 28, 1883, and were engaged four months later. The couple seemed to fulfill each other's need for intellectual companionship. Woodrow would soon abandon law in favor of graduate study in politics and history, with plans for a career as a college professor.

Woodrow and Ellen remained apart for the majority of their two-year engagement. After the first year, Ellen's father died in an asylum under questionable circumstances. Reverend Axson, who suffered for years from severe depression, may have committed suicide; however, the exact cause of death was not recorded by asylum officials. Ellen offered to break off the engagement, but Woodrow refused. In an interesting move for a woman of her era, Ellen decided to use the money from her father's estate to resume her own studies at the liberal Art Students League in New York City, rather than joining her fiancé in Baltimore, where he was studying history and politics at Johns Hopkins University. Although she only spent one year in New York, that experience evidenced an independent streak—a sign of Ellen being a "new woman" who was interested in expanding her opportunities beyond the domestic sphere and preserving a sense of independence and self-reliance.

In October 1884, Ellen moved to New York City and began taking classes at the Art Students League. The league was "regarded as radical, based as it was upon a student-run, nonauthoritarian society with equal status accorded to women and men" (Saunders 1985, 49). She took classes from some of the top American impressionists of the period, and won a spot in the league's exclusive life class that employed live models, some nude and some draped. Her work was widely praised by her instructors and peers. Ellen took advantage of her time in New York, often touring museums and attending the theater during her free time. She also found time to devote to volunteer work, which she viewed as part of her Christian duty.

Ellen's interest in social reform can be traced to her days in New York. While taking classes, she volunteered at a mission school, located over a barroom in one of the city's "slum areas," where she taught African American children basic reading, writing, and math, along with Bible studies. Fiancé Woodrow questioned her volunteer work at the mission, particularly the location of the school, in a letter dated February 9, 1885:

> It will not add to my piece of mind on Sabbaths that you have undertaken missionary labours. . . . One who is not a New Yorker must be exposed to risks in the work to which city-wise and city-hardened persons would not be subject. I entirely sympathize with your feelings in the matter, but I can't help questioning the wisdom of the arrangement. (quoted in McAdoo 1962, 122)

Ellen responded the next day, February 10, 1885, by arguing that it was "her duty" to teach at the school: "To think first of any small risk or unpleasantness connected with teaching there does not seem right. . . . The mere possibility should not keep me from trying to do something" (quoted in Link et al. 1966, 233–34). Despite her fiancé's concerns, she continued her work at the mission. This insistence on working outside the home was a vital part of Ellen's "new woman" persona. Her commitment to working at the mission and her independence would later inspire her daughter Jessie to become involved in the settlement house movement.

Ellen married Woodrow in June 1885. For two decades, Ellen focused on her roles as a professor's wife and mother to three daughters. The Wilsons' first daughter, Margaret, was born on April 16, 1886; sister Jessie was born on August 28, 1887; and youngest child Eleanor arrived October 16, 1889. In each of her husband's increasingly important positions, first as president of Princeton University and later as governor of New Jersey, Ellen acted as Woodrow's trusted advisor, honing their political partnership. And as a university president's and governor's wife, she was able to begin her work as an advocate for social issues, which she would continue during her time in Washington. All of this would prepare Ellen for the multiple roles she would perform as first lady.

The Road to the White House

Early on, when Woodrow was being touted as a candidate for the democratic presidential nomination in 1912, Ellen served as an informal, yet very shrewd, campaign manager. She watched the papers for any mention of the candidates, especially her husband. Official Wilson biographer Ray Stannard Baker states: "Mrs. Wilson followed indefatigably, as she had been doing for years, everything in the press that she thought would interest or assist her husband . . . and clipped out everything related to the campaign." But her work did not end with clipping articles. As Baker explains, "She would go over the assortment with Mr. Wilson every day, often giving him suggestions as to people to see, Mr. Wilson making memoranda in the little book he carried always in his vest pocket" (1931, vol. 3, 114). Those clippings, numbering in the hundreds, can be found today in the Wilson Papers at the Library of Congress.

Examples of this aspect of Ellen's involvement in her husband's campaign are also found in their correspondence. In May 1911, when Woodrow was on a speaking tour out west, Ellen urged him to throw his hat into the ring as an official candidate:

> How very interesting the story about the telephone from Denver! The New York reporter asking "what is the news in Denver" and the answer: "the town is wild over Woodrow Wilson and is booming him for President" . . . By-the-way-, please don't say again that you "are not thinking about the presidency." All who know you well know that that is fundamentally true, but superficially it can't be true; and it gives the cynics an opening which they can seize with glee. The "Sun" of course had an outrageous little editorial about it. (WW Papers)

A few days later on May 15, 1911, she shared some important information regarding his chances at the nomination, including some reassuring comments from the press:

> News from Washington that Bryan has now conceded your nomination. Whether true or not I do not know. I enclose today's editorial from the "True American." I think it handles that remark of yours which caused so much comment very well. Another paper defended you well too. It said that your mind was occupied not with an office but with principles and that you were equally ready to work for them as a leader or in the ranks. (WW Papers)

During the campaign, Ellen continued to keep track of the press responses, and she used this information to help her husband formulate his campaign speeches and comments to the press (Boller 1998, 222). She also intervened on her husband's behalf in at least one campaign conflict involving Colonel Harvey, the editor of *Harper's Weekly* and a strong early supporter of Wilson's campaign. In a previously unpublished letter to an influential cousin, Judge Robert Ewing, sent on January 12, 1912, Ellen asks him to straighten out the misunderstanding between Woodrow and Harvey regarding his candidacy: "His speeches and editorials about Woodrow have all been wonderful and are among my dearest treasures. In short, this matter involves something more important than politics, viz. friendship" (Wilson-McAdoo Papers). In the spring 1912, Ellen also accompanied her husband on a campaign trip through her home state of Georgia, helping him garner important southern votes (Saunders 1985, 223).

There are even indications that it was Ellen Wilson who kept her husband from conceding during the tedious balloting process at the Democratic Convention, thus indirectly helping him win the presidential nomination.[5] It appeared at one point that Wilson did not have enough votes to gain the nomination and was advised to release his delegates and allow them to vote for one of the other candidates. Wilson, who was at home at Sea Girt with his family, reportedly considered conceding. Ellen's brother Stockton Axson states in his memoirs: "Governor Wilson wrote out a message of withdrawal, showed it to Mrs. Wilson. She immediately flashed back: 'What do you gain by doing this? You must not send it.' After some argument, he deferred to her opinion." This story was told to Axson by Wilson's secretary Joseph Tumulty. He notes that "it never occurred to me to doubt it—nor unfortunately to confirm it. If it is true, and nothing but documentary evidence to the contrary could convince me that it was untrue (it was like her, and what earthly reason had Tumulty to manufacture the story, with all sorts of detail, for me?), then she quite literally as well as spiritually made him president" (Axson 1993, 106).

While advising her husband, Ellen also began to pursue her interests in social reform. During her husband's tenure as governor of New Jersey, Ellen had the opportunity to become actively involved in numerous causes. Since the state did not provide a year-round governor's mansion, Ellen had few social obligations, allowing her more time to read newspapers and analyze political issues. She also devoted time to volunteer efforts, including taking an active role as honorary director of the New Jersey State Charities Aid Society. During the summer 1911, the Wilsons conducted an inspection trip of state institutions, including veterans' homes, mental institutions, reform schools, hospitals, and prisons (Saunders 1985, 213). Ellen continued to conduct such inspection trips on her own. She would continue this type of hands-on social work during her tenure in the White House.

Establishing an Artistic Career

Ellen's duties as a university president's and later governor's wife, as well as a mother to three children, left Ellen little time to devote to her youthful ambitions to be a professional artist. Thus, during the early years of the Wilson's marriage, art became simply a hobby for Ellen. But the death of her brother Eddie in 1905 brought her back into the world of art in a more professional way. In an effort to restore his wife's spirits, Woodrow arranged for the family to spend the summer in Old Lyme, Connecticut, home to a community of artists. During this first summer, Ellen worked in watercolors and oil, focusing on landscapes in the tradition of the popular American Impressionist movement of the time. She befriended several prominent American painters, some of whom had been fellow students from her Art Students League days. From this point on, Ellen would never again abandon her art. In fact, she would pursue a career as a professional artist that would continue until her death.

After spending several summers as part of the artists' communities at Old Lyme, Connecticut, and Cornish, New Hampshire, Ellen Wilson amassed a collection of original paintings, mainly landscapes, that fellow artists encouraged her to show (Griswold Papers).[6] In November 1911, aware that her husband's name was becoming nationally known, Ellen submitted one of her canvases for exhibition in New York under the name "W. Wilson" of Metuchen, New Jersey. The painting won a spot in the show, yet she was still reluctant to show her work (Saunders 1985, 256). By the spring 1912, at the same time her husband was beginning to campaign for president, Ellen was finally convinced by friends to hire a professional art agent. In a previously unpublished letter dated May 25,

1912, she wrote to prominent New York gallery owner and art dealer William Macbeth:

> My friends have been urging me for some time to send my pictures for exhibition to the Pennsylvania Academy, etc., etc., but I am excessively shy about them. . . . As I am sending a few into New York anyhow to be framed, I am going to ask you to do me the great favour of looking at them and telling me what you think of them. (Macbeth Papers)

Macbeth replied on June 22, 1912, that the paintings were "all most happy in composition and have much fine quality. I think they would hold their own very well in any public exhibition" (Macbeth Papers). In a follow-up letter, Wilson asked him to be her agent, and he agreed. In the fall 1912, he helped her select several paintings to submit to shows. Her paintings were accepted at shows at the Art Institute of Chicago, the John Herron Art Institute of Indianapolis, the Pennsylvania Academy of the Fine Arts, and the National Academy of Design in New York. Meanwhile, five of her landscapes were selected for exhibition by the Association of Women Painters and Sculptors, which she joined upon invitation. She was also offered membership in The Pen and Brush Club, founded in 1893 for professional women writers and artists that is still active today. She is listed on the organization's website as a "more well known" member along with Eleanor Roosevelt (Aucella and Hobbs 1993, 7).

Shortly before the presidential inauguration in March 1913, Ellen's one-woman show of fifty landscapes opened at the Arts and Crafts Guild in Philadelphia. The show was successful, selling twenty-four paintings. Ellen donated the proceeds of all of her art sales to the Martha Berry School, a school for needy children in her hometown of Rome, Georgia (Saunders 1985, 257). In a February 21, 1913, review of her one-woman show, an art critic from the *New York Times* wrote, "Mrs. Wilson's paintings show her to be a real lover of nature and the possessor of a fine faculty for interpreting it. . . . The peace and quiet of her scenes are marked by subdued colors and a sacrifice of detail" (5). Unfortunately, because her public success as an artist came at the same time as her husband's political triumph, Ellen had little time to savor the moment. But she continued to paint and sell her artwork while in the White House, thus continuing to pursue her career while performing the duties of the first lady position.

Unfortunately, Ellen only spent a short seventeen months as first lady. She fell ill in March 1914, shortly before the wedding of daughter Margaret, the second Wilson daughter to be married in the White House (her sister Jessie was married four months earlier). While Ellen reportedly suffered a fall just before Margaret's wedding, which required minor surgery, she also suffered from a more serious condition. She never fully recovered and spent much of her time confined to her bed throughout the summer. But she kept busy even during this time, overseeing the plans for a White House "Rose Garden." She died in the White House on August 6, 1914, from Bright's disease. Following a small family funeral in the East Room, Ellen's body was carried by train to her hometown of Rome, Georgia, where she was buried (Saunders 1985, 266–79).

Rhetorical Activities as First Lady

Woodrow Wilson was inaugurated on March 4, 1913. In the spirit of progressivism, the Wilsons chose to forgo an elaborate inaugural ball in favor of smaller gatherings, and rather than focus on social events, they decided to get to work immediately. While Woodrow quickly began tackling legislative measures, Ellen began to establish herself as a first lady interested in more than entertaining. Along with assisting her husband's efforts by researching issues such as tariff reform and the unstable political situation in Mexico, Ellen immediately began to involve herself in social reform efforts, including a controversial plan to address the living conditions of poor residents of the District. She also made certain modifications to her own living arrangements, installing an art studio for herself in the White House living quarters. Despite serving only seventeen months as first lady, Ellen Wilson both continued traditions established by her precursors and broke ground for those who followed her. She served as her husband's advisor on matters personal and political, labored tirelessly as an advocate for a number of controversial social causes, and all the while continued to work as a professional artist. These rhetorical activities mirror, and in many ways surpass, the accomplishments of modern first ladies.

The Presidential Partnership of Woodrow and Ellen Wilson

The Wilsons are arguably the precursor to the modern presidential couple, looking strikingly similar to couples like the Carters and Clintons when viewed from a rhetorical perspective. The study of presidential couples is in its infancy, but as Gil Troy argues, "Presidential historians and political scientists must begin to recognize the importance of studying both members of the presidential couple, separately and together" (2000, xiii). Troy uses the term "co-presidency" to define the relationship between modern presidential couples. Robert Watson in *The Presidents' Wives* makes a similar point, using instead the phrase "presidential partnership" (2000, 29). Their approach is similar to Karlyn Kohrs Campbell's discussion of the rhetorical presidency as a "two-person career" (1996). As mentioned earlier, Ellen Wilson was an active part of her husband's academic and political careers, aiding him in his own pursuits by acting as his advisor and confidante. She also helped him through her own progressive performance of the first lady position.

Like several other notable first ladies, Ellen served an important role behind the scenes at the White House as her husband's advisor. Their twenty-nine-year marriage was a true partnership, with the Wilsons sharing all aspects of their lives. While Ellen educated herself about political philosophy as a young wife in order to understand and assist her husband in his teaching and research, Woodrow learned to appreciate art and poetry when he realized it was his partner's passion. Woodrow found out early that he married the "perfect type of wife" for an intellectual such as himself (Boller 1998, 221). Her German skills came in handy when Woodrow, who struggled with the language, needed to translate manuscripts for his research. In his memoirs, Ellen's brother Stockton Axson notes that "she made digests of many very dull German treatises on government in order to save him the time and energy for his more creative type of work" (1993, 94). He also says: "He read her everything he wrote. She listened attentively (had great power of concentration), criticized, suggested changes—you know what he told me about the 'hit' of his speeches being germinated by her suggestions" (Axson 1993, 105).

While Woodrow Wilson focused on performing the duties of his position, whether as university president or president of the United States, it was his wife who stayed informed of what was going on in the world, particularly in politics. Ellen used her skills as an avid reader to devour newspapers and magazines, clipping any articles that might be of importance to her husband; she also possessed an "extraordinary understanding of political issues and of human nature" (Saunders 1985, 248). According to Wilson's advisor (and son-in-law) William G. McAdoo, of all of the president's advisors, Ellen was "the soundest and most influential of them all" (1931, 285). Another close presidential advisor, Colonel House, writes of his discussions with Ellen regarding political matters, from policy matters to cabinet appointments (Link et al. 1966–1985). After her death, Woodrow told a close friend, "I don't know that I would be here in the White House at all if it had not been for Ellen and the way that she influenced the growth of my career, and yet I sometimes regret that we ever came here, for I almost fear the strain of it all cost my darling's life" (Axson 1993, 226).

An interesting chronicle of Ellen's advisory role exists in the Wilsons' correspondence. During any period of separation of more than a few days, the Wilsons wrote to one another on a daily basis, leaving a legacy of thousands of letters, many of which have been preserved. While the letters are considered to be "among the greatest love letters in the English language," they also record Woodrow Wilson's career and his wife's key role in it (McAdoo 1962, vii). Much of the correspondence contains discussions of both personal and professional issues, proving that the Wilson's marriage was a true partnership.

Just as she had done when her husband was governor of New Jersey and a presidential candidate, Ellen continued to advise her husband when they moved to the White House, primarily by researching topics and keeping track of news reports. An example of this was her assistance in dealing with the Mexican situation. Shortly before Woodrow took office, a revolution in Mexico left General Victoriano Huerta's unstable military regime in power; it was not recognized by the United States and was a thorn in the new president's side (Saunders 1985, 253–54). Ellen served as her husband's primary source of background information on the issue by reading books on Mexican history and articles about the situation (Baker 1931, vol. 4, 244). Woodrow kept Ellen apprised of the situation as it progressed, sharing even confidential information regarding the activities of his attaché John Lind, who was sent to Mexico to negotiate with Huerta. In one letter dated August 16, 1913, she says: "I see Huerta may resign in order to run for constitutional president. Will you please tell me, dear, if your Mexican policy does or does not admit of accepting him on those terms? . . . [I am] anxious to know what message Lind bears as regards that point" (WW Papers). The president shared the most intimate details of this matter with his trusted advisor in his reply dated August 19, 1913: "Lind was instructed to ask Huerta for assurances that he would not be a candidate at the elections" (WW Papers). Ellen was extremely relieved when the matter was resolved. She also played a similar role in her husband's tariff and banking reform efforts, following the news reports and helping to formulate the speeches that Wilson would deliver before special joint sessions of the Congress, which Ellen viewed from the visitor's gallery (Saunders 1985, 248).

Ellen Wilson's involvement in her husband's work is an early example of the presidency as a "two-person career," arguably helping to set the standard for future "co-presidencies." Among other things, Ellen, like several other first ladies, was not afraid to lobby her husband on matters of personal importance. She was influential in convincing her husband to honor William Jennings Bryan, the most prominent Democrat of the time, with a major position in his cabinet, despite the protests of several other advisors. She also supported keeping Joseph Tumulty, Woodrow's personal secretary, on in that role in spite of controversy over the fact that he was a Roman Catholic. To her, Tumulty was not only the most capable person to be the president's personal secretary, but he had over time become part of the Wilson family (Saunders 1985, 256). Yet Ellen's political influence was evident not only privately but publicly as well as she ultimately fashioned her own political identity.

Ellen Wilson's Social Advocacy

One of the hallmarks of the modern first lady is a commitment to social advocacy. Whether performed out of a sense of noblesse oblige or a commitment to social reform, as is the case with Ellen Wilson, first ladies are expected to use their position to work on behalf of a cause. In one of her rare interviews with the press, Ellen was quoted as saying, "I wonder how anyone who reaches middle age can bear it if she cannot feel on looking back that, whatever mistakes she may have made, she has on the whole lived for others and not for herself" (Bicknell 1914, 22). A great deal of her time and energy as first lady was spent acting as a social advocate for various causes. Her views on advocacy were formed mainly by her upbringing as a minister's daughter, but were also influenced by her own commitment to progressive ideals. While we do not have discourse related to these activities, public engagement in them represents symbolic action with persuasive consequences.

Ellen's most significant rhetorical action was her work on the Slum Clearance Bill. Woodrow Wilson was inaugurated on March 4, 1913, and both he and his wife began their work immediately. On March 22, Ellen received Mrs. Charlotte Everett Wise Hopkins, a noted social advocate (the appointment is listed in WW Papers). Hopkins' goal was to make the new first lady aware of the deplorable housing conditions of many of Washington's African Americans who were living in crowded shacks with no water or sanitation in the many alleys surrounding the Capitol (Bicknell 1912, 3–5). Ellen made an appointment with

Hopkins to tour the alleys on March 25. She was driven that day through several alleys, the final stop a shocking slum within three blocks of the Capitol building. After witnessing the problem, the first lady was presented with a possible solution. She was taken to view 109 two-family dwellings constructed as model "sanitary" housing and supervised by a social worker from the National Civic Federation. Without revealing her identity, Wilson spoke with several of the occupants. After the tours, she became a stockholder in the newly organized Sanitary Housing Company, which she contributed to until her death (Saunders 1985, 245).

Part of Ellen Wilson's innovative rhetorical performance of the first lady position involved her public association with political leaders. Women had been fighting for various political change measures for many years, but even prominent female leaders of social movements were disadvantaged by their non-institutional status. Ellen's innovation comes in her use of her institutional position, independent of her husband, to legitimate her participation in the male political sphere. Such a movement from outside the political mainstream to inside the male refuge represents paramount rhetorical action that must become part of the U.S. collective memory.

Ellen quickly involved herself in the housing reform measures, taking on the public role of honorary chair of the housing department of the National Civic Federation's women's department and lobbying congressmen for their support. She designated a White House car for touring alleys and often accompanied congressmen and other interested parties on tours of the slums and model housing. Interestingly, one of the tours in 1913 included the wife of the assistant secretary of the navy, future first lady Eleanor Roosevelt. The politicization of her activities is evidenced by her alliance with political leaders without the accompaniment of her husband. An article in the *Washington Post* (August 7, 1914) noted that Wilson "had become deeply interested in the social welfare of the community, and had worked always without seeking the aid of the President" (WW Papers). The Committee of Fifty, made up of leading men and women from charitable and civic organizations, was soon formed to draft legislation addressing the alley problem. Most notably, the name of "Mrs. Woodrow Wilson" is listed in the congressional record as a member of the committee responsible for this proposal (U.S. House 1914, 37). At a time when a woman's signature was one of the few political powers she possessed (Zaeske 2002), Ellen Wilson used her signature to indicate her political autonomy and to exercise her rights as a citizen, which was a bold rhetorical action for a woman, let alone a first lady, to take.

Ellen's radical and rhetorical signature act was publicized by the Wilson administration, furthering its rhetorical significance. Ellen was an active member of the "50," organizing several lobbying events for the committee, some of which were held at the White House (Saunders 1985, 246; WW Papers). During a meeting of the committee, which included many other prominent members of Washington society, her efforts were publicly applauded by her husband's secretary of state, William Jennings Bryan, who himself evidenced the rhetorical significance of Ellen's entrance into the public sphere on political matters:

The most eloquent speech here tonight is the one that has not been made at all, for actions speak louder than words. The fact that the wife of the President is with her presence here ... lending support to the movement is enough. As crowded as my life is, I feel that if she can find time out of her busy days to be here and to work for this cause, I can too. (quoted in Bicknell 1914, 20–21)

The alley bill was introduced in Congress in February 1914, and was passed shortly before Ellen's death in August of that year (U.S. House 1914).[7]

The rhetorical impact of her signature is further revealed by the legislation's nickname, "Mrs. Wilson's bill," which is how the majority of press accounts referred to the plan. In fact, newspaper accounts of the passage of the bill became linked with reports of Ellen's final hours. According to a *Washington Post* article on August 7, 1914:

She told the president yesterday morning that she would more cheerfully "go away" if the bill for the improvement of the alleys were passed by Congress. A word to leaders from the President's secretary, and the measure was adopted in silence by the Senate and soon reported in the House, where it will be passed today. She learned that the measure would be a law in another day or so, and expressed her satisfaction. (WW Papers)

Joseph Tumulty, Woodrow Wilson's personal secretary, clipped Ellen's obituary from various sources and they may be found in the Wilson papers. Nearly all of these announcements recounted this story and praised her public activity on behalf of the cause, once again evidencing the rhetorical significance of her association with the bill.

At least one source claims that Wilson went beyond offering her signature and actually produced written discourse in the form of essays aimed at persuading people to support reform efforts like the Slum Clearance Act. The obituary that appeared in the August 10, 1914, Dublin, Georgia, *Courier Herald* made a lengthy reference to essays written by Ellen on behalf of social advocacy efforts. The newspaper account notes:

Her most beautiful and forceful passages occur in the papers read before the various civic and charitable institutions of which she was a most enthusiastic and active member. Her interest in children, in the poor women of the slums found frequent expression in powerful written appeals for understanding aid from the country as a whole. Her essays were nearly all expositions of the needs of others. (WW Papers)

Unfortunately, these essays have apparently been lost, and this lone obituary is the only reference to discourse that would give further insight into Ellen Wilson's rhetoric. The essays are not preserved in Ellen Wilson's papers, in her husband's papers, or in the archives of any of the organizations with which she was associated. However, this important reference to her writings has been overlooked even by the few scholars who have studied Ellen Wilson, despite its powerful support of Wilson's unprecedented political activity.

The rhetorical significance of the issue is demonstrated through her public alliance with the bill through her alley tours, her unprecedented signature on the bill, and the bill's nickname which publicly aligned a first lady squarely with a legislative action from within rather than from without the system. No other first lady had ever been so explicitly politically involved, evidencing Ellen's true independence as a new woman, and a new kind of first lady. In the process, she pioneered a new role for the modern first lady, not to be replicated again until Lady Bird Johnson's work on the Highway Beautification Act of 1965. However, first lady scholars continue to mistakenly credit Johnson rather than Wilson for the innovation of the first lady as policy maker (Gould 1996, 510).

Of course, her actions were radical for the time, which spawned criticism. Behind her back, her project was condescendingly dubbed "slumming parties" by her own social secretary, Belle Hanger. Another Washington observer recalled the "sardonic laughter" at the joke that the first lady had joined the "Society for the Prevention of Useless Giving" (Anthony 1990, 346). The bill also faced opposition on the Hill because it threatened vested property interests and involved difficult race relationships (Baker 1931, vol. 4, 467).

Yet for the most part, Ellen was lauded for taking a stand on an unpopular issue that likely would have gone unnoticed if it were not for attention from the first lady. On August 17, 1914, an article in the *Mississippi Star* stated in Ellen's obituary:

> Mrs. Wilson took a great interest in social welfare work and it was due to her personal effort that many needed reforms were brought about in government of the national capital, reforms that made it easier for the poor and needy whose large presence in Washington was scarcely known to the public at large until Mrs. Wilson's several trips through the alleys of that city was given publicity through the newspapers. (WW Papers)

Charlotte Hopkins, who first involved Ellen in the issue, offered her condolences in a letter dated June 21, 1914, to a grieving President Wilson by noting the good his wife had done:

> Mrs. Wilson understood the general situation, grasping at a glance the fact that with 96,000 Negroes, a third of the population, the great crying need was improved living conditions . . . Mrs. Wilson never made any secret to any of the men she took in the alleys that the work she was trying to do in passing the bill was to improve the conditions of the Negroes. Only 2,000 whites live in these alleys. She went to the Colored Social Settlement and gave them money and in all her work her interest centered in what she saw was to improve the living conditions of Negroes. (WW Papers)

Reflecting the remnants of her religious upbringing and the social conventions of the day, Ellen said to her cousin, "The women are so grateful that it is embarrassing. Here they have worked for years and years and could get nothing. I have done so little—only been interested" (Baker 1931, vol. 4, 467–68). But she was also clearly aware of the significance of her work. In a letter to her husband on July 2, 1913, she said that one woman commented that she "had done more good in Washington in four months than any other President's wife had ever done in four years—had completely changed the conditions of life for 12,000 people, or was it 12,000 alleys" (WW Papers). Because of changes to the legislation and legal issues including questions of property ownership, the plan was never implemented. Thus, the first active policy making effort by a first lady is widely forgotten, or misrepresented. However, the failure of the legislation does not diminish the rhetorical significance of Ellen's efforts, which revealed the political power of women and set new precedents for performing the first lady position.

Ellen Wilson, though, did not limit herself to the slum clearance issue. In October 1913, the first lady was appalled at the working conditions of government employees, particularly working women, during an unofficial tour of the Post Office Department. She was particularly concerned with the lack of restroom facilities and other "unsanitary conditions." She brought her concerns to Postmaster General Albert S. Burleson but with no effect (Saunders 1985, 246). So she petitioned her husband's chief advisor, Colonel House, to take up the matter, broaching the matter with him during a luncheon. House recollects in his memoirs that the conversation was not "an exchange of pleasantries," and he hastily promised her to "take it up too and see that something is done along the lines of her suggestion" (Oct. 30, 1913, quoted in Link et al., 476). House describes Ellen's forcefulness in pursuing the matter with him, despite what could be considered an inappropriate setting, as well as an inappropriate request. But as House indicates throughout his memoirs, Ellen was as much of a political force in the White House as her husband, and she felt free to discuss political matters with her husband's closest advisors. The behind-the-scenes lobbying actions of Ellen were not unlike the actions of male political officials whose rhetorical influence was often practiced privately. Yet other actions were public, further politicizing Ellen's role and revealing the political contributions of first ladies.

When she made another unannounced visit to a government office, this time the Government Printing Office, the *New York Times* reported on November 1, 1913, that she was there to inspect the "light, space and air, and other things essential to . . . the health and comfort of Government employees" (WW Papers). She again petitioned her husband's advisors to do something to improve the working conditions in government offices. She was particularly concerned about the women who were working in these offices and the effect these poor conditions were having on their health. Such actions expanded the role of first ladies to matters of the workplace, a common cause of progressive era reformers.

Ellen was also the only first lady to make a public statement on the issue of women's suffrage. Her biographer argues that she personally supported the cause but chose to keep her views to herself because she did not want to hurt her husband's political career. All three of her daughters supported the suffrage movement, with middle daughter Jessie being the most active. Jessie shared her mother's commitment to social advocacy and was working in a Philadelphia settlement house when her father became president. Although Ellen was not a public supporter of the movement, she made an interesting statement in an article published in *Good Housekeeping* just before the inauguration: "The arguments of my Jessie incline me to believe in the suffrage for working women" (Daggett 1913, 323). Although she divested her own views in the arguments of her daughter, Ellen nevertheless made a public statement in favor of suffrage some seven years before passage of the Nineteenth Amendment. Her public voice on the matter further politicizes the first lady role, evidencing her autonomy during a time when many still opposed women's suffrage.

While lobbying for better conditions for city residents and government employees, Wilson also showed interest in other social reform issues, including truancy laws, child labor, care for the mentally ill, drug addicts and neglected children, adult education, and community recreation centers. As first lady scholar Carl Anthony notes, "Previous first ladies had assumed humane projects, but none had ever been so publicly spirited" as Ellen Wilson (1990, 347). And her husband never interfered with her work. While Eleanor Roosevelt is remembered as being the most socially active first lady, Ellen Wilson set a strong precedent for Roosevelt and others during her brief time in the White House. Her work as a social advocate is particularly remarkable considering that most of it was done during her first year as first lady. Her rhetorical actions, particularly her use of the first lady position to promote legislation and social reform efforts independent of her husband, significantly altered the first lady role, expanding the performance of the position well into the political sphere. Yet despite her politicization of the first lady position, her precedent-setting work has not been given the prominence it deserves by scholars. Meanwhile, social advocate was just one of Wilson's roles as first lady. She also made a unique contribution to the institution by continuing her own career as a professional artist while in the White House, another unprecedented step for a first lady.

A Working Artist in the White House

Based on what we know now, no other first lady continued to work while in the White House. Even Eleanor Roosevelt, who wanted to continue to teach and work for various organizations while first lady, was persuaded by her husband to abandon her prior career and focus her efforts on White House–related activities (Gould 1996, 432). Ellen Wilson was an exception, and can be considered the first and only working woman in the White House.

As noted earlier, Ellen had planned a career as an artist, which she continued to pursue even after her engagement to Woodrow Wilson. But, as she explained, "three daughters take more time than three canvases" (Anthony 1990, 343), and thus she put her career aspirations on hold while her children were young. But following her brother's death in 1905, Ellen would spend every subsequent summer focusing on her artwork. Ellen's rise into the ranks of professional artist coincided with her husband's political assent. Her husband's career complicated matters for the aspiring artist, who found herself thrust into the limelight. She also faced other obligations as the new first lady. However, one of her first decisions as first lady was to turn a sunlit third floor room in the West

Wing into a studio. But unfortunately, because of her hectic schedule combined with her failing health, Ellen found little time to paint while in the White House. However, according to her brother's memoirs, she did find time to "slip away" to view paintings at the Congressional Library and other D.C. museums (Axson 1993, 107).

There is some controversy over whether Ellen Wilson can be considered a professional "working woman" while in the White House. During her tenure as first lady, she had an agent, belonged to professional organizations, exhibited her work in juried shows, and sold her work. In her letters to Macbeth, she directs the promotion, exhibition, and sale of her paintings, just as any career artist would do (Aucella and Hobbs 1993, 6–8; Macbeth Papers). Her success at several art exhibitions just prior to her entering the White House, including her own one-woman show at the Arts and Crafts Guild in Philadelphia, established her as a professional artist and allowed her to continue selling her works while she was first lady.

During the summer 1913, rather than stay in Washington, D.C., with her husband, she once again traveled to the artist's community in Cornish where she spent her days painting new canvases and selling her work. That summer, she sold many of her paintings herself and donated the proceeds to one of her favorite causes, the Martha Berry School, mentioned earlier. As she explains in her letter of September 20, 1913, to her husband:

> A Mrs. Barnett, who asked some time ago if she might buy one of my small pictures, which she had heard I would sell for the school, came in the morning and took two—for fifty dollars each unframed. Rather oddly she chose the two from which I have just painted the large ones—which of course suited me exactly. I told her that I used them in that way and she thought it added to their interest. (WW Papers)

During that summer, Ellen actively sought buyers for her artwork as a way of raising money for the Berry School. She discusses her fund-raising scheme in her letters to her husband, for example, in the letter dated September 26, 1913, she writes: "This morning, the son of Mrs. Barnett who bought two of my paintings came and bought one for himself. That makes $350.00 of the $1000 I want to raise myself for the Berry School" (WW Papers). After Ellen's death, Wilson made sure his wife's support for the Berry School would continue. In a letter dated August 25, 1914, to Sarah Caruthers Park Hughes, the school's director, he writes:

> My own judgment would be that it would be best to raise a fund which should be an endowment the interest of which should be used to pay the way through school of mountain boys and girls, because I know this is what Mrs. Wilson would have done if she had the means and opportunity. She was paying for the education of several herself from year to year. It might be called the Ellen Wilson Fund for the Christian Education of Mountain Youth. (WW Papers)

Ellen's decision to use her artwork to raise money for a social cause evidences her commitment to progressive ideals, showing her to be both a woman with independent financial means and a committed advocate of social causes. But her decision, as first lady, to spend several months away from the White House in pursuit of her own career as an artist is a remarkable rhetorical act, one which had not been replicated until recently, when Hillary Rodham Clinton campaigned for Senate while still first lady.

Ellen's artistic talents were recognized not only by her family, her colleagues in the art community, and her patrons, but also by the press during her time as first lady. Almost every article written about her mentioned her artistic talents. One journalist, during Wilson's presidential campaign, wrote: "She has high talent as a landscape painter. Not the kind of thing that goes with a few well-decorated china plates and a plaque to fill wall space; nor the quality that does place cards and an entertaining sketchbook. But a real, big artist talent" (Arnold 1912, 18). The May 1913 issue of the *Ladies' Home Journal* contained full color reproductions of two of her works to illustrate the artistic talents of the new first lady. The press seemed to accept and admire her talent, particularly because it did not interfere with her womanly duties, which were still being touted as traits of the "true woman" in most magazines.

Ellen's continuation of her career as a professional artist during her short time as first lady was a significant rhetorical activity. Her pursuit of her artwork was in no way connected to her role as first lady, thus making her unique in the fact that she was able to retain some level of independence despite the demands and constraints of the institution and the restrictions on upper-class women's employment. Ellen's career as a professional artist clearly represents the intersection of the "new woman" and progressive ideologies. She was independently employed, earning an income that she did not turn over to her husband. Yet, reflecting the progressive ideals of philanthropy and volunteerism, she donated her earnings to a needy cause.

Legacy

When asked to define the role of first lady, Hillary Rodham Clinton described it as a "partner who represents for all of us a view of who her husband is, as well as a symbol of women's concerns and interests at a particular time" (quoted in O'Brien 1992, 72). This definition accurately describes Ellen Axson Wilson's rhetorical performance of the first lady position. Ellen often told her daughters that no one should "rest on the laurels of another person, but must grow to the limits of her own spirit, mind, and ability" (Saunders 1985, 258). She was a woman who took her own advice and in so doing made an indelible mark on the role of the first lady. Even Woodrow Wilson's official biographer, Ray Stannard Baker, commented: "Stimulated by the opportunities for usefulness presented by her new position, she added to the onerous traditional duties of the Mistress of the White House philanthropic and artistic activities" (1931, vol. 4, 462). In this respect, Ellen Wilson was a representative of her age. Her performance as first lady reflected an era of change in which social reform was prized, in which women were expanding their roles beyond the domestic sphere, and in which women felt more comfortable expressing their individuality. She embodied the spirit of the "new woman" who found a way to straddle the public and private spheres and balance the traditional domestic roles with that of advocate and professional. And she did this all in the span of seventeen months.

Following in the rich tradition of her predecessors, Ellen Wilson both extended the scope of the first lady's role and added new dimensions to it, creating opportunities for many of her successors through her rhetorical performance of the position. Her social reform efforts were viewed in the spirit of progressivism and the "new woman," and they would be remembered and mirrored by future first ladies, like Eleanor Roosevelt and Lady Bird Johnson. As noted earlier, Roosevelt participated in one of Ellen Wilson's alley tours. The authors of *The Eleanor Roosevelt Encyclopedia* speculate that "Ellen Wilson influenced E[leanor] R[oosevelt] as First Lady, for when the latter assumed the role, she took an interest in the deplorable housing conditions of African Americans in the District of Columbia as well" (Beasley et al. 2001, 184). Later, Lady Bird Johnson would also take up the cause of clearing the slums and making the District more livable for its residents as part of her beautification efforts. And both Roosevelt and Johnson would actively lobby for legislation as Ellen did with the alley bill. Her advocacy work would also help establish the tradition of first ladies choosing a cause to support. Like Roosevelt, Wilson was credited as having a keen political awareness and being an excellent judge of human character, thus making her a trusted advisor. The Wilsons' marriage was a true partnership, similar to the Carters and Clintons.

Her public support of the alley bill had great rhetorical significance for women in politics and first ladies in particular. She performed a public role by explicitly aligning herself with political officials, by taking congressmen on tours of the slums, helping draft the legislation that was eventually named in her honor, and hosting lobbying events at the White House. She also used the power of her signature, one of the few political actions available to women during this time, becoming the first first lady to formulate policy from within the realm of mainstream politics. Ellen did all of this as the first lady, but independently of her husband. Her actions on behalf of this bill alone politicized the role of the first lady to an extent never before witnessed and seldom seen since.

Another unique contribution of Ellen Wilson to the role of first lady was her work as an artist. Whether or not she is considered a "professional artist," she was still the first and, to date, the only first lady to pursue work while in the White House that was unrelated to her institutional role. Her artwork was completely independent of her first lady position, yet she managed to create, exhibit, and sell her paintings while championing the alley bill and advising her husband. She used the proceeds from the sale of her artwork to support another of her favorite causes, the education of poor children in her home state of Georgia. Her brother Stockton Axson argued: "Perhaps one of the few things she was ever proud of that belonged to her own career as separate from her husband's career was that she was able to sell some of these landscapes for good money, which she gave to a mountain school in Georgia, in which she was very much interested" (1993, 93). Her work as an artist was recognized and applauded by the press, who credited her ability to balance many roles successfully.

All of her contributions added to the evolving construction of the role of first lady, and by recognizing her accomplishments, we can begin to see more clearly the links that bind together past and present, that connect each first lady from Martha Washington to Laura Bush. No link should be forgotten or misrepresented, and more work needs to be done to recover the voices of the first ladies who have been overlooked. Rhetorical scholars are uniquely qualified to do this work. As David Zarefsky notes, "By studying important historical events from a rhetorical perspective, one can see significant aspects about those events that other perspectives miss" (1998, 30). The rhetorical history of Ellen Wilson shows that in little over a year, she contributed a great deal to one of the most unique roles in American society, extending the efforts of her predecessors and setting precedents for those who followed. Through this rhetorical reassessment, we can also reclaim Ellen Wilson's position as a model for the modern first lady. Using Mrs. Clinton's definition, Ellen Wilson represented the progressive political ideals of her husband while at the same time symbolizing the "new woman" who was active in social reform and even pursued a career independent of her domestic duties. Ellen Axson Wilson deserves to be recognized for her contributions to the evolving first lady position. By examining her achievements, we can better understand and appreciate the complexities of the first lady institution.

Notes

The author would like to thank the staffs at the following archives for their assistance: the Manuscript Reading Room staff at the Library of Congress, the archivists at the Archives of American Art in Washington, D.C., and the Special Collections staff at the Carnegie Library of Rome, Georgia.

1. The narrative presented on the placard focuses on Wilson's support of the Slum Clearance Act, which was aimed at improving the housing conditions for thousands of District residents who lived in unsanitary alley dwellings. It is implied that this cause was a form of misguided charity: "The act, as finally passed by Congress, provided for slum areas to be cleared of dwellings and turned into parks, but made no provisions to find or build new housing for those who were displaced." However, the narrative fails to note that the act passed by Congress was very different than the original legislation supported by Wilson, which called for funding for the construction of affordable sanitary housing projects that would become the new homes for the displaced alley dwellers.

2. The discourse generated by Ellen Wilson is limited compared to other first ladies. Her correspondence may be found in Series 2 (reels 3–131) of the Wilson Papers. Most of her archives are comprised of letters to and from her husband, many of which were published by daughter Eleanor Wilson McAdoo in *A Priceless Gift: The Love Letters of Woodrow and Ellen Axson Wilson*. Many of the Wilsons' personal letters were also published in Baker's *Woodrow Wilson: Life and Letters* (Vols. 2, 3 & 4) and Link et al., *The Papers of Woodrow Wilson*. The archives also include letters to other relatives, friends, and business associates, many of which have not been previously published. However, outside of Saunders' biography of Ellen Wilson and limited comments by Baker in his biography of Woodrow Wilson, these letters have not been critically examined, thus re-

sulting in Ellen Wilson being largely overlooked or misinterpreted.

3. Two thorough discussions of women's discourse and the available avenues of action, as well as the gender prescriptions of the turn of the century, can be found in the following works: Eleanor Flexner, *Century of Struggle: The Woman's Rights Movement in the United States*; Karlyn Kohrs Campbell, *Man Cannot Speak for Her: A Critical Study of Early Feminist Rhetoric*, Vol. 1. An interesting look at women's use of letter writing can be found in Lisa M. Gring-Pemble's "Writing Themselves into Consciousness: Creating a Rhetorical Bridge between the Public and Private Spheres" (1998). Susan Zaeske looks at the political power of women's signatures in her article "Signatures of Citizenship: The Rhetoric of Women's Antislavery Petitions" (2000). Finally, the power of "parlor politics" is examined in Catherine Ailgor's *Parlor Politics* (2000).

4. In the only biography written about Ellen Axson Wilson, Frances Wright Saunders follows her life from childhood to death. Her thorough research provides an understanding of the personal world of Ellen Wilson, from her family and friends to her views on a number of issues. The book is organized according to periods in a somewhat chronological order. All of the general biographical information about Ellen Wilson comes from Saunders, unless otherwise noted.

5. This use of letter writing is a common tactic for women involved in political activity during this era. Catherine Allgor, in her research into women's political role in the early years of the United States, argues that letter writing was a primary and powerful form of political activity for women because it allowed them to act publicly without venturing out of the private sphere (2000, 1–3). Allgor argues that many political wives wrote letters on their husbands' behalf, acting as intercessors in touchy political situations. She also notes that first ladies, like Dolley Madison and Louisa Catherine Adams, often served as unofficial campaign managers for their husbands, handling the unpleasantness of politicking so that their husbands could appear above the fray. Ellen Wilson served this very function for her husband.

6. From Florence Griswold's personal papers. The Wilsons stayed at Florence Griswold's boardinghouse, which became a center for the artists who came to Old Lyme each summer. Ellen and Griswold were frequent correspondents, often discussing new exhibitions and the successes enjoyed by their mutual friends. In many ways, Griswold kept Ellen in touch with the activities of the art community during the year. She also discussed her artwork with Griswold. In a letter from Ellen to Griswold on April 20, 1911, she asks for a room at Griswold's boardinghouse for a week in the spring: "I should love to get in two weeks of sketching in that charming season."

7. H.R. 13219, Certain Alleys in the District of Columbia, 1914. Its main provision was: "To promote health, raise revenue, and improve housing conditions in the District of Columbia . . . to regulate and determine the conditions of tenancy and occupancy of any or every building . . . and may refuse to permit the occupancy of any building . . . provided in their judgment such occupancy is or would be a menace to the health, welfare, or safety of the occupants, or to the health, welfare, or safety of neighboring residents, or to the health, welfare, or safety of the general public in the District of Columbia."

References

Allgor, Catherine. 2000. *Parlor Politics*. Charlottesville, Va.: University Press of Virginia.

Anthony, Carl Sferrazza. 1990. *First Ladies: The Saga of the Presidents' Wives and Their Power, 1789–1961*, Vol. 1. New York: William Morrow and Company.

Arnold, Cloe. 1912. The Governor's Lady. *Delineator*, July, 18.

100 *Lisa M. Burns*

Aucella, Frank J., and Patricia A. Piorkowski Hobbs. 1993. *Ellen Axson Wilson: First Lady—Artist*. Washington, D.C.: The Woodrow Wilson Birthplace Foundation.

Axson, Stockton. 1993. *Brother Woodrow*. Ed. Arthur S. Link. Princeton, N.J.: Princeton University Press.

Baker, Ray Stannard. 1927–1939. *Woodrow Wilson, Life and Letters*. 8 vols. Garden City, N.Y.: Doubleday, Page & Co.

Beasley, Maureen H., Holly C. Shulman, and Henry R. Beasley, eds. 2001. *The Eleanor Roosevelt Encyclopedia*. Westport, Conn.: Greenwood.

Bicknell, Mrs. Ernest P. 1914. The Home-Maker of the White House. *Survey*, 3 October, 22–25.

Bicknell, Grace V. 1912. *The Inhabited Alleys of Washington, D.C.* Washington, D.C.: The Committee on Housing, Women's Welfare Department, National Civic Federation.

Boller, Paul F., Jr. 1998. *Presidential Wives: An Anecdotal History*, 2nd ed. New York: Oxford University Press.

Caroli, Betty Boyd. 1987. *First Ladies*. New York: Oxford University Press.

Campbell, Karlyn Kohrs. 1989. *Man Cannot Speak for Her: A Critical Study of Early Feminist Rhetoric*, Vol. 1. New York: Praeger.

———. 1996. The Rhetorical Presidency: A Two-Person Career. In *Beyond the Rhetorical Presidency*, ed. Martin J. Medhurst, 179–95. College Station, Tex.: Texas A & M University Press.

———. 1998. The Discursive Performance of Femininity: Hating Hillary. *Rhetoric & Public Affairs*, 1:1, 1–19.

Daggett, Mabel Porter. 1913. Woodrow Wilson's Wife. *Good Housekeeping*, March, 316–23.

Elliot, Margaret Axson. 1944. *My Aunt Louisa and Woodrow Wilson*. Chapel Hill, N.C.: University of North Carolina Press.

Flexner, Eleanor. 1972. *Century of Struggle: The Woman's Rights Movement in the United States*. New York: Atheneum.

Gould, Lewis L. 1996. *American First Ladies: Their Lives and Legacies*. New York: Garland.

———. 1996. Modern First Ladies and the Presidency. *Presidential Studies Quarterly*, 26, 677.

Gring-Pemble, Lisa M. 1998. Writing Themselves into Consciousness: Creating a Rhetorical Bridge between the Public and Private Spheres. *Quarterly Journal of Speech*, 84, 41–61.

Griswold, Florence Papers. Personal Papers. *Lyme Historical Society Records*. Washington, D.C.: Archives of American Art.

Gutin, Myra G. 1989. The *President's Partner: The First Lady in the Twentieth Century*. Westport, Conn.: Greenwood.

Healy, Diane Dixon. 1988. *America's First Ladies: Private Lives of the Presidents' Wives*. New York: Atheneum.

Hosford, Hester E. 1912. The New Ladies of the White House. *Independent*, 21 November, 1159–64.

Link, Arthur S., David W. Hirst, and John Little, eds. 1966–1985. *The Papers of Woodrow Wilson*. 48 vols. Princeton, N.J.: Princeton University Press.

Macbeth, William Papers. Washington, D.C.: Archives of American Art.

McAdoo, Eleanor Wilson, ed. 1962. *The Priceless Gift: The Love Letters of Woodrow and Ellen Axson Wilson*. New York: McGraw-Hill.

McAdoo, William G. 1931. *Crowded Years: The Reminiscences of William Gibb McAdoo*. Boston: Houghton Mifflin.

Means, Marianne. 1963. *The Woman in the White House.* New York: Random House.
The New Mistress of the White House. 1913. *Current Opinion*, March, 195–96.
O'Brien, Patricia. 1992. The First Lady with a Career? *Working Woman*, August, 72.
Prindiville, Kathleen. 1964. *First Ladies*, 2nd edition. New York: MacMillan.
Saunders, Francis Wright. 1985. *First Lady between Two Worlds: Ellen Axson Wilson.* Chapel Hill, N.C.: University of North Carolina Press.
Troy, Gil. 2000. *Mr. and Mrs. President: From the Trumans to the Clintons*, 2nd edition. Lawrence, Kans.: University of Kansas Press.
Tumulty, Joseph. 1921. *Woodrow Wilson as I Know Him.* Garden City, N.Y.: Doubleday, Page & Co.
Turner, Kathleen J. 1998. Rhetorical History as Social Construction. In *Doing Rhetorical History*, ed. Kathleen J. Turner, 1–15. Tuscaloosa, Ala.: University of Alabama Press.
U.S. House. 1914. Committee on the District of Columbia. *Certain Alleys in the District of Columbia, Hearing on H.R. 13219.* 63rd Congress, 2nd session, 13 and 18 March.
Watson, Robert P. 1997. The First Lady Reconsidered: Presidential Partner and Political Institution. *Presidential Studies Quarterly*, 27, 807.
———. 2000. *The Presidents' Wifes: Reassessing the Office of First Lady.* Boulder, Colo.: Lynne Reinner Publishers.
Wilson, Woodrow Papers. 1973. Washington, D.C.: Library of Congress, Manuscript Collection.
Wilson-McAdoo Collection. Washington, D.C.: Library of Congress, Manuscript Collection.
Winfield, Betty Houchin. 1997. The First Lady, Political Power, and the Media: Who Elected Her Anyway? In *Women, Media, and Politics*, ed. Pippa Norris, 166–79. New York: Oxford University Press.
Zaeske, Susan. 2002. Signatures of Citizenship: The Rhetoric of Women's Antislavery Petitions. *Quarterly Journal of Speech*, 88:2, 147–68.
Zarefsky, David. 1998. Four Senses of Rhetorical History. In *Doing Rhetorical History*, ed. Kathleen J. Turner, 19–32. Tuscaloosa, Ala.: University of Alabama Press.

Chapter 6

Edith Bolling Galt Wilson
Actions Speak Louder than Words

Amy R. Slagell and Susan Zaeske

> I have never made a speech, so I can only wish you well, and say that you are all very good little Americans.
> —Edith Wilson addressing Philadelphia Girl Scout Troop 57

"We have petticoat Government! Mrs. Wilson is President!" shouted Senator Albert Fall pounding his fist on a table during a fall 1919 Senate committee meeting. Fall's was only the loudest of many voices murmuring that Woodrow Wilson had suffered a stroke and that the United States was being run by "presidentress" Edith Bolling Galt Wilson (Anthony 1990, 375). In the aftermath of the crisis in presidential power, Mrs. Wilson maintained vehemently that she had made no decisions and merely had conveyed messages to and from her husband in order to allow him to recuperate. To this day scholars debate whether Edith Wilson usurped the office of the presidency. No matter what one concludes, it is fair to say, as did historian Bernard A. Weisberger, that for two to six months Edith Wilson "had the most absolute power ever exerted by a First Lady" (1993, 20).

That Edith Wilson found herself in a position of immense political power was a historical irony, for throughout her life she displayed little interest in government and as first lady avoided leadership, even in social affairs. In fact, upon announcement of President Wilson's engagement to Mrs. Galt, the *New York Times* reported on November 15, 1915, that Edith "has no ambition to dictate to society at large, or the Administration circle in particular."[1] Even when she allegedly ran the White House, Edith Wilson refrained from granting interviews or speaking in public, as was her practice throughout her tenure as first lady. When in 1915 a *New York Times* reporter approached the soon-to-be first lady for an interview, all Edith would say is "I am very happy . . . but I am of no importance, and the less the newspapers print about me at this time the more I shall appreciate it, and so, I am sure, will the President" (October 8, 1915). Her beliefs that women, even the first lady, should say little in public paralleled those of Woodrow Wilson, who, like Edith, was raised amid the conservative culture of upper-crust Virginia. Before they married, Woodrow shared with Edith his impressions upon attending a session of the 1884 Women's Congress, describing a "chilled, scandalized feeling that comes over me when I see and hear women speak in public" (Caplan 1986, 27). The two seemed to agree that men and women possessed different duties and were repelled by women who attempted to subvert the social order by entering the professions (Caplan 1986). Edith perceived her proper role to be that of loyal partner to her husband, and even found the title "First Lady" disagreeable (Wilson 1938, 127).

Her notions about the proper role of women in society and her commitment to being the wife of Woodrow Wilson rather than the "First Lady" significantly shaped Edith Wilson's rhetorical practices. Hers was a rhetoric not of words, but of actions. Mrs. Wilson, a keen observer, understood the power of actions and appearance. She managed these with utmost care and relied on the media to spell out in words the meanings of her symbolic actions. This tactic enabled her not only to retain the persona of a traditional, feminine woman, but also to exploit the resource of ambiguity. By refusing to make statements on controversial issues such as suffrage, she avoided having to take a stand and, yet, kept the attention of the media and public who continually wondered about her opinions. On those occasions when she wished to convey her ideas more directly, rather than speaking or appearing in print, Edith Wilson issued statements through others. The only exception to her rhetoric of action and appearance, and a major exception at that, was her 1938 volume *My Memoir*, which she published in large part to counter Woodrow Wilson's critics and deny claims that she had taken over the government during his illness.

Biography

Edith Bolling Galt Wilson, second wife of Woodrow Wilson, was born into an aristocratic family of Wytheville, Virginia, in 1872. The seventh of eleven children of Judge William Holcombe Bolling and Sallie White, and a direct descendant of the Native American princess Pocahontas, Edith was educated largely by her father and paternal grandmother. At age fourteen, she entered Martha Washington College in Abingdon, Virginia, to study music but stayed only a year. From 1889–1890, she attended Richmond Female Seminary, more commonly known as Powell's School, but the school closed the next year when the headmaster became ill. In the end, Edith received only two years of formal education.

With her shiny dark hair, flawless skin, fashionable dress, and refined up-bringing, Edith Bolling was known as a charming beauty. While visiting a sister in Washington, D.C., during 1891, Edith Bolling met Norman Galt, owner of a well-established exclusive jewelry store. The two courted for more than four years and were wed in 1896. When Norman Galt died suddenly in 1908, Mrs. Galt carefully selected a trusted employee to manage the family's jewelry business, though she oversaw its daily operation. Steady profits from the business enabled her to travel and engage extensively in social activities and even to become one of the first women in Washington to race about town in an electric car (Gould 1996; Maddox 1973).

In March 1915, thanks to her close friend Alice Gertrude (Altrude) Gordon, who was being courted by President Woodrow Wilson's personal physician, Edith Galt was invited to the White House. There she met the president, who was mourning the death seven months earlier of his wife Ellen Louise Axson Wilson. His grief was acute, for they had been married for nearly thirty years. During her seventeen months in the White House, Ellen Wilson had earned the reputation of playing the role of first lady with dignity and grace. As the *Richmond News Leader* stated the day after her death, "Mrs. Wilson was not a showy woman. She was no slave to her modiste and no captive to her mirror . . . one realized that her poise, her sympathy, her democracy and her frankness were evidence of a spirit which had won peace through inward battles" (August 7, 1914).

Ellen's death devastated Woodrow Wilson. "God has stricken me almost beyond what I can bear," he wrote to a friend (Heckscher 1991, 334). So concerned were those close to Wilson about his depression, especially his doctor, Admiral Cary Grayson, that in hopes of lifting his spirits they facilitated the meeting with the widowed Mrs. Galt. The lonely president was immediately drawn to Edith and she became a frequent guest at the White House. Their relationship intensified not only through dinners and car rides along the Potomac, but also through the exchange of love letters that have been deemed "unique in Presidential history for their passion and zeal" (Tribble 1981, iv). After a courtship of only a few weeks, Woodrow Wilson proposed marriage to Edith, who was sixteen years his junior. Fearing a public scandal would result if the president were to become engaged so soon after the death of his first wife—a scandal that could damage his chances for reelection in 1916—Edith asked Woodrow to wait at least a year. Nonetheless, Wilson threw caution to the wind and not long thereafter urged Galt to marry him despite the potential for gossip (Shachtman 1981).

On October 6, 1915, the White House announced the engagement of President Wilson and Mrs. Galt. Rumors circulated. One held that the president had killed his first wife so he could be with his new love, another accused Wilson's personal physician of poisoning Ellen at the president's request, and others claimed that Wilson was neglecting the grave of his first wife as well as his official duties while pursuing Mrs. Galt (Maddox, 1973). However, the dreaded scandal never seriously materialized and the general public greeted the soon-to-be Mrs. Wilson with admiration and enthusiasm (*NYT* Oct. 9, 1915). Edith and

Woodrow were wed on December 18, 1915, in a private ceremony in her Washington, D.C., home, outside of which crowds gathered to catch a glimpse of the wedding party. The couple was showered with gifts. (*NYT* Dec. 19, 1915). Reflecting public curiosity about Edith's highly publicized hereditary links to Pocahontas, she received many gifts of a Native American theme and from Native Americans such as blankets, and statues and paintings of Pocahontas (Anthony 1990).

Within the first few years of their marriage, the couple navigated a whirlwind of political events, the first being the election of 1916. Due to several concerns such as the timing of the Wilsons' marriage and Edith's unclear stance on women's suffrage, at the recommendation of Woodrow's advisors, Edith played a small role in the campaign though she accompanied her husband to a few major public events. In the end, Wilson was elected to a second term by a narrow margin of the electoral college. Despite his campaign slogan, "He kept us out of war," by April 1917, Wilson reluctantly asked Congress for a declaration of war against Germany and its allies to "make the world safe for democracy." The war significantly altered Edith Wilson's responsibilities both in terms of her private relationship with the president and her public relationship with the American people.

In private, Edith worked closely with Woodrow throughout the war assisting him with correspondence, decoding documents, helping him make decisions, forcing him to take some recreation, and keeping vigil with him as he worked into the night. In her memoir, Edith recalled staying with him in the office after midnight and being rewarded with a kind remark from her husband, such as, "'You don't know how much easier it makes all this to have you here by me. Are you too tired to hear what I have written?'" (Wilson 1938, 92). But she also bore new public responsibilities. She was asked by the War Department to name hundreds of naval craft, many of which she gave Native American monikers. Edith Wilson became the first first lady to christen a ship when on August 5, 1917, she broke a bottle against the Quistconck, the ancient Indian name of the place where the ship was built (*NYT* August 6, 1918; Anthony, 1990). Many of Edith's more public activities on behalf of the war effort centered on the home. The first lady signed a public pledge to ration resources and implemented meatless Mondays, wheatless Tuesdays, and gasless Sundays at the White House and asked cabinet members' wives to do the same. In addition to modeling conservation measures, Wilson worked for the Red Cross and promoted liberty bonds by appearing with celebrities such as Mary Pickford, Charlie Chaplin, and Mabel Normand (Anthony 1990).

Seventeen months after the United States entered the war, the Central Powers requested an armistice and Wilson announced that he would go to Paris as part of the five-member American delegation to negotiate a peace treaty. Edith Wilson accompanied her husband and throughout Europe toured hospitals overflowing with wounded soldiers, attended official dinners, and, on June 28, 1919, witnessed world leaders sign the Treaty of Versailles. Upon returning from Europe, Edith joined her husband on a nationwide speaking tour as he took his case for ratification of the peace treaty and U.S. entry in the League of Nations to the American people. The frenzied pace of the campaign compromised Wilson's already ailing health, and in September 1919, he suffered a paralyzing stroke. At this point in American history, there was no constitutional provision for what should be done in the event that the president became incapacitated. The Twenty-fifth Amendment dealing with "Presidential Disability and Succession" was not ratified until 1967. With her husband physically disabled, yet, by her account, completely competent mentally, Edith embarked on her "stewardship" of the executive office in order to release the president from disturbances that would impede his recovery. Remaining constantly at Woodrow's side, Edith studied papers sent by government officials and functioned as gatekeeper, deciding which matters were worthy of his attention. Although Edith Wilson insisted that she never made presidential decisions, newspapers at home and abroad speculated about her role (for example see, Canton [Ohio] *Daily News*, March 12, 1920 and London *Daily Mail*, Feb. 22, 1920 in WW Papers, reel 505 scrapbook 5, 7, 3; Phiffer 1971).

At the end of Woodrow's term as president in 1920, the Wilsons retired to a brick home on Washington's S Street. The ailing former president died on February 3, 1924, leaving Edith Wilson, at age 51, a widow for the second time. Following a yearlong seclusion, Edith Wilson resumed her world travels and worked for the Democratic Party. She expended much energy in her later years attempting to shape the historical legacy of Woodrow Wilson by collecting his personal papers, obtaining a satisfactory biographer, and campaigning to make his birthplace a national landmark. In 1938, Edith Wilson published *My Memoir*, which is in large part a vindication of her actions during the war, the peace conference, and especially during the president's illness. Though she maintained her policy of avoiding public speaking, Edith Wilson participated in Democratic Party activities until the end of her life. She supported Democratic presidential candidate John F. Kennedy, and, in 1961, attended his inauguration. Later that year, Edith Wilson sat at the young president's side as he signed a bill authorizing a memorial to her late husband. On December 21, 1961, at the age of 89, she died. Ironically, her death coincided with the 105th anniversary of her husband's birth.

Rhetorical Activities as First Lady

Women's Suffrage

From the beginning of her tenure as first lady, Edith Wilson made clear her decision to remain silent on political issues. However, the growing momentum of the women's suffrage campaign and the fact that she was a highly visible woman led to public pressure for her to take a public stand on the issue. Suffragists sent droves of letters urging Mrs. Wilson to act on behalf of their cause, but there is no evidence that she did so. In fact, some scholars have concluded that she opposed women's suffrage. Carl Anthony's standard work on first ladies paints a dire portrait: "Grace Coolidge, like Eleanor Roosevelt, was no suffragette, but neither woman quite so vehemently opposed granting women the vote as Edith Wilson" (1990, 359). To support this judgment Anthony cites Edith Wilson's statement in her *Memoir* that the only speech of her husband's she disliked was one supporting women's suffrage. In addition, Mrs. Wilson referred to the suffragists who picketed the White House as "detestable creatures." In an effort to account for Edith Wilson's apparent aversion to women's suffrage, Marianne Means suggests, "female independence, and traditional male rights such as voting, did not fit into her concept of a Southern lady's proper behavior" (1963, 153). But Edith Wilson's opinion about women's suffrage is more complicated than these summaries suggest.

The American people had every reason to suspect that the financially independent, world-traveling, car-driving first lady supported women's suffrage. This notion was reinforced when Woodrow Wilson released a statement declaring his support for women's suffrage in New Jersey on the same day the White House announced his engagement to Edith. The *New York Times* on October 7, 1915, paired these stories on its front page under a headline proclaiming," President to Wed Mrs. Norman Galt, Intimate Friend of His Daughters; Also Comes Out for Woman Suffrage" leaving readers free to assume that she had liberalized his views on the issue.[2] That the timing of these announcements affected public perception of Wilson's policy making can be seen in a *New York Times Magazine* political cartoon appearing on October 10, 1915; the cartoon shows Wilson seated on the parlor sofa fixated on a caricature of Edith Galt labeled "Woman Suffrage," as hovering Cupid smiles overhead. Outside, but visible through the window, a beleaguered male figure labeled "War" taps on the window, trying in vain to gain the president's attention (Oct. 10, 1915). Media impressions notwithstanding, efforts to get a public statement from the betrothed Mrs. Galt on the subject of women's suffrage were unsuccessful. Consistent with her general rhetorical strategy of refusing to grant interviews or make public statements, Edith refused to say where she stood on the issue (*NYT* Oct. 1, 1915). Instead, she allowed the public to discern her attitude on women's suffrage based on the timing of her husband's press releases and her persona as an independent businesswoman.

Some have interpreted Wilson's strong objections to suffragists who picketed the White House as evidence that she opposed suffrage. This conclusion is problematic. During the later years of the fight for the ballot, the president's inaction led Alice Paul and her National Woman's Party to adopt a strategy of holding Wilson accountable for the Democratic Party's failure to pass the national suffrage amendment. They fought Wilson's reelection and later began to picket the White House and to burn copies of his speeches praising representative democracy. Edith objected to these tactics and even opposed Wilson's pardon of the arrested picketers, but her objection to the pickets did not mean that she opposed suffrage for women. Betty Boyd Caroli accounts for Edith Wilson's negative statements about the National Woman's Party by noting that her attitude "centered on how the issue affected her husband's well-being—not the issue itself" (1987, 147). This conclusion is consistent with Edith Wilson's persistent stance as defender and protector of her husband.

A fact often overlooked in discussions of Edith Wilson's position on women's suffrage is that she was hardly alone in her objections to the picketers. An article in the *New York Times* appearing on August 8, 1918, indicates that mainstream suffragists disagreed with the tactics employed by radicals under the leadership of Alice Paul. "The militant members of the National Woman's Party have again brought the cause of woman suffrage into disrepute without gaining by their tactics a single practical advantage," lamented the head of the New York City Woman Suffrage Party. In its analysis of the 1916 election results where western states had given Wilson the margin of victory, the *New York Times* noted on November 10, 1916, that "the women in San Francisco voted for Wilson three to one. They paid no attention whatever to the attempt of the Women's Party to solidify them as a sex and vote against Wilson in conformity with its wishes." Since women's suffrage supporters themselves disapproved of the tactics of the radical wing of the movement, there is little reason to believe that Edith's disapproval of the pickets meant that she opposed suffrage.

In the absence of any clear public statement from Edith Wilson on the issue of women's suffrage, have we any reason to suspect that she supported enfranchising women? We do indeed. Wilson knew and was willing to be publicly associated with Anna Howard Shaw, former president of the National American Woman Suffrage Association. In fact, during the war she joined Shaw in an effort to protect the morals of American troops abroad (this activity is discussed later in this chapter). More directly, Edith Wilson spoke positively about suffrage while in St. Paul, Minnesota, with her husband on the League of Nations lecture tour. According to the *St. Paul Daily News* on September 9, 1919, during a long conversation with friends, Edith described informing the president that morning that Minnesota had just voted to enfranchise women. Indicating her knowledge of the progress of the campaign, she also mentioned that Minnesota was the fourteenth state to grant women the vote. Mrs. Wilson declared, moreover, that she thought it "a wonderful thing to have something to say about the laws of the land we live in" (WW Papers, reel 505 scrapbook 4, 207). Furthermore, Edith Wilson exercised her newly won right to vote. On October 31, 1920, the *New York Times* made much of the occasion of Mrs. Wilson casting her first ballot, noting that she was among "the first of the great army of women enfranchised by the Nineteenth Amendment to vote in the 1920 election."[3]

While Edith Wilson was no outspoken suffragist, her public discourse—or lack of it—on the issue of enfranchising women was consistent with her overall rhetorical strategy as first lady. She said little about suffrage just as she said little about all other political issues of the day. Yet she never disavowed widespread public perception that she was sympathetic to the suffrage movement. Whether and how this perception influenced others remains unknown.

Contributions to the War Effort

In April 1917, despite President Wilson's campaign promise to keep the nation out of war, international events forced him to ask Congress for a declaration of war against Germany and its allies. On April 6, when the president signed the formal declaration of war with his wife's gold pen, Edith had performed the duties of first lady for just over fifteen months. During the nineteen months to follow, the exigencies of the world war forced her to increase her rhetorical activities. Edith intensified both her behind-the-scenes work, typical of the Wilsons as a couple, as well as her public activity, in which she relied on actions, rather than words, to provide a model of behavior for American women.

A good deal of Edith Wilson's most important wartime activity occurred in private. In her role as the president's cryptographer, Edith Wilson decoded and encoded official messages through which her husband exchanged information with the highest-level U.S. officials in Europe. So secret were these messages that they bypassed the War Department and, in a code developed by Wilson himself, went straight to officials such as Colonel House, whom the president had dispatched to Europe to serve as his eyes and ears. As the president's cryptographer Edith gained a thorough knowledge of war movements and U.S. war policies. So intimately was Edith involved in the president's management of the war that when House returned from Europe in December 1917 and came to the White House for debriefing, she sat in on the meeting thus hearing the latest news about the war and U.S. military strategies.

Edith Wilson also lent her name and image, though not her voice, to public campaigns in support of the war effort. Days before her husband signed the declaration of war, the *New York Times* reported that she had accepted honorary chairmanship of the Women's Volunteer Aid Committee of the District of Columbia Red Cross (March 31, 1917). This step guaranteed visibility and prestige for the organization as it assisted the military with such tasks as outfitting hospitals and running canteens for departing soldiers. Undoubtedly aware that her actions carried significant rhetorical power to encourage other women to participate in the Red Cross, Wilson also volunteered regularly at the Washington, D.C., canteen and was active in producing cloth goods for hospitals. In July 1917, the *New York Times* reported that Mrs. Wilson and Woodrow Wilson's cousin Helen Bones had produced dozens of sheets, pajamas, and other cloth goods and that "their example has been followed by women high in official and diplomatic circles." Edith also invested rhetorical capital in the materials she and Bones produced at the White House by initiating outreach projects such as sending a special shipment of items they had sewn to the queen of Romania for distribution there through the Red Cross. She also sent a large package to the British Red Cross intending to demonstrate "her active and most practical interest in the work of mercy and relief carried on by Red Cross Societies" *(NYT* July 6, 1917).

Wilson employed similar strategies in her attempts to persuade Americans to conserve resources for the war effort. Again aiming to set an example for American women by lending her name, the first lady assisted Herbert Hoover, head of the Food Administration, in launching the war conservation program by being the first citizen to sign a pledge card. It stated: "I am glad to join you in the service of food conservation for our nation, and I hereby accept membership in the United States Food Administration, pledging myself to carry out the directions and advice of the Food Administrator in the conduct of my household, in so far as my circumstances admit." The symbolic value of this gesture was captured by newspapers, which reported that "Mrs. Woodrow Wilson took the lead in getting the women of the country organized when she attached her signature to this pledge." Once Wilson's pledge card had been filed, she was presented with a card upon which was printed a red, white, and blue shield surrounded by heads of wheat. It was posted in the dining room window of the White House announcing that the home was owned by a "Member of United States Food Administration." The first lady's participation in and endorsement of the program were widely reported, creating the opportunity for her actions to serve as examples to other women in hopes of bolstering the conservation campaign (*NYT* July 1, 7, and 9, 1917; Harmon 1918).

Wilson's conservation efforts extended beyond working with the Food Administration. Within ten days of the official declaration of war, she, along with the wives of cabinet members, began a movement to increase domestic efficiency in order to invest more time and money in war relief work. Their plan of action included a cessation of social activities and avoidance of "unnecessary expenditures." As part of the campaign, an unnamed cabinet member issued a statement to the *New York Times* declaring that the women had pledged themselves "to buy inexpensive clothing and simple food and to watch and prevent all kinds of waste." Their hope, the statement explained, was that through increased conservation as well as increased food production the nation would be able "to help those who are in such desperate need." As they set an example of women meeting wartime obligations, the officials' wives also appealed to "all the women of America to do everything in their power along these lines" (April 13, 1917).

Despite her attempts to frame conservation in domestic terms, Wilson's call for participation aroused political controversy. The *New York Times'* praise for the campaign was laced with a cautionary note warning women, even the wives of government officials, against engaging directly—on their own—in public campaigns. "They are too tactful to pose as leaders of a movement, for that would be sure to excite not a little of irritation in a sensitive democracy," the newspaper editorialized. It went on to emphasize the uniqueness of "existing circumstances" and the propriety of "all patriotic families" refraining from indulgences during the war. Of concern was not only the propriety of the women's actions, but also economists' fears that Americans would interpret the statement as a justification for hoarding money (April 14, 1917). Despite the *Times'* endorsement and clarification, Wilson received a pointed letter from Anna Whitson, a spokesperson for the dry goods trade, who expressed her dismay at the first lady's newspaper interview and argued that the conservation pledge would have a terrible effect on the ready-to-wear clothing industry. Wilson's response, issued through her secretary and written in the third person, sidestepped Whitson's arguments about effects on garment workers, and focused instead on the manner in which the first lady attempted to influence the public. "Mrs. Wilson," said the private letter written by the first lady's secretary Edith Benham, "wishes me to say that . . . she has given no 'interview' to the newspapers of the country, for she has made it a rule ever since she has been in the

White House not to be interviewed." She had, the letter explained, issued a statement "in conjunction with the ladies of the Cabinet in regard to the necessity for economy at the present time." Newspaper coverage of the exchange does not record what must have been Whitson's exasperation at this argumentative hairsplitting (*NYT* April 30, 1917).

While raising money for the war effort, Wilson also relied on the press to report her actions and invest them with symbolic value. In a scheme certain to invite publicity, the first lady borrowed a flock of sheep to graze the White House lawn. The sheep not only reduced the labor of grounds keeping, but also proved an innovative means of raising money. At shearing time, the flock produced "White House wool," two pounds of which was sent to each state, where it was auctioned and reportedly raised $50,000 for relief work (Caroli 1987, 148). Likewise, Wilson buoyed efforts to sell liberty bonds by appearing in public with celebrities and with those persons who sold bonds. In April 1918, for example, she reviewed the Women's Liberty Loan Parade of 25,000 marchers (*The Philadelphia Press*, April 21, 1918, in WW Papers, reel 504 scrapbook 2, 79). As the *New York Times* reported, the occasion of reviewing the parade was the "first time that Mrs. Wilson . . . has acted independently of the President as the patroness of a public function" (April 28, 1918).

Nowhere is Wilson's consistent rhetorical strategy of relying upon actions rather than words better illustrated than in her visit to Philadelphia Girl Scout Troop 57 to present them with an American flag for selling more liberty bonds than any troop in America. There she studiously avoided giving a formal speech, declaring, "It gives me great pleasure to present this Flag. I have never made a speech, so I can only wish you well, and say that you are all very good little Americans" (June 27, 1918, *Public Ledger* (Philadelphia) in WW Papers, reel 504 scrapbook 2, 89). Yet it was in the work of fund-raising that Edith Wilson was willing to move beyond symbolic action to write letters to various organizations to laud their efforts, boost morale, and draw press coverage. Her letter to the Aviation Committee of the National Special Aid Society in New York, for example, stated that she felt "the keenest interest in its undertaking" and praised members for their exertions (*NYT* Oct. 9, 1917).

Even in her most discursive statement during the war, Edith Wilson exerted her influence through a traditionally feminine form, alongside another woman, upholding conservative values. Early in February 1918, the first lady and woman suffrage leader Dr. Anna Howard Shaw issued a public letter addressed to the women of the allied countries, distributed by American diplomats, asking them to assist in preserving the morality of American men fighting in Europe. Attempting to establish identification with its readers, the letter opened by acknowledging that the men and women of the allied nations shared deep commitments to democracy and peace. Women, in particular, were united by "a deeper and more subtle bond which makes all women akin," namely, "the yearning of the mother heart of the world for the highest moral and spiritual welfare of children." American mothers, the letter continued, willingly offered their sons on behalf of the noble ideals of democracy, but they asked for help from European women who were in a position to protect their sons from the corruption that too often results from the "unnatural life of the camp." The letter urged all women to rise to the challenges brought on by the war and to do all they could to "conserve the moral forces of society." Taking action now, the writers instructed, will protect "the future home life of our peoples," for a nation's peace and prosperity depended upon the character of its individual citizens as much as the righteousness of its government. Though the letter associated Edith Wilson with suffrage leader Shaw, it reinforced traditional ideas about women's concerns and apparently fit Wilson's idea of appropriate womanly behavior (*NYT* February 6, 1918).

Searching for Peace Abroad

When she landed with her husband in Brest, France, December 13, 1918, a month after the war had ended, the Wilsons became the first American presidential couple to travel abroad while in office. In Europe, the first lady basked in the adoration showered on President Wilson, as parades of thousands of people turned out in several cities in France, Italy, and England to see and cheer the American leader and his wife. Edith's earlier travels in foreign countries, her winning personality and self-confidence served her well through what must have been trying times abroad. Throughout the peace conference, the first lady was required to appear at formal ceremonies with European royalty and her actions were reported widely in the international press. As such, Edith Wilson became for the world a representative of American womanhood and played an important symbolic role in American diplomacy. She carried out these duties in a manner consistent with her domestic persona, appearing as the president's closest confidant and helpmate throughout the arduous negotiations.

At the president's side and on her own, Edith Wilson demonstrated her commitment to the Allied cause by visiting encamped soldiers, and comforting the wounded in hospitals and rehabilitation centers. But whether consoling a blinded infantryman or dining with the king of England, Edith Wilson faced the challenge of cultivating a persona befitting the feminine embodiment of democracy while among European monarchists. Indeed, according to Edith's memoir, an old French duchess disdained the very idea of meeting the common Wilsons until she learned of Edith's ancestral link to Princess Pocahontas (Wilson 1938). Though the duchess found Edith Wilson's royal lineage compelling, the first lady herself made little of it and instead negotiated the issue of status by making it clear that she represented, rather than ruled, the women of America. In addition, she made strategic use of informality in her interpersonal encounters and of fashion choices that modeled democratic womanhood.

Appreciative officials from throughout Europe, and especially in France, greeted the first lady as though she were royalty. When the Wilsons arrived in Paris, for example, they were made citizens of the city. When the president of the Municipal Council of Paris presented Edith Wilson with a diamond broach of peace doves, he spoke to her with deference due a queen.[4] "Madame, Paris is infinitely happy and is touched that you, who have accompanied the president have been good enough to add to this occasion the charm and the grace of your presence," he said and then declared, "Paris, by my voice, acclaims you, and lays at your feet, Madame, the homage of its gratitude and its respect" (unidentified clipping, December 16, 1918, Associated Press in WW Papers, reel 504 scrapbook 3, 153). To bear such praise and public ovation so graciously was no easy task. On several occasions, propriety required that Edith respond fittingly. After receiving from the Orphélinat des Armées a medal commemorating the assistance American women had offered the people of France during the war, Mrs. Wilson issued a public statement which emphasized that in accepting the honor, she spoke not for herself, but rather that she "express[ed] the sentiments of my countrywomen." Acutely aware of the devastation visited upon the French nation, she assured that "this aid was given gladly, our only regret being that we could not have done more to help the soldiers and the women who stood so bravely behind them in this great struggle for liberty in the world." On this occasion and others, Edith succeeded in demonstrating grace, humility, and democratic sensibilities, qualities for which she won accolades abroad and at home (*NY Herald*, Feb. 10, 1919, in WW Papers, reel 504 scrapbook 3, 123).

Edith Wilson's interpersonal interactions with soldiers and civilians blinded and disfigured during the war were the subject of constant press coverage and of repeated praise for the first lady. Newspapers praised her display of "true American informality" when meeting with military officers as well as her natural and unostentatious manner when visiting Red Cross canteens, where, according to news reports, the doughboys grew to worship the "tireless, indefatigable, smiling, keen, alert and natural" first lady (*NY Herald* Paris Edition, April 29, 1919; *Chicago Tribune* Paris Ed., April 12, 1919, in WW Papers, reel 504 scrapbook 3, 256, 211). The *London Chronicle* declared that Mrs. Wilson had become "the living symbol of the American ideal." She was, they continued, "the most picturesque expression of her husband's ideal that it is character which counts and that beside it rank and riches and power are little things" (Dec. 28, 1918, in WW Papers, reel 504 scrapbook 2, 198).

Her words and carriage were important, but Edith Wilson's very appearance, the manner in which she adorned herself, was of utmost rhetorical significance. Newspaper writers, both European and American, commented frequently and extensively on her fashion choices. "She was absolutely stunning in her black spangled gown, which seemed to bring out the blackness of her hair," described the *New York Herald* in its international edition. "And with her sparkling eyes, agreeable smile and gracious manner, it was evident that she really took all before her by storm" (Jan. 3, 1919, in WW Papers, reel 504 scrapbook 3, 6). The French noticed and approved of her "decided preference" for French design. Yet even in her fashion choices, Wilson skillfully negotiated the dilemma between royal and democratic behavior (*New York Herald*, European ed., Dec. 17, 1918, in WW Papers, reel 504 scrapbook 2, 154). While she had visited the most prestigious designers in Paris and the dresses she wore emulated Parisian models, the *Chicago Tribune* noted that all of her gowns were purchased from Worth, an American dressmaker (Paris ed., Feb. 6, 1919, in WW Papers, reel 504 scrapbook 3, 304). She also carefully observed and honored the fashion choices of her royal hosts. When attending a dinner with the English royal family, she took pains to ascertain whether Queen Alexandra and Princess Mary would be wearing gloves, only to learn that the women would not wear them but would carry in their left hands a new pair tied together, held with fingers up. Edith was relieved upon garnering this information and commented that attention to the details of fashion "makes for a sense of stability and relieves a stranger of the embarrassment of running counter to social custom" (Wilson 1938, 196).

Carl Anthony (1990), historian of first ladies, faults Edith Wilson for having delusions of grandeur during the European peace conference due to all of the adulation she received during her travels abroad. Yet, by press accounts, Mrs. Wilson succeeded in negotiating the dilemma she faced as a representative of democracy while in the presence of royalty. Her success was captured by a long article in the *London Chronicle*, which expressed the collective reaction of the English people. "Mrs. Wilson came to London on Thursday as a simple woman of simple ancestry, but as the wife of a great man," it said, noting that the people of London were eager to greet and cheer her husband. Within days, however, reported the *Chronicle*, Mrs. Wilson was cheered not because of her connection to her husband, but rather, "because of her gracious self." Not only had she as an individual won the hearts of the English, but she had also succeeded in upholding democratic ideals. "No queen could have a more queenly manner, no great lady could be more gracious, no woman more utterly winning than President Wilson's wife" (Dec. 28, 1918, in WW Papers, reel 504 scrapbook 2, 198).

The additional credibility Wilson gained through the presence of his energetic and gracious wife is impossible to measure, but it is clear from the newspaper coverage that she reinforced his central message concerning the superiority of democratic government. In addition, as Mrs. Wilson weathered the European trip with her husband she became more intimately familiar with his vision for the future. Her daily presence at dinner when Wilson updated press representative Ray Stannard Baker on the day's events made her privy to the challenges faced by the negotiators. Hidden behind a heavy curtain, Edith witnessed one of her husband's shining moments as he delivered his plea for the League of Nations to a closed session of the all-male peace conference. These experiences deepened Edith Wilson's commitment to the president's vision for world peace and help account for her actions during the most trying period of the Wilson presidency (Wilson 1938).

The League of Nations and "The Presidentress"

The Wilson's were warmly received when they returned to Washington from their final peace trip to Europe, in July 1919. The Woman's Suffrage Club of Cambridge, Massachusetts, greeted Edith "with love and congratulations" for her "invaluable help in 'holding the hands' of our beloved President Wilson" (WW Papers, reel 505 scrapbook 4, 162). Yet the president received a far less friendly reception in Congress for during his absence isolationist Republicans had stirred opposition to American involvement in the League of Nations. Indeed, the president faced an uphill battle in the Senate for the passage of the treaty. In a move associated with the modern presidency, Wilson decided to take his case to the American people by way of a cross-country speaking tour. As usual, Edith traveled with her husband. "I go along with him to take care of him, you know," she purportedly told a *St. Paul News* reporter. "After all, that is a woman's first duty to her family" (Sept. 9, 1919, in WW Papers, reel 505 scrapbook 4, 207).

As the famous couple traveled across the country, thousands turned out to hear the president speak, while millions eagerly read details of their journey. As was her custom, Edith Wilson refused to grant press interviews or answer questions. When reporters from the *Portland Journal* (Oregon) pleaded with the first lady to describe how it was to be the wife of "The Great War President," she flashed her most disarming smile and replied, "I'm sorry but I really cannot tell you" (Sept. 15, 1919, in WW Papers, reel 505 scrapbook 4, 241). In the absence of words from the mouth of Mrs. Wilson, reporters commented on her appearance, and on the crowd's response to her. About her attire they wrote: "every day since the beginning of her trip she has appeared with a new chapeau." Another newspaper reported that "Mrs. Wilson has never worn the same gown twice since she left her home" (*Portland [Oregon] Telegram*, Sept. 15, 1919, *Seattle Times*, Sept. 14, 1919, in WW Papers, reel 505 scrapbook 4, 241, 231). About her personality they declared, "she is most gracious in manner, and quite unaffected, even though she is so recently home from visits to the principal royal places in Europe." In fact, a *Columbus Dispatch* writer stated that Mrs. Wilson could "teach Columbus women of the 'upper crust' just how charming a great woman may be, and yet be the wife of the president of the United States" (Sept. 4, 1919, in WW Papers, reel 505 scrapbook 4, 179).

Though gratified by positive public reception, Edith Wilson was less concerned with the impression she was making than with her husband's deteriorating health. So attentive was she to her husband, that the press took note. In mid-September, *The Oregonian* reported that while the president stood in his car bowing to vast crowds, "his good wife, thoughtful of his welfare, held her white-gloved hand at his back to help steady him" (Sept. 16, 1919, in WW Papers, reel 505 scrapbook 4, 242). Another article entitled, "Mrs. Wilson Is Real Executive on Presidential Train," quoted secret service men who declared: "She sets her little foot down when she sees the president is getting the least bit tired" (*Des Moines Register* Sept. 7, 1919, in WW Papers, reel 505 scrapbook 4). What the reporters were prevented from seeing were the scenes that heightened Mrs. Wilson's worries—the president's inability to sleep well, his persistent headaches, and his intense exhaustion.

On September 25, 1919, as the train moved from Pueblo, Colorado, to Wichita, Kansas, President Wilson suffered a stroke. Years later Edith would recall her feelings at this moment, writing in her *Memoir* that she felt that "something had broken inside me." She realized that from that moment she "would have to wear a mask—not only to the public but to the one I loved best in the world; for he must never know how ill he was, and I must carry on" (1938, 284).

The remaining stops on the League of Nations tour were canceled and the train rushed back to Washington. On October 1, the president suffered another serious stroke that paralyzed the left side of his body. Wilson was confined to a sickroom, unable to make public appearances or attend cabinet meetings (Weaver 1985, 54). Edith did carry on, and thus began what she called her "stewardship."

When the president became bedridden, Edith Wilson played a central role in making two crucial decisions. First, she made no public statements about her husband's condition, and agreed with others in Wilson's inner circle that the truth about the president's condition should not become public knowledge (Walworth 1978). In fact, as Wilson scholar John Milton Cooper argues, there is no evidence that Wilson himself was told that he had had a stroke (Cooper 1994, 82). Second, in consultation with Wilson's doctors, Edith decided that despite his illness, the president should not resign. According to her *Memoirs*, Edith asked Woodrow's neurologist, Dr. Dercum, whether Wilson should resign the presidency, to which he reportedly replied that resigning "would have a bad effect on the country and a serious effect on our patient." Instead, Mrs. Wilson recalled, Dercum instructed that she should have all of the president's business directed to her. After weighing the importance of each matter, he recommended that she consult with cabinet members to address issues rather than bringing them to her husband. "But always keep in mind," Dercum allegedly cautioned, that every new problem she took to him was like "turning a knife in an open wound" (Wilson 1938, 289). Cooper casts doubt on Edith Wilson's recollection, reasoning that it is unlikely that any of Wilson's doctors would offer "such categorical advice about how to run the government," nor is it likely that the "strong-willed" first lady would act so passively. What is more likely, says Cooper, is that Mrs. Wilson devised a system for handling matters of state to allow Wilson to rest as the doctors prescribed (1994, 84–85).

Both her *Memoir* and contemporary news articles describe Edith Wilson acting as a "gatekeeper" during the president's illness. By her account, Mrs. Wilson studied every paper sent to the president, consulted with members of the cabinet, and digested and presented to her husband matters that could not wait or be diverted to others. Contemporary sources comport with her recollections. The *Canton Daily News* reported on March 12, 1920, that Mrs. Wilson was acting as a buffer between the chief executive and a world "pitiless in its demands and limitless in its expectations" (in WW Papers, reel 505 scrapbook 5, 7). Under the headline "President Wilson's Wife Is Heroine of White House Drama," another newspaper reported that "day and night" Edith was at Woodrow's bedside "not only ministering to his wants but reading the mass of memoranda that is transmitted to her and determining what quantity he shall see each day" (in WW Papers, reel 505 scrapbook 4, 286). Rather than allowing callers to see the president, the first lady met with them in her sitting room where she verbally delivered messages from the president. On those occasions when she was unprepared to answer a question, she would enter the adjoining sickroom, discuss the matter with her husband, and return with a statement (Selden 1921; Phiffer 1971).

It remains unclear how long the first lady acted as messenger and gatekeeper for President Wilson. Based on what Edith Wilson told him, the first lady's official biographer wrote that her "regency" lasted six weeks; another biographer claimed that it lasted six months, until the president attended a cabinet meeting on April 13, 1920 (Hatch 1961, 219; Smith 1964, 131). "By any reasonable measure," concludes Cooper, "the United States did not have a functioning president between the beginning of October 1919 and the end of January 1920" (80). Although the length of her "stewardship" cannot be pinpointed, what is clear is that there were those at home and abroad who were alarmed by the first lady's apparent increase in power. In February 1920, *the London Daily Mail* reported: "Nothing more startling has been disclosed in this week of endless sensations at Washington than the fact that the wife of President Wilson has for months past been acting President of the United States" (Feb. 22, 1920, in WW Papers, reel 505 scrapbook 5, 3). In the United States, rumors spread that Edith Wilson was signing her name to state papers and that the nation was in the hands of a woman president (Anthony 1990). Edith's publicly acknowledged role in events such as negotiating, at the president's direction, the appointments of Admiral Benson and John Barton Payne to cabinet positions, as well as her role as one of only a handful of people who saw the president during these weeks, added fuel to the blaze of rumors.

Contemporaries and historians alike have criticized Edith Wilson for exceeding her proper role as first lady and allegedly seizing the reins of American government. Among the harshest recent critics of Mrs. Wilson's actions is Judith L. Weaver, who holds the first lady largely responsible for the failure to get the League treaty approved by the Senate. "Her jealousy of Wilson's advisors mixed with her intense and blind loyalty to her husband's opinion on the Treaty, contributed to its defeat," writes Weaver (1985, 69). Emphasizing that personal rather than political concerns guided Edith Wilson's actions during her stewardship, Weaver faults her for denying trusted advisors Joseph P. Tumulty, Robert Lansing, and Colonel House access to the president as well as putting off for four months the reception of visiting British special emissary Lord Grey, who wished to discuss the League treaty with the president. As a result, Weaver argues, Woodrow Wilson did not receive counsel on the necessity of compromise, leaving him without information to form a proper judgment. Mrs. Wilson erred, Weaver concludes, by being too concerned "for the welfare of her husband" and too little concerned about the welfare of the country (55). In order to avoid upsetting her husband, Edith made sure he "received no reports on public opinion and heard no views except those he wished to hear" (51). The end result, Weaver argues, "was destruction of the Treaty" (51). As evidence that Edith allowed personal rather than political issues to determine the outcome of various issues, Weaver points to the first lady's personal animosity toward Secretary of State Robert Lansing, rather than any inappropriate action on his part, as the cause of Lansing's dismissal in February 1920 (51).

Throughout her life, Edith Wilson stridently denied that during Wilson's illness she had done anything more than take care of routine details of government, insisting that she never took control of the executive branch of the U.S. government. "I, myself, never made a single decision regarding the disposition of public affairs," she wrote in *My Memoir*. "The only decision that was mine was what was important and what was not, and the very important decision of when to present matters to my husband" (1938, 289). Unlike Weaver, Cooper maintains that Edith Wilson "tried scrupulously to avoid infringing on policy matters," adding that if she had attempted to act as the president's surrogate "she would have been well qualified to do so, since he had made her his closest political confidante and shared secrets of state with her even before their marriage in 1915." In fact, Cooper argues that charges of usurping the executive office could more rightly be leveled against Tumulty (1994, 85). Likewise, Robert J. Maddox argues that Edith Wilson was neither "the first Lady President" nor a dictator, but rather that for four or five months she "exercised considerable power on small to middling affairs within the Executive department. She influenced the President personally and in her role as a sort of guardian of the gates." Given that Vice President Thomas R. Marshall was deeply disturbed by the prospect of ascending to the presidency and that he is best remembered for uttering the phrase "What this country needs is a really good five cent cigar," Maddox argues that Edith Wilson's "regency" of the federal executive "seems less unfortunate" (Maddox 1973, 44).

Protecting the Wilson Legacy

With the death of Woodrow Wilson in February 1924, Edith withdrew to a very private life for a time, yet her commitment to her husband and perhaps the interest in political affairs that had awakened within her, pulled her back to activity. Without her husband to stand beside and behind she found herself a conspicuous figure at events such as the Democratic National Conventions. In 1928 she was an honored guest of the convention and even found herself forced to say a few words before a large audience. A few months earlier she had firmly declined a speaking offer from the League of Nations Non-Partisan Association of Texas: "You have evidently forgotten," she wrote, "that I am *not* a speaker, so it seems to me it would be much more effective to send one of your best speakers instead of a person who is never vocal" (letter to Mrs. David E. Waggoner, Dec. 10, 1927). Nevertheless, on the eve of the 1928 convention she agreed to speak at a ceremony for the dedication of a new convention hall in Houston. While the *New York Times* ran a picture of Mrs. Wilson standing at the podium, her speech was so "brief and soft-spoken" and the crowd's ovation so boisterous, that only those nearest her could hear the former first lady speak (June 25, 1928; July 1, 1928, *NYT* picture section, 2). A similar scene was played out the following day when Will Rogers introduced Mrs. Wilson to a breakfast meeting of Democratic women. Though Rogers claimed that she "made an awful nice and appropriate speech," a reporter wrote that she "briefly and graciously although inaudibly . . . expressed her pleasure and appreciation" (*NYT* June 28, 1928; *NYT* June 28, 1928). Although she continued to be asked— even Eleanor Roosevelt pleaded with her to speak on the radio to aid the Democratic Party—Edith Wilson steadfastly avoided speaking in public (Eleanor Roosevelt to Edith Wilson, telegram, n.d. in Edith Bolling Wilson Papers, Library of Congress).

Yet, Edith Wilson was more than willing to write a good many letters to ensure that her husband would be properly remembered by history. During the summer of 1924, only a few months after her husband's death, she sent out hundreds of letters to his relatives, friends, and associates soliciting correspondence as well as other materials relating to him. She also embarked on the all-important task of selecting a biographer. By the end of 1924 she had chosen Ray Stannard Baker, the journalist who had covered the Wilson's sojourns in Europe and had published volumes on the Paris Peace Conference. Baker had corresponded with the president a month before his death about the prospect of writing a biography, and Wilson had stated in writing that "he had confidence in Baker's impartiality and justice" (McWilliams 1984). The task of narrating the story of Woodrow Wilson's life was daunting, and when the entire Wilson collection was shipped to Baker's home, it weighed five tons. Baker spent the next fourteen years writing *Woodrow Wilson: Life and Letters*, which consumed eight volumes. He credited Edith Wilson with giving him complete freedom and immense patience in writing the biography (McWilliams 1984).

When the final volume of the biography was published in 1939, Edith gifted the Wilson collection to the Manuscript Division of the Library of Congress, with whom she had been in contact since her husband's death. She asked both that she have a say in deciding "the importance or unimportance" of documents in the collection and that she have final say over who had access to the papers. The Library of Congress' special custodian of the papers, Kathryn Brand, noted: "Mrs. Wilson in almost every case granted access generously, although she often withheld permission to publish quotations from Wilson's letters." Mrs. Wilson's determination that the library should have all of her husband's papers continued to the end of her life. Repeatedly, she sent to the Manuscript Division papers which had been found in the cupboards, closets, and unused rooms of the S Street house (Brand 1973).

In 1938, a year before Baker published the final volume of Woodrow Wilson's biography, which ended in 1918 with the armistice, Edith Wilson published *My Memoir*. This public utterance departed drastically from her practice of suppressing her voice in favor of allowing others or her actions to speak for her. Yet even in this departure from custom, in the foreword to *My Memoir* she expressed reluctance to make public disclosures, stating that she had "never written a line for publication," and that friends and editors had encouraged her to write. The volume traversed only those years she spent with Woodrow Wilson, including the president's illness and death. She did, however, offer a few chapters to describe her family of origin and establish her persona as an independent though nonpolitical woman. As a whole, Mrs. Wilson's autobiography constituted an apologia, as evidenced by the fact that in the foreword she swore that she had "revealed the truth concerning personal matters which has often been distorted by the misinformed" (1938, vi). She denied any motive to achieve power and fame and emphasized her love and devotion to Woodrow Wilson, depicting herself as a loyal helpmate. Yet while claiming that she worked out of love for her husband, an ostensible purpose of *My Memoir* seems to be to garner credit for the strenuous work she performed in her role as first lady, or, as she would have preferred to be called, wife of the president. Yet she vehemently denied allegations concerning her desire to act as president and accepted no blame for isolating her husband from his advisors. She insisted, instead, that everything she did, she did in order to save her husband's life (Phiffer 1971).

Another apparent purpose of *My Memoir* was to defend the legacy of President Wilson. Time and again she attacked those she believed had wronged her husband. Edith expressed her dismay toward radical suffragists who picketed the White House when the nation was on the brink of war. She depicted artist John Singer Sargent as a pawn of Wilson's political enemy Henry Cabot Lodge and accused him of painting an unflattering portrait of President Wilson. She also denigrated individuals she personally disliked such as Wilson's trusted secretary Joseph P. Tumulty, who had opposed her marriage to Woodrow and whom she distrusted because he was Catholic (Weaver 1985).

Despite the fact that *My Memoir* contains numerous inaccuracies due to the fact that it was written two decades after the events it described and was highly romanticized, it remains the most revealing source we have about the closing days of the Wilson administration (Gould 1996, 366). Though composed to achieve rhetorical goals, *My Memoir* comes across as disarmingly honest. The book invites readers to take a detailed and intimate journey through the couple's courtship, work life, home life, diplomatic travels, and the trying days of the president's illness. Its pages communicate the mind and character of this first lady. They show the good—the tireless worker, the loving wife, the caring stepmother, the avid traveler, and the appreciative witness to world history. And they show the less appealing—an individual unashamed of voicing racial stereotypes, a person willing to engage in *ad hominem* attack, a woman obsessed with fashion, a public figure who often lacked reflection or historical insight. Though ostensibly an autobiography, her story ends with the death of her husband. In this way the memoir aided Edith Wilson in conveying the message that she was "of no importance" to the public except through her marital connection with the president. It was his legacy, she insisted, not hers that must be kept alive.

Legacy

Like many historical figures, Edith Wilson's legacy has been shaped more by the historical context in which she lived, than by the actions she performed. "Her chief anxiety is to keep out of the papers," wrote Woodrow Wilson to a war agency director requesting the first lady's public endorsement (Day 1952, 279). Yet historical circumstances—marriage to a sitting president, the culmination of women's suffrage movement, World War I, and the president's collapse—made it impossible for her to maintain a low public profile. Though she eschewed making public statements, Edith Wilson responded to these exigencies by carefully orchestrating her actions and appearance. Active in wartime conservation and relief movements and assisting her husband in every way possible, with the aid of the press, she succeeded in presenting herself at home and abroad as the symbol of democratic American womanhood.

Her most conscious rhetorical stance was to present herself as the president's wife rather than an independent figure called the first lady. Even Joseph Tumulty, who had every reason to hold a grudge against Mrs. Wilson for coming between him and the president, claimed, "No public man ever had a more devoted helpmeet" (Tumulty 1921, 436). Tumulty also applauded her efforts to protect the president during his illness and found fitting her declaration, "'I am not interested in the President of the United States. I am interested in my husband and his health'" (1921, 438). Her persona of helpmate to Mr. Wilson, who happened to be president of the United States, was perpetuated by the press. As one reporter put it:

> Ask anyone in Washington "What interests has the President's wife?" "The President," is the invariable answer. "But what work appeals to her?" "The President's," is the reply. "Surely she has some pet ambition, some . . .?" "To make the President happy." "Well, has she talents? Hobbies?" "Yes. Her talents are reading aloud, playing golf, discussing human affairs, writing letters, analyzing reports and pardon pleas, hunting up good detective stories, supervising the household, motoring and movies—all with, for and because of the President." (*New York City Evening Mail,* Saturday Sept. 4, 1920, in the WW Papers reel 505 scrapbook 5, 20)

Her interest in and loyalty to her husband did not cease with his death. The backlash against the Wilson presidency (a 1937 survey indicated that 71 percent of Americans believed that the United States should not have entered World War I [Reid 1995]) pushed Edith out of her years of action without words and into the writing of a startling and engaging memoir.

As Lewis Gould (1996) has suggested, the controversy surrounding Edith Wilson's actions during her husband's illness led to heightened awareness of the consequences of the unlimited access and influence a first lady can have over a president. Recent debates over the first lady's role suggest that the American public remains ambivalent about the power wielded by these unelected spouses. It is ironic that Edith Wilson became the first major test case of these issues since she seems to have been one of the least politically ambitious. She clearly had the opportunity to exercise unprecedented executive power, but instead she focused on her husband's health and allowed decisions to be delayed and cabinet members to carry out increasing responsibilities with little guidance. Curiously, her years with Wilson seemed to have awakened a latent interest in politics, especially in perpetuating his legacy even in an era rife with isolationist sentiment. After Wilson's death, Edith was a frequent guest at the White House and she often reminded succeeding administrations of the price America had to pay for turning its back on her husband's vision for attaining world peace.

Notes

1. Newspaper articles are cited only with text references and are not included on the References page. References to the *New York Times* will be abbreviated as *NYT.* Some

newspaper articles were found as clippings in the scrapbooks included in the Woodrow Wilson Papers (1973, cited as WW Papers in the text). In these cases the parenthetical text citations will include microfilm reel number and scrapbook number followed by the page number along with newspaper titles and dates when they are available.

2. Wilson's statement concerning the New Jersey suffrage law indicated his support for a state-by-state approach to the issue as well as his opposition to a national amendment, but many suffragists were nevertheless delighted by this breakthrough.

3. Edith Wilson's voting career was cut short by the death of her husband in 1924. At that time her residency reverted back to Washington, D.C., whose citizens were ineligible to vote in presidential elections until the 1961 passage of the Twenty-third Amendment.

4. Carl Anthony (1990) cites additional evidence of Edith Wilson's royal treatment. For example, when her social secretary Edith Benham was mistakenly identified as "lady-in-waiting" Mrs. Wilson "made no attempt to correct the confusion. . . . In fact, everywhere she went, the American First Lady was treated with the status of a European queen." The Wilsons stayed in castles, traveled in kings' trains, and were showered with flowers by crowds which "acknowledged the First Lady as the Yankee queen. In the European consciousness, it was the first widely public recognition of an American First Lady. And back home, it was reported that Edith was treated 'as the consort of a reigning sovereign and welcomed by queens on a footing of equality'" (366).

References

Anthony, Carl Sferrazza. 1990. *First Ladies: The Saga of the Presidents' Wives and Their Power, 1789–1961*, Vol. 1. New York: William Morrow and Company.

Baker, Ray Stannard. 1927–1939. *Woodrow Wilson, Life and Letters*, 8 vols. Garden City, N.Y.: Doubleday, Page & Co.

Barzman, Sol. 1970. *The First Ladies*. New York: Cowles Book Company.

Bender, Robert J. 1920. Signed—Edith Bolling Wilson. *Collier's*, 6 March, 5.

Brand, Kathryn. 1973. Introduction. In *Index to the Woodrow Wilson Papers*, v–xv. Washington, D.C.: Library of Congress.

Caplan, Judith. 1986. Woodrow Wilson and Women: The Formative Influences on Wilson's Attitudes toward Women. *New Jersey History*, 104:1–2, 22–35.

Caroli, Betty Boyd. 1987. *First Ladies*. New York: Oxford University Press.

Cooper, John Milton. 1994. Disability in the White House: The Case of Woodrow Wilson. In *The White House: The First Two Hundred Years*, ed. Frank Freidel and William Pencak, 75–99. Boston: Northeastern University Press.

Day, Donald, ed. 1952. *Woodrow Wilson's Own Story*. Boston: Little and Brown.

Gould, Lewis L. 1996. *American First Ladies: Their Lives and Their Legacy*. New York: Garland.

Harmon, Dudley. 1918. What Is Mrs. Wilson Doing? The Part the President's Wife and His Daughters Have in the War. *The Ladies' Home Journal*, July, 22, 24.

Hatch, Alden. 1961. *Edith Bolling Wilson: First Lady Extraordinary*. New York: Dodd, Mead & Company.

Heckscher, August. 1991. *Woodrow Wilson*. New York: Charles Scribner's Sons.

Maddox, Robert J. 1973. Mrs. Wilson and the Presidency. *American History Illustrated*, February, 7, 36–44.

Means, Marianne. 1963. *The Woman in the White House*. New York: Random House.

McWilliams, Ruth. 1984. Preparing for the Biographer: A Widow's Task. *Manuscripts*, 26:3, 187–96.

Phiffer, Gregg. 1971. Edith Bolling Wilson: Gatekeeper Extraordinary. *Speech Monographs*, 38:4, 277–89.

Reid, Ronald F. 1995. *American Rhetorical Discourse*, 2nd edition. Prospect Heights, Ill.: Waveland.

Selden, Charles A. 1921. Mrs. Woodrow Wilson: Wife, Nurse and Secretary, Who Kept the President Alive during the World's Greatest Crisis. *The Ladies' Home Journal*, October 3–5, 152, 155–56.

Shachtman, Tom. 1981. *Edith & Woodrow: A Presidential Romance*. New York: G. P. Putnam's.

Smith, Gene. 1964. *When the Cheering Stopped: The Last Years of Woodrow Wilson*. New York: William Morrow.

Tribble, Edwin, ed. 1981. *A President in Love: The Courtship Letters of Woodrow Wilson and Edith Bolling Galt*. Boston: Houghton Mifflin.

Tumulty, Joseph. 1921. *Woodrow Wilson as I Know Him*. Garden City, N.Y.: Doubleday, Page & Co.

Walworth, Arthur. 1978. *Woodrow Wilson*. New York: W.W. Norton.

Weaver, Judith L. 1985. Edith Bolling Wilson as First Lady: A Study in the Power of Personality, 1919–1920. *Presidential Studies Quarterly*, 15:1, 51–76.

Weisberger, Bernard A. 1993. Petticoat Government. *American Heritage*, 44:6, 18–20.

Wilson, Edith Bolling. 1938. *My Memoir*. New York: Bobbs-Merrill.

Wilson, Edith Bolling Papers. Washington, D.C.: Library of Congress.

Wilson, Woodrow Papers, microfilm edition. 1973. Washington, D.C.: Library of Congress.

Chapter 7

Florence Kling Harding
Bridging Traditional and Modern Rhetorical Roles

Ann E. Burnette

> Well Warren Harding, I have got you the Presidency; what are you going to do
> with it?
> > —Florence Kling Harding

Americans today rate Florence Kling Harding as one of the least memorable first
ladies of the United States. Margaret Truman nominated her as the "worst"
(1995, 233); Robert P. Watson said that her performance as first lady was
ranked at the bottom of two significant polls (2000). Yet, Mrs. Harding was a
popular figure in her day and served as a transitional first lady. In many ways,
she reflected the changing values of the early 1920s. During this time women
won the vote and made advances in science, politics, sports, and social reform
work. The first lady celebrated the advances of women and was an accomplished professional woman in her own right. During this time, mass media,
including older print forms and new forms like radio and movies, became staples of American culture. Mrs. Harding used these mass media to advance her
husband's career and sometimes her own views. In an era when women were
negotiating new roles and responsibilities, Florence Harding was a bridge between the traditional, domestic, woman's sphere and a more open, public, and
equal arena for women. But while she expanded the repertoire of first lady in
some important respects, she still adhered to the traditional role of wife and
helpmate. She publicly affiliated herself with some causes, but she refrained

from commenting on many important political issues. She met with reporters but often did not permit them to quote her directly. The influence she exercised on her husband's professional decisions was usually private.

Florence Harding took on responsibilities beyond the traditional feminine sphere, performed many activities that have become expected of modern first ladies, and associated herself explicitly with some public issues and causes. She was a single mother working to support herself and her son when she met Warren Harding. Her marriage to Harding quickly became a business and political partnership. She worked side by side with Warren at the newspaper he had founded, where she exhibited strong business acumen. She was an active agent in her husband's political career, giving him advice, helping him orchestrate his campaign events, and campaigning herself. In the White House, she publicly extolled the achievements of scientist Marie Curie, as well as women reporters and politicians. She also occasionally took public stands on political issues such as veterans' affairs, international famine relief, and the political rights and responsibilities of women.

While some of her work went beyond the domestic role of wife, Florence Harding also framed many of her beliefs and accomplishments in more traditional terms. She described most of her own behavior as an effort to support her husband in his ambitions and protect him from the physical and emotional demands of politics. Throughout her husband's political career, Florence devoted a great amount of energy to serving as a social hostess. Many of her contributions to Harding's political campaigns and his tenure in the White House came from her enthusiasm and popularity in that role. As first lady, her favorite public issues, such as aiding wounded and disabled veterans and supporting animal rights, fit within the caretaking role that had long been deemed appropriate for women.

Florence Harding thus embodied both modern and traditional values. In retrospect she was neither radical enough to redefine the job of first lady nor entirely comfortable within the confines of the traditional role. This may account for the low regard in which she is currently held.

Biography

Florence Mabel Kling was born on August 15, 1860, in Marion, Ohio. Her mother, Louise Bouton Kling, was born and grew up in New Canaan, Connecticut, and her father, Amos Kling, was born in Lancaster County, Pennsylvania, before his family moved to Ohio. After meeting in New Canaan while Amos was traveling, Louise Bouton and Amos Kling were married in 1859. The newlyweds settled in Marion, Ohio, where Amos demonstrated his ambition and shrewd business sense in establishing himself as one of Marion's most prominent and wealthy citizens. Early in his career Kling took advantage of business opportunities during the Civil War, and made a great profit by selling hardware to the Union Army. His hardware store in downtown Marion was successful; Florence was born in an apartment over the store. Florence's father ultimately expanded his business dealings to include real estate holdings and other invest-ments.

The first of three children, "Flossie" Kling was in many respects raised as the son her father had wanted. The Klings later had two sons: Clifford, in 1861 and Vetallis, in 1866. Nevertheless, Amos Kling established a strong relation-ship with his daughter and provided intensive instruction and discipline for Flor-ence as she was growing up. Florence often accompanied her father to the hard-ware store where she learned to handle business transactions and keep accounting records. Amos also frequently took Florence with him as he in-spected his properties and met with the people who rented or leased them. Amos Kling's influence on his daughter was heightened by the fact that Florence's mother was an invalid during Florence's childhood.

In addition to her exposure to her father's business dealings, Florence en-joyed a wide range of activities as a child. She was a talented and accomplished horsewoman who competed in equestrian events and often won. She enjoyed other athletic activities, such as roller-skating, ice-skating, and bicycling. Flor-ence also displayed a talent for music, which her parents encouraged. She at-tended public school in Marion and during her late teens she briefly attended the Cincinnati Conservatory, which had recently opened.

When Florence Kling returned to Marion from Cincinnati, she began a rela-tionship with Henry Atherton DeWolfe, a young man whose family had been neighbors of the Klings. Both Henry and Florence were nineteen when Florence became pregnant. They went to Columbus in March 1880, and announced their marriage. Historian Carl Sferrazza Anthony argued that Florence Kling and Henry DeWolfe were never formally married and that their subsequent divorce was a dissolution of a common law marriage (1998). On September 22, 1880, Florence gave birth to a son, Marshall, in Prospect, Ohio. Henry DeWolfe found employment as the manager of a new roller-skating rink in Galion, Ohio, where the new family settled.

Henry's heavy drinking strained his relationship with Florence, and their life as a family ended when Henry left Florence and their son. Florence filed for divorce on June 12, 1886, and returned to Marion with Marshall. Henry De-Wolfe died just eight years later. Amos Kling refused to take in his daughter and grandson, and Florence supported herself and her son by teaching piano lessons. Henry DeWolfe's father, Simon DeWolfe, helped Florence and Marshall during this time; Amos Kling eventually softened and extended help to Marshall.

In the aftermath of her divorce, Florence met Warren Gamaliel Harding. Harding had been born in Blooming Grove, Ohio, but he and his family had relocated to Marion. Warren Harding had graduated from Ohio Central College and had spent time teaching school, studying law, selling insurance, and work-ing as a journalist. He had bought part ownership of a small Marion newspaper. Although Warren Harding was five years Florence's junior and was only start-ing his career in journalism, Florence was attracted to him. Warren recognized Florence's strong qualities and the two began a courtship. Amos Kling strenu-ously objected to his daughter's relationship with Harding. In spite of her fa-ther's objections, Florence married Warren Harding on July 8, 1891, and the couple began their married life in Marion.

After his wedding, Warren Harding devoted his energies to building his newspaper, the *Marion Star*. Ultimately Harding assumed full ownership of the paper. During this time, he experienced a number of health problems. In early 1894, he suffered a nervous breakdown and checked into the Battle Creek Sanitarium in Michigan for two lengthy stays. While he was incapacitated, Florence stepped in to take over for the *Star* circulation manager, who had quit. She oversaw the circulation of the newspaper by organizing the routes for delivery and managing the delivery boys. Florence formed close relationships with many of the delivery boys, who were known as "newsies." She dispensed guidance and discipline, which sometimes included physical punishment. When Warren Harding returned to work in the fall of 1894, his wife remained at the *Star* and the two worked together on the paper. Florence Harding was not usually involved in reporting, writing, or making editorial decisions; however, many observers gave her much of the credit for the *Star*'s eventual journalistic and economic success. The *New York Times* reported that the *Star*'s success was "aided greatly by Mrs. Harding" ("Harding a Farm Boy" 1923). One of her contributions to the newspaper was her thrift; she "literally saved the pennies, taking the coin home with her until the collection was large enough to be banked" ("Harding a Farm Boy" 1923). Florence's authority was reflected in the lifelong nickname she acquired during this time—"Duchess." The professional partnership between the Hardings at the *Star* foreshadowed their partnership in politics. Florence's role in her marriage was already a departure from the traditional, domestic role of women.

Florence Harding's role as a mother was also atypical. She had supported her son as a single parent early in his life; after her marriage to Warren Harding, she turned her attention to their work at the *Star* and spent little time actively rearing Marshall. She maintained a relationship with him throughout his life, and his new stepfather also regarded him warmly. As he grew up, Marshall divided his time between the household of his mother and stepfather and the home of Amos Kling. Although both Hardings publicly professed a love for children, they never had children of their own.

As the *Marion Star* became increasingly successful, Warren Harding was a prominent booster for Marion interests and became active in politics. He was elected an Ohio state senator in 1899, and held that office until 1903. He served as lieutenant governor for a year, then ran an unsuccessful campaign for governor in 1910. From the beginning, Florence Harding was involved in her husband's political career. She spent part of her time in Columbus during Warren's term as state senator; in 1910, she accompanied him on trips to Washington, D.C., to meet with President William Howard Taft and, in 1911, to celebrate the Tafts' twenty-fifth wedding anniversary. Florence also formed relationships with political advisors around her husband; one of the most enduring was her friendship with Harry Micajah Dougherty, who would ultimately be named attorney general by President Harding. Historian Willis Johnson, a contemporary of the Hardings, argued that it was Florence Harding who was responsible for keeping her husband focused on a political career (1923). When he served in state politics, Harding acknowledged the role his wife played in his political career, stating in a campaign speech in 1910, "I owe allegiance to only one boss—and she sits right over there in that box. She's a mighty good one too" (quoted in Anthony 1996, 373).

In 1914, Warren Harding was elected to the U.S. Senate. When the Hardings moved to Washington, D.C., Florence became involved in the social circle and activities of various women's groups, including the Ladies of the Senate. She participated in a war sewing circle and helped produce clothing for soldiers during the war. She also formed a close friendship with Evalyn Walsh McLean, an heiress whose husband, Edward Beale "Ned" McLean, owned the *Washington Post* and the *Cincinnati Enquirer*. Evalyn McLean was a prominent social figure in Washington, D.C., and the owner of the notorious Hope Diamond. The McLeans were valuable and trusted friends of the Hardings. The Hardings often traveled with the McLeans and were frequent guests at the McLean homes in Washington, D.C., Virginia, and Florida. Evalyn McLean also shared Florence's love of animals and her interest in occult phenomena. Periodically, they would consult an astrologer, Marcia Champrey, who practiced her trade under the name Madame Marcia. According to Champrey, Florence Harding continued her consultations with Madame Marcia during Warren Harding's campaign for the presidency and throughout his administration (Madame Marcia 1938). She was neither the first nor the last first lady to do so—two others were Mary Todd Lincoln and Nancy Reagan.

During this time, Florence Harding was also concerned with other developments in her personal life. Her mother, Louise Bouton Kling, died on June 23, 1894. Her father retained his negative opinion of Warren for years. As a result, he did not welcome his daughter or his son-in-law into his home or have regular interactions with them until 1905, when he finally resumed his relationship with Florence. In 1906, Amos Kling remarried and in 1907, the Klings and the Hardings made a trip to Europe together. Florence's son Marshall married Esther Naomi Neely in 1906 and subsequently had two children. Florence's grandchildren were Eugenia, born in 1911, and George Warren, born in 1914. While Florence had not played a strong maternal role with regard to her son, she maintained a cordial relationship with her daughter-in-law and her grandchildren. Marshall DeWolfe died in 1915, after battling drinking problems and attempting unsuccessfully to establish himself as a journalist and newspaper editor. Florence Harding kept in touch with her daughter-in-law for the rest of her life.

Florence Harding also contended with severe health problems of her own. She had a chronic kidney condition which made her seriously ill in 1905, and again in 1913. During these bouts as well as less severe recurrences she was treated by Charles E. "Doc" Sawyer, a Marion homeopath. Sawyer would later become President Harding's personal physician. Florence battled her kidney ailment for the rest of her life, and her hospital experiences gave her sympathy for others who had been hospitalized. The *New York Times* quoted her as saying, "I was in a hospital for eight months with an open wound that had to be dressed twice a day, and I know what hospital life means to a patient" ("Mrs. Harding

Dies after Long Fight" 1924).

The private relationship between Florence and Warren was another source of concern. Letters released in the 1960s document a long-standing affair that Warren Harding conducted with Carrie Phillips, a Marion resident. Carrie Phillips and her husband James were both friends of the Hardings; the two couples had traveled together. Warren Harding's affair with Carrie had political as well as personal ramifications. Mrs. Phillips developed strong ties to Germany; she lived in Germany from 1911 to 1914. She was vocal in her opposition to the United States waging war against Germany and urged Senator Harding to vote against it. Because of her sympathies toward Germany, the U.S. government investigated her as a possible German informer. In 1920, the Phillipses used Carrie and Warren's extramarital affair to blackmail Harding. The Republican National Committee paid the Phillipses before the election to keep them from publicizing the affair. Carrie Phillips was not the only Marion native with whom Warren Harding carried on a long-term extramarital affair. Nan Britton, who was thirty-one years younger than Warren, engaged in an affair with him while he was senator and president. In 1927, Britton published her autobiography, *The President's Daughter*, in which she claimed that Warren Harding had fathered her daughter, Elizabeth Ann, who was born in 1919.

As his Senate term was coming to an end, Warren Harding considered a run for the presidency in 1920. Accounts differ as to Florence Harding's role in her husband's decision to seek the White House; two pictures emerge from reports by contemporary and later biographers. Some observers discussed Florence Harding's influence on her husband as a positive one and described the Harding marriage as a successful working partnership. According to these accounts, Florence Harding was worried about the strain the presidency might place on her husband, but ultimately supported his decision to run for office. Others, however, cast Florence as an ambitious and overbearing wife who drove her husband to seek an office he did not want.

Many who described Florence Harding as a supportive spouse argued that she did not want her husband to run for president at all. *Life* reported before the Republican National Convention that Mrs. Harding would have preferred her husband to remain a senator and that she regarded "the presidency as too hazardous a job for a family man" (July 1, 1920). Harry Daugherty, a confidant of both Warren and Florence and the manager of Harding's presidential campaign, also maintained that Florence Harding was opposed to the idea of her husband running for president. Daugherty noted, though, that once Harding was nominated, Florence Harding was an "enthusiastic and tireless" campaign worker who posed for photographs and spoke to audiences despite her professed distaste for both activities (Daugherty and Dixon 1932, 58).

Critics of Mrs. Harding argued that she compelled her husband to seek the presidency. Mark Sullivan wrote that Florence Harding was "a kind of nagging ambition for her husband" and greatly influenced his decision to run (1937, 46). Reporter Robert T. Small wrote in 1923, that Warren Harding did not want to run for president, but preferred to remain in the Senate. Florence Harding, though, "ever a dominating influence in his life, prevailed and Mr. Harding continued in a pre-Convention fight which appeared to him as all but hopeless" (Small 1923).

At the 1920 Republican National Convention, Warren Harding was not the favored nominee for the presidential ticket, but, during the party's negotiations, Harding emerged as the compromise candidate who was the least offensive to everyone. *Life* magazine reported that "the delegates . . . finally fixed on Harding because there was less objection to him than to anyone else" (July 8, 1920). Behind the scenes, Florence helped her husband make a sensitive decision; before the Republican delegates selected the presidential nominee, Warren had to decide whether or not to file for reelection as a senator. Daugherty advised him that if he filed for the Senate race he would be perceived as a weaker presidential candidate. Florence argued that he should file for the Senate race despite the risks of doing so, and Warren filed for that race on the eve of the selection of the Republican candidate.

As Warren Harding kicked off his presidential campaign, his wife was an integral part of it. Harding conducted much of his campaign from the front veranda of his Marion, Ohio, home and called it his "front porch" campaign. He used that location to deliver speeches to voters and the press and to grant interviews with reporters. Florence Harding was at his side during many of his appearances and even stage directed some of them for better effect (Anthony 1998, 206). Sometimes she made news herself. In one instance, she addressed a group of former "newsies," who had come to the front porch. "How many of you boys have I ever spanked?" she asked, "Put your hands up." A *New York Times* reporter wrote, "half a dozen raised their hands, amid laughter from the rest" ("Harding Will Meet Cox at Unveiling" 1920). Mrs. Harding also became famous for serving homemade waffles to reporters.

When the candidate traveled, Florence often went with him. Campaign manager Daugherty believed that the appearances she made with her husband helped him win the votes of women, who were voting in their first presidential election. Daugherty recounted, "in a quiet, efficient way Mrs. Harding worked wonders with the women of the West" (Daugherty and Dixon 1932, 57). Senator Harding's support of women's suffrage had been lukewarm, but historian Carl Sferrazza Anthony (1998) argued that in her informal speeches to women during the campaign, Florence Harding most likely urged women to make their vote count by joining a political party. The Hardings also greeted representatives of the National American Woman Suffrage Association and the National Woman's Party on their front porch (Anthony 1998). Nevertheless she was careful to circumscribe the topics she would address on the record during the campaign. In response to a question about the League of Nations, she said, "You know you really shouldn't ask me to talk about politics. My husband will do that. I'm leaving it to him" (Daugherty and Dixon 1932, 57).

Florence Harding participated in another public dimension of the campaign: the endorsement of the candidate by popular entertainment figures. Movie stars including Al Jolson, Ethel Barrymore, Lillian Gish, and Lillian Russell visited Marion during the campaign to proclaim their support for Harding. Florence was often photographed with these celebrities during their appearances. In addition to these promotional activities, Florence worked with a campaign publicist and was "an eager partner in shaping and promoting her public persona" (Anthony 1998, 205). She posed for photographs with her husband that were circulated by the campaign to the print press. "I want the people to see these pictures so that they will know we are just folks like themselves," she explained (*The Mirrors of Washington* 1921, 6).

Privately, meanwhile, Florence was adamant about another decision made during the campaign. When allegations surfaced claiming that Warren Harding was partially of African American descent, the campaign was split as to whether or not he should respond to them. Harding himself wanted to issue a response, but Florence prevailed, insisting, "I'm telling all you people that Warren Harding is not going to make any statement" (Murray 1969, 64). The candidate did not respond publicly to the rumors.

Florence Harding was the first American woman to help elect her husband president by voting for him on November 2, 1920. The women's vote was beneficial to Harding; more women voted for Harding than for his Democratic opponent James M. Cox. Overall, Harding won 60 percent of the popular vote. His platform of "a return to normalcy" and his stand against the United States entering the League of Nations struck a responsive chord with voters. As Harding entered the White House to succeed President Woodrow Wilson, many observers remarked on the contrast between the frail and ailing man who was leaving office and the robust and vigorous man who was entering office. Both Hardings sought to capitalize on the theme of renewal and freshness.

Whether as a loyal wife, an equal political partner, or a controlling decision maker, Florence Harding played a significant role in her husband's political success. One White House employee reported an incident that indicated the new first lady's sense of accomplishment. Upon the Hardings' arrival at the White House, Mrs. Harding said to her husband, "Well Warren Harding, I have got you the Presidency; what are you going to do with it?" (Jaffray 1927, 87–88). Predictably, her influence on her husband did not end with his election to the presidency.

Rhetorical Activities as First Lady

Once in the White House, Mrs. Harding continued her life as a political wife; she was the most visible political wife in the country. Her life in the White House included many of the usual feminine responsibilities as well as some less conventional activities. She received acclaim for her skills as a hostess. News accounts of the day praised her for opening the White House to the public. Florence remained a strong partner of her husband; she continued to give him advice and to make public appearances with him. She also influenced key personnel decisions in the White House. Mrs. Harding used a variety of communication strategies, including public speeches. The first lady also continued to cultivate her relationship with the press. In this regard, she engaged in some unorthodox behaviors for first ladies; she published letters in newspapers, met with reporters, and posed for movie cameras. She still tried not to overstep the bounds of convention, however. She often did not allow reporters to quote her directly, so the public record of her statements is less rich than it might otherwise be. Finally, she affected some of the president's policy decisions, and she adopted public issues of her own.

Social Duties

As the first lady, Florence Harding followed the tradition of serving as the hostess of the White House. The style of entertaining during the Harding administration was a departure from previous administrations. One of the first acts of the Harding White House was to reopen the institution to American citizens. Florence Harding had pledged to Marion citizens during the front porch campaign that the White House would never be closed to the American people and that the people of Marion would be especially welcome to visit the president during the Harding administration. In a *New York Times* profile of the newly elected president and first lady, Florence said, "There'll be no formality at the White House while we are there" ("A Glimpse of Mrs. Harding" 1920). As part of the inauguration festivities, President and Mrs. Harding received well-wishers on the lawn of the White House. On the evening of the inauguration, the crowds remained on the White House grounds, and many tried to look inside the residence. The first lady accommodated them by having the blinds opened. "Let 'em look if they want to," she explained, "It's their White House" (Adams 1939, 211). The opening of the White House to the public was noteworthy because social activities had diminished during the Wilson administration due to the war and to President Wilson's illness. Reporter Edward Lowry wrote in *The New Republic* that the first lady's effort to make the White House accessible "has proved to be as tactful and effective a gesture as could have been devised to indicate that a page has been turned in our political history" (1921).

Florence Harding was instrumental in setting the social tone of the new administration. She wanted White House events to be livelier and less formal than those in previous administrations. Newspapers and periodicals of the day noted that the new first lady's preference for entertaining would be simpler than past administrations. A reporter for *The Delineator* wrote that one event was "a sign that the Hardings' official dinners will be as small as possible, not as large as possible, as was the case in the McKinley administration" (Wade 1922). In addition to traditional state events, the president and Mrs. Harding often hosted large gatherings on the White House grounds. They reestablished several traditions, including the annual Easter egg roll, the Christmas reception, and the New Year's Day reception. At several of these functions, the Hardings made a particular point to welcome and honor veterans, whose cause Florence Harding would champion throughout her time in the White House. On New Year's Day, 1922, the Hardings hosted a reception where they greeted everyone who wanted to come through the receiving line. The Hardings received visitors from 11:00 a.m. until 5:00 p.m. and shook hands with over 6500 people. According to one account, the president appeared tired but even when the first lady had to stop using her right hand she declared, "my left hand is good for two hours yet!" (Johnson 1923, 128). The *Washington Post* wrote of the White House garden parties, "Mrs. Harding . . . has literally shaken hands with tens of thousands of persons, in a steady streaming line through the White House gates," and concluded, "No President's wife in the memory of the Capital has displayed such endurance" (Jeffries 1960, 314). Florence Harding's enthusiastic reception of White House visitors enhanced her popularity with the American public (Murray 1969, 419).

Even when she was not hosting parties, Florence Harding enjoyed meeting visitors in the White House and sometimes led tours through the executive mansion. One journalist estimated that the first lady welcomed more than one hundred visitors a week (Wade 1922). The nation also read about the first lady's wardrobe, her favorite color (dubbed "Mrs. Harding blue"), and the decisions of citizens to name everything from newborn babies to a variety of sweet pea after the first lady.

Through these activities, Florence Harding enacted the traditional role of wife, homemaker, and hostess during her husband's administration. *The Outlook* concluded a profile of the first lady by noting, "The family is still the ideal unit of American life. . . . Warren and Florence Harding have continued this fine tradition in a way that has commanded the respect and admiration of their countrymen and countrywomen" ("Mrs. Harding" 1922). These accounts underscored the picture of the nation's first lady and first hostess. Mrs. Harding adapted to this role with great energy, but in this domain her activities were highly traditional. The first lady's efforts "were a real political benefit to Harding" (Trani and Wilson 1977, 37).

Partnership with Her Husband

The relationship between Florence and Warren Harding was a subject of public discussion during the Harding administration. After Harding's election, the *New York Times* predicted that "responsibility for the White House, politically as well as domestically, will rest on four shoulders during the next four years" ("A Glimpse of Mrs. Harding" 1920). The newspaper described the relationship between the new president and the first lady as an intense working relationship:

> Even more than her husband, Mrs. Harding is a leader. She likes to sway the crowds. She is aggressive and forceful. The two Hardings have blended their qualities and personalities perfectly through long experience in working together. Theirs has been a partnership of their work. Together they made their newspaper, *The Marion Star*. Together they entered politics. Mrs. Harding in the background, devoted, confident and forward looking, while her husband furnished the generous, amiable qualities that made him popular. ("A Glimpse of Mrs. Harding" 1920)

The first lady's partnership with her husband was evident in her relationship with his advisors, her public appearances with the president, and her influence on some of her husband's political decisions.

One dimension of the first lady's influence on her husband was her relationship with some of his advisors. She was close to Harry Daugherty, who, after successfully running Harding's presidential campaign, served as attorney general in the Harding administration. She was also close to "Doc" Sawyer, the homeopath whom the Hardings installed as the personal physician to the president. The decision to appoint Sawyer was a mutual decision on the part of the Hardings. Mrs. Harding was influential in the president's selection of Colonel Charles R. Forbes as the head of the Veterans Bureau (Sullivan 1937, 144). The first lady also formed a friendship with New Mexico senator Albert B. Fall, who became the secretary of the interior. Florence Harding's effort to maintain relationships with these and other members of the Harding administration caused the president to remark, "Mrs. Harding wants to be the drum major in every band that passes" (Waldrup 1989, 259).

Mrs. Harding often appeared with her husband during ceremonies at the White House and when he traveled on official duties. The major newspapers and periodicals of the day published frequent photographs and reports of President and Mrs. Harding conducting business at the White House together. Florence Harding also traveled with the president frequently. Perhaps the most significant example of this was when she accompanied him on his "Voyage of Understanding" tour in 1923. Late in the tour, President Harding became ill and, in the later stages of his illness, the first lady would sometimes act as a surrogate and briefly address the crowds that had gathered to hear the president. In response, the San Francisco *Journal* referred to her as the "acting President" (Anthony 1998, 442).

Occasionally, the first lady also made direct suggestions to the president regarding policy. Samuel Adams wrote that Florence edited President Harding's inaugural address (1939, 245). Attorney General Daugherty described one instance when she disagreed with a position her husband had expressed in a speech he was preparing. Both Hardings were opposed to the League of Nations, but in this section of his speech the president had indicated that the United States might ultimately join the League. The first lady objected and helped persuade the president to change that section (Daugherty and Dixon 1932, 171–76). Florence also disagreed with her husband's decision to grant amnesty to jailed Socialist Eugene V. Debs in 1921. And when the president had the opportunity to designate a donated house the official residence of the vice president, his wife objected. The vice president did not receive an official home during the Harding administration.

The public response to this active first lady was again mixed. While Florence Harding received praise for her active partnership with her husband, she also was the subject of criticism. Sherman Cuneo wrote in 1922: "Mrs. Harding is well fitted for the duties of a President's wife, has a mind of her own, [and] is a true helpmate" (67). By contrast, a cartoon published in *Life* the same year expressed the sentiments of her critics; it depicted both of the Hardings with the caption "The President and Mr. Harding" (Anthony 1998, 344).

Communication Strategies

On the campaign trail and in the White House, Florence Harding delivered short, usually informal speeches to various audiences. Anthony observed, "Mrs. Harding was the first First Lady of her century to give regular speeches" (1998, 325). She addressed audiences from the White House balcony and from the back of the train when she was traveling with her husband. These speeches were generally impromptu, and only one full text of any of her speeches exists (Anthony 1996, 1998). The record of the first lady's public speeches, therefore, is primarily a product of what was recorded in the press. Because of Florence Harding's frequently expressed desire not to be quoted in the press, this record is meager.

As was the case during her husband's presidential campaign, Mrs. Harding had a multifaceted relationship with the press once she was in the White House. She protested that she should not be a subject for interviews, but she used a variety of strategies to publicize her views. She often conducted meetings with reporters, although she usually did not permit them to quote her. However, she often allowed newspapers to print letters that she had written to individuals and organizations. She also demonstrated an understanding of the power of visual symbols by posing for photographs and newsreel footage.

The first lady, who referred to reporters as "my boys" or "us girls," arranged events where she would talk to reporters off the record. Accounts of these events sometimes appeared in major newspapers, although without substantive quotations from Mrs. Harding. Since she considered herself a "newspaper woman," she planned activities specifically for women reporters. She initiated a series of regular meetings with women journalists at four o'clock tea soon after her husband's inauguration (Anthony 1998). On one occasion, the first lady invited a group of female journalists for a cruise with her on the presidential yacht, *Mayflower*.

In September 1922, her kidney ailment flared up again and she spent several days close to death and weeks afterwards recovering. In February 1923, she called for a meeting with thirty women reporters and discussed her illness and answered questions. The meeting resulted in a flattering report of the first lady and her determination to recuperate fully. The *New York Times* commented on the first lady's press savvy, noting, "Like her husband, Mrs. Harding has learned through experience and newspaper training what not to say as well as what to say" ("A Glimpse of Mrs. Harding" 1920).

Sometimes, rather than talking directly to the press and allowing herself to be quoted, Florence Harding sent letters and telegrams to organizations or meetings and allowed the letters to be read and become part of the proceedings. Often newspapers printed these letters; in this way she found a forum for some of her views. In one letter published in the *New York Times*, she thanked the Women's Harding and Coolidge Club for their help with her husband's campaign. She concluded the letter by writing, "I look to the women of America; I pin my faith on the women of America; [and] I believe in the women of America" ("Mrs. Harding Is Grateful" 1920). She also released a letter of congratulations that she had written to Alice Robertson, who was elected to Congress from

Oklahoma. In 1922, Florence Harding wrote other letters that became public to the national convention of the Girl Scouts of America and to the newly formed New York Women's Newspaper Club. The next year, she sent a telegram of support to the New York Housewives' Sugar Committee, a group organized to protest high sugar prices. In some of these public statements, the first lady addressed topics that were within the traditional realm of concern for women. And when she recognized the political strength of women—as campaign workers or as candidates—she directed those messages to other women.

Florence Harding's skill in dealing with press extended to photographs as well as written accounts. She professed to dislike being photographed. During the Harding presidential campaign, she remarked to press photographers, "I always take a frightful picture and I hate this. But I know you've got to do it" (Daugherty and Dixon 1932, 58). When she was in the White House she met with an artist who was doing portraits of prominent political figures and who wrote of her experiences for the magazine *The Delineator*. The artist reported that "Mrs. Harding and I had a long talk. . . . But because she hates publicity, I did not sketch her" (Jacobs 1922). Out of respect for the first lady's wishes, the author included neither a sketch nor any quotations from her interview with Harding. Despite her distaste for being photographed, she learned to pose for still photographs and newsreel footage. Anthony wrote that Florence Harding began the tradition of the White House "photo opportunity" (1996, 378).

The news coverage of Florence Harding's illness in the fall 1922, marked a different kind of reporting on first ladies. While she was sick, newspapers reported on her condition in great detail, with some newspapers publishing the record of her vital signs daily. *The New York Times* reported, "Mrs. Harding's optimistic nature, her indomitable will and the manner in which she is helping in the fight for life are all on her side" ("Mrs. Harding Still in Critical State" 1922). The paper also noted that the president was distraught about his wife's condition and that the first lady, despite her illness, was committed to helping her husband: "Ill as she is, she is interested in everything that pertains to her husband and doing all in her power to relieve his overwhelming anxiety" ("Mrs. Harding Still in Critical State" 1922). This coverage of Florence Harding's illness was unusually frank and detailed. This was a departure from the delicate way in which Mrs. McKinley's illness was treated by the press.

Positions on Issues

When Warren Harding won the presidential election, the *New York Times* said of the first lady, "she likes politics. She likes to participate in activities until recently regarded as men's spheres" ("A Glimpse of Mrs. Harding" 1920). Speculation about the new first lady's degree of political involvement was widespread, some of it fueled by Florence Harding's previous accomplishments and some of it fueled by the new political status which women had gained with the right to vote. *The Ladies' Home Journal* argued that the new first lady would have a unique influence on her husband because of her status as a voting citizen.

The publication predicted that in this capacity Florence Harding would "lay her emphasis on social justice and public welfare" (Rinehart 1921).

Indeed, Florence Harding did take overt stands on a number of issues. Some of the issues she embraced were extensions of traditional feminine concerns, such as defining women's role or taking care of the sick or wounded. But she also broke new ground by addressing issues that had not been part of women's sphere.

Florence Harding had been a supporter of women's suffrage. Once suffrage was won, the first lady also engaged in the debate about how women should best organize to consolidate their new political power. Some women believed that the National Women's Party would best represent the interests of women. Others argued that women should become as active as possible within the already established political parties. Mrs. Harding sided with the second view; in a letter she released to the *New York Times*, she said that "the effective organization of women in affiliation with established political parties" was the most worthwhile strategy for women ("Mrs. Harding on Politics" 1921). In a letter to the president of a Republican women's club, also published in the *New York Times*, Florence Harding urged, "Surely we women will not permit it to be said that because we came into the full obligation of citizenship our contribution served to lower the standard of civic responsibility." She added, "we Republican women shall devote our utmost energies to that work of organization, education and advancement which is so well typified in your own aggressive and efficient club" ("Partisan Loyalty Urged upon Women" 1922).

Because of her interest in expanding opportunities for girls and women, Florence Harding was made an honorary president of the Girl Scouts of America and a member of the Camp Fire Girls. She endorsed both organizations because of the physical and moral training they provided for girls. She also sponsored the first women's tennis tournament on the White House lawn. The first lady also publicly supported the efforts of individual women to achieve excellence in their fields. She lent her support to a drive by American women to purchase a gram of radium worth $100,000 for scientist Marie Curie to use in her research. Florence Harding, together with her husband, presented the radium to Curie in May 1921, at the White House.

Florence Harding expressed a commitment to veterans' issues throughout her time in the White House. She visited veterans in the hospital, she invited them to receptions at the White House, and she kept a close eye on those who were appointed to oversee veterans' affairs. The first lady also participated in and publicized international relief efforts. One of Florence Harding's early acts as first lady was to inform the American Committee for the China Famine Fund that she would eliminate one course from White House meals and donate the resulting savings to the fund. The first lady also publicly endorsed Armenian relief efforts.

The first lady was renowned for her love for animals and her desire to help protect animal welfare. The Hardings' Airedale terrier, Laddie Boy, was almost as famous a resident of the White House as the Hardings themselves. Americans saw Laddie Boy depicted in numerous photographs and political cartoons. Laddie Boy appeared as a character in a political column where he commented on White House activities. The dog even sat in on cabinet meetings in a chair specially carved for him and joined the president and first lady in greeting official visitors. After President Harding's death, the members of the Newsboys Association pledged to donate pennies that would be melted down and made into a sculpture of the dog.

Florence Harding enthusiastically supported the efforts of the Animal Rescue League. In one instance in 1922 she tried to intervene personally in the case of an old farm horse whose owner was afraid he could no longer maintain the animal. She offered $100 to the owner of the horse, the reverend Dr. Myers, to help support the horse. In a letter published in the *New York Times*, she wrote, "I hope 'Clover' will long continue to be the oldest horse in the world, and that somehow there will grow an impression that the loving God never intended either dumb friends or self-sacrificing men to be consigned to mother earth merely because the most and best of their strength has been exhausted in human service" ("Mrs. Harding Gives $100" 1922). This generous move drew criticism as well as praise, however, when people questioned why a horse might be worth that amount of money when there were people who also needed financial help (Anthony 1996, 379).

In addressing issues such as the political role of women or the need to protect the welfare of people in poverty, American veterans, or animals, Florence Harding could still stay within woman's sphere. But she also expanded the role of first lady by commenting on issues that were not traditional concerns of women. In 1921, she wrote a letter to the women who attended a meeting of the Southern Tariff Association in Atlanta in which she announced her belief in the need for protectionist trade practices and appropriate tariffs. The *New York Times*, in an editorial titled "Nobody Calls It Meddling," supported her right to express her views because "hers is the pen of a voter—of a citizen with as much right as anybody else to have and to urge her views on the tariff or whatever seems to her interesting or important" (1921). The editorial also commented on her political shrewdness by observing that she "refrains from an exact definition of what she wants in the way of duties. . . . Not without acquisition of wisdom has she lived long in a political atmosphere" ("Nobody Calls It Meddling" 1921).

While Florence Harding did publicly associate herself with some political issues, she did not take public stands on the debate that began when several scandals in the White House came to light. In January 1923, President Harding learned that Charles Forbes, the director of veterans affairs, had engaged in conspiracy and profiteering. Harding confronted Forbes, and he resigned in February. The Senate began an investigation the same month. In March 1923, Albert Fall, the secretary of the interior, resigned amid evidence that he had taken advantage of his position to profit in oil leases in Elk Hills, California, and Teapot Dome, Wyoming. Florence Harding felt betrayed by these actions—she had considered Forbes and Fall friends and supporters—but she did not make public statements about these matters while she was first lady.

Legacy

Florence Harding's tenure as first lady came to an untimely end when Warren G. Harding died in office on August 2, 1923. The Hardings had embarked on their "Voyage of Understanding" tour in June of that year and made their way through midwestern and western states and ultimately to Alaska. When the presidential party began their return trip, the president became ill before arriving in Canada. Initially, the president's personal physician, Charles Sawyer, attributed President Harding's sickness to a case of food poisoning. The president seemed to begin recuperating and the tour continued, although he could not always make his scheduled appearances. When the tour arrived in San Francisco, the president's illness became worse. He died on August 2, 1923, in the Palace Hotel in San Francisco. The attending physicians officially listed the cause of death as a cerebral hemorrhage, although the symptoms were more consistent with a heart attack.

Florence Harding lived for just over a year after her husband's death; she died in Marion, Ohio, on November 21, 1924. In the brief period of her widowhood, she did not fade entirely from public view. She received praise for her role in her husband's administration and for her stoicism after his death. However, she also made some controversial attempts to protect her husband's legacy, and this behavior further fueled the debate over her role in her husband's political career. Was she a concerned wife who was trying to protect her husband's reputation against spurious criticism, or was she a domineering woman who was inappropriately trying to create her own version of history?

Immediately after her husband's death, Florence Harding made the funeral arrangements and comported herself with efficiency and dignity. Although she permitted Warren Harding's body to lie in state at the Capitol, she insisted that his burial in Marion be a simple ceremony. During the funeral proceedings reporters quoted her as saying, "I am not going to break down" ("President Harding Dies Suddenly" 1923; "The Death of President Harding" 1923). According to *The Outlook*, as mourners in Marion lined up to pay their respects to the deceased president, Florence said, "Don't stop the line; let them come until daylight" ("The People Honor Their Dead Leader" 1923). The public responded positively to these behaviors, but Mrs. Harding made other decisions that ensured that she would be a figure of controversy. She refused to allow an autopsy to be performed or a death mask made. For several days after the funeral, Florence Harding retreated to the McLeans' estate in Virginia and burned many of her husband's papers. One of her motives may have been her belief that the scandals caused by cabinet members were unrelated to her husband and would only sully his reputation. The result, though, is that many primary documents concerning Florence and Warren Harding have been lost to posterity.

Florence Harding's immediate legacy was positive. During her widowhood and in the wake of her death, news stories and editorials on the widowed first lady praised her stoicism and grace. The nature of the situation meant that it was unlikely that mainstream opinions about her would be negative; it would be unseemly to criticize a woman so soon after her husband's death. However, many of the obituaries of Warren Harding and Florence Harding specifically addressed her unique role in the White House and the nature of her working relationship with her husband. A *New York Times* editorial asserted that Florence Harding had struck the right balance between having political opinions and being a traditional first lady:

> Mrs. Harding was the President's wife and she knew how to maintain the dignity of that relation, but she knew as well that in our system of government there is no such person as "Mrs. President." If she had anything of political influence, it was exercised in the strictest privacy, where it belonged. ("She Knew Her Place and Kept It" 1923)

After Florence Harding's death the periodical *The Outlook* also commented on her contributions to her husband's career:

> No one will know how great a part of the career of Warren Gamaliel Harding was her career. Yet it seems certain that she shared largely in building the structure of his life, his fight was her fight, and his triumph hers. ("Mrs. Harding Dies" 1924)

These eulogies also contained the conventional expressions of respect for the dead. Beyond these conventions, however, these tributes demonstrate that Florence Harding's conduct as first lady had been noteworthy.

As the constraint of propriety subsided, a negative backlash against both Hardings began. Two shocking exposés were published that contributed to the backlash. Nan Britton, in her 1930 book *The President's Daughter*, asserted that Warren Harding had fathered her illegitimate child. The same year former Secret Service agent Gaston Means published *The Strange Death of President Harding*, coauthored with May Dixon Thatcher, in which he made a series of startling allegations. He asserted that Florence Harding had known about her husband's affair with Britton, that she had nearly caught the two lovers together in the White House, and that she had hired Means to keep Britton under surveillance. Most shockingly, he implied that the first lady, believing her husband would have been impeached if he had lived, poisoned him in San Francisco so that he might die "in honor" (1930, 264). Although critics rushed to impugn the books (in fact, Means's coauthor recanted), they cast a negative light on both the president and the first lady.

Less sensational, but also negative, was a portrait of Florence Harding in the February 1932 issue of *Good Housekeeping* that was written by "a well-known woman politician." The author styled Mrs. Harding "the exploiter wife" and depicted her as an ambitious, conniving woman whose scheming was responsible for Warren Harding's successful career. The article noted that Florence Harding answered reporters' questions about housekeeping "poorly," but "if these writers had asked for her opinion on patronage, on wire-pulling, she might have amazed them" ("The Other Presidents" 1932).

In evaluating her long-term legacy, it is important to note that Florence Harding bridged two worlds. She demonstrated ambitions and capabilities that went beyond the traditional female role of helpmate to her husband. Yet, she often portrayed her behaviors and interests as typical domestic concerns. She was the first first lady to vote for her husband, and she made a determined effort to communicate her vision of the new role that women could define for themselves as citizens. She was an unapologetic career woman. She was actively involved in her husband's campaigns and presidential administrations. She took stands on political issues, including the new civic responsibilities of women as well as other issues that were beyond women's traditional concerns. She managed a successful relationship with the press and supported women journalists in particular. But she could not define herself as too far outside the women's sphere, and she was careful not to do so. She was careful to present herself primarily as a supportive wife. Although she sometimes expressed her beliefs directly to audiences, she usually did not speak directly to the American people through newspaper profiles or interviews. She favored indirect methods of conveying her views, such as allowing reporters to quote letters or telegrams she had sent particular groups. The degree to which she was successful at bridging the traditional and modern duties of first ladies gives us insight into Americans' expectations of first ladies, the political and social norms of that era, as well as the character of Florence Harding herself. While many contemporary observers commented positively on the job she did, her innovations as first lady did not set a bold new course for the position. While she helped shape the office of first lady into the form we know today, she pales in comparison to more outspoken women who have held the position. Nevertheless, Florence Harding deserves credit for the contributions she made to the American political culture.

References

Adams, Samuel Hopkins. 1939. *Incredible Era: The Life and Times of Warren Gamaliel Harding.* Boston: Houghton Mifflin Company.

Anthony, Carl Sferrazza. 1996. Florence (Mabel) Kling Harding. In *American First Ladies: Their Lives and Their Legacy*, ed. Lewis L. Gould, 368–83. New York: Garland.

————. 1998. *Florence Harding: The First Lady, the Jazz Age, and the Death of America's Most Scandalous President.* New York: William Morrow and Company.

Boller, Paul F., Jr. 1988. *Presidential Wives.* New York: Oxford University Press.

Britton, Nan. 1930. *The President's Daughter.* New York: Elizabeth Ann Guild, Inc.

Caroli, Betty Boyd. 1987. *First Ladies.* New York: Oxford University Press.

Chapple, Joe Mitchell. 1920. *Warren G. Harding—The Man.* Boston: Chapple Publishing Company.

————. 1924. *The Life and Times of Warren G. Harding, Our After-War President.* Boston: Chapple Publishing Company, Limited.

Cuneo, Sherman A. 1922. *From Printer to President: The Story of Warren G. Harding.* Philadelphia: Dorrance & Co.

Daugherty, Harry M., and Thomas Dixon. 1932. *The Inside Story of the Harding Tragedy.* New York: The Churchill Company.

The Death of President Harding. 1923. *The Outlook*, 15 August.

A Glimpse of Mrs. Harding. 1920. *New York Times*, 14 November.

Gutin, Myra G. 1989. *The President's Partner: The First Lady in the Twentieth Century.* New York: Greenwood.

Harding a Farm Boy Who Rose by Work. 1923. *New York Times*, 3 August.
Harding Will Meet Cox at Unveiling. 1920. *New York Times*, 27 September.
Jacobs, Leonebel. Seeing Things with a Pencil. 1922. *The Delineator*, June.
Jaffray, Elizabeth. 1927. *Secrets of the White House*. New York: Cosmopolitan Book Corporation.
Jeffries, Ona Griffin. 1960. *In and Out of the White House: From Washington to the Eisenhowers*. New York: Wilfred Funk, Inc.
Johnson, Willis Fletcher. 1923. *The Life of Warren G. Harding: From the Simple Life of the Farm to the Glamour and Power of the White House*. William H. Johnston (private copyright).
Kohlsaat, H. H. 1923. *From McKinley to Harding: Personal Recollections of Our Presidents*. New York: Charles Scribner's Sons.
Life, 1920. 1 July and 8 July.
Lowry, Edward G. 1921. The Great Emollient. *The New Republic*, 23 March.
Madame Marcia. 1938. When an Astrologer Ruled the White House. *Liberty*, 9 April.
Means, Gaston B., and May Dixon Thatcher. 1930. *The Strange Death of President Harding*. New York: Guild Publishing Corporation.
The Mirrors of Washington. 1921. New York: G. P. Putnam's Sons.
Mrs. Harding. 1922. *Outlook*, 20 September.
Mrs. Harding Dies. 1924. *Outlook*, 3 December.
Mrs. Harding Dies after Long Fight. 1924. *New York Times*, 22 November.
Mrs. Harding Gives $100 to Save Old Horse's Life. 1922. *New York Times*, 14 August.
Mrs. Harding Is Grateful. 1920. *New York Times*, 5 November.
Mrs. Harding on Politics. 1921. *New York Times*, 5 May.
Mrs. Harding Still in Critical State; Shows Slight Gain. 1922. *New York Times*, 10 September.
Murray, Robert K. 1969. *The Harding Era: Warren G. Harding and His Administration*. Minneapolis, Minn.: University of Minnesota Press.
Nobody Calls It Meddling. 1921. *New York Times*, 20 January.
The Other Presidents. 1932. *Good Housekeeping*, February.
Partisan Loyalty Urged upon Women. 1922. *New York Times*, 15 January.
The People Honor Their Dead Leader. 1923. *Outlook*, 22 August.
President Harding Dies Suddenly. 1923. *New York Times*, 3 August.
Rinehart, Mary Roberts. 1921. A New Citizen in the White House. *The Ladies' Home Journal*, March.
Russell, Francis. 1968. *The Shadow of Blooming Grove: Warren G. Harding in His Times*. New York: McGraw-Hill Book Company.
She Knew Her Place and Kept It. 1923. *New York Times*, 4 August.
Sinclair, Andrew. 1965. *The Available Man: The Life behind the Masks of Warren Gamaliel Harding*. New York: Macmillan Company.
Small, Robert T. 1923. Warren Harding—Stranger to Hate: Correspondence from Washington. *Outlook*, 15 August.
Smith, Ira R. T., and Joe Alex Morris. 1949. *"Dear Mr. President": The Story of Fifty Years in the White House Mail Room*. New York: Julian Messner.
Sullivan, Mark. 1937. Our Times: The United States, 1900–1925. New York: Charles Scribner's Sons.
Thompson, Charles Willis. 1929. *Presidents I've Known and Two Near Presidents*. Indianapolis, Ind.: Bobbs-Merrill Company.
Trani, Eugene P., and David L. Wilson. 1977. *The Presidency of Warren G. Harding*. Lawrence, Kans.: Regents Press of Kansas.
Truman, Margaret. 1995. *First Ladies*. New York: Random House.

Wade, Margaret. 1922. White House Parties: Official Washington Follows Time-Honored Rules and Precedents. *Delineator*, March.

Waldrup, Carole Chandler. 1989. *Presidents' Wives: The Lives of 44 American Women of Strength*. Jefferson, N.C.: McFarland & Company.

Watson, Robert P. 2000. *The Presidents' Wives: Reassessing the Office of First Lady*. Boulder, Colo.: Lynne Rienner Publishers.

White House Joins Fight on High Sugar. 1923. *New York Times*, 8 May.

Chapter 8

Grace Goodhue Coolidge
Articulating Virtue

Janis L. Edwards

> There was a sense of detachment—this was I and yet not I, this was the wife of the President of the United States and she took precedence over me; my personal likes and dislikes must be subordinated to the consideration of those things which were required of her.
>
> —Grace Coolidge

Historian Robert P. Watson describes the first lady position as a "highly public institution, where image and public speaking competence are important" (2000, 127). Examined from a contemporary perspective such as his, Grace Goodhue Coolidge appears to be a paradoxical first lady because she was highly visible in her era, yet silent, and she was relatively invisible in history. By her own admission, she felt little need to keep a diary of her time in the White House. She chose not to record what she experienced; presumably, she did not believe her experience was relevant to any historical account of the Coolidge administration that might be written at a later time. Interestingly, a citizen she had never met presented her with a scrapbook, thereby preserving for her some small account of her tenure. More important to her were traditional feminine duties, and here she set a new standard for performing the ceremonial aspects of the first lady role.

In most respects, Grace Coolidge was a very modern woman in a modern time. She was the first presidential spouse to graduate from a standard, coeducational university, and she was also the first to pursue a professional career prior to marriage, a calling to which she remained committed in other ways throughout her life. Her youthful demeanor and lively personality were not incommensurate with the mien of the politically liberated "new woman" of the 1920s. Significantly, the first presidential ticket offered to women after the passage of the Nineteenth Amendment featured her husband, Calvin Coolidge, as the vice-presidential nominee.

In another sense, however, Grace Coolidge projected an image of "ideal womanhood" that, as Allgor (2000) argues, eighteenth-century politicians of the new republic as well as twentieth-century business executives found fitting for their purposes. The ideal woman was a partner in her husband's pursuits by "humanizing" his image (Walsh 2001). Grace's interest in music and domestic management were those familiar to young ladies and matrons of prior centuries, and, although she assisted her husband socially and established a range of public, ceremonial traditions for future first ladies,[1] her performance of the first lady role excluded speaking formally in public, granting interviews, or influencing her husband in political affairs. As such, Grace Coolidge might be said to embody the paradoxical nature of the 1920s, a period that first lady scholar Betty Boyd Caroli characterizes as a combination of exuberance and restraint (1987). Although the Coolidges were both modest and restrained by the values of their Protestant New England upbringing, restraint served Coolidge's attempts to restore dignity to the presidency following the Teapot Dome scandal that defined the Harding years.

The Coolidges must have been quite successful at projecting this image of decorum, at least according to Alice Roosevelt Longworth, who said, approvingly, that the Coolidge White House was "as different (in style) as a New England front parlor is from a back room in a speakeasy" (Miller 1987, 395). Grace's style and demeanor must have contributed to this impression. Profilers writing in the national newspapers were complimentary, and there is a consensus among her biographers who describe her as a "model of decorum," contrasting her to the more outspoken Florence Harding and the perceived political meddling of Edith Wilson. Perhaps, this sense of restraint on her part is why presidential scholars rank Mrs. Coolidge near the bottom in fitness for office, activism, and presidential partnership, but very high on personality and charisma (R. Watson 2000, 183–86). Ironically, Mrs. Coolidge was a tireless advocate for several issues in and out of the White House, but her advocacy was performed largely out of public view.[2]

In her imprint on the symbolic role of first lady, Grace Coolidge shared similarities with a first lady who came to prominence nearly half a century after the Coolidge years: Jacqueline Bouvier Kennedy. Like Jackie Kennedy, Grace Coolidge was a much-photographed, fashionable celebrity[3] who pioneered efforts to restore the White House interior and offered a courageous demeanor in the face of family tragedy. Like Jackie Kennedy, Grace also eschewed the "white glove pulpit," not only during her husband's tenure as president, but throughout most of her life, even as she remained involved in national and community issues.

The central question of this chapter is: How are we to regard the rhetoric of a public person who "did not choose to talk?"[4] Although Grace took lessons in elocution and participated in speech competitions as a college student, no evidence of significant public speech in an official capacity remains, whether related to political matters or to her duties as president of the governing board for the Clarke School of the Deaf in Northampton, Massachusetts, a position she held for nearly twenty years following her husband's death. In addition, it was her "unbroken policy not to give interviews," even in her later years, as she insisted to a newspaper reporter (McGaffin 1955). The absence of recorded speeches during her administrative tenure with the Clarke School suggests that her silence came from a core vision of her position in life as much as from her husband's wish to keep family life and political life separated. To evaluate the rhetorical persona of Grace Coolidge as first lady requires a broader interpretation of rhetorical action, as well as a broader interpretation of the first lady role.

Despite her public silence, Grace was nonetheless a highly visible first lady, in terms of social standing and media coverage. Later, she offered a written description of her performance of the first lady role in her memoirs, an autobiography that focuses on personal, rather than political, events. From this perspective, examination of Mrs. Coolidge's rhetoric as a first lady highlights the many contradictions that have infused the office throughout the twentieth century. It also defines the first lady role as one that transcends the boundaries of a historically contained political context. The first lady is not affected by political tides and political legacy in the way a president is. Once out of office, the president loses power, but power and politics are not the first lady's trade. Unless she is widowed, a first lady is able to continue her private role as spouse, as well as any public advocacy activities, for they are consistent with a private citizen of her class. Therefore, in a sense, a first lady holds her symbolic office for life.

Biography

Like her husband, Grace Anna Goodhue Coolidge was a New Englander, born in Burlington, Vermont, to Andrew Issacher and Lemira Barrett Goodhue, in 1879. An only child, Grace's arrival marked the eighth generation that was descended from a fifteenth-century Massachusetts pioneer. Her New England ancestors included a member of the first Congress. Grace Goodhue was raised within a comforting environment of security, tradition, and positive attention. As she wrote in her autobiography, "the sun, moon, and stars, in the opinion of my parents, revolved around my infant head," (Coolidge 1992, 4) and, despite household thriftiness (her father worked as a mechanical engineer), Grace was provided with the material playthings and cultural opportunities of a typical middle-class child and young lady of the nineteenth century. She was also provided with the close company of her parents and their friends, which may have instilled Grace's subsequent poise and social ease. Portraits from the family photo album suggest Grace was a serious child and adolescent, but that image is countered by her own stories of a lively, if sheltered, youth. The Methodist Church provided a "church home" in Burlington that functioned equally as a

center for social life, and, in her autobiography, Grace remembered her participation in class meetings, church suppers, and socials enthusiastically.

Although she paints a modest and self-deprecating verbal portrait of herself
and her small-town upbringing, disavowing any particular social popularity
(Coolidge 1992, 22), Grace was also a vivacious and fun-loving young woman
with a friendly manner. At school, she chose the loneliest girl in her class for her
best friend and began her first tender forays into girlhood romance. As an adolescent Grace studied piano and elocution, and was sufficiently adept at public
speaking that she was chosen as a commencement speaker for her high school
graduation class. She went on to attend a coeducational college (the University
of Vermont) at a time when few girls did so. An ardent baseball fan, she also
participated fully in the social activities and cultural pursuits available to young
women from nice families, such as taking part in school musicales and drama
productions and being a founding member of her college sorority. The *New York
Times*, in an approving editorial of her performance as first lady, would later
point to Grace Coolidge as an example of the value of college education for
young women in terms of their traditional roles as mothers and members of the
community.

Through the influence and example of a close family friend, June Yale,
Grace Goodhue became interested in the work of the Clarke School of the Deaf
in Northampton, Massachusetts, and secured a teaching position there in 1902,
that lasted for three years. While in Northampton, she met Calvin Coolidge, a
promising lawyer and graduate of nearby Amherst College, who was already
involved in local Republican politics. The initial encounter became a piece of
family lore. As their son John Coolidge described it,

> My mother was watering flowers outside Baker Hall when she happened to
> look up at the nearby house where she noticed a young man standing in the
> window shaving. He wore a derby hat and appeared to be dressed only in a un-
> ion suit. She burst out laughing, then turned away and continued sprinkling the
> flowers. Apparently, her spontaneous laughter was heard by my father. He in-
> quired about her. [Later] he explained to her that the reason he wore a hat while
> shaving was to hold down an unruly lock of hair. (Clarke School 1998)

Although Grace was not politically inclined, her relationship with Calvin
was infused with politics. Their first date was attending a Republican rally at
Northampton's city hall. While they shared many aspects of their backgrounds,
particularly the fact that they were native Vermonters and shared New England
values of hard work and unpretentiousness, the contrast between their personalities was evident to outsiders. Where Grace was friendly and outgoing, Calvin
impressed others as aloof and humorless, but Grace discovered and appreciated
in Calvin a ready, dry wit (Miller 1987).

Grace Anna Goodhue and Calvin Coolidge were married in a small ceremony in 1905, in her family home, and they lived in Northampton while Calvin
climbed the political ladder in various city and state offices, until he became lt.
governor, then governor, of Massachusetts. The Coolidges remained domiciled
in Northampton even then, with Grace managing their home (and two young

sons) while Calvin took the weekend train home from Boston, or, alternatively, Grace traveled with the boys to Boston for short visits.

Grace's view of marriage has been expressed in the metaphor of a "double harness" (Coolidge 1992, 32) but it was not a pairing of equals. She submitted happily to her husband's lead. Of marriage, she wrote,

> If it is to be a going concern it must have a head. That head should be the member of the firm who assumes the greater responsibility for its continuance. In general this is the husband. His partner should consider well the policies which he advises before taking issue with them. (Coolidge 1992, 34–35)

Her words explain much about her role as a partner in political life and her acquiescence to her husband's wishes on her public (in)visibility. Whether or not Massachusetts sought a symbolic role for the wife of its head of state, Grace Coolidge apparently served in no official ceremonial capacity, except as a member of the Massachusetts social scene. At this, she was popular and impressed many leaders in politics and industry with her gregarious manner. As one influential industrialist, Frank Stearns, noted to Dwight Morrow in 1919, "She (Grace) will make friends wherever she goes, and she will not meddle with his conduct in office" (Ross 1962, 232).

Calvin's tenure as governor set the stage, inadvertently or by design, for the demarcation between the domestic and the political that was to characterize the Coolidge White House years. Mrs. Coolidge was to prioritize her roles as mother first, then wife, then first lady, but met with social approval in all. At the same time, she maintained strong associations with other women through her college sorority, participating in a round-robin correspondence throughout her life. Grace organized many of her public events in the White House in connection with organizations for girls and women.

By 1921, Calvin Coolidge had been elected vice president. The Coolidges were vacationing in Vermont at Calvin's parental homestead in August 1923, when President Harding died. Calvin's father, John Coolidge, a justice of the peace, administered the oath of office to his son.

The Coolidge term, following scandals that marked the Harding administration and sandwiched between the First World War and the onset of the depression, seems relatively uneventful in retrospect. Watson describes Coolidge's approach to the presidency as "passive" (2000, 133), and, because the president discouraged his wife from assuming a public role and from delivering public speeches (Miller 1987), her tenure as first lady also seems unremarkable, although she made a sharp contrast with her older, less fashionable, and physically inactive predecessors.

Although Grace Coolidge's involvement in public affairs as first lady seems markedly limited, her vivacity and charm as the social center of the White House is evident in many anecdotes of the era. Biographers reveal a woman of wide interests and a playful nature, a woman who "enjoyed herself so much that people enjoyed just being with her" (Prindiville 1941, 251). She answered all of her personal letters and invited or met with a steady stream of visitors to the White House. Photographs demonstrate her famous love of animals, as she was pictured with several family dogs (which she liked to dress up at parties), a pet raccoon, and with her cat draped around the shoulders of a White House visitor. Initially, her autobiography was to include an entire chapter on the Coolidge menagerie, but it was subsequently omitted, perhaps indicating the balance between high spirits and sober duty that the first lady embodied. The enduring assessment of Mrs. Coolidge was that of a warm, friendly, and beloved woman, who "deferred to her husband in public, but in private . . . was the foundation upon which the President rested, [who] helped define his presidency and touched nearly every person with whom she came into contact" (Emery 1999, A4).

Undoubtedly, the Coolidge's mutual heritage bound them together in shared values and informed their lives more than any other aspect. "All the strength and simplicity of New England Vermont went into their life," wrote one biographer, "into the training of their sons" (Prindiville 1941, 232). The modesty and simplicity inherent in the Coolidge's common heritage tempered Grace's liveliness and made Calvin's famous extravagance towards his wife's wardrobe seem out of character.

The Coolidges spent just over six years in the White House. During that time their younger son died from blood poisoning that developed from a blister, a particular blow to the president, who had lost his mother and sister at an early age. The president did not choose to seek reelection following his first full term (a prescient decision in light of the subsequent stock market crash and its effect on the Hoover legacy). Afterwards, Grace and Calvin Coolidge returned to their home in Northampton, Massachusetts, where, following her husband's death in 1933, Mrs. Coolidge was elected to the board of the Clarke School of the Deaf. Although she maintained a low public profile, she was devoted to the cause of education for deaf persons, and she supported other civic and social issues, including U.S. refugee relief in World War II. Due to the effects of declining strength and health, Grace resigned as president of the Clarke School board in 1952. She died of heart disease on July 8, 1957, at the age of 78, two hours after the anniversary of her younger son's death thirty-three years before.

Rhetorical Activities as First Lady

A first lady potentially plays a number of roles. Grace Coolidge fulfilled only one traditional role, that of hostess. The absence of public speeches by this first lady would seem to deny the existence of significant rhetorical activities, but that view would also disregard the symbolic attachments that generated from her image. Despite her reticence in the political sphere, she was very much a public person within the confines of White House sociability and ceremony. Even the role of White House hostess was less "traditional" for a first lady of her time than one might assume. More than half of presidential spouses before 1900 delegated the role of White House social mistress to someone else, in whole or in part, and few participated in public ceremonies. As O'Connor, Nye, and Assendelft (1996, 844) point out, "For a long period of time, the nation's image of a first lady was one of a woman out of sight." Grace was very much a visible presence in the unofficial structure of the White House domestic sphere and in ceremonial affairs. She embodied Allgor's description of the perfect woman of the early republic: "Although [the first lady] was educated [she] was essentially a domestic being, able to be lively and articulate without calling attention to herself, and astute enough to appear politically null" (2000, 31).

Mrs. Coolidge enjoyed tremendous popularity, a public affection that enhanced the presidency in its own way. For one thing, Grace's vivacity and warmth balanced her husband's stern demeanor, inviting more positive public regard for the Coolidges than the president could have mustered on his own. With the expansion of the mass media, the public at large became acquainted with Grace Coolidge through the hundreds of pictures and newsreels she appeared in, often with family pets or visiting children, and through her appearances at official events such as parades, luncheons, and ceremonies. In this sense, Grace Coolidge was far more "public" than her predecessors. The camera liked her as well. Calvin's famous frugality did not extend to his wife's appearance; her fashionable wardrobe enhanced the sense of a real and engaging woman in both official portraits and candid news shots. Grace took her job seriously and to heart, although being first lady was not without its stresses.

Biographers who comment on Grace's adjustment to the White House note the constraints she felt and those imposed by her husband. Three weeks into the presidency, Grace herself acknowledged, "Being wife to a government worker is a very confining position" (Miller 1987, 395). A famously indefatigable walker, Grace now had to be escorted by the Secret Service, with all the complexities that sort of scheduling entailed. She had little opportunity to indulge in a favored pastime, reading, amidst the White House social demands. In her autobiography, Grace recounted a remark from a White House visitor,

> "How wonderful it must be to live here and be able to take a book out under those lovely trees and read!" I replied, "Yes, I think I have read one book since I came." She looked at me in surprise, shaded in pity, and I am sure she went away with the idea that I did not care for reading. (Coolidge 1992, 74)

The president was not immune from similar feelings of restriction. In a letter to his father, he remarked, "Great power does not mean much except great limitations. I cannot have any freedom to go and come" (Miller 1987, 395).

In the White House, Grace adapted to the familiar role of domestic partner, raising her two sons and providing an engaging contrast to her taciturn husband's demeanor. Her "balancing and compensating personal style" evidently endeared her to those who found Calvin stern and humorless (Heckler-Feltz 1984, 187). Grace, herself, remarked that the couple held "vastly different temperaments and tastes" (Coolidge 1992, 32).

Early in their marriage, Mr. Coolidge discouraged overlap between politics and family life. "Having a wife who did not divulge her opinions on any important matter fitted in with his image of the president as corporate head" (Caroli 1987, 167). Grace did not oppose her husband's wishes. "If I had manifested any particular interest in [political affairs], I feel sure that I would have been put properly in my place," she later remarked (Coolidge 1935, 181).[5] Grace was, nevertheless, a young, active, stylish, and popular leader in Washington society. While her public demeanor was impeccable, it was infused with a resounding sense of fun. She enjoyed sports, hunting, and fishing, and was an indefatigable walker. She was, by all accounts, the perfect White House hostess, presiding over ceremonial functions, teas, and musicales, and frequently hosting breakfast or luncheon guests. She especially went out of her way to invite groups of women and girls to events in the White House and encourage their efforts. She posed for photographs filling out her ballot to promote women's newly acquired right to vote, and she ceremonially opened the Women's Worlds Fair in Chicago, which showcased women's achievements in nontraditional occupations (Miller 1987, 398–99). The Coolidges entertained an unprecedented number of White House visitors, including noted actors, performers, royalty, political leaders, and American icons Will Rogers and Charles Lindbergh. Such entertaining was continued even as the Coolidges moved their household to summer residences and a temporary Washington domicile necessitated by the renovation of the White House.[6] Because the Coolidges owned little furniture of their own, Mrs. Coolidge is credited with some of the first efforts to restore the White House as a living museum by locating permanent furnishings of historical significance as renovations were under way.

All in all, the image of Grace Coolidge was that of an utterly natural woman, whose unpretentious personality was easy for the average person to identify with. She was dubbed, "The First Lady of Baseball" by an official of the Boston Red Sox, due to her enthusiasm for the game ("Considered 'First Lady of Baseball'" 1957, A1). The Coolidge family was the recipient of at least one dog as an official gift who joined a household of pets, including a White House raccoon. They were often used during Mrs. Coolidge's "photo-ops," as she posed in stylish, expensive clothing that was paid for by her reputedly frugal husband. Perhaps, he was mindful of the symbolic role of women and the usefulness of material display in creating a positive impression of his status and political potency.

Not that the Coolidge administration was one long, lively social affair. Their teenage son, Calvin Jr., died in the summer of 1924 from a minor foot wound that developed into fatal septicemia, which prompted Grace to write (and subsequently publish) verse that revealed her pious Protestant upbringing. This tragic event stands out in a public life that seemed otherwise unremarkable.

Grace Coolidge's compliance with her husband's injunction against public speech was clearly not the product of the first lady's shyness. "I don't think anyone ever accused mother of being shy," noted her son John (McGaffin 1955). She willingly appeared with her husband at formal ceremonial occasions and entertained influential people on behalf of her charitable concerns. While Grace chose a traditional, domestic role for herself, she was not "old-fashioned." She was as gregarious and effervescent as she was modest and gracious. Where her predecessors Mrs. Harding and Mrs. Wilson were, in first lady scholar Diana Dixon-Healy's terms, defined by their influence on presidential affairs, Mrs. Coolidge was the "national hugger" (Dixon-Healy 1988). Thus, one wonders whether Mrs. Coolidge's popularity and esteem stemmed, in part, from the symbolic contrast she provided to her predecessors Edith Wilson and Florence Harding, who were seemingly more actively involved in presidential affairs,[7] and who inspired remarks of a "petticoat government" in the White House (Dixon-Healy 1988). Grace was regarded favorably, especially in contrast to her husband. Apart from Calvin's uncharacteristic generosity in providing stylish fashions for his wife, the Coolidge ethos discouraged self-aggrandizement and self-promotion. Their approach to public service was dutiful more than egotistical. Such an attitude, as much as anything else, may have discouraged Grace's adoption of the "white glove pulpit," but it did not deny her a rhetorical role.

Rhetoric is not merely artifactual; it is a public process of self-revelation that occurs in response to exigencies. Grace Coolidge's unexpected plunge into Washington's politically steeped social milieu called for an appropriate response from her as a public person. As Gould notes, she became "a celebrity in her own right, part of the public image of the Coolidge presidency" (quoted in Hand 1992, 103). Grace's rhetorical response—her sociability, her fashion presence—followed traditional lines of performance. Her activities were subsumed under her husband's role, and she restricted her personality to that of a domestic partner. She performed as an elite republican (e.g. upper class) lady who maintained the home environment, entertained socially, and, when appropriate, accompanied her husband in the ceremonial performance of his "business" affairs. If the media highlighted her activities, it was not due to Grace Coolidge's arrangements. She sought no unique or independent role as first lady, even though she could not escape the public nature of her status. Coverage of the first lady in the newspapers centered on the quotidian, reporting on her attendance at public events or travels, her clothing, her skills at fishing and operating motion picture cameras, and her minor illnesses. The closest the *New York Times* came to ascribing policy to the first lady was when they reported on (and affirmed) Mrs. Coolidge's belief that colds were contagious.

However low the profile Grace Coolidge maintained in performing her role, her chosen performative attitude spoke volumes. Media approval and deference to Grace Coolidge were prompted by her "natural" demeanor, in contrast with Florence Harding's "artifice" (Caroli 1987, 170). She easily remembered the names of people attending official receptions, she put guests at ease, and, in published photographs with pets and children, she was revealed as loving, playful, and affectionate. Her personality was as lively as her husband's was cool, a contrast which undoubtedly generated her affectionate public regard. As biographer Betty Boyd Caroli has noted, "Her exuberance generated so many stories that the public felt an acquaintance with her as with few other first ladies" (1987, 170). Certain representative anecdotes appeared in print to be repeated in biographical material on the Coolidges: a shopping trip where she teased a clerk who recognized her, her prowess at fishing, and her indulgence in forbidden (by her husband) pleasures such as dancing, smoking, and horseback riding (Caroli 1987, 170–71) Despite her liveliness, Grace was never perceived as vulgar or irreverent. As first lady, as a woman of warmth and spirit, she was "public," if not overtly political. People read about her in newspapers and magazines such as the *New Yorker*, and she was the only nonprofessional listed among *Good Housekeeping's* most admired women, an honor that is now bestowed upon first ladies with regularity.

Despite her personal lack of pretensions, Grace's own expressed view of her position was reverent and monumental. "To me the home of the presidents is sacred ground hallowed with the memories of those men whom our country has chosen to the high office," she later wrote. "To live in it is to live in a shrine . . ." (Grace Coolidge 1992, 70–71). To Grace Coolidge, the office of first lady was not a platform for action or individual identity, it was a civic monument. The responsibility of a first lady was to maintain and preserve that monument against the potential impact of words or deeds by a presidential wife who acted outside her conventional role. While a woman might become first lady by way of politics, the office itself was apolitical. In turn, Grace remained unaffected by the ideal the office represented. She performed her duties as her authentic self. Inside or outside of the White House, her role and persona seemingly remained unchanged. She was not passive, she was a partner, but in marriage, not politics, although the effect of a pleasing wife and hostess on her husband's presidential ethos was undeniable. As one Washington observer remarked, Grace Coolidge was "the administration's greatest success" (Miller 1987, 396).

Grace Coolidge was not heard, but she was seen as a charming woman who provided a model for modern womanhood that reaffirmed the traditional values of a conventional wife and rejected the possibility of a woman more actively involved in her husband's political affairs. It was a role that became increasingly associated with first ladies in the twentieth century, even as American women became increasingly independent of their domestic roles and involved in public affairs and activities.[8]

Legacy

Grace Coolidge's legacy does not stem from a designated cause or project that she used to make an impact as first lady. Rather, it stems from the way in which she assumed her role as a natural extension of her domestic identity.

As Grace Coolidge declined to shape the first lady role, it was shaped for her by others. Leaving the White House did not mean leaving the "white glove pulpit," because Grace had never constructed one for herself.[9] Instead, her role as first lady fused with her domestic role in such a way as to eliminate a demarcation between life in and life out of the White House. Even as she resumed active involvement with the Clarke School where she had taught before her marriage, her rhetorical persona was expressed through traditional virtues of female domesticity that she had displayed as first lady. "The traditions and old customs of the White House had a strong appeal for me," she wrote in her memoirs, "and I endeavored to carry them out as far as changing conditions would permit" (Coolidge 1992, 90).

In Gutin's paradigm of the first ladyship as a communication activity, Grace Coolidge hardly registered in terms of verbal expression. However, she embodied the idea of performance as rhetoric. With the advent of film newsreels and the broadened distribution of photogravure features in the print media, nondiscursive presentation was becoming instructive in constituting the rhetorical persona of people in the public eye. The developing impact of the media on the White House was evident in the president's rhetorical activities. He institutionalized the presidential press conference, appeared in newsreels, and was the first president to address the public on radio (Nelson 1996, 136). These media practices brought a sense of immediacy to White House affairs, and the first lady's presence was noted, even if "she was known for . . . moving out of the view of the camera when she saw one near" (Parnass and Mitchell 1999, A7). Her own fascination with motion pictures was duly noted in the newspapers when she acquired a camera and learned to operate it. The first lady may have been drawn to the background, but cameras put her in the scene. Her visual presence had symbolic currency, an effect that has remained for other first ladies.

Grace Coolidge's rhetorical persona was further expressed in her autobiography. Although it was published after her White House years, the writing of it signaled the importance of the first lady position as one of lifelong significance. Because first ladies are more removed from politics than their husbands, their public image often benefits from polite, if not affectionate, regard when they leave the White House. At the same time, their loss of "public-ness" provides an opportunity to reflect more candidly on their own lives. In her examination of autobiographies of women activists, Martha Watson argues that autobiographies are useful rhetorical texts that "enlarge the rhetorical spaces suitable for a discussion of women's roles and rights by offering their lives as evidence for their claims" (1999, 118). Similarly, an autobiography written by a first lady characterized by her public silence as much as her public visibility provides the weight of her voice (in Martha Watson's terms) to her rhetorical persona. Like the women authors of autobiographies that Watson studied, Grace Coolidge "depicts [herself] as an agent who acts in specific ways (agency) in particular circumstances (scene) to accomplish a clear end (purpose)." In Coolidge's case, the purpose was to serve honorably and virtuously as first lady. The concept of civic ideal was apparent in the opening paragraphs of her White House narrative, as she attempts to describe her feelings on moving into the White House:

> There was a sense of detachment—this was I and yet not I, this was the wife of the President of the United States and she took precedence over me; my personal likes and dislikes must be subordinated to the consideration of those things which were required of her. (1992, 62)

Grace Coolidge's deference to the role, as she perceived it, set aside any potential she might have had to make her mark on a civic ideal; she preserved the first lady role, not as a mutable framework for action, but as a concretized monument. Although the domestic scene of the White House seemed unfamiliar initially (she remarked elsewhere on her lack of social experience which would be required of a White House hostess), she quickly found her rhetorical persona in authenticity. The White House was a place where she could fulfill her purpose by being "Mrs. Coolidge" rather than "Mrs. President." Any contrast between the two roles was inconsequential. "I found that the domestic problems of the mistress of the White House were not different from those of the housewife of any well-run household," she noted (Coolidge 1992, 63.)

The first part of the White House narrative reiterates the theme of unremarkable normalcy. Those events that call attention to the first lady role are small departures from habit: a round-robin letter she shared with her sorority sisters was filed along with other papers as a matter of course rather than forwarded, guests pocketed room decor as souvenirs, she had little time to indulge in reading. The image of normalcy, which continued after her return to Northampton, had its effect on the public perception. As one news report was to describe it, "She shopped plain, as the man said, 'Like your mother or mine'" (Parnass and Mitchell 1999, A6). Although her everyday manner was authentically rooted in her unpretentious persona, Coolidge might also have used such an approach in her autobiography to create identification with her readers, a strategy sometimes necessitated by the need of the "exceptional" public woman to "overcome the charge that they are highly unusual . . ." (M. Watson 1999, 20). But the creation of an image of virtuous domesticity belies Grace's access to unfolding history, and her potential role as part of that history. Tellingly, the idea of "history" never encroaches upon the narrative unless it concerns the history or decor of the domicile. Political personalities are almost absent in the tale. "I kept no diary," she reports, and the consequence is a narrative that seems to float in atmospheric displacement from historical or political specificity.

The public connotations of the first lady role and its potential to merge with political affairs did not find development in the Coolidge years. Rather, the role itself was treated by both Coolidges as a national icon, protected from the vagaries of public life by confinement to the domestic sphere. Mrs. Coolidge, through her appearance and demeanor, symbolically communicated a feminine ideal of virtuous domesticity that reassured a country newly faced with the potentials, uncertainties, and consequences of female emancipation.[10] A presidential administration is fixed and historical, but the first lady role expands those constraints. As first lady historian Carl Anthony has noted, "One of the keys to understanding Grace Coolidge is to realize there's a timeless quality to her personality. . . . She helped make the role of the first lady" (Anthony 1999). Coolidge helped make the role of first lady transcend the historical boundaries that apply to former presidents. It allows for a sustained aspect to their rhetorical influence, whether through spoken words, written words, or the performance of deeds.

Grace Coolidge's performance as first lady critically shaped contemporary expectations and attitudes toward that role in three ways. First, she began to bring the role into sharper focus as a virtuous embodiment of a civic and cultural ideal, as expressed in the now-standard position of first ladies on lists of admired women. Further, the role, in its ahistorical evolution, became a template for identification with the common experiences of women, expressed through subsequent autobiographies and personal narratives, exemplified by Betty Ford's public battles with breast cancer and substance addiction. Finally, the first lady became a more visible partner in the presidency by participating in a ceremonial agenda and setting the tone of fashion, exemplified by Jackie Kennedy's memorable sense of style. Although Americans still experience tensions over a first lady who dares to act independently,[11] we expect the first lady to be an active, if ceremonial, adjunct to the presidency. Grace Coolidge helped to set this standard as figurehead of ceremonial symbolism and social grace, as no first lady other than Dolley Madison has done. Although largely unknown in public memory (outside of Vermont and Northampton, Massachusetts), Grace Coolidge's legacy lives on in our social expectations that the woman should rise to the role of first lady without overwhelming it. Her expressed interest in the "traditions and old customs of the White House" refixed them in a time that, in many ways, centered on change and upheaval. As one historian suggests, Grace's apolitical formula "reassured those concerned over the private exercise of public power by those neither elected nor appointed to public office" (Hand 1992, 102), but it presents an unresolved legacy for the "first of the modern first ladies" (Parnass and Mitchell 1999) and for the idea of a more activist role for political wives and political women.

Notes

The author is grateful for the assistance of Donna Meehan of the Clarke School of the Deaf, Cindy Bittner of the Calvin Coolidge Foundation, librarians at the Northampton Library Coolidge Room, and Professors Carolyn Anderson and Jane Blankenship at the University of Massachusetts for their assistance in providing relevant materials for this study. Completion of this essay was assisted by a grant from the College of Fine Arts and Communication at Western Illinois University.

1. Most particularly, with the advent of motion picture newsreels and mass circulation of print media, Grace Coolidge became a groundbreaking and featured player in the presidential photo opportunity.

2. For example, Grace often welcomed organizations for girls and women to the White House, and she worked on behalf of war relief during the 1940s. Most importantly, the former first lady served on the board of the Clarke School of the Deaf for many years, even lobbying then-senator John Kennedy on a related matter. The New England taciturn heritage of the Coolidges might be featured here. Miller reports that the Coolidges intentionally worked behind the scenes on their favored cause in the belief "that promoting a cause so important to them might appear a matter of self-interest" (1987, 394).

3. As an example of her celebrity power, the Baldwin Piano Company sent Mrs. Coolidge a piano for the White House, mindful of the first lady's interest in music and the publicity value of linking her name to their product.

4. "I do not choose to talk" (McGaffin 1955), was her explanation for declining interviews, although, according to biographers (Caroli 1987), her reticence stemmed from her husband's admonition during his political career.

5. After her husband's death, she remarked to a friend, "Nobody is going to believe how I miss being told what to do. My father always told me what to do. Then Calvin told me what to do" (Miller 1987, 404).

6. Mrs. Coolidge wrote of their many temporary residences during the White House years in an article for *The American Magazine* upon their return to private life in Northampton, Massachusetts, in 1930.

7. Robert P. Watson characterizes Florence Harding and Edith Wilson as "full partner" and "partial partner," respectively, to their political husbands (2000, 143).

8. The contrast between two ways of being is illustrated by a comparison with Grace Coolidge's younger contemporary, Anne Morrow Lindbergh. Although she raised a family, Mrs. Lindbergh also accompanied her husband on daring adventures in aviation and established an independent career as an author, to great public admiration. A first lady's independence continues to instigate public criticism and disdain, whereas Mrs. Coolidge's conventional wifely role was the source of her public regard.

9. A number of petitioners did attempt to gain political favor or influence via Mrs. Coolidge, but there is no evidence that she ever followed through on such requests.

10. Although women gained some social freedoms along with the right to vote, there were also declines in women's career opportunities. As Caroli (1987) notes, the number of female physicians and female college students declined during the 1920s, and few women exercised their voting rights.

11. As Edwards and Chen (2000) found, even the most socially liberal political cartoonists routinely disciplined first ladies who attempted to speak independently, upsetting the equation in a zero-sum presidential marriage. Serious social criticism follows the wife who does not defer to the chief.

References

Allgor, Catherine. 2000. *Parlor Politics: In Which the Ladies of Washington Help Build a City and a Government.* Charlottesville, Va.: University of Virginia Press.

Anthony, Carl. 1999. Grace Goodhue Coolidge: Northampton to the White House. Keynote Address at Smith College, Northampton, Mass., 30 July.

Caroli, Betty Boyd. 1987. *First Ladies.* New York: Oxford University Press.

Clarke School of the Deaf. 1998. Coolidge Legacy Lives on at Clarke. *Clarke Speaks/Today,* 31.

Coolidge, Grace Goodhue. 1930. Home Again! *The American Magazine,* 20–21 January, 119–23.

———. 1935. The Real Calvin Coolidge. *Good Housekeeping,* February.

———. 1992. *Grace Coolidge: An Autobiography.* Ed. Lawrence E. Wikander and Robert H. Ferrell. Worland, Wyo.: High Plains Publishing Company, Inc.

Considered "First Lady of Baseball." 1957. *Daily Hampshire Gazette,* 8 July, A1.

Dixon-Healy, Diana. 1988. *America's First Ladies: The Private Lives of the Presidential Wives.* New York: Athenaeum.

Edwards, Janis L., and Huey-Rong Chen. 2000. The First Lady/First Wife in Editorial Cartoons: Rhetorical Visions through Gendered Lenses. *Women's Studies in Communication,* 23:3, 367–91.

Emery, Theo. 1999. "I Know What I'm Doing": Grace Coolidge's Gentle Influence Remembered during Retrospective. *Daily Hampshire Gazette,* 1 August, A1, A4.

Fuess, Claude M. 1940. *Calvin Coolidge.* Boston: Little, Brown, & Co.

Galbraith, Archibald V. 1957. Education of Deaf Children Preoccupation with Grace Coolidge since 1902. *Daily Hampshire Gazette,* 12 July, n.p.

Gutin, Myra G. 1989. *The President's Partner: The First Lady in the Twentieth Century.* Westport, Conn.: Greenwood.

Hand, Samuel B. 1992. Grace Coolidge and the Historians. *Vermont History News* (November-December), 98–103.

Heckler-Feltz, Cheryl. 1984. *Heart and Soul of a Nation: How the Spirituality of Our First Ladies Changed America.* New York: Doubleday.

McCoy, Donald R. 1988. *Calvin Coolidge: The Quiet President.* Lawrence, Kans.: University Press of Kansas.

McGaffin, Bill. 1955. "I Do Not Choose to Talk." *Chicago Daily News*, n.p.

Miller, Kristie. 1987. Grace (Anna) Goodhue Coolidge. In *American First Ladies*, edited by Lewis L. Gould, 385–408. New York: Oxford University Press.

Nelson, Michael. 1996. *The Presidency*. New York: Smithmark.

O'Connor, Karen, Bernadette Nye, and Laura Van Assendelft. 1996. Wives in the White House: The Political Influence of First Ladies. *Presidential Studies Quarterly*, 26:3, 835–53.

Parnass, Larry, and Phoebe Mitchell. 1999. In Praise of Grace Coolidge. *Daily Hampshire Gazette*, 30 July, A1, A6.

Prindiville, Kathleen. 1941. *First Ladies*. New York: Macmillan.

Ross, Ishbel. 1962. *Grace Coolidge and Her Era*. New York: Dodd, Mead.

Walsh, Mary Williams. 2001. So Where Are the Corporate Husbands? *New York Times*, 24 June, 3, 13.

Watson, Martha. 1999. *Lives of Their Own: Rhetorical Dimensions in the Autobiographies of Women Activists*. Columbia, S.C.: University of South Carolina Press.

Watson, Robert P. 2000. *The Presidents' Wives: Reassessing the Office of First Lady*. Boulder, Colo.: Lynne Reiner Publishers.

White, William Allen. 1938. *A Puritan in Babylon*. New York: Macmillan.

Chapter 9

Lou Henry Hoover
Mining the Possibilities as Leader and First Lady

Ann J. Atkinson

> Don't let amusement hours "just happen." For your future is almost as dependent on what you do in your periods of re-creating, a recreation, as in those of your creating efforts.
>
> —Lou Henry Hoover

Lou Henry Hoover experienced great high and low moments during her life with her husband, particularly during their years in public service. But through all of the peaks and valleys, she displayed an adventurous nature, a pioneering spirit, and was efficient, flexible, and exacting. As an adventurer, she journeyed to China the day after she was married to be with her husband as he developed his career as a mining engineer. She had grown up riding horses, hunting, and fishing with her dad, so her love of adventure had been instilled and encouraged in her early life. As a pioneer, she was the first woman to graduate from Stanford University with a degree in geology. Her classmates, all men, questioned whether she would be able to do the fieldwork required in some of her courses. She used the skills learned in her recreational hours as a child to put her classmates' doubts to rest as she negotiated difficult terrain to examine geological forces at work or to trek to mining sites.

Her efficient nature combined with her pioneering spirit held her in good stead as she became a leader in the Girl Scouts of America. She taught the girls in her charge to make productive use of their free time—not to let their amusement hours "just happen"—and to love the great outdoors. She demonstrated an ability to be flexible as she traveled throughout the world and adapted to her husband's changing roles, from engineer to public servant. Some of her skills had been honed as she camped with her dad and completed fieldwork for her undergraduate degree.

In her role as a hostess during the White House years, she was both efficient and exacting, employing a system of hand signals for the White House staff to respond to during state and other types of dinners in an attempt to ensure that the elaborate organizational plans not seem obtrusive to their guests.

To provide a political context for the high and low moments, it is important to offer a brief discussion about the Hoovers' road to the White House. When Lou's husband decided to run for president in 1928, he was one of the most admired men in America. He had accumulated a fortune as a young, hardworking mining engineer with Lou traveling to numerous foreign locations with him until the birth of their first son. While Herbert administered the mines, Lou steeped herself in the culture of the places, learning to speak five languages during these years. He and Lou then designed and delivered an impressive relief effort to feed the people of Belgium during World War I. That extraordinary achievement led Herbert to a stint as food administrator during the Wilson administration. He served as secretary of commerce during the Harding and Coolidge administrations, working tirelessly to define the fledgling cabinet post. During these years, Lou developed her skills as a hostess, which greatly helped her husband, who was not at all socially adept, preferring to work in settings that allowed him to act as leader and to hold forth about executing plans.

In his *first* run for an elected office, which happened to be for the highest office in the land, he defeated New York's governor, Al Smith, in a landslide. On Inauguration Day, March 4, 1929, Hoover delivered his address in a downpour. (Even the weather served to illustrate the highs and lows at work on this political landscape.) He said, "In the large view, we have reached a higher degree of comfort and security than ever existed before in the history of the world."[1] Seven months after the hopeful inaugural speech was delivered, the stock market crashed. By 1930, the country found itself in the midst of the Great Depression.

The differing usages of the family name to define circumstances serve as a dramatic example of the change, which became politically devastating for Herbert Hoover and a source of profound sorrow for Lou Hoover. During his tenure as food administrator, a cabinet-level post throughout World War I, his surname came to mean efficiency and conservation. People went without wheat on their dining tables on Wednesdays and without meat on Fridays (wheatless Wednesdays and meatless Fridays, as the days were labeled) in their efforts to *hooverize*. As a leader in the Girl Scouts of America, Lou Hoover dispatched the members of the organization to aid in the effort.

The surname was altered for ironic effect during the Great Depression, with makeshift villages being called *Hoovervilles* and large cardboard boxes used for shelter by the homeless being referred to as *Hoover hotels*. In 1932, the American people voted Hoover, the common man who had achieved uncommon heights of power and acclaim, out of the presidency and out of their lives.

From 1899, when Lou Henry and Herbert Hoover married, they developed a mutually beneficial partnership during many of these high and low moments. As we consider the accomplishments of Lou Henry Hoover, the notion of extremes can also be used to describe her placement between Grace Goodhue Coolidge and Anna Eleanor Roosevelt as first lady. Grace Coolidge was a first lady who, except in rare instances, was silent according to her husband's wishes while Eleanor Roosevelt, the "eyes and ears of FDR" after her husband's bout with polio, was the most vocal and publicly present of all first ladies in her time and, with the possible exception of Hillary Rodham Clinton, of all time.

Who is this figure, Lou Henry Hoover, who endured extremes in her public life and who, while not as reticent as Grace Coolidge was encouraged to be, has not been placed as prominently in the public mind as her immediate successor, Eleanor Roosevelt? To answer this question, I will present a biographical sketch of Lou Henry Hoover's life, her rhetorical activities during her years as first lady, and the way she is placed by scholars and in the public memory.

Biography

Lou Henry Hoover liked to take things apart and put them back together again. She prided herself in her ability to pack efficiently for trips, and in her lifetime, she packed and unpacked often. She traveled with her husband as he honed his skills as an engineer, then as he achieved great goals as a public servant, and also by herself as she assumed various leadership positions. She enjoyed setting up an encampment—figuring out how to live in nature with the bare essentials.

When she was traveling by ship with her young sons, Herbert Jr. and Allan[2], to join Herbert in one of his many engineering endeavors, she'd give the boys clocks to take apart with screwdrivers, hoping they would stay entertained during the long voyages and learn something about how things work.[3] We see, in this particular example that she also believed in making productive use of one's free time. Camping—the creating of temporary, efficient spaces—was another favorite activity that provided opportunities for fun *and* learning.

Lou Henry Hoover was born in Waterloo, Iowa, on March 29, 1874. Her father had hoped he would have a son. Lou did not disappoint him in terms of the interests she cultivated while in his care. She fished and hunted, developed a lifelong enjoyment of camping, and became an expert horsewoman. The family lived in northeastern Iowa for just ten years, moving to California for the sake of her mother's health. Here we see just how early in her life place and relationships became closely intertwined. The move to Whittier, California, and then to Monterey, California, was accomplished to find a climate that would allow her mother to gain control of her asthmatic condition and a place that would be good for her father's business. Lou and sister Jean's immediate needs were less important than their parents' needs, so the girls would have to find ways to adapt to the change needed to sustain their loved ones. They did, and in future years the ability to adapt became a trait that friends and family admired about Lou.

She went to normal school after high school and graduated in 1894, prepared to be a teacher, but a presentation given by a professor from Stanford University changed all that. She was most impressed by John Casper Branner of the Department of Geology and Mines and his lecture called "The Bones of the Earth." Following the speech, she enrolled at Stanford and, in 1898, was the first woman to graduate from that university with a degree in geology. She enjoyed the freedom of the research, of being in the outdoors camping and exploring mines, dressed in what would have been called men's clothing during this era. Her father had encouraged her to pursue interests that would have been deemed nontraditional, even unacceptable by many parents during this time. This closeness to one's father is a hallmark of many American women who achieved acclaim for their achievements in the 1800s and early 1900s (suffragist Elizabeth Cady Stanton, labor leader Florence Kelley, and Secretary of Labor Frances Perkins, to name a few).

The courtship of the Hoovers began with a chance meeting at a geology laboratory at Stanford University while they were students there. Herbert was working for Professor John Casper Branner as a laboratory assistant. Branner, the teacher whose presentation had provided the impetus for Lou to attend that university, introduced them. Herbert would remember in later years how pleased he was to have met a woman who shared his interest in the peripatetic life of a mining engineer and one whose earliest memories had also been created in Iowa. He had been born in a two-room house in West Branch, a village about one hundred miles from Lou's hometown of Waterloo. Orphaned by the age of ten, he had been separated from his siblings in a move to California to be raised by relatives.

Lou and Herbert spent time together during Herbert's senior year of college. Then he was off to be employed as a mining engineer. He secured a post in Australia after working briefly in California. Soon after Lou's graduation from Stanford, he cabled her a marriage proposal and an invitation to journey to China with him as he assumed his position as director of mines there. She returned his cable with a one-word response, "Yes." Theirs had not been a passionate courtship but rather one that had begun with a mutual interest and matured into a relationship marked by mutual respect. Of Hoover's time at the Henry home before the wedding, Lou's mother, Florence, said, "We had made up our minds not to like him very well as he was going to take Lou so far away, but after he had been here a few days—(he stayed with us nine days before they were married, as Lou said she would not go until just before they sailed) I think we all liked him about as much as Lou did" (Honors and Awards, LHH Subject File).

Their marriage, in an unusual turn of events, was performed by a Catholic priest. Herbert was Quaker and, at the time of their wedding, Lou Henry was Episcopalian, though she had told Herbert she was "determined to join the Quaker faith" (Hoover 1952, 36). The local minister was not available to officiate at the wedding, but a friend of the family, a padre of the old Spanish mission in Monterey, was. He agreed to preside over the ceremony at which both Lou and Herbert chose, quite by coincidence, to wear a brown suit. The next day, they sailed for China. This adventurous start to the marriage was made more so, when, a year after their arrival in China, the Boxer uprising broke out.[4] Lou

Henry Hoover dodged bullets during this conflict while riding her bicycle to help the wounded in a nearby hospital (Caroli 1995, 175).

She indicated, in later years, that on mornings during the uprising, she would sweep spent shells off the porch of their accommodations. But lest biographers make more of the adventure than was exactly true, she wrote to Mrs. Koverman in 1928, to correct that author's errors in a biographical piece about Lou. She wrote,

> Unfortunately, too, the matter of standing on a wall to protect the foreigners from the Chinese is a much favored tale, quite without foundation, that has gone round the world many times ever since its first appearance in the San Francisco papers of 1900. The fact that I should have been quite *willing* to have done my share of actual work, if any were necessary, does not alter the fact that my share of protection lay much more toward the region of the kitchen and dining room. Just as Mr. Hoover's share was in building barricades, providing food, water, etc. and not in running a machine gun! (Honors and Awards, LHH Subject File)

During her years in this region, she learned to speak Chinese and started a book about China.

Between 1907 and 1912, she and her husband translated an important book about mining technology, *De Re Metallica*, from Latin.[5] The author of the text, Georgius Agricola, had invented words for mining practices. The Hoovers performed experiments to determine the specifics of the practices and then translated accordingly. The Mining and Metallurgical Society of America rewarded the translation effort with a prize for excellence.[6] While Herbert assisted with the experiments, Lou did all of the translation work. Here again, we have evidence of Lou Henry Hoover's love of taking things apart, seeing how they worked, and then putting them together again. The effort was also a way for Lou and Bert to spend leisure time together, especially during long ocean voyages, engaged in a productive activity, not letting amusement hours "just happen."

After the stint in China, Herbert became a partner in Bewick Moreing with three other men. The company had its headquarters in London, England. Herbert was in charge of scouting and selecting suitable locations for mine development and, after setting up necessary business arrangements, overseeing the day-to-day operations. Hard times hit the firm in 1902, when it was discovered that one of the firm's partners had embezzled close to one million dollars. The Hoovers, who by this time had become frustrated with the firm's practices apart from this recent disaster, initially thought they would assume their share of the company's losses and depart for a more suitable opportunity. They then considered the investors. Fearing for their financial outcomes, Herbert and Lou decided they should stay to attend to the company's debt (Allen 2000, 41). During these years, Lou was a member of the Society of American Women in London, enjoying her time with other American women and serving as one of the club's leaders for several years (Allen 2000, 63).

In 1908, with the slate at Bewick Moreing wiped clean, Herbert left the company to venture out on his own and form a consulting engineer company with offices in London and in San Francisco. His promise to the engineer who bought his interest in Bewick Moreing not to compete for business anywhere in the British Empire set the stage for a most impressive travel schedule. During the next six years, the consulting firm's business took the family, now increased to four with the births of their two sons, to Burma, Korea, Nicaragua, Newfoundland, Siberia, California, the Caucasus, and Peru (Allen 2000, 48). Sometimes Lou and the children would accompany Herbert and, at times, Herbert would make the journeys alone, with Lou, Herbert Jr., and Allan, keeping the home fires burning at the Red House, near Kensington Gardens in London.

The travels, while exciting and productive for the consulting firm, also served to provide the Hoovers with a vivid global understanding of political events. During 1914, soon after they both experienced a personal high moment with the awarding of the gold medal for their translation of *De Re Metallica*, they knew they would have many low moments ahead as they witnessed the coming of World War I in Europe.

When war was declared, many Americans were stranded in London. Lou and Herbert launched an effort to secure passage home for these Americans, offering their organizational skills and their own monies to achieve the goal. Early in the effort, Lou observed that women traveling alone were intimidated by some of their soon-to-be fellow travelers. She appealed to her husband to form two organizational committees—one for men, one for women. He agreed. From her previous club work in London with the Society of American Women, Lou had an established organizational structure from which to work. When their goals were met, the Hoovers returned to California.

Herbert's stay there would be brief. The tactics of war in Europe were effectively cutting off food supplies to Belgium, a country that did not have a military or political stake in the conflict and yet, with this imposed situation, was in danger of having its citizens starved. Walter Page, America's ambassador to Britain, appealed to Herbert Hoover to organize food shipments through a blockade to save the Belgian people. Hoover agreed and was given an assurance that the shipments would not serve to help the German armies but would travel safely to Belgium. Soon after he began his work on this project, named the CRB—Commission for the Relief of Belgium, he contacted Lou and asked her to take part. She gave speeches asking Californians to contribute money to the cause, contacted friends, and organized local committees (Allen 2000, 64–65). Her efforts, in support of her husband's brilliant plan, were hugely successful.

Later, in 1916, Lou helped to market fine Belgian lace, so that the painstaking efforts of many of the women in Belgium would not be lost to the blockades of war. Just as lace is identified by its patterns, we see a pattern of behavior emerging, with Lou Henry Hoover understanding the specific needs of women as she had in London before World War I and marshaling her organizational skills, economic resources, and persuasive talents to meet those needs.

As the United States moved closer to entering World War I, the Hoovers decided to make their return to the states a permanent one, with their sons leaving British schools to be enrolled in American ones. In April 1917, with the United States now at war with Germany and her allies, President Woodrow Wilson asked Herbert Hoover to head up the effort to administer food distribution in the United States. As in his efforts to feed the Belgians, one of his first actions was to contact Lou and ask for her help. She gave speeches encouraging food conservation and promoted a cutback on home delivery of items which may have coined the phrase "cash and carry" as the label for a preferred alternative. She also created the "Hoover apron," which was a cotton housedress designed to be worn over an everyday dress with an end to reducing laundry bills (Allen 2000, 75). Once again, the Hoover name was being used to describe efficiency and the saving of money and resources.

At war's end, Lou thought the family could finally put down roots in California. At this time, she became involved in the Girl Scouts of America and the National Amateur Athletic Federation. In addition, she worked hard on behalf of her and Herbert's alma mater, Stanford University, and she was raising two sons. The return to Palo Alto, however, was not to be. President-elect Warren G. Harding asked her husband to be secretary of commerce and Herbert accepted. The Commerce Department was the newest of the cabinet posts, and Hoover spent long hours establishing regulations for radio, a new medium, and forging cooperative arrangements with industry.

When Harding died, Hoover stayed on in the Coolidge administration as cabinet secretary, at the new president's request even though Coolidge was not as enamored of Hoover's administrative skill as many others had been.[7] In these years, Lou Hoover served as a capable hostess. And, again, she was a model of efficiency. In one instance, she was able to convince cabinet spouses that the custom of the wives of high Washington officials calling on each other in person and leaving cards four or five afternoons a week was a waste of precious time, time that would be better spent doing the work of such organizations as the Girl Scouts of America, the League of Women Voters, the Campfire Girls, and the General Federation of Women's Clubs (Boller 1998, 277).

When Calvin Coolidge announced that he would not seek reelection, the Republican Party needed to find a leader to fill the void. While Lou Henry Hoover was not thrilled by the idea of her husband seeking elected office, she believed his talents as a manager would guarantee his success in the presidency should he prevail in the contest. While he was an organized manager, he did not prove to be an effective political leader.

Lou was both a good manager, as evidenced by her ability to transport her family and set up homes all over the world, and she was an effective leader, as displayed in her work in a variety of volunteer organizations. Prior to her years as first lady and after her term in the White House, she was very active in the Girl Scouts of America, serving as president of the organization from 1922 to 1925, and again from 1935 to 1937. She had become acquainted with Juliette Gordon Low, founder of the Girl Scouts of America, during the efforts to provide relief to the Belgians during World War I.[8] Other first ladies were supportive of Girl Scouts such as Florence Harding, Grace Coolidge, and Eleanor Roosevelt, but none was as actively involved in the development and daily workings of this organization as Lou Henry Hoover.

She also helped found the National Amateur Athletic Federation. From

1923 to 1928, she served as president of the women's division of that organization. During her tenure, she argued that sport should be pursued for its health value and for the sake of camaraderie, not just for competitive ends. Here we see the beginnings of an argument for the importance of lifelong sports, now well understood on the American scene.

Rhetorical Activities as First Lady

What principles guided Lou Henry Hoover's thinking and helped her to be such a successful leader in volunteer organizations—most prominently, in the Girl Scouts of America—and a successful scholar, translator, mother, and first lady? To discover the principles that guide a person's life, one can examine texts— structures of a sort—for consistent themes or arguments that represent a consistency in one's thinking. Such consistent themes can serve as predictors, not in the sense of a crystal ball, but rather as keys to explain a person's behaviors and actions.

In Lou Hoover's work with the Girl Scouts, there is an opportunity to study speeches given to the girls and to some of the other women in leadership positions in the organization. In these speeches, she emphasized three themes about the hopes and aspirations of girls.[9] She asserted that girls were limited only by their imaginations in terms of what they could accomplish. As they were studying for their chosen fields, they should learn to be responsible citizens so they could be capable wives, mothers, and homemakers (Mayer 1990, 692–93). This logic parallels the notion of republican motherhood expressed in the sentiment, "The hand that rocks the cradle rules the world." Mothers, after the Revolutionary War in the United States, were to be educated so that they would be well prepared to raise the next generation of leaders, then all male. Their wisdom would serve to ignite their sons' lights.[10]

Lou Hoover also emphasized the importance of camping for girls. She said, in a speech given in Savannah, Georgia, home of Juliette Gordon Low, in January of 1922:

> To me the Outing part of scouting has always been the most important. The happiest part of my own very happy childhood and girlhood was without doubt the hours and days, the sometimes entire months, which I spent in pseudo-pioneering, or scouting in our wonderful western mountains with my father in our vacation times. So I cannot but want every girl to have the same widening, simplifying joy-getting influences in her own life. (LHH Speech, Girl Scouts in Articles, Addresses and Statements, LHH Subject File)

The juxtaposition of the words "widening" and "simplifying" gives an indication of the tenets that guide her in her thinking—openness, and the desire to reduce the complexities of life to that which is essential.

And in a speech given over the radio in the White House to 4-H Clubs on November 7, 1931, there is evidence of the principle that was employed as she encouraged her own children to take things apart during playtime and as she produced the prize-winning translation effort with her husband. (It is worthy of note that Lou Hoover often placed commas and dashes next to each other in her handwritten speeches and had them typed in that fashion. Perhaps she was using punctuation marks to remind her to pause or to highlight the section in some way.) She said,

> And, as I think I said when I talked with you at that amusing banquet of ours over two years ago, when you sat here in Washington and I at the Rapidan,— don't also neglect to plan your future joy hours, as well as for your achieving, working hours. Don't let amusement hours "just happen." For your future is almost as dependent on what you do in your periods of re-creating, a recreation, as in those of your creating efforts. (LHH Speech, 4-H Clubs in Articles, Addresses and Statements, LHH Subject File)

All moments of work and play in Lou Henry Hoover's world, were moments from which to learn.

Another principle that informed the way she spent work and amusement hours was the value she placed on nurturing relationships. (As she places her talk on the page, it looks more like a poem than a speech.) She says, to the Girl Scout grown-ups in Chicago, during her second stint as president of the organization:

> Relationships.
> Human relationships?
> All the world is just relationships, isn't it?
> Except for the hermit.
> Yes, and even for him, it is.
> So that talking about human relations is just a new wording for being able to talk about any or all of life's problems.
> The theme gives us a free field to talk about anything that concerns the affairs of the Girl Scouts. From Cookie Sales to Golden Eaglets,—From Uniforms to "Citizenship."
> (LHH Speech, Girl Scouts in Articles, Addresses and Statements in LHH Subject File)

When she came to the White House she had traveled all over the world and acted as a public servant in her own right. She was comfortable in Washington, D.C., and had definite ideas about how to impose her style and priorities upon the White House. As first lady, she maintained, created, and broke traditions. In accomplishing the tasks associated with these three missions, she employed effective interpersonal skills, demonstrated a complex understanding of group dynamics, and delivered both epideictic and deliberative speeches to communicate her messages which were largely about helping others in need. Further, in the instances of creating and breaking traditions, she became an advocate for education and civil rights.

Specifically, Lou Hoover was an able hostess, maintaining that long-standing expectation. She was creative, bringing an arts program to the White House, cataloguing the furnishings, broadcasting speeches over the radio, and creating the first Presidential Retreat, which also resulted in the creation of a school for the children in the nearby region.[11] And she was an agent of change, discontinuing the tradition of the president and first lady greeting the public on New Year's Day and creating a stir by altering the protocol for entertaining congressional spouses.

Maintaining Tradition

In her role as hostess in the White House, she helped her husband feel comfortable talking about life's problems with political figures and leaders of industry. She also helped their guests experience the grandeur of the house. Herbert Hoover did not make conversation easily, unless he was talking about ways to manage, mine, or administer. He did, however, enjoy having many guests for dinner even though he was known to say few and, on occasion, no words at elaborate dinner parties. Lou Henry Hoover made her guests feel welcome, engaged them in the topics of the day, and lent a formal air to gatherings. As an example, she did not speak directly with the White House staff who served the dinners, preferring instead to employ an extensive set of hand gestures to indicate how and when courses would be served and cleared from the table or tables. David Kennedy, writing in *Freedom from Fear*, said of Lou Hoover, "She was a formidable woman who was his [Herbert Hoover's] lifelong shield against the intrusive world, the organizer of punctiliously correct dinner parties at which Hoover [Herbert] took refuge behind a mask of decorum and formality" (Kennedy 1999, 45).

A clip from the C-SPAN series about American presidents shows an instance where Lou's skill as a hostess and leader is better suited to politics than her husband's no-nonsense managerial style. We see Herbert, Lou, and other members of the Republican leadership coming together publicly to announce the decision of the party to name Hoover the Republican candidate for president in 1932. Lou is smiling and nodding to several of the people assembled. Herbert Hoover looks serious and is interacting with no one. After the brief announcement where a Republican senator says, "We're going to keep you," Hoover nods and says nothing. Someone whispers to him and then a voice is heard, "Say something." Lou smiles at her husband encouragingly. After several awkward moments pass, Hoover says, "I scarcely know whether to thank you for your good suggestion or not, but I do appreciate the character of the meeting which the party has had."[12] It is a stunning moment, one where Herbert Hoover is unaware of his immediate audience or the audience who will see the film at a later time, many of whom will vote in the next election.

At Christmas time in 1930, Lou Hoover employed creativity and her ability to get to the heart of things when she selected gifts that she would send to personal friends and White House attachés. During a renovation of the White House to replace original timbers, Lou Hoover learned that the original timbers were going to be destroyed. She had some of the wood salvaged and made into wooden boxes, bookends, bookmarkers, letter openers, and pen trays. With each gift, she included a poem that she had composed about the wood:

A pine tree on the hills of Maryland,—through many summers' heats and winters' snows,
Felled, carted, quartered, sawn,—a metamorphosis within a week.
And then a century buried deep within the White House walls,—unseen, unsung,
but one of myriads holding firm together the storied structure.
Until,—a new age came and replaced steel for wood.
Then months upon the dump-heap,—the dump cart actually arrived for one last ride,
—And then, a rescue. Now here I rest upon your desk for a short space; until,—
the wastebasket and the fire.
Then once again I'll go,—free smoke before free wind,—to touch again the hills of Maryland.
("Recollections of a Piece of Wood," White House, LHH Subject File)

Creating Traditions

Lou Hoover believed in music appreciation and demonstrated that value as she created the White House Arts Program which included thirty-minute concerts after state dinners and an afternoon series of Lenten Musicales. She insisted that these events be used to showcase American artists, both established and fledgling talents (Kirk 1994, 104–5). Her pioneering spirit was evident as she created the program and determined the type of talent that would define the program. Further, as Elise Kirk notes, "[s]he was the earliest first lady to bring black artists to the White House at a time when they were struggling to gain recognition in American theaters" (1994, 100). Hers was not a restrictive definition of "American talent," but an all-encompassing one.

She worked to preserve the architectural and design choices of the White House so its history would be accessible to those who followed her as first lady. To that end, she purchased exact reproductions of furnishings for the White House permanent collection. William Seale, who has written a two-volume history of the White House, indicates that the Monroe Room, formerly known as the Rose Parlor, was the "first historically 'restored' room in the White House—and one of the few ever attempted" (1994, 94).

With her interest in research and categorization, she compiled an inventory of the important holdings in the House, including photographs and descriptions, that is indispensable for presidents and first ladies as they work to keep the White House in good repair (Mayer 1994, xi). Years later, Jacqueline Kennedy was lauded for her restoration efforts that were made easier with the use of Lou Hoover's inventory.[13]

Lou Hoover's interest in architecture, in decorating, in reconfiguring spaces as she did in the houses she inhabited throughout her life, suggests a relationship between scene and purpose and its effects on the actors, in this case, the Hoovers.[14] When she came to the White House, she documented the furnishings. This is a historic site, one that is occupied by its residents, never owned. Lou Hoover had a particular appreciation for her role as a custodian of the White House, since she spent so much of her life, especially after her marriage to Herbert, moving all over the world. She cared for places, insured that her family was content in them and then moved on. And from the White House, she would move on in four to eight years, but not before the site's furnishings were organized as historical documents.

The idea of a retreat for the president of the United States began with the Hoovers.[15] Lou Hoover oversaw construction of Camp Rapidan in the Blue Ridge Mountains so that her husband would have a quiet place away from the business and relentless responsibilities of Washington, D.C. The location was also a cool escape from the summer heat of the capital. In a letter to friends on January 27, 1929, Lou Hoover outlined her thoughts on the camp project before construction began:

> My husband's idea was to have a camp down on one of the tree-covered flats beside a stream or at the junction between two streams. He likes to be near enough to hear the water murmuring. A spot might be found where part of the camp could be down there and part of it a hundred feet or so higher on one of the broad benches giving a distant view. (Letter to James Y. Rippin in Properties and Lots, LHH Subject File)

The following discussion is offered to illustrate how one of Herbert Hoover's preferences was attended to architecturally by his wife. He liked to dine with others, though he was often silent during these dinners. Understanding this trait in her husband, Lou Hoover talked about her ideas for one of the cabins in her letter to the Rippins:

> Conditions necessitate a rather biggish establishment. There must be room for 18 to 20 people to eat, with a feeling of spaciousness,—architecturally not gastronomically. And for the same number or more to sit in another portion of the same structure,—probably the two to open into each other, or to be a part of the same "room," to help with this feeling of spaciousness. (Letter to James Y. Rippin in Properties and Lots, LHH Subject File)

He ate quickly, even when he was at the camp relaxing, maintaining the habits he developed at the White House, particularly as economic conditions worsened after October 1929. Yet, he wanted to be in the company of others even if only in a visual sense and Lou Hoover ensured that he was, both at the White House and at Camp Rapidan.

She was concerned with every detail of the camp, even with what flowers and shrubs should be added to the landscape: "The President is very fond of color in gardens so where possible and appropriate to the species, arrange the flowering shrubs and flowers so as to give mass effects of color" ("Flowers and Shrubs for the President's Camp" in Properties and Lots, LHH Subject File).

Historian William Seale noted, "Mrs. Hoover's view on decorating and building seems to have been this: When one decorates, be subtle and artistic; when one restores, stick to the facts" (1994, 92). To that assessment I would add, when Lou Hoover decorated she considered how relationships could be sustained; when she designed and restored, she recorded the excavation and translation process so that others could benefit from it—goals which require attention to group dynamics and to rhetoric, in this instance, in the determination of architectural first principles.

As she was overseeing the construction of the camp, she became acquainted with the people who lived nearby and learned that the children did not go to school. That sad fact was soon rectified. Lou saw to it that a school was built with an apartment for a teacher, and one who was trained at Berea College was hired. The Herbert Hoover Mountain School opened on February 24, 1930 (Lambert 1971, 90–1). As an especially good neighbor, she was also demonstrating her commitment to universal education.

Perhaps the most dramatic example of her pioneering spirit is in her being the first first lady to broadcast a speech over the radio. This groundbreaking event occurred on April 19, 1929, when she dedicated Constitution Hall (Colbert 1998, 78). And she was first to speak on the radio from the White House, offering messages which stressed the importance of helping others. Historian Lewis L. Gould notes that "Mrs. Hoover's use of the radio to communicate her views on the Depression was her method of promoting the president's position that volunteerism and individual initiative, rather than government relief programs, were preferable responses to the economic distress" (1994, 66).

In addition to the messages about ways to pitch in during the Great Depression, there is the voice of the first lady on the radio leading the way in the use of technology. She was very familiar with radio, having listened to her husband grapple with the regulatory implications of the medium during his years as secretary of commerce. And she had a talent for it. In November 1931 a reporter noted,

> Mrs. Herbert Hoover is one of the best radio speakers on the air today, according to radio engineers. Her voice has a certain zip and tone quality which make it easy to handle. If she were not the President's wife, but was merely an American woman looking for a job, radio broadcasting would offer a secure future for her. (Clippings 1931, LHH Subject File)

Breaking Traditions

One of the expectations of a first lady at the time was that she entertain congressional wives for tea. On June 12, 1929, Lou Hoover presided over such an event as she had many times before, except this time Mrs. Oscar DePriest of Chicago was among the group of honored guests. All assembled were cordial to each other. The next day newspapers in the South were harshly critical of the afternoon tea because Mrs. DePriest, an African American, had been invited to the White House for a social event. Before the criticism subsided, Mrs. Hoover had been censured by the state legislatures of Florida and Texas (Gutin 2000, 40–41). While she was startled and upset by the strength of the attacks, she never faltered in her belief that her definitions of hospitality and protocol were the appropriate ones. The Harlem Registration League's resolution explains why the action was right: "Be it further resolved that . . . she [Lou Hoover] be appraised of the fact that we applaud her action in inviting Mrs. Oscar DePriest to the White House . . . and that it is our belief that the true American sentiment of the people of the United States will sustain her in this action" (DePriest Incident Approving Mrs. Hoover's Action, LHH Subject File). Here we see the first lady as a champion of civil rights.

During New Year's Day 1933, the Hoovers were away enjoying the holiday privately after the grueling election campaign. Lou Hoover did not believe standing for hours on end to shake the hand of thousands and thousands of citizens who came to the White House on New Year's Day to get a glimpse of the president and first lady was a productive use of time. Further the Hoovers would be leaving the White House in March 1933 on the orders of the citizenry. Lou had demonstrated her willingness to be an agent of change during the Harding administration when she challenged the practice of leaving cards, arguing that time could be spent more wisely. She took a decisive action again, and the New Year's Day tradition ended during the Hoover administration.

Legacy

After the White House years, Lou was ready to settle into the home that had been a dream of hers for many years, a home largely designed by her. While the Stanford House was nearly completed in 1921, the Hoovers did not spend much time there after Herbert was appointed secretary of commerce.[16] In 1933, a "permanent" return to California was possible. During a ten-day vacation in the Florida Keys shortly after Roosevelt's inauguration in March 1933, Herbert told Lou he did not want the Stanford House to serve as their primary home. National political action occurred on the East Coast. He didn't want to be away from it (Kirk 1994, 114). He took an apartment at the Waldorf Towers, a part of the Waldorf Astoria in New York City. They both traveled extensively in the years between 1933 and 1940 with Lou preferring California as home base and Herbert preferring New York City.

Lou Henry Hoover died at the apartment in New York on January 7, 1944, soon after her return from a concert by her friend, Mildred Dilling, an acclaimed harpist who had performed as part of the White House Arts Program. At the funeral, heads of state and celebrities who came to pay their respects were seated *behind* many girls dressed in green uniforms—Girl Scouts all (Mayer 1994, x, xii, 47). So, in the ritual of paying one's respects to the departed, she was publicly identified primarily for her accomplishments apart from her husband, the former president, and secondarily for the role she had played as his partner.

Several newspaper stories focused on the numbers of people at the service. (The count varied from 1000 to 1500 to 2000.) *The Palo Alto Times* reported Ray L. Wilbur's words. The chancellor of Stanford University said his friend was one of the American women "who took conditions as they found them and moulded them for a better future. There is no finer example of how to live than was given to us by Lou Henry Hoover" (Clippings 1944, Death of Mrs. Hoover, LHH Subject File).

Journalist and author Marianne Means's assessment of the role of the first lady informs how Lou Hoover was able to adapt to the myriad of changing circumstances in her life: "Every day hundreds of proud American mothers look at their new-born sons and reflect on the almost hopeless cliché, 'He may grow up to be President.' But I will wager that not a mother in history has held her infant daughter and dreamed that some day she might become First Lady. A woman usually marries the man she loves, and what happens to him will determine her life as well" (Means 1963, xii). Lou Henry married a man she cared about and with whom she would share world travel and an abundance of adventures in the pursuit of having her life make a difference.

In these pursuits, she excavated her way to what she could label the essential view, whether that was a moment in her translation efforts, or in her labors to categorize the holdings in the White House, or in her decision to invite Mrs. DePriest to tea at the White House. She got to the bones of a structure, to the essence of that particular structure, whether it was a structured encounter or a structure called home.

And, even in a hobby like collecting, she was interested in distilling practices to ascertain if any were universal. She noted that all civilizations had two things in common—the practice of employing servants and the use of weaponry. She decided to collect the weapons that were used in the countries she visited and resided in. She had always been comfortable with guns, having hunted as a young woman. During the Boxer Rebellion, she carried a sidearm.[17]

She had been accustomed to being first—she was the firstborn, the first woman to earn a geology degree from Stanford University, the first woman to win a prize from the Mining and Metallurgical Society of America. And then she became the first lady. The title of "first" was bestowed upon her in this instance because of her relationship with her husband in his political capacity as the president. And yet, even in this role, she also recorded some firsts. She was the first to categorize the holdings in the White House. She was first to acquire and design a retreat for the president. She was first to broadcast a speech on radio.

It is interesting to observe the persona Lou created when she was in her husband's company and when she was not. When she was in the picture *without* Herbert, she was a leader who moved the agenda forward, who was beloved as she performed the tasks expected of her as was evidenced by her election to positions of leadership in the Society of American Women, Girl Scouts, and the National Amateur Athletic Federation. A journalist who covered the Girl Scout convention held in Minneapolis in 1936, said, "After watching Mrs. Herbert Hoover move about among people for three days, I can quite understand why women who knew her well always spoke of her as 'Lou Henry Hoover' instead of 'the wife of the President' during those years she was the first lady of the nation" ("Simplicity of Mrs. Hoover Just One of Many Graces" by Bess M. Wilson in Articles, Addresses, and Statements, LHH Subject File).

After her death the Girl Scouts named their conservation projects for her, calling them the Lou Henry Hoover Memorial Forests and Memorial Wildlife Sanctuaries. The published tribute concludes by saying:

> The majority of people who loved their youth and are grateful for it want to
> pass on to younger girls and women what they themselves learned. Lou Henry
> Hoover was even wiser. She wanted to give to youth the places and conditions
> where the wise things are best learned. The woods, the rivers, the trails, the
> hills, the fire-ring in the dark—all to be lived in and learned by, in fun and
> companionship. ("Lou Henry Hoover: A Tribute from the Girl Scouts, 1944" in
> Girl Scouts and Other Groups, LHH Subject File)

She was politically astute, understanding and responding well to the needs of her
constituents, be they children or adults.

When she was in the picture *with* her husband, she seemed to dress the stage
to suit her husband. As a geologist, she had a sophisticated understanding of the
substance of things, an understanding that informed her definition of her role,
which was to support her husband's predictable patterns of behavior, even if she
would have made different political choices had she been in charge. That is not
to say she did not have a deep respect for her husband's talent and energy. In a
letter to their sons in July 1932, she wrote:

> I have watched him at close range ever since he went out into the world from
> college, and with the very slight exceptions of the times at the very first, when
> he was the least important employee of his group, and was concerned primarily
> with making bread and butter and room rent for himself while he worked a
> typewriter in a mining engineer's office or swung a pick and shovel under-
> ground,—with those very early and absolutely essential exceptions, the main
> motives of his activities have been for other people, for people less fortunately
> situated than himself. (Personal Correspondence, 1929–33, LHH Subject File)

As she was leaving the White House on Inauguration Day in March 1933, she
told the staff, "My husband will live to do great things for his country" (Allen
2000, 154). The hurt was for him. She did not share, in this moment, how she
was feeling but rather how much she believed in him. She was her husband's
helpmate.

And she helped future first ladies. Eleanor Roosevelt witnessed Lou Henry
Hoover's organizational skill, especially as they both worked to develop the Girl
Scouts of America. Jacqueline Kennedy could have read of Lou's work to bring
the arts to the White House. Certainly her catalogue of the furnishings in the
White House would have informed Kennedy's restoration efforts.

As scholars mine her papers, her contributions are there to be found, to be
discovered anew. Though she and Herbert Hoover understood the importance of
archives for historical research and even started one that is now known as the
Hoover Institution on War, Revolution, and Peace, Lou Hoover did not seem to
be concerned that her contributions would be of great use to posterity. Add to
that her husband's decision to have her papers available for study twenty years
after his death and you have a forty-year gap in the record, with the exception of
Helen Pryor's 1969 biography.

Historian Betty Caroli notes that a comment made by Lou near the end of
her life is startling. Lou says, "I have been lucky to have my trail move alongside that of such exceptional men and boys" (Caroli 1995, 184). In her tribute to

her family, she leaves her trailblazing contributions out of the picture, privileging the notion of republican motherhood, as she also did in her role as a leader in the Girl Scouts of America. She is both ahead of her time and a product of her time, using her considerable leadership abilities to bring people together to help each other and not to shine the light on herself.

Notes

I would like to thank the Herbert Hoover Presidential Library Association for awarding me a travel grant in June 1999 to examine Lou Henry Hoover's Papers at the Herbert Hoover Presidential Library and Museum in West Branch, Iowa. Special thanks to archivists Dwight M. Miller, now retired, and Dale C. Mayer for their willingness to answer my questions and to help me use my time with the documents efficiently.

1. *Public Papers of the Presidents of the United States: Herbert Hoover* 1974, 1.
2. Lou Henry and Herbert Hoover had two sons. Herbert Clark Jr. was born on August 4, 1903. Allan Henry was born on July 17, 1907. Herbert Jr. grew up to work for TWA, Transworld Airlines, and in 1940, he founded the United Geophysical Company, an oil exploration firm. Allan ran several ranches owned by his father and developed one of the first farm shipping operations in the United States, Anne Beiser Allen (2000, 161).
3. The section of the museum exhibit about the world travels of the Hoovers notes that Herbert Jr. and Allan took clocks apart with screwdrivers during ocean voyages, Herbert Hoover Presidential Library and Museum, June 1999. Helen B. Pryor, M.D. writes about the boys working on the clocks on a "long train trip from New York to San Francisco" (1969, 80).
4. The uprising had begun as a turn against Christians and particularly the foreign missionaries who had encouraged the Chinese to convert. It became an indictment of all foreigners, with Chinese peasants fearful that the north of China would become a colony of the West. The ranks of the Boxers grew, in part, because of an unrelenting drought. With no work to do, young men could do little but wait for rain. During idle days, many in the north watched the Boxers practice—an activity that was part maneuver, part ritual, part theater—and, intrigued by the activity, ended up joining the new association. This social movement, enlarged by the dry climactic conditions, was changed—and ultimately diluted—because the members of the association were not always linked by a sense of common goal (Esherick 1987, 271–313).
5. The translated book, *De Re Metallica* that earned the Hoovers the prize was dedicated to the professor who had introduced the two of them to geology and to each other, and who, near the end of his career, served as president of their beloved Stanford University, Dr. John Casper Branner.
6. It is interesting to note that the article in the *New York Times* (March 10, 1914, 11), which reported the awarding of the gold medal by the Mining and Metallurgical Society of America, was titled "Miners Honor a Woman." The lead for the story at this point in time was that a woman was honored, not that the work was recognized for its brilliance.
7. Lou Henry and Herbert Hoover were with the Harding party in Alaska when Warren G. Harding fell ill and died.
8. Juliette Gordon Low had hoped to work for Herbert Hoover on the Belgian relief effort. By the time her citizenship status was properly defined—American not British—all the jobs were filled. But during this time, she began a lifelong friendship with Lou Hoover, later expressed in their shared commitment to the Girl Scouts (Shultz and Law-

rence (1958, 335).

9. These themes are detailed in a document called "Outlines for Speakers." The document, prepared by members of the leadership of the Girl Scouts of America and revised regularly, divides each speech outline into the following categories: subject, purpose, note, talking points, references, and quotations. This resource would have been a useful guide for leaders as they were preparing remarks and would have served to ensure that the Girl Scout message be consistent ("Girl Scouts Speakers Kit, 1934" in Girl Scouts and Other Groups, LHH Subject File).

10. For an extended discussion of the notion of republican motherhood, see Linda K. Kerber's *Women of the Republic* (1986).

11. Camp Rapidan is now cared for by the U.S. Park Service and is called Camp Hoover. The school buildings are no longer there.

12. *American Presidents: Herbert C. Hoover* (1999).

13. The catalogue of the White House furnishings, while it was not published, is of publishable quality.

14. Kenneth Burke discusses the pentad—act, actor, scene, purpose, and agency—as a way to understand what motivates people to take action, see *A Grammar of Motives* (1969, 3–20).

15. Camp Rapidan serves as the first instance of a retreat for the president that was intended to be a permanent contribution to the office of the presidency. The Coolidges used an Adirondack Great Camp as the Summer White House from July 7 to September 18, 1926. Franklin Roosevelt built Shangri-La, which is now known as Camp David. The Hoovers built this first recreational facility with federal and personal funds and deeded it to the government at the end of Herbert Hoover's term of office as president. It was not used extensively or at all by any subsequent president.

16. The home in Palo Alto, California, referred to as the Stanford House, now serves as the residence for the president of Stanford University.

17. Many of the weapons collected by Lou Henry Hoover during the family's years abroad are held at the Herbert Hoover Presidential Library and Museum.

References

Allen, Anne Beiser. 2000. *An Independent Woman: The Life of Lou Henry Hoover*. Westport, Conn.: Greenwood.

American Presidents: Herbert C. Hoover. 1999. C-SPAN, 8 October.

Boller, Paul F., Jr. 1998. *Presidential Wives: An Anecdotal History*, 2nd ed. New York: Oxford University Press.

Burke, Kenneth. 1969. *A Grammar of Motives*. Berkeley, Calif.: University of California Press.

Caroli, Betty Boyd. 1995. *First Ladies*, expanded edition. New York: Oxford University Press.

Colbert, Nancy A. 1998. *Lou Henry Hoover: The Duty to Serve*. Greensboro, N.C.: Morgan Reynolds.

Esherick, Joseph W. 1987. *The Origins of the Boxer Uprising*. Berkeley, Calif.: University of California Press.

Gould, Lewis L. 1994. A Neglected First Lady: A Reappraisal of Lou Henry Hoover. In *Lou Henry Hoover: Essays on a Busy Life*, ed. Dale C. Mayer, 63–77. Worland, Wyo.: High Plains Publishing.

———, ed. 1996. *American First Ladies: Their Lives and Their Legacy*. New York: Garland Publishing.

Gutin, Myra G. 1989. *The President's Partner: The First Lady in the Twentieth Century.* Westport, Conn.: Greenwood.

———. 2000. Ten Defining Moments in the History of the American First Lady. *National Forum*, 80:1, 40–44.

Hoover, Herbert. 1951–1952. *Memoirs.* New York: Macmillan.

———. 1962. *On Growing Up: His Letters from and to American Children.* New York: William Morrow.

Hoover, Irwin Hood (Ike). 1934. *Forty-two Years in the White House.* Boston: Houghton Mifflin.

Hoover, Lou Henry Papers. LHH Subject Files. Herbert Hoover Presidential Library and Museum, West Branch, Iowa.

Kennedy, David M. 1999. *Freedom from Fear: The American People in Depression and War, 1929–1945.* New York: Oxford University Press.

Kerber, Linda K. 1986. *Women of the Republic: Intellect and Ideology in Revolutionary America.* New York: Norton.

Kirk, Elise. 1994. Lou Henry Hoover: First Lady in the Arts. In *Lou Henry Hoover: Essays on a Busy Life,* ed. Dale C. Mayer, 99–112. Worland, Wyo.: High Plains Publishing.

Lambert, Darwin. 1971. *Herbert Hoover's Hideaway.* Luray, Va.: Shenandoah Natural History Association.

Mayer, Dale C. 1990. An Uncommon Woman: The Quiet Leadership Style of Lou Henry Hoover. *Presidential Studies Quarterly,* 20:4, 685–98.

———, ed. 1994. *Lou Henry Hoover: Essays on a Busy Life.* Worland, Wyo.: High Plains Publishing.

Means, Marianne. 1963. *The Woman in the White House: The Lives, Times and Influence of Twelve Notable First Ladies.* New York: Random House.

Miners Honor a Woman. 1914. *New York Times* 10 March, 11.

Museum Exhibit, 1999. The Herbert Hoover Presidential Library and Museum, West Branch, Iowa.

Parks, Lillian Rogers. 1961. *My Thirty Years Backstairs at the White House.* New York: Fleet Publishing.

Pryor, Helen B. 1969. *Lou Henry Hoover: Gallant First Lady.* New York: Dodd, Mead.

Public Papers of the Presidents of the United States: Containing the Public Messages, Speeches, and Statements of the President. 1974. Herbert Hoover—March 4 to December 31, 1929. Washington, D.C.: U.S. Government Printing Office.

Randolph, Mary. 1936. *Presidents and First Ladies.* New York: D. Appleton-Century.

Reviews of Books—Georgius Agricola: *De Re Metallica.* 1914. *American Historical Review,* 19:2, 597–99.

Seale, William. 1986. *The President's House: A History,* Vol. 2. Washington, D.C.: White House Historical Association.

———. 1994. Lou Henry Hoover and the White House. In *Lou Henry Hoover: Essays on a Busy Life,* ed. Dale C. Mayer, 79–97. Worland, Wyo.: High Plains Publishing.

Shultz, Gladys Denny, and Daisy Gordon Lawrence. 1958. *Lady from Savannah: The Life of Juliette Low.* Philadelphia: J. B. Lippincott.

Walch, Timothy, and Dwight M. Miller, eds. 1998. *Herbert Hoover and Franklin D. Roosevelt: A Documentary History.* Westport, Conn.: Greenwood.

Watson, Martha. 1999. *Lives of Their Own: Rhetorical Dimensions in Autobiographies of Women Activists.* Columbia, S.C.: University of South Carolina Press.

Wilson, Joan Hoff. 1975. *Herbert Hoover: Forgotten Progressive.* Boston: Little, Brown.

Chapter 10

Eleanor Roosevelt
A Rhetorical Reconstruction of First Ladydom

Lisa R. Barry

I am in a position where I can do the most good to help the most people.

Women, whether subtly or vociferously, have always been a tremendous power in the destiny of the world and with so many of them now holding important positions and receiving recognition and earning the respect of the men as well as the members of their own sex, it seems more than ever that in this crisis, *It's Up to the Women!*

—Eleanor Roosevelt

Eleanor Roosevelt was a prolific speaker and writer. Thousands of speech transcripts, writings, and articles are housed in the Franklin Delano Roosevelt Library, the Franklin and Eleanor Roosevelt Institute, the Library of Congress, and in books and periodicals. Many scholars have dedicated their careers to examining Mrs. Roosevelt's activities and legacy as a first lady.[1] Rather than re-create their studies, this chapter focuses on the ways in which Mrs. Roosevelt used both oral and written rhetoric to educate women who were recently enfranchised.

Mrs. Roosevelt's rhetorical strategies took many forms. At times, she spoke only to women, such as during her three hundred press conferences that were open only to female reporters. This rhetorical action helped at least some women gain meaningful careers. She also spoke directly to women through a variety of columns such as *My Day* and *If You Ask Me,* which provided Mrs. Roosevelt a means of educating women about civic responsibility. Her press conferences help us understand how she supported women's work outside of the home, while her other writings, collected in book form as *It's Up to the Women,* help us understand her belief that women are necessary for a healthy public sphere.

Eleanor Roosevelt took her role as first lady seriously, turning it into a position with long-term effects. According to presidential historian Doris Kearns Goodwin, "She was the first president's wife to hold—and lose—a government job, the first to testify before a congressional committee, the first to hold press conferences, to speak before a national party convention, to write a syndicated column, to be a radio commentator, to earn money as a lecturer" (1994, 10). She effectively changed the role of the first lady from a predominantly social hostess role to a social activist. Indeed, "She shattered the ceremonial mold in which the role of the first lady had traditionally been fashioned, and reshaped it around her own skills and commitments to social reform" (Goodwin 1994, 10).

Mrs. Roosevelt's many speeches and articles often addressed women's special ability to recognize social issues such as racism and working conditions and their capacity to solve these problems.[2] Because cameras were often focused on her, Mrs. Roosevelt worked hard to ensure that she was surrounded by women. Thus, in many photographs she is shown meeting with women of all races, classes, and professions. Together, these artifacts speak to the special emphasis she placed on the importance of women in the public sphere and demonstrate her commitment to social feminism. Ultimately, she worked to educate the nation about its immense potential made possible only through the inclusion of women and the recognition that all individuals in a society are important to its health, happiness, and success.

Eleanor Roosevelt's personal investment in the success of the individual drove her rhetoric, which was neither as polished nor as smooth as her husband's. She was an ordinary person speaking to and with ordinary people.[3] A close analysis of *It's Up to the Women,* one of her key monographs, demonstrates how Mrs. Roosevelt achieved a balance between the personal and political that made her such a viable and important first lady. She used neither speechwriters nor ghostwriters, so a close analysis of her edited compilation of speeches and columns provides insight into her stance on key issues and her rhetorical skill in articulating them. My analysis illuminates the rhetorical strategies she used to construct an identity consistent with, but separate from, her husband's. This identity encompassed many elements, including the traditional roles of wife, mother, and especially educator. Importantly, she taught school before embarking on what was to become a respected political career.

Eleanor Roosevelt has garnered much scholarly attention, however, scholars have not interpreted her many writings, interviews, and speeches as a rhetorical attempt to educate the nation. Most scholars agree that she was more involved in politics and in her husband's decisions than any first lady before her.[4] This chapter seeks to demonstrate that Mrs. Roosevelt's political involvement not only fulfilled her personally, as Maurine Beasley (1987) claims, but also enabled her to educate the nation about the importance of all its people—women, minorities, the underprivileged, the ill—in the development of a peaceful and equitable society. *It's Up to the Women* is a particularly useful text for illuminating how she incorporated her beliefs into all that she wrote and said and, in so doing, became the nation's teacher. The analysis of her book provides an opportunity to explore how Mrs. Roosevelt rhetorically reconstructed the role of first lady as she negotiated her public and private personae.

Biography

Born Anna Eleanor Roosevelt on October 11, 1884, Eleanor Roosevelt was the only daughter of an alcoholic father and a beautiful, but often aloof, socialite mother who publicly criticized her daughter's homely and unattractive appearance. Eleanor was insecure about her appearance and her future, especially whether she would be able to achieve the social status of her mother. Her home life was somewhat unstable as her father frequently traveled for business or attended medical facilities because of his alcoholism. Despite this, Eleanor and her father were emotionally very close. When her mother died in 1892, Eleanor and her siblings went to live with their grandmother who was better able to care for them. Her father died two years later, and her grandmother, Mary Hall, became her guardian (Gould 1996, 424). Because of her father's death, Eleanor felt empty, alone, and unsure about her grandmother's ability to guide her. However, her grandmother sent her to London's Allenswood Academy in 1899, a school that proved extremely influential in setting her future course.

Eleanor studied under Mademoiselle Marie Souvestra, "a bold, articulate woman whose commitment to liberal causes and detailed study of history played a key role in shaping Eleanor's social and political development" (Gould 1996, 424). Eleanor considered the three years spent at Allenswood the happiest of her adolescence; she formed close friendships that lasted throughout her life, studied subjects such as language and history, "learned to state her opinions on controversial political events clearly and concisely" (Gould 1996, 424), and gained confidence and independence. When Eleanor returned to New York, she joined the National Consumers League and became active in other social movements. Her devotion, enthusiasm, and commitment to these political activities garnered her a reputation in New York reform circles as an asset to their causes. These activities also gave her practical political experience and helped refine her political beliefs.

Eleanor was reacquainted with her cousin Franklin Delano Roosevelt (FDR) during the summer of 1902, and, after a year of secret meetings, the two announced their engagement on November 22, 1903. Franklin's mother disapproved and attempted to separate the couple, but they married on March 17, 1905. President Theodore Roosevelt, Eleanor's uncle, gave her away in the ceremony. She spent the next eleven years as a dutiful wife during which she bore six children, one of whom died in infancy. She admitted that she had not been prepared for nor had she understood what being a loving wife and mother entailed, but she dutifully attended to both. Her marriage was not ideal, though, and when she mistakenly opened a letter to her husband that revealed his romantic affair with her former social secretary Lucy Mercer (in whose arms he later died), she offered to divorce him. He refused, and their relationship became a formal one that took on the characteristics of a business partnership. This proved to be advantageous for both; FDR had a trusted confidante and Mrs. Roosevelt had the opportunity to pursue her own political and professional interests.

Although she had placed her political career on hold while she raised her children, Mrs. Roosevelt resumed it when FDR served in the New York senate, 1911–1913. During her husband's tenure as assistant secretary of the navy, she continued to hone her political skills. When he was paralyzed with polio in 1921, she became active in the women's division of the State Democratic Committee; her purpose was to maintain *his* political interests by becoming an integral member of a powerful political team.

Mrs. Roosevelt shocked the nation when she said that she would not leave her job if her husband were elected to the presidency. "During [FDR's] four years in the Albany statehouse, Eleanor had traveled down to New York City to teach three days a week at her school on East Sixty-fifth Street, and she saw no reason why his transfer to Washington should alter her schedule or stop her from doing what she 'enjoyed more than anything I have ever done'" (Caroli 1987, 185). Prior to her husband's election, she had formed two business partnerships with other women: "one to operate a school in New York City and the other to manufacture furniture at Hyde Park" (Caroli 1995, 189).

FDR was elected to the presidency in 1933, and, because of his physical condition and her political and social knowledge, she became his eyes and ears. During World War II, Mrs. Roosevelt traveled the world and reported to her husband. Her travels resulted in widespread public admiration for a woman who truly cared about the American people. The many photographs taken during her travels demonstrate her commitment to people; she was often seen with people of color and with women.

Mrs. Roosevelt delivered many speeches, wrote daily columns that appeared in newspapers and magazines, wrote several books, and compiled her speech transcripts and columns into other books. She held regular press conferences, as we have seen, limiting attendance to female journalists in an effort to help them gain entry into an otherwise male-dominated industry. These rhetorical activities provided an opportunity for her to speak out against racism, segregation, and sexism. She was particularly vocal about her opposition to Jim Crow and her support of women's rights. When she equated American racism with fascism and argued that segregation would lead to Aryanism, J. Edgar Hoover— then director of the Federal Bureau of Investigation—attempted to silence her. She was not silent, however, and continued to educate American citizens about the plight of marginalized groups in the United States. Part of this effort included capitalizing on photo opportunities by surrounding herself with women and people of color.[5] Mrs. Roosevelt was not always popular; her opposition to racism and her support of social advancement and education for colored people earned her many enemies.

Although Mrs. Roosevelt spoke publicly about her opposition to existing social and political practices, she was careful not to publicly challenge her husband's New Deal policies. She was very influential during his presidency, and some reporters speculated about whether she ran the White House instead of her husband.

As mentioned earlier, Mrs. Roosevelt engaged in a variety of rhetorical activities, many of which she compiled into books. For purposes of clarity, this analysis focuses on her press conferences and her book *It's Up to the Women*. Rather than examining specific press conferences, I will discuss their general themes and show how she used the press conference as a rhetorical tool. I will also offer a close analysis of *It's Up to the Women*, because she selected the contents carefully to represent her political and philosophical beliefs.[6]

Rhetorical Activities as First Lady

Despite her childhood insecurities, Eleanor Roosevelt became a confident woman concerned with the rights of all people regardless of race, creed, religion, class, or gender. She learned a considerable amount from her political activities when her husband was senator of New York and assistant secretary of the navy. Her friendship with reporter Louis McHenry Howe and later with Lorena Hickok also enabled her to attain the skills she needed to address audiences as well as the knowledge that fueled her activism. When she entered the White House in 1933, she was prepared to embark on a personally fulfilling public political career.[7]

Women's rights was a key issue that Mrs. Roosevelt tackled during her years in the White House. As first lady, she held approximately 300 press conferences, restricting attendance to female reporters. She knew that news organizations would have to hire women in order to gain access to her. Other issues she addressed include the rights of African Americans, subsistence farmsteads, and World War II. She also campaigned on behalf of her husband's New Deal and sought ways to improve the quality of life for the less fortunate; the letters she received from her constituents influenced her deeply. She addressed these issues in approximately 1400 speeches, lectures, radio broadcasts, and short statements that she delivered between 1933 and 1945, as well as in magazine and newspaper articles, books, and autobiographies (Gutin 1989, 97). She also "wrote, without a ghost writer, four autobiographies, seven monographs, seven children's books, and more than 550 articles. . . . In February 1933, she began a monthly column, which existed in a variety of forms until her death in November 1962. On December 30, 1935, she began 'My Day,' a 500-word column published five days a week, which ran continuously until September 27, 1962" (Black 1999, 2). As we have seen, she condensed what she believed were the most telling aspects of her speeches and columns (many of which were also collected in other book-length manuscripts) in *It's Up to the Women*. All of these texts may be viewed as distinct rhetorical artifacts that demonstrate Mrs. Roosevelt's abiding interest in social issues and her passion for teaching— persuading—all Americans to understand their importance.

She believed her projects could resolve social issues and was thus able to convey a sincerity that her audiences readily perceived. Because many of the issues she cared about fell comfortably under the purview of women's concerns (nurture, domesticity, peace), she furthered feminist causes while she simultaneously presented herself as the country's matriarch and the nation's educator. Beasley acknowledges that Mrs. Roosevelt "assumed the role of an instructor for American women on various social topics during [her] press conferences." Her skill at "disguising" her politics enabled her to "[establish] herself at the center of a network of those involved in women's causes" even "if governmental action or policy changes did not result from the issues discussed" (Beasley 1987, 59). She was a feminist fighting for feminist causes years before doing so was fashionable.[8]

Press Conferences

As a first lady who refused the traditional constraints associated with the role of first lady, Eleanor Roosevelt made certain that her public activities were newsworthy and used them as an opportunity to educate her constituency. Mrs. Roosevelt's press conferences helped to establish female reporters as worthy of more than social news. Media historian Maurine Beasley states, "many of the thirty-five women reporters who assembled for Mrs. Roosevelt's first press conference had struggled against the handicap of their sex to attain journalistic careers" (1987, 38). Mrs. Roosevelt limited attendance at her press conferences to only one female reporter from each of the Washington newspapers (Beasley 1987, 41). As a result, many Washington newspapers scrambled to hire female reporters so they could gain access to the first lady. They hoped she would reveal insights about her husband's political agenda, but they believed that she would also contribute information that readers of the social columns would find interesting. Many male reporters believed the press conferences would be social gatherings and disregarded them entirely.

Commonly referred to as "newspaper girls," Mrs. Roosevelt attempted to alter the inequities that many of the thirty-five reporters in attendance faced. They were not allowed membership in the National Press Club where prominent figures often appeared, so they created their own professional group, the Women's National Press Club. However, they still had difficulty gaining access to prominent figures and were often consigned to soft news stories such as social functions. Because Mrs. Roosevelt limited attendance at her press conferences to women, she attempted to provide them the same opportunities afforded to their male counterparts.

Beasley claims that the publication of a well-known photograph taken at the second press conference, March 13, 1933, prompted resentment and contempt by male reporters who perceived the conferences as social gatherings disguised as political meetings. This photograph showed Mrs. Roosevelt with the female reporters gathered around her—some standing, some sitting on the floor near her feet.[9] Although the photograph was intended to promote the legitimacy of women's work and the value of female reporters, "The pose prompted masculine competitors to dub the group 'the incense burners,' and gave them an excuse to scoff at the gatherings, which they initially had scorned" (Beasley 1987, 47).

Although the press conferences appeared to be entirely social, they were not, nor were they simply for show. Mrs. Roosevelt agreed to have weekly personal contact with reporters, which broke all precedents for a first lady's press relations, and her reasons for doing so had significant implications. At the first press conference, held March 6, 1933, Mrs. Roosevelt was nervous, unsure as to how much she should play the role of hostess, the traditional role most first ladies had enacted. She was, however, clear about her purpose: she wanted the reporters to use their articles for educative purposes to teach the American public—especially women—how the government worked. At that meeting, Mrs. Roosevelt labeled female reporters "interpreters to the women of the country as to what goes on politically in the legislative national life and also what the social and personal life is at the White House" (Beasley 1987, 38). Mrs. Roosevelt recognized the value of these reporters as a means to communicate directly to U.S. women; she claimed that a female reporter's job was, "to make her impressions go to leading the women in the country to form a general attitude of mind and thought" (Beasley 1987, 38).

Clearly, Mrs. Roosevelt saw herself as a teacher charged with educating U.S. women about civic responsibility, and the reporters were the means by which she distributed her lessons. At one conference, Mrs. Roosevelt taught women how to read a newspaper properly and encouraged them to read three newspapers with opposing viewpoints on a daily basis, so they could form their own opinions and reach their own conclusions about social and political issues. Personally, she feared she would lose her political identity as the result of her husband's election, so she used the press conferences to construct a public persona, one related to, but separate from, the president's.

Mrs. Roosevelt worked to "disguise" her political involvement during press conferences, hoping to maintain what Beasley (1987, 61) classifies as, "the conventional fiction that a president's wife should remain aloof from politics." Yet, by the time her husband was elected, she already had a well-established political career. Not only had she raised a family, taught school, and managed a business, she had also, "coordinated statewide and national political campaigns, chaired investigative committees and statewide reform organizations, became a respected lobbyist, launched a career as a journalist, and . . . developed a reputation in her own right as a skilled politician who refused to abandon her commitment to democratic ideals" (Black 1999, 2). She did not want to abandon these activities to become merely a social hostess. Doing otherwise, however, would too obviously challenge established beliefs about the proper role and activities of a first lady. The press conferences offered her the opportunity to act politically while at the same time appearing to adhere to the constraints of first ladydom.

Because she limited attendance to female reporters, male reporters and editors dismissed the conferences as soft news, social gossip, and so on. Under this disguise, Mrs. Roosevelt championed women's right to work, to do so with equal pay, and women's role in politics, among other political and social issues.

According to historian Allida Black (1999, 2), "Although other first ladies had been active behind the scenes, they had concealed their influence from the public, leaving [Mrs. Roosevelt] no overt precedent to follow for public activism on behalf of social change and public policy." Mrs. Roosevelt saw herself as a teacher and the press conferences as "classes" of a sort, and so her activities were consistent with those in women's traditional sphere of teaching. Thus, she was able to perform a traditionally feminine activity while she simultaneously challenged and enlarged the role of the first lady. She was able to balance the feminine and the feminist in ways that often went unchallenged.

Presidents traditionally hold press conferences, but Mrs. Roosevelt was the first first lady to make herself available to the press on a regular basis. She was encouraged by her husband and his advisors to discuss only social issues such as parties and gatherings, but Mrs. Roosevelt refused. She did mention social events occasionally, but only if they provided a means by which to approach other more political issues. Clearly, her press conferences were the first attempt at political communication by a first lady, and as the conferences progressed, Mrs. Roosevelt became increasingly skilled as a rhetor.

The press conferences benefited both Mrs. Roosevelt and the journalists who became her close friends. Often the reporters gave her advice about how to conduct the conferences, and in time several helped her plan them to ensure they would have news to report that would impress their male counterparts. Sometimes, "they planted questions, proposed topics, and coached on the wording of statements. Sometimes Mrs. Roosevelt accepted their advice; other times she did not" (Beasley 1987, 51). Together, they worked to educate women of the country about politics, human rights, civic responsibility, and at times, about Mrs. Roosevelt's personal life.

Mrs. Roosevelt's press conferences were an effective rhetorical tool for teaching the country about certain issues, but they did not neatly present the entirety of her political and philosophical beliefs. Moreover, reporters sometimes edited or characterized her comments in ways Mrs. Roosevelt did not always agree with. As a result, her press conferences alone do not adequately represent her efforts to educate the nation's women. Therefore, it is necessary to examine her personal writings; in particular, her 1933 book, *It's Up to the Women*, which she presented as a tool for women to use as they worked to establish new roles and identities. It covered much of the same material as her press conferences, but in a more succinct manner. Because Mrs. Roosevelt authored and compiled the book, we can assume that it accurately reflects her personal philosophy on life, love, and politics in ways her press conferences could not.

It's Up to the Women

"Rushed into print in November 1933, the book contained a compilation of Mrs. Roosevelt's speeches and articles urging women to sacrifice, volunteer and become politically active to make the best of hard times" (Beasley 1987, 72). Although it might be argued that all of Mrs. Roosevelt's speeches, columns, letters, and articles sought to educate the citizens of this country, this monograph in particular reads like an educational tool and is consistent with her early attempts to appear as if she were adhering to conventional feminine activities.

Because she had successfully raised a family and cared for a sick husband, she possessed an identity consistent with societal norms and expectations for women. She fulfilled her roles as mother and wife, only then did she turn to projects that enabled her to fulfill her own needs and desires. Her work enabled her to create a separate identity that was consistent with her own personality; at heart, she was an activist and educator as well as a mother and wife. Importantly, as a teacher she chose to focus her lessons on issues that were consistent with society's beliefs about women and women's concerns. Thus, she was able to further a feminist agenda by encouraging women to read and think while simultaneously "disguising" that agenda through her choice of subjects and her persona as the country's matriarch.

It's Up to the Women covers many of Mrs. Roosevelt's beliefs, especially her strong belief in the role that women must play to help the country survive the Great Depression. She attributes that belief to historical precedent, that is, the role women have already played in helping the pilgrims survive starvation and our fledgling forces overcome the British during the Revolutionary War. She argues that the first winter in New England was devastating, "a real battle in which many women and children paid with their lives for their heroism" (viii). Although she admits that the Great Depression is different from other crises faced by the United States, she insists that women can pull the United States out of its current crisis, and her book is dedicated to that purpose: "Perhaps we need again a little of the stern stuff our ancestors were made of. In any case, it will do us no harm to look at ourselves somewhat critically in relation to some of the problems that confront us to-day [sic]" (x).

Mrs. Roosevelt suggests many ways that women might contribute to the country's success, not the least of which is to discuss women in relation to various jobs. Yet she recognizes that the only way for women to gain and retain a job outside the home is to maintain their duties inside the home (this double bind persists today). Mrs. Roosevelt argues that women are fully capable of doing both.

The book offers twenty chapters that deal with various concerns women have and the challenges they face, including budgets, time management, recreation, and health. Of particular importance for this analysis are those chapters that address women and jobs, education, family life, working conditions, and peace. These chapters will be discussed in the order they appear in her book.

In the first chapter, "To-day's Challenge to Women," Mrs. Roosevelt establishes a matriarchal identity, offering motherly advice in a way that not only makes sense, but also comforts us. In an attempt to reinforce an identity that audiences would be comfortable with, she focuses on what was known about her; she relies on her reputation as a devoted mother and wife. She draws upon that as she uses the book to counsel women to look beyond a man's earning power and focus on his qualities as a person when choosing a spouse.

The Great Depression factors heavily in this discourse, but Mrs. Roosevelt is able to convey motherly concern and wisdom as she encourages all people to focus on their roles as spouse, parent, neighbor, and citizen. At the same time, she sets the stage for commentary about women's work and their ability to contribute to the family income. Thus, she uses a rhetorical strategy whereby she conforms to societal expectations, but, at the same time, works to develop a constituency of women who will be motivated to take action on their own behalf and on behalf of others. Mrs. Roosevelt also invites the audience, both men and women, to perceive themselves as able to contribute to the country's well-being, regardless of their economic status. She offers the kind of faith in our potential that is typical of motherly and teacherly advice, and we embrace it.

The next chapter of interest in the book is chapter 8, "Modern Family Conditions." In it, Mrs. Roosevelt addresses family composition and divorce. She recognizes that the increasing number of women holding professional jobs is changing traditional expectations and understandings of the family. She does not advocate divorce, but counsels acceptance when it is the best course of action. Making marriage more difficult to enter into, she claims, might be the answer: "I personally think that probably it would be wiser if marriage were made far more difficult" (124). Here she might be reflecting her own marital unhappiness, hoping that the younger generation will not marry out of necessity or tradition, but rather for reasons far more meaningful. In this chapter, she also recognizes the need for society to understand and accept men in general and women's work. In fact, she claims that she *expects* women to work; this point she makes in the chapter's last sentence when she says that women are now more likely to hold jobs outside the home.

Mrs. Roosevelt uses her position as first lady as a platform for advocating women's rights, just as she uses her matriarchal persona to discuss the family with regard to marriage and divorce. She advocates tolerance of societal changes, but she insists that the family will persist. She counteracts the nation's concerns with a discussion of Russia, where a movement occurred in which children were to grow up in professional homes and the family was to become obsolete. Even there, she claims, the family persisted and the movement died. Knowing that U.S. society holds the family in high regard, she argues that women's ability to hold jobs outside the home need not necessarily compromise the family and, with a little tolerance and acceptance, the family will persist. Mrs. Roosevelt thus "camouflages" a political issue—women's rights—with a discussion grounded in the family, nurture, and tradition. She does not call attention to her discussion as political, but works toward political ends. She constructs an identity that appears concerned with life, love, happiness, and trust—a persona befitting the country's matriarch. At the same time, she constructs an identity that demonstrates knowledge and wisdom, and offers guidance and counsel—a persona befitting the nation's educator.

Of particular importance in the book is the chapter that discusses types of positions women should pursue and subtly restates her views on women's work. Chapter 11, "Women and Jobs," begins with a tacit acknowledgment of societal concerns, "Nowadays there is a great deal of agitation as to whether married women should work or not and in order to consider the question, I think we should go back a little bit further and consider whether women should work at all" (142). Mrs. Roosevelt neatly articulates the issue and uses it as a starting point for a discussion of women's "proper" role in society, societal assumptions, equity, and women's rights. She writes about a time when very few women worked outside the home, when society paid little attention to them, when their work was taken for granted, and when they received only food and lodging as compensation. She contends that women have advanced from this condition, but only as they have gained economic independence for themselves and, in turn, provided financial help in their homes. She thus claims that society must consider the question of whether or not women should work "not as an academic question, but as an actual situation which is with us to stay in the industrial world and in the average family" (143–44).

Mrs. Roosevelt claims that, although society may believe that single women work so they can be wasteful and indulgent, many work to help support their families. She maintains that single women must have the opportunity to work, so they can support their families (parents, siblings) and/or themselves. Of more importance, though, is her belief that married women should be given equal opportunity to work outside the home. She attempts, through her writing, to demonstrate the possibility of balancing family and career. She argues that family and career need not be oppositional. We recognize in this chapter that her commentary is based on her own experiences as a devoted mother and wife, who also assumed a "career" as first lady when her husband was elected president. She invites her readers to recognize their own special talents, needs, and desires, and to consider that just as men must sacrifice certain aspects of their lives when they get married, so must women. This statement of equality—Mrs. Roosevelt's belief that women are in most respects just like men—establishes her as a political activist and feminist. Interestingly, although she advocates women's rights, she also recognizes love and marriage, and a woman's interest in and duty to her family. She therefore balances the personal and political in a way that does not call attention to her discourse as political.

Later in this chapter, Mrs. Roosevelt defines the work women have done historically, and demonstrates that this work is similar to the work being done by contemporary women. She attempts to link home and work, family and career, by demonstrating that today we purchase many items that women made previously in their homes. Thus, she invites her readers to support and encourage women's desire to do the same kind of work outside their homes. In addition, Mrs. Roosevelt argues that by working outside the home, women become more interesting to their families:

> The very best thing that comes to a woman with a job is the fact that she has to use her brains in order to find the time for both her job and her home duties. This keeps her brain from stagnating. She has something new to talk to her husband about and he never will get the feeling that she is just like the old chair, which he has always sat in—comfortable, but thoroughly familiar and never very interesting in consequence. (148–49)

Clearly, Mrs. Roosevelt seeks to improve women's status both inside and outside the home. Some women, she insists, may not be very good at performing some caretaker roles: "There is no use in closing your eyes to the fact that women do not become satisfactory nurses and governesses simply because they have brought children into the world" (152). On the other hand, some women with children might be better suited to work outside the home, and we should give women the opportunity to discover their true talents. She invites the audience to perceive themselves as players in the drama she presents and, in so doing, to accept her views. In this way, she adheres to traditional standards of womanhood, while attempting to extend them.

Chapter 12 presents "Various Occupations for Women." Although Mrs. Roosevelt discusses only two in detail, she begins with a list of those occupations available to women that she believes are worthwhile. She writes, "We can be librarians, secretaries, stenographers, newspaper reporters, photographers, hostesses on planes; in the professions we can be lawyers, doctors, scientists of various kinds, and in the arts women have excelled as sculptors and we have good women poets, writers, painters, playwrights" (153). Notably, she does not restrict the list to those traditional occupations that seem well suited for women. Instead, she expands it to include not only the more traditional roles of secretaries, librarians, and hostesses, but also newspaper reporters, lawyers, doctors, scientists, and artists. However, Mrs. Roosevelt limits her extended discussion to follow to two vocations that she believes are particularly important: teaching and nursing. She discusses the specialized fields of nursing that require advanced education and training, but cautions, "I do not believe that any one who does not really care about alleviating the suffering of humanity can become a good nurse" (168). She thus links nursing with the more traditional roles of women, which include nurturing and caring for others. She argues that women can find complete and utter satisfaction as nurses, but acknowledges that the physical and emotional rigors of that occupation can wear a woman out. She urges women to set money aside for their later years, when they will no longer be able to sustain the demands of that career.

The vocation to which Mrs. Roosevelt devotes most of the chapter is teaching, and it is here that she truly establishes her identity as the nation's educator. She begins by stating that historically, "Women became teachers long before they entered any other gainful employment because it was the one occupation which tied in with the life of the home closely" (154). She states that many enter the profession without any real aptitude, "because we who constitute the public have given so little thought to what we wish to produce in our teachers and to what we expect from our private and public education" (154). She then turns to a discussion of what distinguishes great teachers from others. According to Mrs. Roosevelt, "The quality which makes men or women great teachers is the ability to inspire with curiosity the youthful mind" (156). She subtly argues that women are well suited for careers in teaching because, traditionally, they have concerned themselves with children's lives and well-being. In this way, she placates those who might object to women teachers by framing such outside work as consistent with women's traditional roles.

Mrs. Roosevelt compares European models of education and declares the

English model to be best because of its focus on culture. She claims that our country should follow the English model and argues that doing so will help to prevent another world war, which would surely wipe out our civilization. She maintains that women are superior teachers, not only because we are better able to understand and inspire children, but also because we are more concerned with peace, self-preservation, and the betterment of humanity. Therefore, for the sake of world peace, her argument goes, women should be teachers, and beliefs that prevent women from working outside the home as teachers must be changed. Mrs. Roosevelt thus disguises the political nature of her comments by building on traditional assumptions that women are not only concerned with nurturing children, but also peace and the preservation of humanity.

Mrs. Roosevelt champions equal pay for equal work in her discussion of teaching. She claims:

> Year by year, however, what with sports and college and coeducational courses, girls are finding themselves less and less handicapped and I believe for that reason that the day will come when places will be filled by people who are capable of filling them quite regardless of their sex. This is the goal for which every woman who is now working should be striving, for no one wants special privileges these days, but an equal chance, and for equal work, equal wages should be paid. (166–67)

Mrs. Roosevelt therefore demonstrates her belief in the value of an education that will enable women to perform well in their places of employment. Rather than receiving "special privileges" because of their gender, she believes woman can take their part in the workforce and should be paid equally for doing so. Her position seems progressive—to be very much ahead of its time.

In chapter 14, "Women and the Vote," Mrs. Roosevelt addresses political issues and does so directly. She reviews the benefits accorded women with the passage of the Nineteenth Amendment and the responsibilities associated with it. Because Mrs. Roosevelt believes in the importance of civic action, she champions the right to vote for all people regardless of gender, race, or class. She works to educate everyone about the benefits of following politics and voting. In this chapter, she claims that the right to vote provides direct power for women— something they had not previously possessed—and acknowledges those individuals who worked to provide women with that right. She references key figures of the suffrage movement and emphasizes the unselfish devotion that is considered traditionally feminine. She insists that unselfish devotion to a cause is noble and encourages us to devote ourselves not only to our families (if we have them), but also to other social and political issues that affect humanity.

Although the power of the vote provides women with the opportunity to act unselfishly toward the betterment of humanity, Mrs. Roosevelt is forced to consider what women have achieved with the power they have been given. She does not disguise her politics; rather, she recognizes that women have not accomplished all that the suffrage movement hoped they would. She then muses about what might be possible if women exercise their right to vote. In this way, she emphasizes civic virtue and works to develop a constituency that will enact civic

duty. Clearly, her position as first lady enables her to address what might otherwise be considered a touchy subject, but does so by celebrating the efforts of
those who came before her and by using an educational perspective to encourage
her audience to read the works of those individuals who fought publicly and
politically to secure women's right to vote.

Mrs. Roosevelt then turns to a discussion of the responsibilities of citizenship. She claims that women may think they have little time for anything but to
earn a living. However, for the men and women of this country, "Their good
citizenship consists in leading their lives so as to make them as productive of
good for all around them as they can be, and their public duty is expressed by
using their vote as intelligently as possible" (191). While the only intelligent
vote is a knowledgeable vote, Mrs. Roosevelt claims that women often vote
according to what others tell them. She encourages women to seek out the information that will help them become more informed and to compare a candidate's agenda with his or her personal needs and experiences. She also claims
that party affiliation should not be the result of family tradition, but of careful
consideration of the platforms and issues associated with candidates. She then
provides the names of agencies (such as the League of Women Voters) that offer
a means for women to obtain the knowledge they need to be responsible, intelligent voters. This endorsement politicizes Mrs. Roosevelt's discourse differently
from earlier chapters. However, since she claims only to want to educate
women, this politicization is minimized.

Mrs. Roosevelt wants her readers to become informed voters. Unfortunately, she admits that many people are not interested in casting their votes
intelligently: "The vast majority of women," she laments, "remain as indifferent
to the vote and how they use it as are the vast majority of men" (192). In this
respect, Mrs. Roosevelt maintains women are not inferior, but rather are as indifferent about politics as men are. The problem, she claims, is that we are all
happy to let others think for us. She does mention a few women who worked to
educate themselves about politics and who entered the political realm, and she
expresses a hope that others will follow. She also mentions her efforts to educate
women about how political decisions affect every facet of our lives. She recognizes, though, that women have as yet made no significant changes in politics.

Although women have not yet acted on their right to vote, Mrs. Roosevelt
still believes they are at least thinking about voting and about issues. She pre-
dicts that women will run for office despite the fact that "many women have
dreaded the give and take of a campaign, they have dreaded the public criticism,
they have not learned to discount the attacks of the opposition; but business and
professional life is paving the way and this reason will not deter them much
longer" (199). By articulating some of the challenges of politics and the difficulties involved in running for political office, Mrs. Roosevelt attempts to educate
her audience about them and to encourage women to rise to the challenge.

Mrs. Roosevelt then turns her attention to the future and reemphasizes civic
virtue by envisioning a democracy that offers more than material compensation
to its citizens. Again, she incorporates "social problems" into her discussion,
which realigns her comments with traditional expectations about women. She

argues that women have to work together first and foremost. This focus on constituency and consensus is political, while her focus on social issues is traditional. Thus, she balances the personal and political through her carefully constructed arguments. At the same time, she reveals the political nature of her comments as she incorporates the New Deal into her discussion, a political issue to which she was as devoted as her husband. Once again, although her comments are political, they are in line with traditional expectations of the president's wife and as an advocate of her husband's agenda.

Mrs. Roosevelt also offers a discussion of a political nature in chapter 15, "Women in Public Life." Throughout the chapter, she discusses the need for women to educate themselves about the various public positions they might obtain by starting at the bottom and working their way up. In this way, women will be able to learn about all aspects of a position, so they will understand that political life is, at times, sordid, and "that human beings are disappointing" (211). This is essential for a complete understanding and acceptance of the responsibilities associated with public life.

Mrs. Roosevelt then turns to a discussion of another political issue—the presidency. This discussion is complex and filled with text and subtext. On the surface, she acknowledges that women will be unable to hold the office of president until sex is no longer an issue; she also implies that some men who hold the office will be unworthy, but they will be less scrutinized than women would be in the same position. She contends that the sex of a candidate should not matter, but because it does, she encourages women not to run for the presidency or for any other office until they have gained the experience necessary to succeed. This includes education of the sort that she addressed in earlier chapters such as voting, learning about issues and candidates, and working their way up from the bottom to higher positions.

The subtext is even more political than the text. For instance, although Mrs. Roosevelt claims that a woman will not be president until a worthy candidate appears, she also implies that when a woman does run for president she will likely be a more worthy candidate than the man she runs against. This stems from her belief that women are more concerned with humanity and that such concern necessarily makes them more capable of holding positions that have the power to affect society on a grand scale. She may also have in mind her own experiences in the political arena, experiences that afforded her the opportunity to see the underside of politics. Mrs Roosevelt also implies that women will be judged more harshly than men, and that any woman who might consider running for political office should be sure she is capable of filling it. Women must thus be more intelligent, articulate, responsible, civic-minded, and willing to suffer the sneers and judgment of those who will oppose their candidacies. This implication relates to her earlier discussion about the importance of education. It reinforces Mrs. Roosevelt's persona as educator, because all that she says in *It's Up to the Women* is designed to educate women for life—civic and economic.

Mrs. Roosevelt closes this chapter with an editorial on civic virtue that emerges, if we read the subtext, from her personal experience. Mrs. Roosevelt was not popular when she began to speak publicly about political issues. Many around her, including her husband and the FBI, attempted to silence her or at least convince her to speak about issues traditionally befitting a first lady and social hostess. She persisted, however, and her success as a politically involved first lady resulted from her ability to disguise the nature of her discourse as political. In this discussion, Mrs. Roosevelt seems to draw on her experience as she recognizes that people who enter public life are open to criticism and accusation, but encourages them to make up their own minds and stand firm in their positions. Ultimately, their convictions will prevail and, although they may not win friends, they will win respect. It was her strong convictions that eventually won her the respect and admiration she deserved. At times, her convictions may have benefited not only her, but her husband's administration as well.

Another chapter worth examining is chapter 17, "Women and Working Conditions." In this chapter, Mrs. Roosevelt devotes attention to working conditions generally, and the discrimination that women who work outside the home face. Again, she supports equal pay for equal work. She also provides evidence for her claim that women deserve equal pay when she insists that machinery has enabled everyone to accomplish the work that must be done. More important, however, is her tacit support for women's work outside the home; she discusses it as if it is an unquestionable fact. Again, Mrs. Roosevelt balances the scales by demonstrating that women are equal to men in the work they do. Although not explicit, she argues that women should be afforded the right to pursue work outside the home, to expect equal pay, and to have the opportunity to pursue their interests. At the same time, she addresses a very dangerous topic—unions and unionization.

Mrs. Roosevelt does not champion existing male-dominated and male-run unions for women; rather, she encourages women to create women's trade unions designed to protect their special needs. She placates those who might object by focusing on the differences between men and women. Although she worked throughout this book to demonstrate the many ways in which women are equal to men, here she differentiates women to provide special protections based on their physical abilities. In addition to better working conditions, she argues that women deserve equal pay, a minimum "living" wage, and time off for childbirth. This appears to be an important and notable precursor to the contemporary Medical and Family Leave Act championed by Hillary Rodham Clinton, one that recognizes women's unique ability to bear children. By demonstrating the need for such accommodations, Mrs. Roosevelt appeals to traditional societal expectations and, in subtle ways, disguises the political nature of her discourse. At the same time, she challenges the legitimacy of male-dominated unions—a move that was dangerous for her husband's administration—by arguing that they do not provide the special protections women need. While she addresses explicitly political issues, however, she works to foster a constituency that, if educated about social issues and motivated to vote responsibly, could ultimately have benefited the Roosevelt administration.

A final chapter worth examining is chapter 18 in which Mrs. Roosevelt addresses "Women and Peace." In a move that appears designed to return to traditional expectations and assumptions about women, she discusses the many ways women can work to maintain peace both at home and abroad. Mrs. Roosevelt claims, "One of the things in which women are vitally interested to-day [sic] is the abolition of war as a means of settling disputes between nations, and I feel that this is particularly a question which is up to the women" (237). As she did at the beginning of the book, Mrs. Roosevelt contends that women are particularly concerned about the preservation of humanity and that women are uniquely able to address these issues. In another move designed to disguise the political nature of her comments, Mrs. Roosevelt demonstrates the way women can work toward peace when she states, "As I see it there are two things which women must do. One is to create a *will to peace* in all things and the other is to make adventurous some other things in life besides war. The will to peace will have to start with women and they will have to want peace sufficiently to be crusaders on the subject" (238).

The will to peace that Mrs. Roosevelt describes can only be achieved through education, the type of education that women are expected to provide—a mother's education. Women have the unique ability to affect children's lives and attitudes by virtue of bringing them into the world and assuming the role of primary caretaker. Because she champions motherhood as much as she champions women's rights, it makes sense that she would return to the virtues of motherhood—explicitly or implicitly—at book's end. It makes more sense that she would allude to the special power mothers have to instill a will to peace in their children, just as they might instill a will to succeed. Importantly, Mrs. Roosevelt encourages women to become crusaders on the subject. This politicizes her discussion, but only subtly, as it nevertheless focuses on womanhood traditionally conceived. She then turns to a brief discussion of Joan of Arc who, although a peasant, possessed a vision of freedom, and she encourages U.S. women to possess a similar vision of world peace.

Mrs. Roosevelt continues by acknowledging the thrill of adventure and argues that war appeals to youth because the sacrifice and patriotism associated with it are exciting. Her solution is the excitement of working to organize a new social order based on democracy. "This challenge to organize a new social order not in one place, but all over the world, has possibilities of adventure and excitement, a society which of itself should take the place of the old glamour surrounding war. Only the women and the youth of any country can initiate this change" (246–47). Motherhood, then, provides the means by which women can affect change by instilling certain values in their children. Thus, motherhood is politicized, and the personal becomes political. However, because it appears to adhere to the constraints of tradition, its politicization is disguised and its threat to tradition is diminished.

In chapter 20, her conclusion, Mrs. Roosevelt oscillates between contemporary issues and established tradition. She discusses from where women have come and where women might go. She shares a hope that women will embrace her words and act responsibly in the world. After recounting a story about her grandmother who expected her to be more thoughtful and sensible than her brothers, she claims that women of that generation accomplished a great many things "by working through the men when they hardly knew they were being influenced" (262–263). She closes the book with a challenge to women wherein she contends, "women, whether subtly or vociferously, have always been a tremendous power in the destiny of the world and with so many of them now holding important positions and receiving recognition and earning the respect of the men as well as the members of their own sex, it seems more than ever that in this crisis, 'It's Up to the Women!'" (263). In this final statement, Mrs. Roosevelt marries the personal and the political. She claims that women have always had power and the ability to affect the world around them. She challenges women to use their power. She does so, however, by remembering traditional expectations and arguing that even within the constraints of tradition women have had power. She thus challenges women to act both within and outside societal constraints to change the world.

It's Up to the Women was written during the Great Depression and dealt with many of the issues facing both men and women. Throughout, however, Mrs. Roosevelt maintains the belief that only women have the power to help the United States overcome the crisis. How they can do it is the impetus for the book, and Mrs. Roosevelt cleverly oscillates between the virtues of womanhood and the virtues of feminism. In sum, the book argues that womanhood provides a power not available to men, a power that can change the current social order in the United States and in the world. By discussing feminist power as an element of traditional womanhood, however, Mrs. Roosevelt disguises the political nature of her arguments, thereby enacting a rhetorical persona best understood in terms of social style. By focusing on education—as a vocation and as a means to demonstrate women's power—and on womanhood, especially, motherhood, she both celebrates and enacts an identity consistent with societal expectations. As a result, her rhetorical identity is strategically social in that it is not explicitly political (except in a few instances), and it relies for its validity on her position as the president's wife. Her role as first lady gives her a voice, but limits its power because of traditional assumptions about wifedom. Clearly, this book was a balanced political endeavor, as were most of Mrs. Roosevelt's rhetorical activities.

Legacy

When Franklin Delano Roosevelt died on April 12, 1945, Mrs. Roosevelt was prepared to move forward with her political career, although she did not intend this kind of future. After her husband's death, she told a reporter, "The story is over" (quoted in Anthony 1990, 513). Within a week of his death, she coordinated his funeral and moved out of the White House. She also hosted a farewell reception for the women's press corps, where she answered questions about her political and journalistic career, which she implied would end.

Mrs. Roosevelt's political career did not end with the death of her husband, however. In fact, "Over the next decade and a half, she continued to be the most effective woman in American politics" (Chafe 1980, xvi). She was appointed to the first American delegation to the United Nations where, as the U.S. representative to the Social, Humanitarian, and Cultural Committee of the General Assembly, she helped draft the Universal Declaration of Human Rights (Black 1999, 10). Mrs. Roosevelt considered this document to be her greatest achievement, both personally and politically. In many respects, it serves as the most articulate statement of her beliefs and vision of the world. Her rhetorical activities during her husband's presidency were less conspicuous than those after his death. Although she publicly disagreed with her husband often, she nevertheless felt obliged to support his political agenda. She therefore limited her disagreements to those issues that did not directly challenge his New Deal policies. After his death, she more clearly articulated her own beliefs, and texts such as the Universal Declaration of Human Rights are indicative of them.

Mrs. Roosevelt's rhetorical activities as first lady helped reshape the way the public thought about this important, if unelected role. Moreover, she helped pave the way for first ladies who followed by demonstrating that they could be politically active. She did so, however, without appearing to be political. As her husband's eyes and ears, she fulfilled traditional expectations by functioning as a devoted wife, while at the same time promoting her political beliefs and agenda, that is, educating the nation about the importance of all its people, and laying the foundation for what was to be a long and satisfying political career.

Eleanor Roosevelt championed many causes during her lifetime, especially during her tenure in the White House, but none seems as important as the role of women in society. Although not politically popular during the Roosevelt administration, she believed in the rights of all people regardless of race, class, and gender. Underneath her many causes was a personal drive to succeed that manifested itself in the form of a feminist perspective that still resonates with those who read her works today.

It's Up to the Women is particularly interesting because it enables Mrs. Roosevelt to educate her audience, in a concise and articulate manner, about issues of concern to her. The monograph outlines many issues of concern to Americans during the depression, and argues throughout that women are uniquely able to solve the problems she addresses. She arranges her arguments in a manner that enables her to "disguise" her feminist perspective by using traditionally feminine images. Thus, her argument that women should be encouraged to work outside the home appears as an editorial about how such work might enhance a marriage by providing conversation that is lively and new. Similarly, she bases her argument on behalf of women's involvement in politics on the ability of women to recognize social ills and to work for the betterment of humanity.

Not only did her monograph support women's rights, so did her presence both within and outside of the White House. Indeed, when the United States was involved in World War II, Mrs. Roosevelt "insisted that the struggle would not be worth winning if the old order of things prevailed" (Goodwin 1994, 10). Her argument that women should receive equal pay for equal work eventually led to commentary about how women accepted the challenge to support the war effort. This was supported by a variety of photographs in which she was surrounded by women. These were not idle women, though; they were photographed at their places of employment. As Goodwin notes, "Ultimately, 350,000 women would serve as members of the Women's Army Corps and the WAVES (Women Accepted for Voluntary Emergency Service in the Navy)" (1994, 415). Mrs. Roosevelt celebrated the women who rose to the challenge by visiting with them and describing her visits in her many columns and articles. This seems to have been a way for her to celebrate women's work outside the home and to demonstrate that the "lessons" presented in her books, columns, press conferences, and speeches were worthwhile and valuable.

According to Allida Black, Mrs. Roosevelt's "legacy as first lady, delegate to the United Nations, Democratic Party leader, humanitarian, and social activist made her an icon to millions, many of whom would agree on nothing other than their respect for her" (1999, 1). Her husband's death enabled her to speak her mind about issues that were important to her, including Democratic domestic policies. She also began to address more vigorously international issues with which she disagreed such as human rights issues. She believes these were not confined only to the free world, but also existed in communist countries such as the Soviet Union and China. Her humanitarian interests resulted in her appointment to the first American delegation to the United Nations by Harry Truman.

Mrs. Roosevelt strongly believed that this was the most important position of her life—more important than that of first lady—and she dedicated much of the rest of her life to promoting and defending the United Nations and its policies. She guided the writing of the Universal Declaration of Human Rights and worked for its adoption as the U.S. representative to the Social, Humanitarian, and Cultural Committee of the General Assembly (Committee III). This was no easy task, as the committee consisted of delegates with diverging political agendas. However, her grace and determination resulted in a unanimously supported document. Although she admitted that there was no official recourse for countries who failed to uphold the declaration's principles, she believed that its completion and adoption was her finest achievement.

As with her time in the White House, Mrs. Roosevelt was not always popular. In fact, J. Edgar Hoover continued to monitor her activities, believing her to be a communist sympathizer. Her FBI file indicates that the agency closely monitored her columns as well as articles written about her for signs or clues that she was spreading communist propaganda. She eventually was one of the most outspoken opponents of Senator McCarthy's communist witch-hunt that was the Red Scare. She was particularly outspoken in her speeches and her columns about the practices of the House Un-American Activities Committee (HUAC). She claimed that Senator McCarthy was engaging in the very same politics of fear in which he accused the communists of engaging. In addition to her opposition to Senator McCarthy's tactics, Mrs. Roosevelt outraged southern politicians when she publicly supported *Brown v. Board of Education* and the Civil Rights Acts of 1957 and 1960. "[A]s she became more familiar with the unique problems African Americans faced, [Mrs. Roosevelt] abandoned her position as a defender of equal treatment to become a staunch advocate of integration and nonviolent protest. She had joined the board of directors of the National Association for the Advancement of Colored People (NAACP) in 1945"

(Black 1999, 13). She continued to agitate for the right to vote, fair housing, quality education, and the right to organize in protest against discriminatory practices. When students, both African American and white, were attacked on the Freedom Rides, she was outraged and likened the actions of the white mobs to those of the Nazis against the Jews during World War II.

Mrs. Roosevelt was outspoken and dedicated to her causes, but continued to foster a matriarchal persona in the media. Beasley agrees that, "She herself continued to present to the public an image of a gracious, dignified lady with a motherly concern for oppressed peoples everywhere" (1987, 167). This reinforced and strengthened public support for her and her causes, which the media regularly monitored. Most of the mainstream media delighted in praising her, often implying that she was able to retain her womanly attributes while matching wits with men. In 1948, *Time* called her "perhaps the best known woman in the world" (Beasley 1987, 177). *The Saturday Review of Literature* in 1951 named her both the "greatest living American woman" and "the greatest woman in the world" (quoted in Beasley 1987, 177). She did not adhere to traditional societal expectations for women, though, and was often censured. This included criticism from those who believed she was responsible for her children's string of unsuccessful marriages. Yet, she continued to provide a role model for women who wanted to combine feminine qualities with the type of power and influence usually attributed to men. Her grace and dignity, combined with her dedication to her causes and her determination to fight for human rights made her a role model that many women (Hillary Rodham Clinton, for example) admire today.

Published late in her life, *You Learn by Living* is a monograph that articulates her philosophy of life. In it, she claims that women are uniquely well equipped to adjust to new situations because they are constantly forced to adjust to the lives of their husbands and children. This book is evidence that Mrs. Roosevelt refused to give in to her old age and her ailments. Her appointment as a visiting lecturer at Brandeis University is further evidence that she intended to remain active. This appointment also reflects her passion for teaching, something that was evident throughout her life. She thus embodies the most feminine qualities at the same time she uses them with a cunning that only the most successful men to that time had exhibited.

Mrs. Roosevelt created an identity separate from her husband. According to Beasley "Heywood Broun, a popular columnist, compared Mrs. Roosevelt to Nora, the heroine of Ibsen's play, *A Doll's House*, who sought to be a human being rather than a plastic creation of her husband. He contended, 'Neither marriage nor the last national election can obliterate the fact that Eleanor Roosevelt is an individual.'" She was perceived as the country's matriarch whose family was the entire country. She emerged as the nation's educator and believed, "Teachers are more important than anything except parents in the lives of children" (quoted in Hershan 1993, 140).

Eleanor Roosevelt expanded the political possibilities for first ladies by speaking out on issues, asserting her right to earn money independently, and developing a journalistic career with journalistic admirers who, as a result, treated her fairly in news reports about her. She did so within the constraints of a patriarchal society that defined what was and was not acceptable for women—especially the first lady. The preceding analysis has helped to illuminate how Eleanor Roosevelt created an identity that simultaneously championed women's rights and placated patriarchal unease. Admittedly, much of what she did and many of her causes are considered philanthropic and therefore appropriate for upper-class women. "What was revolutionary about Mrs. Roosevelt was . . . [her] ability as first lady to inspire the public with a message that reinforced traditional values at the same time it enlarged them" (Beasley 1987, 81). Democracy, she believed, relied for its success on the participation of all individuals in a society. She was passionately devoted to democratic principles, even when those around her appeared not to be. Democracy was—and is—the basis for all social change. Ultimately, Mrs. Roosevelt believed that social change was up to the women. And it still is.

Eleanor Roosevelt died from a rare form of tuberculosis on November 7, 1962. She was seventy-eight years old. She left a legacy that is unique among first ladies.

Notes

1. Some of the most prominent scholars are Black (1996), Cook (1992) and Beasley (1987). Presidential scholars such as Goodwin (1994) and first lady scholars such as Gutin (1989) have devoted a great deal of attention to Mrs. Roosevelt's influence during her husband's tenure as president.

2. Scholars such as Black (1995, 1996, 1999), Chadakoff (1989) and Roosevelt (1946) among others support this claim. Often considered the preeminent Eleanor Roosevelt scholar, Black has compiled many of Eleanor Roosevelt's essential speeches and writings. I have used her compilations and insights throughout this essay as a springboard for many of my own arguments.

3. Beasley (1987) claims, "Admirers accepted the triteness of her comments, both written and spoken, as her way of identifying with ordinary people" (74). However, Mrs. Roosevelt claimed (and Beasley agrees) that she addressed people the only way she knew how. Later in her career—both during her White House years and afterward—Lorena Hickok acted as Mrs. Roosevelt's editor and helped her refine her prose.

4. See, for instance, Beasley (1987), Black (1995, 1996, 1999), Chafe (1980), Eaton (1956), Goodwin (1994), Gould (1996) and Youngs (1999). In their introductions or biographical narratives, all of these scholars acknowledge that Eleanor Roosevelt acted politically and publicly. In addition, most agree that this was the result of Franklin Delano Roosevelt's paralysis. Regardless, all acknowledge that Mrs. Roosevelt changed the role of the first lady through her actions and her willingness to champion issues important to her.

5. Many well-known books such as Goodwin (1987) and Beasley (1987) include press photos in which Mrs. Roosevelt is surrounded by women and people of color. The Franklin D. Roosevelt Library website also includes a page of copyright-free photographs, which present Mrs. Roosevelt with dignitaries, her husband, women (many in their places of employment such as pilots and nurses at military hospitals during the war), and children (such as those at a "Negro Nursery"). Other photographs include Mrs. Roosevelt surrounded by her close friends (such as Lorena Hickok). All photographs of Mrs.

Roosevelt appear to demonstrate the lessons she distributed in her writings.

6. Eleanor Roosevelt was a rhetor in the most traditional sense, and her rhetoric encompasses a range of activities of the sort studied by rhetorical scholars. However, it is not enough to study only her speeches and press conferences, or her letters and columns. A careful critic must also examine her autobiographies and monographs, which she filled with insights, hopes, and convictions so strong that they demand sustained meditation. Indeed, many scholars study a variety of her texts from different perspectives; to date, however, no sustained examination of her monographs exists. It seems to me that her monographs offer the most focused statements of her political beliefs and, as such, deserve critical attention. This kind of study is outside the scope of my present essay.

7. The use of "public" in this statement is specific and intentional. Although other first ladies engaged in political activities behind the scenes, mostly influencing their husbands during private conversations, Eleanor Roosevelt chose to make her activities public and, in so doing, radically changed the way the public saw the first lady and her importance to what Karlyn Kohrs Campbell calls "the presidential corporation" (1996).

8. This argument is based on a belief that the fight for women's suffrage was not fashionable; moreover, it recognizes that the suffrage movement was made up of different constituencies, each with their own ideas about methods and goals. For more about the women's rights movement, see Flexner and Fitzpatrick (1996).

9. This photo is published in several scholarly books, including Beasley (1987) and more popular works, including Mayo (1996).

References

Anthony, Carl Sferrazza. 1990. *First Ladies: The Saga of the Presidents' Wives and Their Power 1789–1961*, Vol. 1. New York: William Morrow.

Beasley, Maurine H. 1987. *Eleanor Roosevelt and the Media: A Public Quest for Self-Fulfillment*. Urbana, Ill.: University of Illinois Press.

Black, Allida, ed. 1995. *What I Hope to Leave Behind: The Essential Essays of Eleanor Roosevelt*. Brooklyn, N.Y.: Carlson.

———. 1996. *Casting Her Own Shadow: Eleanor Roosevelt and the Shaping of Postwar Liberalism*. New York: Columbia University Press.

———, ed. 1999. *Courage in a Dangerous World: The Political Writings of Eleanor Roosevelt*. New York: Columbia University Press.

Campbell, Karlyn Kohrs. 1996. The Rhetorical Presidency: A Two Person Career. In *Beyond the Rhetorical Presidency*, ed. Martin J. Medhurst, 179–95. College Station, Tex.: Texas A & M University Press.

Caroli, Betty Boyd. 1995. *First Ladies: An Intimate Look at How 38 Women Handled What May Be the Most Demanding, Unpaid, Unelected Job in America*. New York: Oxford University Press.

Chadakoff, Rochelle, ed. 1989. *Eleanor Roosevelt's "My Day": Her Acclaimed Columns 1936–1945*. New York: Pharos.

Chafe, William H. 1980. Roosevelt, Anna Eleanor. In *Notable American Women, the Modern Period: A Biographical Dictionary*. Cambridge, Mass.: Belknap-Harvard University Press,

Cook, Blanche Wiesen. 1992. *Eleanor Roosevelt: A Life*, Vol. 1. New York: Viking.

Eaton, Janette. 1956. *The Story of Eleanor Roosevelt*. New York: William Morrow.

Edens, John A. 1994. *Eleanor Roosevelt: A Comprehensive Bibliography*. Westport, Connecticut: Greenwood.

First Ladies. 2000. www.firstladies.org/anna_roosevelt.

Flexner, Eleanor, and Ellen Fitzpatrick. 1996. *Century of Struggle: The Woman's Rights Movement in the United States*. Cambridge, Mass.: Harvard University Press.

Goodwin, Doris Kearns. 1994. *No Ordinary Time. Franklin and Eleanor Roosevelt: The Home Front in World War II*. New York: Simon & Schuster.

Gould, Lewis L. 1996. *American First Ladies: Their Lives and Their Legacies*. New York: Garland.

Gutin, Myra. 1989. *The President's Partner*. Westport, Conn.: Greenwood.

Hershan, Stella K. 1993. *The Candles She Lit: The Legacy of Eleanor Roosevelt*. Westport, Conn.: Praeger.

Mayo, Edith P., ed. 1996. *The Smithsonian Book of the First Ladies: Their Lives, Times, and Issues*. New York: Henry Holt & Co.

Roosevelt, Eleanor. 1946. *If You Ask Me*. New York: Curtis.

———. 1933. *It's Up to the Women*. New York: Frederick A. Stokes.

Scott, Anne Firor, and William H. Chafe, eds. 1986. *The Papers of Eleanor Roosevelt, 1933–1945*. Frederick, Md.: University Publications of America.

Youngs, J. William T. 1999. *Eleanor Roosevelt: A Personal and Public Life*. New York: Longman.

Chapter 11

Bess Wallace Truman
"The Boss" from Independence

M. Heather Carver

> She is my chief advisor. I never write a speech without going over it with her. I
> have to do that because I have so much to do and I never make any decisions
> unless she is in on them. She takes care of my personal mail.
>
> —Harry S. Truman

> I've been in politics for more than twenty-five years.
>
> —Bess Truman

Elizabeth Wallace Truman, known by her nickname, Bess, was a first lady who
did not deliver any speeches during her husband's eight years as president of the
United States. She held no press conferences, abandoning a practice begun earlier by her predecessor, Eleanor Roosevelt. Many reporters did not approve of
this woman whose inaccessibility signaled a lack of respect for the nation's
interest in her. Instead, she preferred to stand by her husband's side, to support
him in ways that she felt were appropriate for a wife. Refusing to engage in
platform rhetoric, she still managed to make a rhetorical impact through her
activities as a hostess and especially by all of the help she gave her husband
behind the scenes.

When Bess Truman moved from Independence, Missouri, to Washington,
D.C., she was a homemaker, mother, and helpmate to her husband. For many
years, Bess had worked hard behind the scenes to advance her husband's political career. In various ways, she contributed to Harry Truman's campaigns,

speeches, and policy decisions. When Harry S. Truman was a senator, she ran his office. She participated, in her own way, in his 1948 presidential campaign. She traveled with her husband during each of his campaigns, but never spoke at rallies. On his famous whistle-stop campaign, Harry would conclude his speech by introducing Bess to the crowd as "The Boss," and their daughter Margaret as "The Boss's Boss." Bess would smile and wave as the train faded into the distance. This is the image that most people have of her as first lady: a supportive wife and mother, who silently stood by her husband's side. That was the image Bess wanted, and that was the one "The Boss" achieved.

Bess stands out in the twentieth century as a presidential wife who successfully resisted the demands of the public and the press. She did not believe that her public role as first lady was anything more than a social one. She firmly believed that Harry was the elected public official, not her, and the active role she played behind the scenes in his political life was none of the public's business. She stuck to her roles as wife and mother in public, no matter how much pressure she must have felt from popular opinion and the press.

Eleanor Roosevelt, Bess's immediate predecessor, was enormously popular and her dedication to public service widely admired. Whoever followed Mrs. Roosevelt would have faced high expectations for what the first lady should be and do. When Bess Truman completely shunned the public nature of the role, skeptics began to question her intelligence, social capabilities, and ability to "handle" the role of presidential wife, even though it was a position still not clearly defined after nearly two centuries. That the first lady was and continues to be an undefined position is not news, but how her identity is constructed raises several interesting questions, two of which are raised in this chapter: How did Bess Truman use rhetoric to construct her role as first lady? How did the public and press view the image Mrs. Truman projected as a first lady?

This chapter examines a publicly distant first lady whose usual response to questioning was "no comment." The public rhetoric of Bess Truman during her tenure as first lady includes a few extremely brief written interviews and presidential engagements, for only in these rare instances did she allow her opinion to be heard by the general public. Because sources of her public persona are so limited, other information becomes important in understanding how she shaped her role as first lady. This chapter examines the surviving correspondence of "The Boss" and other personal narratives for clues about her opinion of her role as first lady.

As Lewis L. Gould notes, "The ways in which a president uses or manages the political and cultural assets that a First Lady provides says a great deal about the style and impact of an administration" (1996, 678). Harry was quick to grow angry at any negative press coverage of his wife, but Bess was untroubled and always calmed him down before he went out and "gave 'em hell." Harry S. Truman was a straightforward, down-home, plain-speaking man from the Show Me State, and his wife's stubborn defiance of public attention fit right in with his administration's style. Bess Truman approached her role as first lady with a Midwestern work ethic, did her "job" as *she* defined it, and eagerly brought her husband back to Independence, Missouri, their lifelong home when the job was done. Her public rhetoric may have been kept to a minimum, but her indirect rhetorical influence on the Truman presidency was great. As her husband admitted, she was part of every significant decision he ever made.

Biography

Bess Truman's childhood dramatically influenced her communication practices, on both a private and public level. Her family occupied a high status role in the Independence, Missouri, community, due to her mother, Margaret Gates's, side of the family. As Margaret Truman notes in her biography of Bess, "for women, life in Independence revolved around culture, the family, and the church. By and large, the churches reflected the social scale. The so-called best people were Presbyterians. . . . Farther down the scale were the Baptists, the Mormons and the Catholics" (1986, 5). From the beginning, the social hierarchy of Independence was emphasized as an important structure in Bess's life.

As the first child born to David and Margaret (Madge) Wallace, Bess was responsible for taking care of her siblings. She had two younger brothers, Frank and George, and a little sister who died at the age of three. The care she took of her siblings, however, did not make Bess a sedate homebody. She excelled in tennis, baseball, ice-skating, horseback riding, and basketball. According to her family, Bess was also the "peacekeeper" on the block, as her ability to whistle quite loudly, without using her fingers, "struck terror" into the neighborhood misfits' hearts. Bess also used her whistle for more friendly purposes, such as calling her friends over for ice cream (Truman 1986, 8). Bess's mother was a strongly opinionated and domineering figure in her life. She was the first to educate Bess on the principles of being a proper lady. While Madge may have let Bess engage in sporting activities, she still taught her the importance of etiquette and "social graces." Bess took dancing lessons and learned how to properly host a party. This early training was very influential on how she would handle the role of being the first lady of the United States.

Bess was a very good student throughout her school years. After high school, several of her friends made plans for college, but due to Bess's father's financial troubles, she did not join them. The family's money problem was not a fact that was publicly discussed. Bess's mother was shamed by her husband's lack of financial prowess, and she took great pains to hide their situation. Madge also tried to cover up David's growing drinking binges as well. Eventually, Bess's father's depression and alcoholism led to what was to be a defining moment in her life—his suicide. On June 17, 1903, just four months after Bess's eighteenth birthday, David Wallace arose from bed, went into the bathroom, and shot himself in the head.

The disgrace of her father's suicide was only compounded by the town's reaction. Two days after the traumatic event, a local newspaper published a front page article about David Wallace's suicide. Hundreds of people attended the funeral. Margaret Truman notes that all of the attention was "mortifying beyond belief" for Madge as it "flung her from the top of Independence's social hierarchy to the bottom" (1986, 19). Bess's mother was reported to completely fall apart over the disgrace, and it shattered the lives of everyone in the family. Bess's later distrust of the press was probably due to all of the damaging negative publicity surrounding her father's suicide. She simply refused to fall prey to another scandalous press attack on her family.

David Wallace's premature death influenced Bess's life in many ways, and his suicide greatly contributed to her communication strategies, particularly on an interpersonal level. Margaret Truman notes that Bess recognized that her mother's "lady-like" ways of communication were ineffective in sustaining a happy marriage. Truman writes, "If she ever found a man she could trust—Bess Wallace vowed she would share his whole life, no matter how much pain it cost her. She rejected absolutely and totally the idea of a woman's sphere and a man's sphere" (1986, 20). After her father's death, it was not long before Bess took charge of the household. She assumed this leadership role out of necessity, and her keen sense of responsibility and direction helped build the role that she is known for in history: the Boss.

When she was twenty years old, Bess attended the Barstow School in Kansas City, a women's finishing school that provided a rigorous academic experience for its students. Bess excelled in the camaraderie of her classmates and made very good grades, including an A+ in literature. Bess also became the star forward on the basketball team and won first place in shotput at a track meet (Truman 1986, 22). At the end of the year, as many of her classmates went eastward to pursue their bachelor's degrees, Bess once again returned home to Independence. Even though she did not attend college, Bess's interest in reading, writing, and learning never diminished. Her literary education at Barstow proved to be a valuable tool that she used for the rest of her life. Bess did not return home to sit around and mope, but rather she began to engage enthusiastically in the social life of the community.

Harry Truman insists that he fell in love with Bess at first sight, at the age of six, when he first began to attend school at the First Presbyterian Church. Five-year-old Bess hardly gave Harry a second glance that day, or in the next twenty years that followed. Margaret Truman notes that the "Trumans were far beneath the social world inhabited by the Wallaces and the Gates. . . . They were country folk and newcomers in the bargain" (1986, 11). Needless to say, Bess was still wary of Harry's continued interest in her two decades later, when at the age of twenty-five, she accepted his request to call on her.

Harry had been a bank teller in nearby Kansas City, before he returned to Grandview, Missouri, to help run the family farm. Because Harry's journeys to see Bess usually took at least a couple of hours, they began to correspond through letter writing. Truman writes that Harry quickly realized how much Bess enjoyed a good laugh, and he began to write to her about funny stories and events (1986, 36). While he amused her, she still turned down his first proposal of marriage a year after their courtship began. Harry dug in his heals and worked harder to convince her. After two and a half years of trying, it finally paid off when Bess told him that if she were going to be married, it would probably be to him. A long series of family troubles for the Wallaces and the Trumans held up the would-be marriage, and then Harry enlisted to fight in World War I. The couple continued to write letters until the war was over and Harry returned home. After a nine-year courtship, Bess and Harry were married on June 28, 1919. Bess was thirty-four and Harry was thirty-five.

Harry and Bess did not begin their married life in their own home, quite the contrary. The couple moved into the same home that Bess had grown up in at 219 North Delaware, the heart of downtown Independence. Harry wanted to make money to support his new wife and set out to do so despite the continual put-downs from his mother-in-law that he would never amount to anything. Bess dutifully continued to take care of her mother while helping Harry with the bookkeeping of his new haberdashery business.

The first year of their marriage was successful financially, but Bess was crushed when she suffered a miscarriage. She worried that at age thirty-five, she may have waited too long to bear children. Unfortunately, their early financial success gave way to ruin over the following year as the economy began to deflate (Truman 1986, 84). Harry contemplated a career in politics that frightened both Bess and her mother, for it was David Wallace's political career that had contributed to his downfall. According to Margaret Truman, Bess "managed to suppress her negative feelings and support her husband's decision" (1986, 86).

Bess's family connections helped Harry's early political efforts. Truman notes that Bess, herself, contributed to a new political force in the county—women voters. Her family friends canvassed Independence door-to-door to persuade women to vote for Harry Truman (Truman 1986, 88). While Harry beat the pavement and campaigned all over the county, Bess stayed home to take care of herself and the new baby on the way. Unfortunately, Bess suffered another miscarriage during the summer of 1922. Then, on August 5, Harry won his first election, and Bess became the wife of a Jackson County, Missouri, judge.

Harry Truman may be remembered for his Missouri stubbornness, but he certainly met his match in Bess. She may have been supportive of his interests, but she had no intention of deferring to Harry about important matters. The birth of Margaret Truman is a telling example of Bess's steadfast convictions. Because Bess had already had two miscarriages and one of her friends had a still-born baby, she refused to prepare the household for the potential arrival of a new child. During her third pregnancy, Bess did not buy any baby clothes or a bassinet. "When the infant girl arrived in the middle of a snowstorm on February 17, 1923, she was packed with blankets into a bureau drawer until Judge Truman could plow through the snow to purchase a long list of baby items" (Truman 1986, 93). Bess's reluctance to prepare for the baby's arrival was an understandable psychological defense against potential despair. The stubbornness of both Trumans truly shone through when their disagreement about the baby's name lasted over the next several years, until they settled on Mary Margaret Truman. In the meantime, Harry successfully won the Democratic nomination for presiding judge of Jackson County. He and Bess were in politics for good.

Bess certainly fit the old cliché that you can take the gal out of the small town, but you can't take the small town out of the gal. Many of her decisions about how she would be as a first lady were determined by the values she had learned while growing up in Independence. She was not taught to look down on others, but she was simply to "behave" better than others. Madge Wallace taught her the "proper" and the "improper" ways of doing things as a hostess. Margaret Truman explains the control that Madge had over the home, particularly noticeable in the evening dinner ritual:

> Dinner always emphasized for me that we were living in Madge Wallace's house. She and my father sat at opposite ends of the table. Whether she sat at the head and he at the foot or vice versa was anybody's guess. I sat between my mother and grandmother, on her left, and Fred [Bess's younger brother] sat opposite us, on her right. The atmosphere was always very formal. My manners were expected to be perfect, and so was everyone's costume. (1986, 109)

Bess's training from her mother was transferred to disciplining her own daughter. Margaret Truman notes how she became a "Daddy's girl" as her mother was usually the strict disciplinarian. In addition to learning how to conduct herself properly within the home, small-town life taught Bess how to behave socially. She learned ways to "make do" in a pinch, rather than tell others her troubles. A proper lady was well-groomed, gracious, hospitable, and tasteful, and the last thing a small-town gal would want would be to have others make a "fuss" over her. Bess was able to maintain this level of "proper" behavior during the first part of Harry's political career, and she would do her best to adhere to such standards when she moved to Washington, D.C., with the new senator from Missouri.

Bess was never pleased with Harry's decision to run for the Senate. Truman writes that her parents' marriage was a union of two strong people; often such a union required the woman to surrender herself to the man, but "Bess Truman never did that" (1986, 129). Bess did not surrender herself, but she did keep her wedding vow to support Harry, and "when he announced his candidacy for the U.S. Senate, she was there beside him. No one, except the candidate, was aware of the reluctance and doubt in her troubled heart" (Truman 1986, 29). The race for the Senate was grueling. Harry took lots of hits over his relationship with Tom Pendergast, the head of the Kansas City political machine. He campaigned heavily all over the state, often giving more than a dozen speeches a day. Bess set her precedent for political rhetoric during this campaign—she was to have no part in public speaking. She would help write his speeches and appear by his side, but delivering speeches herself was not her "style." Truman writes that Bess once stated that "A woman's place in public is to sit beside her husband, be silent, and be sure her hat is on straight" (1986, 132).

Even though Bess initially resisted Harry's rise in politics, by all accounts, she enjoyed the time that Harry was a senator. She worked very closely with him, so hard that he put her on the payroll. Truman writes that for Bess, being a senator's wife, "was a perfect combination of being near the center of the political stage while remaining more or less anonymous to everyone but a circle of chosen friends" (1995, 73). That would all change when Harry decided to run for vice president in 1944. After Harry's nomination, the Trumans were barraged with attention, requiring several policemen to maneuver them through crowds. Bess, displeased with the commotion, asked Harry, "Are we going to have to go through all this the rest of our lives?" (Truman 1956, 68). It was just the first flicker of the spotlight that was to shine on the Truman household for the next eight years.

The 1944 campaign was nearly as painful for Bess as she had anticipated. Fortunately, her biggest fears were not realized, as the press did not seize the moment to rehash her father's suicide. Instead, she was humiliated by such indignities as a *Life* magazine article on her family home that described it as a "gloomy Victorian" and a reporter's labeling of her as "Payroll Bess" because of her status as a paid employee of her husband (Truman's Wife on U.S. Payroll, Keeley Papers, Box 1, HST Library). In her defense, Harry was extremely protective of his wife's hard work in his senate office:

> Certainly my wife works for me. And she earns every cent I pay her. She is my chief advisor. I never write a speech without going over it with her. I have to do that because I have so much to do and I never make any decisions unless she is in on them. She takes care of my personal mail. (quoted in McNaughton 1945, 183)

The Trumans weathered the campaign and soon moved into the vice president's residence. Bess Truman's mother was still being proved wrong about her daughter marrying a man who wouldn't amount to anything.

Madge Wallace's training of her daughter to be a lady would soon make its mark in history, when Franklin Roosevelt died in 1945, and Bess became the first lady of the nation. On a local level, Bess's lifestyle choices fit well with the expectations of the upper echelon of her small community. Her behavior had been proper as a senator's wife, and, for the most part, she was ignored as a vice president's wife. On a national level, however, Eleanor Roosevelt had dramatically changed the expectations for a presidential wife. No longer was hostessing tea parties and attending society functions all the public expected to see, or hear, from the first lady. Bess, however, had no interest in letting others dictate how she was to fulfill her role as wife, mother, woman, or first lady. Harry may have "given 'em Hell," but Bess gave the press and public what she thought they deserved, and that was not much.

Rhetorical Activities as First Lady

> [Bess] told someone that her favorite first lady was Elizabeth Monroe . . . because of her success at virtually disappearing from the White House for most of her husband's two terms. (Truman 1986, 76)

Bess began her work as first lady by supervising state dinners, social teas, and attending charity functions. These were activities for which she had the requisite training and experience. She was very fearful, however, of the weekly press talks Eleanor Roosevelt had given, and she was therefore quite relieved to learn that the practice was totally up to her. Bess quickly wielded her power as first lady to stop these press conferences and began her term as a distinctively different first lady. Truman writes that Bess "struggled to give some shape and coherence to her role as First Lady in the shadow of her famous predecessor" (1986, 75). That shadow was quite large and impressive, but Bess was simply not interested in pursuing the same types of activism and did not want the public attention or scrutiny upon which Eleanor had thrived.

This section focuses, first, on Bess Truman's unique rhetorical relationship with the press and other aspects of the role that she found difficult and, second, on the activities that she felt well-suited to perform. In the end, her most enduring role as first lady from her perspective was as a political partner for her husband. When she felt estranged from Harry and his work, she grew very unhappy, but when she was involved in executing the tasks of "their presidency," she did an excellent job by using both her interpersonal communication skills and her writing ability.

The Washington press, of course, was extremely unhappy with Bess's decision to abandon the press conferences. As a result, they quickly dubbed her: "No Comment Bess." The press corps that followed Eleanor was mostly comprised of women reporters who had found a way, through Mrs. Roosevelt, to enter the world of political reporting, no matter how marginal the first lady's affairs may have been, compared to the actions of the president. Being denied regular meetings deprived them of a key source of information and made it difficult for them to satisfy their audience of women readers who were interested in White House affairs. Needless to say, Bess's decision evoked an immediate negative response from reporters, many of whom became relentless in calling the office of the first lady to ask (beg) for details of Bess's everyday business. The more the press harped on her inaccessibility, the more Bess dug in her heels. Truman writes that when a reporter called to ask what Bess was wearing to a reception, "she was blunt: 'Tell her it's none of her business'" (1986, 76). Staffers had to try and put such comments more gracefully to the press.

Bess's "compromise" to the press was to offer a session in the Green Room of the White House every two weeks at which her staff secretaries, Edith Helm and Reathel Odum, reported any activities that she or Margaret wanted to make public. The secretaries also noted questions that the press wanted Bess to answer. Bess's answers were often quick and to the point. Most of the questions centered on her likes and dislikes about clothing, food, hobbies, and interests. Close-ended questions such as "Did she go to college?" or "Does she like gardening?" were usually met with a simple "Yes" or "No." Even an open-ended question such as, "What would you like to do and have your husband do when he is no longer President?" received a three-word retort of "Return to Independence." Perhaps her most well-known answer was to the question, "What qualities, innate or acquired, does Mrs. Truman think would be the greatest asset for the wife of a President?" Bess's response was, "Good health and a well developed sense of humor" (Press Meetings with Mrs. Helm and Miss Odum, Box 4, Odum Papers, HST Library).

Bess's irritation with the press was obvious in her lack of interest in speaking with them personally. Her secretaries mediated all requests from reporters and only forwarded certain items to the first lady. Bess's attitude shines through in one particular note responding to a letter from Reathel Odum. Her personal secretary's official letter to Bess read:

> Mrs. Truman:
> Betty Beale, one of the reporters, telephoned me and asked what is keeping Margaret in Independence. She said Margaret is missing the Junior League provisional course—and that you had told them she would not be back before Nov. 1. Miss Beale insisted that I ask you the reason for Margaret's staying in Missouri—and said she would telephone me in the morning for the answer. R.O.

In her own handwriting on the bottom of the letter, Bess scrawled out her reply:

> Finishing a course in voice lessons—Better tell her. God only knows what they may be saying—I'd prefer telling her it's none of their d--- business. (Bess Truman to Reathel Odum, Box 4, Odum Papers, HST Library)

Regrettably for Bess, her first public appearance as first lady was the press's business, and she made headlines. Bess was asked to christen an airplane at the Washington National Airport on May 30, 1945. Because the nose of an airplane is a great deal softer than a ship and because the first champagne bottle had not been cut, Bess swung the bottle at the plane eleven times—all to no avail. She then went over to christen another plane and, with a second powerful swing, showered champagne all over herself and a nearby naval officer. One article noted that the unraveled Bess "smilingly" posed for a picture next to the plane and remarked, "Well, let's make a picture of the bottle that won't break." When the president was reported to have laughed and suggested that "the First Lady ought to have pushed back her hat, spat on her hands, and let fly with a mighty swing as she used to do when they played sandlot baseball as kids," Bess replied, "I'm sorry I didn't swing that bottle at you" (Means 1963, 233). This situation was quite humiliating and undoubtedly reinforced her distain for public appearances and press coverage throughout the rest of her tenure as first lady.

In the fall of 1945, Bess Truman's firm decision that she was not an elected official and thus did not have to behave as one, made headlines. It was a significant controversy and Bess's response to the situation was released to the press. The incident became a turning point in discussions of the role of the first lady in setting an example for the country. The new wife of New York congressman Adam Clayton Powell, Hazel Scott, was denied the use of Constitution Hall in Washington, D.C., to give a concert because of her race. The hall, owned and operated by the Daughters of the American Revolution (DAR), had rules that forbade all nonwhites from performing. On October 1, Powell sent Truman a telegram asking for his assistance with the racial discrimination that barred his wife from the hall. Truman did not send an official response; so, on October 11, Powell sent another telegram to the president and one to Bess.

Six years earlier, Eleanor Roosevelt had resigned from the DAR, when another African American performer was not allowed to perform in the hall. Her resignation was "a further symbolic statement by Eleanor Roosevelt of her abhorrence of racial discrimination, and it was received in black communities with considerable gratitude and respect" (Hamilton 1991, 165). Soon before Hazel Scott's rejection from Constitution Hall, Bess had accepted an invitation to tea with the DAR. Powell's telegram on October 11, reminded her of her predecessor's reactions to a similar incident and requested her to cancel her acceptance to the tea to "publicly denounce the DAR's action." Bess responded that she did not see a relationship between her previous acceptance to a tea and the Constitution Hall incident. Her telegram, released to the press, stated:

> In acknowledging your telegram of October eleventh, may I call your attention to the fact that the invitation to which you refer was extended and accepted prior to the unfortunate controversy which has arisen. Personally I regret that a conflict has arisen for which I am in nowise responsible. In my opinion my acceptance of the hospitality is not related to the merits of the issue which has since arisen. I deplore any action which denies artistic talent an opportunity to express itself because of prejudice against race or origin. (Bess Truman Vertical File, HST Library)

For his own part, President Truman's telegram responded that the government could not place demands on a private institution such as the DAR to host Powell's wife. Harry noted that "One of the marks of a democracy is its willingness to respect and reward talent without regard to race or origin . . . I am sure that you will realize however the impossibility of any interference by me in the management or policy of a private enterprise such as the one in question" (Bess Truman Vertical File, HST Library).

Congressman Powell responded by calling Bess "the last lady" of the land, and Harry was furious. He did not tolerate criticism of his wife or his daughter. The incident went no further, but Harry never invited the congressman to the White House again, even to ceremonial parties for members of Congress and their wives. Hamilton (1991) notes: "each man was protecting the honor and integrity of his wife, with racial prejudice at the center of the antagonism" (165). One Missouri woman wrote to the *Washington Post* in support of Bess's actions, stating that she ought to be able to make her own decisions, just like her predecessor:

> Because Mrs. Roosevelt liked politics, and herself was born to the prestige of public life, and herself seemed to like a good fight is no reason why Mrs. Truman must follow in her footsteps unless she desires to do so. Many may have criticized Mrs. Roosevelt's point of view but I seem to remember nobody tried to deprive her of the right to think for herself. Those who violently disagreed with her at times granted her the right to such individuality, and I think, in the long run, respected her for being herself. (Murray, Bess Truman Vertical File, HST Library)

While there were many letters, telegrams, and editorials aimed at the first lady's decision, it had become clear that Bess was going to make up her mind, for right or wrong, and for good or bad publicity.

The *New York Times Magazine* ran a story on Bess on June 9, 1946, and gave the full text of Bess's only speech on record:

> Good Afternoon. I take great pleasure in introducing Franklin D. Roosevelt (FDR), Jr., whom I am happy to have as my guest in the White House in place of his mother. He will preside at today's broadcast. (27)

Bess's brief introduction of FDR Jr. was given at the March-of-Dimes campaign. Franklin Jr. was filling in for Eleanor who had suddenly been sent to London as the only United States woman delegate to the United Nations Assembly. Clearly, these were two very different first ladies.

Press relations, including coverage of the Powell incident, were not the only factors that made the first years of the presidency hard on the Trumans. Other pressures on Harry limited the couple's time together, and this had a negative effect on Bess. In *First Ladies*, Margaret Truman writes:

> Never has any President in American history had to learn more about the problems facing him—and make world-shaping decisions about them faster—than Harry S. Truman. . . . In this avalanche of decisions and events, Bess Truman played little part. More and more, she began to feel that the presidency had virtually dissolved the political partnership that had been at the heart of her relationship with her husband for so many years. (1995, 75)

As Harry devoted more and more time to the Oval Office, Bess grew increasingly angry with him and with her role as first lady. In 1945, Bess and Margaret first escaped Washington six days before Christmas to spend the holidays at home in Independence. Because he was embroiled in foreign policy negotiations, Harry did not arrive until Christmas day. The weather across the country was quite severe, but Harry had his official plane, the Sacred Cow, make the treacherous journey. Bess did not greet him with open arms and warmth toward his gesture. "So, you've finally arrived," Bess said, "As far as I'm concerned, you might as well have stayed in Washington" (Truman 1986, 280). Harry could only stay until December 27, when he rushed back to the White House.

Margaret Truman relates the next events between her parents that demonstrate the importance of their partnership. After returning to Washington, Harry was so distraught over Bess's chilly demeanor at Christmas that he angrily wrote her a letter and sent it special delivery. He phoned Margaret the next day to ask her to retrieve the letter and burn it. He wrote another letter, describing how much he valued Bess, noting, "You can never appreciate what it means to come home as I did the other evening after doing at least one hundred things I didn't want to do and have the only person in the world whose approval and good opinion I value look at me like I'm something the cat dragged in" (Truman 1986, 78). According to Margaret, this letter had a lot to do with Bess's better mood and attitude when she returned to Washington in 1946. No matter the weight of the presidency, Bess was to be included, not excluded, from her husband's life. They were partners before the presidency, and Bess simply would not tolerate any changes in this aspect of their relationship.

When Harry decided to run for his own term as president in 1948, Bess was unhappy that she would not be returning to Independence. She did not express this displeasure by leaving Harry's side, but traveled with him on his famous whistle-stop campaign. A reporter traveling on the Truman train wrote that Bess was "a one-woman Gallup Poll and audience-reaction tester, keeping a sharp watch on the crowds which listened to her husband's oratory. She was also the careful censor of the President's occasional lapses into humorous over exuberance" (Means 1963, 229). President Truman often received his loudest applause when he would introduce Bess and Margaret to the crowds as "The Boss" and "The Boss's Boss." Washington reporter Bess Furman posed several written questions to Bess for her book on the role of the first lady. Bess Truman hand wrote her answers after each question:

> Q: If it had been left to your own free choice would you have gone into the White House in the first place?
> A: Most definitely, would *not* have.
> Q: Now that the position of President's wife is an old story, is it really enjoyable?
> A: There are enjoyable spots, it's true, but they are in the minority.
> Q: Does returning to the Midwest each summer help in keeping a proper perspective on world affairs and or life in the White House?
> A: Returning to Mo. each summer is just a trip "*home*" and everything that means to anyone.
> Q: Does a peaceful world seem closer to you or farther away than when the Truman administration started?
> A: We were still in the midst of a shooting war when the T. administration started. (Bess Truman to Bess Furman, Odum Papers, Box 5, HST Library)

Truman pulled off the election, defeating John Dewey. He even went to bed early on election night, while Bess and Margaret stayed up all night waiting for the election results, which eventually showed that it would be four long years before "The Boss" would be able to return home to Independence.

If Bess Truman disliked and avoided some aspects of being first lady, she enjoyed and excelled at others. One of her best characteristics was as a communicator at the interpersonal level. She was a dedicated supporter of her family, friends, and husband—and they knew it through her words to them and her actions. Bess was also highly praised by those who met her for being a warm and gracious hostess. Her memory for names and faces was quite impressive. Means writes that "she once sent a note down the head table to the President to remind him that the shy dinner partner he was ignoring was Dr. Lise Meitner, the noted atomic scientist" (1963, 226). Her interpersonal skills are also reflected in press coverage of White House affairs. On November 15, 1945, Bess held a dinner party for over one hundred press women at the White House. Betty Hynes of the *Washington Times-Herald* wrote that Bess:

> proved again last night that no First Lady ever made guests feel more at home. She wandered between the tables chatting now here, now there, revealing her rare gift of making each guest believe that she had her personal interest and happiness very much at heart. (November 16, 1945, 47)

Another reporter invited to the dinner party, Austine Cassini, noted that Bess

was as vigilant a hostess of the large group as she would have been at an intimate supper in her Independence home. In "These Charming People," he wrote:

> When one latecomer arrived, Mrs. Truman jumped up, crossed the room to
> greet the embarrassed girl, and find her a seat. Conversationally, Bess did more
> listening . . . However, don't be deceived. She's not all "motherly home-
> body"—she's smart, knows the score, and never misses a trick! (Bess Truman
> Vertical file, HST Library).

A *Time* magazine article describes how Bess decided to entertain members of
Congress at two teas instead of a large state dinner:

> She greeted all 400 guests with enthusiasm, fumbled nary a name. Introduc-
> tions over, she worked hard to keep everybody milling in the huge state dining
> room while a red-coated Marine band played familiar airs. . . . Everybody de-
> clared the party a big success. Bess Truman had made a good start as first lady.
> ("The Presidency" 1945, 17)

The White House staff also enjoyed Bess's warmth and good humor. She
pushed them to be more tidy and efficient, but spoke to them more as equals
than as a superior. J. B. West, chief usher at the White House during the Truman
administration, noted that Bess and Harry would introduce their house staff to
company, a practice never before kept by previous residents.

Bess's written communication was also abundant. She thought of her letters
as personal, however, and was dubious of strangers reading what she had written. One letter to Harry early in her marriage began "Sweetie," and then in pa-
rentheses it read "Burn this in the stove" (Truman 1986, 90). Twenty-five years
later, Bess assured herself that her letters to Harry would not be seen by others.
Margaret Truman tells the story:

> Around Christmas time of that year, [1955] Dad walked into the living room
> and found Mother sitting before the fireplace, in which a brisk blaze was crack-
> ling. All around her were piles of letters. As she finished one, she tossed it into
> the fire. "Bess," Dad said. "What are you doing?" "Burning our letters," she
> said. "Bess," Dad said, "Think of History." "I have," Mother said, and tossed
> another letter on the fire. (1986, 404)

Bess did not burn as many of Harry's letters to her, but rather "with that
determination to stay in the background that was the essence of her role in their
partnership, she burned almost all of her letters" to him (Truman 1986, 404).
Unfortunately, her desire to keep her personal life private has made researching
this unique first lady more difficult.

Perhaps, Bess Truman's largest contribution to the rhetorical role of the first
lady was as her husband's political partner. Harry often referred to Bess as his
"helper." Truman writes: "As senator he said he never made a report or a speech
without her editing it" and when he ran for vice president, Bess told a reporter
that she would help with his speeches "because we've done that so long, it's a
habit" (1995, 83). West writes: "the full impact of Bess Truman's contribution

to the history of America, and, indeed, of the world, will probably never be measured" (1974, 127). He adds that her vision of the role of first lady as a background support system kept her "keen intelligence, calm reasoning, and unswerving devotion" to Harry out of the limelight, so that "few people knew . . . she was his full partner, in every sense of the word" (1974, 127).

Ten years after the Trumans left the White House, Harry was interviewed by Marianne Means for her book, *The Woman in the White House*. He said, Bess was "a full partner in all my transactions—politically and otherwise" (1963, 217). He explained that he consulted her about every decision he had ever made, including the United States' involvement in Korea, the use of the atom bomb, and the initiation of the Marshall Plan. "I discussed all of them with her. . . . Why not? . . . Her judgment was always good . . . She never made a suggestion that wasn't for the welfare and benefit of the country and what I was trying to do. She looks at things objectively, and I can't always" (217).

Bess Truman may have shunned the spotlight, but she did not shun hard work. She may have preferred her role as wife and homemaker, but when her husband became president and home became the White House, the meaning of those roles changed dramatically. Bess worked hard on a number of charitable causes to support needy citizens. She was a member, sponsor, patron, honorary member, or honorary president of over eighty organizations from 1945 to 1947. In Washington, D.C., Bess became active in the H Street USO, the Red Cross, and the Congressional Club. She served as an honorary president of such organizations as the Girl Scouts, the Women's National Democratic Club, and the National Achievement Award Committee. She was an honorary member of the American Newspaper Women's Club, Business and Professional Women's Club, Daughters of Colonial Wars, Sulgrave Club, United Nations Club, Red Cross Motor Corps, and the Women's National Farm and Garden Association. In Missouri, Bess was a life member of the Women's City Club of Kansas City, an honorary member of Independence's Pioneer Chapter and vice president of the Jackson County Welfare Board (Odum Papers, Organizations of Mrs. Truman, Box 5, HST Library). Bess may have been characterized as a housewife, but she spent a great deal of time outside of the home, helping others.

A typical week of activities for Bess would include two or three receptions, teas, or luncheons a day, several state or honorary dinners, and at least two benefits or receptions of special groups (Mrs. Truman's Engagements to Be Given to the Press, Odum Papers, Box 2, HST Library). While Bess may have avoided the press, she certainly did not "hide" from the public or what she defined as her official duties. In his book, *Mr. Citizen*, Harry Truman wrote: "I hope some day someone will take time to evaluate the true role of the wife of a President, and to assess the many burdens she has to bear and the contributions she makes" (quoted in Means 1963, 218).

Legacy

There was a sign on President Truman's desk: "The Buck Stops Here." However, we knew that the buck didn't stop there. He packed it in his briefcase every night, took it upstairs, and discussed it with "The Boss." (West 1974, 127)

Bess Truman demonstrated her communication skills as first lady mostly through her well-developed interpersonal skills and her role as White House hostess. Her ability to put people at ease at large government gatherings was very helpful in smoothing out her husband's abrupt entry into the presidency. Bess's legacy as first lady, however, is that she refused to live her life by anyone else's opinions or rules. She held stubbornly to her own idea of what the role of the president's wife ought to be, and neither sought, nor accepted, the opinions of others. In addition, while she lived the principle that a first lady's job is to help the president, she also made it clear that her own emotions and welfare were second to none.

Helen Erskine wrote an article about Bess for *Collier's* that was published February 9, 1952, and titled, "The Riddle of Mrs. Truman." This article began by stating that despite the first lady's attempts to remain obscure, she was an important part of the political scene. The first lines of the article state:

> Mrs. Harry S. Truman is a mystery to the American people. Under other cir-cumstances, that might not matter. It happens, however, that we are all directly or indirectly influenced by what the wife of the President of the United States thinks, says, and does. We ought to try to understand her. The first lady has de-liberately sought obscurity. But the position she occupies is a public position, and she cannot retreat from its demands without failing her husband—which her pride never would allow her to do. She must stay in the picture of the Tru-man administration. She has no choice but to play her part in it as long as it lasts. (1952, 11)

The article discusses various aspects of Bess's life, most notably her public appearances, dealings with the press, and interviews with friends. Erskine quotes one acquaintance of Bess's who explained that she avoided public scrutiny be-cause of her shyness, and that "she is perplexed by her dilemma of being the wife of the President of the United States. Independent as the day is long, origi-nal in her views, she has a certain amount of philosophy, and is sensitive. That makes her shrink from people" (Erskine 1952, 60). The anonymous source also explains how extremely fearful Bess was for Harry's safety and that her reaction to this worry was to repress her feelings publicly, which in turn made her a tar-get for people hungry for another Eleanor Roosevelt. Perhaps it was a reaction to such misunderstanding that made Bess become even more withdrawn from the press, or perhaps she was only trying to protect herself and her family from negative publicity. Whatever her reasons, Bess Truman was quite successful throughout her years as first lady in distancing herself from public scrutiny.

Bess Truman felt, rhetorically, that Harry's words were more important than her own to the public interest. However, that did not mean she thought her opinions were less important behind the scenes. As far as Bess was concerned, Harry had chosen to be the politician, not herself. She shaped the role of the first lady, making it clear that she would not be a dupe at the hands or pens of the press. Bess's strategies of resistance set a new precedent for the first ladies' staff. It became their job, not that of the first lady, to brief the press and provide fodder for their stories. The first lady did not have an official press secretary until Jackie Kennedy, but Bess Truman's staff was indispensable in the often cantankerous relationship between their boss and the press.

While Bess may have shunned her mother's perspective on how a "wife" behaves, her lack of interest in dealing with the media was directly in line with Madge Wallace's moral standards of what was appropriate behavior for a "lady." Bess may have been a more modern presidential *wife*, but she embodied the values of a traditional *lady*. Troy writes that it would be illogical to trace the transformations in the role of first lady in tandem with the rise of feminism in the country (1997, 1). Perhaps the individual women themselves are not to be characterized alongside the development of feminism, but rather each woman's redefinition of the role that "lady" played in her position as the president's partner. For in their exalted status, first ladies often appear to set the standards of what constitutes ladylike behavior.

Bess Truman did not want to be a business partner with her husband, as her predecessor Eleanor Roosevelt had become, but she wanted to be a full marriage partner. For her, this meant that Harry should be as thoroughly involved in her life as she was in his. Bess would not be satisfied unless her husband was just as interested in making her happy as she was in pleasing him. For example, she was not about to sacrifice her own happiness by staying away from Independence for long periods. She stood by Harry as he took the job, but that didn't mean that she had to suffer. Both members of the couple were unhappy when they were apart, and Bess saw her needs as "equally" important as Harry's. This was not a traditional "Victorian" marriage by any means, but a union of equal partners. This partnership was how Harry got into office in the first place, and he never forgot it. On one of the rare occasions that Bess gave a full answer to one of the questions that reporters submitted, she acknowledged the importance of public communication for a first lady. A reporter inquired: "If such a thing were possible, what special training would she recommend to prepare a woman for the role of First Lady?" Bess responded, "Skill in public speaking very helpful [sic]" (Press Meetings with Mrs. Helm and Miss Odum, Box 4, Odum Papers, HST Library). Bess had been trained from her early childhood in the art of being a warm and gracious hostess, but she had never been taught how to speak in public. Her intelligence and wit made her an extremely helpful editor for Harry's speeches, but she, herself, did not have the experience necessary to feel comfortable speaking to audiences. The neat, tidy, and perfectly tailored Mrs. Truman was not interested in letting public rhetoric get the best of her. In every aspect of her performance as the first lady, Bess Truman clearly showed her independence.

Notes

Original letters, notes, and transcripts were obtained from the Harry S. Truman Presidential Library, Independence, Missouri. I would like to acknowledge the help of their staff in locating them. Materials cited come from the Mary Paxton Keeley Papers, the Reathel Odum Papers, and the Vertical File on Bess Truman as indicated.

References

Anderson, Alice E., and Hadley V. Baxendale. 1992. *Behind Every Successful President: The Hidden Power and Influence of America's First Ladies.* New York: Sapolsky Publishers.

Anthony, Carl Sferrazza. 1990. *First Ladies: The Saga of the Presidents' Wives and Their Power 1789–1961,* Vol. 1. New York: William Morrow.

———. 1991. *First Ladies: The Saga of the Presidents' Wives and Their Power 1961–1990,* Vol. 2. New York: William Morrow.

Auster, Bruce B. 1986. The First Lady Picks Her Battles. *U.S. News and World Report,* 2 September, 26.

Barzman, Sol. 1970. *The First Ladies.* New York: Cowles Book Company, Inc.

Beasley, Maurine. 1989. Harry's Silent Partner: The Papers of Bess Truman. In *Modern First Ladies: Their Documentary Legacy,* ed. Nancy Kegan Smith and Mary C. Ryan. Washington, D.C.: National Archives and Records Administration.

Behind Mrs. Truman's Social Curtain. 1947. *Newsweek,* 10 November, 16.

Bess Truman Vertical File, Harry S. Truman Library, Independence, Mo.

Boller, Paul F. 1988. *Presidential Wives.* New York: Oxford University Press.

Brown, Margaret W. 1952. *Dresses of the First Ladies of the White House.* Washington, D.C.: Smithsonian Institution.

Caroli, Betty Boyd. 1987. *First Ladies.* New York: Oxford University Press.

Daniel, Clifton Truman. 1995. *Memories of Harry Truman: Growing Up with My Grandfather.* New York: Birch Lane.

Erskine, Helen W. 1952. The Riddle of Mrs. Truman, *Collier's,* 9 February, 11.

Feinberg, Barbara Silberdick. 1998. *America's First Ladies: Changing Expectations.* New York: Franklin Watts.

Ferrell, Robert H., ed. 1983. *Dear Bess: The Letters from Harry to Bess Truman, 1910–1959.* New York: Norton.

Foreman, Norma Ruth Holly. 1971. *The First Lady as a Leader of Public Opinion: A Study of the Role and Press Relations of Lady Bird Johnson.* Austin, Tex.: University of Texas.

Furman, Bess. 1946. Independent Lady from Independence. *New York Times Magazine,* 9 June, 20.

———. 1951. *White House Profile.* Indianapolis, Ind.: Bobbs-Merrill.

Gould, Lewis. 1996. There's History to Role of First Lady. *Quill,* March, 29.

Grimes, Ann. 1990. *Running Mates: The Making of a First Lady.* New York: William Morrow.

Gutin, Myra G. 1989. *The President's Partner: The First Lady in the Twentieth Century.* New York: Greenwood.

Hamilton, Charles. 1991. *Adam Clayton Powell Jr.: The Political Biography of an American Dilemma.* New York: Atheneum.

Hay, Peter. 1988. *All The Presidents' Ladies: Anecdotes of the Women behind the Men in the White House.* New York: Viking.

Healy, Dianna Dixon. 1988. *America's First Ladies: Private Lives of the Presidential Wives.* New York: Atheneum.

Helm, Edith. 1954. *The Captains and the Kings.* New York: Putnam's.

Hynes, Betty. 1945. Ladies of Press are Guests of Mrs. Truman. *Washington Times-Herald*, 16 November, 47.

Keeley, Mary Paxton Papers. n.d. Truman's Wife on U.S. Payroll. Box 1. Independence, Mo.: Harry S. Truman Library.

McCourt, Kathleen. 1977. *Working Class*. Bloomington, Ind.: Indiana University Press.

McCullough, David. 1992. *Truman*. New York: Simon & Schuster.

McNaughton, Frank. 1945. *This Man Truman*. New York: McGraw-Hill.

Means, Marianne. 1963. *The Woman in the White House: The Lives, Times and Influence of Twelve Notable First Ladies*. New York: Random House.

Odum, Reathel Papers. 1945. Organizations of Mrs. Truman. Box 5. Independence, Mo.: Harry S. Truman Library.

————. 1945. Press Meetings with Mrs. Helm and Miss Odum. Box 4, December 6. Independence, Mo.: Harry S. Truman Library.

————. 1946. Bess Truman to Reathel Odum, Box 5, October 11. Independence, Mo.: Harry S. Truman Library.

————. 1948. Bess Truman to Bess Furman. Box 5. Independence, Mo.: Harry S. Truman Library.

————. 1948–1949. Mrs. Truman's Engagements to Be Given to the Press. Box 2. Independence, Mo.: Harry S. Truman Library.

Paletta, Lu Ann. 1990. *The World Almanac of First Ladies*. New York: World Almanac.

The Presidency: Tea for 400. 1945. *Time*, 17 December, 17.

Prindiville, Kathleen. 1932. *First Ladies*. New York: Macmillan Company.

Robbins, Jhan. 1980. *Bess & Harry: An American Love Story*. New York: Putnam's.

Rosebush, James S. 1987. *First Lady, Public Wife*. New York: Madison Books.

Sadler, Christine. 1963. *America's First Ladies*. New York: MacFadden.

Troy, Gil. 1997. *Affairs of the State: The Rise and Rejection of the Presidential Couple since World War II*. New York: Free Press

Truman, Margaret. 1956. *Souvenir*. New York: McGraw-Hill.

————. 1986. *Bess W. Truman*. New York: Macmillan.

————. 1995. *First Ladies*. New York: Random House.

Wallace, Chris. 1986. *First Lady: A Portrait of Nancy Reagan*. New York: St. Martin's Press.

West, J. B. 1974. *Upstairs at the White House*. New York: Warner.

Chapter 12

Mamie Geneva Doud Eisenhower
Reflecting the Mood of the Nation

Kathleen M. German

> It would have been Colonel Dwight David Eisenhower, if it weren't for Mamie.
> —Kevin McCann, Eisenhower aide

Known more for her signature pink, curled bangs, and charm bracelets than for her political views, Mamie Eisenhower has been regarded as a traditional first lady. By the time she entered the White House in 1953, she had served as a military wife for much of her marriage. In spite of this semipublic role into which her husband's career thrust her, Mamie's aversion to the public spotlight and political participation was well known. Still, she dominated lists of most admired women and continued to be one of the most popular first ladies of the twentieth century.

Perhaps the best explanation for her popularity is that she reinforced the traditional profile of women. As President Carter reflected upon her death, "To generations of Americans, in war and peace, she embodied sincerity and traditional values" (1979, 2074). Mamie regarded herself as primarily a supporter of her husband, minimizing her role as a leader of public opinion. In this guise, Mamie Eisenhower reflected the mood of the nation. In many ways, her public image constituted a metaphor for her times. She reinforced the traditional values of family life and served as an inspiration to many Americans desperately striving for normalcy in the aftermath of World War II.

Among Americans, public expectations were framed by the postwar as soldiers reclaimed their jobs, women returned to their homes, and patriotism flourished. Traditional gender roles, temporarily disrupted by the crisis of war, returned with force. To the extent that the presidency mirrors the mood of the nation, the Eisenhower presidency reflected a nation single-mindedly seeking to rebuild domestic life disrupted by years of war and threatened by global communism.

Mamie Eisenhower perfectly fit the era. Her role as first lady was dominated by her understanding of her place as helpmate and hostess ("Mamie Leaves the Politics to Ike" 1954). The military model that shaped the Eisenhower's early marriage and served well during the political campaign remained unchanged during the White House years. As historian Betty Boyd Caroli summarizes it: "The First Lady's favorite color fit well America's mood in the 1950s when femininity meant opinionless dependence. . . . Mamie Eisenhower did not invent that model of femininity, but she represented it well, making clear by her every public utterance that she thought a wife's role entirely secondary and supportive" (1987, 210–11). Mamie was, according to one enthusiastic supporter in 1944, "a true symbol of the American wife and mother" (Miller 1944, 114). She enacted middle-class values of frugality, sincerity, loyalty to family (Gould 1986). As her son John put it, "No women's libber, she consciously developed a philosophy of always putting her husband on center stage" ("Six Former First Ladies" 1977, 52).

As a first lady, Mamie Eisenhower symbolized the private life, personalizing her husband's presidency by adding the dimension of family life to his political image. Throughout the Eisenhower years, the symbolic dimension of private life was expressed primarily through Mamie's role as a traditional first lady. In particular, Mamie Eisenhower's cultivation of her role as White House hostess, reticence in public communication, and loyalty to her husband (in spite of compelling evidence that she was quite different in private) mark her tenure as first lady.

Mamie Eisenhower was preceded in the White House by the reclusive Bess Truman and followed by media magnet Jackie Kennedy. But she was nothing like them. Unlike Bess Truman, Mamie enjoyed public attention as the country's hostess. In contrast to Jackie Kennedy, Mamie appeared almost dowdy. This chapter will explore facets of her early life, the transition from military wife to political life, her rhetorical activities, and Mamie's legacy as first lady.

Biography

When Barbara Walters asked for the secret of their fifty-year marriage, Mamie Eisenhower replied, "Well, I don't know what it is for everyone . . . but I'll tell what it is for us. We have absolutely nothing in common!" (1974, 64). From all apparent evidence this statement captures the essence of the Eisenhower marriage and aids our understanding of their partnership in the White House.

Dwight Eisenhower and Mamie Doud came from distinctly different social classes. His father was a financial failure in several ventures and Dwight was raised with his four brothers in a rented house in the rough part of Abilene, Kansas. In contrast, the Doud family had been members of the landed gentry in England and came to the New World in 1639 to become leading citizens of the community, making additional fortunes in the process. Her father, John Sheldon Doud, was so successful in the meat packing business that he was able to retire at age 36. Her mother, Elivera Mathilda Carlson, whose father owned farms and flour mills, was also raised in a propertied family. Married at sixteen, Elivera had four daughters, Eleanor, Marie, Eda Mae, and Mabel Frances ("Mike"), before she was twenty-five. Marie ("Mamie") Geneva Doud was the second daughter, born in Boone, Iowa, on November 14, 1896. The family settled in Denver when Mamie was six, and she attended public elementary and high schools. As proper for other young women of means, Mamie ended her formal education with a year of finishing school at Miss Walcott's School.

Although marred by the deaths of sisters Eleanor from heart disease and Eda Mae of nephritis, Mamie's childhood was happy. Family life for the Douds was comfortable, and they commanded social prominence. Mamie was popular among her peers with innumerable friends and gentlemen callers. Former admirers often compared her to Lillian Gish, a contemporary Hollywood actress. As was the custom, Mamie received callers at the family home during early evenings chaperoned by her parents. Sunday afternoon drives through town in the family Packard were also frequent. In the winters, the Douds traveled to San Antonio to escape the cold.

While her family was visiting the Hunter Harris family in October 1915, Mamie met Second Lieutenant Dwight Eisenhower who was assigned to the 19th Infantry at Fort Sam Houston. "He was the handsomest man I ever laid eyes on," Mamie recalled (quoted in Gould 1996, 466). He convinced Mamie who hated walking to accompany him on guard duty rounds; but because her social calendar was so full, he was unable to arrange a formal date until a month later. Persistence and his presence at the family home scared away other, more timid callers and the couple was married on July 1, 1916, when Ike was twenty-five, and Mamie, nineteen.

Biographers note the clash of social class from the beginning of the marriage. Mamie had never learned to cook except for fudge—hardly a staple. The Eisenhowers ate at the officers' mess in spite of its prohibitive cost of $60, one-third of their monthly income. Meanwhile, Mamie enrolled in a basic cooking course. Even though she learned to make mayonnaise, Mamie later told friends "I was a cooking-school dropout" (David and David 1981, 65). Ike eventually became an accomplished cook, noted for his four-inch steaks, pot roast, Mexican style chicken, and vegetable soup. Although Mamie's Million Dollar Fudge was featured in many magazine articles during the presidential years, there is little evidence of other culinary skills.

The clash of social class was also apparent in Mamie's reliance on others for transportation. Although she apparently could drive her family's electric Packard, she never learned to drive the couple's Pullman. She made a few attempts to learn but gave up in the mid-1930s and relied on chauffeurs afterwards. The Eisenhowers established their relationship long before they entered political life. Mamie managed the family finances with close scrutiny and coordinated each relocation required by military duty. This meant uprooting the household twenty-seven times in thirty-eight years, living in the Canal Zone, Europe, the Philippines, and in army posts across the United States. Their only permanent home was a farmhouse purchased in 1949 but not lived in until after the White House years.

Perhaps because this marital rootlessness clashed with her early strong family ties, domestic life was always the central concern for Mamie. Nevertheless, it was not without tragedy. Their first child, Doud Dwight Eisenhower, born at Fort Sam Houston died of scarlet fever in 1921, at four years of age. A second son, John Sheldon Doud Eisenhower, born in 1922, served as an infantry major in the Korean War and produced three grandchildren. He later became an author and served as ambassador to Belgium.

Mamie's reluctance to step into the public spotlight was obvious from the beginning of their relationship. Instead, she excelled at dealing with people interpersonally, particularly as a hostess. She was herself an informal person—vivacious and pretty, poised and friendly. She organized social gatherings, even renting a piano in the early days of their marriage so that other young officer couples could gather and sing in the evenings. As a result of this talent, Mamie is credited with winning "a great deal of good will for Ike among the top brass as well as among junior officers" (Boller 1988, 336).

Although she often smoothed the way for her husband socially, Mamie did not express her thoughts on military or political matters. During World War II, unlike other generals' wives whose publicized opinions sometimes caused public controversy, Mamie did not make comments for newspaper and magazine articles. In the years following the war, her role was inconspicuous. She offered loyal, but silent public support for her husband.

However, there were several occasions when her domestic management caused some public controversy, although short-lived. For example, Ike was assigned living quarters in a chateau near Paris while stationed at NATO headquarters. Mamie rejected the chateau known as Villa Trianon, once home to Marie Antoinette, in favor of a two-story house in Villa St. Pierre. French designers assigned to help her redecorate their house were dismissed and Mamie decorated in her favorite colors, pink and green. She even ordered a plot of corn planted outside to remind her of home. The French were aghast and unfortunate publicity followed. To make matters worse, her refusal to purchase clothing at fashionable Parisian salons also deeply offended the French, especially when she forthrightly explained that her wardrobe was purchased mail order from home, much of it for $10.00 or less (David and David 1981; Wallace 1952).

Some biographers argue that although Mamie was opposite Ike in almost every respect, the contrast complemented him. Mamie served as hostess and polished Ike's rough edges so that he became adept at moving in ever higher military and political circles. Mamie may have provided an understanding of social graces that a poor boy could not have experienced in his early life. John Eisenhower, Ike's brother, noted, "She takes full credit for smoothing the edges off the rough-and-ready Kansan and for teaching him some of the polish that later put him in good stead" (quoted in Neal 1978, 36). Kevin McCann, Eisenhower aide, concluded, "It would have been Colonel Dwight David Eisenhower, if it weren't for Mamie" (Neal 1978, 36). She introduced him to a more sophisticated way of life and instilled a deep confidence that he had not acquired in the narrow social structure in Abilene and West Point.

Mamie also contributed to normalizing Ike's otherwise public life. She insulated him from the pressures of office by demanding private dinners and evening time. Her responsibility for making their home perhaps gave Ike a safe harbor during his otherwise unsettled life. Her insistence on relaxation is credited with Ike's recovery after his first-term heart attack and his ability to continue the duties of the presidency in spite of a serious heart condition ("'Rocking Chair' Routine" 1955).

The Transition from Military to Political Life

Before she became first lady, Mamie promoted Ike's election, at the same time, honing her own rhetorical skills. On the campaign trial, Mamie was a constant feature although decidedly in the background. Her primary duties were to pose with Ike for press cameras, to answer hundreds of letters each week, and to avoid becoming entangled in public issues. She did not make speeches and when cornered, her longest public comments did not exceed twenty words. Usually their substance was an expression of gratitude. Summarizing Mamie's contribution to the campaign effort, a *Life* reporter who followed the candidates on the campaign trail wrote, "No one will ever find Mamie seeking attention or involved in any controversy, nor will she be found aloof and unapproachable. She will have all the highly commendable dignity of Bess Truman enlivened with a touch of Ethel Merman on the side" (Wallace 1952, 158). The article included a photo that symbolized the Eisenhower relationship. The photographer captured Mamie in dark silhouette sitting quietly behind while Ike, illuminated by spotlights, spoke at the podium. Always in the background, Mamie was Ike's most loyal supporter.

The 1952 Republican Convention in Chicago was, by many accounts, mean-spirited and often nasty, but it allowed Mamie to establish a distinct public image (Sillars 1958). Dorothy Brandon, who covered the women's social dinner, wasn't prepared for the "outright daggerishness" of the members. Mamie, who politely refused to address the group after her introduction, even though someone yelled "speech" from the audience, was followed by Hedda Hopper, Hollywood columnist, as the main speaker. Hopper's criticism of her was met with Mamie's polite smile. Later, Hopper commented, "That Mamie's quite a woman. I thought I'd make her sore, but instead she asked my pardon for laughing" (Brandon 1954, 282).

The press reception later the same day provided another test of Mamie's ability to handle pressure. Her first impromptu press conference yielded nothing controversial. Until this point, Mamie had avoided public statements of any kind, staying out of print and off the airwaves. One question was potentially troublesome and popped up in many newspaper columns in the next few days. When asked how she felt about her son, Major John Eisenhower, leaving shortly for combat duty in Korea, Mamie replied, "I am an Army wife and mother, that is true. Like the mother of every other veteran in that dreadful war, I will be anguished every minute he is gone. No woman, no matter how many times she has waited for a loved one at war, becomes used to the empty uncertainty" (Brandon 1954, 284). When asked about Ike's chances for the nomination, her reply was equally diplomatic. Mamie said, "I know that whatever happens will be for the best" (Brandon 1954, 284). Another reporter summarized her performance this way: "Mamie took the fuss . . . calmly emerging from her first venture into public life with a new reputation as a poised, pleasant and bright-eyed woman who appeared younger than she was (55)" ("Mamie Emerges as Poised Campaigner" 1952, 23). Her public image as honest and tactful was established. Her good natured responses to attacks during the convention and impromptu press conferences cemented her congenial public image.

In letters to close friends and family members, Mamie does not mention details of the incidents noted by news reporters, but she does describe the difficulty of the convention. Her most blunt assessment appears in a letter to Louise Cannon, wife of one of Ike's military associates. Sandwiched amid comments about the inappropriateness of her wardrobe for the season, visits from the grandchildren, and other family news, Mamie writes: "The last two months have been so hectic that I really can't know where to start to say anything except that it has all been a nightmare in many ways" (Personal Letter, July 30, 1952).

In addition to establishing herself as amiable, Mamie was able to support Ike's candidacy through her personal contacts. Much of Mamie's correspondence promotes her husband's political career. In a letter to Alma Peake, for example, Mamie refers to a prediction that Alma's husband apparently made regarding Ike's nomination, "Al certainly was right that Ike would be nominated on an early ballot. It really could not have been earlier. We both thank you for all the work you did on the pre-convention campaign. Please try to keep on working until after November. Certainly our Army friends have gone all out to help us" (Personal Letter, August 3, 1952). It appears that Mamie enlisted their network of military friendships for political support. The sheer volume of her correspondence suggests that although she was seldom heard in public, Mamie mobilized the vast number of Ike's military contacts.

Following the convention, Mamie agreed to write an article for the November 1952 issue of *Good Housekeeping* magazine. The title of the article captures the diplomatic tone Mamie had maintained throughout the campaign, "Vote for my husband or for Governor Stevenson, but *please vote.*" In the article, Mamie takes a personal tone, explaining her reluctance to write even though she was urged to do so. She includes the letter from "Jeanie C" that changed her mind. Jeanie, a high school senior, like many other Americans is old enough to fight for her country, but not to vote for its leaders. Her concern that half of eligible voters don't exercise this right sparked her commitment to baby-sit, wash dishes, or otherwise help out so wives and mothers could go to the polls.

Mamie endorses Jeanie's commitment and urges everyone to exercise their voting right. She reminisces about an experience while she and Ike were in Paris while he was supreme allied commander in Europe. A window box of flowers was not only pretty but upon inspection commemorated young lives lost in the war. Mamie concludes, "I believe one way to keep it from happening is to use your vote. Whether your ballot goes for an Eisenhower or a Stevenson, cast it. Cast it while you thank your stars you live in a land where you have the privilege of declaring your choice" (1952, 13). The ostensibly neutral tone of the article emphasizes patriotism and American values above partisanship, a theme that previously surfaced in Mamie's comments to the press at the GOP convention.

In spite of her public reticence, Mamie was an invaluable campaigner on the cross-country railroad tour. Her initial role was to supervise menus, to provide time for Ike to relax between stops, and to answer hundreds of letters. However, Ike soon realized that Mamie was one of his strongest assets. Crowds requested her. After that, his speeches ended with "Here's my Mamie." One incident has been often retold. An eager photographer snapped a photo of the couple very early one morning and other reporters were disappointed to find out they'd missed it. Mamie cooperated and restaged the pose so that everyone could get similar shots.

That Mamie proved an asset during the campaign is surprising in many ways. With the exception of one impromptu press conference and the *Good Housekeeping* article, she was completely silent. Yet, she provided an incredible advantage to Ike. As James Reston wrote in *The New York Times*, "Mamie must be worth at least 50 electoral votes" (quoted in Boller 1988, 343). Perhaps the most important reason for her value in the campaign was the image she helped Ike project—she anchored him as a family man. Mamie was wife, mother, and supporter. So, even when she appeared on the rear platform of the campaign train in bathrobe and hair rollers, she verified the average American. This image resonated with the public during a period when the nation was seeking normalcy. The shift of attention to the domestic sphere required more than a military hero as president. In this way, Mamie helped to recast Ike as a family man (Parry-Giles and Parry-Giles 1996). Her public persona reflected the values of the baby boom era when the family dominated American lives.

Mamie was Ike's political partner long before the couple entered the White House. Although Mamie appeared completely noncontroversial in public, she voiced opinions in private on more than one occasion. Most importantly, her fondness for Pat Nixon seemed to grow out of Pat's stoic support for Richard Nixon. This, in turn, earned the Nixons a valuable ally in the Eisenhower camp. While the versions of the millionaire's fund scandal surrounding Richard Nixon vary, two Eisenhower historians speculate that her approval of Pat Nixon may have sparked Mamie's intervention on behalf of Richard Nixon. When Ike's brother Milton urged him to replace Nixon on the 1956 ticket, Mamie again interceded on Nixon's behalf. They conclude, "It is probable that Nixon owed his job, and his subsequent rise to the Presidency, to Mamie's intervention" (David and David 1981, 19).

Mamie also contributed to the image of Ike as a down-to-earth, guy-next-door. She listened to and critiqued his campaign speeches, urging Ike to be himself and to throw away the speechwriters' texts (Boller 1988). While there are no records of her involvement with his speaking during the White House years, it is reasonable to expect that this relationship continued. Mamie certainly attended most of his public speaking appearances, providing later feedback.

Rhetorical Activities as First Lady

Even though Mamie Eisenhower refused to take the public podium in any form, she functioned rhetorically in other ways—as hostess for the newly emerging world power, as political partner for her husband, as tireless correspondent, and as representative to the press.

Hostess

The need for international diplomacy in the aftermath of World War II, plus the advantages of air travel never before available, changed official hospitality in the nation's capital. The White House evolved from the hub of Washington, D.C., social life to the center of world attention. The Eisenhowers entertained an unprecedented number of heads of state, leaders of world governments, and foreign officials. These changes increased the public role of first lady as a hostess in obvious ways. The need for coordination of state dinners, balls, and other official functions expanded her role, making Mamie less a Washington society figure and more essential to national functions. Mamie was well prepared for this facet of her role since she already was acquainted with European heads of state and members of royalty and was at ease in their company.

Mamie's improvements to the White House introduced a number of changes in traditional customs that brought the attention of the press. For example, she replaced the horseshoe-shaped table arrangement for state dinners with an E-shaped table with the president and the first lady sitting together at the head of the table. This change brought a swell of press coverage with both supporters and detractors. This arrangement allowed Mamie to spend more time with her husband and it symbolized the strength of the Eisenhower marriage.

Mamie brought several talents to the role of first lady that evolved from her years as a military wife (Dwight. D. Eisenhower 1963; Furman 1952). She managed the White House budget on strict military lines, maintaining the separation of personal and political expenditures. She revealed to Barbara Walters, "There was never a Coca-Cola or any sort of a soft drink or anything that was used on our floor [the living quarters of the White House] that wasn't paid for by us. And we never used anything of the government's—except, naturally, for state affairs. I don't know what other people do, but that was our way of doing it" (1974, 66). Mamie and Ike later underwent public scrutiny as allegations were made about donations to their Gettysburg farm, including farming equipment, federal labor used in renovations, and cattle. In her turn, Mamie criticized Jacqueline Kennedy's handling of the budget as frivolous (Anthony 1991). Mamie claimed that she could account for every nickel spent during the years she resided in the White House. It appears that her fierce guardianship of the budget was a matter of personal pride.

As her prerogative, Mamie ruled the White House staff, some suggest in a none-too-gentle fashion, supervising even the most minute jobs like looking for dust over door jambs and demanding that rugs show no signs of footprints (Boller 1988; Caroli 1987; David and David 1981; Gould 1996; Watson 1997). She considered it an important contribution, stating: "Well, being a homemaker, which has always been my forte, I think probably trying to manage three sets of servants a day, three different shifts—it's pretty hard to run a house like that" (Walters 1974, 66).

In addition, as Doris Kearns Goodwin argues, "one of the important functions in the past that I think first ladies performed for their husbands was to allow them to relax" ("The Role of First Lady" 1994). That relationship was established early in the Eisenhower marriage so that by the war years, Mamie was both anchor and harbor for Ike. Her insistence on his presence at evening meals and their quiet time together allowed him to relax. Much of this role is revealed in Mamie's personal letters to friends and acquaintances. She comments repeatedly on Ike's ability to get in a few rounds of golf or to slip away from the responsibilities of the presidency to fish. Her letter to Ike's brother Earl is typical of her correspondence: "Ike and I had a delightful and most restful vacation. This forthcoming trip will be such a hard one and I am so pleased he had the opportunity for some relaxation at this particular time" (Personal letter, November 24, 1959).

In spite of her high public ratings for managing the White House, there were mistakes. While Mamie apparently enjoyed shaking hands and talking with sometimes 600–700 women each day, after complaints from the Daughters of the American Revolution, Mamie changed the reception line at the White House and did not personally shake hands with everyone in attendance. As one report on the controversy summarizes the new procedure, "It lets everybody get a look at the first lady, but it cuts them all out of a handshake" (Cowan n.d.). Among others, the members of the Society of Navy Sponsors were furious because Mamie mixed their group with the wives of Dental Surgeons (Gordon n.d.).

Among more serious improprieties to catch national press attention, Mamie made a diplomatic blunder when she offended the General Federation of Women's Clubs by refusing to honor them with a reception. Mamie later made a few remarks during one of the group's sessions, expressing her gratitude and inviting them to visit the White House. When members appeared at the White House the next day, Mamie failed to show up. A more serious gaffe occurred when Mamie failed to show appreciation for an expensive gift from Mrs. Lopez Mateos, wife of the president of Mexico (David and David 1981; "Mamie's Working Hard for Ike" 1953).

In spite of these mistakes, Mamie's sincerity and genuine interest in people made her a valuable asset in the White House. Her role is reflected by *U.S. News & World Report*, which notes that "As the President's wife, Mrs. Eisenhower has the big job of keeping the country content about home and social life in the White House" (1953, 52). Mamie accomplished this task.

Private Partner

Mamie was a highly popular first lady, probably because she fulfilled the public expectations of the 1950s that women should remain in the domestic sphere (Anthony 1991, 118). In this climate, Mamie's aversion to speaking in public was not a barrier to her service as a first lady. And, it explains why Mamie gave only a single press conference while residing in the White House.

Like others, Francis T. Miller (1944) was rebuffed when attempting to round out a biography on Ike with family history. He comments about Mamie, "In her letters to us, she expressed cordial cooperation with the wish that all the attention be focused on the General and that she be left in the shadows" (114–15). Miller completed his biography relying on public records to fill in the gaps and Mamie remained out of the spotlight.

Mamie's aversion to publicity stems from two sources. Fundamentally, she considered politics inappropriate for herself and probably, considering her disapproval of more visible first ladies like Eleanor Roosevelt, Jacqueline Kennedy, Rosalynn Carter, and Betty Ford, for women in general ("Mamie's Working Hard for Ike" 1953; Van Zwaluwenburg 1998). Her insistence that "Ike took care of the office. I ran the house," suggests a commitment to strict roles (Boller 1988, 345). Robert Wallace reaffirms Mamie's reluctance to enter the spotlight as a matter of principle ("They Like Mamie, Too" 1952). To Mamie, the American people had elected her husband. He alone was responsible for running the country. In addition, she was perfectly satisfied to be known as a housewife, never expressing other ambitions.

On a personal level, there are indications that Mamie probably suffered from some degree of stage fright. Several instances imply this condition. At the opening session of the 1952 Republican National Convention, someone asked for a speech after Mamie was introduced to candidates' wives and women delegates. Avoiding the request, Mamie nodded and pointed to one of the candidates (Brandon 1954). A year later during the White House press conference, Mamie alluded to her feelings of discomfort. She also had difficulty projecting her voice adequately ("Press Conference Transcript" 1953). The promise of additional press conferences was not fulfilled. And, in 1959 Mamie was awarded an honorary degree by St. Joseph College in Emmitsburg, Maryland. Ike conveyed her gratitude because she had an attack of "mike fright" (Caroli 1987). Stage fright, in addition to her belief that she was not an elected public figure, probably kept Mamie from seeking a public forum for her opinions.

There is every indication that Mamie stayed out of public political decision-making, visiting the West Wing of the White House only three times in eight years "because she didn't want to get involved" ("The Role of the First Lady" 1994). And, those visits, Mamie proudly proclaimed, were by invitation. The press records "As a President's wife, Mrs. Eisenhower is, in this era, a new type.

She is completely nonpolitical. She would not dream of taking positions on disputed issues or leading social movements, as did Mrs. Franklin D. Roosevelt. She does not shrink from the social obligations of her position as did Mrs. Harry S. Truman" ("Mamie's Working Hard for Ike" 1953, 55). Ike confirmed those public perceptions commenting that "she was very much against pushing forward into public view" (quoted in Gould 1986, 533).

Even so, there is considerable speculation that Mamie made her views known to Ike privately, particularly on budget and personnel matters (Bourne 1987). As a strong-willed and often forceful woman in personal situations, this is consistent with her personality. The public separation of East and West Wing of the White House was probably not practiced in the private lives of the Eisenhowers (O'Connor, Nye, and Van Assendelft 1996). Her intervention on behalf of Richard Nixon is just one example. Kevin McCann and James C. Hagerty, close associates of Ike, both confirm that Mamie possessed an iron will and strong opinions, certainly never glimpsed in public. Hagerty, Ike's press secretary, concluded, "She'd argue with him plenty of times about his policies, but upstairs, in the privacy of their living room in the White House" (quoted in David and David 1981, 19). In public, her attractiveness and vivacity, particularly her warm smile received favorable responses. Mamie seemed genuinely happy with her role and the American public with her.

Correspondence

As many examples attest, Mamie's primary rhetorical contact was through correspondence. She maintained a "pen pal relationship" with the American public responding to thousands of letters, often in longhand (Gould 1996, 471). Strangers felt comfortable confiding their problems and asking for her advice. Mamie faithfully responded. She once commented, "I get up with letters. I go to bed with letters. I guess I'm what you would call a well-lettered woman" (quoted in Boller 1988, 353).

In many ways, Mamie's reliance on letter-writing reinforces her contribution to personalizing the presidency. She sent thousands of individual congratulations, birthday greetings, special wishes, and thank-yous. They often contained personal comments and details such as apologizing for an awkward letter because Mamie was "green at this dictating" or inquiring after the health of a family member (Personal Letters to Mrs. C. Craig Cannon and Woodrow Wirsig). Such letters probably provided many Americans with a private connection to the White House otherwise unavailable. Senator Stuart Symington wrote to Mamie: "You always write as if you meant it—I suppose that is one of the reasons you have the country in the palm of your hand" (quoted in Gould 1996, 472).

The content of the letters revealed that many perceived Mamie as a friend. For instance, she received hundreds of requests, some of them polite and others not, that she change her curled bangs. The letters began to arrive during the campaign and her bangs continued to be contentious even after the election. One example, a relatively diplomatic letter from editor Chloris Maynard stated, "It is the consensus here in the *Life* picture department that you are by far the best looking first lady we have ever had. We feel, however, that a slightly different hair-do should show your face to better advantage. . . . We hope that you will realize that we are doing this, not as a spur of the moment practical joke, but out of sincere interest" (Maynard 1953). The letter was accompanied by a photo of an alternative hair style. Mamie's reply thanked the editorial staff for their thoughtfulness, but as later photographs reveal, Mamie did not follow their suggestion. Her bangs remained throughout her life—because Ike liked them.

Press Relations

The Eisenhower administration was the first to hire an advertising agency (Batten, Barton, Durstine, & Osborn) during the 1952 political campaign. The pitch aimed at the stay-at-home voter since Republicans were in a minority. The primary appeal was Eisenhower's "frankness, honesty and integrity, his sincere and wholesome approach" (Morant 1976, 756). After the election, the administration continued to manage its relationship with the public using a public relation's model. That is, press glimpses into the Eisenhower's private life were choreographed through official White House channels. It is clear from archives that staff members provided written responses to questions reporters submitted in advance. Certain themes, such as seasonal wardrobe selections and daily schedules, were addressed in detail while potentially political questions were avoided ("Press Releases" n.d.).

Not surprisingly, Mamie's relationship with the American public followed a similar pattern. She was managed primarily through print media especially press releases and photographs. Her first and only White House press conference was held on March 11, 1953. As *Time* reported, "The First Lady looked radiant and chic in a grey suit, handled herself with aplomb . . . as if she had done it a thousand times before" ("The White House Ladies' Day" 1953, 19). The press conference was conducted with the first lady seated at a desk, questions were approved in advance, and responses were written out and rehearsed. A primary component of the conference was Mamie's engagement calendar including the guest list for a tea for Mary Pickford.

During the press conference, Mamie also described the conversion of Bess Truman's sitting room into her own bedroom, newly painted green walls and pink furniture. *Time* reported, "Adroitly sidestepping a political question (she was in favor of tax reduction, 'as who isn't?'), the First Lady gave the impression of a busy, happy household manager" ("The White House Ladies' Day" 1953, 19).

For routine press stories, reporters submitted questions in writing to the White House press staff. Written responses to their questions were usually formulated by her secretary, often after consultation with Mamie. Recurring topics include statements about fashion, the White House as a residence, Mamie's relationship with Ike, her duties as a hostess, and her health. A typical list of questions was submitted by Ruth Montgomery prior to the publication of a *Look* magazine article. Montgomery asked thirty questions ranging from Mamie's weight to whether she took vitamins, still smoked Philip Morris cigarettes, or used the White House swimming pool (Montgomery n.d.). In general, questions regarding fashion comprise the bulk of press inquiries. They include hemlines, new purchases for the fashion season, and outfits for events ranging from Mamie's inaugural ball gown to her Easter ensemble.

Although Mamie had opportunities to speak out, particularly on the condition of women, she did not. For example, reporter Betty Beale sent questions to the White House for a newspaper article following the Geneva Conference. Among them, Beale asked, "Did the President discuss with you beforehand his electrifying proposal for mutual inspection of armaments?" and "Did you feel that the oft repeated statements about the unpopularity of Americans in Europe is a myth? If not, did any ways of correcting that unpopularity occur to you while there?" (Beale 1955). Consistent with her past, Mamie did not respond to these potentially political questions.

While there is no direct evidence, it is likely that the White House public relations team also managed the pictorial depiction of the folksy, traditional Eisenhower family often present in the press. It is conveyed through a family album style of images that encouraged national identification with the first family. As *U.S. News & World Report* summarized it, "Mrs. Dwight D. Eisenhower, a President's wife with important work to do, is concentrating just now on how she best can provide her husband's Administration with a social and family background that will help its prestige the country over" (1953, 52). In the accompanying photographs, Mamie is pictured with the grandchildren, babysitting, attending a movie, ordering supplies for the White House pantry, arranging flowers, planning menus, and suggesting recipes to the White House staff. A similar story in a *Better Homes and Gardens* series on how to raise children concluded that Mamie's background was perfect for producing another first lady (Scott and Usher 1955).

Mamie's role in press management was especially critical during the days following Ike's heart attack on September 25, 1955. Mamie served to reassure and encourage Americans because she was constantly at her husband's side during the recovery period, answering letters and cheering him. Her support was featured in press coverage, assuring Americans that there was no threat to national security. The president's heart problems perhaps heightened national sensitivity to the health of the first couple (Crispell and Gomez 1988).

Ironically, it was Mamie's health rather than her much more seriously ill husband that received the most public attention. Mamie's health was the subject of conjecture about whether Ike would run for a second term. The speculation was triggered by Mamie's mother who commented to a reporter that White House life was just too hard on Mamie and that she couldn't stand another four years in the White House (David and David 1981). Mamie's practice of conducting business while in bed also contributed to the speculation that she was not a well woman. One reporter wrote: "Mrs. Eisenhower finds the social obligations of her White House role more and more wearing. It is not unusual for her to spend a large part of the morning in bed. Both her mother and her husband have been concerned at the drain upon her strength" ("The Story" 1955,

40). The article pronounced a less than normal health rating for Mamie.

Mamie's health claimed further notice when Democratic National Chairman Paul Butler intimated that President Eisenhower would not seek reelection for personal reasons. When asked to explain, he elaborated, "Newspaper reports indicate that Mrs. Eisenhower's health is not too good. I believe that could affect the President's decision on making another White House bid" ("The Presidency" 1955, 15). The ensuing controversy included members of the Senate who addressed the issue from the floor. Arizona Republican Barry Goldwater attacked the use of personal smear tactics by Democrats and defended the president and Mamie with his own obvious allusion to Franklin Delano Roosevelt. Goldwater stated, "Our distinguished President and his wife . . . are in sound healthy and vigorous condition—in vivid contrast to the condition of the man who ran for a fourth term and withheld information of his mortal sickness from the nation" ("The Presidency" 1955, 15).

Senate Majority Leader Lyndon Johnson's retort included these words, "it seems passing strange to me . . . that my delightful friends on the other side of the aisle should be so disturbed in this year 1955. In previous Administrations they talked about the President's health, the President's wife, the President's daughter and the President's piano, and everything else they could think of which concerned the President" ("The Presidency" 1955, 15). While this exchange only drew further attention to Mamie's condition, it ended several days later with the report of White House physician Howard M. Snyder that Mamie was fine except for a slight heart condition contracted in childhood from a bout with rheumatic fever. In addition, Mamie had Meniere's disease or carotid sinus, an inner ear problem that affected her balance. Together, these conditions may have contributed to her lack of stamina and dizziness that sometimes constrained her activity. They also fueled rumors that Mamie's frequent trips to visit her mother in Denver were really drying out spells (Caroli 1987). Others defended her, and Mamie did not publicly reply to these or other accusations until 1973 ("Why Mamie Takes it Easy" 1955).

By August 1957, when Mamie underwent routine surgery, referred to as "appropriate to women of middle age," public discussion of her health had faded (Caroli 1987). Mamie wrote to Mrs. E. N. Eisenhower, "I do not have time to tell you all the details of my operation, but it was exactly as the papers reported. There was no malignancy, and the doctors said it just takes a long time to get over it. I am only now beginning to feel better, but for the past three weeks have been out of the house only three times—once for a short drive and twice on the Barbara Anne" ("Personal Letter" 1957). Perhaps, there was no longer any need for an issue to deflect attention from Ike's heart condition and, thus, Mamie's health did not gain much press coverage (Ferrell 1992).

Legacy

In January 1961, the Eisenhowers left the White House for their Gettysburg farm. Eight years later on March 28, 1969, Ike died of heart failure. His last words "I've always loved my wife" were quoted in Richard Nixon's eulogy. Mamie lived for another ten years, continuing to manage his image and promote his legacy.

During the final decade of her life, Mamie remained in touch with many first ladies who followed her. She visited the White House when invited and on special occasions that warranted her presence. For example, Mamie spent three Christmas seasons with Pat Nixon, accompanying her to the dedication of the Eisenhower Hospital in Palm Springs. Early in the Kennedy administration, she attended a luncheon for the Japanese premier and also toured the White House. Mamie served with Jacqueline Kennedy as honorary cochair of the National Cultural Center fund-raising drive. She was guest of honor at 1966 and 1967 Senate Wives Luncheons and took an active interest in Lady Bird Johnson's china pattern selection (Anthony 1991).

At times, Mamie voiced her disagreement with the actions of other first ladies. She was particularly critical of Jackie Kennedy, and she found fault with Rosalynn Carter for imposing her decisions when she wasn't elected. Although Mamie personally liked Betty Ford, she clearly didn't understand and probably didn't approve of her public statements (Anthony 1991).

During the years following her husband's death, Mamie became increasingly public, although never to a great degree. Her persistent reticence was overcome by the desire to establish a legacy for her husband. As she aged, Mamie became more outspoken as she assumed the role of Keeper of the Flame: "Tentatively at first, always with the understanding that she was doing so for Ike's memory, Mamie also began to make public speeches at the age of seventy-nine" (Anthony 1991, 245). In 1972, Mamie narrated the short film *Tribute to My Beloved Ike* shown at the Republican National Convention.

Her first public speech was at the Eisenhower College commencement. It is not surprising that Mamie shared Ike's memory with the graduates in personal terms, recalling the strength of his hands. She recounted, "Every knuckle was broken from football or whatever, but I always felt in all the years we were married that I could grab onto them when I felt sick or worried, and nothing was ever going to happen to me" (quoted in Waldrup 1989, 309). The most remarkable thing about the address is that apparently Mamie had come to terms with her fear of speaking in public.

No treatment of the Eisenhower years would be complete without some attention to the Summersby scandal. While other scandals erupted during her life, the allegations of Ike's wartime affair with his pretty Irish driver, Kay Summersby, were the most persistent. It began with rumors among officers and their wives and gained momentum when *Stars and Stripes* published photos featuring Ike and Kay. While Mamie was publicly silent, speculation still persists that her war letters to Ike questioned him about Summersby (David and David 1981). The letters have never been found. Despite this, the Summersby affair dogged Mamie until her death.

Reports faded until 1973, when Merle Miller's book *Plain Speaking*, based on a series of conversations with Harry Truman, resurrected the controversy.[1] Shortly afterwards, Kay Summersby's account, *Past Forgetting*, was published posthumously. Several scholars have concluded that Summersby, hounded by debt and life-threatening illness, sensationalized an account of the affair to stimulate book sales. Whatever her motivation, Summersby's death left many unanswered questions. Even after the publication of *Past Forgetting*, Mamie refused to acknowledge the rumors and reiterated her husband's devotion to her. Nevertheless, speculation continued and ABC network aired a miniseries based on the affair.

Finally, Mamie dealt with the scandal during a national televised interview and authorized her son John to use personal letters from Ike. The resulting book, *Letters to Mamie*, based upon about 400 letters, revealed a homesick husband separated by war from his beloved wife. With the help of John, Mamie continued to fortify Ike's memory as a devoted husband. During the years of speculation, Mamie reinforced her role as a traditional woman, allowing others to come to her public defense (Caroli 1987).

Mamie Eisenhower suffered a stroke in October that ended her life several days later on November 1, 1979. As Lyndon Johnson summarized, "To me— and I am certain to countless others—Mamie Eisenhower has been one of the most affectionately regarded women of our times" (Johnson 1980, 84). One reason for such widespread sentiment is certainly that Mamie captured the imagination of the 1950s postwar period when the importance of family dominated the national agenda. She resonated with the mood of the nation, personalizing a general-turned-president at a time when the nation was healing from war. Her gift for conveying a sense of spontaneity and sincerity brought with it a closeness to the presidency seldom felt in prior administrations.

During her tenure in the White House from January 1953 to January 1961, Mamie dominated the lists of most admired American women, ranking no lower than fourth in the top ten (Gutin 1989). Although Mamie does not fair as well among historians, who ranked her thirteenth among first ladies in a 1982 poll, she has retained a measure of popularity (Caroli 1987). A 1980 *Good Housekeeping* poll of readers credits Mamie with improving the White House (ranked third) and inspiring women (ranked fifth) (Caroli 1987). Upon examination, the reasons for public perception of these qualities are clear: Mamie excelled in her role as hostess for an emerging world power, as her husband's political partner, as correspondent, and as the embodiment of a traditional woman in the media.

During her lifetime, the tension between the traditional role of women and the public nature of first lady became more pronounced as the United States moved into a position of world leadership. Even so, Mamie Eisenhower staunchly remained in the background during her eight years in the White House. As historian Caroli puts it, "The old conflict between private 'person' and public 'personage' would continue to trouble all who took the job. . . . Curiously enough, it was Mamie Eisenhower, generally perceived as the least shrewd . . . who pointed out in 1977 how completely the job of First Lady had changed in the twenty years since she left Washington. Reticence and a place on the list of 'Most Admired Women' no longer sufficed" (1987, 219). Still, Mamie Eisenhower stood for the private life, personalizing her war hero husband by adding a dimension of domesticity. As Mamie is frequently quoted as saying,

"Ike runs the nation; I turn the lamb chops" (David and David 1981, 17). Little did it matter to Americans that Mamie's only culinary achievement was fudge. Her public image eclipsed the reality.

Notes

1. As Miller (1973) recounts, Truman stated, "Why, right after the war was over, he wrote a letter to General Marshall saying that he wanted to be relieved of duty, saying that he wanted to come back to the United States and divorce Mrs. Eisenhower so that he could marry this Englishwoman" (339). The ensuing correspondence between Marshall and Eisenhower disappeared because as Truman revealed, "one of the last things I did as President, I got those letters from his file in the Pentagon, and I destroyed them" (340).

The book generated responses, both supporting and denying Truman's account. Among the most staunch defenders of Ike and Mamie, Boller (1988) concludes: "The Truman story must surely be put down to the faulty memory of an aging former President who was still rankling over Ike's charge in the 1952 campaign that the Truman administration was riddled with corruption" (341).

References

Anthony, Carl S. 1991. *First Ladies: The Saga of the Presidents' Wives and Their Power, 1961–1990*. Vol. 2. New York: William Morrow.

A Rare Picture Visit: The First Lady at Home. 1958. *Life*, 20 October, 60–65.

Beale, Mrs. B. L. 1955. Personal Letter to Mrs. Eisenhower. Box 3, 28 July. Abilene, Kans.: Dwight D. Eisenhower Library.

Boller, Paul F. 1988. *Presidential Wives*. New York: Oxford University Press.

Bourne, Russell. 1987. When the First Lady Speaks Her Mind. *American Heritage*, 27 September, 108–9.

Brandon, Dorothy. 1954. *Mamie Doud Eisenhower: A Portrait of a First Lady*. New York: Charles Scribner's Sons.

Caroli, Betty B. 1987. *First Ladies*. New York: Oxford University Press.

Carter, Jimmie. 1979. Death of Mamie Eisenhower. *Weekly Compilation of Presidential Documents*, 2073–74.

Cowan, R. n.d. Mamie Saves Mitt from Wringer. Box 9. Abilene, Kans.: Dwight D. Eisenhower Library.

Crispell, Kenneth R., and Carlos F. Gomez. 1988. *Hidden Illness in the White House*. Durham, N.C.: Duke University Press.

David, Lester, and Irene David. 1981. *Ike and Mamie: The Story of a General and His Lady*. New York: G. P. Putnam's Sons.

Eisenhower, Dwight D. 1963. *Mandate for Change: The White House Years 1953–1956*. Garden City, N.Y.: Doubleday.

Eisenhower, Mamie. 1952. Vote for My Husband or for Governor Stevenson, but Please Vote. *Good Housekeeping*, November, 13.

———. 1952. Personal Letter to Mrs. Albert Peake. Box 32, 3 August. Abilene, Kans.: Dwight D. Eisenhower Library.

———. 1952. Personal Letter to Mrs. C. Craig Cannon. Box 6, 30 July. Abilene, Kans.: Dwight D. Eisenhower Library.

———. 1954. Personal Letter to Woodrow Wirsig, Box 35, 13 January. Abilene, Kans.: Dwight D. Eisenhower Library.

————. 1957. Personal Letter to Mrs. E. N. Eisenhower. Box 13, 27 September. Abilene, Kans.: Dwight D. Eisenhower Library.

————. 1959. Personal Letter to Mr. and Mrs. Earl Eisenhower. Box 13, 24 November. Abilene, Kans.: Dwight D. Eisenhower Library.

Ferrell, Robert H. 1992. *Ill-Advised: Presidential Health and Public Trust.* Columbia, Mo.: University of Missouri Press.

Furman, Bess. 1952. Keeping House at the White House. *New York Times Magazine,* 28 December, 7–9.

————. n.d. Memo from Bess Furman, *New York Times* to Murray Snyder, White House Press Room. Box 35. Abilene, Kans.: Dwight D. Eisenhower Library.

Gordon, E. P. n.d. There's Some Disagreement about Mamie's Entertaining. Box 15. Abilene, Kans.: Dwight D. Eisenhower Library.

Gould, Lewis L. 1986. First Ladies. *American Scholar,* 528–35.

————. 1996. *American First Ladies: Their Lives and Their Legacy.* New York: Garland.

Gutin, Myra G. 1989. *The President's Partner: The First Lady in the Twentieth Century.* New York: Greenwood.

Johnson, Lady Bird. 1980. Mamie: A Touching Tribute. *McCall's,* January, 84.

Kellerman, Barbara. 1981. *All the President's Kin.* New York: Macmillan.

Kutner, N. 1953. The Story of Mamie. *Women's Home Companion,* July, 25.

Mamie Emerges as Poised Campaigner. 1952. *Life,* 4 October, 23.

Mamie Leaves the Politics to Ike. 1954. *U.S. News and World Report,* 15 October, 64–65.

Mamie's Working Hard for Ike—Teas, Receptions, Handshakes. 1953. *U.S. News & World Report,* 21 August, 52–55.

Maynard, Chloris. 1953. A Personal Letter to Mrs. Dwight D. Eisenhower, Box 28, 10 November. Abilene, Kans.: Dwight D. Eisenhower Library.

Miller, Francis T. 1944. *Eisenhower: Man and Soldier.* Philadelphia: John C. Winston Co.

Miller, Merle. 1973. *Plain Speaking: An Oral Biography of Harry S. Truman.* New York: G. P. Putnam's Sons.

Montgomery, Ruth. 1954. An Intimate Portrait of Our Vivacious First Lady after One Year in the White House. *Look,* 23 February, 31.

————. n.d. Questions Submitted by Ruth Montgomery, Article for *Look.* Box 29. Abilene, Kans.: Dwight D. Eisenhower Library.

Morant, Stephen. 1976. *The Glorious Burden.* Lenox, Mass.: Authors Edition, Inc.

Neal, Steve. 1978. *The Eisenhowers.* Lawrence, Kans.: University Press of Kansas.

O'Connor, K., B. Nye, and L. Van Assendelft. 1996. Wives in the White House: The Political Influence of First Ladies. *Presidential Studies Quarterly,* 835–53.

Parry-Giles, T., and S. J. Parry-Giles. 1996. Political Scopophilia, Presidential Campaigning, and the Intimacy of American Politics. *Communication Studies,* 191–204.

The Presidency: Heat about a Cold. 1955. *Time,* 21 March, 15–16.

Press Conference Transcript. 1953. Box 35 Abilene, Kans.: Dwight D. Eisenhower Library.

Press Releases. n.d. Box 35. Abilene, Kans.: Dwight D. Eisenhower Library.

"Rocking Chair" Routine: It Will Be New, Strange. 1955. *U.S. News & World Report,* 7 October, 64.

The Role of the First Lady. 1994. Public Broadcast Featuring Doris Kearns Goodwin, Stephen Hess, Gil Troy, and Suzanne Garment, 14 May. www.pbs.org/thinktank.

Scott, R. B., and A. Usher. 1955. How Would You Raise a First Lady? *Better Homes and Gardens,* June, 70–71.

Sillars, Malcolm O. 1958. The Presidential Campaign of 1952. *Western Speech*, 94–99.

Six Former First Ladies: What Their Lives Are Like Now. 1977. *U.S. News & World Report*, 20 June, 52.

The Story of Mrs. Eisenhower's Health: White House Duties Are Causing a Strain. 1955. *U.S. News & World Report*, 25 March, 40.

U.S. News & World Report. 1953. No title, 21 August, 52.

Van Zwaluwenburg, P. J. 1998. First Partner: First Ladies and Their Roles. In *Presidential Frontiers: Underexplored Issues in White House Politics*, ed. R. J. Barilleaux, 195–225. Westport, Conn.: Praeger.

Waldrup, C. C. 1989. *Presidents' Wives: The Lives of 44 American Women of Strength*. Jefferson, N.C.: McFarland & Co.

Wallace, R. 1952. They Like Mamie, Too. *Life*, 13 October, 149–58.

Watson, R. P. 1997. The First Lady Reconsidered: Presidential Partner and Political Institution. *Presidential Studies Quarterly*, 805–18.

Walters, Barbara. 1974. Mamie Eisenhower: The Ike I Remember. *Ladies Home Journal*, April, 148.

The White House: Ladies Day. 1953. *Time*, 23 March, 19–20.

Why Mamie Takes It Easy. 1955. *U.S. News & World Report*, 13 May, 46–47.

Chapter 13

Jacqueline Kennedy
The Rhetorical Construction of Camelot

Elizabeth J. Natalle

> If you fail your husband and your children . . . that really is the role
> that means the most to me. I am an old fashioned wife.
>
> The first lady should preserve the traditions and enhance [the White
> House] and leave something of herself there.
>
> There will never be Camelot[1] again.
>
> —Jacqueline Bouvier Kennedy

Jacqueline Kennedy, wife of thirty-fifth president John Fitzgerald Kennedy, was
the thirty-ninth woman to serve in the role of first lady or its equivalent in the
United States. Although she occupied this role for only one thousand days from
January 20, 1961, to November 22, 1963, Mrs. Kennedy left an enduring legacy
that indisputably ranks her as one of the most popular first ladies both at home
and abroad. She has, in fact, achieved iconic status among the American people,
in popular culture, and in artistic and fashion circles. Known for her regal
beauty, her fierce protection of her family's privacy, and her stunning sense of
aesthetics, Mrs. Kennedy was also a behind-the-scenes influence on diplomatic
protocol and foreign policy through her interpersonal and letter-writing skills.

Veteran UPI correspondent Helen Thomas credits Mrs. Kennedy with
changing the way first ladies were covered by the press corps: "In large measure, she made our coverage hit the front pages more often than not, and she set

the tone for full-time coverage of first ladies that persists to this day" (1999, 244). Several factors contributed to this change in coverage, but the power of televised media was the most important during the Kennedy administration. Mrs. Kennedy was quickly catapulted to the most photographed woman in the world, to be surpassed only by Princess Diana in the 1990s. Thus, visual imagery is a central tenet in the overall iconography of Jacqueline Kennedy and calls for semiotic consideration. This is a significant departure from traditional approaches to first lady scholarship, which tend to be more text-based rhetorical analyses.[2]

Mrs. Kennedy's skillful rhetorical-semiotic construction of what became known as Camelot will be the focus of this chapter. Through her strategic choice of causes, primarily the White House restoration project and the infusion of new cultural standards for the executive branch, Mrs. Kennedy influenced American life as no other contemporary first lady. Her courageous demeanor throughout her husband's funeral cemented her place in the heart of the American public and influenced the interpretation of President Kennedy's legacy as well. The challenge in analyzing Mrs. Kennedy's rhetorical role as first lady lies in the fact that she gave no substantial personal interviews during her residency in the White House, nor did she release during her lifetime a memoir or personal reflections on her role.[3] This chapter seeks to understand the juxtaposition of public and private persona in Mrs. Kennedy's role as first lady as the key to her rhetorical impact. This analysis also affords the opportunity to explore the intersection of rhetorical and semiotic analysis in the understanding and effect of public icons.

Biography

Jacqueline Lee Bouvier Kennedy Onassis, was born to the aristocratic parentage of Janet Norton Lee Bouvier (Auchincloss) and John Vernou "Black Jack" Bouvier III on July 28, 1929, in Southampton, Long Island.[4] She died from non-Hodgkin's lymphoma on May 19, 1994, in New York City. Jacqueline grew up surrounded by wealth, horses, fashion, and the privilege of a high society education including study at The Chapin School in New York and Miss Porter's School in Farmington, Connecticut. Her life revolved around society activities in New York, Newport, and suburban Washington, D.C. She was named Debutant of the Year by the *New York Times* in 1947, attended Vassar from 1947–1949 as a literature major, studied during her junior year in Paris, and graduated from George Washington University in 1951. Although she won the *Vogue* Prix de Paris prize in 1951, she chose not to accept the prize of becoming a *Vogue* junior editor. Clearly, up to this point, Jacqueline's introduction to art, literature, poetry, fashion, and French culture provided a framework for her to develop an aesthetic perspective that would guide her decision-making as both first lady and as a private citizen. The year in Paris and her three-month European trip with her sister in 1951[5] stand out as the single most important influence from which she crafted an integrated sense of American and French ideals in her personal aesthetic. In fact, she wrote in her self-portrait for the *Vogue* prize competition what would prophesy her life:

> Last winter I took my Junior Year in Paris and spent the vacations in Austria and Spain. I loved it more than any year of my life. Being away from home gave me the chance to look at myself with a jaundiced eye. I learned not to be ashamed of a real hunger for knowledge, something I always tried to hide, and I came home glad to start in here again but with a love for Europe that I am afraid will never leave me. (quoted in Brenner 1994, 253)

While still living with her parents, Jacqueline enjoyed a brief stint with the *Washington Times-Herald* as a photographer, where she met Senator John Fitzgerald Kennedy of Massachusetts when interviewing him for her column entitled "Inquiring Camera Girl." Jacqueline married Jack on September 12, 1953. For the next seven years, Mrs. Kennedy played the role of senator's wife, entertaining in their Georgetown home and concentrating on her preferred role throughout her adult life: mother. She had difficult pregnancies. A daughter was stillborn in 1956, Caroline Kennedy was born in 1957, and John Jr. in 1960. In spite of her pregnancy, Jackie campaigned during her husband's 1960 bid for the presidency, and they entered the White House two months after John Jr.'s birth. A son named Patrick died several days after birth in 1963.

During the three years (1960–1963) that the Kennedys occupied the White House, Jackie Kennedy rose to iconic status in the eyes of both the American public and the world at large. Although she did not engage a public speaking schedule to promote causes as first lady, Mrs. Kennedy's personal plan and fund-raising effort to restore the White House launched a national agenda to see the White House and the presidency take on near-royal status. Through the adept use of television, strategic interviews, and personal correspondence, Jackie Kennedy established an aesthetic ideal for the pure art of living. The overwhelming success of the televised tour of the restored White House in February 1962, along with her fashionable appearances at official functions and international visits catapulted Mrs. Kennedy into a global spotlight that continued until her death.

Jacqueline Kennedy considered her primary roles in the following order: mother, wife, and public figure. Shunning the title of first lady, she preferred to be called "Mrs. Kennedy" and made every effort not to make the role of first lady a series of public appearances to greet visitors to the White House. Ironically, her White House restoration project, her stunning Oleg Cassini wardrobe, her ability to charm political dignitaries with her skill in French, Italian, and Spanish, her wit and intelligence, and her choice of artistic entertainment fascinated the American public to the extent that she became the most public of contemporary first ladies.

On November 22, 1963, President Kennedy was assassinated in Dallas, Texas, and Jackie, widowed at age thirty-four, orchestrated one of history's most famous funerals, which she patterned after the protocol established at President Lincoln's funeral. It was in the 1963 interview with *Life* correspondent Theodore White that the legacy of the Kennedy presidency was named with Jackie's reference to her husband's favorite musical, *Camelot*.

Five years after President Kennedy's assassination, Jacqueline married Greek shipping magnate Aristotle Onassis, which dismayed the American public. Her popularity, however, never waned, and her period as fashion icon and jet-setter from 1968–1975 reinforced her image as an international star. Mrs. Onassis did not remarry after the death of her husband; she returned permanently to her Fifth Avenue apartment in New York, and worked as a book editor for Viking and, subsequently, Doubleday Press. Her children, John Jr. and Caroline, remained close by, and she spent time in the company of financial advisor and diamond dealer Maurice Tempelsman. In addition to her work as an editor, patron of the arts, and advocate for public landmarks such as Grand Central Terminal, Mrs. Onassis concentrated on the pleasures of mothering and grandmothering, thus retaining a role that she always considered a primary responsibility.

Jacqueline Kennedy Onassis's death in May 1994 brought an unexpected, yet not surprising, reaction from the public. She is the only former first lady to have complete television coverage of her funeral, and fittingly, she had chosen to be buried in Arlington National Cemetery with John F. Kennedy and their two children, the unnamed baby girl, and Patrick Bouvier Kennedy. John F. Kennedy Jr., who was killed in a plane crash in July 1999, was buried at sea rather than at the Kennedy gravesite in Arlington.

The Sotheby's auction of personal items selected for sale by her children in April 1996 drew a record $34.5 million (Gray 1996), and is yet another indicator of the literal "craze" that the American people continue to have for Jacqueline Kennedy Onassis. Many of these items were from the Kennedy White House or the Georgetown home occupied during John Kennedy's years as senator, including an oak rocking chair, golf clubs, the Louis XVI mahogany desk on which JFK signed the Nuclear Test Ban Treaty in 1963, and a three-strand pearl necklace that Jackie wore in a famous photograph with John Jr. *USA Today* dubbed the auction "Camelot for Sale" (Williams 1996), and a recurring theme among the media throughout the period of the auction was the desire of the American public to literally own a piece of Camelot. In some sense, the auction was the largest public revelation ever of a private life that Jacqueline Kennedy Onassis sought to protect throughout her lifetime. To date, the copyright and sealed protection that are in effect regarding her personal papers hamper the Kennedy Library from systematically offering materials to the academic community. Each year more personal papers are released by the Kennedy Library for public access, but Mrs. Kennedy's wish to protect her own and her family's privacy while retaining the status of a very public icon continues to be a theme.

Rhetorical Activities as First Lady

Jacqueline Kennedy's rhetorical activities as first lady have been described as "emerging" by communication scholar Myra Gutin (1989, 41). That is to say, Mrs. Kennedy was the first "television" first lady, which meant increased coverage and scrutiny of her daily activities; she was the first to appoint her own press secretary; she staged elaborate state dinners and cultural entertainment; and she traveled officially overseas as first lady unaccompanied by her husband. Yet, she spent much time avoiding the press in an attempt to protect the privacy of her family, and she set no formal agenda to engage in political or social activities to change the lives of ordinary American citizens. Her public speaking was limited to extemporaneous, ceremonial remarks, for example, brief speeches in India and Latin America. Most of her time as first lady revolved around two agenda items: caring for her family as wife and mother and, according to documentary filmmaker Suzanne Bauman (1999), using art to elevate politics. In other words, Jacqueline Kennedy rhetorically constructed the ideal aesthetic presidency that would become known as Camelot to satisfy her own belief that art and politics are intertwined. Perhaps the best example of this was the fact that she persuaded French minister of culture, André Malraux, to bring the *Mona Lisa* to the United States in 1963, as a gesture of friendship. This was the first time the *Mona Lisa* officially had left French soil since da Vinci brought it to France in 1516 (Folliard 1963); therefore, the gesture represents a significant rhetorical statement regarding the political relationship between France and the United States at that time. The loan of the *Mona Lisa* also serves as the exemplar of how Mrs. Kennedy engaged communication as a visual, that is, semiotic form of persuasion. It is the ultimate cultural statement to be made about the mutual taste of the United States and its allies.

In this chapter, Mrs. Kennedy's rhetorical activities are divided topically, yet each type of activity is based on an aesthetic form, and each is a component of Camelot. The analysis that follows includes fashion as persuasion, the White House restoration project, White House entertainment, the orchestration of President Kennedy's funeral, and interpersonal diplomacy. The least important type of rhetorical activity was public speaking, therefore, only brief remarks will be included regarding Mrs. Kennedy as a formal public speaker.

Fashion as Persuasion

Before Mrs. Kennedy even entered the White House as first lady, the press and the public began what became known as "Jackie Watching." Much of the gaze was turned on her clothing and hair, and she and her personal couturier, Oleg Cassini, created what became known as "The Jackie Look" (Cassini 1995, 22). Jacqueline Kennedy herself was the rhetorical object, and her ability to heighten the ethos of the Kennedy administration through her personal presentation is unmatched by any other first lady. Although other first ladies, such as Ida McKinley, enjoyed beautiful and expensive clothes, it is Mrs. Kennedy who elevates the iconography of fashion (Barthes 1990) to its central position in relationship to how first ladies present themselves and are received by the American public. Fashion is not whimsical or trivial, indeed, as the Smithsonian Institution exhibition on first ladies demonstrates. When curators redesigned the Smithsonian First Ladies exhibition from its focus on inaugural ball gowns to a wider ranging exploration of "political role and public image" (Mayo and Meringolo 1994), there was a public backlash against the fact that so many of the first ladies' gowns were removed from the public view. I have visited the first ladies exhibition several times in its new format, and the ball gowns still draw the largest groups of people who spend more of their time viewing the dresses than other artifacts on display. One need only remember the public's view of Rosalynn Carter as dowdy, and their subsequent praise of Nancy Reagan for returning the look of the first lady to designer clothes, to know that the appearance of the first lady is largely a rhetorical act that influences the perception of the presidency.

In the exhibition showing in 2001–2002, entitled "Jacqueline Kennedy: The White House Years," the Kennedy Library has collaborated with the Costume Institute of the Metropolitan Museum of Art to renew the public's knowledge and interest in Mrs. Kennedy as *the* icon of twentieth-century American style and fashion. In this stunning exhibition commemorating the fortieth year since she became first lady, over eighty ensembles are displayed within the contexts of the 1960 presidential campaign, the inauguration, White House style, and travel. Hats and riding habits are also on display along with other artifacts such as videos of both the president's and Mrs. Kennedy's public speaking. Metropolitan director, Philippe de Montebello, appropriately described the impact of the exhibition as I witnessed it: "Thus, in our galleries, these garments held by the Kennedy Library, and valued in that context for their historical associations, have the expanded implications of an aesthetic response to the highly public and ceremonial role of first lady" (Bowles 2001, vi).

Mrs. Kennedy's rhetorical action could literally be termed "fashion diplomacy." Over 300 dresses were hand sewn for her during the time she occupied the White House, including more than 100 dresses during the first year. Unlike the previous several first ladies, thrity-one-year-old Jackie was five feet seven inches tall, slender, and carried herself with perfect posture. Her dark hair, striking eyes, long neckline, and beautiful collarbone structure were physical attributes that Cassini capitalized on as he created a personal wardrobe for Mrs. Kennedy that rivaled and copied the haute couture creations of European designers such as Givenchy, who designed a strikingly similar wardrobe for film star Audrey Hepburn. In fact, there is evidence that Mrs. Kennedy would have preferred to wear Givenchy designs, which she did at her discretion (Bowles 2001). As an American first lady, however, she was under pressure to wear "American" couture.

Cassini reports that he had a particular philosophy that governed the "Kennedy Look":

> For the daytime, there is a bit of the military and menswear approach to the clothes—slightly severe but comfortable. For evening, the Egyptian theme predominated because of the strength of Jackie's shoulders. Often her chiffon dresses were inspired by hieroglyphics. I saw Jackie as a geometric goddess. (1995, 33)

Cassini's "architectural" concept of minimalism consisted of A-line cuts, sheaths, one-shouldered or strapless gowns, deep cut backs with a "covered look" for the front bodice, and sumptuous fabrics such as dupioni silk, silk peau d'ange, silk gazar, Swiss double satin, chiffon, silk velvet, silk brocade, and silk crepe de chine. In addition to the Egyptian leitmotif, many of Mrs. Kennedy's ensembles echoed military themes with the use of double rows of large buttons, fringed or tasseled decoration, cockades, and piping. Evening clothes were sometimes decorated with beading, but very few patterns were evident overall. Most often, a single bow provided accent, and she often wore a triple strand of pearls. Monochromatic color and geometric lines prevailed. Her choice of colors reflected her knowledge and interest in painting and history, according to Cassini. Although she preferred white and black, Veronese green, Nattier blue, "old master" yellows, pinks, reds, greens, and blues were also favorites. Finally, Mrs. Kennedy was one of the last first ladies to regularly wear hats, and her famous pillbox style sitting back on her bouffant styled hair was, according to Cassini's interpretation (1995), inspired by images of Nefertiti of Egypt.

Cassini's aim was to orchestrate glamour through clothing that would allow Mrs. Kennedy to stand out from everyone else in the room. He aimed at a royal look, and he succeeded from the first outfit he designed for Mrs. Kennedy. The white Swiss double satin gown she wore to the inaugural gala was so stunning that it is reported President-elect Kennedy wanted the lights turned on in the limousine as they rode through the city "so they can see Jackie" (Thayer 1971, 62). Cassini correctly analyzed that "nobody suspected back then, not even the President, that Jackie was to become his best public relations tool" (1995, 33). Starting with the first trip abroad in May of 1961, where Mrs. Kennedy was photographed with Royal Canadian Mounted Police in a red wool suit that complemented their uniforms, to the Givenchy-designed gown for an evening with President de Gaulle at Versailles, to the chiffon gown she wore for the unveiling of the *Mona Lisa* at the National Gallery of Art in 1963, she epitomized the American version of royalty. The public was mesmerized, and as Cassini flatly states, "There was nobody to touch Jackie in using style as a political tool" (1995, 178).

From a visual perspective, Jackie Kennedy became what David Halberstam (1979) would call part of the supporting cast in her husband's recognition that television conflated theatre with politics. In an astute analysis of the influence of media on the presidency, Halberstam argues that Kennedy was the man with the appropriate instincts to exploit media coverage so that "style became in some ways as important as substance, and on occasion *more* important" (1979, 389). The star power of President Kennedy included the constellation of family, particularly Jackie, as both a glamorous first lady in haute couture, but also as a mother photographed with the adorable Caroline and John. Much of the visual imagery was an attempt to control the tension between public access and the protection of privacy,[6] but there is absolutely no doubt when looking at the dazzling array of photographs from 1961 to 1963 that Mrs. Kennedy was at her best in evening gown entertaining heads of state, artists, and other important people.

In both popular and academic measure, only Princess Diana of Wales comes close to matching Jacqueline Kennedy's status as fashion icon. In her analysis of American fashion, entitled *Looking for Jackie*, Kathleen Craughwell-Varda classifies a fashion icon as a woman with a personal style whose imitated look across class lines "permanently [alters] the American cultural landscape" (1999, 9). She sees first ladies as a clear category of icon and Jacqueline Kennedy Onassis as the epitome of the phenomenon:

> Despite the current ubiquity of fashion-conscious celebrities, it is safe to say that no single figure has emerged in the last forty years who can rival the appeal and impact of Jacqueline Kennedy. That no contemporary woman has taken Jackie's place in the public consciousness is perhaps a reflection of our unwillingness to find a replacement for her; to do so would mean relinquishing the mythical appeal of the golden era of Camelot. (1999, 198)

In the popular press, Jackie Kennedy has remained, even after her death, as one of America's most admired fashion icons of the twentieth century (Collins 1994; Keogh 2001; Pogoda 1996; *Vogue* 1999). Academic analysis of women's magazines (Wang 1987) also documents Mrs. Kennedy, along with Princess Diana, as fashion leaders of their times.

White House Restoration

Nonverbal communication scholars who study impression management (Leathers 1992) often argue that one's personal body and, by extension, one's home are the two sites where individuals have control over the image they wish to present to the public, therefore influencing the outcome of the communication situation. Mrs. Kennedy, indeed, presented herself and the White House as aesthetic aspects of the Kennedy administration, with the result that the American public has consistently rated the Kennedys and the Kennedy White House years as one of the most popular and effective presidencies ("American Opinion" 1999; Gallup 2000; Watson 2000, 179–95). The single most cited agenda item of Mrs. Kennedy's is undoubtedly her White House restoration project. The Smithsonian First Ladies exhibit posts a placard which reads: "Jacqueline Kennedy marked a pivotal transition in the role—after her, first ladies would be expected to have significant agendas of their own." The agenda in question pertains to her restoration project and the subsequent congressional legislation she saw passed that insured the preservation and protection of White House artifacts. Mrs. Kennedy's greatest contribution to American history is the transformation of the White House itself to a museum quality building that represents an accurate portrayal of presidential life, including authentic artifacts and furniture representing some of our most important presidents. Although presidential libraries convey historical pictures of individual presidents, it is the White House itself that provides the larger context for the life of the president and first family in regard to both private living and state entertainment. Mrs. Kennedy's knowledge of history, art and antiques, and her aesthetic sense in general converged as she set her agenda to make the White House an American rival to European houses such as Versailles.

Mrs. Kennedy unveiled the restoration project in some detail to *Life* magazine correspondent Hugh Sidey in an interview accompanied by seven photographs published in September of 1961. Two important things are established in this interview. First, Mrs. Kennedy's academic approach to the restoration was clear when she stated, "Everything in the White House . . . must have a reason for being there. It would be sacrilege merely to 'redecorate' it—a word I hate. It must be *restored*—and that has nothing to do with decoration. That is a question of scholarship" (Sidey 1961, 57). More importantly, in this interview Mrs. Kennedy reveals the restoration project as a long-term vision she brought with her to the White House. In other words, she came with an agenda that would give the Kennedy administration a place in history:

> I knew the White House would be one of my main projects if he won . . . How could I help wanting to do it? she asks. I don't know . . . is it a reverence for beauty or for history? I guess both. I've always cared. My best friends are people who care. I don't know . . . when you read Proust or listen to Jack talk about history or go to Mount Vernon, you understand. I feel strongly about the children who come here. When I think about our son and how to make him turn out like his father, I think of Jack's great sense of history.[7] (Sidey 1961, 62)

To achieve the restoration, Mrs. Kennedy created a White House Fine Arts Committee to advise her and assist with the work. Membership included David Finley, chair of the National Commission of Fine Arts and Henry Francis Dupont of the Winterthur Museum. Lorraine Pearce became the first curator of the White House. Jacqueline Kennedy established a permanent association between the White House and the Smithsonian by persuading her husband to support legislation she had introduced to Congress by Representative J. T. Rutherford and Senator Clinton Anderson. The legislation proposed that the Smithsonian store all White House objects not in use at any given time and provide a permanent curator for the White House. Behind the scenes she used the advice of French interior designer Stephane Boudin, although there is some evidence that his presence was a source of controversy regarding the amount of French influence needed for an American design project (Klein 1996; Truman 1995).

Mrs. Kennedy further established the White House Historical Association (JFK Library website; Salinger Papers) as a body that would raise funds for the restoration through donations and the publication of the first White House guidebook. She wrote the introduction, approved the text, selected photographs, and designed layout for *The White House: An Historic Guide*, which was published in 1962, and became a success with visitors. This editorial endeavor was a precursor to Jacqueline Kennedy Onassis's career as an editor from 1975 until her death in 1994. The restoration project itself was the first of a number of restoration projects she became involved in during her lifetime, including redesign of the Rose Garden, saving historic homes on Lafayette Square from demolition, saving the War, State, and Navy Building from demolition to be remodeled and renamed as the Old Executive Building, and, as Helen Thomas reports (1999), she assisted with the redesign of Air Force One by enlisting the help of designer Raymond Loewy. Again, these activities foreshadowed her lifelong interest in historic preservation. In later years, she campaigned to save Grand Central Station and preserve portions of Central Park, and she assisted with the establishment of the Costume Institute at the Metropolitan Museum of Art.

In addition to bringing historic preservation to the attention of the American people, Mrs. Kennedy chose to present the restored White House through a one-hour televised tour on February 14, 1962. It is one of two events in which she spent a sustained period of time communicating with the American public. (The other event was the funeral of President Kennedy, where her communication was entirely nonverbal.) Several sources document the tour, including the CBS copy of the program itself, a summary of the tour linked to the JKF Library website, and a fascinating book entitled *A Tour of the White House with Mrs. John F. Kennedy* by Perry Wolff in conjunction with CBS. Wolff sums up the essence of the rhetorical situation: "A woman spoke for an hour and the White House once more became the central symbol of America" (1962, 10). Camelot was visually and firmly established for America as a result of the tour. The number of viewers who saw the tour[8] runs from one-third of a nation (Wolff 1962, 9) to 48 million (Thomas 1999, 245) to 50 million (JFK Library website) to 80 million (www.geocities.com/~newgeneration/tour.htm). The Nielsen rating was 28.3 million homes (Thayer 1971, 330), so calculations vary based on number of people estimated per home. Whatever the actual number, it is the most significant public speaking Mrs. Kennedy did as first lady.

Wolff (1962) reported that CBS shot the tour over a three-day period in January. Mrs. Kennedy was on set about seven hours to produce a one-hour documentary comprised of approximately 100,000 electronic images. Correspondent Charles Collingwood served as the interviewer, but much of the final footage is Mrs. Kennedy herself explaining the purpose of various rooms and the historic significance of the furniture and artifacts in each room.

Several features characterize Mrs. Kennedy as a public speaker. Most noticeable visually is Jacqueline Kennedy as a "perfect model of American manners," to use a description offered by Arthur Schlesinger Jr. (1999). She appears impeccably dressed in a two-piece wool suit with a bouffant hairstyle, and her posture is absolutely perfect throughout the broadcast. She is poised and polite to Mr. Collingwood, and she confidently leads the way through the White House without ever erring in direction or control. In reality, the tour is a videotape with 190 splices in the master tape, that is, about 95 scenes were inserted (Wolff 1962, 243). However, few retakes were needed for the live taping. Wolff reported, "It was obvious that her intensity about the White House and her work was communicable" (248). When President Kennedy makes a brief appearance, his commentary appears to flow in tone and content with the rest of the tour. In reality, the president's appearance was taped twice since he did not like the impact of his words on the first take, according to Wolff (1962, 233).

Vocally, Mrs. Kennedy had a high-pitched, breathy style of speaking that, by today's standards, would be considered detrimental to a woman's public speaking impact. Her vocal quality has been described in various ways: "softly in a whispery voice" (Gutin 1989, 58), "little girl whisper" (Klein 1996, 5), and by her sisters-in-law she was jokingly referred to as "Babykin, a popular talking doll" (Klein 1996, 124). The *London Observer*, however, called her voice "a phantom intimacy" (quoted in Anthony 1991, 72), which was clearly meant as a compliment. For the 1960s, Mrs. Kennedy's voice was not a liability overall; rather, it epitomized her femininity while masking the interior strength and control that she needed as first lady. To further enhance her natural movement and voice, she was fitted with a hidden microphone under her suit jacket. Her spontaneity appeared flawless.[9]

Finally, Mrs. Kennedy spoke on camera from memory. The level of detail she mastered regarding historical fact was rather incredible and greatly impressed the American public. It certainly enhanced her ethos and proved that she was not only physically attractive, but highly intelligent as well. This was a winning combination for the Kennedy administration. *The White House Tour* was a sensation. It was broadcast in Europe and Asia and received an Emmy Award. A reported 10,000 letters came into the White House after the initial broadcast, and tourists increased between one-third and one-half from the previous year (Thayer 1971). *The Guide*, selling for one dollar, appears to have financed much of the restoration project. After the televised tour, Camelot was firmly entrenched in the American public's visual memory. The White House was seen as a kind of American royal palace or "national shrine" (UPI 1964, 70). This is an important distinction because the White House and the Capitol vie with the Statue of Liberty as perhaps the most important icons of democracy in the world.

White House Entertainment

During the tour of the White House, CBS correspondent Charles Collingwood has the following exchange with Mrs. Kennedy:

> CC: Mrs. Kennedy, this administration has shown a particular affinity for artists, musicians, writers, poets. Is this because you and your husband just feel that way or do you think that there's a relationship between the government and the arts?
> JK: That's so complicated. I don't know. I just think that everything in the White House should be the best—the entertainment that's given here and, if it's an American company that you can help, I like to do that. If it's not, just as long as it's the best. (Wolff 1962, 78–79)

The evasiveness of the remark is not genuine. Mrs. Kennedy knew very well that she wanted a relationship between the government and the arts in a manner that emulated her observations of French culture and government. First ladies scholar Carl Anthony (1991, 27–43) offers a marvelous analysis of her cultural agenda, and he gives her credit for her intelligence regarding her reasoning for a government agency to promote the arts and for a Washington National Cultural Center patterned after Lincoln Center in New York. The Johnson administration would follow through with the National Endowment for the Arts and the National Endowment for the Humanities. The Kennedy Center opened in her lifetime, but during her service as first lady, the arts flourished inside the White House. Interestingly, Mrs. Kennedy's first caller at the White House was George Balanchine, choreographer and director of the New York City Ballet, while one of President Kennedy's first callers was poet Robert Frost (Thayer 1971). Literally, the stage was set for what would come in the next three years.

Immediately upon JFK's election to the presidency, Jacqueline assembled members of a team who would assist her to literally transform White House style in entertaining. Letitia Baldrige, an old friend from Vassar and an experienced mistress of etiquette, was appointed social secretary. Shortly after, Pamela Turnure was hired as Mrs. Kennedy's press secretary (although her title was Assistant Social Secretary for the Press) and Oleg Cassini as her couturier. J. B. West was already in place as the chief usher of the White House, Providencia Parades served as Mrs. Kennedy's maid, and George Thomas was the president's valet. After an initial disastrous dinner party, French chef Rene Verdon was hired to bring truly good food to all White House guests. In a delightful book entitled *In the Kennedy Style* (1998), Letitia Baldrige describes six of the most memorable state dinners from the Kennedy administration, and Rene Verdon includes menus and recipes for each event. Ms. Baldrige's observations, however, run deep regarding the rhetorical-semiotic effects of the first lady's decisions. The total sensual appeal of sight, fragrance, taste, and sound made White House galas communication extravagances that boosted everyone's ethos. As novelist William Styron noted on one occasion, "even Republicans were gaga" (Baldrige 1998, 90).

Given how badly the White House needed to be restored, it is not surprising that the public rooms, particularly the State Dining Room, were not conducive to entertaining. The lighting was poor, the colors and furniture were unsightly and uncomfortable, and the general feeling was cold and dismal. Mrs. Kennedy was already a seasoned hostess and knew social protocol. She told Letitia Baldrige, "The entertaining is going to be very important to us . . . There are many things that can be done to make it [the White House] warmer, more gracious, more distinguished" (1998, 21). Indeed, Mrs. Kennedy made several strategic choices that changed the entire nature of the communication during a White House event. According to Baldrige, round tables seating eight or ten replaced horseshoe or rectangular tables. Walls painted white or yellow and pale blue tablecloths lightened the rooms and the mood. Flemish style flower arrangements were plentiful and of low height to provide fragrance (to mask the smells of cigarettes and cigars) and color without obscuring sightlines. Intimate and lively conversation was now possible. Given the age of the Kennedys, it is not surprising to know that one aim of their entertaining was to have fun. Dancing, alcohol, and smoking were permitted.

Communicatively, Mrs. Kennedy used seating charts and room arrangements to enliven the possibilities for conversation. At large dinners, two dining rooms were necessary. She presided in one while her husband hosted in the other. Husbands and wives were separated (a break in tradition) by room and tables so that each could meet different people and have something to talk about after the party. Guests of honor were usually seated at the president and Mrs.

Kennedy's tables, but the guest lists were so innovative that each table seated interesting people. Pierre Salinger (1966) reported that Mrs. Kennedy would literally spread out the seating charts on the floor of her sitting room and plan seating. For a dinner of 120 guests, typically forty people would be seated based on government protocol, and she would decide where to seat the other eighty. The Kennedy's were a glamorous couple, and they invited glamorous people to mingle with heads of state and government officials. Depending upon the events of the evening, the Kennedys often had guests of honor to their family quarters before or after dinner for private conversation.

The White House truly took on the persona of Camelot a short time into the Kennedy administration. Mrs. Kennedy wore her Cassini gowns, sometimes accented with a tiara or sunburst brooch, and the president greeted dignitaries in formal white tie. Three entertainments are well known for their extravagance or innovation regarding the celebration of arts and culture. The most ambitious event ever undertaken was an outdoor dinner for 132 guests staged at Mount Vernon to honor the president of Pakistan on July 11, 1961. The president and his guests sailed down the Potomac River to Mount Vernon and dined under a gigantic tent. For Mrs. Kennedy, the dinner was reminiscent of the evening when she and the president were entertained at Versailles by President de Gaulle. Mount Vernon represented a historic monument that the American people could show to their guests, and the site truly represents a consistent theme with the Kennedys: history is important because it is the story of the United States. Again, Mrs. Kennedy selected a visual icon, Mount Vernon, as the symbolic presentation of America to the president of Pakistan.

The most remembered artistic evening in the White House was November 13, 1961, when Pablo Casals gave a concert after a dinner for 155 guests. It was a stunning coup to persuade Casals to come dine and entertain the president. At a time when an invitation to the White House catapulted the recipient to unequaled social status (Baldrige 1998, 67), Casals declined the first invitation to come because he continued to boycott U.S. support of Francisco Franco during the Spanish civil war. In the end, Casals did perform in the United States for the first time since 1928 in the company of the governor of Puerto Rico and composers such as Samuel Barber and Leonard Bernstein. Casals' worldwide fame as a cellist boded well for the Kennedys. After a thirty-three-year hiatus from performing in the United States, Mrs. Kennedy is credited with renewing our country's relationship with one of the world's most gifted musicians.

Finally, there was the party for "the brains," which was Ms. Baldrige's code name for the dinner honoring the American Nobel Laureates on April 20, 1962. This was the evening where, among the 175 guests, Linus Pauling waltzed impromptu after marching on the White House earlier in the day to advocate banning the atom bomb. The evening with the American intelligentsia highlights the focus on intellect that the Kennedys were known for, but also adds to the list of "firsts" for White House entertaining, among them poetry readings, opera, ballet performances, youth concerts, and the first reception ever for Congressional Medal of Honor recipients (Baldrige 1998, 87). The rhetorical impact of these events was not lost on the rest of the world. Like the great European palaces, the

United States could now boast that we, too, appreciated music, art, intellect, and politics as part of our great traditions. The presence of such important people in the White House symbolically demonstrated the value of American culture and succeeded in elevating the history and the passion of this country. Mrs. Kennedy's strategy endures as art and politics continue to mix at the White House.

Orchestration of President Kennedy's Funeral

On November 21, 1963, Mrs. Kennedy traveled to Texas with her husband as part of a strategy to strengthen Democratic allegiance to the president. It was her first trip since suffering the loss of Patrick, a son born in August who died within three days of a premature birth. Most analysts agree that the Kennedys were at a turning point in their personal relationship and looked forward to a stronger marriage as a result of their family loss. Mrs. Kennedy's popularity was as strong as ever, marked by the comments President Kennedy made when she arrived fashionably late to a breakfast in Forth Worth on the morning of November 22. He quipped that "nobody wonders what Lyndon and I wear" (Office of the Federal Register 1964, 888), when she entered the dining room in a Cassini pink suit and matching pillbox hat. Approximately four hours later President Kennedy was assassinated in Dallas, presumably by Lee Harvey Oswald. To this day, one of the most enduring images of November 22, 1963, is Jacqueline Kennedy wearing the blood-splattered pink suit as Lyndon Johnson took the oath of office on Air Force One and, later, as she descended from the plane to accompany the coffin to Bethesda Naval Hospital. Most astonishing, however, is the calm dignity with which thirty-four-year-old Mrs. Kennedy carried herself from November 22 until the close of the funeral on November 25. Upon reflection, *Look* correspondent Laura Bergquist wrote, "Last November she showed her quality. It was her toughness and discipline that carried a nation through the trauma with a transcendent dignity" (1964, 36).

Margaret Truman's analysis may be most accurate:

> Aristocrats also have a sense of their own stature, as well as life's depths. They have been trained to speak and behave in a style that fits the occasion, no matter what their private feelings may be. Jackie's previous three years, in which, behind her various masks, she had forged her own unique identity as First Lady, became a resource on which she drew to sustain not only herself but the American people in this tragic ordeal. . . . Jackie's dignity, her sense of history, enabled the nation to focus on its grief. (1995, 44)

Mrs. Kennedy had the presence of mind to think rhetorically even as she returned to Washington, D.C., aboard Air Force One sitting next to her husband's coffin (Smith 1964, 33). Instructions were given to research the details of President Lincoln's funeral, and by the next morning, the iconography of the Kennedy funeral began to reflect the formality of a national protocol inclusive of several presidential funerals, most notably Lincoln's, but also laden with military imagery reflecting the superpower status of the United States. The extensive television coverage allowed the American people, as well as citizens around the globe, a constant image bathed in black against the sound of muffled drums. This message lasted from Saturday through Monday, during which time Mrs. Kennedy did not speak publicly, yet appeared as the symbol of our national grief. Not once did she lose control in front of a television camera.

Several rhetorical gestures characterize President Kennedy's funeral. Black bunting in the East Room, where the president lay in state on Saturday, was similar to the Lincoln funeral (UPI 1964, 45). In the Capitol rotunda, Kennedy's coffin laid on the same catafalque that held the coffins of Presidents Lincoln, McKinley, and Garfield. During the eulogy in the Capitol on Saturday, Mrs. Kennedy and her daughter Caroline approached the flag-draped coffin and kneeled down, Jacqueline kissing the flag and Caroline touching the coffin. This was a poignant moment of grief for families everywhere. On Monday, the day of the funeral, John F. Kennedy Jr., on his third birthday, saluted his father's coffin as it came down the steps of St. Matthew's Cathedral. The photograph is, perhaps, the most well known and enduring of the funeral itself, and it was his mother who prompted John to salute. The funeral procession included six horses drawing the caisson, three of them riderless, and behind the coffin, a black riderless horse with boots inserted into the stirrups backwards as the symbol of a lost leader (UPI 1964). Finally, Mrs. Kennedy selected an eternal flame to grace the graveside in Arlington National Cemetery, where she chose to have President Kennedy buried (rather than in his home state of Massachusetts) because she reasoned "he belongs to the country" (UPI 1964, 99). The eternal flame was an extremely important choice because it symbolically continues the Kennedy legacy forward in history. For those of us who witnessed the events of November 1963, the flame is both a reminder of tragedy, but also a symbol of endurance and hope.[10] President Kennedy will not be forgotten, and Jacqueline Kennedy's orchestration of his funeral was the final rhetorical act of the Kennedy administration.

Interpersonal Diplomacy

Although Mrs. Kennedy did not speak in public as part of her role as first lady, other than ceremonial remarks, it is clear in hindsight that she engaged a kind of interpersonal diplomacy that is fitting to her view of politics. I want to argue here that she had a keen sense of interpersonal relationships and how to maneuver within the constraints of the patriarchal social protocol of the 1950s and 1960s. It has been said (Gutin, 1989) that Jacqueline Kennedy had no interest in politics, that, in fact, politics bored her and that she did not care to participate in politics.[11] I do not believe this to be entirely true, and there is evidence that, for example, during the Cuban Missile Crisis Mrs. Kennedy was present during some of the conversations of the president's inner circle (Anthony 1991, 81). Further, Margaret Truman (1995) reports that Mrs. Kennedy used her intelligence and good judgment to smooth the relationships between President Kennedy, Indian prime minister Nehru, and U.N. Ambassador Adlai Stevenson. She also sent political observations from her trips to India and Italy in personal letters to her husband.

No first lady can divorce herself from politics since it is at the core of White House life. Mrs. Kennedy was an intelligent, well-read woman who shared with her husband a keen sense of history (Sidey 1961; White 1963). They discussed history often, she made mention of history in public remarks, and she knew that the relationship of the president to the American public was one of the most documented relationships in American history. Although she may not have been interested in discussing publicly particular policy issues, there is no doubt that she was very aware of politics and a role that she might play as a first lady. Historian Carl Anthony (1990; 1991) documents Mrs. Kennedy's role as campaigner, speech advisor, listener, sounding board, debate partner, and historical consultant to her husband from his senator years until his death. However, it is clear that Mrs. Kennedy chose to exercise her knowledge and power behind the scenes in terms of President Kennedy's formal political agenda.

She clearly was not an Eleanor Roosevelt regarding an activist agenda, nor was she the housewifely Mamie Eisenhower. For the public record, Mrs. Kennedy claimed the following in a written interview with journalist Helen Thomas: "When I asked her what was the best thing about living in the White House she responded, 'Seeing my husband be a great president,' but politics, to her, took a backseat to being a mother to her children. 'The official side of my life takes me away from my children a great deal,' she said. 'If I were to add political duties, I would have practically no time with my children and they are my first responsibility. My husband agrees with me'" (1999, 58–59). Mrs. Kennedy, however, understood the value of politics, as evidenced by this response in a televised interview:

> I think politics is one of the most rewarding lives any woman can have—to be married to a politician. I think every woman wants to feel needed, and in politics you are—so much more than in other areas. You're always living in a state of crisis. You're always being demanded to meet a challenge, and when you meet it, it's a great satisfaction to you. (The World of Jacqueline Kennedy 1962)

She did find a way to engage politics, even if she did not set an official political agenda.

Specifically, Mrs. Kennedy used three rhetorical strategies to aid her husband's presidency: first, her fashion diplomacy was a calculated persuasive strategy to present the best face of the presidency. Her iconic beauty and sophisticated interpersonal style particularly paid off in smoothing the relationships between President Kennedy and French president Charles de Gaulle, and more importantly, President Kennedy and Russian president Nikita Khrushchev. Her skills in French allowed her to serve as the translator between de Gaulle and her husband on their 1961 trip to Paris, which was a highly unusual position for a first lady, but which solidified Mrs. Kennedy's position as the pivot on which French–American relations were strengthened. One of President Kennedy's most quoted lines is, of course, the statement he made to a press luncheon after the first two days of their visit: "I do not think it altogether inappropriate to introduce myself to this audience. I am the man who accompanied Jacqueline Kennedy to Paris, and I have enjoyed it" (Blair 1961, 1). In 1962, she journeyed to India on a highly successful state visit to bolster her husband's credibility and U.S. influence over India's foreign policies regarding Pakistan, Portugal, and China. President Kennedy and Prime Minister Nehru had not seemed compatible when Nehru visited the United States, yet Kennedy was very interested in supporting India as a pivotal site of Asian interest (Schlesinger 1965). Mrs. Kennedy's diplomacy accomplished the goal.

Her second persuasive strategy concerned protocol. By redesigning the staging for state dinners, White House cultural entertainment, and informal parties, Mrs. Kennedy was able to widen the number of people who came into contact with the president, bring people together for behind-the-scenes politicking while enjoying highbrow cultural entertainment, and she solidified the inner circle of influence by hosting frequent private lunches and parties for both friends and key political figures whose company the president and first lady desired. Even on the day of her husband's funeral, Mrs. Kennedy had the poise to host a receiving line in the Red Room of the White House for international heads of state (Baldrige 1998), and over 200 people were members of this group (UPI & *American Heritage Magazine* 1964).

Mrs. Kennedy's third persuasive strategy was her use of handwritten, personal letters and notes. She is, in fact, known for her handwritten memos to staff on yellow legal pad paper and her colorful handwritten notes to friends and family, in which she often included drawings and lines of poetry (Salinger 1966). Although she very often used such notes as follow-ups for a job well done by her personal staff, she also wrote to heads of state and other important people, including her own husband. Biographer Margaret Thayer reported that whenever Mrs. Kennedy traveled, her personal maid hand carried a briefcase that contained "writing paper; information about places on the itinerary; and list after list, with brief profiles attached, of the important and interesting people Mrs. Kennedy would meet" (1971, 277). She was never out of touch with people and used her letter-writing skills as a preferred form of communication.

Given the tense nature of American–Russian diplomacy during the Kennedy administration, it is worth noting that Jacqueline Kennedy may have served to restrain not only the personal awkwardness between President Kennedy and Mr. Khrushchev (as was evident in Vienna in 1961), but she also may have aided in restraining the diplomatic animosity between the two countries. It is evident that Mr. Khrushchev was quite fond of Mrs. Kennedy, and it is clear that she saw the importance of preserving a civil relationship between the United States and the Soviet Union.

In June 1999, President Boris Yeltsin released approximately forty declassified documents to President Clinton, one of which is a copy of a top secret cipher telegram from Russian ambassador Anatoly Dobrynin dated December 4, 1963 (U.S. Dept. of State, LS no. 0692061-27). In this document, Ambassador Dobrynin sends to the Kremlin the contents of a personal letter from Jacqueline Kennedy to Nikita Khrushchev. Dobrynin explains that the letter is handwritten ("considered here [the United States] to be a sign of particular respect for the addressee") on small pages with the stamp of the White House. The text of the letter contains 367 words in which she thanks Mr. Khrushchev for sending a representative to President Kennedy's funeral and then writes an extremely personal and political message which reads in part:

> I am sending it [this letter] only because I know how much my husband was concerned about peace and how important the relations between you and him were to him in this concern. He often cited your words in his speeches: "In the next war, the survivors will envy the dead."
>
> You and he were adversaries, but you were also allies in your determination not to let the world be blown up. You respected each other and could have dealings with each other. I know that President Johnson will make every effort to establish the same relations with you. The danger troubling my husband was that war could be started not so much by major figures as by minor ones.
>
> Whereas major figures understand the need for self-control and restraint, minor ones are sometimes moved rather by fear and pride. If only in the future major figures could still force minor ones to sit down at the negotiating table before they begin to fight.
>
> I know that President Johnson will continue the policy my husband believed in so deeply—the policy of self-control and restraint—and he will need your help. I am sending you this letter because I am so deeply mindful of the importance of the relations that existed between you and my husband, and also because you and Mrs. Khrushchev were so kind in Vienna.

Mrs. Kennedy's political savvy is astute. According to the telegram, even President Johnson and Secretary of State Dean Rusk were not aware of the contents of this letter, yet Mrs. Kennedy sets the stage for the Johnson administration to enter into American–Russian diplomacy on a positive note. Further, her ability to show interpersonal consideration for Mr. Khrushchev and his wife is a strategic stroke of genius given that, by all accounts, beginning with the 1961 meeting in Vienna, Kennedy and Khrushchev did not personally get along. Khrushchev, however, was smitten with Mrs. Kennedy as evidenced by a *Life* magazine (1994) photograph in which he adoringly smiles at Jackie. She probably also knew about the secret correspondence between her husband and Khrushchev that served as a means to negotiate within the tense context of nuclear threats during this phase of American–Soviet relations (Salinger 1966).

Jacqueline Kennedy's interpersonal skills also intervened to soften the relationship between President Kennedy and his own vice president, Lyndon Johnson. Katharine Graham reports in her autobiography (1997) that right from the 1960 Democratic Convention, when Johnson was selected as Kennedy's vice-presidential running mate, there was tension between Johnson and the Kennedy family as a whole. Johnson is reported to have said that Jacqueline Kennedy was the only person from the Kennedy clan who was nice to him, and she speaks highly of him in her oral history for the LBJ Library (Onassis 1974). Apparently, she was genuinely kind to him throughout the Kennedy administration, even when she was delegating unwanted public appearances as first lady to Mrs. Johnson (Anthony 1991; Truman 1995). In a recent release of telephone tapes from the LBJ Library (Tape No. WH6409.02), the American public was astonished with the fact that President Johnson asked Mrs. Kennedy if she would serve as ambassador to Mexico for the Johnson administration. She graciously declined the offer. Pierre Salinger reported (1995) that President Johnson asked him to carry a personal message to Mrs. Kennedy in 1964 requesting her acceptance of an ambassadorship to France; however, she declined once again. Clearly, Mrs. Kennedy's diplomatic skill and her facility in Spanish and French impressed Lyndon Johnson, however inappropriate an invitation to become ambassador might be for the new widow of a former president.

Although much of the public's perception of Mrs. Kennedy's achievements as first lady was contained in images that reflect her use of fashion diplomacy and protocol, the written and oral forms of communication she employed are less known. Her public imagery as mother and fashion icon are a subtle form of political influence and, perhaps, should even be characterized as social-cultural influence on the shaping of American life. But, a look behind the photographs indicates that, like other first ladies, Mrs. Kennedy exercised considerable political power through her strategic use of silence and discretion. Mrs. Kennedy's private persona, called the most "complex" of recent first ladies by White House usher J. B. West (Anthony 1991), balanced the public image of glamour that the press insisted on creating during the Kennedy administration. Ironically, Anthony notes that the public's "adulation was often insulting to her intelligence. Her celebrity intruded on her privacy, and consequently her ironclad limitations on her role began to serve as refuge from the intensity of global fame" (1991, 44). It is not surprisingly, then, that first ladies scholars have not been able to ascertain fully how politically influential Mrs. Kennedy actually was given that her husband's assassination cut short her role as first lady and that the press coverage insisted on glamour images whenever possible. Since she was the first "television" first lady, the true tension between public and private in a first lady's life may be epitomized by Jacqueline Kennedy. The fact that she chose to remain an enigma for the rest of her life only increases the ambiguity of her personal politics.

Mrs. Kennedy as Public Speaker

Contrary to the usual starting point for analyses of first lady rhetoric, I selected to privilege visual forms of communication over public speaking in regard to Mrs. Kennedy. I do so because Mrs. Kennedy herself did not shape her role as first lady through her public speaking. In fact, she chose to shun the public platform once in the White House. It is clear from those close to the Kennedy Senate and presidential campaigns (O'Donnell and Powers 1970; Salinger 1966) that Jacqueline Kennedy was very good at campaigning. She retained good cheer, was genuine to people whom she met, listened to what voters had to say, and spoke with enthusiasm when asked to take the stage on her husband's behalf. Kennedy confidants Ken O'Donnell and Dave Powers even tell an amusing story in which Jackie Kennedy borrowed the manager's microphone in a supermarket to tell people about her husband during the 1960 presidential campaign. She also wrote a column entitled "Campaign Wife," distributed by the Democratic National Committee (Anthony 1990). In this column she covered a range of observations about her husband as a presidential candidate out on the trail, but also offered her point of view on such serious issues as education and medical care for senior citizens ("Jacqueline Kennedy: The White House Years" 2001).

We do know that Mrs. Kennedy assisted her husband with his speech writing, primarily by suggesting quotations or discussing books with him. It is reported that she even translated French books on Indochina and read passages from de Gaulle's *Memoires* that later influenced her husband's thinking (Schlesinger 1965, 103).

Mrs. Kennedy's low priority for her own public speaking is also reflected in the fact that there is no systematic documentation for a "speaking schedule" or speech texts. During the White House years, she spoke rarely and always on ceremonial occasions. Her speeches were short and extemporaneous. The videotape archive at the JFK Library contains the best documentation of her public speaking, although the occasions are not always dated or places cited. The arts, for example, were one of her priorities as first lady, and she spoke on several occasions to support art patronage (e.g., *Accent* 1961). However, most interesting is Mrs. Kennedy's preference to give speeches in French or Spanish, or to speak in front of an international audience. Anthony (1990) documents the radio tapes and brief remarks she made in Spanish to voters of Latin, Hispanic, and Spanish descent during the 1960 presidential campaign. She continued this trend while in the White House.

I have documented (translated on occasion) thirty public speeches/press interviews by Mrs. Kennedy,[12] but this must be considered incomplete as it is the first attempt to piece together a chronology. One of the highlights is her taped interview in French that aired on French television the night before she and President Kennedy arrived in Paris in May 1961. In the interview she is remarkably charming, even coy, as she speaks to Monsieur Crenesse about the history of the White House, including some links to France through artifacts such as a Cezanne painting in the Green Room. She also discusses her role as a mother, the importance of family, and the way the Kennedys relax by listening to music. This interview was a highly successful public relations strategy (Salinger 1966). Helen Thomas (1999) reported that while in France, Mrs. Kennedy snubbed American reporters, but obligingly spoke in French to French reporters.

On the Latin American state visit in 1961, she spoke briefly in Spanish in Venezuela, concluding: "You know my husband's profound desire to help those who need help. I am sure that with your collaboration, he will be successful." In Mexico, she spoke at a luncheon honoring President and Mrs. Mateos on June 30, 1962. The text (Moreno, n.d.) contains 177 words and carries a message in which she tells the Mexican people to retain their culture and spirit even as they gain material progress: "Your profound faith in the dignity of man has been expressed in your art and literature over the centuries. . . . The ancient spirit of Mexico has not changed. . . . material progress can make a change without destroying the values of the heart and the human mind."

Even on the trip to Texas, she delivered a seventy-three-word speech in Spanish to the League of United Latin American Citizens in Houston (Thayer 1971). Her most unusual speech, other than a badly done interview she conducted with the captain of the U.S. Olympic Equestrian Team in 1963, was delivered in December of 1962 at the Orange Bowl in Miami to the brigade of rebels left from the Bay of Pigs (Schlesinger 1965). In an odd political statement that links the bravery of the rebels to teaching her son the story of the Bay of Pigs, she compliments the rebels in Spanish for their courageous fight for democracy.

Film footage from her trip to India and Pakistan in 1962 shows her speaking comfortably—in English—from a balcony overlooking Shalimar Gardens in which she makes the following speech:

> I must say I am profoundly impressed by the reverence which you in Pakistan have for your art and your culture and for the use which you make of it now. My own countrymen, too, have a pride in their traditions. So, I think, as I stand in these gardens, which were built long before my country was born, that that's one more thing that binds us together and always will. (Invitation to Pakistan, 1962)

Note that Mrs. Kennedy was predisposed to short greetings or compliments that contained references to culture, particularly art and literature. She always tried to link the audience to her husband or the United States to show a positive and mutual relationship.

Altogether it is not unfair to say that Jacqueline Kennedy enjoyed the ethos of first lady most often when projecting the presidency to audiences who were not American born, and for this reason, she could be called our most "international" first lady. At the 1963 reception for the three branches of government, Speaker of the House John McCormack toasted Mrs. Kennedy as "a great diplomat and a great Ambassador—who has given an image of America which has made the world smile again" (quoted in Thayer 1971, 190). After three years in the role of first lady and official trips to Canada, France, Austria, England, Latin America, Italy, India, and Pakistan, Mrs. Kennedy earned such high praise from Speaker McCormack, and it is no wonder that President Johnson sought to honor Jacqueline Kennedy as an ambassador. As much as she celebrated the best of the United States, Mrs. Kennedy's public persona is international in scope, particularly when analyzed from the perspective of the public speaking she engaged in as first lady.

Legacy

At his mother's funeral on May 23, 1994, John F. Kennedy Jr. told the mourners that he and Caroline had discussed three themes that had influenced his mother's life: "love of words, emphasis on family, and desire for adventure" (Gould 1996, 494). Clearly, Jacqueline Kennedy's love of words is a chief theme in her life, but it is a personal more than a public theme. She read voraciously and in several languages. She wrote poetry, memos, and letters virtually every day. She edited books. She spoke often and with a great sense of intelligence and wit in private conversation. For public consumption, little is recorded to give a coherent view of this complex first lady. Rather, the public thrived on the imagery of a beautiful woman who brought to the White House a sense of modern style that was copied the world over and continues to influence fashion and popular culture.

Jacqueline Kennedy's emphasis on family translated into the primary tension she had to negotiate while living in the White House, that is, how to protect her family from the overzealous press. Helen Thomas summed it up, "Jackie was more elusive, due I think to her shyness, and as time went on her antipathy to the press grew in proportion to her fear of a loss of privacy" (1999, 58). Mrs. Kennedy was known as a woman of many masks. She had two children under the age of five when she entered the White House, and she had a husband who came from one of the most patriarchal clans in the country. Her priority was to protect her family even when it cost her on a personal basis. One of her strategies was to employ her own press secretary. Pamela Turnure described her duty as "to help preserve Mrs. Kennedy's privacy and not to create publicity" (quoted in Thayer 1971, 32). This is an odd position for a press secretary, and it worked only partially. As the first modern press secretary appointed to a first lady, Ms. Turnure was really under the direction of Pierre Salinger, President Kennedy's press secretary, even though Mrs. Kennedy outlined an extended plan in her initial memo regarding policies. Mr. Salinger was really the one to deal with the public–private tension on Mrs. Kennedy's behalf, but he did stay true to her wishes: "minimum information with maximum politeness" (Thayer 1971, 34). Mrs. Kennedy was, indeed, an expert at avoidance strategies, or as she termed it "the polite brush-off."[13]

What first lady does not have at least a small desire for adventure? Jacqueline Kennedy may have had more than the average woman, but she was born and lived in material circumstances that allowed her to fulfill her dreams. Her love of travel, language, history, art, and culture motivated her to seek adventure as far away as Cambodia, but during the White House years she was the first modern first lady to represent the United States to the pope and the prime minister of India without her husband by her side. This signaled the beginning of a new strategy for first ladies to become international ambassadors on behalf of the United States. But, beyond adventure or ambassadorship, Mrs. Kennedy translated her ability to connect nations on a cultural level into tremendous influence on her husband. In an exhibit entitled "Jacqueline Kennedy Travels Abroad" (2000) at the JFK Library, it was astounding to see a three-page memorandum she wrote to JFK outlining a complete plan to save the temples of Abu Simbel during the time that Egypt was struggling financially to create the Aswan Dam and preserve its monuments. The United States was a ten-million-dollar contributor to the preservation project. This type of power was simply not known to the public. Nevertheless, Mrs. Kennedy paved the way for other first ladies, such as Rosalynn Carter and Hillary Rodham Clinton, to engage in international "goodwill tours" as an appropriate domain for first ladies.

It is difficult to draw a single conclusion about a first lady as complicated as Jacqueline Kennedy. It is easy to overstate her case as the ultimate female American icon of the late twentieth century. The dialectical tensions between public and private, imagery and silence, modesty and stardom, intelligence and restraint all characterize this first lady. Her communication choices were extremely difficult given the media fishbowl that surrounded her at a young age. Had she not come from an aristocratic family, she may not have survived the White House years, particularly the assassination of her husband, with the dignity that she demonstrated. Perhaps her most effective communication choice was the strategic use of silence. She used image rather than words to convey messages that allowed public satisfaction while preserving her privacy as an individual. She thus became the female archetype, or idealized self, that every woman aspires to (Brenner 1994).

In this chapter I have argued that Jacqueline Kennedy executed a rhetorical-semiotic series of strategies to construct the legacy of Camelot. These strategies included what I have termed "fashion diplomacy," the restoration of the White House as a symbol of the presidency and a site for all pilgrims of democracy, a restructuring of entertainment protocol, and interpersonal diplomacy. Earlier in this volume, Kari Anderson argues that several first ladies have achieved political agency without violating norms of femininity by cultivating what she calls a "social political style." Like Dolley Madison, Jackie Kennedy knew how to throw a good party and, likewise, she did translate the role of hostess into diplomat. In fact, the placard at the JFK Library that leads visitors into the exhibit entitled Ceremonial and State Events reads: "They used social and diplomatic occasions at home and abroad to express important national values; to celebrate American history, culture, and achievement; and to enhance the role of the arts in national life."

But, I want to resist Anderson's frame of containment rhetoric in regard to Jacqueline Kennedy. Anderson argues that first ladies used social style as a political strategy against cultural constraints (i.e., containment) to liberate themselves and exercise power. Although her argument is noble, political agency was *not* Mrs. Kennedy's primary goal. Unlike Eleanor Roosevelt and Hillary Rodham Clinton, who clearly articulated political agendas, Jacqueline Kennedy's agenda was a more complicated mix of personal achievement and political participation. Mrs. Kennedy did not need the role of first lady to achieve her life goals. Her stature and position in society would have allowed her to create a life of social and cultural contribution with or without politics. She was not interested in a formal political agenda, so she did not need to circumvent the kind of containment described by Anderson. I would argue that Mrs. Kennedy's training placed her in a "comfortable" position regarding her goals as first lady. Her difficulties were based much more in the relentless invasion of her privacy from the press and the overt sexism from the Kennedy family that often left her in compromising or humiliating personal circumstances. If, however, first ladies represent a unique rhetorical strategy that conflates social and political style, then Jacqueline Kennedy is the epitome of such a strategy, but *not* because she used it to achieve a political agenda. Her strategy was based more on class and gender within the context of the historical period in which she lived. No other modern first lady has come from such an aristocratic background. As such, it places Jacqueline Kennedy in a unique position and may account for the public's fascination and willingness to see the Kennedy administration as the myth of Camelot.

Notes

1. Making the choice to frame Mrs. Kennedy's rhetorical activities as Camelot was a difficult point of scholarship. Pierre Salinger, press secretary to JFK and close friend of Jacqueline Kennedy throughout her life, claims (1995) that the media was guilty of *Camelotization*, which was not reflective of Mrs. Kennedy's view. Nevertheless, it *was* Mrs. Kennedy who evoked the name in her interview with Theodore White in 1963. (It is very clear in White's notes from the interview that she wanted *Camelot* to be known to the public.) After the word *Camelot* appeared in White's two-page remembrance in *Life* magazine, it became the synonym that the public has consistently used to describe the Kennedy White House years. At this time in history, it is more than a name; it evokes a clear mythology and symbolism about the Kennedy presidency and the role Jacqueline Kennedy played during those years. Because rhetorical activities of first ladies are judged by the public, I have selected the public perspective as the primary mode for analyzing Jacqueline Kennedy.

2. For those readers who are not familiar with semiotic analytical techniques or vocabulary, I will argue here that it is a necessary expansion of traditional rhetorical analysis. Because Mrs. Kennedy does not allow for a straightforward text-based analysis of her words, it is crucial to see her as a visual sign who actually signifies Camelot. She stands for, or signifies, the cultural aspects of Camelot. Additionally, as a cultural icon, she is the object that the general population attempts to simulate with regard to style and fashion. Semiotics is the study of signs, hence I will analyze Jacqueline Kennedy as a sign (icon) with communication value when considering the very idea of a first lady. *See* Wendy Leeds-Hurwitz's *Semiotics and Communication* (1993) for an excellent introduction to semiotic methodology.

3. Both the JFK Library and the Oral History Archive at the LBJ Library contain written and spoken materials from Mrs. Kennedy. Interestingly, the LBJ Library interview is available, while much of the oral material at the Kennedy Library is designated to be released to the public at various times, for example, some will not be unsealed until sixty years after her death in 2054. The oral history at the LBJ Library, a copy of which is also available at the JFK Library, is confined to comments about the relationships of the Johnsons and Kennedys. Lewis Gould (1996) reports that Mrs. Kennedy kept no diary. Pierre Salinger quotes Jackie Kennedy Onassis as saying, "I want to live my life, not record it," when asked why she hadn't written a personal memoir (1995, 209).

4. The following biographical sketch is a compilation of cross-checked references from at least eight biographies on Jacqueline Kennedy, including Anthony (1991), Boller (1998), Caroli (1996), Gould (1996), Gutin (1989), Mills (1999), Thayer (1971), and Truman (1995). Although there are several dozen biographies of Mrs. Kennedy, which vary from the academic to the tawdry, only the works of M.V.R. Thayer and Carl S. Anthony claim cooperation from Mrs. Kennedy.

5. In 1974, Jacqueline (Onassis) and Lee Bouvier published a delightful memoir of their trip entitled *One Special Summer*. It is actually the exact journal that the two of them constructed as a gift to their mother. Jackie created the drawings, poems, and narratives on Rome and Spain, while Lee wrote the journal entries describing the boat trip on

the *Queen Elizabeth* and their activities in London, Paris, Venice, Rome, and Florence. This book is a microcosm of the Bouvier style and, importantly, captures the personal style that Jacqueline used throughout her adult life. Prose and poetry are mixed together in witty, highly personal expression. The handwriting is large and dramatic, and drawings are crammed into any free space.

6. The issue of releasing photographs was a difficult one for Mrs. Kennedy. The public adored her children and wanted to see or take photographs. She had press secretary Pierre Salinger schedule photography sessions in the private quarters of the White House to appease the public and control the imagery of the first family.

7. In my view, this quotation sums up the essence of Jacqueline Kennedy. It contains references to all of the things she consistently cared about throughout her life: beauty, history, French literature, her husband, and the legacies left to children.

8. Although CBS was the official network, the program was simultaneously broadcast on CBS and ABC, according to Wolff (1962). Thayer (1971) reports that CBS broadcast the tour on February 14 followed by both NBC and ABC on February 18.

9. At least two people disagree with this assessment of Mrs. Kennedy's performance. Communication professor Mary Ann Watson charges that "any observer with a modicum of objectivity could not deny that she seemed awkward and stilted" (1987, 124). The other cynic, Norman Mailer, whose criticism of Mrs. Kennedy was published in his unkind essay in *Esquire* of July 1962, labeled her a "royal phony." Arthur Schlesinger (1965) reported that Mrs. Kennedy took no offense at Mailer's comments and probably agreed with him!

10. In October of 1997, I flew out of Washington National (now Ronald Reagan International) Airport just as darkness set in. As the plane rose, I looked out of my window and was taken aback to see below me the blackness of Arlington National Cemetery. In the center of the blackness was the eternal flame burning on Kennedy's grave. I spontaneously cried at the sight, remembering clearly the events of 1963, but also recognizing the hopeful symbolism of the flame. I will never forget that image as something that *is* contemporary America.

11. There is also ample evidence that Mrs. Kennedy did a good job as a campaigner during her husband's Senate race in 1958 and again during the presidential bid in 1960. Although she probably would not have put campaigning high on a list of favorite activities, she could do it and may even have enjoyed small doses of campaign activities ("Kennedy's Wife" 1960).

12. No major speeches given. Chronology for ceremonial remarks and interviews that follows was compiled from documentary evidence at the JFK Library and cross-referenced with *The New York Times*.

July 14, 1960	Press Conference, Hyannis Port, Massachusetts
March 16, 1961	Televised Remarks on National Gallery of Art 20th Birthday
April 11, 1961	Remarks at White House Women's Press Luncheon
May 5, 1961	Opening of Annual Flower Mart, Washington, D.C.
May 10, 1961	Interview with French Television Journalist, M. Crenesse (in French)
June 1, 1961	Press Interview and Receiving Line at U.S. Embassy in Paris
June 20, 1961	National Women's Press Club Dinner, Washington, D.C.
October 27, 1961	Presentation of President's Cup at Washington International Horse Show
December 16, 1961	Greetings at La Morita Agrarian Reform Project, Caracas, Venezuela (in Spanish)
December 17, 1961	Dinner Speech at San Carlos Palace, Bogota, Colombia (in Spanish)

February 14, 1962	Televised White House Tour
March 15, 1962	Presentation of Children's Art Carnival Gift to Indira Ghandi, India
March 21, 1962	Remarks for All-India Radio
March 22, 1962	Shalimar Gardens Speech, Pakistan
March 26, 1962	Farewell Message from Karachi, Pakistan
May 8, 1962	Christening of Submarine U.S.S. Lafayette, Groton, Connecticut
June 21, 1962	Opening of White House Library
June 28, 1962	Opening of White House Treaty Room
June 28, 1962	Ceremony Marking Publication of White House *Guide*
June 30, 1962	Luncheon Address at the Hotel Maria Isabel, Mexico City (in Spanish)
August 23, 1962	Message of Sympathy to Earthquake Victims, Ravello, Italy (broadcast in Italian)
September 11, 1962	Presentation of National Culture Center Model, Newport, Rhode Island
November 29, 1962	Closed-Circuit Broadcast of National Culture Center Benefit, Washington, D.C.
December 29, 1962	Cuban Brigade Speech, Orange Bowl, Miami, Florida (in Spanish)
June 20, 1963	Jacqueline Kennedy Interviews Captain of U.S. Olympic Equestrian Team Recorded at the White House
November 21, 1963	Dinner Speech to League of United Latin American Citizens in Houston, Texas (in Spanish)
January 14, 1964	Televised Thank-You Speech to the Nation Broadcast from Attorney General RFK's Office, Washington, D.C.
May 29, 1964	JFK Memorial Telecast, Hyannis Port, Massachusetts
June 5, 1964	Testimony to Warren Commission
November 17, 1964	Memoir of JFK for *Look* Magazine

13. Although the public wanted to hear all about family and children, the press releases in Pierre Salinger's Papers on file at the JFK Library are all geared toward the White House restoration project and formal White House entertainments such as dinners, teas, concerts, and theatre events. Interestingly, the restoration project press releases were most numerous and are highly detailed regarding expenditures, committee membership, acquisition of pieces, identification of donors, etc. Entertainment press releases always contained menu, guest list, entertainment program, and a precise description of the flowers in the table arrangements.

References

Accent. 1961. 20th Birthday of National Gallery of Art. JFK Audiovisual Archives Code TNC: 57.

American Opinion in the 20th Century. 1999. *USA Today*, 15 December, 8A.

Anthony, Carl S. 1990. *First Ladies: The Saga of the Presidents' Wives and Their Power, 1789–1961*, Vol. 1. New York: Quill/William Morrow.

———. 1991. *First Ladies: The Saga of the Presidents' Wives and Their Power, 1961–1990*, Vol. 2. New York: Quill/William Morrow.

Baldrige, Letitia, with Rene Verdon. 1998. *In the Kennedy Style: Magical Evenings in the Kennedy White House.* New York: Doubleday.

Barthes, Roland. 1990. *The Fashion System.* Translated by Matthew Ward and Richard Howard. Berkeley, Calif.: University of California Press.

Bauman, Suzanne. 1999. *Jackie: Behind the Myth.* PBS Television, 29 November.

Bergquist, Laura. 1964. A Lonely Summer for Jacqueline. *Look,* 17 November, 36–37.

Blair, W. Granger. 1961. Just an Escort, Kennedy Jokes as Wife's Charm Enchants Paris. *New York Times,* 3 June, A1.

Boller, Paul F., Jr. 1998. *Presidential Wives: An Anecdotal History.* 2nd ed. New York: Oxford University Press.

Bouvier, Jacqueline. 1950. Prix de Paris Essay. Rpt. 1994 in *Vogue,* August, 255, 302.

Bouvier, Jacqueline, and Lee Bouvier. 1974. *One Special Summer.* New York: Delacorte Press.

Bowles, Hamish. 2001. *Jacqueline Kennedy: The White House Years—Selections from the John F. Kennedy Library and Museum.* [Exhibition Catalogue]. New York: The Metropolitan Museum of Art/A Bulfinch Press Book/Little, Brown and Company.

Brenner, Marie. 1994. The Unforgettable Jackie. *Vogue,* August, 246–53, 300–302.

Caroli, Betty Boyd. 1996. Jacqueline Kennedy. In *American First Ladies: Their Lives and Their Legacy,* ed. Lewis L. Gould, 476–95. New York: Garland.

Cassini, Oleg. 1995. *A Thousand Days of Magic: Dressing Jacqueline Kennedy for the White House.* New York: Rizzoli.

Collins, Amy Fine. 1994. JKO. *Harper's Bazaar,* August, 148–51.

Craughwell-Varda, K. 1999. *Looking for Jackie: American Fashion Icons.* New York: Hearst Books/Fair Street-Welcome.

First Ladies: Political Role and Public Image. Washington, D.C.: National Museum of American History.

Folliard, Edward T. 1963. Escorting Mona Lisa to America. *National Geographic,* June, 838–47.

Gallup Opinion Presidential Poll. 2000. *CNN Headline News,* 21 February.

Gould, Lewis L. 1996. *American First Ladies: Their Lives and Their Legacy.* New York: Garland.

Graham, Katharine. 1997. *Personal History.* New York: Alfred A. Knopf.

Gray, Paul. 1996. What Price Camelot? *Time,* 6 May, 66–73.

Gutin, Myra G. 1989. *The President's Partner: The First Lady in the Twentieth Century.* New York: Greenwood.

Halberstam, David. 1979. *The Powers That Be.* New York: Alfred A. Knopf.

Interview with French Journalist (M. Crenesse). 1961. Film, 10 May. JFK Audiovisual Archive Code FON 10C.

Invitation to India. 1962. USIS Film. Washington, D.C.: JFK Audiovisual Archive Code USG: 1–10.

Invitation to Pakistan. 1962. USIS Film, 15 min. Washington, D.C.: JFK Audiovisual Archive Code USG: 1–14.

JBK Interviews U.S. Olympic Equestrian Team Captain. 1963. Film, 6 min., 20 June. Washington, D.C.: JFK Audiovisual Archive Code IFP: 200.

Jacqueline Kennedy: The White House Years. 2001. Exhibition, May 1–July 29. New York: Metropolitan Museum of Art.

Jacqueline Kennedy Travels Abroad. 2000. Exhibition, May 27–November 1. Columbia Point, Mass.: John F. Kennedy Library and Museum.

John F. Kennedy Library Website. 1998. *Jacqueline Bouvier Kennedy: First Lady.* www.cs.umb.edu/jfklibrary/jbkexhi.htm, accessed 31 December.

———. 1998. *The Wedding of Jacqueline Lee Bouvier and John Fitzgerald Kennedy.* www.cs.umb.edu/jfklibrary/jbkwed.htm, accessed 31 December.

Kennedy's Wife Finds Campaign Exhilarating. 1960. *New York Times,* 20 April, 29.

Keogh, Pamela Clarke. 2001. *Jackie Style.* New York: HarperCollins.

Klein, Edward. 1996. *All Too Human: The Love Story of Jack and Jackie Kennedy*. New York: Pocket Books.

LBJ Library Telephone Tape Collection. Conversation with Pierre Salinger. December 23, 1963. Tape No. K6312.16, Program No. 5.

LBJ Library Telephone Tape Collection. Conversation with George Reedy. September 2, 1964. Tape No. WH6409.02, Program No. 1.

Leathers, Dale M. 1992. *Successful Nonverbal Communication*. 2nd ed. New York: Macmillan.

Leeds-Hurwitz, Wendy. 1993. *Semiotics and Communication: Signs, Codes, Cultures*. Hillsdale, N.J.: Lawrence Erlbaum Associates.

Magic Moments. 1962. USIS Film, 13 min. JFK Audiovisual Archive Code USG: 1-1.

Mailer, Norman. 1962. An Evening with Jackie Kennedy. *Esquire*, July, 57–61.

Mayo, Edith P., and Denise D. Meringolo. 1994. *First Ladies: Political Role and Public Image*. Washington, D.C.: Smithsonian Institution.

Mills, Jean. 1999. *Moments with Jackie*. New York: MetroBooks.

Moreno, Maria Eugenia. 1962. *Jackie, Mexico: 1962*. N. P. Columbia Point, Mass.: JFK Library.

O' Donnell, Kenneth P., and David F. Powers (with Joe McCarthy). 1970. *"Johnny, We Hardly Knew Ye": Memories of John Fitzgerald Kennedy*. Boston: Little, Brown, and Company.

Office of the Federal Register, National Archives. 1964. *Public Papers of the President: 1963*. Washington, D.C.: United States Government Printing Office.

Onassis, Jacqueline Kennedy. 1974. Interview I with Joe B. Frantz for LBJ Library Oral History, January 11. Transcript available, Library, Columbia Point, Mass.: John Fitzgerald Kennedy Library.

Pogoda, Diane. 1996. Who's Got Style. *Women's Wear Daily*, 8 August, B2.

Salinger, Pierre Papers. n.d. Press Releases from the Office of Assistant Social Secretary for the Press. Columbia Point, Mass.: John Fitzgerald Kennedy Library.

———. 1966. *With Kennedy*. Garden City, N.Y.: Doubleday and Company.

———. 1995. *P. S.: A Memoir*. New York: St. Martin's Press.

Schlesinger, Arthur M., Jr. 1965. *A Thousand Days: John F. Kennedy in the White House*. Boston: Houghton Mifflin Company.

———. 1999. Guest Appearance on *Face the Nation*, CBS Television, July 25.

Sidey, Hugh. 1961. "Everything Must Have a Reason for Being There." *Life*, 1 September, 56–57, 62–65.

———. 1994. Introduction. In *Remembering Jackie: A Life in Pictures*. New York: Warner Books.

Smith, Merriman. 1964. Eyewitness Account. In *Four Days: The Historical Record of the Death of President Kennedy*, edited by United Press International & *American Heritage Magazine*, 32–33. n.p.: American Heritage Publishing Co.

Thayer, Margaret V. R. 1971. *Jacqueline Kennedy: The White House Years*. Boston: Little, Brown and Company.

Thomas, Helen. 1999. *Front Row at the White House: My Life and Times*. New York: Scribner.

Truman, Margaret. 1995. *First Ladies*. New York: Random House.

United Press International & *American Heritage Magazine*, eds. 1964. *Four Days: The Historical Record of the Death of President Kennedy*, n.p.: American Heritage Publishing Co.

U.S. Department of State. Top Secret Cipher Telegram. [Letter from Jacqueline Kennedy to Nikita Khrushchev.] L.S. no. 0692061-27. Received from National Archives, October 1999.

Valentino. 2001. Introduction. In *Jackie Style* by Pamela Clarke Keogh. New York: HarperCollins.

Vogue supplement. 1999. "The People in *Vogue*." n.p.

Wang, Whei-Fang. 1987. An Investigation of Fashion Leadership of Princess Diana (English 1981–1985) and Mrs. Jacqueline Kennedy Onassis (American 1961–1965) as Shown in Selected Publications. Unpublished Ph.D. diss., University of North Carolina at Greensboro.

Watson, Mary Ann. 1987. An Enduring Fascination: The Papers of Jacqueline Kennedy. *Prologue* 19, 117–25.

Watson, Robert P. 2000. *The Presidents' Wives: Reassessing the Office of First Lady.* Boulder, Colo.: Lynne Rienner Publishers.

White House Website. 1998. *Jacqueline Lee Bouvier Kennedy Onassis, 1929–1994.* www2.whitehouse.gov./wh/glimpse/firstladies/html/jk35.html, accessed 31 December.

———. 1998. White House Tour. www.geocities.com/~newgeneration/tour.htm, accessed 31 December.

White, Theodore. 1963. For President Kennedy: An Epilogue. *Life*, 6 December, n.p.

White, Theodore Papers. 1963. The Camelot Documents, item III-A, dated 19, December: Interview with Jacqueline Kennedy on November 29, 1963. Transcription of Notes (carbon copy) from Columbia Point, Mass.: John Fitzgerald Kennedy Library.

Williams, Jeannie. 1996. Camelot for Sale: Auction Catalog Opens a Window on Jackie's Life. *USA Today*, 8 March, D10.

Wolff, Peter. 1962. *A Tour of the White House with Mrs. John F. Kennedy.* Garden City, N.Y.: Doubleday.

The World of Jacqueline Kennedy. 1962. Film, 56 min. JFK Audiovisual Archive Code TNN: 1.

Chapter 14

Lady Bird Johnson
The Making of a Public First Lady with Private Influence

Diana B. Carlin

> The Constitution of the United States does not mention the First Lady. She is
> elected by one man only. The statute books assign her no duties; and yet, when
> she gets the job, a podium is there if she cares to use it. I did.
> —Lady Bird Johnson

Jacqueline Kennedy's tenure as first lady resulted from her husband's triumph at
the polls and began amidst the inaugural glamour that ushered in what was
called a new Camelot. Her successor, Claudia Alta (Lady Bird) Taylor Johnson,
became first lady at a somber swearing-in ceremony that ushered in an era
marked by assassinations, racial tensions, an unpopular war, social unrest, and
changing social mores.

In the diary she began the day President John F. Kennedy was assassinated
(November 22, 1963), Lady Bird Johnson expressed her sentiments during a
time of national tragedy: "I feel I am suddenly onstage for a part I never rehearsed" (Johnson 1970, 16). The reality, however, was that her many years in
Washington as the wife of a politically active man who served as a congressional aide, member of Congress, Senate majority leader, and vice president,
ultimately made her one of the best-prepared presidential partners. She had been
a surrogate campaigner for Jackie Kennedy during the 1960 campaign and had
filled in for Mrs. Kennedy at numerous functions since Mrs. Kennedy "frequently refused to appear on ceremonial or political occasions" (Caroli 1987,
236).

Added to her Washington savvy was what her daughter Luci described as "a calm soul who smooths [sic] us down, and makes all of us feel closer together" (Boller 1988, 379). During a time of growing unrest, Lady Bird Johnson not only calmed her family and brought them together but she did the same for the country. She weathered the jeers and signs of protesters, who appeared frequently, and she enthusiastically boarded a whistle-stop campaign train to travel through hostile political territory championing her husband's election and causes that she believed were right. The respect she showed to those who opposed her husband enabled her to fulfill her mission and earned her admiring crowds and standing ovations. She even found time in her demanding schedule during difficult times to embrace a cause of her own and in doing so made us all more aware of the fragility of the environment and our need to be good stewards of the earth.

Margaret Truman asked the question, "Has there been a First Lady who did it all—who was a flawless White House hostess, a loving and protective wife, an astute political partner, and an admired public person in her own right?" Truman answered her own question by noting that "a remarkable consensus of historians, reporters, and average Americans[1] seem to agree that there has been one First Lady who came close: Claudia Alta Taylor Johnson, better known to the world as Lady Bird" (Truman 1995, 169).

Lady Bird Johnson was indeed a first lady well suited for the challenges posed by a changing and tumultuous time. The rise of the rhetorical presidency[2] and the increased presence of television brought with it more demands on first ladies as public figures with a rhetorical role as well as a social one. By the time Mrs. Johnson became first lady, it was becoming more difficult for a presidential partner to avoid the limelight. How first ladies approached their rhetorical roles has differed greatly, as this book illustrates. However, after Lady Bird Johnson it would become more difficult for a Bess Truman or Mamie Eisenhower to occupy the White House. While the public would not want a copresident, as Hillary Rodham Clinton learned, it did expect a first lady to be "a reliable sign of the values or underlying beliefs of her husband" (Campbell 1996, 181). Jackie Kennedy's appointment of the first press secretary for a first lady was a signal that presidential wives would have difficulty *not* making news of their own. Lady Bird Johnson's move to expand the role of her press office and take the first lady from the society page to the front page firmly established the rhetorical presidency as what Karlyn Kohrs Campbell called it: "a two-person career" (180).

Viewing the first lady as a partner in a rhetorical presidency forms the basis for this essay on Lady Bird Johnson. To fully understand Mrs. Johnson's rhetorical activities and legacy, both in terms of defining the role and responsibilities of a modern first lady and in projecting a public agenda, it is important to begin with a brief biography of her life. Her background clearly influenced her values, interests, and rhetorical activities as first lady. Those activities included an active campaign agenda, promotion of her husband's issues, development of her own environmental agenda, and private influence on her husband's decisions and rhetorical activities.

Biography

Claudia Alta Taylor was born on December 22, 1912, in the East Texas town of Karnack. Biographers differ as to when she was given the nickname by which the world came to know her, but they agree on who gave it to her. Somewhere between the time she was an infant and two years of age, a nurse, Alice Tittle, claimed that she was "pretty as a ladybird." The name stuck, and the official White House Historical Society biography of the first ladies notes that, "perhaps the name was prophetic, as there has seldom been a First Lady so attuned to nature and the importance of conserving the environment" (Klapthor 1989, 80).

Her father, Thomas Jefferson Taylor, was a successful and wealthy businessman who operated a general store. Her mother, Minnie Pattillo Taylor, was a native of Alabama who died as the result of an accident when Lady Bird was five. Her mother's unmarried and somewhat sickly sister, Effie, was enlisted to move to Karnack and assist Mr. Taylor and the servants in raising her. Aunt Effie "initiated her niece into the pleasures of literature and nature, [but] she left other areas untouched. 'She never taught me how to dress or dance,' Lady Bird remembered, and her weakness and frailty presented a model of what to avoid, rather than what to attempt" (Caroli 1987, 231). Thus, Lady Bird's father, who showed physical strength and business acumen, became her role model.

Most biographical accounts of her early years indicate that her childhood was lonely and caused her to retreat to nature. According to one biographer, "Her father's money and her mother's absence made her an outsider, the subject of both envy and pity by her friends" (Russell 1999, 68). She came to enjoy quiet, solitary time on Caddo Lake or in fields of flowers.

She was an excellent student throughout elementary school and high school. When the time came for graduation from Marshall High School in 1928, she realized that if she finished in the top two in her class, which she surely would, she would have to give a speech—something she feared greatly. She also thought she might risk the loss of one of her closest friends, Emma Boehringer, who was also in contention for a top spot. She purposely let her grades slip and "prayed if she came in first or second in her class that she would be struck by smallpox" (Russell 1999, 69). Her plan to lower her class ranking did succeed, and she finished in third place by half a point behind Emma and another girl.

Having graduated from high school at the age of fifteen, she was considered by her family to be too young to leave for college. Her goal to leave Karnack, however, took her to her mother's family in Alabama where she enrolled in summer school at the University of Alabama. She missed Texas and her friends, so she decided to return home. The brief stint in Tuscaloosa, however, was something she would use to establish identification with the people of Alabama when she visited the state and university as first lady. When she returned to Karnack she asked to be allowed to accompany another friend to Dallas for two years of junior college at a boarding school, St. Mary's Episcopal School for Girls. Although her father and uncle both opposed the move—her father because it was an unlikely place for her to find a husband and her uncle because he failed to see the value of a college education—she was firm in her decision (Russell

1999, 70). Her father finally agreed and sent her to Dallas in a car of her own with a monthly allowance and charge accounts.

She compiled an excellent academic record at St. Mary's and began working on her shyness in public by playing small roles in the school's theatrical productions. It was during her time at St. Mary's that she converted to the Episcopal faith.

At the conclusion of her junior college years she enrolled at the University of Texas. She received a bachelor of arts degree, majoring in history, in 1933. She took an additional year to earn a journalism degree in 1934, and "perfected her typing and stenographic skills" (Caroli 1987, 231). She aspired to be a newspaper reporter but also had made sure that she had the necessary courses for a teaching certificate. She was prepared for a multitude of possibilities and opportunities. However, the opportunity that presented itself almost immediately after she graduated was marriage.

In September 1934, she met Lyndon Johnson and married him on November 17, 1934, after a whirlwind courtship of seven weeks. The courtship was conducted primarily long distance through mail and phone calls. Lyndon Baines Johnson, four years her senior, was secretary to Congressman Richard Kleberg. A friend introduced Johnson to Lady Bird during one of Johnson's trips back to Texas. Their first date took place at breakfast the day after they were introduced. Johnson, who had decided immediately upon meeting her that Lady Bird was special, used the breakfast to tell his life's story—including his financial status down to the size of his life insurance policy. Lady Bird told an interviewer when she was first lady that the encounter left her knowing "I had met something remarkable, but I didn't know quite what" (Janeway 1964, 64). When Johnson returned to Texas intent on leaving only with Lady Bird beside him as his wife, he had support from her father and eventually a willing bride.

After a brief honeymoon, Lady Bird found herself in Washington embarking on a fast-track political education that would serve her for the rest of her life. Her life centered on Lyndon and his political friends, who showed up at their apartment usually unannounced and expecting a meal. She learned how to cook and to budget his salary to cover their expenses and save money as well. And while she attended to the domestic sphere, she learned the intricacies of politics by listening and observing.

Three years after their marriage, a congressional seat opened in Texas when a congressman died. Lyndon decided to run. Lady Bird entered the fray with him and exhibited for the first time the political savvy and quiet, behind-the-scenes influence that would be instrumental in Johnson's successful political career. She visited Alvin Wirtz, a former state senator, attorney, and political insider, for advice. She wanted to know what Lyndon's chances were for winning and what it would take to lodge a successful campaign.

Wirtz gave her an honest assessment and a dollar amount that would help launch a campaign to create the necessary name recognition he needed. She then called her father and asked for a $10,000 campaign loan from her inheritance from her mother. Her father, who did not like politics and thought the amount was too much, finally consented. The money was in the bank the next day, and

Johnson was the first to announce in the special election. Johnson campaigned tirelessly, and while Lady Bird "criticized herself for being too timid to get out and campaign with him" (an activity that was not expected of wives at the time), she "pushed herself to work harder behind the scenes" (Russell 1999, 131). When Johnson had an emergency appendectomy two days before the election, Lady Bird was with him, but she spent election day making phone calls to get out the vote. He won the election, and their political partnership was firmly launched.

The role that Lady Bird played in the partnership grew with the start of World War II. Johnson volunteered for active duty in the navy immediately after the attack on Pearl Harbor. For the eight months her husband was on active duty, Lady Bird managed his congressional office without compensation. He wanted her in charge instead of one of his aides because she had "the authority of his name" (Russell 1999, 135). Such recognition of the surrogate role a political wife could play was atypical. This was an era in which wives usually remained in the background of everyday politics or at best at their husbands' sides smiling, waving, and saying little.

The experience of running the congressional office gave Lady Bird a first-hand view of what was expected of an officeholder and an appreciation for the need to be at the service of constituents. The experience caused her to become more involved in meeting with constituents, talking with them, and taking them on tours of Washington sites. In the process, she gained valuable information for her husband about what was happening back home.

Lady Bird learned the ways of Washington and Capitol Hill society early on as a congressional wife. She participated in a ritual of the times that required congressional wives to make official calls on other wives. Mrs. Johnson described the practice as being "like a business" in which the wife was equipped with her personal calling cards and those of her husband.

> On Mondays, she called on the wives of the Supreme Court justices. On Tuesdays, she went to visit other congressional wives. Wednesdays were reserved for cabinet wives. Thursdays for the Senate wives, and Fridays for the Diplomatic Corps. She went to the White House whenever invited. (Russell 1999, 134)

She did this because it was expected, but her shyness caused her, as she indicated in interviews later, to hope the women weren't in so that all she had to do was leave her calling card for the wife and Johnson's for the husband (Russell 1999, 134).

Her tenure in Johnson's office, however, gave her confidence that she could do things on her own, and made her aware of the need for income beyond a congressional salary to advance LBJ's career. She looked for a way to invest the inheritance from her mother and uncle to secure their financial and political futures. In late 1942, using part of her resources and an additional loan, Lady Bird bought a bankrupt Austin radio station. It became the foundation for a family broadcasting business that made her a multimillionaire. Neither the initial purchase nor the expansion of the business into television came without controversy, however. There was a political battle for the license that included a conservative Austin newspaper owner who was a vocal opponent of President Roosevelt. FCC Chairman James Fly, a fellow Texan and FDR supporter, blocked the application and opened the way for Lady Bird's successful rival bid. Including only Lady Bird's name on the licenses finessed conflict of interest charges, but, understandably, questions were raised. When Lady Bird applied for a license for a television station in Austin several years later, she was the only applicant. This fact raised some eyebrows over the years, but biographers and observers point to no clear evidence that federal agencies favored the Johnsons. The best explanation that was given for the lack of competition was simply that when word got out that the senator's wife was applying, no one else decided to challenge (Caroli 1987, 234).

After the purchase of the radio station, Lady Bird spent time in Texas hiring a staff and overseeing daily operations. She maintained oversight through close communication with the staff and visits to Austin. She also claimed that LBJ took an active interest in the business and that she did not build the empire alone. Giving recognition to her husband was important for Lady Bird. According to biographer Russell, "Lady Bird invested her time and money in helping to create a grand persona for LBJ. She helped build his reputation as a great man, a Texas rancher, a wealthy businessman, as well as a member of Congress—someone worthy of the whole nation's leadership" (1999, 143).

Although much went well for the Johnsons, their lives were not without setbacks, disappointments, rumors, and challenges. In 1941, Lyndon waged an unsuccessful race for a Senate seat. Lady Bird suffered a series of miscarriages before finally giving birth to their first child, Lynda Bird in 1944, and Lucy (later changed to Luci) Baines in 1947. When Johnson suffered a heart attack while serving as majority leader in the Senate in 1955, Lady Bird once again found herself overseeing the office until his return. The heart attack was a reminder to Johnson of his mortality and also made him realize how important Lady Bird was to him. The significance of the role she played in being by his side during recovery and also overseeing his office again was made greater by the fact that rumors of his unfaithfulness were prevalent throughout much of their marriage.

Lyndon was a demanding husband who was known to criticize his wife's clothes or makeup in public and even to embarrass her with his often-crude manner. She tolerated the negative side of his personality with dignity publicly and showed devotion and loyalty to him both publicly and privately. Her behavior spoke volumes about her shared vision of the significant and historical role he could and would play as a public official and her own view of a wife's duty. In an interview in *American Heritage*, she acknowledged that her traditional view of a wife might have been unacceptable to some, but she adopted a traditional role because "I really wanted to serve my husband and serve the country, and if that sounds—geesy, well . . ." (Klaw 1980, 7).

Lady Bird balanced dedication to her husband, children, and country as LBJ's career continued its ascent in 1948, during his successful campaign for the U.S. Senate. Even with small children to care for and a broadcasting busi-

ness to run, Lady Bird was determined to find ways to extend her role in Johnson's campaign and do more than she had in 1941. She found someone to help
with management of the business and worked from her home to organize a
women's division for the campaign. She sat in on strategy sessions and made her
first campaign speeches. She worked the main streets of towns throughout
Texas. "She enlisted the services of friends and former high school and college
classmates, arranged teas for her husband in the little towns they visited together, went over speeches with him and suggested phrases to use in them"
(Boller 1988, 384). As she had done in his first campaign in 1937, she also organized the get out the vote activities in the waning hours of the campaign.

Initial vote counts had Johnson's opponent, former Texas governor Coke
Stevenson, ahead by a slight margin. Johnson eventually won the election by a
highly suspicious eighty-seven-vote margin achieved from one ballot box in
South Texas. The count was challenged by his opponent but was upheld in the
courts.

Johnson's election to the Senate and his growing prominence later as majority leader set him up for a presidential race in 1960. While he had given some
thought to retiring from political life after his Senate term ended, he decided to
make a run for the ultimate political office and challenge. When LBJ failed to
get the nomination and then accepted the second position on the ballot with John
F. Kennedy, Lady Bird's political life took another major step.

Although she had taken a more public role in LBJ's Senate campaigns, most
of her work was still confined to a support function. In 1960, she knew she
would have to expand her public role. Because Jackie Kennedy was pregnant
with John F. Kennedy Jr. and had to restrict her campaign activities, Lady Bird
was called upon both to campaign as the vice presidential candidate's spouse
and to assist the Kennedy women in organizing and waging their own campaign.
She introduced the president's mother, sister Eunice, and sister-in-law Ethel to
Texas politics at a tea in Houston. Given the importance of Texas and the Kennedy's East Coast roots and Catholic faith, Lady Bird's efforts were instrumental in helping to win over Texas women's votes. She also worked with the Kennedy campaign to fill in for Jackie when needed.

Soon after the Los Angeles nominating convention and at the age of 48, she
decided to take a speech course to help her meet the demands of the campaign. It
was a wise decision. During the campaign she traveled 35,000 miles. She made
16 campaign appearances in 11 states on her own and accompanied her husband
on 150 stops. She traveled a total of 35,000 miles in two months.

Her second wise decision was to hire Liz Carpenter, a Texan who co-owned
a Texas newspaper chain and a Washington news bureau, to assist her with the
press and her part of the campaign. Carpenter would later serve as Mrs. Johnson's press secretary and chief of staff in the White House. It was Carpenter's
advice two weeks after Lady Bird became first lady that helped her create the
rapport with the media that enabled her to succeed in getting the media's coverage and cooperation to promote her causes. Carpenter advised Mrs. Johnson that
the media's request in her dealings with them was simple: "'Be Available' and
'Never Lie—tell us you can't tell us, but never lie'" (Johnson 1970, 15). She

followed the advice assiduously, and the results quickly became apparent as she garnered her own political coverage and compliments from the Washington press corps.

During the vice presidential years, Lady Bird was often called on to pinch-hit for Jackie Kennedy who disdained most aspects of political life. Anything Jackie Kennedy did not want to do would be given to her social secretary, Letitia Baldrige, with the instructions: "Give them to Lady Bird" (Russell 1999, 210). In her first year as second lady, Lady Bird substituted for Mrs. Kennedy at fifty official events along with keeping her own schedule.

When the Kennedy assassination thrust the position of first lady upon her, Lady Bird instinctively knew what to do even as she expressed doubts about her preparation. The entry for November 23, 1963, in *A White House Diary* shows a woman whose primary concern was "the million and one things to be done—just the simple things that are part of going on living, if one is among those who are going to go on living. Lyndon will be wrestling with the very big business of making the country go on living" (Johnson 1970, 8).

As first lady, Mrs. Johnson also followed the advice former president Harry Truman gave her when the two of them attended the funeral for King Paul of Greece. She asked him, "What is the best thing a wife can do for her husband in the White House?" to which Truman replied, "Protect him. Don't let people use you. If people bring you some sort of proposition they want you to talk to the President about, it's all right to tell him, but if you have doubts about them be sure and tell him that" (Johnson 1970, 83).

Lady Bird did not hesitate to voice her opinion about any issue her husband addressed, as is evident in her diary, papers, and biographies of her life. Perhaps her adherence to Truman's advice was best seen in her taking charge of a highly volatile situation during the 1964 campaign. Johnson's longtime friend and aide, Walter Jenkins, was arrested on a morals charge. As the incident became public, LBJ listened to advisors who told him to ask for Jenkins' resignation and distance himself from him. Johnson was in New York where he had a full schedule of speeches when he learned of the problem. He consulted his advisors and mulled over his options. He orchestrated what needed to be done to bring about Jenkins' resignation; he removed his personal and business files that were in Jenkins' keeping, and he helped create a new position in Texas for Jenkins.

Lady Bird, however, disagreed with the advice to put politics above loyalty to friends and expose Jenkins to more public embarrassment and scrutiny than she thought was necessary. She swung into action to diffuse the potentially explosive political and personal situation. She and Liz Carpenter penned a three-sentence statement supporting Jenkins and delivered it to the media—a group that included many Jenkins supporters. The statement read: "My heart is aching today for someone who has reached the point of exhaustion in dedicated service to his country. Walter Jenkins has been carrying incredible hours and burdens since President Kennedy's assassination. He is now receiving the medical attention he needs" (Russell 1999, 268). The approach worked and the story died quickly with no damage to the president and his campaign.

Throughout the entire diary one finds evidence of a woman who balanced concerns about her husband's health—physical, emotional, and political—and her desire for the family to live as normal a life as possible with the demands of her multifaceted position. She saw her official role as contributing to what it took for everyone to go on living, and "living" required her to be a "participant in 718 different ceremonial activities [that comprised an estimated] . . . 75 percent or more of her time on official duties" (Gutin 1989, 118–19).

Nancy Kegan Smith who worked as an archivist at the Johnson Library and dealt with Mrs. Johnson's papers best summarizes the extent of her activities as first lady:

> She gave over 164 speeches. She founded and chaired the First Lady's Committee for a More Beautiful Nation's Capital, served as the honorary chairman of the Project Head Start program, was a member of the Committee for the Preservation of the White House, and acted as the president's representative on the committee responsible for the planning and building of the Johnson Library. She established and hosted the Women Doer Luncheons [a series of 16 luncheons to highlight women's achievements] and presided over countless White House dinners, teas, luncheons, receptions, tours, and presentations. To highlight President Johnson's "See the USA" program and while accompanying her husband on foreign visits, she traveled hundreds of thousands of miles. (1989, 111)

After leaving the White House in 1969, the Johnsons returned to Texas. Lady Bird worked on her book, *A White House Diary*, which was published in 1970. She continued to assist her husband in his postpresidential pursuits until his death in 1973. She was instrumental in helping plan the Lyndon Baines Johnson Library in Austin. She founded the National Wildflower Research Center in 1982, and served as a trustee on the board of the National Geographic Society. She also returned to active involvement in the family business from which she retired in 1996, giving way to daughter Luci's management. At the turn of the century and the start of a new millennium, she was nearing ninety. She continued to live on the family ranch where LBJ is buried and to devote time to her family and to the environmental causes that were born out of her youthful need to embrace nature as a way to go on living.

Rhetorical Activities as First Lady

The increased attention to the role of first lady in recent years has resulted in numerous books about the evolution and current status of the position.[3] In reading any of these books, one point becomes immediately clear: since Martha Washington, every first lady has, in her own way, exerted influence on both the position of first lady and on the man to whom she was married. There is no denying that occupants of the White House share a unique kind of partnership, with some first ladies in the background as silent partners influencing the president quietly or concentrating on the hostess role. Others are seen as independent spokeswomen for their own causes, as openly influencing their husbands, or as making their own views on issues publicly known whether they are in concert with his or not.

Karlyn Kohrs Campbell (citing the work of sociologist Hanna Papanek on careers that place "institutional demands on a married couple") argued that the presidency epitomizes a "two-person career" or one that "precludes a traditional public–private spousal division of labor and requires their cooperative efforts if it is to be pursued successfully." As such, Campbell claimed that "the First Ladyship is a vital part of the presidency," worthy of study by presidential scholars, and that first ladies' rhetoric provides insight into how their enactment of the role contributes to the institution of the presidency (1996, 180).

Historian Carl Anthony noted that soon after becoming first lady, Lady Bird's staff "sent out a statement of her 'duties' and though 'hostess' was first, it listed a primary one as 'advancement of the President's programs'" (1991, 110). Mrs. Johnson told Liz Carpenter when she hired her as press secretary for the 1960 campaign that she wanted to be a "doer" not a "talker" (Russell 1999, 191), and she reaffirmed that commitment as first lady. However, doers require talk or rhetoric to accomplish what they want to do, and the act of "doing" itself has symbolic power. Lady Bird Johnson knew that better than most. Thus, her tenure as first lady was marked, as noted previously, by a heavy speaking schedule, committee work, travel with and on behalf of her husband, and social events with a political purpose. Her "doings," which included activities such as visiting poverty-stricken parts of the country to highlight her husband's War on Poverty or Head Start program were also intended to open the eyes and minds of Americans about the problems facing the country so that they would act also (Anthony 1991, 110). The rhetorical nature of her "doings" is indisputable, as is their direct relationship to her husband's goals.

Based on an acceptance of the argument that the presidency is a two-person career and that a study of a first lady's rhetoric provides insights into a presidency, Lady Bird Johnson's rhetorical activities are examined to determine how they enhanced Lyndon Johnson's presidency and furthered the development of the role of first lady. Terlip (1986) identified seven criteria that are commonly used by critics and the public to evaluate a wife's effectiveness as a political partner. They are: (1) she conveys support of her husband's positions and activities, but also demonstrates independence and strength; (2) she influences her husband, but doesn't actually affect his policies or positions; (3) she addresses issues, especially "women's issues," but not in a way that makes her more expert than he is; (4) she is both a traditional and a modern woman; (5) she selects an appropriate cause; (6) she has a good relationship with the press; and (7) she is careful about discussing personal problems. These criteria are considered in analyzing Mrs. Johnson's rhetoric and legacy.

Given the extent of Lady Bird's rhetorical activities, it is impossible in a single chapter to do justice to the length and breadth of her achievements as first lady. As a means of providing representative examples of how her rhetoric enhanced her husband's presidency, this section examines her campaign rhetoric during the 1964 whistle-stop tour, her beautification campaign, and her behind-the-scenes influence on her husband's rhetoric.

The 1964 Whistle-Stop Campaign

Abigail McCarthy, who was married to Senator Eugene McCarthy, reflected on her campaign experiences and noted, "A candidate's wife making a speech is, by the very nature of things, at a terrible disadvantage. . . . It is only a very dull woman who is unaware of the speculative curiosity mixed with hostility with which her every platform appearance is greeted" (McCarthy 1972, 5). Lady Bird Johnson was anything but a dull woman and knew that she could be an asset to her husband if she took risks to break out of the traditional role of observer and take to the platform. As noted previously, Lady Bird learned to control her fear of public speaking and began taking an active part as a campaigner in the 1948 Senate campaign. After the 1960 campaign, she was a seasoned veteran who was ready to face both the cheers and jeers that greeted both her and her husband during a tumultuous period of American history.

A political wife giving a speech does face a difficult rhetorical situation, as McCarthy observed. The wife simultaneously creates an identity for both herself and her husband. She asks audiences to identify with her as a means of identifying with her husband. Her credibility is affected by her husband's, and she, in turn, can enhance or hurt his. In essence, "her every word is scrutinized in the belief that she is a reliable sign of the values or underlying beliefs of her husband. Accordingly, she becomes a lightning rod for discontent with his administration or opposition to its stands on particular issues" (Campbell 1996, 181).

Given these realities, the task that Lady Bird Johnson undertook in the 1964 campaign was one of the most difficult assigned to any first lady—her own whistle-stop campaign tour. In a memorandum to President Johnson on August 18, 1964, presidential staffer, Douglass Cater, commented on Mrs. Johnson's appearances in several western states and provided the arguments for having her campaign independently:

> Mrs. Johnson represents a political asset for the campaign, which is unique in Presidential history. She is highly appealing and effective on the platform. She comes across as intelligent and knowledgeable and *unlike* Eleanor Roosevelt thoroughly feminine. She maintains grace under the most hectic conditions. Politicians and reporters alike felt she would be more sought after than the Vice Presidential nominee for many occasions. The consensus was that she should make a number of treks apart from you—that she could give extra push in critical states, visiting communities that lie outside the Presidential circuit. (Cater 1964, 1)

Of all the country, the one region that was eventually determined to be outside the presidential circuit was the South. Passage of the 1964 Civil Rights Act under the leadership of a Democrat president from the South, made it nearly impossible for either Lyndon Johnson or his running mate, Hubert Humphrey to visit the South and "get in and out . . . with their hide on—or they couldn't take the time to visit because it was a lost cause" (Carpenter 1970, 145). The South, however, could not be ignored and holding ground was a crucial part of the strategy. In the end, half of the South held for the Johnson–Humphrey ticket, and Lady Bird's whistle-stop campaign was credited with helping.

Between October 6 and October 9, the nineteen-car Lady Bird Special carried 300 passengers including media, staff, supporters, Southern political wives, and the Johnson daughters. It traveled 1682 miles with 47 stops and 4 "slow downs." The trip was carefully planned with input from the president and first lady regarding the stops. Topics were suggested by staffers, including one that would associate her with an issue that was commonly considered a "women's issue" but held the key to the South's future—education. The memo noted, "She would be a natural talking about education . . . TVA was FDR's dream for the South. Education can be the new dream and the ingredients are already at hand" ("Whistle-Stop" 1964, 1)

Mrs. Johnson personally called southern governors and members of Congress to invite them to be on the train with her when she arrived in their states. Many of them provided feeble excuses, such as a hunting trip that could not be canceled, to avoid being seen with anyone close to the administration. She persevered, however, and found enough high-profile supporters to lend credibility to her message.

From the first stop in Alexandria, Virginia, to the last stop in New Orleans, Lady Bird gave speeches that showed pride in her southern roots, acknowledged her locale, recalled great southerners and their accomplishments, called on her audiences to find those things that unify Americans, and asked her fellow southerners to accept the new law and their responsibility in ensuring equal rights for all of us.

The words were largely hers and represented what she called "a journey of the heart." In notes she dictated while preparing for the trip, she acknowledged that her feelings "may not always be politic or wise ones. Some thread of this, however, will have to bind together whatever I say . . . or else it won't be natural" ("Whistle-Stop" 1964, Folder 3). Many of the random thoughts in her memorandum appeared almost verbatim in each of the speeches to explain why she was there and what she expected of all Americans. This excerpt from the first stop in Alexandria set the tone and the theme:

> I want to tell you from Alexandria to New Orleans that to this President and his wife the South is a respected and valued and beloved part of the country. I know that many of you do not agree with the Civil Rights Bill or the President's support of it, but I do know the South respects candor and courage and I believe he has shown both. It would be a bottomless tragedy for our country to be racially divided and here I want to say emphatically, this is not a challenge only in the South. It is a national challenge—in the big cities of the North as in the South. (Smith 1989, 115)

With those words she sought to identify with her audience and to show that their values were her husband's. She showed support for her husband but also demonstrated her own convictions by taking on a challenge that was even too big for the president. She assuaged any feelings southerners might have that they were being singled out for blame by identifying the racial divide as a national problem, not a southern one.

At every stop she made a comment about the locale and local politicians and related personal connections to the location to establish identification. This opening in Valdosta, Georgia, illustrates her strategy:

> I understand from Mrs. Sanders, the wife of your governor, that this is a fisherman's paradise. I just hope I can come back some leisurely time and try it.
> This is a campaign visit, but it is also a sentimental journey. From the time I was six until I was twenty-one, my summer times were spent in Alabama with side trips to Georgia. Georgia strains run strong in my family and my husband's family—his great grandfather, Jesse Johnson, came from Oglethorpe County. (Johnson 1964b, 1)

In developing the substance of the speeches, Mrs. Johnson did not attempt to show her expertise on the issues of race, education, or other localized topics. She accomplished her goal of representing her husband and not influencing him or representing her own views by framing the issues within a value system representative of the South and her husband. This allowed her to make a subtle argument that LBJ's positions were a natural outgrowth of him as a person—a southerner who had his home region's needs and best interests at heart.

Later in her speeches, she attempted to transcend the issue of the legislation itself by looking at the larger issue of the nation, its future, and the important role the South would play:

> I'm even more proud of the new South, the spirit of growth, advances in the economy and progress in education, and I share the irritation when unthinking people make snide jokes about us. None of this is right. None of this is good for the future of our country. We must search for the ties that bind us together, not settle for the tensions that tend to divide us. (Carpenter 1970, 156)

Throughout the four days, the spirit of the South was exhibited in one small town after another. High school bands played, signs waved, crowds cheered, as plastic train whistles, paper engineer hats, and saltwater taffy were distributed from the train to the crowds that grew larger with each stop. The media coverage intensified interest in the campaign and helped demonstrate the strength of a soft-spoken daughter of the South when some crowds inevitably turned ugly.

In Colombia, South Carolina, a group of hecklers yelled out "We Want Barry! We Want Barry!" as soon as the governor finished his introduction of Lady Bird. She waited, then she calmly raised a hand and said, "My friends, in this country we are entitled to many viewpoints. You are entitled to yours. But right now, I'm entitled to mine" (Carpenter 1970, 162). That quieted the crowd, and the film of the incident that aired on the evening news caused the Goldwater camp to denounce the tactics. The belief that it would be difficult to attack a southern woman in the South where women are respected, if not revered, proved correct. Southern chivalry was not dead and was evidenced as more male political leaders joined the train and praised Lady Bird and Lyndon.

The steel magnolia, who showed courage under fire and respect for a dissenting opinion, found a way to make the crowds listen and the message did get through. A reporter asked one man at a stop in Charleston, South Carolina, about his candidate preference, and he replied, "Johnson, because I'd rather stand beside a Negro in a factory than stand behind a white man in the soup line" (Carpenter 1970, 163).

At the final stop of the tour, a buoyant Mrs. Johnson expressed her belief that the trip had been a success:

> Eight states, sixteen hundred miles, and 47 speeches ago, when we left Alexandria, I said that this was a journey of the heart. And truly it has been that. . . . This was, however, not only a sentimental journey, but also a political trip. I came because I wanted to say that for this President and his wife, we appreciate you, and we care about you, and we have faith in you.
> We have too much respect for the South to take it for granted and too much closeness to it to ignore it.
> I am aware that there are those who would exploit its past troubles to their own advantage. But I do not believe that the majority of the South wants any part of the old bitterness. And the more I have seen these past few days, the more I know that is true. (Johnson 1964c, 1)

By the time the Lady Bird Special reached its final stop in New Orleans, to be joined by the president, the atmosphere was such that Lyndon Johnson could build on what his wife had done and give a speech from his heart as well to end the journey. In a departure from his prepared text, Johnson hit the race issue head-on and redefined civil rights into something other than a "Negro" issue. In a folksy manner reminiscent of his early campaigns, he rolled up his sleeves and told a story about a southern politician at the end of his career who bemoaned:

> I wish I felt a little better. I would like to go back home and make 'em one more Democratic speech. I feel like I have just one more in me. The poor old state. They haven't heard a Democratic speech in thirty years. All they ever hear at election time is nigger, nigger, nigger!
> After gasps and then applause led by the Blacks in the crowd, Johnson said in his own voice: "There is only one real problem that faces you. It isn't an economic problem. It isn't a Negro problem. It's whether you're going to live or die!" (Carpenter 1970, 170)

Without Lady Bird leading the way, Johnson would not have been in New Orleans to make such a pronouncement. A newspaper story illustrated the partnership that was the whistle-stop tour, the larger campaign, the Johnsons' political lives, and the Johnson presidency: "Together, the President and the First Lady made an assault on the heart and the mind of the South that must be the most remarkable joint campaign effort in American political history" (Carpenter 1970, 170).

The Beautification Campaign

While Lady Bird Johnson's whistle-stop tour during the 1964 campaign signified a major shift in the role a first lady would play in the public sphere, the rhetorical activities for which she is best known are those related to the environment and her beautification program. Given the scope of her environmental advocacy, only a cursory treatment is provided here. Lewis L. Gould's *Lady Bird Johnson and the Environment* (1988) and *Lady Bird Johnson: Our Environmental First Lady* (1999) provide a thorough study of Mrs. Johnson's beautification and environmental activities. Given the availability and extensiveness of Gould's work, this analysis concentrates on the strategies she used in promoting the issues and how they demonstrate the Johnsons' political partnership and complementary agendas.

Lady Bird's decision to adopt a cause was made soon after the 1964 election was over. The choice of the environment and beautification was one that evolved gradually and naturally out of a series of events in which she and the president participated in his early months in office and during the 1964 campaign.[4] Selection of the environment and beautification was strategic rhetorically in and of itself.

It was a comfortable topic for Lady Bird since her affection for wildflowers and nature began during her youth in Texas. Thus, it was not just something that was selected for public relations or publicity purposes. The timing of the choice was also excellent. Lady Bird became first lady when environmental issues were gaining attention through books such as Rachel Carson's 1962, *Silent Spring*, which called attention to the environmental harms of pesticides. It was also a time when the city of Washington needed a major face-lift.

The environment could be viewed as a natural issue for a political wife—it merged the more traditional domestic sphere interests of a political wife with policy initiatives. Gould noted, "When Lady Bird Johnson launched her campaign for natural beauty in 1964–65, she was taking her place among other female advocates of the environment in the United States who had been a positive force in improving the quality of the nation's life since the late nineteenth century" (1988, 1). Among the women Gould discussed in his book were those who led beautification programs of major cities. She could be an advocate in a very public sense without appearing to directly take on a "presidential" issue. Finally, it was an issue of concern to LBJ and one that related to initiatives such as his Great Society program, the "See the USA" tourism promotion to keep U.S. dollars in the country, and the broader environmental agenda that began surfacing soon after he was elected.

The way that Lady Bird developed her campaign demonstrated her adept organizational and rhetorical skills. She wrote in her diary, "How many things are launched in the name of a tea!" (Johnson 1970, 240). Her beautification program began with meetings at the Texas ranch and with teas and social gatherings at the White House designed to enlist the key people she needed to provide the political and financial clout to make her projects work.

She sought advice from many sources on the scope and content of her project. "Lady Bird Johnson rarely limited herself to one set of advisors or to one line of action" with the result being a decision to start with a beautification campaign for Washington, D.C., that would relate to her husband's Great Society goals of improving the overall quality of life. She would chair a committee to give awards for preservation and beautification of cities, and she would promote initiatives to remove unsightly junkyards and billboards from the nation's highways to better highlight the country's natural beauty (Gould 1988, 52–54).

It was also decided that her efforts in Washington, D.C., would combine public and private funds and would involve all interest groups as well as environmental experts. She provided opportunity for input and shared ownership from the beginning. Without widespread support and cooperation, she would not have succeeded. Once all of the decisions were made and her plan was in place, she went public through an interview in *U.S. News and World Report*. The result of her Washington, D.C. project and the national publicity she received was a nationwide campaign to improve the quality of cities and the landscape nationally.

One of the major problems with the campaign was the name itself—"beautification"—which was seen by some as "superficial" and "cosmetic" (Gould 1988, 64). Mrs. Johnson, however, dealt with the criticisms head on. Through her speeches, she defined what she meant, demonstrated the impact of the issue on everyone in a community, provided examples of legal and public policy actions related to her cause, and challenged her listeners—regardless of their professions—to acknowledge the relationship of the environment to their own lives. She elevated the issue of beautification to something that was not cosmetic but had major public policy, economic, and social implications.

A speech at the Yale Political Union in 1967, illustrates how she recast the issue:

> The word "beautification" doesn't really convey the full sweep of the concept. It embraces all of these questions:
>> How can we rebuild the core of our cities?
>> How can we create new towns, pleasant and functional?
>> How can we bring order rather than chaos out of our highways and transit systems?
>> How can we provide parks and open space to let our cities breathe and our people relax?
>> How can we control the waste we pour into our air and water?
> To me, in sum, "beautification" means our total concern for the physical and human quality of the world we pass on to our children. (Johnson 1967)

While she continued to have her critics and detractors even with clarifications such as these, she had a major impact in Washington, D.C., and nationally.

In Washington, D.C., millions of bulbs, flowering plants, and shrubs were planted. Trees and shrubs were trimmed. Statues were scrubbed, schools were cleaned up, and recreation areas were installed in the inner city. To honor her efforts, her committee arranged to have a million daffodils and twenty-five hundred dogwood trees planted in an area on Colombia Island, on the route to Reagan National Airport. The area was named "Lady Bird Johnson Park" (Anthony 1991, 160), and the results can still be seen today.

Nationally, individuals and organizations embraced the cause. "Civic groups long advocating similar themes hitched themselves to her work. Lady Bird was pitted against "Litter Bug" when—as a tribute to her—Keep America

Beautiful, Inc., sent out one thousand informational packages to state and local officials suggesting community programs and role models" (Anthony 1988, 133). Thousands of letters poured into the White House offering support and advice, and she received more speaking invitations throughout the country than her schedule could accommodate. She logged over 100,000 miles on behalf of her cause. Her efforts to promote U.S. tourism, especially in the national parks, resulted in increased numbers of tourists, including a tripling of visitors at Big Bend Park (Anthony 1988, 134).

The public support and interest in the campaign prompted Lady Bird to work with the West Wing to introduce legislation, the Highway Beautification Bill. Through a combination of her charm and her husband's well-honed skills in pushing through legislation, the bill became law. She did incur criticism along the way from Republicans in the Congress, such as Kansas senator Robert Dole, who questioned the appropriateness of Lady Bird's activism (Russell 1999, 279). Opposition also came from many small businesses that relied on billboard advertising, and she even took on the Defense Department's billboards. But she was unrelenting in her advocacy and weathered the political cartoons and other slings and arrows. After the legislative victory, she returned to public appeals for support and refrained from further congressional lobbying.

In the course of promoting her environmental cause, Lady Bird recognized that "the environment, after all, is where we all meet; where we all have a mutual interest; it is one thing that all of us share. It is not only a mirror of ourselves, but a focusing lens on what we can become" (Johnson, 1967, 5). Just as she understood the importance of creating identification during her whistle-stop tour, she also recognized the role identification could play in her advocacy for environmental issues that went far beyond simply planting flowers and cleaning up neighborhoods. She spoke to the need to find answers to questions that "will reveal our quality as a civilization" and that she anticipated would be answered "in the next two decades" (Johnson 1967, 5). Twenty years after Lady Bird embraced the environment as her "cause" she very likely considered herself a success in light of Earth Day celebrations, less litter on highways, community recycling projects, the establishment of an Environmental Protection Agency, and clean air and water legislation. All of these would, most likely, have come into existence without Lady Bird Johnson, but no movement succeeds without some degree of consciousness raising by those who have access to a bully pulpit and know how to use it to motivate others.

Private Influence

According to Margaret Truman, Lady Bird Johnson was "an implementer, an embellisher and translator of her husband's ideas" (Truman 1995, 179). Often those actions occurred outside of the public eye. As a political advisor to LBJ, she furthered her husband's agenda and influenced his decisions and actions. Carl Anthony described her as "her president's political partner" (Anthony 1991, 114) and quoted an academic, Eric Goldman, who was "hired to advise and observe the administration" as indicating that LBJ respected the "'judgment of his wife in all matters'" and "'talked politics, all aspects of it, on a basis of equality.'"

The 1964 campaign provides several important representative examples of Lady Bird's role as an advisor and her influence on LBJ throughout his career. In 1964, she played an important role in his decision to run, his acceptance of the nomination, and his handling of a controversy at the convention.

Soon after becoming president, LBJ had to decide if he would run in 1964. Knowing that the years ahead would be difficult, he engaged in serious soul-searching about what was best for the country, his family, and himself. In May, as the president neared a decision, Lady Bird consulted with two physicians who were going to examine the president to determine his physical and emotional readiness for a campaign and a potentially difficult four-year term. While she waited for them to arrive at a friend's home in Virginia where she was visiting, she wrote, "a nine-page analysis of what I thought his situation was. First, in case he definitely decided that he wanted to use it, there was a suggested announcement that he wasn't going to run again. . . . I hope he won't use it—that's that! Then I put down the alternatives" (Johnson 1970, 138). The alternatives included a frank discussion of what they all would face—both the opportunity for triumph and its satisfaction and the pain of failure and hostility. She stated her belief that he would win and made a realistic assessment of a life for him without politics and power. She asked the two physicians to deliver it to him and then met with them to discuss "the possibilities for Lyndon" (Johnson 1970, 140). In drafting the analysis, she exhibited an understanding of what drove Lyndon Johnson and also what demons he had to conquer to continue. Only she could have written such a candid analysis and given him the freedom to make the choice he ultimately made.

Three months later, Lady Bird discovered that her husband was still haunted by self-doubts. After the opening of the 1964 Democratic National Convention on August 25, 1964, Lyndon Johnson considered withdrawing his name as the party's nominee. While he had brought the nation through a difficult period following the Kennedy assassination, he questioned his suitability to lead the country at that point in its history. He drafted a withdrawal statement and shared it with Lady Bird. She responded by writing him a letter telling him that,

> You are as brave a man as Harry Truman—or FDR—or Lincoln. You can go on to find some peace, some achievement amidst all the pain. . . . To step out now would be *wrong* for your country, and I can see nothing but a lonely wasteland for your future. . . . I am not afraid of *Time* and lies or losing money or defeat.
>
> In the final analysis I can't carry any of the burdens you talked of—so I know it's only your choice. But I know you are as brave as any of the thirty-five. (Johnson 1970, 192)

The combination of words that were once again crafted to bolster his confidence, challenge him, and appeal to his sense of duty worked, and "Johnson credited his wife with his decision to stay in the race" (Heckler-Feltz 1997, 88).

That was not the only example of her influence during the convention, however. The president was confronted with a credentials challenge to the all-white delegation from Mississippi. Civil rights leaders wanted the president to support the challengers. When it came time for him to make a decision, he asked Lady Bird to draft something for his consideration. She wrote a statement that supported the elected delegation, but confirmed the president's support of civil rights:

> I believe the legal delegation ought to be seated. I am not going to bend to emotionalism. I don't want this convention to do so either. The election is not worth that.
>
>   I am proud of the steady progress that has been made in the area of human and equal rights. In 1957, in 1960, and again in 1964, I was in the leadership to bring equal rights and decent progress to the Negro. I would not change a line of what has been passed or written. So long as I am President I will continue to lead the way within the guidelines of the law and within the framework of justice. (Johnson 1964a)

A compromise made it unnecessary for Johnson to respond publicly, but "the document is important . . . because it shows that President Johnson so valued Mrs. Johnson's advice that he asked for her guidance on a potentially explosive key issue" (Smith 1989, 114).

Throughout Lady Bird's diary and within the thousands of boxes of her papers are additional insights into her influence on her husband's speeches and decisions. She was one of the few around him who could offer candid criticism and constructive advice. One of the most frequently referenced examples of her teacherlike critiques was one captured on tape in the first few months after he became president. Lady Bird took four pages of handwritten notes while watching her husband speak that served later as promptings for the critique of the news conference. At the top of the first page is a bold "B I"—the grade she gave his performance—followed by notes on delivery ("Perhaps slightly fast & not enough change of pace") and content ("De Gaulle answer not really good—Viet Nam answer good—Answer on Lodge good") (Museum Display 1964).

The tape revealed that LBJ welcomed the critique but also became defensive and that Lady Bird knew exactly how far to push him, when to insert flattery, and when to revert to her role as wife. It was this balance of roles that made her effective in her dealings with her husband and in the execution of her duties. This excerpt demonstrates her political insights, political savvy, and agility in dealing with her husband:

> Mrs. Johnson: I thought your answer on Lodge was good. I thought your answer on Vietnam was good. I really didn't like the answer on DeGaulle because I think I've heard you say, and I believe you actually have said out loud, that you don't believe you ought to go out of the country this year . . .
> President Johnson: Uh . . .
> Mrs. Johnson: . . . so I don't think you can very well say that you can meet him anytime it's convenient for both people.
> President Johnson: Well, when it can be arranged. I'm not goin' out of this

country. I didn't say where I'd go. (Long pause) I didn't say I'd go out of the country at all, there . . .

Mrs. Johnson: Uh, no, I guess you . . .

President Johnson: Yes, I reaffirmed that I wouldn't go.

Mrs. Johnson: I see. Uh huh. Well, I didn't hear . . . I didn't get the meaning out of it that everyone else did. I think the outstanding things were that the close ups were excellent. . . .

In general, I'd say it was a good B+. How do you feel about it?

President Johnson: I thought it was much better than last week.

Mrs. Johnson: . . . It will be interesting to hear everybody else's reaction. And we've, uh, got the Thornberrys (sp?) anyhow are wanting a reasonably early dinner with us, and I got my 10 o'clock date and you can do anything you want to about getting another couple or two to eat with us and let me know. I love you very much. (Telephone Conversation 1964)

This taped interaction is useful in providing understanding of their personal relationship and political partnership. The written record is equally helpful in identifying her skills as a rhetorician and strategist for her husband. Speech drafts in the president's files literally show her hand and confirm the comments in her diary about the active role she played in the speech writing and vetting processes. She wrote comments in the margins of drafts, provided analyses on notepaper, and wrote new sentences in cursive or shorthand. The shorthand comments reveal her penchant for taking notes during meetings she attended— something most of her biographers commented on as being necessary because of LBJ's reliance on her to remember names and details.[5]

While she underplayed her role and referred to it as "infiltrating" (Anthony 1991, 114) rather than overtly influencing, the historical record suggests otherwise. She had a powerful influence on the president, his words, and, ultimately, the presidency. She described the ideal first lady as one who could argue issues with her husband but remain quiet in public about those issues (Anthony 1988, 115). Her ability to reach her own definition of ideal is what added to her power behind the scenes.

Legacy

Lady Bird Johnson said of her husband, "Lyndon stretches you. He always expects more of you than you're really mentally or physically capable of putting out" (Truman 1995, 174). It can be said of Lady Bird that she stretched the role of first lady to be a composite of the roles played by her predecessors. Lady Bird Johnson clearly achieved the characteristics of Terlip's effective political wife. She demonstrated that a first lady can be a consummate hostess, wife, and mother who provides the atmosphere a president needs to withstand the rigors of the job while simultaneously pursuing her own policy interests. She recognized that any event that took place in the White House or involved the first lady had potential political and rhetorical implications, and she took advantage of every opportunity to advance her husband's agenda. Her understanding of her husband and her own political instincts made her a valued and valuable advisor.

She built on the legacy of Eleanor Roosevelt and expanded the public role of the first lady into an independent and interdependent position. After Lady Bird Johnson, presidential candidates' wives became more active campaigners. She demonstrated to future political wives how to use their own experiences to build identification with an audience and then transfer that identification to their husbands.

She took on an issue—the environment—in a way that advanced positions expressed in her husband's speeches but also put her own mark on it. Her selection of the environment, while criticized in some circles, proved to be an issue with longevity. Anyone who lives in, works in, or visits Washington, D.C., today benefits from her efforts. She helped raise the national consciousness about the environment—a consciousness that eventually produced Earth Day, legislation, and efforts by average citizens to be good stewards of the earth through recycling and other measures.

Her environmental work also taught a lesson about the importance of language and how things are named. The word "beautification" sounded frivolous and expensive at a time when the nation was embroiled in divisive issues and costly social and wartime pursuits. It produced public criticism and derision of her as a first lady. However, her speeches reflect her understanding of how to address a problem as she redefined the nature of her campaign and linked environmental interests with LBJ's promotion of domestic tourism. These strategies overcame some criticism and demonstrated the advantages of linking a first lady's issues to her husband's.

Finally, Lady Bird Johnson undoubtedly made Lyndon Johnson, the politician, possible. If ever there was a wife who balanced her husband's temperament, supported and challenged him equally, and enabled him to do what he could not do himself, it was Lady Bird Johnson. Whatever the legacy of the administration of Lyndon Baines Johnson, it is a legacy shared with Lady Bird. Initiatives with long-term impact such as the 1964 Civil Rights Act and Head Start were issues she embraced along with her husband.

Although Karlyn Kohrs Campbell did not mention Lady Bird Johnson in her chapter on the presidency as a two-person career, she could have. If there was ever a couple that embodied the concept, it was the Johnsons. If there was a woman who helped shape the modern first ladyship, it was Lady Bird Johnson. Meg Greenfield recognized Lady Bird's reshaping of the office within two years of her becoming first lady. She wrote:

> What Lady Bird Johnson has done is to integrate the traditionally frivolous and routine aspects of the East Wing life into the overall purposes of the administration and to enlist the peculiar assets of First Ladyhood itself in the administration's behalf. They are assets no one fully understood until Mrs. Johnson moved into the White House—or at least no one fully understood their potential political clout. (Greenfield 1965, 29)

Future political wives would be wise to study Lady Bird Johnson's record of her White House years and follow her example.

294   *Diana B. Carlin*

Notes

Diana Carlin would like to thank Nancy Kegan Smith for sharing files and insights about Lady Bird Johnson.

    1. Numerous polls of primarily presidential scholars ranking both presidents and their spouses rank Lady Bird Johnson among the best. Robert P. Watson (2000, 179, 188–89, 195) in his book *The Presidents' Wives: Reassessing the Office of First Lady* includes several measures that show Mrs. Johnson ranked sixth on two, fourth on another, and seventeenth on a third. A Gallup Poll cited by Watson showed that Lady Bird remained on the list of most admired women through 1974. Betty Boyd Caroli (1987, 385–90) includes earlier surveys in *First Ladies* that rank Mrs. Johnson third among all first ladies and second among twentieth-century first ladies among scholars and first in a public survey.
    2. See James W. Ceaser, Glen E. Thurow, Jeffrey K. Tulis, and Joseph M. Bessette, "Rise of the Rhetorical Presidency"; Jeffrey K. Tulis, *The Rhetorical Presidency*; and Martin J. Medhurst, editor, *Beyond the Rhetorical Presidency.*
    3. See Carl Sferrazza Anthony, *First Ladies: The Saga of the Presidents' Wives and Their Power 1789–1961*; Betty Boyd Caroli, *First Ladies*; Myra G. Gutin, *The First Lady in the Twentieth Century*; Margaret Truman, *First Ladies*; and Robert P. Watson, *The Presidents' Wives: Reassessing the Office of First Lady.*
    4. See Gould (1988, 37–50) for a chronology of speeches given by both President and Mrs. Johnson prior to and during the 1964 campaign that related to the environment and beautification that formed the basis for the selection. According to Gould (39), "The Johnson administration's impulse to promote natural beauty in 1964 was part of a general revival of the conservation movement that had begun in the late 1950s and had gathered momentum during the years of the Kennedy presidency."
    5. See Anthony, *First Ladies: The Saga of the Presidents' Wives and Their Power 1961–1990*, Vol. 2., Paul F. Boller Jr., *Presidential Wives*, and Jan Jarboe Russell, *Lady Bird: A Biography of Mrs. Johnson.*

References

Anthony, Carl Sferrazza. 1990. *First Ladies: The Saga of the Presidents' Wives and Their Power 1789–1961*, Vol. 1. New York: William Morrow and Company.
———. 1991. *First Ladies: The Saga of the Presidents' Wives and Their Power 1961–1990*, Vol. 2. New York: William Morrow.
Boller, Paul F. 1988. *Presidential Wives*. New York: Oxford University Press.
Campbell, Karlyn Kohrs. 1996. The Rhetorical Presidency: A Two-Person Career. In *Beyond the Rhetorical Presidency*, ed. Martin J. Medhurst, 179–95. College Station, Tex.: Texas A & M University Press.
Caroli, Betty Boyd. 1987. *First Ladies*. New York: Oxford University Press.
Carpenter, Liz. 1970. *Ruffles and Flourishes: The Warm and Tender Story of a Simple Girl Who Found Adventure in the White House*. Garden City, N.Y.: Doubleday & Company.
Cater, Douglass. 1964. Memo: Douglass Cater to Bill Moyers, 18 August. EX PP5/Johnson, Lady Bird 7/15/64–10/1/64. Box 62, LBJ Library.
Ceaser, James W., Glen E. Thurow, Jeffrey K. Tulis, and Joseph M. Bessette. 1981. Rise of the Rhetorical Presidency. *Presidential Studies Quarterly*, II, 158–71.
Greenfield, Meg. 1965. The Lady in the East Wing. *Reporter*, 15 July, 28.

Gould, Lewis L. 1988. *Lady Bird Johnson and the Environment*. Lawrence, Kans.: University Press of Kansas.

———. 1999. *Lady Bird Johnson: Our Environmental First Lady*. Lawrence, Kans.: University Press of Kansas.

Gutin, Myra G. 1989. *The President's Partner: The First Lady in the Twentieth Century*. New York: Greenwood.

Janeway, Elizabeth. 1964. The First Lady: A Professional at Getting Things Done. *Ladies' Home Journal*, April, 64.

Johnson, Lady Bird. 1964a. Draft Statement by Mrs. Johnson, 31 August, EX PP5/Johnson, Lady Bird. Box 62, WHCF, LBJ Library.

———. 1964b. Press Release: Remarks of Mrs. Lyndon B. Johnson, Valdosta, Ga., 8 October. Mrs. Johnson—Press Release Copies of Mrs. Johnson's Speeches, LBJ Library.

———. 1964c. Press Release: Speech by Mrs. Lyndon B. Johnson, Depot at New Orleans, 9 October. Mrs. Johnson—Press Release Copies of Mrs. Johnson's Speeches, LBJ Library.

———. 1967. Press Release: Remarks by Mrs. Lyndon B. Johnson, Yale Political Union, New Haven, Conn., 9 October. Mrs. Johnson—Press Release Copies of Mrs. Johnson's Speeches, LBJ Library.

———. 1970. *A White House Diary*. New York: Holt, Rinehart and Winston.

Heckler-Feltz, Cheryl. 1997. *Heart and Soul of the Nation: How the Spirituality of Our First Ladies Changed America*. New York: Doubleday.

Klapthor, Margaret Brown. 1989. *The First Ladies*. Washington, D.C.: White House Historical Association.

Klaw, Barbara. 1980. Lady Bird Johnson Remembers. *American Heritage*, 13 December.

McCarthy, Abigail. 1972. *Private Faces/Public Places*. Garden City, New York: Doubleday & Company.

Medhurst, Martin J., ed. 1996. *Beyond the Rhetorical Presidency*. College Station, Tex.: Texas A & M University Press.

Museum Display. 1964. Taken from an Envelope dated 7 March, CTJ Diary Collection, LBJ Library.

Russell, Jan Jarboe. 1999. *Lady Bird: A Biography of Mrs. Johnson*. New York: Scribner.

Smith, Nancy Kegan. 1989. A Journey of the Heart: The Papers of Lady Bird Johnson. In *Modern First Ladies: Their Documentary Legacy*, ed. Nancy Kegan Smith and Mary C. Ryan, 109–20. Washington, D.C.: National Archives and Records Administration.

Telephone Conversation. 1964. Lyndon B. Johnson and Lady Bird Johnson, 7 March, at 4:10 PM, Citation #2395, WH6403.05, PNO 8, LBJ Library.

Terlip, Laura A. 1986. Communicating Ideals: The Role of the Politician's Wife. Conference Paper, Central States Speech Association, Chicago, April.

Tulis, Jeffrey K. 1987. *The Rhetorical Presidency*. Princeton, N.J.: Princeton University Press.

Truman, Margaret. 1995. *First Ladies*. New York: Random House.

Watson, Robert P. 2000. *The Presidents' Wives: Reassessing the Office of First Lady*. Boulder, Colo.: Lynne Rienner Publishers.

Whistle-Stop October 13–16. 1964. Memo, n.d., p.1, Box 11, Liz Carpenter's Subject Files, White House Social Files, LBJ Library.

———. Box 12, Liz Carpenter's Subject Files, White House Social Files, LBJ Library.

Chapter 15

Pat Nixon
Wisdom to Know the Difference

Linda B. Hobgood

I believe that even when people can't speak your language, they can tell if you
have love in your heart.

—Patricia Nixon

Socrates: Tell me, then: you say, do you not, that in the rightly developed man
the passions ought not to be controlled, but that we should let them grow to the
utmost and somehow or other satisfy them, and that this is a virtue?
Callicles: Yes; I do.
Soc.: Then those who want nothing are not truly said to be happy?
Cal.: No, indeed, for then stones and dead men would be the happiest of all.[1]

Henriette Wyeth Hurd painted the official portrait of Patricia Nixon. The woman
depicted is serene, almost sad. She appears fragile, yet brave. Above all, the face
that gazes from the canvas understands—the wisdom in her eyes reflects that
sense of tribulation bequeathed by experience. Both the painting and the subject
reflect "calm at the center." It is an insightful portrayal of the American first
lady known to the world as "Pat."

As the wife of a man who was by the time he became president one of the
most well-known public figures of the twentieth century, Pat was herself a familiar face. Richard Nixon featured his family in every political contest he entered, and by 1968, the nation knew the Nixons—even their dog, Checkers.
Television, as a medium of news, burst on the scene to coincide with Richard

Nixon's rise in national politics. As the visual medium expanded press coverage, any privacy that political families once may have enjoyed could no longer be presumed. This explains in part why so many of our memories of Pat are the indelible photographic images of her across more than four decades of American history.

Remarkable for their similarity are the terms used—both complimentary and critical—to describe Pat Nixon. Those who paid tribute to her upon her death praised the same qualities in her character. She seemed to embody all the virtues of Reinhold Niebuhr's familiar prayer, the very qualities revealed in her official portrait: serenity to accept what she could not change, courage to change what she could, and wisdom to know the difference.

What is striking about Pat Nixon's image is that while nearly everyone of her era recognized her familiar face, she remained a mystery. The life beyond the range of the camera's lens was a private one that Pat worked hard to protect. What the public did not know was left to speculation and caricature. Pat's response to such characterizations—even those that were blatantly false—was always a perspicacious silence. Faith that the truth as she knew it would have the final say gave Pat the confidence to refrain from elaboration and sustained her during the most trying times of her life. The temptation to publicly respond to criticism during or after her White House years was something Pat Nixon resolutely resisted.

We often forget that Pat Nixon was a wartime first lady. Undeclared and far away, the Vietnam conflict cast a shadow over the Nixon presidency that never lifted. American lives were sacrificed in the jungles of Southeast Asia for more than thirteen years, five and a half of which comprised the Nixon administration. Entrenched fears of the Cold War, mistrust of the Soviet Union and of its communist rival the People's Republic of China, Soviet aggression in Eastern Europe and the quashing of liberty in Czechoslovakia, heightened tensions between East and West Berlin, and the perilous aftermath of the six-day Arab–Israeli war combined to make Nixon's a more tremulous diplomatic and complex international challenge than the presidency had been since the Second World War.

Discontent with the Vietnam War led to violence at home. The sounds of protest in Lafayette Park across the street were the voices to which Pat Nixon awakened every morning of her White House stay.[2] Increasingly stark ideological differences between the two political parties in Congress were compounded by resentment over the narrow majority by which Richard Nixon won the presidential election of 1968. Finally, there was Watergate and, following an overwhelming victory in 1972, the unprecedented resignation of the president. Through it all there was the quiet calm of Pat Nixon.

Discernment seemed almost inherent in Pat. She had an instinct for what mattered and what, in the long term, did not. This "wisdom to know the difference" was complemented by two additional qualities in her character—a rigidly demanding definition of public service and an unwavering sense of self-discipline. These two qualities may have strengthened her capacity to withstand political battles that would have overwhelmed almost anyone else. At the same time, they gave rise to perceptions hardly compatible with the person friends and family knew her to be. The uncertainty that lingers regarding the stoic figure of so many press photographs reveals a failure of press and public to penetrate her silence to appreciate her sense of duty or share her regard for privacy. Pat's own supposition that these predilections should not need explaining may have contributed to her persona as an enigma. In the vacuum, otherwise implausible portrayals of Pat Nixon in print and film nourished a fungible narrative[3] easier to believe than to question. Lack of inquiry, however, deprives us of an understanding of Pat Nixon's indomitable strength and steadfastness that are hallmarks of her life and legacy as first lady.

Because by choice she gave so few publicly recorded remarks, the informal expressions and the activities of Pat Nixon form the basis of my analysis. If indeed they "speak louder than words," the actions of this first lady are valid assessments of her rhetorical effectiveness. This study begins with a biographical overview that records Pat Nixon's lengthy public career, examining especially the advantages and constraints of its duration and high profile. My study culminates in a critical look at Mrs. Nixon's White House years and the remaining two decades of her life.

Biography

In 1960, *Time* magazine featured the nation's second lady on its cover. In the accompanying story, headlined "The Silent Partner," author Burt Meyers wrote:

> Along with her bottomless energy, Mrs. Nixon has formidable reserves of poise and aplomb, and a notably retentive mind. . . . Since her abrupt debut into public life, there have been many occasions to test her serenity, and she has never failed to meet the test.
>
> Pat Nixon's stamina and courage, her drive and control have made her into one of the U.S.'s most remarkable women—not just a showpiece Second Lady, not merely a part of the best-known team in contemporary politics, but a public figure in her own right.
>
> She earned that right the hard way—in a tough childhood that knew little luxury. (Meyers 1960, 25)

Lessons in self-discipline, explicit and inferential, accompanied the meager circumstances into which Thelma Catherine Ryan was born. Nicknamed "Pat" because her birth came on the eve of St. Patrick's Day 1912, she adopted the name officially to honor her father's memory upon his death. The third child and first daughter born to Will and Kate Ryan, Pat inherited her father's love of reading and adventure. A sailor and then miner, Will moved his family from Ely to Artesia, California, to try his luck at farming when Pat was just a year old. Money was scarce, and Pat learned at an early age to be content with little—to accept the things she could not change.

Before she was in school, she already knew how to suppress her tears and keep her head high. One of her earliest memories is of riding into the little southern California town of Artesia with her farmer father to buy the weekly staples. While Will Ryan shopped, his four-year-old daughter waited patiently, perched on the high seat of the family buggy. "I would never ask for anything," she remembers, "but how I hoped! I'd watch the corner to see if he came back carrying a strawberry cone. That was the big treat." If there was no cone, the little girl understood that her father had no money left for treats, and she stifled her disappointment. "I just waited and hoped" (Meyers 1960, 25).

Pat knew better than to ask for such luxuries. Not wishing to add insult to the injury of Will Ryan's struggle to provide for his family's needs, Pat seemed to dread the thought of causing or adding undue misery even unintentionally. She therefore learned to read not just the printed word, but people as well. She developed an instinct for recognizing others' underlying emotions and responding with sensitivity. Years later, as first lady, Pat's "way with people" was the trait staff and visitors alike recalled best. Susan Porter Rose, who served as Mrs. Nixon's appointments secretary, recalled the White House reception for a group of Appalachian quilters, who were so overwhelmed by actually being at the White House and shy in the presence of the first lady that many began weeping uncontrollably.

> When [Mrs. Nixon] walked into the Diplomatic Reception Room to greet the quilt makers and heard the sobbing, she simply went around the room and wordlessly gave each of her guests a hug. Susan remembers that as the tension eased she was so moved that she felt tears spring into her own eyes. (Eisenhower 1986, 84)

Neither economic circumstance nor age seemed to make any difference in Pat's ability to anticipate and respond to others' needs. As first lady her "way" with children became almost legendary.

> Once, when a little crippled boy came to the White House for a photo opportunity with the First Lady, Pat saw the youngster was terrified and tried everything to help him relax, to no avail. Suddenly, he blurted: "This isn't your house!"
> "Why do you say that?" Pat asked.
> "Because I don't see your washing machine."
> Pat solemnly conducted him to the third floor and showed him the washing machines in the laundry room. He returned to the first floor holding her hand, as contented and cheerful as if he were with his own mother. His awed parent said that it was the first time he had ever been at ease with a stranger. (Truman 1995, 192–93)

Her mother died of Bright's disease and cancer of the liver when Thelma Ryan was thirteen. The details of Kate Ryan's life, her family, her faith, her favorite things, and the advice and hopes she no doubt had for her daughter were never conveyed. Pat recalled: "We were so busy on the farm. It was always a struggle. We didn't have much time to talk. And when you're thirteen you do not ask questions about philosophy or family" (Eisenhower 1986, 27).

In the years that followed, Pat assumed household responsibilities, attended school where she excelled academically, and found time for extracurricular activities such as debate and drama. She put off college to nurse her father through silicosis until he died in 1930. Then the youngest Ryan, who had taken care of her father and brothers since the time of her mother's death, was on her own to pursue an education and her dream to travel. Both necessitated constant employment.

Her degree in merchandising from the University of Southern California, with teaching and office administration certifications, was financed by research assistantships and work as an x-ray technician, jobs that included serving food in the cafeteria, checking books at the library, and performing bit parts as a movie extra. One faculty member commented on Pat Nixon's ubiquity on campus because of her numerous people- or service-oriented occupations. Another professor wrote of Miss Ryan's "splendid attitude towards young people, with her buoyant enthusiasm for life in general." The assessment by the teacher who supervised Pat Ryan's practice teaching is telling: "Her students are very fond of her and she gets good results from them" (quoted in Eisenhower 1986, 48).

The opportunity to travel presented itself when an elderly couple asked Pat if she would chauffeur them in their Packard from California to Connecticut. Such an offer, coming at the onset of the Great Depression, must have seemed especially exciting. She traversed dangerous mountain highways, learned to change flat tires, and reached the East safely in the fall of 1929. Her payment was a bus ticket back to California, but Pat decided to see as much of the East Coast as possible before returning to complete her undergraduate work. She visited relatives she had never met, saw the nation's capital for the first time, and toured the White House. Pat's Aunt Kate, a nun with the Sisters of Charity, worked at Seton Hospital in New York. She offered Pat a position that autumn working with the patients who suffered from tuberculosis. In one of many letters to her brother Bill back in California, Pat wrote: "I love to help others. . . . It's funny but even a cheerful smile uplifts them. . . . Sometimes I feel that I should like to spend my life just working for the afflicted unfortunates—helping them to be more happy. Too, I enjoy hospital work" (Eisenhower 1986, 37).

Pat avoided sharing with her brothers that the Seton patients would soon die of the very disease that had taken Will Ryan's life. Years later, Pat's daughter Julie asked her mother if she had been afraid that she too would contract the illness while caring for these patients, but Pat claimed she had not been afraid. Pat showed the same courage to care for others in difficult conditions when she was first lady. Her first solo mission to a foreign country was to Peru to bring comfort to the many victims of a devastating earthquake. She also visited soldiers wounded in Vietnam, becoming the first president's wife to enter a designated combat zone on foreign soil. Photos of Mrs. Nixon at the bedsides of amputees and wounded servicemen, often on her knees so that they might whisper private messages for her to convey, reveal a woman singularly focused on the face of each of the suffering and completely oblivious to self.

Pat returned to California to complete her studies as the summer of 1934 came to an end. Her brother Tom financed the bus trip home, and to save money Pat shared an apartment with her brothers for the remainder of her college years.

Upon graduation, she accepted a teaching position at the local high school in Whittier, California. An earnest sponsor of extracurricular activities, Caroli's biography suggests that Miss Ryan's willingness to support the students' pursuits beyond the classroom was mutually rewarding. She writes:

> Her students found her so lively and likable that they selected her to advise the Pep Committee, organized to arouse school enthusiasm. Robert C. Pierpoint, who later covered the White House as a correspondent for CBS, was a member of the Pep Committee, and he remembered Miss Ryan of his Whittier student days as: "approachable, friendly, and outgoing. She was happy, enthusiastic, sprightly. Her disposition was sunny, not intermittently but all the time. . . . We liked her enormously." (Caroli 1987, 246; David 1978, 40)

Pat also found an opportunity to pursue acting, from high school days a source of enjoyment. The decision to join a local theatre group changed the course of her life. In February 1938, Pat went to a tryout for the Whittier Community Players and met Richard Nixon. Their daughter, Julie Nixon Eisenhower, recounts that for her father it was love at first sight. He actually proposed that evening, in a manner of speaking.

A young attorney in Whittier's Wingert and Bewley law firm, Richard Nixon was highly regarded in the community. Awarded a scholarship to Harvard upon graduation from high school, Nixon had been forced to turn down the offer because his family lacked the money for his travel and boarding expenses. He had instead attended nearby Whittier College where he excelled and was elected president of the student body. His high academic achievements continued at Duke University Law School where Nixon was inducted into the Order of the Coif (the law equivalent of Phi Beta Kappa) and served as president of the Duke Law School Student Bar Association. Back home in Whittier, he was a member and future president of the 20–30 Club (sponsored by the Rotary), an active Kiwanian, and the town's deputy city attorney. But in 1938, his attentions turned to the popular and attractive Miss Ryan. His spontaneous proposal was followed by a courtship that lasted more than two years. Dick and Pat discovered common interests and marked similarities in background beyond their mutual Irish heritage.

In 1940, they were married. Within two years, America was at war. The couple moved to Washington, D.C., where Dick had been hired in the new Office of Price Administration (OPA). Pat volunteered as a secretary for the Red Cross until also finding employment with the OPA. Richard Nixon's service in the navy included duty overseas during which time Pat was employed in a bank in Iowa and then again with OPA as a price analyst in San Francisco. When Dick returned home, his military obligation situated the couple for a brief time in Baltimore. It was there that Richard Nixon received a message from associates in Whittier asking him to return and to consider a congressional candidacy in the upcoming 1946 election against the incumbent House member. Nixon ran and won, against formidable odds.

Pat gave birth to the Nixons' first child in February 1946, just one month after the couple had returned to California. She also managed her husband's campaign office by herself while he stumped across the district to win first the Republican nomination and then the November election. Dick's mother Hannah Nixon cared for their baby Tricia during the day while Pat performed secretarial, accounting, and other campaign duties at the headquarters. In her introduction to campaigns, Pat was exposed to the dark side of politics. A break-in occurred at the Nixon campaign headquarters. Pat, who had sold her small inheritance of land so the couple could afford to produce and distribute campaign pamphlets, reacted with a kind of hurt and disbelief over the loss of all their campaign materials. It was particularly disheartening to her that there was so little press or public outcry, something that, years later, struck her as ironic. It was a sobering lesson. The upset victory, hard fought and hard won, probably overshadowed the loss of political naiveté that accompanied the campaign of 1946. Nixon won reelection two years later, and it was during that campaign that their second daughter Julie was born.

In 1950, Richard Nixon's bid for the U.S. Senate, also viewed as an uphill race, was successful. His unlikely victories in a crucial state, his prominence on the House subcommittee investigating Alger Hiss, and his relative youth made Nixon a popular choice for vice president on the 1952 Republican ticket alongside presidential hopeful Dwight Eisenhower. Their candidacy was a successful one, but charges made in late summer that the vice presidential candidate operated a secret fund for purposes unreported drew sufficient press attention as to demand a response from Nixon. Republicans and Democrats alike called for an explanation, and there were suggestions that Nixon should withdraw from the ticket. For Nixon, this was tantamount to an admission of guilt. Determined to answer charges he viewed as deliberately false, Nixon was granted airtime on national television to give his side of the story. He determined that the only way to fight the fund allegations would be to disclose his finances entirely and to reveal—as no candidate had ever done before—all personal and family expenses, investments, and debts. Naturally a private person, Pat's exposure to three campaigns had only intensified her inclinations toward protecting the family's privacy. That she supported so resolutely the need for her husband to respond to the fund accusations and agreed with the way he chose to respond is an indication of her own hierarchy of values. Only the injustice of the situation as she perceived it permitted such a violation of their personal life. And though Pat did not know exactly what her husband planned to say, she was by his side at the broadcast. Earlier in the day, he had spoken of quitting the race, but Pat insisted that he defend himself and give the American people the truth they deserved.

The Checkers Speech is one of the most remarkable events in the history of American political campaigns. Nixon spoke directly to the camera for thirty plus minutes; he urged his audience to contact the Republican National Committee to voice their opinions as to whether he should be kept on the ticket. He bared his political and financial soul, listing the costs of his car and his mortgage, his assets and his debts. While his wife didn't have a fur coat, but instead wore a "good Republican cloth coat," he unabashedly asserted, "she'd look good in anything." And he acknowledged that the family had accepted one gift from a supporter in Texas: "It's a dog, a black and white spaniel, and our daughter Tricia named it Checkers and no matter what they say we're going to keep it."

Response was overwhelmingly supportive and Nixon was kept on the ticket. Eisenhower even boasted about his running mate at subsequent campaign rallies. But in the nearly fifty years since the event, those who recall the speech remember that though it was Nixon who spoke so unconventionally and Checkers for whom the event was named, the lasting image is that of a poised Mrs. Nixon. Press accounts at the time described her as cool and collected, but a watching public recalls another Pat. Seated on the stage of the El Capitan Theatre in Los Angeles just a few feet from Nixon she set her unblinking, unflinching gaze on her husband with a somber, tight-lipped smile that barely masked the personal indignation she felt toward what had become politics at its nastiest and most intrusive. The pain in her expression was so palpable that the television viewer could feel it; the camera seemed a heartless trespasser. A half-century later with such supposed sophistication toward the television medium, her image still has that effect on the viewer.[4]

The Checkers Speech would be a key recollection of that 1952 campaign, but another incident, all but forgotten, also left indelible memories. During the Republican National Convention, on the night Richard Nixon accepted the vice presidential nomination, reporters, anxious for a story, brushed past a bewildered baby-sitter in the Nixon home where their daughters were sleeping. They wakened Tricia, six, and Julie, four, making them pose for pictures in a frenzied haste to get the girls' reaction to their father's nomination. The flashbulbs scared the youngsters to tears. The incident was not considered newsworthy, but this was the part of politics neither Pat—nor any mother—could easily forget. It could hardly help but leave a lasting impression regarding the behavior of particular reporters and the press in general.

The 1952 GOP ticket won in a landslide and repeated the victory in 1956. One of the well-known photographs of those years was taken at the 1957 Inaugural Ball. In the picture, the Nixons are smiling and waving to supporters from their box seats, but the new vice president's wife is looking sideways at a yawning daughter Julie. The photo is emblematic of the dual existence that characterized this stage of Pat's life. For the next eight years, Nixon and his wife were put to work on behalf of the administration at home and overseas. Ruth Cowan's feature article on Pat, published at the outset of her husband's vice presidency, is typical of the favorable coverage Mrs. Nixon enjoyed in that era.

> Mrs. Richard Nixon as second lady of the land is beginning an exciting new chapter in a life that already has been as dramatic as any story out of Hollywood in her home state of California. In fact, her life story as a movie could "pack 'em in." The plot is the kind Americans really like—a pot of gold at the end of the rainbow that was reached only after a lot of ups and downs. (Cowan 1953, S3)

During both Eisenhower terms, concern for the president's health limited his activities, and the Nixons assumed diplomatic responsibilities, especially those involving travel to foreign countries. There seems to have been little question but that Mrs. Nixon would accompany her husband, though the decision involved leaving their two young daughters. Her biographers indicate this was a wrenching choice. Nevertheless, response to her activity as an ambassador of goodwill and surrogate on official state occasions was uniformly positive. Members of the media who accompanied the vice president and his wife marveled at Pat's stamina. Julie Eisenhower's biography of her mother, which provides the most comprehensive account of the second lady's travels, includes the impression recounted by Robert Hartmann of the *Los Angeles Times*, following the attack on the vice president's motorcade by violent mobs of communist-inspired insurgents during the couple's 1957 trip to South America:

> At the American Embassy, reporter Bob Hartmann, who had watched the attack from the press truck, was one of the first to talk to my parents and to file a dispatch back to the United States. Part of his report read, "Pat Nixon was magnificent today"; at the end of her ordeal, "she still had a stiff upper lip, but when newsmen cheered her, tears welled in her eyes." (Eisenhower 1986, 176)

In these diplomatic and political duties, Pat Nixon reportedly welcomed opportunities for direct interaction despite the time and energy required. Helen Thomas listened to Richard Nixon describe what became a pattern:

> I remember through all of our campaigns, whether it was a receiving line or whether it was going to a fence at the airport, she was the one that always insisted on shaking that last hand, not simply because she was thinking of that vote, but because she simply could not turn down that last child or that last person. (Thomas 1975, 165)

Support of her husband's political philosophy was by all accounts genuine; Pat appears to have enjoyed demonstrating that support as his traveling partner. Following a press reception in Belgrade, a Yugoslav reporter concluded her story: "I wondered whether I was talking with the wife of a politician or with a woman who is herself a politician. I again remembered the words of Dwight Eisenhower: 'The Nixons are a team'" (Eisenhower 1986, 300). Pat was developing a penchant for informal opportunities.

In all their travels, Pat made it her special purpose to extend goodwill beyond officialdom to citizens of the countries they visited despite age, health, or economic circumstance. Beyond embassy security she came face-to-face with the danger of their ambassadorial role. By far the most dramatic episode occurred in Caracas on the 1957 trip to South America. Communist insurgents had inspired and fomented anti-American sentiment and sympathizers congregated to stimulate protests at points along the planned motorcade routes. The protests quickly became riots and local government officials were unwilling or unable to curb the demonstrators. Hostility greeted the Nixons at every stop, but as the visit progressed the violence increased. Anger culminated at the airport where protocol demanded, despite the danger of the situation, an official departure ceremony. Julie Eisenhower describes the accounts of eyewitnesses:

> When the Venezuelan national anthem was unexpectedly played at the entrance to the terminal, causing my parents to stand immobile in respect for their host

country, the screaming crowd on the observation deck directly above them showered them with a sustained rain of spit and some garbage. At first the spit looked like giant snowflakes, but it turned to foul, dark blotches when it hit my mother's red suit and the clothes of those standing with her. Then, with the aid of the Secret Service, my parents walked through a shouting, spitting mob to the motorcade. At the car Don Hughes hurriedly rolled up the windows and then pulled out his handkerchief and wiped the saliva off the seat my mother would occupy. And yet, as Americans read in their newspapers the next day, reporters saw Pat Nixon ignore the final onslaught and stop to hug a child who had given her flowers. They also saw her lean across a barricade to pat the shoulder of a young girl who had just cursed and spit at her. The girl turned away in shame. (Eisenhower 1986, 84)

Secret Service and military channels of communication from Caracas were blocked that day. News of the rioting interrupted regular television programming back in the United States. The president and official Washington obtained their first glimpse of the trouble by tuning in, as did the Nixon daughters, who attended public school in their Washington, D.C., neighborhood and were home for lunch. The TV program the girls were watching was interrupted by film showing the smashed automobiles that had transported their parents through the dangerous streets. Dramatic voice-overs gave no indication as to whether the vice president and his wife had escaped harm. Attempts to reassure the Nixon daughters were, upon returning, their mother's heavy-hearted task.

Pat no doubt gained during these years an acute sense of the strain public service may bring to the families and personal lives of those who serve. That she nevertheless urged active involvement in public service at informal gatherings and the few formal settings in which she spoke belies Pat's fundamental faith in the value of representative democracy. She had, by her mid-forties, observed a sufficient number of alternative forms of government to endorse knowledgeably, even with its flaws, participatory government and the American system.

Domestic travel was as much a part of the Nixons' schedules as were their foreign assignments. While Pat did not go on every campaign swing, she kept a wearying pace in the campaign for reelection in 1956, and accompanied her husband to assist Republican candidates for House and Senate in the non-presidential election years. During one campaign season, Republicans coined a slogan "Let's Make a Clean Sweep," designed to inspire the recapture of a majority in the November election in both houses of Congress. At a scheduled campaign stop in Cleveland, Ohio, the Nixons emerged from their plane and were greeted by an unexpectedly large crowd of supporters. They enthusiastically chanted the clean sweep slogan and waved scores of brooms, the vast quantity of which had been supplied by a member of the Ohio congressional delegation, George Bender. More than a dozen years later, First Lady Pat Nixon was the special guest at a Congressional Club reception in Washington, D.C., at which a replica of her inaugural gown was to be unveiled. Spotting Senator Bender's widow among the invited guests, Pat approached her and exclaimed suddenly "The brooms!" The first lady then clasped Mrs. Bender's shoulders and said earnestly "You cannot imagine how much that reception meant and what those brooms did for our spirits." Taken completely by surprise at this recollection, Mrs. Bender was overwhelmed by Pat's memory and genuine thought-fulness (Hobgood 2001).

Victorious in five consecutive elections, a proven leader in presiding over the U.S. Senate and in his role as presidential surrogate, and an impressive defender of American values and interests overseas, the vice president was considered a significant asset in assisting GOP candidates for office. He was so visible and influential that columnist Murray Kempton nicknamed the 1950s the "Nixon Decade." It was a foregone conclusion that Richard Nixon would seek to succeed Eisenhower as president; Pat, whom many thought had lost her love of campaigning in the years following the Checkers Speech, summoned her energies and approached the coming contest with customary dedication and enthusiasm. Pat had, by 1959, learned to martial her talent for recollection and her interest in others with so little apparent effort that she could be counted on to recognize former acquaintances as she made new ones. The famous and not-so-famous were treated alike as is demonstrated by one exchange in Idaho that proved typical:

> Danny Kaye stopped to chat for a moment, and Art Linkletter, in a shaggy bearskin serape, got a guffaw from Dick Nixon, and a comment: "Is this man or beast?" Then a stocky man in a blue-and-white Norwegian sweater came by. "I'm Bob Bennett," he said. "I'm sure you don't remember me, but I'd like to shake your hand." Replied Pat, without a moment's hesitation: "Of course I remember you. You were our campaign manager in Tulare County in 1950. After that big meeting we had there, we went to your house. You raise oranges." Muttered Bennett in wonderment as he walked off: "It's been ten years." (Meyers 1960, 24)

At some point in her husband's political career, Pat Nixon deliberately limited the ways in which she would express her political views, at least stateside during a campaign season. According to her daughter Julie, it was during the first congressional campaign in 1946 that Mrs. Nixon determined the extent of her own political activity:

> My mother had an innate sense of what would or would not be politically appropriate for her. She knew that she would never be comfortable with a public speaking role, so she confined her remarks to brief "greetings" in which she thanked the volunteers for their efforts. She felt strongly also that there should be only one voice on issues in the campaign—the candidate's. (Eisenhower 1986, 89)

On one occasion in 1956, when the flu kept Richard Nixon from delivering prepared remarks, Pat filled in with a three-minute speech at a stop in Oklahoma City. Julie Eisenhower's biography traces the otherwise faithful twenty-eight-year maintenance of this policy and Mrs. Nixon reiteration of it in response to reporters' questions. In one instance, Julie combines her mother's response to one of the many "why no policy pronouncements from the First Lady" with an assertive call by Mrs. Nixon (one of many informal exhortations) to citizen involvement:

She avoided policy statements, telling Vera Glaser of the North American Newspaper Alliance, "I don't think one person can speak for another. The candidate should speak for himself." Repeatedly, she declared that individuals could make a difference. "Get involved. Instead of complaining, go to work. People should participate in local political groups. Each community has some kind of organization in which it is possible to become active. Work for a candidate whom you believe to be qualified—they are the ones who can take a problem to the top. Indicate interest to your Congressman or Senator." (Eisenhower 1986, 243)

Here is clear indication that Mrs. Nixon's reluctance to speak publicly on issues did not reflect a lack of interest or concern. And according to Julie Eisenhower, "[t]hat philosophy—the individual can change the quality of life—would be the theme of her White House years" (Eisenhower 1986, 243). Nevertheless, this combination of inclinations creates a challenge for a first lady who evidently enjoyed interacting with people in almost any situation but that of making a formal address. As one who held to certain values including the need to support her husband's positions, and who felt that attitudes or beliefs could and should be supported by action, her sense of propriety restricted expression. The rhetorical dilemma for Pat Nixon was, therefore, one of her own making. Having eliminated the option of speaking formally to effect persuasion, she limited the number of available and appropriate rhetorical options by which to exert influence. In the 1960 election, this dilemma called for creative alternatives.

Columnist Ruth Montgomery, writing in her syndicated column, asserted that "for the first time in American history one woman could conceivably swing a presidential election." According to Julie Eisenhower:

Another reporter evoked historical precedent when she pointed out that Pat Nixon was the first woman around whom a separate campaign was being built. The Republican National Committee's women's division decided to sponsor a Pat Week beginning October 3, during which Mother would attend coffees and mini-rallies in her honor, and precinct workers would canvass the neighborhoods. (Eisenhower 1986, 189)

Pat was reportedly uncomfortable with these efforts and her permission had not been sought in advance. She would not have approved activities that distracted from the candidate himself, and she may not have fully realized the extent to which she herself was viewed as an asset by her husband's campaign organizers.

The 1960 campaign and election proved physically and emotionally draining. Richard Nixon had, by age 47, run for office twice nationally, five times successfully. Any discussion of losing was viewed as tantamount to admitting defeat during the campaign, so between Pat and Dick there was no speculation about this possibility. They maintained a grueling schedule, ignoring illness and strain. The president was judged by First Lady Mamie Eisenhower too ill to stump for Nixon; Ike's absence from the campaign was easily misinterpreted. The first televised debates took place between Kennedy and Nixon; the unprecedented role and impact of the visual medium created exigencies that families and supporters of both candidates had to face abruptly. When it became clear on election night that the outcome was the closest in U.S. history and that Richard Nixon appeared to have lost, Nixon ignored reports of voting fraud incidents and irregularities and made a swift decision to concede. Supporters who jammed the Ambassador Hotel ballroom in Los Angeles, dismayed at his admitting defeat so early, chanted to the Nixons as they entered the room "Don't give up!" "You're still going to win!" As the vice president and his wife stood at the microphones waiting for the applause to subside, Pat Nixon, whose poise had come to be presumed, looked out at the crowd of friends and supporters of fourteen years and more and lost her composure. Again there is the unforgettable photo of Pat whose face bore all the shock and strain and disappointment of months spent exhausting themselves only to face this first defeat.

The Nixons remained in Washington until the summer 1961 when their daughters completed the school term, but it was a difficult time. Julie Eisenhower writes:

> In a sense those months in Washington marked another turning point in my mother's attitude toward politics. Nineteen sixty disillusioned her beyond redemption. She saw a stolen election and could not understand why so many were indifferent. Gradually she resolved to channel her energy into the new life awaiting us in California." (Eisenhower 1986, 204)

It was time to change the things she could.

More likely for reasons of party loyalty and anxiousness to avoid the almost inevitable split that subsequently occurred among California Republicans, Richard Nixon was less than two years later a candidate for governor of his home state. Pat had grave misgivings as to the outcome, and her fears were well founded. In the famous press conference that followed his humiliating defeat, Richard Nixon bade farewell to politics with the bitter promise "You won't have Dick Nixon to kick around anymore." Pat, watching via television, reportedly cheered, counting on this to be a promise kept.

One can therefore hardly comprehend Pat Nixon's thoughts as she came to the realization that she would be returning to the political scene. The family had moved to New York where Richard Nixon practiced law. He traveled extensively for his firm, campaigned for Republican candidates, and addressed the 1964 GOP National Convention, but the family remained close, indulging in long-postponed visits with treasured friends. On at least one of these visits, the notion of a second run for the presidency was discussed. Pat's closest friend Helene Drown recalled for Julie Eisenhower: "I sensed strongly that Pat still had a deep belief in your father's unique talent. She was sure that he alone was capable of solving some of the problems we were facing in the country then" (Eisenhower 1986, 232). As to her mother's attitude in 1968, Julie reflects: "It took courage to re-enter public life as spiritedly as she did." And she wisely notes: "She had no illusions about campaigns or Washington; no confidence that success lay at the end of the rainbow" (235).

Pat understood the odds. They did not have vast wealth, her husband steered a moderate course, he had been tagged a loser, or a has-been, and they had no way of knowing whether he still had a real political following. At the same time, foreign and domestic crises had reached a critical point. The significance of Julie's observation is that the campaign of 1968 seemed to be an experience Pat thoroughly enjoyed. She appeared buoyant and lighthearted after years away from the limelight. She obliged the demands of campaign protocol in such a way that they seemed second nature, almost fun. She paced herself and her activities. Her happiness did not appear to depend on the election outcome. Her children had reached adulthood, there was a degree of family financial stability and, except for what he considered a minor bout with phlebitis, Dick and Pat Nixon enjoyed extraordinary good health.

The outcome in 1968, was again razor thin, but this time the edge went to Richard Nixon. Acknowledging to supporters that "Winning's a lot more fun," the president-elect and his family prepared for the wedding of daughter Julie to David Eisenhower, and their return to Washington. Daughter Tricia was married to Edward Cox in the White House Rose Garden in June 1971. Nixon was re-elected president in 1972, by the largest landslide to that time. Then, exactly six years and one day following his 1968 acceptance of the Republican presidential nomination, Richard Nixon became the first president in American history to resign from office, under threat of impeachment. The former president and first lady retired to La Casa Pacifica, their home in San Clemente, California, where Pat Nixon suffered a stroke in June 1976, from which she never fully recovered. The Nixons moved back to New York and New Jersey to be near their children and four grandchildren. Pat Nixon died on June 22, 1993, the day following her fifty-third wedding anniversary and was buried on the grounds of the Nixon Library in Yorba Linda, California, next to the home that was her husband's birthplace. Her epitaph[5] reads: "I believe that even when people can't speak your language, they can tell if you have love in your heart."

Rhetorical Activities as First Lady

That Patricia Nixon took living in the White House seriously yet did not take herself too seriously created a blend of character that was recalled fondly by those who helped her perform the duties of first lady. In the brief months that I served on her staff, I asked my coworkers questions on every conceivable subject, but the answer to "What is the event or occasion you remember best?" was always the same: "The POW Dinner." The White House staff, used to entertaining, was less accustomed to planning a gala of this size and scope. Returning from imprisonment in Vietnam, the 591 servicemen were invited along with their families to an evening of supper and entertainment on the South Lawn of the White House in May 1973. Preparations for the event were unprecedented, but what her staff recalled uniformly was that Mrs. Nixon seemed especially moved by the bravery of these men and the fortitude of their families. The suffering they had endured was matched by the gratitude they expressed, and the celebration was carefully designed to honor them in a way they would remember for the rest of their lives.

To combine a dignified reserve with a genuine sense of caring that transcended age, language, and cultural limits is uncommon. My first observation of Mrs. Nixon entertaining a little boy in the White House Library convinced me that the combination of gentleness and encouragement I witnessed was something rare. In greatest detail, the child, who was afflicted with a disease for which there was then no known cure, described losing his tooth the evening before. Mrs. Nixon knelt beside him so that from his seated position he could show her the empty space in his mouth that had so recently housed his tooth. She listened attentively, oblivious to the presence of the others in the room. His spontaneous embrace came as no surprise, and she returned it warmly when it was time for him to leave. Such moments occurred regularly, but nothing about Mrs. Nixon's demeanor on these occasions could be considered routine. Carl Anthony likened her to Grace Coolidge: "As teachers, they focused on children requiring special attention. . . . Children seemed to respond to Pat Nixon as openly as she did to them, embracing, kissing, and leading them by the hand because she felt like it" (Anthony 1991, 165).

As a teacher, Pat was fastidious in all manner of contact with others. Her staff—four key assistants plus their respective teams—was well acquainted with her rules regarding correspondence. In the wording of letters, vagueness, jargon, trite or clichéd terms were to be avoided. She checked every letter she signed for spelling, punctuation, and grammatical errors. It was explained to me that while we might become accustomed to seeing White House letterhead there were citizens worldwide who cherished the only letter from the White House they might receive in a lifetime. Pat had seen letters from the White House framed and hung in homes' most special places. It was considered our responsibility to treat each piece of stationery, funded by the taxpayer, with utmost care.

Pat Nixon did her homework. She spent weeks and months prior to state visits, studying culture and customs, the people and politics with whom she expected to visit. William Safire recalls how well her extensive preparations served her when she was in Moscow for the 1972 summit and was seated next to Aleksei Kosygin at an official dinner. He quizzed her specifics of American government and the number of women holding elective office, inquired as to names of members of the traveling White House press corps, compared views of Russian theatre, and the Moscow subway system versus the one proposed for Washington, D.C. They discussed the Orlov Diamond and the clamor of fire engines outside the Soviet Embassy in New York City. Kosygin wryly suggested that the reason Americans had a grain surplus was because they didn't eat enough bread. Pat Nixon replied to all his jokes and queries. She had noted all the names (present and past) of the places in which he had spent his childhood and asked him to tell her of his youth. He recalled famine and hardship as a young boy and went on at great length because the American first lady seemed somehow to understand. Safire recounts the conversation as evidence "of a First Lady doing her job—nothing dramatic, but a bit of flavor that rarely makes the reporting of great events" (Safire 1975, 609–10). This was just as Pat Nixon would have wanted it.

Every Pat Nixon biographer alludes to the keen sense of duty and dedication maintained throughout her career in public life: "She believed that publicly the First Lady must always be an unquestionable example of high virtue, a symbol of dignity, yet refused to fall prey to the trappings (Anthony 1991, 165). She had a kind of sixth sense, however, about when to uphold the standards of decorum and when it was actually more appropriate to "be flexible" in ceremony and protocol. Perhaps because of this otherwise strict adherence to appropriateness, it was always a special delight to see Mrs. Nixon "let down her guard." Children, pets, and holidays accommodated perfectly such occasions. So too, did the presence of another first lady, the widowed Mamie Eisenhower, who Pat welcomed into the life of the Nixon family and White House. Mamie lent a kind of "impish" grandmotherly presence to executive branch officialdom. Pat brought her as the surprise guest to a reception for the staff one summer evening in 1973, and a colleague invited me to come with him to meet her. We introduced ourselves, and my colleague Bill Fillmore informed Mrs. Eisenhower that he was planning to marry that fall. "Do you have any advice for newlyweds?" he inquired. Mamie, who to that point had been quietly demure, looked tiny next to her interlocutor. Suddenly, standing on tiptoe and grasping the lapels of Bill's jacket, she looked him in the eye and admonished "You tell her she'll get a lot further with honey than she will with vinegar!" Pat, standing nearby, laughed heartily as we struggled to maintain our composure.

There were times when Pat had to conceal her own surprise. Seated next to Chou en Lai at dinner during the historic trip to China, Mrs. Nixon reached for a cigarette case that was wrapped in tissue decorated with panda bears. Pat fingered the wrapping and commented to the premier that she had "always loved them."

"I will give you some," he replied.
"Cigarettes?"
"Pandas."

That is how the National Zoo in Washington, D.C., became home to the Chinese pandas, one of the most popular tourist sites in the nation's capital.

Pat was asked to define at various times her "cause" as first lady. While she launched the "Right to Read" literacy program, championed the arts and American artists in particular, and drew attention to volunteerism nationwide, she often simply alluded to her affection for people. Others viewed this as a special gift and her greatest talent—"her boundless compassion for humanity"—but she herself never saw it as anything other than being herself. On one or two occasions she did refer to her "personal diplomacy." If it can be called a style, it was one that began well before her husband became president and it remains a viable model of rhetorical effectiveness for a "silent partner."

Too prudent to be drawn into gratuitous confrontation, she apparently perceived as a violation of decorum the spouse-as-spokesperson, which seemed to her to disregard the fact of who was the candidate in an election. What enjoyment a president's family might find in the perquisites of a presidency was, she believed, balanced by concomitant obligations and sacrifice. Mrs. Nixon probably understood better than most the rhetorical risk of a voice with two faces, the danger of intended harmony being perceived instead as contradiction. As she was inclined to support almost all of Richard Nixon's expressed views, allowing any possible confusion that might undermine his efforts by something she might say was considered counterproductive, politically and personally.

There was public support for her conduct. Throughout the more than five years of the Nixon presidency, Pat routinely led national and international popular opinion polls (Truman 1995, 192). Her style as a first lady was perceived as consistent with her four predecessors[6], and, importantly, with herself. By 1969, when she entered the White House, Pat Nixon was hardly a stranger in the popular sense. She had been a familiar face to the general public for nearly two decades, since the Hiss case had propelled her husband into the national spotlight. In the 1968 presidential race, supporters and opponents alike looked for anything that might hint of a distinction between the "new" Nixon and the "old" Nixon as a strategy to gain voter support. Patricia Nixon may have surmised that 1968 was not the time for a departure from personal conduct she viewed as having been appropriate; after all, no one had blamed her for her husband's defeats of 1960 and 1962 (or, for that matter, any of his personal and political setbacks). She, therefore, adhered to an image with which the public appeared both familiar and comfortable. The value of this can best be appreciated in its historical context. Images that pervaded print and electronic media in the early 1970s, those of Vietnam War protesters or increasingly agitated demonstrators, presented a stark contrast to any coverage of Mrs. Nixon's daily routine. The drama provided by one set of photographs easily overwhelmed and obscured the predictable appearance of the other. One gathers an impression that she would still have opted for a "safe rather than sorry" course of action.

Apart from consideration of day-to-day public opinion, Pat Nixon was no doubt aware of longer-term shifts in social and cultural perspectives regarding institutions and values. They included the presidency, the notion of privacy, and the roles and rights of women in public and corporate spheres.

Richard Neustadt's redefining of the power of the presidency as the power to persuade had proven valid and to Lyndon Johnson's advantage. His War on Poverty and civil rights legislation both owed their support to the persuasive force of that one individual. But it could also backfire. Vietnam had become Johnson's war; it then threatened to become Nixon's. A personalized presidency posed the risk that anyone close to the president might become an issue and a problem for which the chief executive could and would be held accountable. The woman whose cloth coat and cocker spaniel had dogged her since 1952 was sensitive to what may become news and grounds for criticism. Her solution appears to be based on the adage: be mindful of unintended consequences.

Privacy in the era of Franklin Delano Roosevelt bore no resemblance to the brand of the late 1960s. Respect for the personal lives of public figures, violated infrequently, and accepted by Americans of the World War II era, had evanesced by 1969. The ways in which personal and family concerns had become public fare during the Johnson administration, detailed reporting of the Johnson daughters' social experiences and the tragedies and misfortunes of Johnson family friends, no doubt alerted the Nixon family (inclined to be private anyway) to be even more cautious before making public statements. Even so, Pat Nixon must have known that any effort to protect privacy came at a price. Her rhetorical approach, if at one time fitting, was not as conducive to increasingly staccato press coverage of the day. She needed to address the possibility that the mediated audience might perceive her as keeping the public at arm's length or lacking candor. The risk of having her disciplined nature viewed as Callicles' "dead men and stones" did in fact, occur. An unflattering image of a stiff and dispassionate consort was occasionally used to characterize Mrs. Nixon from the 1950s until the end of her husband's presidency in 1974. But reports of Pat Nixon taking any public position in contrast to the administration were, as she desired, nonexistent.

It was on the issue of women's rights that Mrs. Nixon gave the only indication of being more liberal politically than her husband. While she had indicated (via family and friends) that she favored initiatives in the 1968 and 1972 Republican Convention platforms which endorsed the Equal Rights Amendment, and that she supported the nomination of a woman to the Supreme Court, she must have been keenly aware of three constraints. First, there was little national consensus on these issues and her position would not resolve that. Second, her expressed sentiments would not likely change feminist opposition to the Nixon agenda. And third, the expanded world audience to which her husband was so keenly attuned included vastly divergent sentiments regarding the treatment of women in general and the outspokenness of political spouses in particular.

These factors, in addition to her personal preferences already noted, presented a tantalizing challenge to someone of Mrs. Nixon's political awareness and experience. She began with a savvy understanding that effecting political persuasion is not confined to registered or even eligible voters. While taking into account the breadth of an expanded world audience, she may have assessed those with whom interaction was personally most fulfilling. Already, she had defined her role as first lady, as she had consistently throughout her husband's public life, from the perspective of her status as a wife and mother. If such exemplification was not enthusiastically received by members of the media or politicians, neither did it spawn detractors in and of itself. Those inclined to like Mrs. Nixon approved the example she set; those politically opposed to her, or more precisely, to her spouse, took exception to other things. Criticism focused mostly on her manner: "reserve" became "robotic." In the popular press the term, "Plastic Pat" typically signified an unflattering news item. But for her, a domestic countenance appears to have been a natural and rewarding representation, one that permitted, even encouraged reaching out to others. Genuinely comfortable with young and old alike, and imbued by her upbringing with the demeanor of a caregiver, Pat Nixon was what Margaret Truman called "a small *d* democrat in her bones, someone who always preferred to iron her own dresses, wash her own clothes, who instinctively sympathized with the poor and unlucky of this world" (Truman 1995, 190).

A final aspect should not be casually dismissed. The office of first lady has come to convey a measure of dignity and distance that inspires curiosity, even awe. In her presence, an ordinary citizen might expect the display of gracious hospitality or pleasantness, but not necessarily the easy warmth of a friend. If members of the public had, in addition, any preconceived notions of a reticent Mrs. Nixon, they encountered a paradox that forced choosing between the "plastic Pat" they had read about and the laughing first lady who was patting their shoulder or squeezing their hands. An expression or spirit of unconditional warmth and acceptance takes on an implausible and therefore special significance when it originates in one who is perceived by an audience to be shy and reserved. This unintended aid may have been the secret to whatever success Pat Nixon's "personal diplomacy" enjoyed. As the advantage of the so-called "stealth bomber" is its ability to fly low, undetected by radar, so the strength of "personal diplomacy" may have been that it was so obvious and came to be taken so for granted, that reporters often missed its effects completely. Two incidents in particular come to mind.

From the time of her departure following her husband's assassination, Jacqueline Kennedy had not returned to the White House. The official portraits of President and Mrs. Kennedy, painted by artist Aaron Shikler, were finished in 1971. Mrs. Nixon extended a hand-delivered invitation to Mrs. Kennedy and her children, inviting them to view privately the official portraits and to spend an afternoon in their former home. Surmising accurately that Mrs. Kennedy would not wish the press to be informed, she promised the former first lady privacy and not a word to the media. When Mrs. Kennedy accepted the invitation Mrs. Nixon did not share the reply with her press secretary Helen Smith, so that in the event the press might suspect or learn of the visit, Helen would be able to—and indeed, did—respond honestly that she knew nothing of the get-together. The three Kennedys arrived without fanfare, viewed both paintings and commented appreciatively on the prominent locations selected for each. Mrs. Nixon, who admired her predecessor's extensive efforts at White House restoration, briefed her on the progress in recovering White House antiquity. Mrs. Kennedy expressed admiration for the work of curator Clement Conger and Mrs. Nixon that was continuing based on Mrs. Kennedy's initiative. The Nixon daughters showed Caroline and John Jr. the family quarters and the rooms that had been their own. All three Kennedys wrote afterwards, thanking the Nixon women effusively for their gracious hospitality and more important for making every effort to guarantee the privacy of their visit. Jacqueline Kennedy wrote: "The day I always dreaded turned out to be one of the most precious ones I have spent with my children" (Eisenhower 1986, 310). Only later, by mutual agreement, was news of the event made public. Personal diplomacy admits loyalty and trustworthiness to an unusual degree. Mrs. Nixon could have violated the wishes of her predecessor and choreographed a press and photo opportunity without equal. Instead, she incurred the wrath of the press corps for withholding information. Helen Thomas, dean of the White House press corps and a personal favorite of Pat's had suspected something, leaked her suspicions, and felt betrayed by the White House's reluctance to confirm. Pat Nixon chose the path that hurt others least and paid the price herself.

In May 1972, the first lady accompanied her husband to the Moscow Summit and there is evidence to suggest that events occurred as a consequence of

Mrs. Nixon's personal diplomacy. According to *U.S. News and World Report*, "[Mrs. Nixon's] friendliness seemed to captivate the Russians" ("Pat in Moscow: A Busy Week," 19). *Newsweek* reported:

> Three months ago she charmed them in Peking with her unfailing cheerfulness and tact. And last week in Moscow, Pat Nixon turned in another virtuoso performance as a goodwill ambassador extraordinaire, handling the people-to-people aspects of the Moscow summit trip with aplomb. . . . As a former schoolteacher herself, Mrs. Nixon seemed happiest while visiting children's ballet classes and Soviet classrooms. ("Ladies Day in Moscow," 31)

Washington Post reporter Robert G. Kaiser cited unprecedented media coverage to the summit by the Soviet media:

> Thirteen minutes of the 15-minute main news program was devoted to the Nixons' visit. . . . Such elaborate coverage is extremely unusual here, and it contradicts predictions by Soviet journalists who said that no big fuss would be made over the visit. On the contrary the Nixons have been given the sort of attention that is reserved for extraordinary events. . . . The impact of all this on ordinary Russians cannot be described with certainty. But there is no doubt that they will get the message that this visit is regarded as an extremely important event. (1972, A12)

Of Mrs. Nixon's impact specifically Kaiser wrote:

> Pictures of a smiling Mrs. Nixon at a Moscow school and in the city's subway system put the First Lady in a sympathetic light for Soviet citizens. Her neatly-coiffed good looks are a far cry from the hook-nosed snarling Uncle Sam who often represents America in Soviet cartoons. (1972, A12)

In mid-1973 Soviet officials, in the spirit of détente, reversed an earlier decision with the surprise announcement that the children's cast of the Bolshoi Ballet, with whom Mrs. Nixon had visited the previous spring, would be permitted to accept the invitation to perform in the United States for the first time. The *New York Times* reported that Mrs. Nixon had invited the entire membership of the ballet, young and old, to a reception at the White House when the tour came to Washington.

Preparations for the August event focused on the children. Fruit punch and an array of sweets adorned the buffet in the State Dining Room. The Marine Band played and the White House seemed unusually festive. But the arrival of the ballerinas signaled a change in mood. Huddled together, the young members of the troupe appeared apprehensive and skeptical. One of the chaperones whispered to a member of Mrs. Nixon's staff that a newspaper's unfavorable review of the previous evening's performance had been shared with the girls.[7] They had taken it personally and doubted whether their American hosts really wanted to be friends after all.

A receiving line was quietly formed, and invitations to eat and tour the house were extended. But as the children shook hands with the first lady their manner was dutiful and their expressions wooden. The reception looked to be a disaster. As one child extended her hand to greet the first lady, the interpreter standing beside her remarked, "Today is Zuhra's birthday." Mrs. Nixon brightened. Grasping the child's hand with both of her own and smiling at the young ballerina, she asked the interpreter "How old?" Before the interpreter could put the question to Zuhra, Mrs. Nixon had released the child's hand and ventured a guess as to her age, using her fingers. Zuhra responded almost immediately, holding up all ten fingers, and then raising a hand again to show one finger alone. As everyone in attendance watched, Mrs. Nixon reflected the gestured "eleven" response and then, in an almost seamless movement enfolded Zuhra in her arms. Zuhra clung to the first lady. Personal diplomacy had found expression in a birthday embrace for a child 5,000 miles from home.

But that was only the beginning. Ballerinas who had proceeded through the line abruptly turned and ran back to Mrs. Nixon, intent on "equal time." Chaperones tried in vain to restore the orderly procession of little girls, but they held tight to Mrs. Nixon who, laughing, made no move to stop the children. The reception became a birthday party, no one wishing to leave. The personification of an American mother, the first lady in fact, accompanied by the symbolic potency of a universal gesture, otherwise known as a hug. Détente, from that vantage on an August afternoon, seemed destined to succeed.[8]

Legacy

As the subject of rhetorical analysis, the wife of the thirty-seventh president is easily overlooked. She never sought the limelight; occasions at the podium were rare. To deflect attention she engaged in brevity, but her responses were purposeful and according to members of the media assigned to cover her, successful in the way she was able to connect with her audience for more than three decades in the public spotlight. Once asked to identify her favorite cause, the one with which she would endow the prestige and influence of her position, Patricia Ryan Nixon replied simply: "People are my project" (Eisenhower 1986, 267). Dean of the White House Press Corps and UPI reporter, Helen Thomas declared: "She was the warmest First Lady I covered and the one who loved people most" (Thomas 1975, 165).

The record of accomplishment set by Mrs. Nixon as first lady (1969–1974) is impressive. It includes restoration of White House antiquity, providing inspiration for illuminating federal buildings and monuments of the nation's capital, becoming history's most traveled first lady as an official guest of eighty-three countries, and the first to enter a designated combat zone on foreign soil. She was repeatedly honored by service organizations for revitalizing a spirit of volunteerism nationwide. Between 1959 and 1979, she climbed fourteen times to the heights of the Gallup "Most Admired Women" survey (Watson 2000, 179). And when she died in June 1993, friends and columnists paid tribute to her qualities of character and communicative behavior. Suzanne Fields recalled her "person-to-person attentiveness, her personal touch" (Fields 1993, E1). Ellen Goodman attributed to her a "steadfast" quality and stoicism: "Pat Nixon formed our classic image of the political wife. She was the woman who campaigned once with three broken ribs and another time with a swollen ankle. And she never mentioned it" (Goodman 1993, 33). Chris Matthews eulogized: "Through it all, the great power of Pat Nixon was the simple nerve" (Matthews 1993, F3). But because Mrs. Nixon was by nature reluctant to make herself the subject of conversation, Goodman began her memorial column: "We never knew her. Not really" (Goodman, 1993, A-11).

Ellen Goodman's statement prompts a question: Was Mrs. Nixon's approach, which entailed the preservation of a measure of personal privacy, worth what it cost her image? Though additional factors are attributed to the perception of Mrs. Nixon as remote, biographers, including Eisenhower, Thomas, Caroli, and Anthony all acknowledge to some degree in their biographies the truth of Margaret Truman's assessment that "Pat Nixon is the First Lady nobody knew" (Truman 1995, 188). Gutin goes so far as to suggest that Pat Nixon shirked her responsibility as first lady: "Pat Nixon never impressed her image on the consciousness of Americans. The consummate traditional political wife, she was a nondescript cypher, a woman who preferred to be neutral rather than committed. She was a woman who understood the enormous potential of her position and yet generally rejected it" (Gutin 1989, 61)

This is a difficult assertion to substantiate when applied to specific situations. Guests at the White House, treated to Mrs. Nixon's low-key, personalized approach, did not leave feeling shortchanged. Media access to these events, with rare exceptions, was not limited. Interestingly, however, it was a style so characteristic and expected of Mrs. Nixon that it was taken for granted and not often considered newsworthy.[9] If the ability to "make news" is the primary gauge of one's speaking style, Gutin may have a point. But relying exclusively on such a measure may cause critics to miss the wisdom of a strategy that reaches beyond conventional structural boundaries of a political and rhetorical situation to become uncommonly effective.

As a study of ethos, this essay has focused on two of the three qualities ascribed by Aristotle: character and goodwill. The third component, knowledge or expertise, is every bit as critical. In Mrs. Nixon's case, experience had given her a heightened understanding of people from varied backgrounds and nationalities. In her role as first lady, she put her knowledge to use. Though Caroli suggests that Mrs. Nixon's emphasis on domestic matters was excessive, the fact that fifteen years later Barbara Bush extolled Pat Nixon's style as one to emulate suggests recognition of qualities both endearing and enduring (Weinraub 1989, A20). What is meaningful for this study is that her conduct was grounded in her field of expertise, reflected her probity, and demonstrated her benevolence. It "revealed her character" and enhanced her credibility both nationally and internationally. It was not uniformly understood or appreciated, although somewhere in Russia a former ballerina (and now her children) probably recalls, with a certain fondness, the lady who embraced her on her birthday.

Personal diplomacy was a sophisticated rhetorical strategy, but there is nothing about Mrs. Nixon's demeanor to indicate that it was calculated. She appears to have possessed a capacity, if not instinctive, then impeccably disciplined to respond to heartfelt need. It is fair to say that by adulthood this is who Pat Nixon was as a human being. She did acknowledge in at least one interview: "I'm a perfectionist. I won't do a thing without trying to do it well" (Meyers 1960, 24).

She never aspired to the role of first lady, or a life in politics. Within the framework of public service she sought—and found—those who needed her. The inherent motivation that Kenneth Burke locates in human action is at least implied in Meyers' account of a rare, unguarded moment:

> Recently a young friend asked about the rigors of public life. Pat's eyes suddenly filled with tears. "I've given up everything I ever loved," she blurted, and looked out the window until composure returned. Then she continued: "The people who lose out are the children. Any of the glamour or reward in it comes to the grownups. It's the children who really suffer." (Meyers 1960, 25)

Patricia Nixon adhered rigidly and dutifully to protocol, traditionally understood and personally endorsed. But there were key moments in her career, a few described in this essay, when compassion overruled her strict sense of duty. Her impulsive departure from the decorum of the moment may have been persuasive in part because she so assiduously maintained strict decorum so much of the time.

Attention to the significance of balance may be what a study of Mrs. Nixon's self-styled personal diplomacy most strongly suggests. Her penchant for privacy has been noted. In her rhetorical demeanor, it extended beyond a sense of personal decorum to set a tone of conduct that appears to have satisfied a public need. Pat Nixon's image provided an equilibrium and fortitude when compared with that of her spouse in the era they shared. Edwin Black has written of the former president: "Experienced and skillful as he was a rhetor, he was never quite able to sequester his private life in the way that other public figures routinely do, or at least did prior to Nixon's presidency" (Black 1999, 1). Pat was, however, enabled or compelled by the events of Nixon's turbulent career to master the skill. Black notes that Richard Nixon himself recalled in two separate autobiographies the devastating effect that exposing personal and family financial details as part of the Checkers Speech defense in the 1952 presidential campaign had on Pat. Black keenly observes:

> Hannah [Nixon's mother] and Pat embodied privacy for Nixon, but they were not alone in their sensitivity to the pain of his disclosure. Anyone with a reverence for the privacy of family matters and a commitment to the pieties of the public-private allocation may have regarded Nixon's financial divulgence as an act of voluntary mortification, a brave and painful conquest of inhibition in the service of a higher candor. For an audience imbued with the values of privacy, the Checkers speech was a trial by embarrassment through which Nixon triumphantly passed before their very eyes. (Black 1999, 12)

Pat Nixon appeared to complete her husband's triumph. Her embodiment of the value of privacy with which many Americans identified certainly contributed to the pathos of the Nixons' financial disclosure episode in 1952. Her stoic dignity became an undeviating stance in times of crisis. Emotion overcame her only once, at Nixon's concession in Los Angeles the morning following the 1960 presidential election. Print and broadcast journalists conspicuously included mention of her stoic demeanor in reporting events of Nixon's political career. It signaled such a distinct contrast to her warmth and effusiveness that it served as a cue. Viewers observed the same resolute expression of the Checkers Speech broadcast in the gaze she maintained during her husband's resignation as he bid his staff farewell on August 9, 1974. It had become a demeanor on which the public could rely; its persuasive value may have been derived from its consistent maintenance.[10]

This demeanor continued to reflect Pat Nixon even after she left the White House. It was a period marked by silence. Prior to the debilitating stroke in 1976, she neither wrote nor commissioned a personal memoir. Her daughter Julie published the most comprehensive biography, but key staff members whose admiration for her was profound appear to have followed Mrs. Nixon's lead and are thus far content to let events of her life speak for themselves. Yet events encompass and contain facts. David Zarefsky (1998, 20) reminds those who would "do" rhetorical history, "Facts cannot speak for themselves; they must be spoken for."[11] A fuller understanding and appreciation of Mrs. Nixon's persuasive capacities will depend on the willingness of those who knew her well to share their recollections. Insufficient source material for comprehensive appraisal hinders any opportunity to appreciate forgotten virtues.

Civic virtue is persuasive, so long as it is perceived as genuine. But even in that event, it may be taken for granted and go unnoticed. Its short-term effect is apt to be confined to the context in which it occurs. If one's behavior as part of a rhetorical strategy needs to attract a certain attention, it is an inappropriate demeanor. If perceived as feigned, any appearance of integrity will likely prove counterproductive.

In the long term, however, the exemplification of civic virtue still has the capacity to ennoble a culture and its people, provided the virtues themselves continue to be valued and recorded as such. "The eyes of the beholder" or the identification that may occur between critic and subject will influence who emerges as heroic according to timeless and timely criteria. Socrates' dignity still inspires, but so too does Quintilian for preserving Socrates as he does: "he preferred that what remained of his life should be lost rather than that portion of it which was past. . . . he committed himself to the judgment of posterity [by] conduct honorable to his character as a man" (Watson 1856, Bk. II, ch. 11, p. 1). The persuasive effect of conduct may likewise depend on "the judgment of posterity." More than we realize may hinge on Zarefsky's "fourth sense" or as someone close to Patricia Nixon once said: "who writes the history" (Hobgood 1974e).

Notes

Portions of this essay were presented as "Conduct Becoming: Pat Nixon and the Rhetoric of Personal Diplomacy," at the Southern States Communication Association Convention,

Lexington, Kentucky, April 7, 2001.

The author extends appreciation to Welford D. Taylor, Jerry Tarver, and Kathleen J. Turner for their valued suggestions and superb editing. Julie Eisenhower, Jinny Bartlett, and Joe Bartlett, who provided similar assistance, graciously shared their knowledge and recollections of Pat Nixon as well. My deepest thanks.

1. From Plato's Gorgias (Bennett 1993, 98–99).

2. Even before the Nixons moved into the White House, security had required the parking of buses, bumper to bumper, so as to surround the White House grounds to protect the first family from the more violent demonstrators.

3. The term "fungible narrative" was, to my knowledge, first provided by Craig Allen Smith in his text *Political Communication* (1990, 94–95). It refers to the fact that what we do not know "about human motives, problems, relationships, and their resolutions," we infer from entertainment, from dramas we've seen. In other words, what we have no way of knowing about Pat Nixon, we "absorb" (hence, fungible), much as a sponge absorbs moisture, from such sources as Oliver Stone's film *Nixon* or reruns of *Saturday Night Live*. Eventually, what we know to be true and what we have inferred from entertainment sources become blurred—too blurred to make distinctions.

4. Professor Kathleen Turner, who served as panel respondent at the SSCA Conference in Lexington, Kentucky, April 2001, described her own reaction watching Pat Nixon during the Checkers Speech. Members of the panel audience nodded a unanimous agreement as she was apparently voicing their own impressions of the actual or taped broadcast.

5. Epitaph on cemetery monument at Mrs. Nixon's grave.

6. Though Lady Bird Johnson delivered 164 speeches during her husband's presidency, Betty Caroli writes: "Unlike Eleanor Roosevelt, Lady Bird did not thrive on the controversies inherent in politics, and she disapproved of First Ladies who involved themselves in issues that might divide the country" (1987, 237, 241). That Johnson's position was more the expected norm for first ladies by the public audience of her era is implied.

7. The review actually praised the children's ballet performance, but found the adults' performance less than impressive (Lewis 1973, D3).

8. The reception was hardly noted by the media. The best account is Tom Shales (1973, D1, D3).

9. On one occasion in particular during the summer of 1974 when this author was especially moved by Mrs. Nixon's gesture of kindness to a visitor, her press secretary Helen McCain Smith rejected apologies for display of emotion saying, "No, it's good to be reminded of Mrs. Nixon's rare qualities. We see them so frequently, we can become too accustomed to her unique way with people."

10. It failed her only once as has been noted, during Richard Nixon's November 9, 1960, concession speech at the Ambassador Hotel in Los Angeles, shortly after midnight following his presidential election defeat. She learned from the experience. On the final day of Nixon's presidency, his family was unaware until they arrived on the main floor of the White House, that there was to be media coverage of the staff farewell. Pat Nixon acknowledged almost no staff members who were assembled in the East Room of the White House. When her husband finished speaking, the family proceeded to the South Lawn for departure. Afterward, she placed a call to Helen Smith. In her determination to retain composure, she had failed to say good-bye.

11. Similar commentary by Richard Weaver is: "The supposition that facts will speak for themselves is of course another abdication of the intellect" (1948, 58).

References

Anthony, Carl Sferranza. 1991. *First Ladies: The Saga of Presidents' Wives and Their Power, 1961–1990*, Vol. 2. New York: Quill/William Morrow.

Bennett, William, ed. 1993. Plato on Self-Discipline: Selections from *Gorgias*. In *Book of Virtues*. New York: Simon & Schuster.

Black, Edwin. 1999. Richard Nixon and the Privacy of Public Discourse. *Rhetoric and Public Affairs*, 2:1, 1–29.

Burke, Kenneth. 1954. *Permanence and Change: An Anatomy of Purpose*. Los Altos, Calif.: Hermes Publications.

———. 1969. *A Grammar of Motives*. Berkeley, Calif.: University of California Press.

Caroli, Betty Boyd. 1987. *First Ladies*. New York: Oxford University Press.

Cowan, Ruth. 1953. Pat Nixon's Story Pales Movie Script Writers' Best Try. *Washington Post*, 18 January.

David, Lester. 1978. *The Lonely Lady of San Clemente*. New York: Crowell.

Eisenhower, Julie. 1986. *Pat Nixon: The Untold Story*. New York: Simon & Schuster.

———. 2001. Interview on CNN's *Larry King Live*. Broadcast 20 June.

Fields, Suzanne. 1993. First Ladies' New First. *Washington Times*, 28 June.

Goodman, Ellen. 1993. Pat Nixon Was the First Lady of Virtue, Loyalty, and Family. *Richmond-Times Dispatch*, 26 June.

Gould, Lewis L. 1996. *American First Ladies: Their Lives and Their Legacy*. New York: Garland.

Gutin, Myra G. 1989. *The President's Partner: The First Lady in the Twentieth Century*. New York: Greenwood.

Hobgood, Linda. 1974a. Interview with Susan Dolibois, June.

———. 1974b. Interviews with Susan Porter Rose, June and July.

———. 1974c. Interview with Gwen King, July.

———. 1974d. Interview with Helen Smith, July.

———. 1974e. Interview with Richard M. Nixon, 5 August.

———. 2000. Interview with Mrs. William Broomfield (Jane), 26 October

———. 2001. Telephone Interview with Virginia B. Bartlett, 11 July.

Kaiser, Robert G. 1972. Soviet Media Play Up Nixon Visit. *Washington Post*, 24 May, A12.

Ladies Day in Moscow. 1972. *Newsweek*, 5 June, 79.

Lewis, Jean Battery. 1973. Less Than Inspired. *Washington Post*. 4 August, D3.

Matthews, Chris. 1993. Dignity and Grace in a Cloth Coat. *Washington Times*, 25 June.

———. 1997. *Kennedy and Nixon: The Rivalry That Shaped Postwar America*. New York: Simon & Schuster.

McPherson, Myra. 1975. The Blooming of Betty Ford. *McCalls*, September.

Meyers, Burt. 1960. The Silent Partner. *Time*, 29 February, 24–26.

Pat in Moscow: A Busy Week. 1972. *U.S. News and World Report*, 5 June.

Safire, William. 1975. *Before the Fall*. New York: Doubleday.

Sattler, William M. 1947. Conceptions of Ethos in Ancient Rhetoric. *Speech Monographs*, 55–65.

Schamber, Jon F., and Russell W. Vinyard. 2000. Cicero Revisited: A Look Back on Citizenship for the Rhetorician. Paper presented at the National Communication Association, Seattle, Wash., 9 November.

Shales, Tom. 1973. Stealing the Show at the White House. *Washington Post*. 4 August, D1, D3.

Smith, Craig Allen. 1990. *Political Communication*. San Diego: Harcourt Brace Jovanovich.

Thomas, Helen. 1975. *Dateline: The White House.* New York: Macmillan.

Truman, Margaret. 1995. *First Ladies.* New York: Random House.

Watson, John Selby. 1856. *Quintilian's Institutes of Oratory: Or Education of an Orator.* London: Henry G. Bohn.

Watson, Robert P. 2000. *The Presidents' Wives: Reassessing the Office of First Lady.* Boulder, Colo.: Lynne Rienner.

Weaver, Richard. 1948. *Ideas Have Consequences.* Chicago: University of Chicago Press.

Weinraub, Bernard. 1989. A Down-to-Earth Tenant for an Exclusive Address. *New York Times,* 15 January, A1, A20.

Will, George. 1975. Calculations. *National Review,* 12 September, 984.

Zarefsky, David. 1998. Four Senses of Rhetorical History. In *Doing Rhetorical History,* ed. Kathleen J. Turner, 19–32. Tuscaloosa, Ala.: University of Alabama Press.

Chapter 16

Betty Ford
A Certain Comfort from a Candid First Lady

Nichola D. Gutgold and Linda B. Hobgood

Being ladylike does not require silence.

—Betty Ford

Her White House stay was short-lived, but the lessons of Betty Ford's experience remain vividly instructive. By accident of a national political crisis which catapulted her to the rank of first lady in 1974, Mrs. Ford's tenure lasted a brief two years until her husband, Gerald R. Ford lost his bid for reelection. During that time, she developed a relationship of candor with the press and public. She spoke her mind on social and moral issues that were at the forefront of public debate. The positions she took were not always popular with the majority of Americans, many of whom complained bitterly especially after her notorious interview on CBS's *60 Minutes*. Indeed, Mrs. Ford's rhetorical responses between 1974 and 1976 show how difficult it can be for a well-meaning public figure who must learn—"onstage"—to fill the role into which she had been so abruptly cast.

Taking full advantage of the considerable visibility and influence of the office of first lady, Betty Ford became a voice for the causes she supported. But public backlash and her reply are reminders that taking part in a controversy, even inadvertently, exacts a price. The risks taken by Mrs. Ford illustrate possible consequences when endearing traits of a first lady's character "collide" with the enduring values of many of her fellow citizens. An unintended effect of Mrs.

325

Ford's experience demonstrates that presidential campaigns do prepare candidates and their wives for interaction with a national audience that is eager to know them. Unfortunately, Mrs. Ford did not have this benefit.

Mrs. Ford's persuasive efforts as first lady grew in sophistication as she gained experience in that position; she continued to build upon what she had learned from being the wife of a politician and the other roles she had played. We begin with an account of Mrs. Ford's childhood, education, work experience, and marriage to show some of the qualities of character that she brought to the office of first lady. We trace her experiences as the wife of a senator and mother of four children to indicate how "ready" she was rhetorically to assume the position of first lady. Using articles in print media and personal interview accounts, we discuss the role expectations that many Americans held for a president's wife at the time when Mrs. Ford was called to serve. Finally, we show how all of these factors came into play when she spoke her mind candidly to the American public. We use excerpts from Mrs. Ford's speeches, but focus primarily on CBS's televised interview on *60 Minutes* between Mrs. Ford and interviewer Morley Safer. Aired on Sunday, August 21, 1975, this interview prompted thousands of letters, most of them negative. The way Mrs. Ford chose to answer her critics speaks to her own strength of character and her capacity to "measure up" and become accustomed to the demands of her position. Her rhetorical choices reveal an uncommon consistency. By virtue of those choices she was able to regain the admiration of an impressive majority of Americans, whose support she maintained through difficult times following her years as first lady. Indeed, over time Betty Ford learned to put her candor to use for the public good.

Biography

One can almost hear the enthymeme:
Betty Ford is so honest and forthright, so humble and friendly!
Well, of course—look where she's from!

To fully appreciate the character of Elizabeth Bloomer Ford requires understanding what it means to be "Midwestern." People from the Midwest are thought to be "comfortable with who they are. They have a common decency." There is more to it than mere birthright, though by virtue of her place of birth, Chicago, and her childhood home of Grand Rapids, Michigan, Betty Ford certainly qualifies as Midwestern. And despite subtle differences between, say, Hoosiers and Minnesotans, the similarities outweigh the differences and symbolically unify those who belong to the America's geographical "middle." If there is a single identifying attribute among all of those born "Midwesterners," it seems to be candor, including an appreciation for those who are straightforward in manner and speech.

New York Times reporter Jane Howard recalls:

When the President [Ford] promised "straight talk among friends" in his Inaugural Address, he was speaking at least as much for his wife, whose low-key candor quickly surpassed his own. She was full of surprises, this kindly matron from Michigan. (Howard 1974, 64)

Betty Ford scholars (Anthony, Caroli, Gould, Gutin, and Truman among others) all highlight her frankness, but to this most attach another trait, a genuine sense of concern for and about others. They tend to assign regional distinction to this virtue as well. Observes Howard:

> In many ways she is ordinary, well schooled in the midwestern arts of assuaging and consoling. Her thank you notes are prompt and heartfelt. Nice gestures come naturally. . . . "Betty Ford was nice to me," recalls the ex-wife of one controversial Senator, "when other people weren't." But she's not just nice. No. The merely nice bypass the truth when it makes them or anyone else edgy, and that's something Betty Ford doesn't do. She never has. (Howard 1974, 64)

At least two additional qualities are implied in the kindness attributed to Betty Ford: a matter-of-fact, bedrock honesty, and a sense of humility. One of her friends, Jane Broomfield, who is the wife of a colleague of Gerald Ford's, offers tribute to this blend of honesty and self-effacement: "People in the Midwest are just open. Well, at least in Michigan they are. . . . They [the Fords] are great 'truth-tellers.' But she [Betty] could feel terrible and you'd never know it. There was no small talk about herself—ever" (Hobgood, 2000b). Biographer and daughter of another president, Margaret Truman, compared the preferences of two first ladies: "what Betty Ford shared with Bess Truman was a midwestern dislike for any and all kinds of pretentiousness" (Truman 1995, 133).

Mrs. Ford was not the first first lady to be embraced by "the folks back home" who claimed to know her best. For example, Lady Bird Johnson has, for many years, symbolized to Texans and non-Texans alike many of the qualities for which that state is so proud. But it is striking that Mrs. Ford is repeatedly viewed as personifying those same four virtues of frankness, concern for others, honesty, and humility. And while it is allowed that those qualities seem particularly evident among those whose origins are Midwestern, they are used in regard to Betty Ford in an apparent effort to associate her with qualities that are quintessentially American, too. Historian Lewis Gould, who calls her "outspoken—but never strident," assigns her other highly valued aspects of the American character such as an independent spirit and a sense of humor (1996, 553). Carl Anthony uses the first lady's own typically American tendency to convey her forthright attitude: "When somebody asks you how you stand on an issue," explained Betty Ford of her policy of candor, "you're very foolish if you try to beat around the bush—you just meet yourself going around the bush the other way" (1991, 553).

Mrs. Ford's character is thus clearly and uniformly understood, both by those who have known her and those who have studied her. According to Gutin, "Betty Ford is more sharply defined in the minds of Americans than most First Ladies" (1989, 122). One of the reasons for her popularity was the generally held opinion that this particular lady of the White House was the same person in

Washington political circles as the one who had grown up in Grand Rapids and who had raised a family in the suburbs of Alexandria, Virginia. But as Anthony notes, perhaps wryly, there were occasions when "the private person collided with the public persona" (1991, 225). The events she considered significant in her own life and the people Betty Ford most admired might help to explain such "collisions."

Evident in both of her memoirs, *The Times of My Life* (1978) and *A Glad Awakening* (1987), is Betty Ford's genuine fondness for people. But she reserves highest praise for a special few among them, such as her parents. Born in 1918, she was the only daughter of parents she describes as attractive, hardworking, and devoted to each other. Her father's sales career meant constant travel; Betty recalls with tenderness that her mother wrote him every night when he was away. Betty's mother was "rather formal" and protectively firm. She insisted her daughter wear hat and gloves when they went shopping and while Betty didn't object to the accessories, she tried to explain to her mother that other girls went without them. Mrs. Bloomer was adamant, and Betty comments almost as an afterthought that her mother might not always approve the more lenient approach Betty used with her own daughter. In her first memoir, *The Times of My Life*, Betty remembers her mother's resolve, this time in the midst of a rainstorm:

> I can still feel my mother's arms around me, holding me as she stood on the porch and we watched a storm come rolling in across the lake, waves swelling, thunder crashing, lightning slicing the sky, and my mother telling me how beautiful it was. I found out later she was scared to death, but she taught me not to be afraid; I was safe in those arms. (B. Ford 1978, 7)

Later, she tried to emulate that resolve with her own children.

As an adolescent, Betty Ford enjoyed school and loved dancing classes. "Dance was my happiness," she wrote, and she dreamed of a professional dancing career. Her father's sudden, accidental death when Betty was sixteen meant, "It was rougher for everybody after that. . . . he was gone and we'd loved him" (B. Ford 1978, 22). Betty's dream of training in New York to further her career seemed extravagant and to her mother too risky for Betty at the time. "It wouldn't have done me any good to fuss, and I wasn't the kind to run away; the bond between my mother and me was strong" (23). Betty was, however, permitted to spend summers at the Bennington School of Dance in Vermont. It was there that she met Martha Graham, arguably one of the strongest and most lasting influences on Mrs. Ford's life. She says:

> It's almost impossible to describe the impression made by Martha Graham on a girl who came to her straight out of high school. I worshipped her as a goddess. She was a tough disciplinarian. . . . But, as I've said before, I admired that kind of strictness. You can't be a dancer without it; not only your body, but also your mind must be disciplined. (B. Ford 1978, 24)

Betty went to New York to study with Martha Graham's troupe, and she also found work as a fashion model. But at her mother's urging she returned to

Grand Rapids where she taught dance. She married a friend from childhood, but it did not last. After the divorce, Betty devoted herself to a career in retail fashion at a local department store. In 1947, she met a very disciplined young man, Gerald R. Ford, whom Betty called "the most eligible bachelor in Grand Rapids" (B. Ford 1978, 47). She clearly admired his determination. In October 1948, they were married and within a month her husband defeated an incumbent congressman in his first election bid to the U.S. House of Representatives.

Neither Ford imagined that the victory in 1948 was the beginning of twenty-eight years in the nation's capital. The beginning of their marriage and the start of Jerry Ford's congressional career coincided. Betty recalls that she eagerly became dedicated to both. She was convinced that her husband's political success was made more likely by her support and involvement, but this did not always translate into traveling together back to the district, or routinely accompanying him on endless rounds of political and diplomatic engagements. In Betty's case, this meant remaining behind, managing a household flawlessly, and performing the role of both mother and father in the absence of her husband.

During these years, the Ford family grew to include three sons and a daughter, each of whom maintained an increasingly active schedule. Betty coordinated these schedules, provided all necessary transportation, and accepted the many volunteer tasks that school and extracurricular involvements demand of parents (B. Ford 1978, 64–69, 92–95). In addition, she did what many congressional spouses do to augment the constituent service provided by the congressional offices. She mastered the layout and schedule of activities in Washington, D.C., and became a travel guide for visitors from the Michigan district and elsewhere (B. Ford, 1978, 63). Furthermore, as her husband's stature and rank on the minority side of the aisle grew, so did Betty's understanding of the potential reach and influence of legislators' wives who volunteer in Washington-area civic and philanthropic activities. As her husband rose to the position of House minority leader, Betty's volunteer activities increased, and she helped to raise funds by drawing media attention and public support to a vast array of worthy causes (B. Ford 1978, 121–22). She goaded the wives of fellow Republican senators and congressmen into participating as models in charity fashion shows. Her own account is illustrative of her outlook:

> Since Jerry had become an important Republican, I had taken it upon myself to shake up the Republican wives. I thought the Democratic wives were more effective. "If anybody asks you to do anything, say yes," I advised my peers. "Get off your duffs. It's always the Democratic wives who model in the fashion shows for Multiple Sclerosis or the Heart Fund." I coerced a lot of women who'd never done any modeling in their lives into chasing up and down runways for charity, and they got so they liked it. Nobody made me take on these jobs; I was convinced it was my duty. (B. Ford 1978, 121–22)

Betty's role as an active wife and mother sounds remarkably typical for a congressional wife of the '60s and early '70s. But the degree to which she succeeded is not. What is more typical in political situations such as hers is the gradual loss of attention to some aspect of life or another. The balance of family life and political involvement can be daunting; the noteworthy element in this phase of Betty Ford's career while her husband served in Congress is her singular talent in achieving that balance. She was both model political partner and dedicated mother, and she remained as popular with congressional wives and with old friends in Grand Rapids as with the neighbors on Crown View Drive in Alexandria, Virginia. She had proven that she was a dedicated political partner who had even discovered ways to fit that lifestyle to her own particular talents. In some ways she appears to have thrived on the challenge of the balancing act. Had it not been for the aggravation of a pinched nerve that eventually led her to seek help from a psychiatrist, she might have survived painlessly, even triumphantly, a most demanding time (B. Ford 1978, 174–78).

In part, because of her physical discomfort, Betty had exacted a promise from her husband to retire from Congress. Watching his dream of becoming Speaker of the House grow dim in the early '70s, Jerry Ford had agreed to run one last time in 1974, and then retire. As minority leader he was attending more than 250 engagements annually and time with his family had become too infrequent. But the resignation of Vice President Agnew in the fall 1973 altered abruptly the Fords' plans. Instead of looking to retire, Gerald Ford was named Agnew's successor by President Nixon. Ten months later, Nixon resigned the presidency and on August 9, 1974, Gerald R. Ford was sworn in as president of the United States and Betty Bloomer Ford became first lady.

In the aftermath of the Watergate crisis, Gerald Ford made every effort to distance himself from former president Nixon and all that had characterized his presidency. Early on, he issued statements to indicate the kind of administration he intended to set up. The hallmark of his presidency, he vowed, would be a spirit of honesty and openness. Betty concurred in this commitment and tried to do her part. Both Fords were determined to be truthful and to them this meant being candid, even spontaneous in their interactions with the press. While not an uncommon initial approach for some candidates and their wives, political campaigns have a way of tempering this communication objective.

According to Jules Witcover in *No Way to Pick a President* (1999), national campaigns are essential to the electoral process. They help citizens assess candidates' fitness for office, and they help candidates articulate what values and initiatives to pursue. Campaigns also groom the teams of people closest to the candidates—family, staff, and aides—all of whom benefit from their interaction with media and public. They gather insights into national audience values and can then adapt their positions accordingly. Gerald and Betty Ford, thrust as they were into office by unusual circumstances, had no opportunity to learn from such national campaigns.

Gerald Ford, however, was accustomed to campaigning for state office; indeed, his seniority in Congress had been earned by twelve successful campaigns for the Michigan House seat. His constant travel on behalf of Republican colleagues had made him a familiar face across the country as well. But when Betty Ford considered what a national constituency might expect from her as a first lady, her thoughts turned to Grand Rapids and Crown View Drive. She had no familiarity whatsoever with any constituency beyond the Michigan congressional district. Her Alexandria neighbors who knew her best liked her just as she was. Historian James T. Baker wrote: "Untrained to be a President's wife, she could be just the one to turn the First Lady into a human being at last" (Baker 1976, 864). And Anthony quoted Mrs. Ford as saying "I've spent too many years as me. . . . I can't suddenly turn into a princess" (Anthony 1991, 224).

Rhetorical Activities as First Lady

"What state dinner?"

Less than twenty-four hours after her husband's swearing-in Betty Ford received a call informing her that within the week she was scheduled to host a White House dinner for King Hussein and Queen Alia of Jordan. For events such as these, Betty's years as a Washington hostess came in handy. "I've been coming up through the ranks, so it isn't like being thrown into the front lines straight from Grand Rapids," she reminds readers in her 1978 memoir (162). By experience thus mobilized, the new first lady and her husband made known their intended modus operandi, a policy of availability and openness. President Ford, addressing a joint session of Congress on August 12, "[told] legislators he [did not] want a honeymoon with them. 'I want a good marriage. . . . My office door has always been open and that is how it is going to be at the White House'" (B. Ford 1978, 163).

In this spirit, members of the Ford family made themselves accessible to the media. Statements made by the Ford children, however, promptly placed the president in the position of accounting for their remarks and dissociating himself from some of their more extreme statements. Ford explained that his children had always been encouraged to speak their minds, though he did not always share their views.

Betty, too, was eager to meet with members of the press and did so in the East Room of the White House less than a month after her arrival. In what Gutin calls the first official press conference by a first lady in twenty-two years (Gutin 1989, 131), Mrs. Ford answered questions and echoed her husband's acknowledgment that as parents they made no attempt to regulate their children's comments. Relaxed and unrehearsed, Betty's maternal persona projected the means by which she sought to identify with the American press and public. Determined to convey accessibility, she announced those programs to which she would direct her attention and presented an agenda of her own. She spoke in favor of ratification of the Equal Rights Amendment and of increased participation by women in public office. On the issue of abortion she expressed support for the pro-choice position.

These were not official positions of the Ford administration. As the president had always emphasized, the first lady had a right to her own opinion and she felt free to offer it. Mrs. Ford herself writes:

> I tried to be honest; I tried not to dodge subjects. I felt the public had a right to know where I stood. Nobody had to feel the way I felt, I wasn't forcing my

opinions on anybody, but if someone asked me a question, I gave that person a straight answer. I've been told that I didn't play it safe enough, but my husband has always been totally supportive. He's never stepped on my toes; he's never turned around and complained, "Well, that was a dumb thing to say." (B. Ford 1978, 205–6)

In any case, it became clear almost from the beginning of Ford's term that the statements coming from the East and West Wings of the White House in this administration might be distinctly different messages.

In mid-September 1974, President Ford issued a pardon for his predecessor, Richard M. Nixon. The pardon overwhelmed all actions prior to and many that followed Ford's decision. Betty recalls, "Jerry's administration had begun with a flood of good will and good wishes from all kinds of people who liked his decency, his friendliness, his accessibility, his ability to laugh at himself" (B. Ford 1978, 180). This amicable atmosphere (note Betty's use of the same "Midwestern" adjectives!) might have continued indefinitely, but President Ford's pardon of his predecessor marked its end. Then another one of those dramatic, unpredictable circumstances intervened to affect public opinion of the first lady in a manner both sympathetic and compelling.

Just weeks after the pardon, a malignancy was discovered during a routine medical examination of Mrs. Ford, and she underwent almost immediately a radical mastectomy. Gratitude for the assured success of the operation merged in Betty Ford's reaction to the ordeal with a sudden awareness of the power she held as a first lady:

> I got a lot of credit for having gone public with my mastectomy, but if I hadn't been the wife of the President of the United States, the press would not have come racing after my story. . . . Even before I was able to get up, I lay in bed and watched television and saw on the news shows lines of women queued up to go in for breast examinations because of what had happened to me. Lying in the hospital, thinking of all those women going for cancer checkups because of me, I'd come to recognize more clearly the power of the woman in the White House. Not my power, but the power of the position, a power which could be used to help. (B. Ford 1978, 194)

It is hard to imagine anything that could have brought this realization into focus with greater clarity or impact.

Recognition of the power of the office coincided with an oversight by the president, which, although pale by comparison, heightened the Fords' sensitivity to image and protocol. In November 1974, not long after Betty's return to the White House following her surgery, President Ford departed for a scheduled visit to Japan. At a formal dinner, he was photographed with Emperor Hirohito. Ford's dress trousers, "left over from college," appeared too short, and he suffered a fair share of ridicule from the media. Betty commented: "Well, if you're going to assume the office, you have to assume the striped pants that go with it. The public expects a president to dress well; he can't just say to hell with protocol" (B. Ford, 197).

As Betty gained experience in the office of first lady, she increasingly understood the purposes protocol serves beyond mere conformity to expectations. She acknowledged this to the Carters who followed the Fords into the White House when she said:

> The news out of the Carter camp was that they were going to do away with protocol, but I think they're gradually coming around to understanding there's a reason for the forms and the ceremonies, a certain comfort in being prepared. (Howard 1974, 68)

The irony of this statement, coming from a woman hailed for her spontaneity and her "impromptu valor" is striking. The context of her statement was intended as commentary on the comparative advantages of coming to the White House from a House or Senate seat as opposed to a gubernatorial position. Nevertheless, after two and a half years and a presidential race that had proved grueling for the Fords, this first lady who didn't stand on ceremony had acquired an appreciation for decorum. Admittedly, she was not a fan of protocol for its own sake, but she wisely recognized its advantages in enhancing incumbency and in sustaining a certain public ethos.

There were times when she intentionally flaunted traditional norms and was heralded for doing so. Congressional wives invited to lunch at the White House were seated by an egalitarian method, reaching for a number in a hat, rather than the routine hierarchical arrangement according to their husbands' level of seniority or leadership rank. On more than one occasion, she impishly clowned for reporters, and they demonstrated their appreciation by showering her with favorable attention. If taking credit for her husband's appointment of a woman, Carla Hills, to his cabinet, or an insistence that her mentor Martha Graham be awarded one of the nation's highest honors for her contribution to the arts seemed effrontery on Betty's part to some, it was praised by others. And when Rabbi Sage suffered a heart attack just as he was about to make a presentation to Mrs. Ford at the 1976 Jewish National Fund Dinner, she spontaneously led the assembled guests in prayer, amazing many by her sensitivity and presence of mind in a crisis. Betty Ford abandoned her prepared script and stated impromptu:

> Can we all bow our heads for a moment for Rabbi Sage? He is going to the hospital and needs our prayers. Would you rise and bow your heads. (Pause) I'll have to say it in my own words. Dear Father in Heaven, we ask thy blessing on this magnificent man, Rabbi Sage. We know you can take care of him. We know you can bring him back to us. We know you are our leader. You are our strength. You are what life is all about. Love and love of fellowman is what we all need and depend on. Please, dear God. Let's all join together in a silent prayer for Rabbi Sage. (Silent prayer approximately 1 minute) Thank you very much. I know it will mean a great deal to him, and I know it means a great deal to me. (Ford Library, 1976)

In the aftermath of her episode with breast cancer, Mrs. Ford was unanimously praised for being so open with the public about her surgery, prognosis, and treatment in the months following the operation. In a phone interview with

Linda Hobgood (2000b), Jane Broomfield emphasized the unprecedented nature of the publicity that surrounded Betty Ford's cancer surgery. Prior to her potentially life-threatening experience, publication of such personal information and private details would have been unthinkable. As with so many events in her life, Betty Ford was denied the luxury of time to consider how she would share the news of her malignancy. Having acknowledged that she had sought help from a psychiatrist and benefited from his assistance, she must have judged breast cancer to be at least as important. Moreover, the first lady's experience might help to allay fears about cancer in other victims. Her decision to allow such publicity is one of several examples of what Gould refers to as "the combination of personality and circumstance [that] made Betty Ford a valuable First Lady who could not have been more in touch with her times" (Gould 1996, 553). After speaking with Mrs. Ford in a telephone interview, Nichola Gutgold (1998) calls this a reflection of Betty's "impromptu valor."

Still, there were those "collisions" noted by Anthony among others. Less than a year after her bout with breast cancer, Betty Ford began receiving, instead of the thousands of encouraging greetings from well-wishers around the world, expressions of indignation and resentment from those whose support the president most needed. This unfriendly mail, and the less-than-kind editorials that appeared in late August and September 1975, seemed something other than signs of a woman "in touch with her times."

Eleven days following Gerald Ford's official announcement that he planned to run for president in the upcoming 1976 election, CBS-TV promised "an unusual interview with an unusual woman . . . completely frank as she discusses her attitudes toward her role" for its popular Sunday evening program *60 Minutes* on August 21, 1975. Gerald Ford had just marked the first anniversary of his swearing-in as president. Morley Safer, in an exclusive interview with Mrs. Ford in the family quarters of the White House, selected a series of questions, some never before asked of a sitting first lady. According to Anthony:

> She expounded on past revelations, speaking of seeing a psychiatrist, and on the Supreme Court Roe v. Wade judgment. The First Lady said it was "the best thing in the world . . . a great, great decision. . . . She thought smoking marijuana had become as routine for youth as the "first beer" had been for her generation. The one answer of Mrs. Ford's that would spin the nation's TV antennae, however, was not a view she'd previously expressed. When asked about whether it was immoral for young people to live together before marriage, she retorted, "Well, they are, aren't they?" She thought it might even limit the high divorce rate. Then Safer followed up with "the question." "What if Susan Ford came to you and said, "Mother, I'm having an affair?" For a brief second, Betty was silent, then calmly replied, "Well, I wouldn't be surprised . . . she's a perfectly normal human being . . . if she wanted to continue . . . I would certainly counsel and advise her on the subject." (Anthony 1991, 248)

Betty Ford described what followed in a wry understatement: "My stock with the public did not go up. It went down, rapidly" (B. Ford 1978, 206). *Newsweek* reported that *60 Minutes* received more mail following the Betty Ford interview than at any time in the history of the CBS program. According to journalists Peer, Whitmore, and Whitman, "by October, the mail totaled more than thirty-three thousand pieces, with letters opposing her opinion outnumbering those supporting it by two to one" (1975, 19). Gould called the reaction to the interview "astonishing" (1996, 548), and Anthony listed a variety of organizations and individuals who took issue with Mrs. Ford's comments: "the Los Angeles Police Department [and] a Texas minister [W. A. Criswell who] called it [a] 'gutter type mentality'" (1991, 250). Betty Ford became the first first lady since Frances Cleveland to be censured by the Women's Christian Temperance Union (Peer et al. 1975, 19). President Ford himself anticipated fallout: "Jerry remained his usual dear funny self," recalled his wife. "He told the press that when he first heard what I'd said he thought he'd lost ten million votes. 'Then when I read about it, I raised that to twenty million'" (B. Ford 1978, 208). Prominent individuals including evangelist Billy Graham and popular entertainer Bing Crosby took exception to Mrs. Ford's comments. The governor of Georgia, Jimmy Carter and his wife Rosalynn were asked the same question about their daughter and reported they would be shocked by the circumstances that would not have surprised Mrs. Ford.

While most who registered a negative response cited disagreement with specific positions taken in the interview, at least one magazine, *Newsweek*, reported the obvious: "Not all Americans share Betty Ford's views—especially those who believe a First Lady should exemplify moral rectitude in speech as well as behavior" (Peer, Whitmore, and Whitman 1975, 19). Another editorial writer objected to her comments as representing "a manifest abuse of her position as First Lady. They constituted a failure of taste that reflected a failure of understanding":

> the issue is therefore, one of propriety. As First Lady, Mrs. Ford enjoys a wide audience and some cultural power. This circumstance prescribes a sense of restraint. Mrs. Ford ought to know that it is not up to her to rewrite the Ten Commandments over nationwide TV. At the very least she ought to realize that many Americans entertain very different convictions on drug use and abortion. . . . What this suggests on this and previous occasions, is not so much a beguiling "candor" as the desire to exploit her position in order to establish a particular public personality. ("This Week" 1975, 922)

Weighing the prospects for incumbent Ford and his major challenger for the Republican nomination, Ronald Reagan, columnist George Will quipped: "If Reagan supporters had their way, Mrs. Ford would have a prime time television talk show" (Will 1975, 984).

In her own defense Betty Ford wrote: "Morley Safer caught me off balance" (B. Ford 1978, 207). She had expected to be asked questions about women's rights, especially about the ratification of the Equal Rights Amendment (ERA). In early 1975, thirty-four states had ratified the amendment, which was four short of the number needed for its passage. Several state legislatures were in the midst of considering the measure. Mrs. Ford was an active proponent of the ERA, lobbying actively for its passage in several states such as North Dakota, Illinois, Nevada, Missouri, North Carolina, Indiana, and Arizona. Members of her staff provided her with background and tips on key legislators, whom she contacted and asked for support. With phone calls, letters, and telegrams, she laid out the case for the ERA (Gutin and Tobin 1993, 628).

After the interview, according to Gutin, Mrs. Ford was terrified by the reaction to her remarks. While Betty had vowed that nothing would interfere with her defense of women's rights, several of the questions posed by Safer had less to do with women's rights and more to do with parental responsibility. Such issues went to the heart of public sentiment in 1975; these were among the key values around which emerging candidates for the presidency were developing positions on which to run for office. If Betty was terrified, it was due to the growing certainty that her remarks might be a political liability for her husband (Gutin 1989, 132).

It was clear to all who knew her that Betty Ford was, above all else, a supportive spouse. That her answers to Safer's questions might have negatively affected President Ford's standing in public opinion surveys was anathema to her intentions. Anthony has observed that many Americans did not actually watch the Sunday night program, but instead heard or read sensationalized interpretations of it the next day (1991, 250). Stories about her comments far exceeded the dramatic impact of her own statements, removed as they were from their context. Betty had not experienced firsthand the epidemic influence of a news story in which she was the main figure; no sooner had she been buoyed by praise for her courage in facing cancer than she was cast into disfavor for frankness unbecoming to her stature.

In a personal interview with Linda Hobgood (2000a), Joe Bartlett, senior Republican staff officer of the House of Representatives who worked closely with Gerald Ford as minority leader, recalls Betty as "gracious always, to an incredible degree. . . . If she had an agenda it certainly was not obvious and it was not something that she brought into your presence. When you saw her you didn't see her as someone advocating a program. What you saw was a supportive wife." Her candor on *60 Minutes* was more a rhetorical slip easily attributed to Betty Ford's limited experience in such media settings and to her impulsive frankness, suddenly more a liability than an asset. The incident was hardly a premeditated declaration of values she chose to present. It represents a classic example of "gotcha" in televised interview technique extending to the wife of a sitting president.

If it is true that being an asset to her husband mattered most to Betty Ford and if she further believed that the causes she supported would fare best by returning her husband to the White House, the interview itself merits a second look. An "old friend" of the Fords told Jane Howard of the *New York Times*: "Jerry's always turned to Betty for the sensitive point of view. . . . He's often said she was the smart one when it came to politics because she sees the forest instead of the trees" (Howard 1974, 66). Agreeing to chat with Morley Safer was wholly consistent with Mrs. Ford's policy of openness with the media. However, the timing of the taping on August 10, immediately following a demanding trip to Eastern Europe with her husband was poorly planned by her staff. Press accounts of the European summit included speculation as to Mrs.

Ford's health and were based on obvious signs of exhaustion in Belgrade, Warsaw, and Bucharest. In addition, she admitted that the sheets of papers Safer held were filled with questions that "terrified" her, and she claimed that the fact that "they were taping" made her feel forced to answer the questions posed. Her reply to Safer's leading, even amphibolous question about people living together outside marriage—"Well, they are, aren't they?"—was actually very savvy, and shrewdly noncommittal. It established a rhetorical stance and cued her interviewer that she did not intend to use the interview to stand in judgment of others. Safer shifted, realizing he was eliciting the most "newsworthy" material from questions about her personal experience—the same realm in which she was notoriously loath to dwell. If she was uncomfortable with "small talk about herself," she was not about to speak for the actions of her adolescent and grown children. She defended their capacity for making wise choices and went on record as saying she would be there for them in the event of unwise choices. She allowed youth a certain immaturity.

There is reason to believe that Betty Ford was eager to identify with, rather than alienate, as many Americans as possible. In her support of women's rights, for example, she presented herself as a traditional wife and homemaker who also had a career outside the home and understood the challenges of women in the workplace. She saw herself as an ideal spokesperson because she could be a bridge between women's traditional values and those values favored by advocates of the Equal Rights Amendment or proponents of the pro-choice decision rendered by the Supreme Court in *Roe v. Wade*. It is arguable that no two issues sparked more controversy among women in the latter half of the twentieth century, and they both reached an inflammatory tenor during the Ford administration. Whether she wished to be or not, Betty Ford found herself near the center of power when women in America were becoming more politically divided than ever, at least in a public way. This may be why, beyond matters of decorum that change over time, public figures—especially in a democracy, and particularly unelected leaders in a democracy, that is, first ladies—are well advised to maintain a certain distance. But this distance is contingent, of course, upon a first lady's desire to contribute to her husband's political success. There was no question as to Betty's devotion to Gerald Ford's success as president, but in trying to relate to and unite such disparate constituencies she instead drew attention to their differences. There is something paradoxical in Betty Ford's approach: those who admired her traditional life found fault with the liberal views she expressed, while those who favored her liberal views may have had little in common with her traditional lifestyle. When Mrs. Ford was first lady she was truly located at an unusual cultural crossroad of values.

Had any other woman leader of her day made remarks similar to Betty Ford's it would not have made news. Betty Ford had probably expressed many, if not all of these opinions before. That as first lady she expressed these thoughts and did so in public where young and old alike could see and read her comments sparked the charges of impropriety and irresponsibility. First ladies, Baker observed, are eminently imitable (Baker 1976, 863).

Anthony contends: "to present political motivation . . . one must at least attempt to understand human motivation" (Anthony 1991, 18). In 1975, *60 Minutes* sought an interview with Betty Ford because she was the first lady and, not incidentally, the wife of a newly declared presidential candidate. But this woman, so comfortable with her own identity, knew better than most that "First Lady" was a title she just happened to hold. How long she would be a first lady was, she understood, beyond her control. As Mrs. Ford put it in a conversation with Jane Howard: "I don't feel that because I'm First Lady I'm any different from what I was before. It can happen to anyone. After all, it has happened to anyone" (Howard 1974, 87). The fact that she was not subdued by the position may have angered and irritated many. But beyond the causes she espoused and the husband she clearly admired and adored was an incorrigible "Midwestern" honesty. There was also that sense of common decency; Betty may well have known friends or neighbors who had struggled as parents with the very issues Safer raised in his interview. She had no intention of permitting anything she might say to hint of condemnation. Friendship meant a great deal to Betty Ford, and on those rare occasions when being first lady and being a friend appeared to necessitate a choice, Betty Ford invariably chose the latter.

The public came to see and value that. By the end of 1975, national polls showed the first lady's popularity was rising. From a dismal approval rating of 50 percent, she had soared in less than three months to 75 percent. *Newsweek* called her "Woman of the Year." The manner in which she and her staff were able to bring about this change in public perception clearly shows their growth in rhetorical acumen. One of the ways Betty Ford changed negative perceptions was to answer every adversarial letter she received in the aftermath of the *60 Minutes* program. Significantly, her carefully worded reply was intentionally shared with the press. An excerpt, in which she defended her actions as reflective of any "mother next door" who is coping with the challenges of raising children in changing times, read:

> We (Betty and Jerry Ford) have come to this sharing of outlook through communication, not coercion. I want my children to know that their concerns—their doubts and difficulties—whatever they may be, can be discussed with the two people in this world who care the most—their mother and father. (Truman 1995, 140)

Legacy

Gerald Ford came tantalizingly close to winning the presidential election of 1976. Results were not known until well into the night, and Ford, having lost his voice in the final hectic days of the campaign was unable to speak above a whisper. Betty, who had exhausted herself throughout the long campaign, was by family consensus elected to read Ford's concession speech the following morning in the White House pressroom. The departing president and first lady retired to Rancho Mirage, California.

Failure to appreciate what Mrs. Ford described as being "an ordinary woman who was called onstage at an extraordinary time," dims regard for the remarkable stamina and resiliency imbued in the character of this nation's forty-second first lady. Any one of the major crises of these years—the suddenness of taking office, cancer and chemotherapy, the pardon of Richard Nixon, the hostility of the Equal Rights Amendment debate, the unanticipated political schisms that erupted over *Roe v. Wade,* and the *60 Minutes* interview and backlash—might easily have defeated someone with less fortitude. That her daughter Susan could say, following a White House state dinner that she looked across the room and saw "the same old Mother" is undoubtedly the compliment Betty Ford would most cherish.

Betty Ford is one of a handful of first ladies whose lives after leaving the White House has been enriched. But before her life became better, it first became bleak. Mrs. Ford acknowledged, in 1978, her addiction to alcohol and prescription medication. Her treatment, like so many things in her life, was public knowledge and led to greater national awareness of this life-endangering disease. The Betty Ford Clinic serves a worldwide clientele in the struggle to overcome substance dependencies. For her part in drawing attention to these challenges without drawing attention to herself, Betty Ford has, like her mother in the midst of a raging storm, sought to calm fears and lend a certain comfort. What Betty considered so "ordinary" about herself—her outspoken candidness—turned out to be an "extraordinary" part of her legacy to the institution of first lady.

Notes

The authors wish to thank the administration of the Gerald R. Ford Museum and Library who supported this research with a travel grant to visit the collection in Grand Rapids and Ann Arbor, Michigan. Sincere thanks also to Mrs. Betty Ford for granting a phone interview and to her staff for providing follow-up materials.

Chronology of Major Speeches

March 22, 1975	Gridiron Dinner, Washington, D.C.
October 10, 1975	International Women's Year Conference, Cleveland, Ohio
November 7, 1975	American Cancer Society Dinner, New York City
March 26, 1976	American Cancer Society's Courage Award, White House
April 8, 1976	*Ladies' Home Journal* Woman of the Year Award, New York City
June 22, 1976	Jewish National Fund Dinner, New York City
October 14, 1976	Martha Graham Medal of Freedom
November 1, 1976	Paul Harris Rotary Fellow Award and Rally, Harrisburg, PA
November 3, 1976	Concession Speech for Gerald R. Ford
December 1, 1976	American Cancer Society Communicator of Hope Award, New York City
December 19, 1976	University of Michigan Commencement, Ann Arbor, Michigan

References

Anderson, Karrin Vasby. 1998. Complicating Political Identity: A Rhetorical Biography of First Lady Hillary Rodham Clinton. Unpublished Ph.D. diss., Indiana University.

Anthony, Carl Sferrazza. 1991. *First Ladies: The Saga of the Presidents' Wives and Their Power, 1961–1990*, Vol. 2. New York: William Morrow & Company.

Baker, James T. 1976. The Former Miss Betty Bloomer of Grand Rapids. *The Christian Century* 13 October, 863–65.

Betty Ford Gaffe. 1975. *National Review*, 29 August, 920–22.

Caroli, Betty Boyd. 1987. *First Ladies*. New York: Oxford University Press.

Contest of the Queens. 1976. *Time*, 30 August, 31.

First Ladies of the United States of America. www.whitehouse.gov/wh/welcome.html, accessed 27 October, 2000.

Ford, Betty, with Chris Chase. 1978. *The Times of My Life*. New York: Harper and Row.

———. 1987. *Betty: A Glad Awakening*. New York: Doubleday and Company.

Ford, Gerald. 1979. *A Time to Heal*. New York: Harper and Row.

Gerald R. Ford Library. www.fordutexas.edu/, accessed 10 March, 1999.

Gould, Lewis L., ed. 1996. *American First Ladies*. New York: Garland.

Gutgold, Nichola. 1998. Phone Interview with Betty Ford, 16 September.

Gutin, Myra G. 1989. *The President's Partner: The First Lady in the Twentieth Century*. New York: Greenwood.

Gutin, Myra, and Leesa Tobin. 1993. You've Come a Long Way, Mr. President: Betty Ford as First Lady. In *Gerald Ford and the Politics of Post-Watergate America*, ed. Bernard J. Firestone, 625–32. New York: Greenwood.

Hobgood, Linda B. 2000a. Personal Interview with Joe Bartlett, 13 October.

———. 2000b. Phone Interview with Jane Broomfield, 26 October.

Howard, Jane. 1974. Forward Day by Day. *New York Times Magazine*, 8 December, 36, 64–72, 86–94.

McPherson, Myra. 1975. The Blooming of Betty Ford. *McCall's*, 101, 93ff.

Mrs. Ford Speaks Her Mind. 1975. *Christianity Today*, 29 August, 28.

National First Ladies Library. www.firstladies.org.

Peer, Elizabeth, Jane Whitmore, and Lisa Whitman. 1975. Woman of the Year. *Newsweek*, 29 December, 19–23.

Salmans, Sandra, Jane Whitmore, and Thomas M. De Frank. 1975. The Strain on Betty. *Newsweek*, 18 August, 21–24.

60 Minutes. 1975. Interview with Morley Safer. CBS, 10 August.

There's No Gilded Cage for Betty. 1975. *Time*, 1 December, 22.

Thimmesch, Nick. 1976. Ten-Four, First Mama. *Saturday Evening Post*, September, 62–65, 82–83, 120.

This Week. 1975. *National Review*, 27.33, 917–25.

Thomas, Helen. 1999. *Front Row at the White House: My Life and Times*. New York: Scribner.

Tobin, Leesa. 1990. Betty Ford as First lady: A Woman for Women. *Presidential Studies Quarterly*, 20:4, 761–67.

Truman, Margaret. 1995. *First Ladies*. New York: Random House.

Weidenfeld, Sheila Rabb. 1978. *First Lady's Lady*. New York: G. P. Putnam.

Will, George. 1975. Calculations. *National Review*, 12 September, 984.

Witcover, Jules. 1999. *No Way to Pick a President*. New York: Farrar, Straus, and Giroux.

Chapter 17

Rosalynn Carter
Crafting a Presidential Partnership Rhetorically

Diane M. Blair and Shawn J. Parry-Giles

There is no end to what I can do in the White House.

—Rosalynn Carter

More so than any first lady before her, Rosalynn Carter entered the White House keenly aware of the rhetorical opportunities for significant influence afforded a twentieth-century first lady. She reflected in her autobiography, "Before going to the White House, I knew that some First Ladies had had special areas of interest and, because of their influence, had been able to accomplish worthy goals" (1984, 270). In his book on first ladies, Carl Sferrazza Anthony concurred, "she had no doubts about her capabilities, no fears that she couldn't accomplish everything she wanted to" (1991, 278). First Lady Rosalynn Carter began her tenure in Washington, D.C., with an ambitious agenda for herself. Two months into her husband's administration, she proclaimed, "There's no end to what I can do in the White House" (Stroud 1977, 19). The Carters came to Washington with high hopes and expectations for making a difference, but by the end of their four-year term, the Carter presidency was facing a number of political crises from not only the Republicans but also from within their own party as well. Despite their best efforts, the Carters would be forced to leave the White House before they could follow through on many of their goals for improving the nation.

Although the Carters experienced many disappointments as the nation's first couple, historians generally judge Rosalynn Carter's first ladyship as more successful than that of her husband's administration (Caroli 1987, 271). She was a political advisor, an international ambassador, a tireless campaigner for her husband and other Democratic candidates, and an advocate in her own right for a number of social causes. She regularly attended cabinet meetings and met with the president for weekly "working lunches." She served as her husband's political surrogate on a trip to Latin America, and she played a supporting role during the historical Middle East Peace Summit at Camp David. Rosalynn Carter also became a central spokesperson during her husband's political campaigns. While her husband tended to his languishing presidency, Rosalynn appeared in towns and cities across the United States telling voters why her husband was the kind of leader the country needed. Even the news media depicted her as the "spearhead" of the 1980 campaign (Avery 1979, 39). Rosalynn Carter's rhetorical activities and public discourse, thus, were a central component of the Carter presidency. In almost every way, Rosalynn's rhetorical activities—her image as a political advisor, her role as a political surrogate, and her own activist agenda—contributed to the creation of one of the closest working partnerships the White House has ever seen.

Biography

Several significant factors from Rosalynn Carter's biography help explain her broad rhetorical performance as first lady. These factors include: her religious upbringing and sense of moral obligation to help others, her view of herself as her husband's partner and equal, and her personal commitment to progressive social reform.

Eleanor Rosalynn Smith was born the oldest of four children in Plains, Georgia, on August 18, 1927. The town of Plains was small, only one square mile with a population of 600. According to Rosalynn, "We had no movie theater, no library, no recreation center, in Plains. Occasionally someone would open a restaurant, but it would never last long. The social life of the community revolved around the churches" (Carter 1984, 10).

Like many southern towns at that time, religion played a central role in the lives of its residents. Rosalynn was also raised in a devoutly religious family. Her grandmother was Lutheran, her grandfather was Baptist, and her parents were Methodist. Rosalynn attended all three churches and explained, "God was a real presence in my life." The vision of God that Rosalynn grew up with cultivated a sense of doing right by others, if not out of love, then out of fear of displeasing God. She wrote, "We were taught to love Him and felt very much the necessity and desire to live the kind of life He would have us live to love one another and be kind to and help those who needed help, and to be good. But we were also taught to fear God, and though I loved Him I was afraid of displeasing Him all my young life" (Carter 1984, 10).

The Carter family, like many other families, saw hard times during the 1920s and 1930s. Her father lost his savings when the Plains bank failed in 1926. The family grew their own food and her mother made most of the family's clothes. Even so, Rosalynn claimed she and her siblings were unaware of any hardship. She remembered, "Our family didn't have much money, but neither did anyone else, so as far as we knew, we were well off" (Carter 1984, 12).

The Carter family suffered even further at the loss of its patriarch. When Rosalynn was thirteen, her father died of leukemia. Her father's death was a traumatic loss for her. According to Rosalynn, "My childhood really ended at that moment" (Carter 1984, 17). Her mother began to depend on Rosalynn to help with the younger children and to run the household. Rosalynn reflected, "She put me on my best behavior because I was the one she depended on to make all the right decisions" (Carter 1984, 19). This sense of personal responsibility and moral obligation also stemmed from her desire to honor her father's memory. She wrote, "Whenever I was faced with a decision or even a temptation, I would think about whether Daddy would like it or not" (Carter 1984, 19). As a teenager Rosalynn stayed away from alcohol and cigarettes and graduated valedictorian of her high school class. She had dreams of seeing the world beyond Plains, but she was forced, for lack of funds and family obligations, to attend Georgia Southwestern, a local junior college close to home.

When Rosalynn was seventeen, she fell in love with her best friend's brother. Ruth Carter kept a picture of her older brother, Jimmy, pinned to her bedroom wall. Jimmy Carter was three years older than Rosalynn and a midshipman at the U.S. Naval Academy. While on leave in the summer of 1945, Jimmy and Rosalynn went on a double date with Ruth and her boyfriend. He asked her to marry him the following Christmas leave. At first she refused, believing she was too young to marry, but a few months later she accepted. The couple was married on July 7, 1946.

The Carters' marriage was grounded in a sense of equality and interdependence. It was a partnership that would grow and expand as their lives developed and changed. In a 1976 campaign interview, Jimmy Carter characterized Rosalynn as "fully equal to me in every way in our relationship, in making business decisions, and she makes most of the decisions about family affairs" (Richardson 1998, 54). At the same time, he conceded that early in the marriage he was by far the more dominant person, and he suggested that "it was a struggle for her to achieve this degree of independence and equality in our personal relationship" (Richardson 1998, 54).

Indeed, Rosalynn Carter began her married life as a fairly traditional navy wife and mother of three young boys: John William (Jack), born 1947; James Earl Carter III (Chip), born in 1950; and Donnel Jeffrey (Jeff), born in 1952. Navy life, however, required that Rosalynn learn to manage a household on her own since Jimmy was absent at sea four to seven days a week. She came to love the independent life that she had achieved. Although military life took the family to such places as Virginia, Pennsylvania, Connecticut, Massachusetts, Hawaii, and New York, Jimmy Carter decided to leave the navy upon his father's death. It was at this time that the Carters moved back home to Plains so that Jimmy could take over his father's peanut business. The decision devastated Rosalynn. She remembers it being the most serious argument of their marriage, "Never had we been at such cross-purposes, I thought the best part of my life had ended" (Carter 1984, 36). Although Rosalynn resisted the move, she soon found herself taking on new responsibilities within the family business. She took on still more responsibilities as her husband's business partner when he began his political career.

Jimmy Carter started his political career on the local school board and then quickly moved to the state senate. Rosalynn's early involvement in her husband's political career was limited to mailing out campaign literature and posing for family photographs. In 1966, he ran for governor and lost the election, but he was determined to make another run for the governorship in 1970. During the second governor campaign, Rosalynn, now the mother of three sons and a three-year-old daughter (Amy was born 1967), wrote letters, kept files, and clipped news articles for Jimmy's campaign. Significantly, Rosalynn forced herself to overcome her fear of public speaking, which was so severe it caused her to become physically ill on occasion. She recalled, "The idea of standing up in front of people absolutely terrified me, even though I had had no difficulty speaking before my class in high school and actually enjoyed one-on-one political conversations at luncheons or receptions—even interviews with reporters" (Carter 1984, 69). She persisted, and before the end of the campaign she was making brief speeches frequently. The Carters were successful, and Rosalynn became first lady of Georgia in 1971.

The transition from Plains to Atlanta was a difficult challenge and a significant growing period for Rosalynn. She believed the move to the White House was much easier compared to this initial move. She wrote in her memoir, "Overnight, it seemed, we had become 'public' persons living in a fishbowl at the mercy of the press and sometimes the public" (1984, 91). She also reported that she used her husband's governorship years to gain confidence in her social and administrative abilities (Caroli 1987). During these years in Atlanta, Rosalynn developed an appreciation for what government could do to improve people's lives. She was determined to be a modern and socially involved first lady, "I didn't want to spend all my time taking care of that big house" (Carter 1984, 77). While first lady of Georgia, Rosalynn cultivated Special Olympics programs throughout the state. Inspired by Lady Bird Johnson, she started the Georgia Highway Wildflower Program. Rosalynn also met Betty Ford during the governorship years; she remembered, "I was anxious to meet her, for I had heard that Mrs. Ford and I had many things in common" (Carter 1984, 99). Another concern of Rosalynn's was the state's prison system, its inadequacies and inequalities. She worked with the Women's Prison Committee for the Commission of the Status of Women to improve prison housing conditions, and she helped create a Work Release Center. By the end of their stay in the governor's mansion, Rosalynn was an accomplished speaker and advocate, and she put those skills to work on behalf of her husband and his political agenda during his run for the presidency.

During the 1976 campaign, Rosalynn campaigned actively for her husband. Her days began at dawn and included between six or eight speeches, up to eighteen interviews, and three or four press conferences (Angelo 1976). The Carters believed that they could "cover more ground" if they campaigned separately

(Caroli 1987, 265). Rosalynn was accompanied only by her good friend and her son's mother-in-law, Edna Langford, when she campaigned for the first time across the state line into Florida (Carter 1984, 112). Her strategy was to meet as many people and to get as much press coverage as possible "by knocking on the doors of radio and television stations and newspaper offices and saying, 'I'm Mrs. Jimmy Carter and I thought you might want to interview me'" (Carter 1984, 113). During the campaign, Rosalynn developed her own itinerary and wrote her own speeches. Careful lists were kept of the contacts made during the trip, and Rosalynn returned home with four campaign hints: "stop at the courthouse, look for large radio antennas, stay in people's homes, and muster the courage to intrude" (Smith 1996, 564). The Carters' diligence paid off, and they moved into the White House in 1977.

Rhetorical Activities as First Lady

Rosalynn Carter entered the White House with the expectation that she would be an active first lady. She told an interviewer for *U.S. News and World Report*, "I learned while Jimmy was Governor that I could help with anything. It didn't matter what it was. It was a position of influence, as the White House would be. You see the needs and you can do something about them" (Avery 1976, 27). Jimmy Carter described his wife as "an almost equal extension of me," and Rosalynn's first ladyship was in many ways an extension of her husband's presidency (Angelo 1977, 12). As first lady, Rosalynn Carter attended cabinet meetings, met with the president for weekly "working lunches," traveled nationally and internationally as a political surrogate, and was recognized as one of her husband's most influential advisors. By 1979, *Time* identified her as the "second most powerful person in the United States" (Sidey 1979, 22).

Mrs. Carter established early on that she had a number of significant goals that she wanted to accomplish as first lady. At the beginning of her husband's term as president, she explained to a reporter during a *Time* magazine interview: "I felt there would be all kinds of opportunities for me if Jimmy became President. And the more I saw all the problems, I thought, if somebody does something, it's got to be us" (Angelo 1977, 12). Her commitment to progressive social reform led to her active involvement in a number of projects and causes, including serving as the honorary chair for the President's Commission on Mental Health, advocating on behalf of the elderly, promoting community volunteer projects, and lobbying for the passage of the Equal Rights Amendment.

Rosalynn Carter was "an extremely active communicator who took maximum advantage of the national podium afforded her" (Gutin 1989, 150). Even though she was a newcomer to Washington, as first lady she compiled "a remarkable list of accomplishments in just four years" (Caroli 1987, 262). Her rhetorical activities, which included political advising, independent advocacy, and campaign surrogate, expanded the role of the first lady in significant ways and cultivated one of the closest political partnerships between a first lady and a president.

Political Advisor

The Carters moved to Washington as an established political team, and they continued to cultivate this image throughout Jimmy's presidency. As first lady, Rosalynn Carter attended cabinet meetings, met regularly with the president to discuss substantive issues, accompanied her husband to the Camp David Middle East Peace Summit, edited her husband's speeches, and advised him on political appointments. She became known as the president's closest advisor (Ayres Jr. 1979). The news media seized on her potential influence early in the presidency. The *New York Times Magazine* anticipated: "Just as Mrs. [Eleanor] Roosevelt was called 'the Assistant President,' Rosalynn Carter could also have an impact on the making of national policy, advising on her husband's programs as well as advocating her own" (Stroud 1977, 19). While her attendance at cabinet meetings was already well established, *The New Republic* renewed attention to this unprecedented role for a first lady when it reported that in the absence of the vice president, Rosalynn Carter, entering a meeting late, quietly slipped into his chair (Osborne 1978). By 1979, *Time* declared, "The second most powerful person in the United States is Rosalynn Carter" (Sidey 1979, 22), and *Newsweek* referred to her as a "one-woman Kitchen Cabinet" (Mrs. President 1979, 22).

The Carters responded to this media image strategically. For example, when Jimmy wanted to promote his image as a "liberated" husband, he frequently emphasized Rosalynn's role as a "very equal partner" and a "perfect extension of myself" (Ayres Jr. 1979, 39). The Carters also argued that while Jimmy was occupied with the responsibilities of the office, Rosalynn's speaking engagements and travels helped keep him in touch with citizens' concerns. For example, he told Barbara Walters in an interview,

> When I am confined to Washington because of pressing duties and she [Rosalynn] goes out within the United States, she has a much easier relationship with people and can bring back to me an accurate assessment of what the hopes and dreams and fears and concerns of the American people are than I could get from any other possible source. She is a full partner in that respect. ("Interview" 1978)

He told the *New York Time Magazine* that "she helps form my positions because she has a sensitive way of understanding what other people feel. Also, she is able to get a much more frank and unbiased expression of criticism from people than I can" (Stroud 1977, 60, 63). Similarly, Rosalynn Carter would reiterate this important role for herself as first lady, "I can get closer to the people than he can, and then I can go back and talk to him about their hopes and dreams" ("Selling True Grit" 1979, 13). She also emphasized this image of a first lady's closer connection to the American people to justify her role in the speech-writing process, "If I can't understand something, then the American public is certainly not going to understand it either" ("I've Never Won" 1978, 13).

Suggesting that Rosalynn was the president's link to the people situated her advisory role squarely in the realm of benevolent helpmate and reinforced traditional gender expectations for the first couple. She could relate the fears and concerns of the public back to her husband who was concerned with the day-to-day business of running the government. This reasoning would also impact Jimmy's decision to have Rosalynn accompany him to the Middle East Peace Talks. Jimmy wanted the wives of the leaders present to help maintain a "more congenial" atmosphere (Carter 1984, 239). While at Camp David, Rosalynn attended the meetings whenever she could, and took copious notes (over 200 pages typed). She also worked closely with Jimmy and Jody Powell (the president's press secretary) on a special international "call to prayer" for the success of the Camp David meetings. The wording of the prayer was delicate, she reflected, because it needed to appeal to and be approved by members of the Christian, Jewish, and Muslim faiths (Carter 1984, 245). Her role at the Camp David meetings and her support of the president was recognized formally when she was invited to join the procession, which included Prime Minister Begin, President Sadat, and the president of the United States, before a special joint session of Congress to announce the historic peace treaty.

In addition to supporting her husband's presidency, Rosalynn employed her image as her husband's closest advisor to boost her own credibility as first lady. When an American reporter asked what made her think she was fit to discuss serious matters with heads of state during her diplomatic tour of Latin America, Rosalynn replied, "I think I am the person closest to the President of the United States, and if I can help him understand the countries of the world, then that's what I intend to do" ("The President's" 1977, 17). Similarly, Rosalynn was not above promoting her personal influence on Jimmy when it came to improving opportunities for women. For instance, she told a group of women professionals,

> I want to assure you that I use my influence at home on behalf of women whenever I can. Now Jimmy and I try not to talk business after hours, but I have been known to, well, mention that he needs—more women on the White House staff—more women in departmental jobs—and a list of distinguished women just in case he finds himself looking for a woman Supreme Court Justice! (Carter 1979i)

President Carter's aides and White House staff also attested publicly to Rosalynn's influence. For instance, presidential aide, Tim Kraft told *Time*, "Jimmy places the greatest stock in her judgments of people. Her word is gospel" ("I've Never Won" 1978). Another unidentified occupant of the West Wing told the magazine, "If you want Jimmy to do something, you'd better get Rosalynn on your side first" ("I've Never Won" 1978, 13). Carter pollster, Patrick Caddell told *The New Republic*, "I think her political perceptions and judgments are very good. She's extremely shrewd, her instincts on people are generally good and during the campaign I found her to be a tremendous help, particularly in problems that needed to be brought to Jimmy's attention" (Osborne 1978, 14). At the same time, other White House staffers tried to temper speculation about her influence. For example, Jody Powell argued, "Her political judgment is very good. She senses repercussions, impact, the way things come across, very well." That said, he qualified, "We respect her judgment, but we don't always agree with her" ("I've Never Won" 1978, 13).

At times Rosalynn also seemed to downplay her influence as a political advisor—possibly as a strategic response to concerns raised about her proper role. As Rosalynn's activities increased, grumblings of "Who elected her?" and the continuing issue of a first lady's "unappointed, unimpeachable status" created some concern that her prominence might be harmful to the Carter image (Troy 2000, 255–56). She told the interviewer for *U.S. News and World Report*, "I think Jimmy does respect my opinions about things that I'm interested in and know about, but I can't advise him on [Ugandan President] Idi Amin and things I don't know anything about." In this interview she emphasized instead her expertise on issues traditionally associated with women and family, "mental health issues, health programs, children, day-care centers, and things like that" ("Change Comes" 1977, 31). Similarly, in an article for *Time*, she insisted, "I don't consider myself a chief advisor, and I don't advise him on things I don't know anything about" ("I've Never Won" 1978, 13).

There were, however, times when her public discourse belied just how much influence she actually had on her husband's political decisions. For example, Rosalynn played a central role in Jimmy's cancellation of a highly anticipated policy address on the energy crisis. Rosalynn read the speech and told Jimmy that it said nothing new, and "nobody wants to hear it." The president then scheduled a series of Camp David sessions with leaders from "every segment of American life" to devise a new approach to energy policy, resulting in his major policy address, subsequently dubbed the "malaise speech," and a major shake-up of the cabinet and White House staff (Carter 1984, 302; Avery 1979). When questioned about the cabinet shake-up, Rosalynn confused her pronouns creating speculation about just who was making the decisions in the Oval Office. *U.S. News and World Report* wrote that in response to a question about the extent of her influence on the Camp David meetings, she responded, "I don't know that I had any. I sat in on the meetings, I listened with him, and then we—and then he made the decisions" (Avery 1979, 40). Similarly, *Newsweek* reported that when badgered with questions about the cabinet changes, she replied, "I just . . . uh . . . we . . . I . . . uh, Jimmy thought, and I agreed with him, that it was better to do it fast" (Mrs. President 1979, 22). Such bumblings may have reflected Rosalynn's effort to downplay her influence at the same time she sought to present a united front with her husband. Rosalynn rarely, if ever, disagreed with her husband in public. She told the press, "We [she and Jimmy] are very close together philosophically." And she suggested that when they do disagree, it is usually "when I don't understand something or when he doesn't understand how I feel" (Avery 1977, 41). Whatever their private debates, the Carters always supported each other's efforts in the public limelight. Rosalynn's support of her husband is also reflected in her own advocacy agenda.

Social Reform Advocate

Rosalynn Carter knew she could create a social and political agenda for herself as the wife of a twentieth-century political leader. When her husband became governor of Georgia, Rosalynn reflected that "A First Lady can pick and choose her projects and do almost anything she wants because her name is a drawing card, she is influential, and although legislators may not always support her, she can always get their attention, as well as the attention of other powerful people" (Carter 1984, 95). Rosalynn Carter understood the power of public discourse. She told an audience of women journalists and advertisers, "I think we are fortunate to be in the communications business—and I would like to include myself in your field today. We can choose our message. We can affect attitudes. We have influence" (Carter 1979i).[1] The problem, according to Rosalynn, was "which causes to be involved in, what to do, and how much to do" (Carter 1984, 95). As first lady, she pursued an advocacy agenda that extended above and beyond a single "pet" project. She advocated on behalf of a number of social reform projects, including mental health reform, issues of the elderly, volunteerism, expanding opportunities and rights for women (including ratification of the Equal Rights Amendment).[2]

While her pursuit of a number of worthy goals was admirable, her inability to concentrate or limit her advocacy was a source of criticism. Her activities were so numerous and her agenda so broad that some journalists believed it diluted her influence and "fuzzied" her public image (Holt 1978). Unlike Lady Bird Johnson who was known for her beautification project, Patricia Nixon who focused on volunteerism, and Betty Ford who was known for her candor in coping with breast cancer and speaking out on behalf of the ERA, Rosalynn was often criticized by the media for having no clear image or agenda (Quinn 1978). Rosalynn addressed her problems with the media directly in her public discourse. In a speech on April 26, 1979, before an audience of women communicators, she expressed her frustration with the media's lack of attention and criticism of her agenda, "I have been told that the problems of the mentally ill, the elderly, the handicapped and the poor are not 'sexy' issues for a First Lady. The media are not very interested. And I cannot tell you how much I dislike these negative attitudes" (Carter 1979i).

What is clear about Rosalynn's own advocacy is how well it complemented her husband's political agenda. Myra Gutin describes Rosalynn Carter's first ladyship and her husband's presidency as a "symbiotic relationship" (1989, 156). Indeed, in many ways their rhetorical activities and philosophies were so closely linked that it was hard to know where one's role performance stopped and the other began. In almost every way, her rhetorical advocacy on behalf of social reform allied strategically with her husband's presidency. She was fully aware that her interests might be relegated to the secondary status of first lady "pet projects," so she blended her agenda with her husband's. This rhetorical coordination can be seen in the social issues she addressed, the political philosophy she espoused, and the strategic linking of her activist agenda to her husband's political policies and accomplishments. Such a rhetorical coordination served both her own activist agenda and her husband's presidency.

The cause for which Rosalynn Carter's first ladyship is most closely allied is mental health. She first became aware of the issues surrounding mental illness during Jimmy's campaign for the governorship. In her autobiography, Rosalynn tells the story of meeting one woman in particular who revealed the difficulties of caring for a loved one with a mental illness. When Rosalynn met with Jimmy later that same day, she slipped into the receiving line to shake his hand and probed, "I want to know what you are going to do about mental health when you are governor." Jimmy immediately replied, "We're going to have the best mental health system in the country and I'm going to put you in charge of it" (Carter 1984, 73). Although Rosalynn was not placed in charge of the Governor's Commission to Improve Services to the Mentally and Emotionally Handicapped that was established during the Carter governorship, she was later named honorary chair of President Carter's Commission on Mental Health. Because of federal nepotism laws, Rosalynn could not be appointed the formal chairperson of the commission, and so had to settle for the "honorary" title.

Rosalynn was excited at the prospect of promoting a substantive issue, and she set out to promote the commission during her very first press conference following the inauguration. The media, however, showed little interest in Rosalynn's new project. Few of the major newspapers featured the commission; instead, they focused on Rosalynn's decision to serve only wine at White House functions (Carter 1984, 173). In spite of the lack of news media interest, Rosalynn persevered. The commission held public hearings, issued position papers, and eventually made 117 recommendations, including 8 "major" ones which resulted in the Mental Health Systems Act of 1980 (Troy 2000, 251). Rosalynn used her rhetorical first ladyship to lobby heavily for the act's passage. She spoke "everywhere I had a chance" to promote the legislation and raise awareness. She even testified before Congress, becoming the first first lady to do so since Eleanor Roosevelt. She explained her purpose, "I wanted to take mental illness and emotional disorders out of the closet, to let people know it is all right to admit having a problem without fear of being called crazy" (Carter 1984, 271). In September 1980, the Mental Health Systems Act became "the first major reform of federal, publicly funded mental health programs since the Community Mental Health Centers Act of 1963" (Carter 1984, 279). Unfortunately, Rosalynn's hard won effort on behalf of mental health would barely get off the ground, before Ronald Reagan's subsequent administration would cut the bulk of the funding for the project. Rosalynn described the fate of the project as a "bitter loss" (Carter 1984, 279).

Rosalynn's interest in "the problems of the elderly" and the "graying of America" came out of her work on the Mental Health Commission (Carter 1984, 281). Among her rhetorical activities on behalf of the elderly, she coordinated a roundtable discussion on aging and lobbied on behalf of several acts of legislation. After meeting regularly with Nelson Cruikshank, the counselor to the president on aging, Rosalynn decided to invite representatives from elderly advocacy groups to a roundtable discussion. Participants at this meeting "put together a brochure with fifteen recommendations of things people could do in their communities to help the elderly" (Carter 1984, 282). This brochure was then distributed to state agencies and local organizations, and Rosalynn often followed up with a visit to those organizations that implemented programs. Rosalynn spoke out on behalf of a variety of legislation intended to protect the rights of and ensure services for older Americans. Among her legislative efforts, Rosalynn lobbied for the Age Discrimination Act, which eliminated any mandatory retirement age in the federal government and raised the age limit from 65 to 70 in the private sector. She also lobbied on behalf of the Older Americans Act, which authorized substantial increases in appropriations for various social services for the elderly. In addition, she publicly supported Social Security reform and the Rural Clinics Act, which expanded medical services to underserved rural areas. She also lent her first lady ethos and public speaking skills to the American Nurses Association's education program for geriatric patients resulting in a training film (narrated by the first lady) entitled, *The Rosalynn Carter Nurse Training Program.*

Rosalynn's interest in mental health and the elderly are both examples of the blending of her own first lady projects with her husband's domestic policies. In her speeches, she frequently remarked on her own efforts in relation to health reform as an introduction to her larger purpose, which was to highlight and praise her husband's policies and accomplishments as president in such areas. For instance, in a prepared speech draft to be presented before a rally on Capitol Hill regarding hospital cost containment, she recounted the accomplishments of her husband's presidency in the first person plural,

> We have won some important fights in the past two and half years and we will win this one too. We won the fight to save the Social Security System. We won the fight for increased housing and other services for the elderly. We won the fight to free older Americans from the tyranny of forced retirement at 65. The battle for hospital cost containment is in many ways the toughest of all. And it is a battle we cannot afford to lose. (Carter 1979e)

Rosalynn's work with improving health services for the elderly also fueled her interest in promoting community volunteer efforts. In speech after speech, she encouraged her audiences to support local initiatives to create more caring communities and to solve their community's problems. Her focus on volunteerism and local community problem-solving also worked hand in hand with her husband's political philosophy of fiscal responsibility. In a preliminary draft of a speech for the Iowa Jefferson-Jackson Day Dinner, Rosalynn explained her plans to stump across the nation, "I want to have a chance to really talk to people about things that we need to do in our country and how we can do them—not how we can get government to do them, but how we can get together and do what needs doing where we are in our own communities" (Carter 1978a). Similarly, in a draft of a speech to be presented at the opening of a new Work Activity Center in Bartow County, Georgia, Rosalynn planned to tell her audience, "I hope we are growing through the mind-set that said, 'Let the government do it,' whatever it happens to be. Local initiative is critical" (Carter 1979j).

Rosalynn Carter's greatest disappointment in terms of her advocacy efforts as first lady was the struggle and failure of the Equal Rights Amendment. She suggested that she did "just about anything [she] could think of for the cause" (Carter 1984, 286). She gave numerous speeches, made phone calls to legislators in various states, wrote letters, attended fund-raisers, and held multiple events and meetings at the White House. She even agreed to be auctioned off at a dance to raise money for the effort. In the fall 1977, she appeared with former first ladies Lady Bird Johnson and Betty Ford at a Houston conference celebrating International Women's Year. Rosalynn fretted that the ERA had a serious image problem. Her rhetorical strategy was to try to draw media attention away from "those supporters who have appeared to be demanding and strident man-haters—mostly urban professional women" (Carter 1984, 287). Instead, she felt the public needed to see that "nice" women, "relatively traditional" women, like herself, supported the amendment, too (Carter 1984, 287, 289). In a speech before the New York Women in Communications she argued, "it is especially important to explain that women like me support the ERA. I am a relatively traditional person. I enjoy my roles as wife, mother, partner, and business-woman. I care how I look—and what I think. I am not threatened by ERA. I feel freed by it" (Carter 1979i).

President Carter benefited politically from Rosalynn's advocacy on behalf of the ERA. Gil Troy argues that Jimmy understood the Democrats' political strategy of deepening the "gender gap" with the Republicans (2000, 251). In fact, Jimmy wasn't above promoting his own politically "liberated" image at his wife's expense. While Jimmy was governor, the ERA came up for a vote before the Georgia state legislature. To a crowd of anti-ERA protesters, Jimmy pro-claimed, "I respect your right to oppose the ERA, but my mind is made up . . . I am for it—but my wife is against it!" Rosalynn was mortified and claimed she "[couldn't] believe he seriously thought I opposed it." When she confronted him about the incident, Jimmy "just grinned" in response to her indignation (Carter 1984, 101). In spite of this early misunderstanding between the Carters, Rosa-lynn frequently used her interest and support of the ERA to talk about her hus-band's accomplishments on behalf of extending opportunities to women. In a draft of a speech to be delivered via telephone to the American Baptist Churches Biennial Meeting, held on the campus of Southern Illinois University on June 7, 1979, Rosalynn and her speechwriters made this link explicit,

> All of you know my concern for women in America . . . I am proud and grate-ful for the progress we have made for women in the last 2 1/2 years. Jimmy is helping to give women a great new chance. Only five women have ever been appointed as Cabinet Secretaries in the history of our country—two in his ad-ministration. Only four women have been appointed as Under Secretary in the history of our country—two in his administration. (Carter 1979a)

The speech manuscript goes on to list the number of prestigious positions now held by women under the Carter administration. Rosalynn was to conclude this section of the address with one final praise for her husband's commitment to women, "In addition there are scores of women in many other strategic positions in the Administration and the government made possible by Jimmy's concern to give women their rightful place in American society" (Carter 1979a).

Perhaps more so than any other first lady, Rosalynn Carter's first lady activ-ism and activities were intimately connected to her husband's presidential image and agenda. This complementary nature of their political agendas and philosophies, along with her established reputation as a close political advisor, enabled First Lady Carter to perform her most significant rhetorical role in the Carter administration—that of a rhetorical and political surrogate for the president.

Surrogate and Advocate for the President

In addition to advocating on behalf of mental health reform, the elderly, volunteerism, and opportunities for women, one of Rosalynn Carter's most important first lady projects was advocating on behalf of her husband's languishing presidency. She served as an extension of her husband, and one of the defining characteristics of Rosalynn Carter's first ladyship was the surrogate function she performed for her husband. One of the best and earliest examples was Rosalynn's diplomatic trip through Latin America. Her rhetorical activities became so central to the Carter presidency that when political necessity confined Jimmy Carter to Washington, Rosalynn Carter became a campaign surrogate for the 1978 midterm elections and the 1980 presidential campaign.

President Carter characterized First Lady Carter as a representative of the nation and his own personal surrogate. He told Barbara Walters and a national audience during a 1978 interview, "we had a special need to strengthen our ties, for instance with Latin America. And Rosalynn went on a full diplomatic mission representing me personally and also representing the nation" ("Interview" 1978). Her surrogate role began with the first lady's tour of Latin America as Jimmy's personal ambassador. According to Rosalynn Carter's autobiography, a few months after her husband's inauguration, "Jimmy came home one night and asked if I would go on a special mission for him." The new president explained that he was busy "setting in motion a host of domestic and foreign policy initiatives," and so he needed someone to take on the much needed task of promoting stronger relationships with our neighbors to the south (1984, 185).

The purpose of Rosalynn's trip was to explain the Carter administration's policies on human rights, nuclear weapons, and arms sales to neighboring nations. She also intended to listen to the concerns of the individual countries and take their messages back to the president. Her journey took her over 12,000 miles to seven different countries. The first lady visited Jamaica, Costa Rica, Ecuador, Peru, Brazil, Columbia, and Venezuela. She was the first high-ranking U.S. representative to visit Ecuador in twenty years. Her schedule was heavier than the president on his official visits because she assumed the duties of an ambassador plus her duties as first lady. Besides meeting with the leaders of each country, Rosalynn also had "receptions to attend, informal lunches with wives, side trips to show my interest in health and education projects, and the inevitable formal banquet held by the government" (Carter 1984, 200). Her dual role of surrogate president and hostess provided a glimpse into what role a woman U.S. president might someday play (Anthony 1991, 274).

Rosalynn's performance as a surrogate generated a lot of news media coverage and was not without controversy. An editor for *The Nation* remarked, "The wives of our Presidents have played all sorts of roles (mostly ceremonial), but never one quite like this" ("The Carters" 1977, 740). Even though Rosalynn sat through twenty-six hours of briefings by scholars and federal officials, some members of Congress and the media were critical of this new role for the wife of a president. According to *U.S. News and World Report*, the president's decision to send his wife "aroused suspicions among Latin Americans that the President does not take their countries seriously" ("Rosalynn's Turn" 1977, 36). Meg Greenfield, a writer for *Newsweek*, was critical of what she perceived to be Rosalynn's only qualifications for the world of policy making—her relationship to President Carter (1977). In response to some of the news media criticism, White House staff emphasized publicly that her role was not to negotiate or create policy with these leaders; rather, her role was mostly an informational gathering and exchange on behalf of her husband's administration (Goldman 1977).

Post-trip evaluations were also mixed. A national poll gave her a 74 percent approval rating for her role as "ambassador," and 72 percent considered her "a better source of diplomatic information for the president than the State Department" (Anthony 1991, 274). A writer for *Time* suggested that "she achieved her goal of convincing top leaders that President Carter wants to improve long-neglected relations with Latin Nations" ("Rosalynn Takes a Message" 1977, 26). Others were less enthusiastic. According to a *Washington Post* exposé, one former White House staffer claimed that Rosalynn's trip was ineffectual because South American leaders "treated 'her exactly as they would any wife of an American President: politely and nothing more'" (Quinn 1978, K3). Still others expressed concern not over her effectiveness as a surrogate but over whether or not such a responsibility was even proper for a first lady. In an opinion editorial for *Newsweek*, Meg Greenfield argued that Rosalynn's trip to Latin America in her husband's stead raised a fundamental question about the role of a president's wife. She told readers, "What we have here, in other words, is not an 'uppity woman' issue, but rather a question of the proper role in government of un-elected kin of elected officials" (1977, 100).

Rosalynn's reflection on the controversy was that she had always been Jimmy's partner, and so it was only natural for him to turn to her "to take on a challenge that was special and personal to him" (Carter, 1984, 188). She continued in this role as Jimmy's personal ambassador and surrogate throughout his presidency. Drafts of her speeches frequently begin with a comment similar to this one expressed in her remarks at Harlem Church, "Jimmy wanted very much to be here. He sends his love, and wanted me to express his deep regret that he could not come" (Carter 1979d). In the draft of her testimonial for Governor Averell Harriman, she began, "Jimmy sends his greetings to you. And of course I am pleased that he sent me to be his special representative to honor America's most distinguished 'special envoy' Governor Harriman" (1979b). Her surrogate role was such a prevalent part of the Carter partnership, that First Lady Carter was granted the privilege of being the first woman to speak at the Gridiron Dinner for the president, and she began once again (this time for humorous effect) by addressing her role in her husband's absence:

Jimmy really wanted to be here tonight with his friends in the press. Only matters of the highest and most urgent national importance could have kept him away. He just had to go to a town meeting in Elk City, Oklahoma. Actually, Jimmy was invited to the Gridiron by your former President Al Cromley of the Daily Oklahoman and Jimmy thought tonight's dinner was being held in Al's home state. Jimmy just called me from Elk City before I came over here, and he was pretty upset. He said he was the only person in Frankie's Diner who's dressed in white tie and tails. (Carter 1979g)

One of her biggest coups as Jimmy's surrogate came when she was given the privilege of officially greeting Pope John Paul II for his U.S. visit in 1979, an honor Vice President Mondale desired ("Playing" 1979).

Rosalynn Carter's surrogate role soon extended into the realm of political campaigning on behalf of the Democratic Party during the 1978 midterm elections and Jimmy Carter's 1980 reelection bid. In September 1978, she logged a cross-country campaign schedule speaking in support of Democratic candidates. According to Myra Gutin, the first lady was considered a superb campaigner and an effective fund-raiser. Gutin claimed she was "considered a Democratic heavy-weight" (1989, 153). *Newsweek* reported that constituents claimed that of the two, "she's the most acceptable Carter to have at this time" ("Rosalynn on Road" 1978, 33). With her husband's presidency never quite finding its stride, Rosalynn's central goal for her public discourse seemed to be boosting her husband's image. She was, however, politically astute enough to offer the Democratic candidates "some distance from the ailing administration by calling each Democrat 'his own man' who would stand up to the President if necessary" (Troy 2000, 262).

Drafts of Rosalynn's "stump speech" suggest that she reminded her audience of the problems the nation was facing *before* Jimmy was president—highlighting the theme that her husband's administration "inherited a mess, but we are getting it under control" (Carter 1978b). She then reviewed the actions Jimmy took as president to resolve the problems, and she highlighted his accomplishments. For instance, on the issue of unemployment she pointed out that "there are more than six million more Americans on the job today than there were on Election Day 1976. That's the fastest increase in our nation's history" (Carter 1978b). After thoroughly covering domestic policies (the Farm Bill, Social Security reform, the Civil Service Reform Bill, plans to curb fraud and abuse of welfare and Medicaid programs), the speech draft reveals that Rosalynn turned her attention to foreign policy issues. She covered such topics as the Panama Canal treaties, efforts to control nuclear proliferation, human rights policy, and efforts for international peace. As a mother, she emphasized that she was particularly proud "that no American has died in battle anywhere in the world during Jimmy's presidency" (1978b). Her attention to both domestic policies and foreign affairs suggests that as first lady, Rosalynn Carter did not feel confined to a particular topic. Such a broad approach to her public discourse enabled her to expand her role as political surrogate beyond that of traditional topics of expertise for first ladies. It also enabled her to take on an even larger surrogate role for her husband, who by the end of his first term in office found himself facing numerous political crises—at home and abroad.

First Lady Carter's championing of her husband's presidency increased to a new level of responsibility during the 1980 election campaign. Her role as the president's surrogate would play a central role in the administration's campaign strategy. Rosalynn had encouraged Jimmy to hire public relations specialist Gerald Rafshoon to help with the president's image. Rafshoon recognized the value of the first lady for the president's campaign—"she could boast of his accomplishments in a way that Jimmy could not" (Anthony 1991, 303). Rosalynn Carter was designated the central traveling spokesperson for her husband's second presidential bid. *U.S. News and World Report* called her the "Spearhead of [the] Carter Campaign" (Avery 1979, 39). According to historian Gil Troy, "the Carters followed the Nixons' and Fords' reelection tradition of politicizing the First Lady and insulating the President" (2000, 268). President Carter was also constrained in his ability to campaign because of the Iran hostage crisis he was facing toward the end of his first term. In early November 1979, Iranian terrorists stormed the American embassy in Tehran taking sixty Americans hostage. The Iranians were demanding the return of the ailing shah who had come to the United States for cancer treatment.

As early as the late summer of 1979, Rosalynn began stumping to raise funds for her husband's reelection campaign. She made nine stops on a four-day tour that took her to Illinois, Arkansas, Texas, and California. She raised approximately $400,000 for Jimmy's "campaign war chest" ("The First Lady" 1979, 9). By October 1980, Rosalynn had appeared in 166 cities and raised $2.5 million. Reporters and political insiders praised her campaign abilities. According to Liz Carpenter, former press secretary to Lady Bird Johnson, "she's the salesman [sic]—a better salesman than he is" (Avery 1979, 39). A Dallas political consultant remarked, "You can't help but like the woman. She's attractive, charming, intelligent and totally committed to Jimmy. People eat up that sort of thing" ("Selling True Grit" 1979, 13). Even Republicans admired her efforts. Said Senator Roger Jepsen of Iowa, "she's the best campaigner Carter has. She represents him well" (Avery 1979, 39).

Not everyone, though, was impressed with Rosalynn's surrogate role. While her messages were generally well received, she did receive some criticism. During her speech before the National Urban League in Chicago, audience members were offended that she repeated the refrain, "he [or] she happens to be black" every time she referenced a person of color in relation to President Carter's appointments. The patronizing tone "drew outright hoots" from the audience, and Vernon Jordan began his keynote speech by stating, "I'm president of the National Urban League and I happen to be black" ("Selling True Grit" 1979, 12; "Mrs. President" 1979, 23). Notes in the speechwriters' subject files suggest that Rosalynn's speech writing team frequently tried to adapt the first lady's speeches in order to highlight the Carters' appreciation for diversity and their understanding of the contributions and needs of ethnic and racial minorities. Various drafts of speech introductions are marked with titles like: "Language on Asian-Americans," "Language for Greek-Americans," and "Language for Irish-Americans" (Carter 1980).

Rosalynn's role as Jimmy's surrogate also created some tension with leaders of the women's movement. Gloria Steinem complained, "She never appears to say anything separate from him. More than any other president's wife I have seen there is no independent thought or phrasing separate from his" (Quinn 1978, K3). Rosalynn's own press secretary, Mary Hoyt, said that the first lady is best understood as an "extension of the President" (Quinn 1978, K3). Journalist Sally Quinn argued that Rosalynn's performance had not lived up to the 1976 Carter campaign promise of a "much more influential role" for the first lady (1978). According to Troy, "Quinn and her colleagues disapproved of Mrs. Carter's loyalty, selflessness and humanity. They missed Betty Ford" (2000, 261).

Rosalynn's public discourse reflected two primary goals: responding to her husband's critics and convincing the American public that they needed to re-elect Jimmy Carter for four more years so that he could finish what he started. The rhetorical themes of her discourse included: making concrete the accomplishments of her husband's administration, testifying to his moral character and principled ideals, and explaining his vision for the future.

Rosalynn Carter responded aggressively to her husband's critics. She chastised them for being naysayers and for thinking him naïve. In her campaign speeches, she asserted, "They accuse him of thinking that any problem can be solved if you just look long enough and hard enough. And they were right. Jimmy Carter did think that. He does think that. He believes with all his heart that this country can solve its problems" (Carter 1978b). She told *U.S. News and World Report* that depictions of her husband as vacillating and weak stemmed from the news media tendency to try to intercept information and report what is assumed or speculated to be the president's position before he actually makes a decision. She defended Jimmy as a thoughtful, deliberate decision-maker who based his positions on his informed convictions. She asserted, "He studies things, and when he makes a decision, it's *his* [her emphasis] decision." She also argued that Jimmy would not be swayed by his critics in his decision-making process, "You cannot make your decisions based on criticisms. You have to do what you think is right" ("Rosalynn Carter" 1979, 49).

Rosalynn believed that in spite of the various crises and obstacles her husband's administration faced toward the end of his first term, "we were having some successes" (Carter 1984, 304). She saw that her job on the campaign trail was to highlight her husband's accomplishments. This goal manifested itself in her discourse as a kind of chronological recounting of Jimmy Carter's accomplishments in office. The draft of her remarks before the Florida Democratic Convention is representative of her political stump speeches for the reelection campaign. Rosalynn began the speech by attending to the hostage crisis in Iran. Her discussion of the crisis reflected her broader goal of highlighting her husband's diligent and patient response to all the crises faced by the nation during his presidency by enumerating the specific steps the president took "to protect our interests and ensure justice" (Carter 1979h).

After the Iran crisis update, she turned her attention to enumerating her husband's accomplishments as president. Her speech covered Jimmy's accomplishments in terms of reducing unemployment, establishing an energy program that lessens the nation's dependence on foreign oil, addressing inflation, cutting the federal budget deficit (a deficit created by Republicans, she notes), increasing federal aid to education by 60 percent and establishing the Department of Education, saving Social Security from bankruptcy, reforming welfare but also making room in the federal budget for necessary programs for the elderly and the poor, and standing up for minority rights. After fully exploring his successes on the domestic front, she turned her attention to foreign policy issues featuring Jimmy's pursuit of world peace through a strong military, the Middle East Peace negotiations, the Panama Canal treaties, the Salt II treaties, and the administration's formal stand against apartheid in South Africa.

Her recounting of Jimmy's political accomplishments and goals were supplemented with depictions of her husband's character. Most of Rosalynn's campaign speeches, both during the midterm elections and the presidential campaign, created a strategic depiction of Jimmy Carter as a hard worker who was both bold in his initiatives and patient in implementing them. For instance, in a stump speech draft, she concluded her speech by stating, "When he [Jimmy] was inaugurated he offered not a new dream, but fresh faith in the old dreams that have made our nation unique among nations, and uniquely blessed. He has pursued that faith—with boldness, and with patience and the day-to-day persistence necessary to make dreams work" (Carter 1978b). She also depicted him as honest and principled—willing to meet difficult challenges regardless of political risk or gain. In her address to the Florida Democratic Convention, she asserted, "For three years he has not ducked or hidden. He has fought the hard battles. He has taken the heat" (Carter 1979h). In her public discourse she contextualized his lack of popularity in terms of his honesty, perhaps indirectly reminding her audiences of previous administrations who were not honest in their dealings with the American public. In a draft of the first lady's remarks to the Florida Democratic Convention, she argued that truth in politics was not always popular and often hard to come by: "Some people did not like what he [Jimmy] had to say. But people heard something that had long been lacking from our nation's leadership—the truth" (Carter 1979h). According to Rosalynn, her husband was willing to face and speak the brutal truth about the state of the nation and the work and sacrifice needed to solve the country's problems. In another draft of a stump speech, Rosalynn stated, "Jimmy has made the tough choices. He has faced our problems head on, rather than letting us bury our heads in the sand. He is always trying to make us see how much we still have left to do—so we tend to forget how much Jimmy has already done" (Carter 1979f). Throughout her speeches, she assured her audience that even though his decisions were not always popular, Jimmy's heart was always in the right place: "Jimmy loves our country. He is working night and day to do what is right for ourselves, our future, and our children. He wants a prosperous America, he wants a secure America, he wants an America at peace" (Carter 1979f).

Finally, Rosalynn's campaign discourse focused on explaining Jimmy's vision for the nation's future. However, her attempt to reassure the voters that the nation was on the right track was sometimes compromised by her rhetoric of self-restraint, sacrifice, and no easy solutions. For instance, even though she attempted to convince her audience that her husband had already accomplished so much, she also sought to remind her audience that "there are no magic cures" (Carter 1978a). She also compared the nation's current state with that of the Great Depression, "During the Depression, our deep problems led many to question whether even democracy could survive. . . . These are similar times." And yet, like the depression era, Rosalynn encouraged her audience, "With the work already begun, if we continue rebuilding our solid base, the 1980's can mean a stronger, more prosperous America. We can put behind us the talk of retreat and limited expectations" (Carter 1979c). In spite of the various domestic and international crises facing the Carter administration and the nation, Rosalynn's public discourse sought to restore her audience's faith in the White House. She told her audiences, "We know that today's problems are not permanent. They are difficult problems. But they are not insoluble. And America has lost none of the underlying strengths needed to solve them" (Carter 1979c).

Legacy

What distinguished Rosalynn Carter's performance of the first lady role from her predecessors was her keen understanding and public admission of how much influence she wielded. She clearly expanded the political power and rhetorical possibilities for the first ladyship, and her rhetorical activities contributed to one of the closest working, publicly acknowledged, presidential partnerships. As Carl Sferrazza Anthony has suggested, "unquestionably, Mrs. Carter had a degree of political power not seen since Eleanor Roosevelt," and as a couple, the Carters also "seemed almost replicas of fellow southerners James and Sarah Polk of the 1840s—pious, hardworking, and political" (1991, 275).

The Carter presidential partnership demonstrated the central, rhetorical role the wife of a president could play in an administration. Rosalynn's role as the president's closest advisor "added a new page to the evolutionary history" of first ladies. Other first ladies had been active advisors to their husbands, but no previous presidential couple was as open in acknowledging the influence of her advice (Smith 1996, 568). Both Carters acknowledged that Rosalynn was the more political of the pair. Although, they almost always put forth a unified front in public, she frequently disagreed with him privately, especially on the timing of announcements for his major decisions. According to Anthony, "Rosalynn was acutely aware that the problems Carter had to address were unpopular and controversial, and she feared the outcome of approaching them head on" (1991, 277). She argued that unpopular decisions should be made in the second term; the primary goal was to win reelection.

With Rosalynn's performance the office of the first lady also became a base for strong lobbying efforts and advocacy on behalf of substantive issues ranging from mental health reform, to age discrimination, to the ERA, to the Panama Canal, and the Salt II treaty. In addition to her numerous speeches, press conferences, and interviews supporting a variety of issues, Rosalynn was only the second first lady to testify before a congressional committee, Eleanor Roosevelt being the first.

Finally, Rosalynn's first lady performance demonstrated the rhetorical and political possibilities for a first lady as presidential surrogate. She took on the unprecedented role of representing the United States on substantive policy discussions with foreign leaders. Her trip to Latin America and her role as the president's representative marked a significant rhetorical development in the role. Previous first ladies, like Eleanor Roosevelt, traveled abroad as the president's representative, but their mission was not to explain American foreign policy to heads of state (Smith 1996, 570). Rosalynn's rhetorical performance was not limited to the "eyes and ears" role of the first lady; rather, she was charged with communicating persuasively the significant foreign policy themes of the Carter administration. In addition to her ambassadorship, her first ladyship also demonstrated the primary rhetorical role the wife of a president could play in election campaigns. Not only did Rosalynn stump for other Democratic candidates at midterm elections, during the 1980 reelection campaign she became the more "visible 'candidate' substituting for the president in the primaries" (Anthony 1991, 308).

Unfortunately, their bid for reelection was unsuccessful. Both Carters had big plans for the nation, but their term in the White House was short-lived. In spite of the miraculous accomplishment of a Middle East Peace Summit at Camp David, the Carter administration was plagued with problems including: the energy crisis; the struggling economy; the Russian invasion of Afghanistan, which forced President Carter to impose a grain embargo and cancel the U.S. participation in the 1980 Olympics; BillyGate; and last but not least, the Iranian hostage situation. In her autobiography, Rosalynn reflected that in spite of the obstacles for reelection, "I was so sure we could beat Ronald Reagan in the general election. I couldn't believe the people would fall for his rhetoric or support the platform laid out at the Republican Convention" (1984, 334). When it became clear that the Carters would not be remaining in the White House for a second term, Rosalynn admitted she was angry and resentful. She wrote:

> I was bitter at what I had seen on television for weeks that I thought was so unfair to Jimmy; bitter about the hostage situation dominating the news for the last few days before the election as the media "celebrated" the anniversary of the hostage capture; bitter at the opposition for deliberately misleading the American people; bitter that they blamed Jimmy for the hostage crisis when they should have praised him for his sound judgment and patience. . . . Yes, I was bitter. (1984, 342)

Neither Carters allowed their presidential defeat to become a personal defeat. Instead, both maintained their sense of civic responsibility and social activism as they returned home to Plains, Georgia.

Both Carters remain actively involved in those causes and concerns that punctuated their time in the White House. Rosalynn Carter, for example, continues to serve as a public advocate for mental health. As a full partner in the Carter Center, she created and chairs the center's Mental Health Task Force, and every year she hosts the Rosalynn Carter Symposium on Mental Health Policy.

She also works closely with a number of national community volunteer efforts including: Last Acts: Care and Caring at the End of Life (a national coalition of individuals and organizations advocating for more compassionate care for the terminally ill), Habitat for Humanity (a volunteer network that builds homes for the needy), Project Interconnections (a nonprofit organization that provides housing for homeless people who are mentally ill), and the Friendship Force (a citizens intercultural exchange program). In addition to her advocacy, Rosalynn Carter has published four books since her stay in the White House: *First Lady from Plains*, her autobiography; *Everything to Gain: Making the Most of the Rest of Your Life*, a book coauthored with her husband about life after the White House; *Helping Yourself Help Others: A Book for Caregivers*; and *Helping Someone with Mental Illness: A Compassionate Guide for Family, Friends, and Caregivers* (coauthored with Susan K. Golant). She continues to travel and speak throughout the world. Most recently she accompanied her husband on a historic visit to Cuba to meet with Fidel Castro.

Notes

The authors are particularly indebted to the archivists at the Jimmy Carter Presidential Library for their guidance in our search for Rosalynn Carter's public discourse.

1. Speech texts and interview transcripts were obtained from the Jimmy Carter Presidential Library, Atlanta, Georgia. Materials cited come from the Speechwriters Chronological File, the Speechwriters Subject File, Presidential Speechwriters File— Achsah Nesmith, and the Staff Office Files. Most of the speech texts cited are written working drafts and not necessarily the texts delivered. When multiple drafts were present, the last draft was cited. The citations in the bibliography include the dates of the drafts from which we quoted in our text. They may not reflect the date of the actual speech given. Even though the texts may not be "as delivered," they do evidence the themes Rosalynn Carter articulated in her public discourse. The Carter archival materials are just now becoming open to the public, and at the time of this essay, written drafts of her speeches were all that were available.

2. Many of Rosalynn Carter's speeches were drafted by Mary Hoyt, her press secretary, but she was also assisted by various members of her staff. According to Myra Gutin, sometimes entire speeches were drafted for the first lady and she merely made a few changes; however, most often the resulting speeches were a combination of Carter's ideas and phrasing and the contributions of her speechwriters (1989, 155); see also Sally Quinn's article in *The Washington Post* (1978). The drafts of speeches in the files at the Jimmy Carter Presidential Library indicate that speech draft suggestions also came from White House speechwriters Bob Rackleff, Rick Hertzberg, and Achsah Nesmith.

References

Angelo, Bonnie. 1976. She's Running for First Lady. *Time*, 11 October, 27.
———. 1977. Rosalynn: So Many Goals. *Time*, 10 January, 11–12.
Anthony, Carl Sferrazza. 1991. *First Ladies*, Vol. 2. New York: William Morrow and Company.

Avery, Patricia. 1976. We've Worked Hard—I've Done All I Could Do. *U.S. News and World Report*, 18 October, 24–25.

———. 1977. Some Surprises as First Lady. *U.S. News and World Report*, 14 November, 40–41.

———. 1979. Rosalynn—Spearhead of Carter Campaign. *U.S. News and World Report*, 5 November, 39–40.

Ayers, B. Drummond, Jr. 1979. The Importance of Being Rosalynn. *New York Times Magazine*, 3 June, 39–50, 56.

Caroli, Betty Boyd. 1987. *First Ladies*. New York: Oxford University Press.

Carter, Jimmy, and Rosalynn Carter. 1995. *Everything to Gain: Making the Most of the Rest of Your Life*. Fayetteville, Ark.: University of Arkansas.

Carter, Rosalynn. 1978a. Iowa Jefferson-Jackson Day Dinner, 22 August. Speechwriters Subject File. Atlanta, Ga.: Jimmy Carter Presidential Library.

———. 1978b. Suggested Stump Speech, 4 October. Speechwriters File—A. Nesmith. Atlanta, Ga.: Jimmy Carter Presidential Library.

———. 1979a. American Baptist Churches Biennial Meeting, 1 June. Speechwriters Subject File. Atlanta, Ga.: Jimmy Carter Presidential Library.

———. 1979b. Averell Harriman Testimonial, 21 June. Speechwriters Subject File. Atlanta, Ga.: Jimmy Carter Presidential Library.

———. 1979c. First Lady's Campaign Remarks, 3 December. Speechwriters Subject File. Atlanta, Ga.: Jimmy Carter Presidential Library.

———. 1979d. First Lady's Remarks at Harlem Church, 4 December. Speechwriters Chronological File. Atlanta, Ga.: Jimmy Carter Presidential Library.

———. 1979e. Hospital Cost Containment Rally, 22 October. Speechwriters Subject File. Atlanta, Ga.: Jimmy Carter Presidential Library.

———. 1979f. Political Speech. Speechwriters Subject File. Atlanta, Ga.: Jimmy Carter Presidential Library.

———. 1979g. Remarks of the First Lady at the Gridiron Dinner, 24 March. Speechwriters Subject File. Atlanta, Ga.: Jimmy Carter Presidential Library.

———. 1979h. Remarks to Florida Democratic Convention, 16 November. Speechwriters Chronological File. Atlanta, Ga.: Jimmy Carter Presidential Library.

———. 1979i. Women and America—Rosalynn Carter Challenges Communicators, 26 April. Staff Office File—Sarah Weddington. Atlanta, Ga.: Jimmy Carter Presidential Library.

———. 1979j. Work Activity Center, 4 June. Speechwriters Subject File. Atlanta, Ga.: Jimmy Carter Presidential Library.

———. 1980. Material for Ethnic Audiences, 19 February. Speechwriters Subject File. Atlanta, Ga.: Jimmy Carter Presidential Library.

———. 1984. *First Lady from Plains*. Boston: Houghton Mifflin Company.

Carter, Rosalynn, and Susan K. Golant. 1996. *Helping Yourself Help Others: A Book for Caregivers*. New York: Random House.

———. 1999. *Helping Someone with Mental Illness: A Compassionate Guide for Family, Friends, and Caregivers*. New York: Random House.

The Carters. 1977. *The Nation*, 18 June, 740.

Change Comes to White House. 1977. *U.S. News and World Report*, 21 March, 31–33.

First Lady Becomes First Defender. 1979. *U.S. News and World Report*, 6 August, 9.

Goldman, Peter. 1977. Out on Her Own. *Newsweek*, 13 June, 15–18.

Greenfield, Meg. 1977. Mrs. President. *Newsweek*, 20 June, 100.

Gutin, Myra G. 1989. *The President's Partner: The First Lady in the Twentieth Century*. West Port, Conn.: Greenwood.

Holt, Don. 1978. Advocate-in-Chief. *Newsweek*, 4 September, 18.

Interview with the President and First Lady. 1978. 14 December. Speechwriters' Chronological File. Atlanta, Ga.: Jimmy Carter Presidential Library.

I've Never Won an Argument with Her. 1978. *Time*, 31 July, 12–13.

Mrs. President. 1979. *Newsweek*, 6 August, 22–25.

Osborne, John. 1978. White House Watch—Rosalynn. *The New Republic*, 19 August, 8–14.

Playing the Rosalynn Card. 1979. *National Review*, 12 October, 1274–75.

President's Closest Emissary. 1977. *Time*, 13 June, 17–19.

Quinn, Sally. 1978. Have You Heard What They're Not Saying about Rosalynn? *The Washington Post*, 25 June, K1–5.

Richardson, Don, ed. 1998. *Conversations with Carter*. Boulder, Colo.: Lynne Rienner Publishers.

Rosalynn Carter Takes on the President's Critics. 1979. *U.S. News and World Report*, 9 April, 49–50.

Rosalynn on the Road. 1978. *Newsweek*, 18 September, 33.

Rosalynn Takes a Message Home. 1977. *Time*, 20 June, 26.

Rosalynn's Turn at Diplomacy "Family Style." 1977. *U.S. News and World Report*, 6 June, 36.

Selling True Grit—and by God She's Good at It. 1979. *Time*, 6 August, 12–13.

Sidey, Hugh. 1979. Second Most Powerful Person. *Time*, 7 May, 22.

Smith, Kathy B. 1996. (Eleanor) Rosalynn (Smith) Carter. In *American First Ladies: Their Lives and Their Legacy*, edited by Lewis L. Gould, 557–82. New York: Garland.

Stroud, Kandy. 1977. Rosalynn's Agenda in the White House. *New York Times Magazine*, 20 March, 19–20, 58, 60, 63.

Troy, Gil. 2000. *Mr. & Mrs. President: From the Trumans to the Clintons*. Lawrence, Kans.: University Press of Kansas.

Chapter 18

Nancy Reagan
Leading Lady, Supporting Actress, or Bit Player

Janette Kenner Muir and Mary Mooney

> I must say acting was good training for the political life, which lay ahead for us.
>
> —Nancy Reagan

Few first ladies can top the devotion that Nancy Reagan has shown over the years to her husband, Ronald Reagan, the fortieth president of the United States. Framed as one of the "great love stories of American politics," their love continues, even as he spirals deeper into Alzheimer's disease. Once a busy socialite with a late-blooming humanitarian bent, Nancy now spends her days caring for "Ronnie," and she continues to work both "on stage" and "behind the scenes" to ensure his place in history.

For many people, Nancy Reagan was and continues to be an enigmatic first lady. As a young woman, she said that her main goal in life was to be married and have a happy family; yet she seems to be disconnected from her two children, Patti and Ron. Even though she knew her actions as first lady were under continual press scrutiny and criticism for "her meddlesomeness," she remained a resolute participant in meetings with the president and his general decision-making. Many in the White House disliked her, and she was often referred to as "the Dragon Lady," yet her social elite friends recognized and appreciated her loyalty to her husband and their circle.

Much has been written about Nancy Reagan, and this chapter offers another perspective—a rhetorical perspective—in the continuing conversation about this former first lady. After providing a brief account of Nancy Reagan's life, from her early years through her role as a political partner in the campaigns of the up-and-coming Ronald Reagan, we consider her initial perceptions of the role of first lady. Unfortunately for her, these role expectations were far different from what she actually encountered, leading her to rethink her actions and words in more pragmatic terms. We discuss the rhetorical strategies she devised to overcome how she had been typecast by the press—as a socialite who was more interested in fashion than with the condition of America's poor and as a political spouse who meddled too much in presidential affairs. We look at Nancy Reagan's personal transformation as she projected a sense of humor at the 1982 Washington Press "Gridiron Dinner" and then became a passionate advocate of drug abuse prevention. Finally, we examine her current role as caretaker and surrogate as she attempts to provide meaning and structure in the former president's daily life, when he is only barely able to recognize her. Leading lady, supporting actress, or bit player? In truth, Nancy Reagan was all three.

Biography

Nancy Reagan's birth date and birth name have both been sources of dispute. A reproduction of her birth certificate, in *Nancy Reagan: The Unauthorized Biography* by Kitty Kelley, states that she was born Anne Francis Robbins on July 6, 1921, in New York City (1991, 1). However, many competing historical sources list her birth as two years later. Confusion about the difference is said to stem from her Hollywood days when it was common practice for studios never to list any female actress's age as more than twenty-five. Named for her two grandmothers, Anne Francis Robbins was always called Nancy for unknown reasons. Further confusion over her name was produced by her mother's name changes, first after divorcing Nancy's biological father and second after remarrying Nancy's adoptive father. It would seem the woman known as Nancy Reagan changed identity several times during the early part of her life.

Nancy's mother, Edith Robbins, was a stage actress who was known for her colorful vocabulary and spirit. Divorced soon after Nancy was born, she took her daughter on the road. Nancy was known as a "backstage baby" —traveling to every town where her mother performed. They parted after two years when the constant travel became too much for the young child. Nancy went to live in Bethesda, Maryland, with her maternal aunt's family. Living there with cousins and pseudoparents was a stable time, but a painful one as well. She saw her mother only occasionally when Edith visited Bethesda, or when Nancy traveled to New York.

Mother and daughter were reunited after six years, in 1929, when Edith married prominent neurosurgeon Loyal Davis and settled in Chicago. Nancy then became Nancy Davis by her own decision when she was fourteen years old. She discussed the adoption process with a judge, who was also a neighbor and friend of the family, then sought support from her biological father who agreed to the adoption.

As Nancy Davis, she was under the influence both of a mother with whom she had not shared a home for a number of years and a new father. These relationships were positive and both parents made strong impressions on Nancy. In her own words: "I learned a lot about how to be a wife, and about many other things from my mother. . . . She had a profound influence on the woman I turned out to be, as did her second husband . . . whom I have always considered my true father" (Reagan with Novak 1989, 66). Nancy's adult years illustrate vividly this influence. Although she eagerly adopted her mother's passion for the stage, she also developed character traits like her father who was "serious, dignified, and principled" (66).

Many stage actors who were friends of her mother also influenced her and helped shape the roles Nancy Reagan would play in life:

> Whenever Mother's old friends from the theater passed through town, they would stay with us. When I came home from school in the afternoon, it wasn't unusual to find Mary Martin in the living room, or Spencer Tracy reading the newspaper, or the breathtaking Lillian Gish curled up on the sofa, talking with Mother. Spencer Tracy stayed with us so often that he became practically a member of the family. (78)

These people greatly affected Nancy Reagan. Though she did not go immediately to Hollywood, they would soon become her friends and colleagues.

Nancy attended Smith College, double-majoring in drama and English. Her inclination toward drama was obvious, but she also shared her father's interest in English. As a doctor and teacher, Loyal Davis was a studied intellectual who wrote a book during Nancy's high school years and sent her silly word limericks while she was away at college. After graduating from Smith, she pursued a film career as Nancy Davis, often getting auditions, though rarely a part, through friends of her mother.

She lived in New York for a short time, then moved to Hollywood and landed a contract with MGM. When she first signed with the studio, she was asked to complete a questionnaire for the publicity department; one question asked her ambition. Answering with words that were telling of the woman she grew to be, Nancy wrote: "to have a successful marriage" (1989, 122). She made eleven movies in her career, including *The Next Voice You Hear*, 1950; *Donovan's Brain*, 1953; and *Hellcats of the Navy*, 1957, with Ronald Reagan. Her film career led to her next role as Mrs. Ronald Reagan.

The Nancy Davis/Ronald Reagan courtship was a love story filled with both modern-day circumstance and old-fashioned tradition. Although it was set in glamorous Hollywood, it was challengingly modern in that Reagan was recently divorced with two children. This was certainly rare in 1950. Ironically, foreshadowing their future in politics, the impetus for Nancy and Ronald's meeting came when her name was printed on a list of communist sympathizers. Ronald Reagan was president of the Screen Actors Guild at the time, and MGM studios suggested he contact her to clear her name.

It was a near miss in meeting, however, because there were several actresses named Nancy Davis in Hollywood, and Ronald was not inclined to pursue the issue. When Nancy stressed her continued worry, Ronald finally met her for dinner—just for reassurance. Nancy stated in her autobiography, *My Turn*, that upon opening the door for their dinner date, her first thought was, "This is *wonderful*. He looks as good in person as he does on the screen!" This event set the real-life stage for their undying attraction to one another (Reagan with Novak 1989, 94). As her memoirs described:

> Ronnie doesn't wait until he's going away on a trip to be affectionate; sometimes he kisses me when he's only leaving the room. He says 'I love you' frequently, and so do I. We are physically affectionate with each other, both in public and in private, and we're always holding hands. A reporter once told me that he and his colleagues were sometimes embarrassed to look at us, especially when I was meeting Ronnie's plane after a trip, because instead of a peck on the cheek, we would really kiss. (Reagan with Novak 1989, 121)

Their early time together was a happy process of discovering many uncanny commonalities, as they attended the Hollywood hot spots and appeared regularly in the press. One of the many qualities they had in common was that neither of them particularly enjoyed life in the "fast lane"; and thereafter they chose to spend quiet evenings together. Nancy made it no secret that she was anxious to marry Ronald, though he was less eager. Nevertheless, in spite of the fact that he was very recently divorced with two children from first wife, Jane Wyman, they were married in 1952. Following the traditional standards of the time, Nancy gave up her career to raise a family and support her husband's political ambitions ("Nancy Reagan Profile," 1). She moved quickly into the role of mother, having their first child seven months after their marriage. Nancy had two children with Ronald Reagan, Patricia Ann and Ronald Prescott and was stepmother to his two children from his previous marriage, Maureen and Michael. Nancy has remained in contact with Maureen and Michael but has been estranged from Patti and Ron. (Both children have, in recent years, softened toward their mother.)

Nancy Reagan's life was significantly shaped by the career moves of her husband. Ronald's acting career diminished over the early years of their marriage as he gradually worked more as a radio announcer and political campaigner than as an actor. In 1964, he came to the nation's attention with his speech for 1964 Republican candidate Barry Goldwater. Reagan's "A Time for Choosing" opened the door to a life in state and national politics that they had never anticipated (Reagan 1998, 11). The Reagans began their preparation for a public political life in 1965, when he ran for governor of California. Nancy was an active participant in this process. Stuart Spencer, a political consultant for all the Reagan political campaigns, described Nancy as:

> A born politician. They were a team. . . . We never held a meeting in the house with Ron and discussed strategic matters—which we did a lot in 1966—that she wasn't present. Listening. And, as time went on, asking questions. . . . Her political skills were better, in terms of what was best for Ron, than even his own. His skills were in the communication aspect and the beliefs and ideology.

She was the personnel director of the Reagan operation. . . . She made a lot of decisions about people coming and people leaving. She was right 90 percent of the time. (quoted in Colacello 1998a, 135)

After the election, Nancy persuaded Ronald that the family should live in the suburbs rather than in the run-down governor's mansion. Citing the children's safety as a concern, the Reagans moved to an English-style country home in the suburbs, paying the rent themselves until a group of their friends bought the house and continued to rent it to them (Reagan with Novak 1989, 140).

At this time in Nancy Reagan's life, being a wife and a mother were the most time-consuming of her jobs, but her early work as first lady of California focused on building an appropriate governor's mansion. Later, her attention turned to humanitarian projects such as hospital visits to soldiers, POWS, the elderly, and children. Her activities were similar during Reagan's second gubernatorial term.

In 1976, Ronald Reagan began his first bid for the presidency. Nancy Reagan remembers the campaign most vividly when she writes: "That campaign was so exciting, so dramatic, and so emotional. . . . that in my mind it almost overshadows Ronnie's four victories" (Reagan with Novak 1989, 178). She goes on to describe the campaign experience:

You move from town to town, and the days and nights become a blur as one place melts into another. . . . But there can be a wonderful spirit of camaraderie in a campaign; everyone is working together and traveling toward the same goal. It reminded me of being on location for a movie. You become an extended family. . . . your whole life becomes those people and the plane you're on. (Reagan with Novak 1989, 184)

There were times though when Nancy would have to say "Enough!" as schedulers would press for more appearances, "Even then I felt the staff was there to look after Ronald Reagan the candidate, but I was there to look after Ronald Reagan the man" (184). While the election turned out to be a disappointment when Reagan did not receive the Republican Party's nomination, he was able to use the enthusiasm and support received during the campaign to pave the way to a landslide victory in 1980.

Rhetorical Activities as First Lady

One might think that being first lady of California would have prepared Nancy Reagan well for her role as first lady in Washington, but in many ways it did not. As she writes in *My Turn*, "I found out the hard way that nothing—nothing—prepares you for being First Lady" (1989, 20). The lack of privacy, continual public scrutiny, and critical press coverage barraged Nancy Reagan. She writes:

My clothes. My friends. My taste in decorating. My relationship with our children. The way I looked at my husband! My entire life was suddenly fair game for comment by the press and the public alike. . . . Washington can be a tough town, and I didn't know how to handle it. (Reagan with Novak 1989, 21)

Everything she did early on in her husband's presidency seemed to receive criticism. As time went on, she began to change her actions and words to better suit the press and public. For example, in what was perhaps a rare effort early on (1981) to control what appeared in print about her, Nancy Reagan authored a column on prisoners of war, missing-in-action soldiers, and their families. Her knowledge of their conditions came from her visits to wounded Viet Nam vets, senior centers, hospitals, and schools. She continued to gain popular support by working for other causes such as finding foster grandparents for handicapped children, described in her book, *To Love a Child* (with Jane Wilkie). In an effort to help the public get to know her, she wrote *Nancy* (with Bill Libby), then continued to explain herself and her actions from her own perspective in *My Turn* (with William Novak), written after she left the White House.

Throughout all of the self-presentations that map her evolution as a first lady, Nancy Reagan saw herself, above all else, as a wife. In her own words:

> I threw myself into the various First Lady roles—spokeswoman, hostess, manager, and friend. I thought all of them were important, but there was one part of the job that outranked them all. Above everything else, the First Lady is the President's wife. (Reagan with Novak 1989, 60)

It was in the role of "wife" that she defined herself most fully as first lady, and it is a role that might prove to be the most challenging as she carries out her wifely duties caring for her failing husband. Yet, to understand better the rhetorical dimensions of her tenure as first lady, we need to examine how she played the roles of political partner, hostess, public relations specialist, and advocate.

Political Partner

Nancy Reagan has often stated that her life began when she met "Ronnie," as she is fond of calling the former president. Indeed, as she described their romance, his reticence to commit, their brief wedding, and the birth of their daughter Patty, it is clear that the most important role in Nancy Reagan's life was being the wife of Ronald Reagan. She was a partner in both his personal life and the political life they came to share. In addition, this partnership made her fiercely protective of him. In a 1987 speech about the role of the first lady, she noted:

> In spite of everything I've learned these past six years, there's one thing on which I'm inflexible. The First Lady is first of all a wife. After all, that's the reason she's there. A President has advisers to counsel him on foreign affairs, on defense, on the economy, on politics, on any number of matters. But no one among all those experts is there to look after him as an individual with human needs, as a flesh and blood person who must deal with the pressures of holding the most powerful position on Earth. . . . I think it's an important, legitimate

role for a First Lady to look after a President's health and well-being. And if that interferes with affairs of state, then so be it. (Reagan 1987, 10–11)

Nancy Reagan's devotion to her husband was based upon the way she defined her role as first lady and this definition generated much press and public commentary, thus creating for her a significant rhetorical exigence. She wanted to be there for him—all of the time—in every aspect of his life. To some, this seemed intrusive, and Nancy had to answer charges that she was running the White House. Although she claimed she never tried to influence policy directly, she did have a strong influence with people close to Reagan, such as James Baker and Michael Deaver. She was responsible for hiring personnel, and both Baker and Deaver understood that they had to be accountable to her. Richard Burt, former assistant secretary of state under George Shultz, commented, "I'd go so far as to say that Nancy Reagan was the most powerful First Lady of the last 35 or 40 years. And she went about it in the right way, the appropriate way—entirely behind the scenes" (quoted in Colacello 1998b, 115). Muffie Brandon, the White House social secretary from 1981 to 1984, noted that even though Nancy Reagan did not want to appear to be in charge, she was much more influential than she cared to have known. According to Brandon, "I once asked her, 'Don't you ever think about your place in history?' She looked at me and she said, 'Oh, no. It's Ronnie. And Ronnie's place in history'" (quoted in Colacello 1998b, 115).

Much has been written about the level of influence Nancy Reagan had on her husband behind the scenes. Some of the president's advisors were particularly critical of her actions, saying that she tended to interfere with the president's schedule and wanted to be too much involved. After the 1981 assassination attempt on Reagan's life, Nancy acknowledged that her attention to her husband increased because no one else was focused on his personal needs.

The assassination attempt played a crucial role in Nancy's attitudes about her husband's work. She began to consult astrologer Joan Quigley because she was terrified that something might happen to him again. To Nancy, "Joan's recommendations had nothing to do with policy or politics—ever. Her advice was confined to timing—to Ronnie's schedule, and to what days were good or bad, especially with regard to his out-of-town trips" (Reagan with Novak 1989, 48). Advisors closest to Nancy and Ronald Reagan were respectful of her concerns and tried to accommodate her. Many times this meant that she went along with her husband on trips. She always believed that if she had been there on March 30, 1981, the day the president was shot, she might somehow have prevented it.

Throughout Ronald Reagan's two terms in office, Nancy Reagan was an active, engaged member of his circle, and there were times when her opinion was the only one that mattered. Her influence on her husband was credited with elevating the role of first lady to the level of "Associate Presidency" (Caroli 1996, 39). When Ronald Reagan was convalescing in 1985 the press reported that there were three people in control: the president, his chief of staff, and the first lady (77).

They were definitely a team. Nancy Reagan not only read newspapers and watched television news reports, but she also used an elaborate telephone network to make things happen. Despite her involvement from the outset, there were some who were surprised that she would have opinions and refuse to be silenced. She noted in a speech to the Associate Press Publishers:

> I'm a woman who loves her husband, and I make no apologies for looking out for his personal and political welfare. We have a genuine, sharing marriage. I go to his aid. He comes to mine. I have opinions. He has opinions. We don't always agree. But neither marriage nor politics denies a spouse the right to hold an opinion or the right to express it. And if you have anything less, it's not marriage, it's servitude. (Reagan 1987, 14–15)

In discussing the ways that women are silenced in their roles as first ladies, Nancy relates her first stage role where she played a character who was kidnapped and kept in an attic. She describes her small part in the second act, drawing the analogy to the treatment of first ladies: "I ran down the stairs, said my one line; whereupon they captured me and took me back to the attic. . . . there are those who think First Ladies should be kept in attics, only to say our lines, pour our tea and then be put away again" (15–16). Here she describes a tension in the public's expectations of first ladies. On one level, they are expected to be neutral standard bearers for their husbands while remaining silent about their own views on policy issues. On another level, however, first ladies are expected to take risks and determine their own places in history. Media constructed images of Nancy Reagan as a conspicuous consumer of material goods and fashions as well as a blind supporter of her husband were difficult for her to overcome. Feminist Betty Friedan criticized Nancy as "an anachronism . . . denying the reality of American women today . . . what they'd like to see a First Lady represent" (Caroli 1996, 334), while other objectors charged her with having little that she stood for on her own.

Even though she was often ridiculed, the important role she played in Ronald Reagan's political world could not be ignored, and many of her husband's advisors agreed on her value to him politically. For example, Michael Deaver said she deserved as much credit for Reagan's success as did he. Both Deaver and James Baker have commented that they often used Nancy as a sounding board and asked for her advice and help regarding the president. Even historians, who have rated Nancy Reagan low as a first lady, have admitted how valuable she was to her husband, and she is still credited with being the one person most skilled at protecting his image (Caroli 1996, 274).

At a state dinner, Canadian prime minister Brian Mulroney, who had developed a friendship with the Reagans, asked Nancy, "What do you think is the most important thing you do?" She remarked: "I protect Ronnie from himself. . . . He trusts everybody, and he doesn't see when he's being blindsided, or when people are acting out of motives that are less than noble. And he never acts upon it once he does. I do" (quoted by Mulroney in Colacello 1998b, 173). In response to criticism about her influence on the president, she noted, "No First Lady need make apologies for looking out for her husband's personal welfare. . . . The First Lady is, first of all, a wife" (McAllister 1988, A1). Nancy Reagan's view of being a good wife involved being concerned about the issues her husband addressed. She commented, "A First Lady should discuss policies with the President. . . . When they go up to their living quarters at night, is she supposed to talk about dresses and hairdressers? Any man who married a woman that vapid shouldn't be President anyway" (A1). Two issues that reflected the extent of Nancy Reagan's influence were the replacement of Donald Regan and the United States–Soviet détente. Both of these areas were highlighted during Reagan's second term.

Donald Regan Dismissal

During Ronald Reagan's second term in office, Nancy took on a broader supporting role, which resulted in increased influence on the president to the extent that some of the president's advisors were afraid of her. Presidential assistant Helene Von Damm noted with surprise Ronald Reagan's unfailing support of Nancy. Above all, Nancy was his protector. She protected his human needs as well as his political image, and, with the president's advancing age and illnesses, she tried to shield him from negative influences. The Iran/Contra Affair was a devastating blow to the president's credibility and suggested that those who surrounded him were not keeping him informed. Nancy's involvement in the dismissal of Donald Regan, Ronald Reagan's chief of staff, was questionable and added to the perception of influence she had over the president. In his 1988 book, *For the Record*, Donald Regan writes that Nancy vetoed dates for the president's trips and news conferences after consultations with her astrologer, kept the president convalescing too long after surgeries, and described her generally as the "dragon lady." Helene Von Damm, who worked for twenty years as Ronald Reagan's secretary and finally as his director of presidential personnel, described Nancy Reagan's role as manipulative rather than supportive in the firing of Regan:

> Though she always claimed that her sole motivation was making her husband look good, I was very distressed by the open fashion in which she attempted to manipulate him over Don Regan's dismissal. Far from making him look good, her practically open interference made him look pathetic and weak. (Von Damm 1989, 229)

Of course, Nancy Reagan's viewpoint on the firing of Donald Regan was quite different. She saw her role, once again, as one of supporting her husband. In *My Turn* she provided excerpts from her daily journal that speak of her anguish and concern over Regan's lack of popularity with the staff and his way of handling the president. Although she knew people believed that she was influencing Regan's removal, she admitted that while she wanted him to leave, it was, ultimately, the president's decision to make. Leaks to the press implied that she was in control, and an article by William Safire underscored the Von Damm position that the first lady had "staged a coup":

> [A]t the time he most needs to appear strong, President Reagan is being weakened and made to appear wimpish and helpless by the political interference of his wife . . . the power-hungry First Lady . . . an incipient Edith Wilson, un-

elected and unaccountable, presuming to control the actions and appointments of the Executive Branch. (Safire 1987, A17)

In her memoirs, Nancy Reagan described this article as the most vicious and unbelievable article ever written about her. Other reporters came to her aide and took exception to his view—specifically the lead editorials in the *New York Times* and a column by Judy Mann, who was usually critical of Nancy Reagan's actions. Mann countered Safire's remark and was quoted in *My Turn*:

> First Lady Nancy Reagan managed to do what nobody else was able to do— namely, rid the administration of someone who was literally crippling the Presidency. White House Chief of Staff Donald Regan hung on in an unprece- dented display of supreme arrogance, placing his own self-interest above that of President Reagan and, certainly, above the welfare of the country. Calls, pleas, messages through the media, and personal visits from Republican leaders could not move the President to replace him. . . . The Republicans and conservative power brokers ought to be sending her bouquets of long-stemmed red roses. In- stead, she's being depicted as a power-hungry dragon lady. . . . The President didn't look like a wimp. He had a wife who understood what had to be done and was willing to do the dirty work. That makes him a pretty lucky man. (Reagan with Novak 1989, 348)

According to Nancy, most people wanted Regan to leave, but no one was will- ing to convince the President that he needed to dismiss him. She spoke to her husband about it, not to the press. Rather than denying her power behind the scenes, she claimed to have merely facilitated an action that others were too afraid to take.

American/Soviet Détente

In a *Vanity Fair* interview, Nancy Reagan discussed her influence on Ronald Reagan in building the relationship between the United States and the Soviet Union. Referring to it as "the whole Russian thing," she said, "I couldn't have influenced this if he didn't really come to believe it. I just felt, here were these two superpowers sitting here, and it was silly not to get together" (Colacella 1998b, 171). Ronald Reagan's position on the Soviet Union was clear from the beginning of his presidency. Massive military buildup, the MX long- range missile system, the Evil Empire Speech, and the Strategic Defense Initia- tive (Star Wars) all revealed Reagan's skeptical position on the possibility of developing a relationship with the USSR.

In 1989, Nancy Reagan referred again to this influence and how it was per- ceived by the media, "You can't imagine how surprised I was to read I was call- ing the shots on the nuclear arms race" (Reagan 1989b). Yet, she did influence the way her husband handled the Soviet Union. In fact, many people credit Nancy Reagan's behind-the-scenes advice as central to the détente that devel- oped between Gorbachev and Ronald Reagan. Though it was a series of talks and a complicated process, the first lady was involved at all times in the details.

Nancy has spoken of her relationship with Raisa Gorbachev, a degreed his- torian, and the perceived competition that developed between the two. Because of the constant media attention, the two women were very self-conscious about meeting and interacting. In Nancy Reagan's memoirs she noted, "Every nuance of my encounters with Raisa Gorbachev was scrutinized. Every meeting between us was treated like a test of wills. Every time we appeared together, we were seen as contestants in some international pageant" (Reagan with Novak 1989, 336). In the end, however, they developed a relatively warm relationship. Said Mrs. Gorbachev at a luncheon during a visit to New York and the United Nations: "I will miss you and your husband. . . . As for the two of us, it was destiny that put us at the place we were, next to our husbands, to help bring about the relationship that our two countries now have" (379).

It seemed impossible that the end of the Reagan era would see the collapse of the Berlin Wall, the breakup of the Soviet Union, and the end of the Cold War. While this occurred over a very long and tedious series of talks, Nancy Reagan was with her husband as his life and political partner throughout the process, pushing from behind the scenes for peace.

Hostess

Just as relentless as the attention paid to the social interactions of Nancy Reagan and Raisa Gorbachev was the daily scrutiny of social affairs the first lady hosted or attended. Meeting high expectations and playing the tireless, hospitable, prepared, and gracious hostess was another important role Mrs. Reagan performed well for her husband and country. The White House itself illustrates this point.

When the Reagans moved into the White House, the building had not been renovated for a number of years. The private living quarters needed painting, the floors needed work, there were cracks in the walls, and there was general disarray. While Nancy Reagan approached the renovations as necessary for reclaiming "some of the stature and dignity of the building" and for meeting the hostess duties of the first lady, she did not expect that it would provoke great anger and controversy. Nancy began a campaign to raise $200,000 for the White House renovations. The greatest contributors to this fund were her friends from California, known as "the Kitchen Cabinet" and criticized by the press as "an exclusive, wealthy club" (Reagan with Novak 1989, 22). While those in the White House were pleased with the changes, others outside were more critical. Reports of the renovations were contrasted with rising unemployment and homelessness. Some critics opined that the renovations had been paid for with public monies. Others thought it inappropriate for the Reagans' personal friends to contribute to the White House renovations (24–25). The press heavily criticized Nancy Reagan for excessive spending and lavish decorations (Caroli 1996, 100). The image of Nancy that emerged was that of a rich woman who needed to acquire expensive things. In reality, however, she was continuing the work of First Ladies Jacqueline Kennedy and Patricia Nixon, who also made renovating the White House a priority. Similarly, Rosalyn Carter made efforts to acquire fine American paintings for the White House collection (Reagan with Novak 1989, 224).

Nancy's successors were also grateful because her renovations made their work easier. New wall and floor coverings, refinished doors, upgraded wiring, and renovated bathrooms were passed on to First Ladies Barbara Bush and Hillary Clinton, so that these women had only minor refurbishing to do. Barbara Bush wrote of her gratitude: "Nancy Reagan got lots of criticism for redecorating the White House when we all should have been on our hands and knees thanking her. . . . As her successor, I was eternally grateful to her for that" (Bush 1994, 165).

From the first lady's perspective, refurbishing the White House was an attempt to bring a sense of dignity and royalty back into it. This effort contrasted directly with the Carter years when the White House was filled with children, grandchildren, and animals. From the socialite following to the lavishly expensive inaugurals, the Reagans appeared to some to be trying to elevate the presidency to a level consistent with its need to entertain foreign heads of state and royalty. Yet in redecorating, Nancy was providing an environment in which she could fulfill the social hostess aspect of her role as first lady as she defined it.

The replacement of the White House china was an example of the perceived opulence surrounding the Reagans' time in the White House. Although the funds to purchase it came from private donations and the china was clearly needed (sets had to be mixed and matched for large dinners), critics argued that donors gained tax advantages and would want special treatment from the White House. For the press, the china served as a symbol for Nancy Reagan's ongoing extravagance during a time of recession.

The manner in which the Reagans dressed directly added to these perceptions, and Nancy Reagan was well known, and criticized, for borrowing expensive dresses from popular designers. To her critics, Nancy commented:

And I wonder: What would have happened if I *had* stopped borrowing dresses and had started wearing only the clothes that I could actually afford to buy? Before long, instead of calling me extravagant, the press would have started referring to me as "dowdy" and "frumpy." And the newspapers would soon have been keeping track of how many times they have seen me in the same outfit. I don't think I could have won this one. (Reagan with Novak 1989, 32)

Although the media have always focused on the way first ladies dress and look, the attention paid to Nancy Reagan's clothing was extreme, dominating much of the coverage of her. The criticism women writers lavished on her may have been due to the campaign of 1980 and the first year of the presidency in 1981. "With few exceptions," she wrote, "they described me as a woman who was interested only in rich friends and fancy clothes, a supercilious and shallow socialite, a lady who loved shopping and going out to lunch. In other words, an airhead" (Reagan with Novak 1989, 35). In some ways, the press descriptions were true. Nancy had (and continues to have) a circle of very rich, supportive friends. When she campaigned with her husband and after his election to the White House, she did wear designer clothes and was rarely seen in the same outfit twice. She definitely traveled in social circles, but she questioned the criticism that was continually directed toward her. In talking about the press coverage at this time, she noted the various names and jokes that were told about her:

> And the *Chicago Tribune* surely deserved a prize for squeezing the greatest number of negative references into a single sentence when it described me as "Queen Nancy the Extravagant, an aloof former debutante and movie star whose main concerns are fashion, decorating and lunching with rich girlfriends, whose idea of hard times is tablecloths that shrink, whose doe-eyed devotion to her husband leads to hard-eyed terrorizing of her aides." I was called more names than I can remember. Queen Nancy. The Iron Butterfly. The Belle of Rodeo Drive. Fancy Nancy. The Cutout Doll. On the *Tonight* show, Johnny Carson quipped that my favorite junk food was caviar. (Reagan with Novak 1989, 36)

Even today, a tension exists in the different ways that first ladies are talked about in the media. Rarely are they discussed without reference to the clothes they wear and the designers who have influenced them. During the 2000 presidential campaign, great emphasis was placed on the clothing and fashion styles of Laura Bush and Tipper Gore. This focus is supported by the Smithsonian Museum of American History's First Lady Exhibit, which focused originally on the inaugural gowns worn by first ladies. Today, the exhibit focuses on the first ladies' political role and public image, although inaugural gowns are still included as a significant part of the exhibit (Mayo and Meringolo 1994).

Public Relations Specialist

In retrospect, Nancy Reagan realized that she was probably responsible for perpetuating many of the press's attitudes by retreating from rather than directly addressing their charges. Many critics viewed her lack of reaction as snobbishness rather than as self-protection. Nevertheless, the image the press projected of Nancy Reagan was supported by her actions during the first year of her husband's presidency.

As we have already suggested, her public image created a significant rhetorical exigence that Nancy Reagan needed to address. To do so, she began to pay more attention to public relations. Her goal was to recover her reputation and shift the negative perceptions that also surrounded her husband's administration.

The contrast between the poor and unemployed Americans and the perception of a wealthy, extravagant White House created great tension for the Reagans. By the end of 1981, Nancy Reagan had the highest *disapproval* rating of any first lady in modern times. The president's economic recovery plan was not working, and from mid-1981 to late 1982 the country underwent the worst economic recession since the Great Depression. Unemployment and homelessness were on the rise. Polls showed that 52 percent of Americans felt Reagan favored the rich (Colacello 1998b, 170). In her memoirs, Mrs. Reagan wrote:

> During Ronnie's first term, I was portrayed as caring only about shopping, beautiful clothes, and going to lunch with my fancy Hollywood friends. During

his second term I was described as a power-hungry political manipulator, a vindictive dragon lady who controlled the actions and appointments of the executive branch. . . . Part of the problem is that while the President's job is clearly defined, nobody really knows exactly what the First Lady is supposed to do. The Constitution doesn't mention the President's wife, and she has no official duties. As a result, each incoming First Lady has to define the job for herself. (Reagan with Novak 1989, 57)

Acting in the role of public relations specialist, Nancy Reagan attempted to overcome these perceptions and develop her own rhetorical persona. Her appearance at the annual Press Gridiron Dinner did just that.

The Gridiron Dinner is considered by Washington insiders to be one of the most important annual events in Washington, D.C., for journalists and politicians. The program is usually the same—members of the press perform skits that poke fun at Democrats and Republicans, followed by speakers from each party and a toast to the president. In 1982, Nancy Reagan found out that someone had planned to do a song about her. Sheila Tate, Nancy's assistant, came up with the idea that she should sing an attack on the press. Nancy refused to do that saying, "If I'm going to do this at all, I think I should make fun of myself" (Reagan with Novak 1989, 39).

The white-tie crowd was definitely surprised when Nancy showed up in a mismatched costume, with yellow rain boots, a boa, and a red straw hat with feathers. She sang "Second Hand Clothes," a parody of Fanny Brice's "Second Hand Rose." The lyrics were:

I'm wearing second-hand clothes
Second-hand clothes
They're quite the style
In the spring fashion shows
Even my new trench coat with fur collar
Ronnie bought for ten cents on the dollar.

Second-hand gowns
And old hand-me-downs
The china is the only thing that's new.
Even though they tell me that I'm no longer Queen,
Did Ronnie have to buy me that new sewing machine?
Second-hand clothes, second-hand clothes
I sure hope Ed Meese sews.
(Reagan with Novak 1989, 41)

As part of the finale, Nancy Reagan smashed a replica of the White House china to pieces. The crowd cheered and cried, "Encore! Encore!" (Caroli 1996, 170). This song, along with her willingness to sing it and make fun of herself, showed the press corps that she was not as humorless and distant as she had been portrayed. Clearly, this rhetorical act directly overcame the exigence characterized by Nancy Reagan's perceived aloofness and royal image. "From that night on," she wrote, "my image began to change in Washington. . . . It is not often in life that one is lucky enough to enjoy a second beginning, but during one five-minute period in the spring of 1982, I was able to make a fresh start" (Reagan with Novak 1989, 38, 41). In her memoirs, she included a quote from the *Washington Post* that described the journalists' reactions to her act, saying, "The sophisticated audience of journalists, politicians and their friends responded to her performance as though she had undergone a major change. A number of those image-makers left the ballroom saying that Nancy Reagan's song-and-dance number had transformed her image" (Reagan with Novak 1989, 42).

In reflecting on this event and the initial impressions she had to overcome when first in the White House, Nancy Reagan discussed her time as first lady in a speech for the Southern California Conference on Women in September 1989. She talked about the highs and lows of those years and the bad publicity she had received over replacing china, remodeling rooms, and wearing designer dresses. Media scrutiny both "hurt and frustrated her." "There was a time when I never wanted to hear the word china again." She explained again that the china and dresses were donated, costing taxpayers nothing (1989b). The turning point for attitudes, however, appeared to be her performance at the Gridiron Dinner. She proved that she could be a good sport, leading some members of the press to soften their stance toward her.

Further determined to help her husband's administration and still wanting to address her own low popularity ratings, Nancy Reagan turned her attention to the fight against drug abuse. She realized she would be the "object of attention no matter what" and wanted to do something positive (Reagan with Novak 1989, 57). Initially her advisors were not pleased with the topic because it seemed too negative and depressing. However, as she noted at an Associated Press publishers' luncheon, a first lady should do whatever she wants because she will "never again be in this unique position to make such a contribution" (Reagan 1987, 17). Nancy Reagan had always had an interest in the drug issue, and if the issue worked with the American public, it could be important for her image. The effort to remake Nancy's image was acknowledged by several advisors who worked directly with her. During an hour-long television program on Nancy Reagan in 1985, presidential aides talked about "working out a plan" and developing a "public relations campaign" to increase Nancy Reagan's appeal to the American public.[1]

Advocate

Nancy Reagan's most public role was as an advocate against drug abuse. To spotlight the "Don't Do Drugs" program Nancy Reagan traveled nearly 250,000 miles throughout the United States and several other countries. She appeared on talk shows such as *Good Morning America*, taped public service announcements, appeared on the situation comedy *Diff'rent Strokes*, wrote guest articles, and visited prevention programs and rehabilitation centers across the country. She also narrated two PBS specials—*The Chemical People* and its follow-up program, *Chemical People II*—which encouraged community members to organize against drug abuse.

The press covered Nancy Reagan's initial efforts, but soon grew weary of the repetitiveness of her message. However, subsequent approval ratings showed that the issue was popular with the American public. Within just a few months of the beginning of the campaign, she had gained twenty points in public approval polls and had a staff of several dozen because the project had grown far beyond what one person and a few volunteers could do (Caroli 1995, 60).

In April 1985, Nancy Reagan expanded her drug-awareness campaign to the international level, inviting first ladies from around the world to attend conferences in Washington, D.C. She went to the Vatican to speak with Pope John Paul II about drug abuse. She continued her crusade by appearing in June 1986 at the World Affairs Council in Los Angeles. The speech, "The Battle against Drugs," was published in *Vital Speeches of the Day* and laid out her basic platform and appeals for involvement in the campaign. She began by acknowledging the privilege of speaking to such an audience:

> I can't tell you how honored I feel to be speaking before the World Affairs Council. I know of great leaders and intellects who have appeared in the place where I am standing today–and it's a little overwhelming. I certainly don't put myself on their plane, but I believe what I want to discuss with you is just as important as anything previous speakers have discussed. (Reagan 1986, 645)

Nancy told the story of how she became aware of the drug issue in the sixties when she was first lady of California. At that time, she received calls from distressed friends whose children were getting caught up in drugs, and she later integrated some of these stories into her speeches.

> [A]ll the statistics, all the clinical studies, all the expert briefings in the world can't match the reality of one deeply suffering young person. When people learned I was interested in drug abuse, I began getting letters that would simply pierce your heart, letters of pain and loneliness and confusion—thousands of them. (Reagan 1986, 646)

She continued to describe the results of her five years of speaking around the country and the world to raise awareness about the dangers of drug abuse. "We now have 9,000 parent groups that are . . . closing down head shops, becoming involved in school drug programs, and forming support groups for one another" (Reagan with Wilkie 1989, 646). Youth peer groups and "Just Say No" clubs were forming to counter the increased pressure to try drugs. Internationally, she commented that the number of concerned first ladies was on the rise. Nancy's primary appeal in this speech was to everyone's moral responsibility to take a personal stand against drugs. The appeal to moral obligation was interspersed throughout the rest of her speech and put drug use and the denial of abuse onto a moral high plain that gave no room for middle ground. She strongly declared:

> Those who believe that people who use drugs aren't hurting anyone but themselves are wrong. Drugs hurt society. The money spent on drugs goes into the

hands of one of the most ruthless, despicable lots ever to breathe—the drug producers. They are often murderers. They are sometimes terrorists. They are always criminals. They represent man at his most debased. They are the people who are financing the death and destruction of our young people. And by doing nothing when you know of drug use, you're conspiring with them as they line their pockets with even more blood money. (Reagan 1986, 647)

In October 1988, Nancy Reagan became the first American first lady to address a United Nations General Assembly. At this gathering she did not lay blame on other countries that import illegal drugs, but admonished the United States for its lack of responsibility in dealing with its drug users. She noted:

It is often easier to make strong speeches about foreign drug lords or drug smugglers ... than to arrest a pair of Wall Street investment bankers buying cocaine on their lunch break. ... It is far easier for the United States to focus on coca fields grown by 300,000 campesinos in Peru than to shut down the dealer who can be found on the street corners of our cities. (Reagan 1988c, 1)

The focus on what the United States should be doing to prevent drug abuse was at the heart of all of Nancy Reagan's speeches. She was most interested in keeping young people off drugs, creating drug-free zones in school yards, and preventing drug abuse from starting. Too much attention, she also argued, was placed on the suppliers. Drug abuse must be stopped by directly decreasing the demand for drugs, and keeping children away from drugs from the beginning would have a definite impact on that demand. As she developed her platform, Nancy Reagan wove in poignant stories from parents and teenagers about their struggles to quit using drugs.

In a speech for the 43rd Session of the United Nations, she appealed to the audience that "as mothers we are concerned, as First Ladies we are committed, and as citizens of the world we pledge to do all that is possible to stop this scourge" (Reagan 1988c, 1). In a description of the various speeches she has given over the years, Nancy claimed, "I have found that there is a powerful, unified international resistance to illegal drugs that is developing. This is a different type of international conspiracy, a conspiracy of compassion" (2). She argued for education and commitment. Countries must become responsible:

My chief concern is for the children—the children of America and of the world—that they will say "no" to drugs, that they will choose life, and learn to live in the world that God made, not in the nightmare world of drugs. The children need our help; and as you carry out your important responsibilities, what better guide can there be than what is best for our children will also be best for our nations. (2)

Nancy Reagan was successful with this cause in many ways. First, parents' groups, student peer groups, and local support groups sprang up all around the country. Second, more first ladies from other nations signed up for the program as the issue progressed over the years when Ronald Reagan was in office. Finally, her image was enhanced because her advocacy work was successful as a public relations effort. This was evidenced by a 1985 NBC report showing that she ranked second only to Jackie Kennedy Onassis among recent first ladies (Caroli 1995, 335).

Legacy

Despite the ups and downs of her relationship with the press and public, Nancy Reagan's legacy as a first lady must include the positive contributions she made to improve social conditions. Although she had received awards of different kinds before she entered the White House, as first lady she received public service awards for her work against drug abuse and numerous humanitarian awards from the American Camping Association, the National Council on Alcoholism, the United Cerebral Palsy Association, and the International Center for the Disabled (Who's Who, 2).

After leaving the White House, she also contributed to the public good by establishing the Nancy Reagan Foundation to continue her work with drug abuse. In 1994, the foundation joined forces with the BEST Foundation For A Drug-Free Tomorrow and developed the Nancy Reagan Afterschool Program, a drug-prevention and life-skills program for youth.

In her speech to the Southern California Conference on Women, Nancy Reagan called her campaign a "five-year battle to convince America that drugs are indeed a national problem" (Wride and Eng 1989, 3). She continued that battle in a testimony before Congress on March 9, 1995, when she noted that the antidrug crusade she had championed "appears to be fizzling because of a lack of leadership and overemphasis on treatment rather than prevention" (Hook 1995, A4). She commented:

> I am not here to criticize or place blame, but after the great strides that were made just a few years back, I'm worried that this action is forgetting how endangered our children are by drugs. . . . Why is it we no longer hear the drumbeat of condemnation against drugs coming from our leaders and our culture? Is it any wonder drug use has started to climb again, and dramatically so? (quoted in Hedges 1995, A1)

Mrs. Reagan's appearance was part of a larger celebration of conservatism on Capitol Hill. Her appearance at this hearing, along with that of former drug czar William Bennett was important in reminding the public of her agenda. Bennett and his former aide, John Walters, commented that President Clinton "is virtually invisible on this issue" and, if trends continue, 1996 would mark "the greatest increase in drug use in American history" (*On Capitol Hill* 1995). This increase in drug abuse was attributed to Clinton's appeal to youth, his famous "I didn't inhale" line, and his general "liberal" attitude ("Nancy's Back" 1995, A4).

Today, the most important aspect of Nancy Reagan's life is her devotion to her husband—placing his life and needs ahead of her own, working to secure his place in history. Feminists have criticized her for "excessive devotion," but others view her focus on marriage as a result of childhood insecurities within her family. Her main goal in life when she moved to Hollywood was to "have a happy marriage" (Leamer 1981, 64), and Ronald Reagan became the object of this goal, leading her into her future roles as helpmate, political partner, social hostess, public relations specialist, and antidrug advocate.

As Ronald Reagan's health wanes, his mind fading under the ravages of Alzheimer's disease, Nancy Reagan still carries his torch, reminding the world of his role in securing democracy and freedom for many in the twentieth century. Now called "the world's most popular caregiver" and "the Grand Dame of the Conservative Movement," it is clear that Nancy Reagan has come into her own. Her presence at the 1996 Republican National Convention provided a personal, poignant moment, reminding people of the Reagan era and legacy. She said:

> Just four years ago Ronnie stood before you and spoke for what he said might be his last speech at a Republican Convention. Sadly, his words were too prophetic. When we learned of his illness. . . . he made the decision to write the American people and the people responded as they always do. I can't tell you what your cards and letters have meant to both of us. The love and affection from thousands of Americans have been and continue to be a strengthening force for Ronnie and me each and every day. . . . As you all know, I am not the speechmaker in the family, so let me close with Ronnie's words, not mine. In that last speech four years ago, he said, "Whatever else history may say about me when I'm gone, I hope it will report that I appealed to your best hopes not your worst fears, to your confidence rather than your doubts, and may all of you as Americans never forget your heroic origins. Never fail to seek Divine Guidance, and never, never lose your God-given optimism. (Reagan 1996b, 1)

Even in that moment of acknowledgment, she used her husband's words to remind Americans of his legacy. Nancy Reagan has become, for many, the pulse of the Reagan era—the person most able to keep his memory alive.

It is not an easy role for the former first lady. Friends describe her as tired and lonely, unable to spend much time away from the man who now barely recognizes her. She attempts to carry on a normal life with Ronnie—arranging golf games and seeing that he spends time at his office and, on occasion, greets tourists at his presidential library. It is a different world for them, one filled with silence and isolation. Once the most powerful man in the world, the Great Communicator who implored Gorbachev to "tear down that Wall," Reagan is now fading into the darkness of disease. Despite the circumstances, the storybook romance lives on, as Nancy Reagan declares that her love for Ronnie grows deeper as they struggle to find meaning and purpose in their lives together. In a speech for the National Alzheimer Association in New York, October 1996, she compares her trials and tribulations to those of Job, explaining that

> Job stops asking and simply commits himself to go on living. It's his wife who shares her incredible understanding of faith and love. . . . I found that too. I found that even though the person I love and have loved for 44 years is slipping away my love for him grows. As he changes, if I stop asking why, and simply love, I do grow. (Reagan 1996c, 2)

Nancy Reagan represented her husband at the dedication of the Ronald Reagan Building and Trade Center, the largest U.S. structure except for the Pentagon (Reagan 1996a). She also represented him at the dedication of the George Bush Presidential Library and in the 2000 presidential campaign. And so it appears that Nancy Reagan is not quite ready for the final curtain call. There is still much to be done and her husband to care for. The elegant parties, the meetings with world leaders, the cheering crowds at political rallies are all sweet memories of the Reagan era. The dreams they relive in old videos and film clips help the former president to remember the past.

After all the pomp and circumstance and the endless photographers and media scrutiny, the first lady is, as she reminds us, a wife. She has played many roles within that spotlight, leading up to and during her tenure as first lady. She has successfully secured Ronald's place in history, and, inevitably, her own as well. She is a model of participation for the roles of political partner, hostess, public relations specialist, and advocate. But, it is as a wife that Nancy Reagan finds her most challenging and rewarding role. Leading lady, supporting actress, or bit player? Actually, Nancy Reagan was all three.

Notes

A sincere thanks to Cate Sewell and others at the Ronald Reagan Library in Simi Valley, California, who generously assisted in the attainment of Mrs. Reagan's speeches. We also wish to acknowledge C. Claire Smith and Eve DeAngelo for their careful proofreading and editing.

1. NBC Documentary on Nancy Reagan, 1985. This documentary featured presidential aide Michael Deaver and White House pollster Richard Wirthlin outlining plans to make Nancy Reagan more appealing to the American public. By the summer of 1985, NBC reported that the plan had worked because an NBC poll showed Nancy Reagan as ranking second only to Jackie Kennedy Onassis among recent presidential wives.

Selected Chronology of Major Speeches

August 15, 1986	The Battle against Drugs
May 4, 1987	Remarks for Associated Press Publishers' Luncheon
June 9, 1988	Remarks for the World Gas Conference
August 15, 1988	Remarks to the Republican National Convention
October 25, 1988	Address to the United Nations
June 3, 1989	White House Memoirs: A First Lady's Perspective
September 5, 1989	Address to Southern California Conference on Women
August 12, 1996	Remarks to the Republican National Convention

References

American Presidency: First Lady—Nancy Reagan. www.gi.grolier.com/presidents/aae/first/40pw.html, accessed 26 May 1999.

Benedetto, Richard. 1998. Reagans Allow Peek at Their Home Life. *USA Today*, 8 June, A7.

Bush, Barbara. 1994. *Barbara Bush: A Memoir*. New York: Charles Scribner's Sons.

Caroli, Betty Boyd. 1995. *First Ladies*, expanded edition. New York: Oxford University Press.

———. 1996. *America's First Ladies*. Pleasantville, New York: Reader's Digest Association, Inc.

Colacello, Bob. 1998a. Ronnie and Nancy. *Vanity Fair*, July, 76–88, 134–42.

———. 1998b. Ronnie and Nancy: The White House Years and Beyond. *Vanity Fair*, July, 110–22, 169–76.

Creative Quotations from Nancy Reagan. www.bemorecreative.co/one/1030.htm, accessed 26 May 1999.

Hannaford, Peter. 1983. *The Reagans: A Political Portrait*. New York: Coward-Mccam.

Hedges, Michael. 1995. Clinton Faces Criticism for Setback on Drug War. *Washington Times*, 10 March, A1.

Hook, Janet. 1995. Drug Crusade Waning. Nancy Reagan Says. *Los Angeles Times*, 10 March, A 4.

Kelley, Kitty. 1991. *Nancy Reagan: The Unauthorized Biography*. New York: Simon and Schuster.

Leamer, Lawrence. 1981. *Make Believe: The Story of Nancy and Ronald Reagan*. New York: Harper & Row.

McAllister, Bill. 1988. First Lady Defends Her White House Role. *Washington Post*, 10 June, A1.

Mayo, Edith, and Denise D. Meringolo. 1994. *First Ladies: Political Role and Public Image*. Washington, D.C.: Smithsonian Institution.

Nancy Reagan Documentary. 1985. NBC.

Nancy Reagan Profile. www.who2.com/nancyreagan.html, accessed 26 May 1999.

Nancy's Back. 1995. *USA Today*, 10 March, A5.

On Capitol Hill. 1995. Newsletter. Securities Industries Association. April.

Radcliffe, Donnie. 1988. Nancy Reagan's Hard Line: At UN Talking Tough on Drugs. *Washington Post*, 26 October, D1.

Reagan, Nancy. 1986. The Battle against Drugs. *Vital Speeches of the Day*, LII: 21, 15 August, 645–47.

———. 1987. Remarks for Associated Press Publishers' Luncheon. 4 May. Simi Valley, Calif.: Ronald Reagan Presidential Library and Museum.

———. 1988a. Remarks for the World Gas Conference. 9 June. Simi Valley, Calif.: Ronald Reagan Presidential Library and Museum.

———. 1988b. Remarks to the Republican National Convention. 15 August. Simi Valley, Calif.: Ronald Reagan Presidential Library and Museum.

———. 1988c. Address to the United Nations. 25 October. Simi Valley, Calif.: Ronald Reagan Presidential Library and Museum.

———. 1989a. White House Memoirs: A First Lady's Perspective. 3 June. Simi Valley, Calif.: Ronald Reagan Presidential Library and Museum.

———. 1989b. Address to Southern California Conference on Women. 5 September. Simi Valley, Calif.: Ronald Reagan Presidential Library and Museum.

———. 1996a. Remarks at the Dedication of the Ronald Reagan Building and International Trade Center. 5 May. Simi Valley, Calif.: Ronald Reagan Presidential Library and Museum.

———. 1996b. Remarks to the Republican National Convention. 12 August. Simi Valley, Calif.: Ronald Reagan Presidential Library and Museum.

———. 1996c. Remarks at the Gala Event for the National Alzheimers Association. 31 October. CNN Morning News. Transcript #96103112V28.

————. 1997. Remarks at the George Bush Presidential Library Dedication. 6 November, Simi Valley, Calif.: Ronald Reagan Presidential Library and Museum.

————. 1998. Forward. In *A Shining City: The Legacy of Ronald Reagan*, ed. D. Erik Felton. New York: Simon and Schuster.

Reagan, Nancy, with Bill Libby. 1980. *Nancy*. New York: Berkeley Books.

Reagan, Nancy, with William Novak. 1989. *My Turn: The Memoirs of Nancy Reagan*. New York: Dell Publishing.

Reagan, Nancy, and Jane Wilkie. 1989. *To Love a Child*.

Regan, Donald. 1988. *For the Record: From Wall Street to Washington*. New York: Harcourt Brace Jovanovich.

Safire, William. 1987. First Lady Stages a Coup. *New York Times*, 2 March, A17.

Von Damm, Helene. 1989. *At Reagan's Side: Twenty Years in the Political Mainstream*. New York: Doubleday.

Who's Who. Academic Universe. web.lexis-nexis.com/universe/, accessed 2 June 1999.

Wride, Nancy, and Lily Eng. 1989. Nancy Reagan Opens Women's Conference: Talk Focuses on Anti-drug Drive. *Los Angeles Times*, 6 September, 3.

Chapter 19

Barbara Bush
Her Rhetorical Development and Appeal

Molly Meijer Wertheimer

> You have two choices in life: You can like what you do, or you can dislike it. I have chosen to like it.

> A more literate America would benefit every single thing I worry about: crime, unemployment, pollution, teen-age pregnancy, school dropouts, women who are trapped into welfare and therefore poverty, etc.
>
> —Barbara Bush

Two weeks before George Bush was elected president in 1988, he predicted that Americans would fall in love with Barbara Bush (Radcliffe 1989, 3). That prediction came true. In the first three months of her taking residence in the White House, she received 35,000 letters (Kilian 1992, 162); by the end of her first year as first lady, she averaged 3,000 letters a week (Anthony 1991, 422) During her next three years as first lady (1991 through 1993), she was ranked number one in Gallup's annual "Most Admired Women" poll, and she continued to rank in the top five throughout the 1990s (Gallup 1999). Today, she remains popular with Americans in her new identity as first mother—the only woman to be both wife and mother of a president in her lifetime.[1]

What is it about Mrs. Bush's enactment of her public roles that continues to interest so many of us? Is it her "naturalness"—that she seems comfortable with herself? Is it her "honesty"—that she calls it like she sees it? Is it her feisty wit—that she uses humor to disarm her opposition? Is it her maternal persona—

that she projects concern for family, friends, and community? Is it her commitment to service—that she works hard to promote family literacy and volunteerism? Is it her endurance—that she continues to campaign even as she grows advanced in years? Those of us who study her rhetorical activities would say that it is all of those projected qualities because she makes such skillful rhetorical use of them.

Barbara Bush was not always a consummate rhetorician. When she first moved to Washington, D.C., in late 1966, the wife of a newly elected member of the House of Representatives, she stayed out of public view. Yet as George Bush's career advanced, she could no longer avoid publicity. Although she had always been "talkative and opinionated in private," she had to learn to speak in public. She had to find the right balance between being candidly "outspoken," but not seeming too "impudent" or "caustic" (Radcliffe 1989, 50, 53). In short, she had to develop skills as a rhetorician. According to first lady scholar Lewis L. Gould, Mrs. Bush learned to manage "the media and her own image with a great deal of deftness" (1996, xviii). By the time of her husband's inauguration, Kati Marton contends, Mrs. Bush was "so skilled . . . at manipulating her image that she gave almost everybody something to like about her (2001, 275). "Media smart" is how biographer Donnie Radcliffe describes her (1989, 50). Mrs. Bush also developed her public speaking skills to the point where she was selected to speak at the Republican National Conventions in 1988 and 1992. Her popularity and political value was so great that she was even asked to campaign by herself during off-election years. One question this essay raises is: How did she become so accomplished?

Barbara Bush developed her public speaking skills through years of experience. At first she used a slide show that she narrated; this device allowed her to extemporize as her staff member advanced the slides. After that, she learned to speak without using the slides by constructing basic speeches and then amplifying her points with stories that she collected and honed. She used her talent as a storyteller—including timing and mimicry—to enliven her presentations. She also perfected her use of humor—using self-deprecating humor to diffuse those who would provoke her with nasty questions or try to entrap her to reveal *her* position on thorny political issues. She also became a master at manipulating the news media for her own purposes. She learned to project a wholesome image of motherhood—of maternal service to others; her "matronliness," says Marton, "was . . . carefully packaged" (2001, 275).

This essay traces some of the "methods" Barbara Bush used to develop her presentational skills as well as commenting on her interpersonal communication skills—her "social style"—developed from long years of participating in social activities both to promote her husband's agenda as well as her own. Her *A Memoir* provides illuminating detail to support her claim that critically important diplomacy happens when political leaders meet informally in social situations (Bush 1994, 87–88). By the time she entered the White House she had been the wife of a man who was a member of the House of Representatives, ambassador to the UN, head of the National Republican Party, liaison to China, head of the CIA, and vice president. During her eight years as second lady Mrs.

Bush—known as a "traditionalist"—did not "sit home and eat bonbons" (Bush 1994, 166). According to her own tally:

> In the 2923 days of the vice presidential years: 1629 days were spent out of Washington traveling, including visiting all fifty states and sixty-five different foreign countries, many of them more than once . . . George and I traveled an estimated 1.3 million miles, which is 54 times around the world . . . when I was in town, I hosted 1,192 events at the Vice President's House and attended 1,232 other events in Washington. (Bush 1994, 167)

Her activity as first lady was every bit as busy. Although these tallies reveal the many opportunities she had to develop and practice her rhetorical skills, they do not reveal how well she performed. A second purpose of my essay is to review her performance and comment critically on the rhetorical legacy she has left the office of first lady, even today as she breaks new ground as "First Mother" of George W. Bush and "First Mother-In-Law" to Laura Welch Bush.

Biography

Barbara Pierce was born in New York City on June 8, 1925, to parents Marvin and Pauline Pierce.[2] The Pierces lived in Rye, New York, a quiet town of eight thousand people just two train stops away from Greenwich, Connecticut, home of her future husband George Herbert Walker Bush. Although an affluent suburb, Barbara's family lived modestly, but well; even during the depression, the children "never wanted for anything." Barbara remembers especially the wonderful food served at her house and mealtimes shared with members of her family. Afterwards, the Pierces would often spend the evenings together "with everyone enjoying a favorite book or magazine."

Barbara's father worked his way through Miami University of Ohio, waiting tables and tending furnaces after his wealthy Pennsylvania family lost their fortune in the 1880s. Described by Barbara as "really bright" and athletic, Marvin Pierce graduated Phi Beta Kappa, receiving nine letters from playing on athletic teams. He met Barbara's mother, Pauline, a "striking beauty" who was studying to be a teacher, and they fell in love. Her family was from Marysville, Ohio; her father was an attorney who served on the Ohio Supreme Court in the 1920s. When Barbara was born, Marvin worked for the McCall Corporation, becoming its president in 1946. Her mother was the disciplinarian of the family and an accomplished gardener who "knew how to keep an exquisite home." She filled her home with antique furniture and china, purchasing it from vendors from all over the country and paying for it on the installment plan. Her hobbies kept her quite busy.

Barbara related to her father and mother differently. She was especially close to her father who often took her side in family squabbles; in *A Memoir* she writes: "some of my happiest times were walking with daddy to the station in the morning," then she would take her own bus to school (5). Her mother was often preoccupied with her younger brother who was in and out of the hospital for years. As an adult, Barbara understood better what her mother was going through, but as a young girl she missed the attention. She learned lessons from both of her parents that she would use when she raised her own children; from her father she learned to teach by example, to give her children a good education, and lots of love. From her mother she learned to appreciate what she had instead of what she didn't have: "She was a lucky women," writes Barbara, "who had a husband who worshiped the ground she walked on, four loving children, and a world of friends. Her ship had come in—she just didn't know it" (Bush 1994, 9).

Outside of school, Barbara played with her friends, cutting out paper dolls from McCall pattern books, riding their bikes, and reading literature and poetry together. They acted out some of the stories they read as plays. Barbara developed a biting sense of humor and an irreverence that became a permanent part of her personality. She could mimic people well, sometimes using the ability to put people down. Years later, she admitted that she shouldn't have behaved this way and she forbid her own children to make fun of others. As an adult, her humor became self-deprecating—she made fun of herself.

Kati Marton attributes the development of Barbara's sharp wit to her size and weight: "As the large-boned daughter of a coolly critical mother and the younger sibling of a thin and graceful older sister, she survived by irreverence . . . [and] a cutting wit" (2001, 281). Whether true or not, twelve-year-old Barbara weighed 148 pounds and was five feet eight inches tall. She remembers her mother telling her thin older sister, Margaret, to eat up, but warning Barbara not to eat any more at meals. An athletic and solidly built young girl, Barbara reminisces in *A Memoir* about the dance classes she and her friends took on Fridays. Probably because she was tall and there were more girls than boys, Barbara often volunteered to take the role of the boy; that way she could avoid being the last girl asked to dance.

Barbara attended public school until she was in sixth grade, then enrolled in Rye Country Day School, a private school, through the ninth grade. For tenth, eleventh, and twelfth grades she went to Ashley Hall in Charleston, South Carolina, an exclusive preparatory school with limited enrollment (150 students) that offered a classical curriculum. At Ashley Hall, she made good grades and always followed the rules; she enjoyed swimming and acting in plays. About public speaking she wrote: "I was so shy at the time and never could have gotten up and given a speech." One of her classmates remembers her as "just the prettiest thing and very outgoing and athletic" (Kilian 1992, 31); by the time she was a teenager, Barbara had grown more slender.

During Christmas vacation in 1941, sixteen-year-old Barbara Pierce met seventeen-year-old George Bush at a dance at the Round Hill Country Club in Greenwich, Connecticut. She describes her reaction to biographer Pam Kilian: "He was the handsomest-looking man you ever laid your eyes on," and "I could hardly breath when he was in the room" (1992, 34). George was smitten with her, too, for he later wrote his mother, "I have never felt toward another girl as I do toward her" (quoted in Marton 2001, 278). During that vacation, they met at another dance and went on a date. They wrote to each other from school, and during spring break, they went to a movie. At the end of George's senior year, he took Barbara to the prom.

George joined the navy in June 1942, becoming the youngest pilot to earn his navy wings (he was eighteen). Barbara wrote to him during her senior year and when she was a freshman at Smith College. She was preoccupied with George's safety since he was on active duty in the Pacific. In the fall 1944, she received a letter from a pilot in George's squadron saying that his plane had been shot down. She spent three anxious days waiting until she heard that he had been rescued. They were married on January 6, 1945; Barbara was nineteen, George was twenty. In commenting about their young age, she writes: "In wartime, the rules change. You don't wait until tomorrow to do anything" (Bush 1994, 22).

During the first eight months of married life, Barbara joined George as his schedule allowed. In three of the twenty-nine moves she would make during their forty-four years of married life, Barbara set up housekeeping in Michigan, Maine, and Virginia Beach; their accommodations were modest—dark rented rooms, a one-room efficiency, a basement apartment—showing the personal financial situation of this young couple from privilege. Barbara learned to cook, clean, and do laundry, she "wandered the streets" when she was bored and read good books. In Virginia Beach, the Bushes relaxed on the beach, and she chased George's golf balls as he and a friend learned to play. She was very much in love. After the bombs were dropped on Hiroshima and Nagasaki, August 1945, George was released from the navy, the recipient of two air medals and a Distinguished Flying Cross. They headed for New Haven, Connecticut, so George could attend Yale (Bush 1994, 24–26).

The Bushes lived in three different places during the two and a half years they were at Yale—some of them involved living arrangements that were quite communal, sharing kitchens and bathrooms. Barbara was not interested in finishing her education, though she could have done so. Instead, she played bridge, went to the movies, worked part-time in a co-op, kept score for George's baseball team, and had her first child, George Walker Bush, "Georgie," known today as "George W." George graduated from Yale after two and a half years, and then he accepted a position with Dresser Industries to work at one of their holding companies, Ideco Oil. He drove to Odessa, Texas, in a red Studebaker his father had given him as a graduation present, sending for Barbara and Georgie after finding a place to stay.

The Bushes lived in Odessa, while George learned the oil business; then, in 1949, they moved to California, living in four different places as George changed positions within Dresser Industries. Barbara became pregnant, and she visited a clinic for prenatal care, the kind of clinic where you see anyone who is on duty. She did not meet the doctor who delivered her daughter Pauline Pierce Bush, "Robin," until the night she was born on December 20, 1949. This experience later helped Mrs. Bush empathize with other women in similar situations. In 1950, the Bushes moved back to West Texas; they lived in a motel, a small house, and then a slightly bigger house. George's career advanced, and at age twenty-six, he formed his own oil company, Zapata Oil, with a neighbor. In

1953, Barbara gave birth to John Ellis Bush, "Jeb."

Also in 1953, Robin was diagnosed with leukemia and died several months later. This was a heartbreaking episode for the Bushes; Barbara was inconsolable. She was in her late twenties and her hair began to turn white. George helped her through this difficult time, as did son Georgie, who was only seven years old. In *A Memoir*, Barbara describes how Georgie cheered her up and helped the family overcome their sadness by using humor. In 1955, Barbara had another child, Neil Mallon Bush, and less than two years later, Marvin Pierce Bush was born; Barbara gave birth to her last child, a daughter, Dorothy Walker Bush, "Doro," in 1959, the same year the Bushes moved to Houston.

For the next ten years, as George continued to build his business, Barbara did "what every mother in America does: taxiing children to the doctor, the dentist, birthday parties, baseball games, tennis matches, and so on" (Bush 1994, 55). She discovered that her son Neil was dyslexic, and spent considerable time learning about the disorder and helping her son learn to read. She set the tone for the family and was the disciplinarian. George W. said she was like a "drill sergeant," while Jeb said she was the family's "chief operating officer" (Kilian 1992, 57, 66–67). She was highly organized, coordinating all of the children's activities and family moves. These were the kinds of experiences she brought with her when George entered politics.

In 1962, George ran for chairman of the Republican Party of Harris County, Texas. Barbara described this first race as a mean political battle. George campaigned in all 210 precincts of Harris County, and Barbara went with him. Although she did no public speaking at this time, she sat on stage and listened to her husband's speeches. In *A Memoir* she writes: "The evenings could be long and tedious. That's when I took up needlepoint," which turned out to be an effective conversation starter with other stitchers at the rallies (Bush 1994, 57). She attended mixers before and after her husband's speeches where she proved a valuable asset because she had an outgoing personality and a good memory for names, faces, and conversations. She also helped her husband "read character," judging who would and would not serve him well. Over the years, George would learn "to rely on her judgment of people." According to Lud Ashley, one of George's close friends, "it is hard to imagine George going as far as he did without Barbara" (quoted in Marton 2001, 281). George won the election, and then turned his attention to a run for the U.S. Senate.

During the 1963 Senate primaries, John F. Kennedy was shot and Texan Lyndon B. Johnson became president. According to Mrs. Bush, "with Johnson at the top of the Democratic ticket, we did not have a chance" Her use of the pronoun "we" here shows that she considered herself very much in the race with her husband as his political partner. That same tone of "politics as a shared ambition" carries through *A Memoir*, each of the Bushes contributing his or her share as dictated by traditional gender roles. Barbara went door-to-door with members of her husband's staff, wearing a name tag that simply read "Barbara." She felt that she could secure more truthful reactions from voters if she remained incognito (Bush 1994, 60; Kilian 1992, 85; Parmet 1997, 109). George lost that election, but he ran three years later for the U.S. House of Representatives and won.

The Bushes spent the next four years very busy in Washington, D.C. (1967–1971). George was appointed to serve on the prestigious Ways and Means Committee, and their social life escalated. Barbara was George's social partner, attending receptions, dinners, and luncheons both with and without him. Early in January, they attended two days of briefings for new Republican members of Congress and their spouses. During the second day session for wives, she learned about protocol as well as tips about dressing. She felt the information was outdated because the speaker talked about calling cards and long white gloves. She "tried everything once," she said, including briefings at the State Department, Republican meetings, Congressional wives meetings, luncheons, and dinners. She joined the International Club II, perhaps because George's mother had been a founding member (Bush 1994, 67–68). Lady Bird Johnson and Betty Ford had also been members of this group. There were plenty of opportunities for "networking" among these political wives, and Barbara "tried hard never to miss one of those meetings."

Barbara also became an active member of the 90th Club, consisting of the wives of members of the 90th Congress. The women met to study issues; eventually, eleven women became close friends. One of these women, Janet Steiger, introduced Barbara to slide shows. Mrs. Steiger used a slide show of the sights of Washington when she was invited to address constituents; she shared the idea with other wives who were often issued similar invitations. According to Mrs. Steiger, Barbara improved the slide show, she "perfected it to the extent that she had a series of shows, one on the gardens of Washington, another on the buildings, and so on. 'I ended up borrowing her slides. They were so much better'" (quoted in Radcliffe 1989, 151).

At first Barbara was fearful of making presentations. She was invited to talk at a garden club in her home district, for example, and she couldn't say no. But she was scared to death. She told her friend Shirley Pettis Robertson that there was no way she could give the speech. According to Shirley, she put much time into those speeches. Often Shirley would see her lights on late at night as she worked on them (Radcliffe 1989, 157). Marion Chambers, another friend, told a story about finding Barbara on her doorstep one day. Barbara had come to Marion's to rehearse a speech: "She stood in front of the fireplace and we both started laughing because we could hear her knees knocking . . . that was the last time I ever heard them knock" (quoted in Radcliffe 1989, 158). With practice, Barbara developed the slide show into an effective campaign tool.

George made many friends as well, and the Bushes often entertained, inviting friends and neighbors for informal lunches on Sundays, much as they had done when they lived in Texas. Apparently, Barbara kept index cards of all the friends they had made throughout the years, and according to Marton, by the mid-1970s she had between four and five thousand cards (2001, 283). In addition to socializing, Barbara's life "settled into a nice routine" that included carpooling, housekeeping, meetings, losing weight, and coloring her hair (Bush 1994, 71). George was busy most of the time and frequently traveled back and forth to Texas. Barbara remained in charge of the children, taking them all over

Washington to see the sights: "every single weekend," she said, "I dragged those poor young people around Washington, taking hundreds of pictures." Later, she used those pictures in her slide shows. "It certainly was an easy way to give a speech," she wrote. "The slides were almost a protective shield, something you could hide behind" (68). During George's second term, Barbara wrote a monthly newspaper column called the "Washington Scene" that was published in Houston newspapers.

In 1968, George was reelected to the House of Representatives, and in 1970, Republican leaders, including Richard M. Nixon, urged him to run again for the Senate. George lost that election, and the Bushes were faced with the question of what to do next. He asked Nixon for a recently vacated position as ambassador to the United Nations. Many were surprised when Nixon said "Yes," because George Bush had no real experience with foreign affairs. But the Bushes had important social skills: "He [George] and Barbara would get to know all the right people, attend all the right receptions, and give all the right parties. . . . Most of all, they, as a team, would do what they did best, and that required no foreign policy skills—make friends." After a round of trips to Europe to orient the Bushes, they moved to New York. "All the evidence suggests," writes George Bush biographer Herbert S. Parmet, "the Bushes succeeded brilliantly" (1997, 150).

"George loved to entertain and came up with extraordinary and fun ideas," wrote Barbara in *A Memoir* (1994, 85). They also went to "several receptions every evening, many dinners, and quite a few lunches." These social functions were heaven for Barbara: "I loved all of that. In fact, I was born to the job: I love people and I adore eating" (Bush 1994, 87). But they were also work. Barbara stressed the diplomatic importance of such socializing: "At the ambassadors' level, much of the real work of the United Nations was conducted at these social functions. Especially if there was a problem between two countries, the only communications the ambassadors had was 'after hours.' Your guest list was often composed of people who wanted to meet but couldn't on an official level" (87–88). When asked if she was ever given any guidelines or told what to do at such functions she said: "Certainly I was given advice on protocol, and occasionally what to wear . . . , but, for the most part, I just depended on the manners my mother taught me" (86). To overcome the language barrier, she said: "a touch, many smiles, much interest, and lots of honest affection were a universal language" (88).

In 1972, both of the Bushes campaigned for Nixon's reelection; Barbara traveled with other cabinet wives and by herself. After his reelection, Nixon recalled George from the United Nations position and appointed him head of the Republican National Committee, a position Barbara did not want him to accept. News about the Watergate break-in and cover-up was coming out, and Bush's job was "to coordinate efforts at damage control" (Gutin 1996, 61; Kilian 1992, 96). George was kept very busy, traveling around the country, holding the Republican Party together. Barbara kept busy, too, working as a volunteer in a nursing home and for the party, and hosting weekly cookouts for twelve to twenty-five people after church on Sundays. Her family presented her with C.

Fred, a cocker spaniel, on her forty-eighth birthday; he eventually became a traveling companion and "coauthor." When Nixon resigned, George asked the new president, Gerald R. Ford, to appoint him the official diplomat to China—the title was "Chief of the U.S. Liaison Office to the People's Republic of China."

The Bushes moved to China, taking only C. Fred, who attracted considerable attention everywhere they went and so functioned as a conversation starter. The Bushes studied the culture and language, and entertained many different groups and individuals from China, other countries, and the United States. For the most part, the Bushes stayed in their quarters in Beijing, but they were also allowed to visit Red China, Hong Kong, and Canton. Ready with her camera, Barbara snapped shots of interesting sights (Kilian 1992, 97–98), gathering material to use as slides later to raise money for charities and to help her husband campaign for president. In Beijing, Barbara toured the Forbidden City, the Great Wall of China, the Ming Tombs, and she peddled her bike around the city often with C. Fred attached by his leash to her handlebars. The Bushes also entertained a constant flow of guests from the United States, including Henry Kissinger and President Ford as well as family members and friends. According to Mrs. Bush, "everyone wanted to come to China. It was all so new and exciting." But the only way an American could travel there was "if invited by the ambassador to stay in his residence" (Bush 1994, 118). After two years and considerable hostessing, President Ford recalled the Bushes and appointed George head of the CIA.

Morale in the CIA was at an all-time low in early 1976, because a tell-all book by Philip Agee, *Inside the Company: CIA Diary*, had blown some of the agents' covers: one was murdered. The Bushes set off on a morale boosting trip, staying with CIA employees in many countries. This trip must have been a learning experience for both of the Bushes, but George's position required much confidentiality, and Barbara found herself closed out of this part of his life. "I was very depressed, lonely and unhappy," she wrote in *A Memoir*. She was fifty-one at the time and probably going through menopause. The women's movement was in full force, and she began to feel that "her life had been wasted," especially since she may have viewed the CIA job as the end of George's political career. Kati Marton also suggests that Barbara may have been fed up with Jennifer Fitzgerald, George's "executive assistant" ("office-wife"), who had accompanied them to China and made the move with George into "the covert operations of the CIA" (2001, 288–89). Nonetheless, Barbara turned her attention to her public speaking engagements and traveled around the country showing her slides of China "to civic groups, schools, and churches . . . at fund raisers for different charities . . . and at political gatherings." According to Barbara, "China was still a 'hot' item. I tried to have a fast-moving program with *no* pictures of George, me, the children, or C. Fred. I wanted to be completely nonpartisan so civic groups would feel comfortable inviting me to speak" (1994, 135). How different this would be from the slide shows she would put together when she campaigned for George for president. When Jimmy Carter defeated Gerald Ford later that year (1976), the Bushes began house hunting for a place in Houston.

In May 1979, George announced that he was a candidate for the presidency; Barbara brought organizational skills developed from years of child rearing and home management to his campaign (Kilian 1992, 102), and she continued to hone her abilities to speak on issues, deal with media, and refine her image.

During 1979 and 1980, "Barbara Bush was on the road almost every day for two years, campaigning for her husband—first for president, then for vice-president. Most of this time, especially in 1979, she traveled with just one aide," Becky Brady (now Beach) who was new to politics herself (Kilian 1992 103, 105). As the wife of a little-known candidate, Barbara did not attract much attention. She and Becky would fly into a city where a local Republican would act as their guide. They would attend five or six one-hour engagements a day. Her typical audience was a handful of Republican women who would meet in someone's living room for tea and coffee (Kilian 1992, 104). Barbara would present her slide show of China, now modified for partisan purposes. At first, she was not very comfortable and used the slides to "get in the swing of making speeches" (Kilian 1992, 104). Her aide Becky said: "She wasn't accustomed to speaking. But she was fabulous. She put the audience at ease. It was new to her and she didn't realize how well she was doing, but they loved it" (quoted in Kilian 1992, 106). Barbara would narrate the slides using her storytelling ability and Becky would advance them; sometimes Barbara extemporized at length, and Becky would hurry Barbara along by advancing a slide (Kilian 1992, 110). She stuck with the China slide show for about a year, "then decided she could speak on her own without it" (Kilian 1992, 111). She worked out "a basic speech with George Bush as the focus, talking about her family life, his accomplishments, and his goals" (Kilian 1992, 106). She and Becky took the speech to every state except Alaska, and all ninety-nine counties in Iowa (Kilian 1992, 109). Although George Bush was not nominated the Republican presidential candidate in 1980, Ronald Reagan invited him to run as his vice president. Suddenly, Barbara Bush was thrown into the national spotlight and would begin campaigning for the Reagan/Bush ticket.

During the primaries, Barbara had grown familiar with her speech material—highlighting George's personal qualities and his stance on issues. She was not familiar, however, with Reagan's views, so she talked about the problems of the Carter administration. Stressing the negative was not what she liked to do, but initially she had little else to say. She was also not very knowledgeable about literacy, a cause she had chosen to advocate since everything she worried about, she said in *A Memoir*, "would be better if more people could read, write, and comprehend" (145).

Invariably, she was put into situations where she was asked to speak about subjects she had not yet mastered. This raises the question of how well Barbara did as an impromptu speaker. She related an incident in *A Memoir* to explain how she tried to make the best of unexpected situations. During a campaign stop at Cardinal Stritch College in Milwaukee, for example, she was greeted by Sister Camille who said: "We are so excited about your visit. I have collected literacy experts from all around Milwaukee, some forty-five of the most informed people, and they are waiting to hear you. We are just thrilled." Sister Camille introduced Barbara to an audience of experts by saying, "Well, here she is. We can't wait to hear what you have to say." Although Mrs. Bush was unprepared, luckily, she said, "it suddenly came to me what to do." She made a few introductory remarks, and then asked her audience a question: "If you were married to the President and had the opportunity to really make a dent in the field of illiteracy, what one thing would you do? How would you go about it? We'll start on the right and go around the room" (145–46). She said that their two hours ran out before she was halfway around the room. Her audience was happy and she learned about literacy from experts. She also invented through desperation a strategy she could use on other occasions.

She tells about other kinds of impromptu speaking situations and how she handled them in *A Memoir*. Over the years, reporters had asked her questions spontaneously and often she was not given the opportunity to present well-considered answers. Probably the most difficult questions included those designed to catch her taking a stance on thorny issues that was different from her husband's, Ronald Reagan's, or the Republican Party platform. For example, she was often asked about abortion. Donnie Radcliffe claimed the only time she ever heard Barbara sound incoherent was when someone asked her about abortion: "In March 1989, when asked by reporters if she thought the Supreme Court should overturn Roe v. Wade," Mrs. Bush replied, "Now listen . . . you can try this every way you know—I am not going to discuss that. But that really—first of all, I don't think it is very presidential. I don't think it's—it's not—I don't think it's—I'm not going to talk about it. I'm not—because, see, if I start talking about one issue, then I'll have to move into another, and another, and another" (quoted in Radcliffe 1989, 187). She was also asked questions about gun control, the ERA, and personal questions such as: "Did she regret dropping out of Smith College? Did she miss having her own career?" (Kilian 1992, 116) At first her answers were "defensive, snippy," but in time she became good humored and sophisticated.

For example, during the 1980 primary in New Hampshire, she was asked by the *Today Show* to put an open microphone on her belt during an entire day of campaigning. The day included a half-hour interview with Jane Pauley who asked her on camera: "Mrs. Bush, people say your husband is a man of the eighties and you are a woman of the forties. What do you say to that?" (Bush 1994, 148). Mrs. Bush described her reaction in *A Memoir*: "Why didn't she just slap me in the face? She was darn lucky I didn't burst into tears and say that was the worst question I had ever heard. I was speechless and heartsick. I finally answered, 'Oh, you mean people think I look forty? Neat!' I went on to say, 'If you mean that I love my God, my country, and my husband so be it. Why, then I am a woman of the forties'" (149).

In addition to Jane Pauley's interview, Barbara was forced to think about the public impact of her physical appearance by other events. Early in the campaign, she was invited to participate in a press conference at the Waldorf in New York with the wives of the other candidates, including Nancy Reagan and Elizabeth Dole. In *A Memoir*, she compares the conference to a cattle show; the wives were not allowed to speak, they just posed for pictures. "I had the best candidate," she wrote, "but in a beauty contest or best-dressed competition, I didn't have a chance." Mrs. Bush wished she could speak about her husband's qualities, so confident had she become in her ability to address an audience. Kati Marton speculates that as a person, Mrs. Bush "didn't want the burden of beauty. . . . [because] she lacked the narcissism required for its maintenance" (2001, 281). Instead, she relied on her wit to develop what would "become her signature style as first lady." She evolved a self-deprecating humor that allowed her "to turn every potential negative into a positive: her age, her weight, her wrinkles, even her privileged lifestyle" (Marton 2001, 275).

The eight years that Mrs. Bush served as second lady were busy: "I believe the busiest of my life" (Bush 1994, 166). Of course, she moved yet another time into the vice president's house, which "needed a lot of work." She helped plan the renovations and raised private funds to pay for them. She also organized renovations of a house the Bushes had purchased in 1980, in Kennebunkport, at Walker's Point. There the Bushes entertained many U.S. and foreign leaders, as well as members of their large family and friends. She also worked on her image by buying new designer outfits and by meeting designers who would make clothes for her, especially Arnold Scaasi (Bush 1994, 160). In Washington, she set up a staff headed by Susan Porter Rose. She also campaigned for Reagan/Bush during the presidential campaign in 1984, and for Bush/Quayle in 1988.

The Bushes' foreign and domestic travel as well as their entertaining performed important social/political functions. Some of the places they visited outside of the United States included a trip to Ghana in honor of the twenty-fifth anniversary of the Peace Corp. They attended the inauguration of President Marcos of the Philippines, the funerals of Anwar Sadat and Brezhnev. In *A Memoir*, Mrs. Bush explained the usefulness of attending these affairs. About funerals, she said, "George met with many current or future heads of state at the funerals he attended, enabling him to forge personal relationships that were important to President Reagan—and later, President Bush." At all of these functions, Mrs. Bush met new people and deepened her friendships with those she had known before. She continued to learn about the problems and challenges facing other world leaders. The same might be said for her travels in the United States and the entertaining she did both at the vice president's house and at Walker's Point. In fact it was a conversation at a dinner with Nelson and Sandy Doubleday that helped her publish her first book.

As second lady, Barbara promoted the cause of literacy both in direct and indirect ways. *C. Fred's Story*, the book she wrote "with" her cocker spaniel to raise money for literacy, was published in April 1984. The project came about when George told Nelson not to kick C. Fred because the dog was writing a book. This prompted Nelson to inquire about the project and to set up Barbara with an editor to help her. Presented like a slide show, the book shows photographs of C. Fred with George and Barbara in many of the places they lived or visited. The text relates humorous "conversations" the dog had with Barbara, and these episodes perform rhetorical functions: they present the Bushes as "cozy" down-to-earth people who have forged warm personal relationships with many international leaders. Surprisingly, the book raised about $100,000—all donated to the Literacy Volunteers of America and the Laubach Literacy Action (Bush 1994, 188). Mrs. Bush held several book signing events in public libraries, and she went on a media tour to promote the book. She appeared on the *Today Show* and was interviewed again by Jane Pauley. In *A Memoir,* she gave a clear indication of how much she had learned about being interviewed:

> She [Jane Pauley] raced on the set, and as she was putting on her mike, she said something like, "Let's make this fun and not talk about literacy." Not talk about literacy? No way. That was what I was there for. Her first question was, "Mrs. Bush, why would a dog write a book?" Knowing that this might be my only chance, my answer was that he was worried about illiteracy in our country, and then I got in as many facts as possible before I let her get another word in edgewise. (1984, 189)

Mrs. Bush promoted literacy in indirect ways as well. For example, in *A Memoir* she described one of the media savvy methods she used: "It struck me that I worked so hard all year long for literacy and got little or no press coverage, and then I would do something frivolous like going up in a cherry picker [to put the star on top of the national Christmas tree] and my picture is seen around the world. So one year I took Rita and Rex Saurus, two puppets who encourage children to read" (1994, 175). Now the media coverage would be put to good use.

Mrs. Bush's work with literacy groups continued throughout George's second term as vice president, as she worked with Harold McGraw to marshal the support of American businesses and corporations (Bush 1994, 215). She also worked with many of the states' literacy councils and with PLUS (Project Literacy U.S.), a public/private partnership between PBS and ABC. She summarized the work she did during her eight years as second lady as follows: "I participated in 537 literacy related events and another 435 events related to volunteerism." Newspaper coverage of these events, together with articles on literacy that were published in popular magazines, helped raise public awareness of illiteracy and of how this problem could be solved (Bush 1994, 218).

Mrs. Bush continued to use the media for her own purposes, but she was not always successful. Or was she? A highly publicized remark of hers raises the question of whether her "slip ups" with the press were strategic, or whether she could save a mistake by the kind of spin she would later put on what she said. On a plane trip to New York, Barbara was in the press section talking to two reporters about the presidential debate the night before when Fritz Mondale had asked President Reagan about his rich, elite running mate. Barbara made a remark to reporters about Mondale's running mate, Geraldine Ferraro, in what she thought was an off-the-record conversation: "That rich . . . well, it rhymes with rich . . . could buy George Bush any day." Of course, her comment made immediate radio and TV news. When interviewed by the press after the story broke, Mrs. Bush added her own spin on the story by telling reporters she had already apologized to Mrs. Ferraro for calling her a "witch" (Bush 1994, 195–96).

About this "slip up," Kati Marton contends: "even her [Mrs. Bush's] slip-ups seemed calculated. Though she apologized profusely to Ferraro, she had made her point. It was an old Nixon trick: putting negative remarks into circulation by apologizing or denying them" (2001, 292).

No sooner was George Bush inaugurated as vice president in 1985, then the Bushes began to think about his run for president in 1988. "For the first couple of years," according to Barbara, "the campaign consisted of getting out and meeting as many people as possible and attending receptions and dinners. By 1987, it was in full swing." George W., the Bushes' oldest son, moved his family to Washington to help with the campaign.

During the Democratic National Convention in July 1988, Ann Richards, then governor of Texas attacked George Bush in her speech in a way that made Barbara feel sick to her stomach (Bush 1994, 225). Once Dan Quayle was announced as her husband's vice presidential running mate, the liberal press "trashed" Quayle; among other things, he was alleged to have had an affair with Paula Parkinson (Greene 2000, 36). Probably, most hurtful for Barbara was that the same accusation was made about George, who was alleged to have had an affair with his executive assistant, Jennifer Fitzgerald (Grimes 1990, 163–74; Bush 1994, 240) What made matters worse was the concurrent criticism of what was called the Bushes' "affection gap"—that they "were not lovey-dovey enough in public." Although their handlers told them to be more affectionate, neither of them took that seriously. At the Republican National Convention, both joked with exaggerated affection at a luncheon given in Barbara's honor, George calling Barbara "sweetie-pie," and Barbara asking the audience "to see if he looks at me as adoringly . . . as I looked at him" (Bush 1994, 227).

Probably one of the most important campaign speeches Barbara made was at the Republican National Convention in 1988. Even though she had been campaigning for years, she still felt nervous when she gave a highly formal presentation. She rehearsed the speech by standing at the podium at the convention center, "because she wanted to get a feel for the speech and the room" and "to combat the nervous sensation that hit her when she thought of addressing the thousands of delegates who would fill the empty room" (Kilian 1992, 143).

During the speech, Mrs. Bush said: "You've probably heard to the point you're sick of hearing it of all the important, big deal jobs George has held." Acknowledging "the tremendous energy and commitment" those jobs demanded, she told the audience that she respected her husband the most because of his performance as a husband and father: "But do you know what I respect about George. . . . In spite of those important, time-consuming jobs, our family has always felt an enormous part of his life." She continued to detail examples of his concern as a spouse, especially when they lost their four-year-old daughter to leukemia, and as a father, for example, when George told a reporter that his proudest accomplishment was that "the kids still come home." She concluded by reminding the delegates, "You should be proud. You have nominated for the presidency a man who is as strong and caring as America herself" (quoted in Inman 1988).

During the last month of campaigning, Mrs. Bush seems never to have stayed in one place longer than a few hours. She used her slides to show George as "a leader and happy family man." "There were also slides of George with world leaders, George at the Berlin Wall, and George at the Wailing Wall. Sometimes there was a videotape of George describing Barbara's life, with an emphasis on the humorous" (Kilian 1992, 137). According to biographer Donnie Radcliffe, Barbara increasingly used humor well. She made "self-deprecating humor an art. Joking about her white hair and her ample silhouette was a deliberate attempt to be funny, get a laugh, warm up a crowd." She thought that jokes about herself were better than jokes about others (1989, 9–10). Eventually, she had a "whole gag bag filled with stories about herself that she could draw from for any occasion. One anecdote poked fun at the allegations about George's affair: "'George Bush sleeps with two girls,' she deadpanned, pausing for effect, 'Millie [her springer spaniel] and me'" (quoted in Kilian 1992, 137–38). Kilian emphasized especially Barbara's use of timing. She became a favorite with campaign audiences.

Throughout the campaign season, there were still those who wanted to redo her, such as the woman who took a picture that had appeared in *Life* magazine, altering the haircut, earrings, necklace, clothes, and makeup (Bush 1994, 243). She told Roger Ailes, George's media advisor, "I'll do anything you want, but I won't dye my hair, change my wardrobe, or lose weight" (quoted in Radcliffe 1989, 4). She talked about the advantages of her drip-dry style: "I wash my hair every day of my life and probably washed all of the color out. But I can exercise, play tennis, I don't ever have to say to George, 'I'm sorry, I can't do that, I just got my hair done.' You have to set priorities in life and that's just not one I have. What you see is what you get." (quoted in Radcliffe 1989, 7) When George Bush was elected president, she carried this line of thinking—packaged with self-deprecating humor—into the White House.

Rhetorical Activities as First Lady

Mrs. Bush had been an incredibly active second lady and she continued this level of activity when she became first lady, leading one of her staff members to conclude that she was probably "one of the busiest first ladies ever" (Gutin 1996, 620). Together with her husband and by herself, she entertained many heads of state and their spouses in the White House, at Camp David, and at Walker's Point; they also visited many heads of state in their own countries, often staying in their homes or with Americans who worked for the U.S. government abroad. One cannot read *A Memoir* without gaining an appreciation of the political importance of such interpersonal relationships, developed over many years by the Bushes' diplomacy of friendship. They also entertained other friends, family, staff, politicians, and members of the press. Early in George Bush's administration, they held a number of dinners and parties for members of Congress to begin the healing process after a tough campaign; they also held other receptions, luncheons, and parties for the press (252–53) Reports of Mrs. Bush's activities in the press were mostly positive, and she quickly rose in popularity with the American public. She promoted her husband's agenda as well as her own through statements to members of the press, interviews, and through hundreds of formal and informal speeches.

If anyone had asked Mrs. Bush during the 1988 campaign to project her postelection popularity, she probably could not have imagined how well she would be received by the American public. The campaign for president had been "hurtful," she said. Less understated, John Robert Greene, author of *The Presidency of George Bush*, referred to the campaign as "jugular politics" (2000, 27–43); Ann Grimes called it "grueling" (1990, 283). Yet Mrs. Bush's political skin had thickened; "she had become media smart," adept at using the press to manipulate her image (Radcliffe 1989, 50). She quickly discovered that, as first lady, she "attracted media attention wherever she went" and "almost everything she or her family did, no matter how insignificant, was of interest to the public" (Radcliffe 1989, 37). In the first one hundred days, she "scooted around the country to some forty solo publicity events . . . in an effort to capitalize on media attention that inevitably would fade" (Grimes 1990, 267). She preferred to draw attention to good causes and constructive people—to points of light—and not to herself.

Both press and public were eager to compare the incoming Bushes to the outgoing Reagans. With her white hair and full figure, Barbara was an easy contrast to the petite, immaculately coifed Nancy. Headlines forecasted their differences: "Bye Bye Glamour" and "Goodbye, First Fashion Plate—Hello First Grandmother" (Brown 1988, 42). At a tribute given to her at the Kennedy Center, Barbara humorously suggested to an audience of nearly six thousand people that she and Nancy had vastly different values: "Giving her 'Bush Blue' Arnold Scaasi jacket a tug and striking a model's pose," she said: "Speaking of glamour . . . I want you all to look at me. Please notice the hair, the make-up, designer dress. Look at me good this week, because it is the only week" (quoted in Radcliffe 1989, 15). These comments defined her style and early set the tone of the administration. Her words and actions carried the subtext "I am not Nancy Reagan" (Gould, quoted in Grimes, 267). Journalists at the *New Republic* called her, "Mrs. Not Nancy Reagan," and Kati Marton claims that the way she distanced herself from Nancy at the inaugural was brilliant: "She presented herself as the unNancy: plain spoken, authentic, and unthreatening" (2001, 274–75).

Another way in which Barbara Bush contrasted herself with Mrs. Reagan was in how she spoke about the White House. She intended to fill the White House with visits from her children and grandchildren, and she did not plan to redecorate. Instead, she talked about the beauty of the White House *as she found it*, about how much she enjoyed *what was already there*. During an interview, she told journalist Charlotte Saikowski of the *Christian Science Monitor* that the White House is "so much more beautiful than I thought." She said, "The food is the most beautiful food you have ever laid your eyes on. Today, I had lunch off of (Woodrow) Wilson's plates, sometimes I have lunch off of Lincoln's plates" (1989, 14).[3] Her comments marked a glaring contrast with Nancy Reagan, whose slim figure indicated that she did not share Barbara's relish of the White House food and whose efforts to procure a new set of China implied her dissatisfaction with what was there.[4] Although Mrs. Bush projected complete satisfaction with her new home, as a matter of fact, she did redecorate three or four rooms, but she never received any negative press. For example, she converted a "beauty salon" to an office/birthing room for her springer spaniel, Millie, as well as making other changes. According to Grimes, she "kept saying she didn't need to change a thing" and quietly made the changes. "That is a masterful political way to handle the situation" (1990, 279).

Barbara Bush also made it clear that she would not become involved in her husband's work except to promote his agenda and that she would not comment on controversial political issues. The press and public had chided Nancy Reagan for meddling in presidential affairs; Mrs. Bush was determined to avoid making the same mistake. She frequently said: "I don't mess with George's office and he doesn't mess with my house" (quoted in Grimes 1990, 325). Of course, no one doubted her private influence on her husband; in fact, "reports of her private influence circulated throughout the Bush tenure; she was christened by some observers as 'the Silver Fox'" (Greene 2000, 148). According to Grimes, she was viewed in Washington as a "key behind-the-scenes operator" (1990, 293) and Kati Marton, quoting Roger Ailes, George Bush's media advisor, said, "She would not express her opinions in public . . . but she was a strong and respected voice inside" (2001, 297).

An early incident reinforced her resolve to refrain from making controversial statements in public, basically to do "what she . . . dubbed 'muzzling' herself" (Grimes 1990, 296). Two weeks after the inauguration, she was asked a question about gun control and told reporters that she was afraid of guns and would not own them. She also said that the AK-47 was and should be illegal. These remarks caused quite a stir since George Bush did not favor a ban on the AK-47. Thereafter, her press secretary announced that she would not be commenting about any controversial issues. Instead, she would only talk about ideas that interested her, such as women, work, and literacy (Kilian 1992, 159–60; Grimes 1990, 298).

Mrs. Bush found an ingenious way to garner press attention on her terms. She used a strategy that may best be described as "deflection." Millie, her springer spaniel, "married" Tug III during the week of the inauguration, and this marriage along with the subsequent "honeymoon," pregnancy, delivery, and White House brood claimed media attention throughout the first hundred days of the Bush presidency. Acknowledging the rhetorical power of the paw, Chuck Conconi, staff writer for *The Washington Post,* called Millie and her pups a "major public relations asset" (1989, E3). John Hughs of *The Christian Science Monitor* contrasted Millie's treatment with Lucky's, the Reagan's dog "who was banished to California because he could not contain himself in the White House" (1989, 18). Kilian put the point well when she said that Millie "filled the anecdote quota during the early weeks of the administration. Her puppies got a stupendous amount of attention; at one point, more than one hundred photographers were on the White House grounds taking pictures" (1992, 160).

Millie not only helped Mrs. Bush with her public relations activities, she also helped with hostessing and diplomacy. As C. Fred had done before, Millie was present during many White House activities and accompanied Barbara to Camp David and Walker's Point. There are many episodes reported in *A Memoir* suggesting how Millie's presence tended to cut through protocol, allowing the Bushes and their guests to interact in more informal ways. According to Grimes: "A dog running around the White House chomping on a tennis ball . . . functions well as an icebreaker and helps cut through protocol pretty quickly" (1990, 283). Millie also helped Barbara raise money for one of her major causes—literacy.

Mrs. Bush understood the power of her position as first lady. Citing Lady Bird Johnson's notion of the first lady's office as a bully pulpit, she assembled a staff and told them her priorities. She retained Susan Porter Rose as her chief of staff and Laurie Firestone as her social secretary; she hired Anna Perez as her press secretary and rehired Julie Cooke as her director of projects (1994, 253).[5] She told her staff: "each day we should do something to help others" (272). Julie Cooke scheduled many events that "either highlighted a need, helped encourage volunteerism, or focused on literacy." To begin with, she wanted to promote George Bush's "thousand points of light," by celebrating all of the volunteers in the country (Radcliffe 1989, 33). But as we have seen, literacy was her chief focus. In *A Memoir*, she explained why: "a more literate America would benefit every single thing I worry about: crime, unemployment, pollution, teen-age pregnancy, school dropouts, women who are trapped into welfare and therefore poverty, etc." (274–75). The Barbara Bush Foundation for Family Literacy became official in March 1989 (Bush 1994, 251).

As first lady, Mrs. Bush promoted literacy all over the United States and internationally. She attended an important meeting in fall 1989 at the University of Virginia. Meeting with governors' wives, Mrs. Bush asked them what they were doing in their states to help the cause (Bush 1994, 309–11). In *A Memoir* she also referred to a literacy meeting held in the White House on February 21, 1991, at which she raised $3 million (398–99). She read to children on the radio during a program called "Mrs. Bush's Storytime." Later, these readings were released on audiocassettes (360). She appeared on the *Oprah Winfrey Show* to discuss literacy, and she authored a *Reader's Digest* article, "Parenting's Best-Kept Secret: Reading to Your Children," that had great exposure (Gutin 1996, 619). Mrs. Bush also opened an international conference on literacy in Ottawa in October 1990 (Bush 1994, 368). And when she visited other countries, she often included trips to local schools to read stories to children. Altogether, she participated in several hundred literacy events. According to Gutin, "she would ask her sponsors what they wanted her to tell the press who would write stories about the event and whether they needed contributions or volunteers" (Gutin 1996, 620). Her presence gave great media exposure to groups whose mission and activities she helped publicize.

Perhaps her most unusual fund-raising project for literacy was *Millie's Book* (1990), a volume she "wrote" with her springer spaniel much like its predecessor, *C. Fred's Story* (1984). *Millie's Book* was released amidst a media blitz that included appearances on the *Today Show, Good Morning America*, and the *CBS Morning Show*. Mrs. Bush also appeared on the cover of *Good Housekeeping*

(August 1990). The publicity worked, and the book's reception was greater than anyone had imagined; it was even ranked number one on the *New York Times* "Best Seller List" and remained on national bestseller lists for many months (Kilian 1992, 23). Over 400,000 copies were sold, raising more than $1 million for literacy. It was translated into Japanese and German and released in paperback. By the summer of 1990, Millie needed her own volunteer to handle her correspondence (Bush 1994, 352). Earlier, when the puppies were born, Millie's mail had also been extensive.

Mrs. Bush, herself, received a great deal of mail: her yearly average was about 100,000 pieces (Bush 1994, 279). She had a staff to help her respond to these letters, many of which were positive and some of which were about "silly things" like George's dislike of broccoli—a theme she later developed as she campaigned for him for reelection. About 100 letters a day were invitations for her to speak. Especially busy was graduation time—her office would be swamped with more invitations than she could accept. Members of Barbara's staff read the letters and attached notes to them, and then she would look them over. She said: "We tried very hard to select those that would represent a cross-section of schools and regions" (335). Once she had selected the schools, Barbara and her staff worked together to write a general speech that represented what she wanted to say as well as allowing room for adaptation to local conditions.

In *A Memoir*, Mrs. Bush described the inventional process she and her staff used:

> My staff and I had been working on *the* [graduation] speech off and on all spring. We asked Ed McNally from George's speech writing department to help. So he joined our brainstorming sessions, which included Susan Porter Rose, Julie Cooke, Anna Perez, Susan Green, Jean Becker and Sondra Haley. We sat around and talked about the things I wanted to say, and tried to choose the theme for this year. They reminded me that I always say, "You have two choices in life. You can like it or not. I chose to like it.". . . . We talked about my dad and the things he told me. . . . I suggested that we end with the marvelous story from one of Robert Fulghum's books about "where do the mermaids fit into a world of wizards, giants, and dwarfs" . . . Somehow, out of all these ramblings, a speech began to take shape. (337)

This was the core of all the graduation speeches Barbara would give that season, even at Wellesley.

While planning the generic graduation speech, Mrs. Bush and her staff became aware of a controversy brewing at Wellesley College, where she was scheduled to present a graduation speech. She was not the students' first choice as a speaker; Alice Walker was, but Walker was not available. Although a majority of the 600 graduating seniors wanted Barbara Bush to speak, 150 signed a petition in protest and presented it to university president Dr. Nan Keohane. The petition read: "To honor Barbara Bush as a commencement speaker is to honor a woman who has gained recognition through the achievements of her husband, which contradicts what we have been taught over the past four years" (quoted in *Chicago Tribune* 1990, 2). The press reported the controversy in articles and editorials, and it also became a subject discussed widely on television news and talk shows. According to Mrs. Bush in *A Memoir*: "That darn Wellesley flap" took on "a life of its own." Homemakers across the United States were offended, and Mrs. Bush received many encouraging letters. She also received a letter from Chris Bicknell, who had been selected to be the student speaker at Wellesley's graduation. She thanked Mrs. Bush for being so understanding of the students' position and for expressing that understanding to the press (338–39). Mrs. Bush had told a small group of reporters over lunch in the White House family quarters: "I thought they were very reasonable. . . . They're 21 years old and they're looking at life from that perspective. . . . I hope they won't opt not to have families, and I hope they won't opt not to be great parents" (quoted in Robinson 1990, 1).

The controversy was boiling when Mrs. Bush and her staff met a second time to refine the graduation speech. "I told my staff," Barbara said, "that I did not want to make a special speech catering to Wellesley. I also did not want to complain, explain, or apologize in any way. By the end of the meeting, we had settled three things I wanted the students to consider: You have to get involved in something larger than yourself; Remember to get joy out of life; Cherish human relationships." She read the speech to her husband, who suggested that she add: "Read to your child." And she added, "Hug your child." She said, "We cut and pasted and were ready to start the graduation trail" (Bush 1994, 377).

Mrs. Bush presented the same basic speech at many locations, including the University of Pennsylvania, St. Louis University, and Wellesley College. She added local color to the speeches, but altered the speech a bit more for the special interests of students at Southeast Community College in Cumberland, Kentucky, the heart of coal-mining country. Most of these students were the first in their families to go to college and they were, to Mrs. Bush, "truly a group of courageous students" (Bush 1994, 337), quite a contrast to the more privileged students at Wellesley.

What seems not well known about the Wellesley speech situation is that Mrs. Bush almost turned down the invitation. The date conflicted with a visit from the Gorbachevs, an event regarded as critically important to U.S./USSR relations. Instead of declining the invitation, Mrs. Bush asked Dr. Keohane if Raisa Gorbachev could also speak to the seniors. This would be a treat for all because it would be Mrs. Gorbachev's first speech in the United States. Moreover, Raisa was a first lady, but she also had an independent career of her own. Once the flap started, bringing Mrs. Gorbachev perhaps signaled to the students that Mrs. Bush was sensitive to their concerns, even if she didn't agree with them.

On the plane ride to Boston, Mrs. Bush took out her speech and went over it "just one more time" (Bush 1994, 340). Despite the protests, the petitions, and the press coverage, she said, "I had just quit worrying about the whole thing once the speech was written because I felt good about what I wanted to say to them" (341). When she arrived at Wellesley, she discovered that a number of students had circulated a second petition and the results were released right before she spoke. The petition praised the choice of Mrs. Bush as the commencement speaker and commended unknown women who had devoted their lives to serving others. The petition also urged Mrs. Bush to support legislation on day care, welfare, and wage equity between men and women (Gutin 1996, 622).

The Wellesley speech is an excellent example of Mrs. Bush's wit and self-deprecating humor with which she was able to win over her audience. During the speech, Mrs. Bush told the group that family is important in life: "As important as your obligations as a doctor, a lawyer or a business leader may be, your human connection with spouses, with children, with friends, are the most important investment you will ever make." She told them: "At the end of your life, you will never regret not having passed one more test, not winning one more verdict or not closing one more deal. You will regret the time not spent with a husband, child, a friend or a parent." Moreover, she told her audience that she knew she was not their first choice as a speaker: "Now I know your first choice today was Alice Walker . . . known for 'The Color Purple.' Instead you got me, known for the color of my hair." She told the audience that she expected great achievements from them and ended by saying: "Who knows somewhere out in this audience may even be someone who will one day follow in my footsteps and preside over the White House as the President's spouse. And I wish him well" (Bush 1990b; 1994, appendix C).

Mrs. Bush's speech was well received by her audience. According to coverage in the *New York Times* (June 2, 1990), audience members interrupted her speech several times with applause and laughter. A headline in the *Washington Post* announced: "Barbara Bush: Wowing Wellesley" (Radcliffe 1990, C1) and their television critic, Tom Shales, called it "a rock 'em–sock 'em smash hit" (Shales 1990, C1). NBC's Tom Brokaw said it was "one of the best commencement speeches I ever heard" and *Boston Globe* staff writer John Robinson reported: "the rave reviews on the nation's front pages and television shows confirmed her victory" (1990, 1). Not only did the press praise the speech, they also commented on the two first ladies' "symbolic summit": "The picture of the two women forging a friendship over live television symbolized the growing potential of women as leaders in the global quest for international cooperation. . . . Some Washington observers are beginning to call the current US-Soviet summit 'Barbara's summit,' a tribute to her contribution to the tone and atmosphere of the event" (Robinson 1990, 1).

Mrs. Bush gave another important speech while she was first lady—at the Republican National Convention in 1992, when George Bush was running for reelection against Bill Clinton. At the time, public opinion polls showed that she had a high approval rating with the American people, while her husband trailed Clinton. Republican Party leaders counted on her to boost her husband's ratings by driving home their message on family values. Even though this prime-time speech was probably the most important one of her career, or at least the one most widely seen and heard with an estimated audience of 26.5 million people (Kubasik 1992, 35), she described it beforehand as a "trifle," "a Mickey Mouse thing," "nothing at all." But this was the 1992 convention and all eyes were on the four women who were "running" with their husbands: Barbara Bush and Marilyn Quayle versus Hillary Clinton and Tipper Gore. Many members of the press drew a sharp contrast between Barbara Bush, a "career" wife and mother and Hillary Clinton, a "radical feminist" (Couture 1992, B5).

Despite her calling the speech a trifle, she and her staff worked very hard on it. I have examined at least five drafts of the speech and many pieces of correspondence related to it in the "First Lady Office, Press Files" at the George Bush Presidential Library and Museum. A letter addressed to George Bush, written by California citizen Jay Wilson, was among the documents. This letter asked President Bush what he meant by "family values" and explained that he lived with several other unrelated people whom he considered his "family." Sent from the president's staff to the first lady's staff, this letter seemed to crystallize the primary exigencies for Mrs. Bush's speech—define "family values" broadly, show how "family values" connects to American values, and illustrate how the Bush family "lives" what they talk about (also see "1992 Events Files, GOP Convention," OA/ ID 07474).

Mrs. Bush and her staff wrote several drafts of the speech, giving great care to the tone and content. They were particularly concerned about what they meant by "family values." Taking great pains not to give the impression that they were only talking about traditional families, they used a series of examples to emphasize the many different kinds of "families" found in the United States today—traditional families, single-parent families headed by men or women, and extended families of grandparents, foster parents, adoptive parents, divorced parents, aunts and uncles, brothers and sisters, even neighbors and communities. They wanted to emphasize the importance of the family through "tough" times and especially the role of the family in passing down the values that are central to the American character.

During the speech (Bush 1992b), Mrs. Bush stated that regardless of the kind of "family" a child comes from, each must learn values such as "integrity, strength, responsibility, courage, sharing, love of God, and pride in being an American." She told the audience that her husband—"the strongest, the most decent, the most caring, the wisest man"—was determined to preserve a nation of strong families and strong communities. She also recognized the many roles that women are free to choose or are forced to play by circumstances. She presented herself as accepting, without regret, the choices she had made in her own life as well as accepting, with respect, the choices of her daughter and daughter-in-law, both of whom worked and had children. She said: "You may be exhausted from working a job, or two jobs, and taking care of your children, or you may have to put your career on hold. . . . Either way, you may wonder, as I did every now and then, am I doing the right thing? Yes, you are." Mrs. Bush introduced her eldest grandson, sixteen-year-old George P. Bush, Jeb's son, whose remarks were part of her presentation. Echoing points she made in her speech, he added: "In a Presidential campaign, it's hard for people to get a sense of what makes the candidates tick. The family is what makes my grandfather tick." He ended his speech with: "Viva Bush" (Bush 1994, appendix D). They were joined on stage by Mrs. Bush's five children, their spouses, and her twelve grandchildren. Making a surprise appearance, President Bush also joined the group.

Mrs. Bush seemed to be saying visually through this assemblage of twenty-four people: "the rest of you may talk about family values, but George Bush and I live them!" *New York Times* journalist Elizabeth Kolbert made this point when she said: "the show of Bush family solidarity . . . presented a triumphantly simple visual . . . the phrase 'family values' seemed to have a clear meaning" (1992, A12). Even Molly Ivans, who described herself as a "salty Democrat," told *USA Today*: "I liked (her) speech. Her political timing is impeccable. I can't help it. I loved it. I even like the tough slightly bitchy side of her" (quoted in Kelly 1992, D4). Kati Marton also highlighted the usefulness of Mrs. Bush to her husband when she wrote: Mrs. Bush "was . . . the source of one of Bush's strongest assets: his image as the patriarch of a large and appealing brood" (2001, 276) First lady scholar Myra Gutin wrote approvingly that this "speech was another triumph for Barbara Bush" (1996, 623).

Mrs. Bush frequently gave other kinds of campaign speeches. Of course, she campaigned actively for her husband during the 1992 presidential race, but she also campaigned for other Republicans during the midterm elections of 1990, including "thirty-three candidates in twenty states and twenty-nine cities" (Bush 1994, 370). She made most of these trips without her husband, as she would continue to do during the 1992 presidential election, when she and George "rarely traveled together" (487). She went on two types of campaign trips, some were big rallies and others were "smaller fund raising lunches or dinners." Mrs. Bush and one of her staff members, Anna Perez, worked on two speeches—"one to be given at the rallies . . . and a second warm and cozy talk for the smaller groups." Like the graduation speech, their approach was to draft a generic or "core" speech and then adapt it to the particularities of the situation. The bulk of this core speech was a list of George Bush's accomplishments as president, with room left mostly at the beginning and end to insert comments about local candidates, campaign organizers, and conditions. Interspersed throughout the speech were bits of humor—about herself and her family—that had become her trademark.[6]

Especially after the Republican National Convention, Mrs. Bush's campaigning increased dramatically. In *A Memoir* she logged visits to "eleven cities in seven states . . . including eight fund-raisers; five school, library, or literacy events; two cultural centers; three rallies, and one fair" (Bush 1994, 489). The last week of the campaign was especially busy, she "literally criss-crossed the country . . . did unending radio, TV, and print interviews," went to mall after mall, and appeared on the *Larry King Live Show* (475). None of this hard work was rewarded because George Bush lost the election to Bill Clinton, and the Bushes had to make plans to leave the White House.

Legacy

First lady scholar Myra Gutin reports that members of Mrs. Bush's staff said "she was probably one of the busiest first ladies ever" (1996, 620). She performed many traditional roles such as hostess, surrogate, and political partner. In addition, she promoted her husband's agenda as well as her own in indirect non-verbal ways as well as by giving literally several hundred informal and formal speeches. A document among Mrs. Bush's papers in the George Bush Presidential Library and Museum lists 455 speeches that Mrs. Bush gave between 1989 and 1992 (OA/ID 08383). The way she performed these activities modified the "institution" of first lady. I will summarize the lessons she has left us as her legacy.

As we have seen, First Lady Barbara Bush was active as a hostess—in the White House, at Camp David, and Walker's Point. She entertained with her husband and alone, both formally and informally with various kinds and numbers of guests. In reading her *A Memoir* as well as the two books she wrote with her dogs, *C. Fred's Story* and *Millie's Book*, it is quite clear that many of the Bushes' political goals were furthered through their interpersonal diplomacy of friendship.

Mrs. Bush also acted as George Bush's surrogate on many occasions, two important occasions that have not been discussed are her visits with Desert Storm personnel and their families[7] and the toast she gave impromptu when her husband became sick during dinner on a trip to Japan.[8] As we have seen, Mrs. Bush was quite the campaigner and she enabled her husband to get his message to many more people by taking that message to them herself. As Lee Atwater told *The Washington Post*: "she's by far the most sought-after surrogate we've got" (quoted in Grimes 1990, 174).

Mrs. Bush was also very much her husband's political partner, helping him get "into office and keep him happy while . . . there" "Publicly," according to Ann Grimes, she carried "out her purely decorative, symbolic role, but behind the scenes, as her children and friends say, she . . . [was] a full partner in the family business of politics" (1990, 324–25). Grimes continues: "few in Washington . . . doubt [her] enormous influence with the president, despite her *pro forma* disclaimers" (325). Yet, her influence was like "Bess Truman['s], . . . who entered into almost every decision Harry Truman ever made" (326). Kati Marton makes a similar point when she writes: "Barbara did not think it in the Bushes' interest for the public to know how influential she was. . . . She had an upstairs/downstairs attitude about voicing her views—not in front of the staff and not in front of the reporters" (2001, 297). In the end, the kind and extent of her influence, especially how much she has had on her husband's policies, remain open and may never be answered fully. Unfortunately, as Betty Boyd Caroli explains, "much of the influence went undocumented and unquantified because it occurred off the record" (1995, 287).

Many people looked to Mrs. Bush as a liberal voice in an otherwise conservative administration. Moderate Republicans were also reassured by her presence, as Marton points out: "through subtle pauses, inflections, [and] body language, she gave [them] . . . a feeling that she was with them, that they had an ally in the Bush White House" (2001, 277). Her private influence on policy may have been to make some issues more visible to her husband such as funding for Aids research, and to move other issues on her husband's agenda upward in priority such as with the AK-47 legislation. Her influence was most obvious when

George Bush signed the National Literacy Act of 1991 into law. As a symbol of how much Barbara Bush had done to bring literacy to the attention of the American public and legislature, President Bush gave her the pen he used to sign the bill, and it is now in the George Bush Presidential Library and Museum. For her part, she credits many people with passage of the legislation, but her words show how proud she was of the achievement: the act was "the first piece of legislation—and to date, the only one—ever enacted specifically for literacy, with the goal of ensuring that every American adult acquires basic literacy skills. . . . But even more than that, the act seeks to strengthen our nation by giving us more productive workers and informed citizens" (1994, 425).

Mrs. Bush also left another kind of legacy with regard to literacy. During her eight years as second lady and her four years as first lady, she promoted literacy in many different ways. One week after becoming first lady, she began the Barbara Bush Foundation for Literacy and worked to raise money so that the foundation could fund needy programs across the country. Her books alone raised more than $1 million, and she continues to promote literacy even after she has left the White House. Her daughter-in-law and former librarian, First Lady Laura Bush, has continued and extended the project to highlight the value of reading to children. When Laura Bush established her own foundation—the Laura Bush Foundation for America's Libraries—Barbara Bush pledged $50,000 and joined her daughter-in-law on June 4, 2002, to listen to papers presented at a White House Conference on School Libraries.

In regard to public image, Mrs. Bush popularized a natural look that reflected the reality of a life spent enjoying good food, sunshine, exercise, and activity. Her look said that she was concerned with her appearance, as she had to be given her position, but she was not *overly* concerned with it. Her white hair and sun-wrinkled skin became trademarks, along with her triple strand of fake pearls. She legitimized the role of matriarch or grandmother, celebrating motherhood right down to her two dogs and Millie's litter. The cover of *Life* magazine (May 1989), coinciding with Mother's Day, captured this persona well: we see a smiling Barbara shown with a smiling Millie who is nestled with her brood of very photogenic puppies. She stressed motherhood as well when she framed her literacy campaign as an effort to teach mothers to read to their children and when she appeared on stage with her children and grandchildren during the Republican National Convention.

In regard to press relations, we learn from Mrs. Bush's experience and her advice. In *A Memoir* she writes: "One of the lessons someone in public life must learn is: THE PRESS HAS THE LAST WORD" (emphasis hers, 442). This statement is especially significant coming from a woman who has been called "our most unflappable First Lady" (Truman 1995, 317). As we have seen, she had to learn to face interviewers' questions both on camera and off. Beginning with an initial tendency to be sarcastic and teasing, she learned to moderate her words, to direct the conversation to areas that furthered *her* purposes, and to poke fun at only herself. She also learned that nothing might be off the record, that the purpose of the interview could be changed, that the interaction during the interview could be misinterpreted. Yet given all of the constraints in dealing with journalists, they also presented vitally important opportunities to promote the cause of literacy. In the end, Mrs. Bush wrote that there were probably many more decent reporters than nasty ones (498–99).

In regard to public speaking, Mrs. Bush's example teaches that everyone can improve as a public speaker through capitalizing on individual personality traits, shaping them artistically for public performance. Mrs. Bush began her career as a speaker by using slides to deflect attention away from herself—this helped with her nervousness. Using slides also helped with speech organization, for once the slides were arranged in trays, the topics and their sequence were easy to remember by virtue of visual clues. Narrating stories about the images projected made excellent use of her storytelling skills, sense of humor, ability as a mimic, and her comedic timing. As she grew comfortable in front of audiences, her presentations became more "oratorical," only in that she stopped using the accompanying images and concentrated more on set speeches. But even here we learn that she and her staff worked out different basic speeches or "speech templates" for kinds of occasions (genres)—graduation speeches, campaign speeches—and they adapted those general speeches by adding "local color." She instructed her staff to keep her speeches short and funny, and she developed her self-deprecating humor to an art. Myra Gutin, first lady scholar and communication professor, has judged Mrs. Bush's public speech very highly. So have two of George Bush's staff members. Pete Teeley, a former press secretary, who has said, "She is a good speaker . . . she's very composed in terms of what she wants to say. She has real presence" (quoted in Kilian 1992, 111). Victor Gold, a senior campaign aid and coauthor of George Bush's autobiography, has said: "In some ways, she was better before an audience than George. 'When she talks to an audience, there is straight projection. The audience feels this is a real person. She is able to assert strength, ideas, and feelings of personal warmth without trying . . . Barbara is a direct link with her audience'" (quoted in Radcliffe 1989, 158).

After leaving the White House, the Bushes relocated to Houston and traveled extensively visiting family and friends in the United States and abroad. Mrs. Bush retained her interest in the Barbara Bush Foundation for Family Literacy, still claiming that making people more literate will solve many social problems. She also became a member at large of AmeriCares and joined the boards of many other institutions (1994, 521–22). She has attempted to keep up with her correspondence. That is one reason why she published *A Memoir*. She made an interesting comment at the end of that book about the lack of funding for first ladies after they leave the White House. Although she didn't think former first ladies should receive funding, she said she wondered "how I was going to answer my mail and cope with public appearance requests." She wrote *A Memoir* to help finance this work (506).

Perhaps her most active role since leaving the White House has been campaigning for her son George W. during his presidential race. Early in Campaign 2000, she was called in for damage control when George W. ran into a flap for his alleged use of cocaine as a young man. Karen Brown interviewed Mrs. Bush in New Hampshire on WMUR, and a portion of that interview was carried nationally on CNN and ABC's *Good Morning America*. Mrs. Bush was still so well liked and respected that it seemed if she said the drug issue was too old to be relevant, then others would agree with her. She also became very active during fall 2000, as she participated in a "W is for Women" campaign swing with Laura Bush and others. Now that W is president, she has achieved something no other first lady has achieved: been first the wife, then the mother of two U.S. presidents in her lifetime. With a family as large as hers and as interested in political service, she may yet achieve other distinctions such as becoming the first women to be a grandmother of a U.S. president, if George P., dubbed the "Ricky Martin of the Republican Party" during the 2000 Republican National Convention, or one of her other progeny chooses that kind of life (Crowley 2000, A18).

Mrs. Bush was presented with many honors when she was first lady, including at least nineteen honorary degrees at many colleges and universities.[9] A rose was named in her honor and presented to her when she visited France (Kilian 1992, 205). Part of her legacy is the lesson she learned from her mother: to appreciate what we have and not long for what we cannot have. About her own life she says: "Imagine knowing heads of every country, on a fairly personal basis in many cases. . . . Or imagine traveling to all those foreign countries. I feel like I have had the best, the most exciting, thrilling life anyone could ever have" (quoted in Kilian 1992, 207). Not even mentioning the heartbreak of losing Robin or the agony of defeat to "draft-dodging, pot smoking" Bill Clinton, Mrs. Bush's rhetorical sense remains strong. All must agree that her achievements have far exceeded what anyone could have expected from a career homemaker and college dropout.

Notes

I would like to acknowledge the generous help of Dr. Robert Holzweiss, archivist, and other staff members of the George Bush Presidential Library and Museum in College Station, Texas. They helped me find texts and audiotapes of Mrs. Bush's speeches as well as relevant files kept by members of her staff.

1. Abigail Adams was the only other woman to be both wife and mother of a president. Mrs. Adams died in 1818, and John Quincy Adams did not become president until 1925.

2. I have used material from Mrs. Bush's *A Memoir* to write this section, supplemented by material from two biographies: Pam Kilian's *Barbara Bush: A Biography* (1992) and Donnie Radcliffe's *Simply Barbara Bush: A Portrait of America's Candid First Lady* (1989). Unless otherwise indicated, the material is from *A Memoir*.

3. She spoke similarly of the White House in *A Memoir* when she said that even the most ordinary events, like lunch, could seem magical: "I ate off President Cleveland's white china with touches of navy blue and gilt." And she said, "The butlers loved trying to make me guess whose china I was using. Imagine being served a meal on dishes that Abraham Lincoln ate from!" (Bush 1994, 277).

4. Defending the purchase, Nancy Reagan explains in *My Turn* that she ordered the china because the White House didn't have enough pieces from any one set for a state dinner. She also explains that the American people did not pay for the china; rather it was a gift purchased by the Knapp Foundation (1989, 27–29).

5. Her final staff consisted of nineteen people: see appendix A in *A Memoir* for their names and positions.

6. There are two drafts of this core as well as an example of how the core was amplified with local material in Anna Perez's "Political Speech Research File" (OA/ID 08737) in the George Bush Presidential Library and Museum. The same file also contains a list of how Barbara should answer questions about George's accomplishments and about his position on various social issues, such as abortion, women's issues, and so on.

7. Mrs. Bush discusses the military bases she visited, both with and without her husband in *A Memoir*. She often met with the wives, mothers, and fathers of soldiers who were killed in action or missing in action; see 385–408.

8. Mrs. Bush was unprepared to present at toast at a dinner held by the prime minister of Japan. Because her husband got sick during the dinner and was rushed out on a stretcher, she was asked to give a toast in his place. She relied on her sense of humor to put a light touch on the otherwise embarrassing event; she simply said that her husband was a poor sport having earlier lost a game of tennis to the emperor of Japan and the crown prince: see *A Memoir*, 448–51.

9. A list of Mrs. Bush's honorary degrees may be found in Anna Perez's "Political Speech Research File" 2 of 3 in the George Bush Presidential Library and Museum.

References

Anthony, Carl Sferrazza. 1991. *First Ladies: The Saga of the Presidents' Wives and Their Power*, 1961–1990. New York: William Morrow & Co.

Brown, Patricia Leigh. 1988. The First Lady-Elect: What She Is and Isn't. *New York Times*, late city final ed., 11 December, 42.

Bush, Barbara. 1984. *C. Fred's Story: A Dog's Life*. Garden City, N.Y.: Doubleday & Co.

———. 1990a. *Millie's Book: As Dictated to Barbara Bush*. New York: William Morrow & Co.

———. 1990b. Choices and Changes: Your Success as a Family. *Vital Speeches of the Day*, 1 July.

———. 1992a. Events Files, GOP Convention OA/ID 07474. College Station, Tex.: George Bush Presidential Library and Museum.

———. 1992b. Family Values: The Country's Future Is in Your Hands. *Vital Speeches of the Day*, 1 September.

———. 1994. *Barbara Bush: A Memoir*. New York: Charles Scribner's Sons.

Butterfield, Fox. 1990. Family First, Mrs. Bush Tells Friend and Foe at Wellesley. *New York Times*, late ed., 2 June, A1.

Caroli, Betty Boyd. 1995. *First Ladies*, expanded ed. New York: Oxford University Press.

Chicago Tribune. 1990. First Lady Represents U.S. on Trip, 8 May.

Conconi, Chuck. 1989. Personalities. *Washington Post*, 4 April, E3.

Couture, Dan. 1992. Convention '92. *Houston Chronicle*, star ed., 20 August, B5.

Crowley, Brian. 2000. He's Hot, He's Hispanic—and He's a Bush; Campaign Finds Nephew an Asset. *Atlanta Journal and Constitution*, home ed., 3 August, A18.

Gallup Organization. 1999. Most Admired Men and Women: 1948–1998. www.gallup.com/poll/specialreports/pollsummaries/polls_this_century_index.asp, accessed, 13 December.

Gould, Lewis. 1996. The First Lady as Symbol and Institution. In *American First Ladies*, ed. Lewis L. Gould, xiii–xx. New York: Garland.

Greene, John Robert. 2000. *The Presidency of George Bush.* Lawrence, Kans.: University of Kansas Press.

Grimes, Ann. 1990. *Running Mates: The Making of a First Lady.* New York: William Morrow & Co.

Gullan, Harold I. 2001. *Faith of Our Mothers: The Stories of Presidential Mothers from Mary Washington to Barbara Bush.* Grand Rapids, Mich.: William B. Edermans Publishing Co.

Gutin, Myra. 1996. Barbara Bush. In *American First Ladies*, ed. Lewis L. Gould, 608-29. New York: Garland.

Hughes, John. 1989. The Bush White House. *Christian Science Monitor*, 20 January, 18.

Inman, William. 1988. Barbara Bush Praises Her Husband. *United Press International*, 18 August.

Kelly, Katy. 1992. Ivans Has Her Say about GOP's Big Guns. *USA Today*, 21 August, D4.

Kilian, Pamela. 1992. *Barbara Bush: A Biography.* New York: St. Martin's Press.

Kolbert, Elizabeth. 1992. The Media and the Message: Campaign Watch; On TV, a Victory in Family Numbers. *New York Times*, late ed., 21 August, A12.

Kubasik, Ben. 1992. No Barbara Bounce on Nielsen Scale. *Newsday*, 21 August, 35.

Marton, Kati. 2001. *Hidden Power: Presidential Marriages That Shaped Our Recent History.* New York: Random House.

Parmet, Herbert. 1997. *George Bush: The Life of a Lone Star Yankee.* New York: Scribner.

Radcliffe, Donnie. 1989. *Simply Barbara Bush: A Portrait of America's Candid First Lady.* New York: Warner Books.

———. 1990. Barbara Bush, Wowing Wellesley; With Raisa Gorbachev on Hand, the Speech Carries the Day. *Washington Post*, final ed., 1 June, C1.

Reagan, Nancy, with William Novak. 1989. *My Turn: The Memoirs of Nancy Reagan.* New York: Random House.

Robinson, John. 1990. Mrs. Bush Replies to College Flap. *Boston Globe*, city ed., 3 May, 1.

Saikowski, Charlotte. 1989. At Home in the White House. *Christian Science Monitor*, 16 February, 14.

Shales, Tom. 1990. The First Lady, at the Head of the Class. *Washington Post*, final ed., 2 June, C1.

Truman, Margaret. 1995. *First Ladies.* New York: Fawcett Columbine.

Watson, Robert P. 2000. *The Presidents' Wives: Reassessing the Office of First Lady.* Boulder, Colo.: Lynne Rienner Publications.

Chapter 20

Hillary Rodham Clinton
Using Her Vital Voice

Anne F. Mattina

> I'm often asked if what I am doing in Washington creates a new role model for
> first ladies. And I always say I don't want to create any new stereotype. I want
> to free women to live according to their own needs and desires. I do not want to
> create a new category that anyone after me must somehow fit into. I want all
> women to be given the respect they deserve for the choices they may make.
> —Hillary Rodham Clinton

Long before she met her husband, Hillary Rodham had established herself as a
public speaker. From the small venue of the Wellesley College commencement
in 1969, to the international stage of the United Nations World Conference on
Women in 1995, Beijing, China, she has contributed no small amount to public
discourse. With her election as senator from the state of New York, we can expect her to continue to use the spoken word to achieve her political and humanitarian goals. While political pundits and media sages have debated her "place"
as a first lady, and her image has undergone numerous revisions in the press,
Rodham Clinton's message has remained unchanged. She has committed much
of her life, her intellect, and her considerable rhetorical skill to empowering
women and improving the lives of children.

Rodham Clinton's public image remains a contested site among scholars,
the press, and the American public. Admired and loathed with equal passion, the
last first lady of the twentieth century is not easy to capture within the confines
of a book chapter. She came of age during a period of massive social upheaval,

when traditional roles, especially for women, were challenged and boundaries expanded. Her life reflects the experience of many other middle-class white women given access to higher education in the latter half of the twentieth century. Taking their cues from the second wave of American feminism, this first cohort of professional women blazed trails into all areas of public life, all the while struggling to maintain familiar roles of wife and mother. While not all such women chose to embrace multiple (often divergent) roles, many, including the young Hillary Rodham, did.

Though she may share similar experiences with other women from the postwar generation, she is unique in significant ways. Obviously, very few women have had the opportunity to inhabit the White House in so visible a manner. No other first lady since Eleanor Roosevelt seized upon the potential power of that nonelected office with quite the same vigor as Rodham Clinton. And no other predecessor has run for a seat in the U.S. Senate (or any other elected office for that matter), while occupying that role. As her husband left the presidency after a tenure marked by both great joy and sorrow, Rodham Clinton began a new phase in her already remarkable life as a U.S. senator from New York.

In what follows, a biography of Hillary Rodham Clinton is presented, which examines early influences on the future first lady. Significantly, she was influenced by her Methodist upbringing and a strong identification with her mother's experiences as a child of divorce. Next, her rhetorical activities during her White House years will be documented, focusing especially on the Vital Voices initiative. Then follows a discussion of several recurrent themes in Rodham Clinton's rhetoric, namely, her passion for promoting women's and children's rights both at home and abroad.

Biography

"I don't believe there's ever been a full portrayal of Hillary Clinton as a person, a full blown painted picture of her as a person," asserted her press secretary, Lisa Caputo, during a televised discussion on the night Senate candidate Rodham Clinton was to address the Democratic National Convention. "She's a transitional figure in history covered by not a consistent press corps, so there is not a context of her, so what you're seeing are all these different snapshots" (*Lehrer Report* 2000). The hackneyed analogy that Rodham Clinton is a "Rorshach test" for the multitude of perspectives on American womanhood is, nonetheless, accurate. Responses to this first lady in the media and other public venues are largely based on the individual's comfort level with women who push the boundaries of social norms.

Who exactly is Hillary Rodham Clinton? She is a highly educated, professionally competent person who is unfailingly devoted to her marriage and child. She is deeply religious and conservative in ways that few people have noticed. She truly believes in the power of government, and she is very much the product of her time.

Hillary Rodham was born in 1947, in Chicago, to Hugh and Dorothy

Rodham. The oldest of three, she described her childhood as "a family that looked like it was straight out of the 1950s television sitcom Father Knows Best" (Rodham Clinton 1996b, 21). Her father, a Republican, owned a small business and her mother did not work outside of the family home.

Hugh Rodham was a significant influence on his daughter's life. His expectations were high and Hillary worked hard for his approval. An oft-repeated anecdote was his response to her straight-A junior high report card. He said, "Well, Hillary, that must be an easy school you go to." His daughter would later write of this experience, "By raising the bar, he encouraged me to study even harder, and in fact, comments like that spurred me on" (1996b, 22). Hugh Rodham required his children to read the newspaper and to participate in dinner conversations about current events (Kennedy, 2000a).

Hillary's mother also had an equally profound influence on her life and her future choices. Dorothy (Howell) Rodham's childhood had been a difficult one at best. Born to young parents who had little in the way of resources, Dorothy and her sister were bereft after their mother and father divorced. The two small girls were sent by train from Chicago to California to live with their paternal grandmother, a "severe and arbitrary disciplinarian," according to Hillary (1996b, 34). They traveled alone; Dorothy, aged eight, was charged with the responsibility of taking care of her sister, aged three. By age fourteen, Dorothy was employed as a live-in domestic at a neighbor's home. In 1937, she moved back to Chicago and married Hugh Rodham in 1942. Her childhood experiences shaped much of her adult worldview, as well as that of her daughter. The roots of Hillary's passion for children may be found in her mother's unhappy past. Indeed, her mother's story is one that Hillary recounts in almost all detailed discussions of her own life.

Raised a Methodist, Rodham Clinton also notes the centrality of church life in her upbringing. "My brothers and I went faithfully to Sunday school," she recalled, "and were usually back at church at least one more time during the week for youth group meetings, athletic competitions, potluck suppers, or play rehearsals" (1996b, 26–27). According to biographer Lewis L. Gould, young Hillary was active in her church youth group and was influenced by her pastor, a man "interested in theology as it applied to the problems of society." In 1962, the church youth group attended a speech by Reverend Martin Luther King Jr., calling for an end to racial injustice. Afterwards, Hillary met the civil rights advocate, an event that left a deep impression (1996, 632).

Her religious upbringing is a fundamental part of her personality and is essential to understanding her rhetoric. "Hillary Rodham Clinton is as pious as she is political," asserts reporter Kenneth Woodward. "Methodism, for her, is not just a church but an extended family of faith that defines her horizons" (1994, 23). Her public advocacy is best understood through the lens of her faith, a subject to be explored further in this chapter.

During her high school days, Hillary Rodham was a student leader and a member of the National Honor Society. She worked on the school paper, was on the debate team, and was a novice public speaker as well. In her sophomore year, she enrolled in a public speaking class, populated largely by the football team. Years later, the first lady recalled how the players had sat in front making catcalls, trying to "rattle her." "After that, Washington was nothing," she joked (Kennedy 2000a). During her junior year, she ran for Student Council president, an event that shocked many in her suburban world, as no other female student had attempted such a feat. Though she lost to the captain of the football team, she expressed satisfaction with the way her campaign had been run and with her speeches (Kennedy 2000a).

Hillary was active in politics at a very young age. Adopting the political leanings of her conservative father, she was a "Goldwater Girl," supporting the Republican candidate in the 1964 presidential campaign.

She was voted "most likely to succeed" by her classmates and ranked in the top of her class. After graduating, Rodham headed east to Wellesley College, where her political views began to change. Though she served as an intern for the House Republican Conference in 1968, she, like so many others of her generation, began to question the status quo. She joined protests of the Viet Nam War and wrote her senior thesis on the community-action programs of Lyndon Johnson's Great Society. Hillary was not, however, a campus radical. She went to the 1968 Democratic National Convention in Chicago, not to protest, but to observe. "She did not want to destroy the status quo," Carl S. Anthony asserts, "she wanted to wake it up and have it take responsibility. She wasn't anti-establishment, she was reestablishment" (1999, 111). Hillary worked within the system, a choice she would make throughout her life.

Hillary was both intellectual and popular at Wellesley. She was elected president of her class in her junior year and represented her school on the nationally televised program College Bowl. Her classmates also chose her to be their graduation speaker in 1969. Though she had prepared a text with input from her classmates, Rodham instead delivered an impromptu rejoinder to the keynote speaker of the day, Senator Edward Brooke of Massachusetts. Questioning the relevance of Brooke's speech, she seized the opportunity to challenge his remarks and offer an alternative to her classmates. Harkening to themes that would emerge during her tenure as first lady, she asserted, "The challenge now is to practice politics as the art of making what appears impossible, possible" (quoted in Gould 1996, 633). Not only did her speech capture the attention of her audience, it also landed her in *Life* magazine, earning her national exposure at the age of twenty-two. "It was an auspicious end to her rewarding undergraduate experience at Wellesley" (Gould 1996, 633). Hillary's acceptance at a top law school was all but assured.

She applied to several, including Harvard. While visiting that campus, however, Hillary met a professor who explained that the law school did not need any more female students *(Current Biography Illustrated)*. Undeterred, she enrolled at Yale. Before beginning her law classes, Hillary took a job in a fish-canning plant in Alaska. She was fired for questioning the manager about the quality of the fish (Anthony 1999, 113).

While at Yale, she served on the editorial board of the *Review of Law and Social Action*. She also worked with the staff of the Yale–New Haven Hospital to help draft guidelines for the treatment of abused children. While working on this project, the future first lady met another person who would play a large role in her life professionally and personally. Marian Wright Edelman, a Yale alumna and the first African American woman to pass the bar in Mississippi, spoke at Yale in the spring of 1970 about her work with the poor and children's rights.

Inspired by the civil rights activist, Rodham joined Edelman's staff of the Washington Research Project as a summer intern. The work was unpaid, so Rodham secured a grant from the Law Student Civil Rights Research Council and spent her time interviewing families of migrant laborers. Upon completing her work, she reported her findings to a Senate subcommittee *(Current Biography Illustrated)*. Rodham's relationship with Edleman continued long past that first summer, providing her with future job and advocacy opportunities throughout her adult life.

Her interest in family law, combined with her work in a legal aid clinic and her experiences at the New Haven hospital, culminated in a book chapter on the relationship between children and the judicial system. Included in *Beyond the Best Interests of the Child*, Hillary's chapter challenged received wisdom regarding adoption, a subject she would continue to work on throughout her adult life.

It was also at Yale where she met Bill Clinton, a classmate. Their courtship began in the law library and soon Hillary and Bill were teaming up for mock trial debates. In the summer 1972, they traveled to Texas to work as organizers for Senator George McGovern's presidential campaign. Hillary registered Hispanic voters in San Antonio, while Bill managed the local campaign. Returning to Yale for her last year of law school, she provided legal research for the Carnegie Council on Children, specializing in the rights of children to education and medical care *(Current Biography Illustrated)*.

After graduating in 1973, the future president returned to his home state to teach at the University of Arkansas law school and to prepare a run for Congress. Hillary added an extra year to her curriculum, studying child development at the Yale Child Study Center. Upon completing this program, she joined the staff of Edelman's Children's Defense Fund in Cambridge, Massachusetts.

In 1974, she went to Washington, D.C., taking a position with the House Judiciary Committee investigating what was to become known as the Watergate scandal. She impressed supervisors and peers with her energy, objectivity, and knowledge of legal procedures. The position ended with the resignation of President Richard Nixon, whereupon Rodham was "deluged with offers of high-paying jobs at prestigious law firms on the East Coast" as well as an offer to return to her position at the Children's Defense Fund *(Current Biography Illustrated)*. Instead, shocking friends and colleagues alike, Hillary traveled to Arkansas to help with Bill Clinton's (unsuccessful) congressional campaign.

By this point in her life, Hillary Rodham had met Martin Luther King Jr. and worked for Marian Wright Edleman. She had earned a Yale law degree and campaigned for George McGovern. She had testified before Congress and played a role in the final chapter of the Nixon presidency. She had appeared in *Life* magazine and on network television. She was twenty-seven years old.

Bill and Hillary married in October 1975, in a small ceremony in Little Rock, Arkansas. Hillary continued to use her birth name, Rodham. The future first lady joined the faculty at the University of Arkansas law school, teaching criminal law.

In 1976, Bill Clinton was elected to the office of attorney general of Arkansas, and then was elected governor two years later. Clinton lost his second term race for that office, and according to Gould, "one source of voter resentment" was Hillary (1996, 636). Evidently, some voters did not agree with her decision to keep her birth name. "In Arkansas, at that time, there was very little appreciation for pushy, uppity women," explained former state senator Jerry Brookout ("The Clintons" 1999). "I've not wanted to upset anybody," Hillary said at the time. "I really thought I was doing it for the right reason. So, I'm thinking of perhaps changing my name to Martha Washington, or something, I don't know," she joked with an audience at the time ("The Clintons" 1999). As her husband prepared for a political comeback, she added his surname to hers. Clinton was successful in regaining the governor's seat in 1982 and held the position until winning the presidency ten years later.

Chelsea Victoria Clinton, their only child, was born in 1980. "Chelsea's birth transformed our lives," wrote Rodham Clinton, "bringing us the greatest gift of joy—and humility—any parent could hope for" (1996b, 9). The Clintons settled in to what would prove to be an active political and professional life. As the governor's wife, Rodham Clinton not only practiced law, she chaired the state's Education Standards Committee and founded the Arkansas Advocates for Children and Families. She launched a preparedness and literacy training program for parents, the Arkansas Home Instruction for Preschool Youth, and served on the board of Arkansas Children's Hospital.

As chair of the education committee, she traveled around the state, holding hearings and getting a sense of the breadth and depth of the issues, again a precursor of things to come. She developed tough policies designed to improve the system, and though they were unpopular, they worked. She was invited to testify before a joint Arkansas Senate–House Education Committee about her plans, and, according to one state senator, she "mesmerized" and "hypnotized" her audience with her command of the issues. Her concluding remarks were met with silence until one wag broke the "spell" by announcing, "Well, boys, it looks like we elected the wrong Clinton." ("The Clintons" 1999) Many observers have noted that it was the success of education reform that catapulted then governor Clinton to center stage at the 1988 Democratic National Convention, where he introduced the nominee, Michael Dukakis. His lengthy prime-time speech made headlines and earned him an invitation to Johnny Carson's *The Tonight Show*, where he charmed the national audience with self-deprecating humor.

Rodham Clinton was named Arkansas Woman of the Year in 1983, and Arkansas Mother of the Year in 1985. She was also named one of the Top 100 Lawyers in America by *American Lawyer* magazine ("Hillary for Senate") While being both very visible and active in Arkansas, she nonetheless maintained that being Chelsea's mother was the most important role she played in her life. Both supporters and detractors alike frequently note her devotion to her daughter and to her husband and marriage, even though the latter two have caused consternation among those same groups of people (Schindehette 1999, 78–88).

Much has been speculated and written about the Clinton marriage, but Hillary herself has been consistent in her support of her spouse. In early 1992, just as the presidential primary season was getting under way, candidate Bill Clinton was faced with the humiliating spectacle of an alleged mistress's "tell-all" confession in a tabloid newspaper, detailing a twelve-year relationship. Going on the offense, the Clintons agreed to an interview on *60 Minutes* with reporter Steve Kroft. "Hillary was really the one in charge," asserts Kroft, "she just really knew what she wanted to do" in the interview ("The Clintons" 1999).

With their political future on the line, the Clintons faced a difficult situation. And while the candidate may have hedged in his responses to direct questions regarding his fidelity, Hillary demonstrated no such hesitation. "I'm not sittin' (sic) here like some little woman standing by my man like Tammy Wynette," she declared. "I'm sittin' here because I love him, and I respect him and I honor what he's been through, and what we've been through together. And if that's not enough for people, then heck, don't vote for him" ("The Clintons" 1999). The door was closed on the subject, at least for a while. All agreed Hillary's unwavering support saved the candidacy of Bill Clinton.

There was a backlash, however, against what people perceived as Hillary's rebuke of traditional women evinced by her offhand country music analogy. The months remaining in the campaign were far from smooth. During the primaries, both she and her husband introduced themselves to the American public as a partnership—"buy one, get one free," was how the marriage was billed early in the campaign. This strategy was not ill advised given their success in Arkansas.

However, they did meet with resistance on the national level, most pointedly in reaction to another quote, taken out of context, which made it appear (again) that Rodham Clinton was belittling traditional female roles. While being pressed by reporters to defend herself and her husband against charges levied by an opponent that she had benefited financially from Clinton's political station in Arkansas, Rodham Clinton responded,

> This is the sort of thing that happens to the sort of women who have their own careers and their own lives. And I think it's a shame but I guess it's something that we're going to have to live with. Those of us who have tried to make a career, tried to have an independent life and make a difference and certainly like myself who has children but other issues, uh you know I've done the best I can to lead my life but I suppose it'll be subject to attack but it's not true and I don't know what else to say except that it's sad to me. (quoted in Jamieson 1995a 27)

Her impromptu response and "fragmented syntax suggests that she is groping for an answer," concludes Kathleen Hall Jamieson (1995a, 26). Next, Rodham Clinton was asked if there wasn't a way to avoid the appearance of conflict, and she replied,

I wish that were true. You know I suppose I could have stayed home and baked cookies and had teas but what I decided to do was fulfill my profession which I entered before my husband was in public life. And I've tried very, very hard to be as careful as possible and that's all I can tell you. (quoted in Jamieson 1995a, 27)

The uproar over her remarks was swift and intense. The tempest subsided a bit, but the furor over the possibility of a feminist first lady, one who had her own career, did not disappear. Rhetorical critic Karlyn Kohrs Campbell tells us that Rodham Clinton holds the "dubious distinction of being the first presidential candidate's wife to be the focus of a major opposition strategy" (1993, 7). Indeed, her tenure as first lady was marked by extremes in terms of press coverage and popularity. Ultimately, she negotiated the difficult terrain on her own terms, becoming the first presidential spouse to win an elective office as a New York senator, simultaneously fulfilling her duties of first lady.

Rhetorical Activities as First Lady

From the moment she entered the White House, Hillary Rodham Clinton made the role of first lady her own. Observed writer Kati Marton, "She sprung out at the beginning with this incredible force that she has. . . . A woman who is that overt about her own intelligence and that level of self-confidence . . . we were not used to that" ("The Clintons" 1999). What we were used to was some degree of public activism by a first lady. In fact, many twentieth-century presidential spouses have used their positions to advocate for various causes. Rodham Clinton's experience was unique, however, as an observer stated, "most modern First Ladies wielded influence behind the scenes" (Thomas and Rosenberg 1999, 28). This was not the way Hillary Clinton would operate.

Early in his first term, President Clinton appointed his wife chair of his task force on National Health Care reform. Much as she had done when appointed to the Arkansas Education Reform Committee, Rodham Clinton began to travel the country holding hearings and speaking directly to all involved constituencies. One of her first official meetings was with a congressional subcommittee, testifying and answering questions for over two hours under the glare of the national press. She was undaunted and impressed everyone with her knowledge and poise. Coverage in the national press was favorable, and her overall approval ratings rose accordingly (Jamieson 1995a, 47; Anderson 1999, 604).

The Clinton administration was not prepared for what came next. Though she enjoyed a brief "honeymoon" with the press regarding this unprecedented foray into policy, her methods and motivations were soon savaged by the media and callers to radio talk shows nationally. The powerful insurance and medical lobbies responded to her efforts with a series of well-crafted television commercials designed to undermine confidence in her plan. Small business owners, one group particularly anxious over proposed changes, also marshaled forces. These combined efforts were very successful, and the backlash was intense. During a speech in Seattle, the first lady was met by an angry group of protestors chanting, "Socialized medicine makes me sick!" and brandishing signs with messages such as, "Nyet Comrad Hillary." The Clinton administration retreated from the fray, health care reform was no longer a viable option for the young administration.

Conventional wisdom holds that Rodham Clinton then receded from public activism, but even the most cursory research proves that false, as *Newsweek* reports,

> After the collapse of her campaign to remake the nation's health care system she was thought to have retreated into the more traditional role of First Lady, visiting hospitals and worrying about her hairdo. In truth, her hairstyles have changed more than her agenda. She is, and always has been a missionary. Her all consuming task is to do good as she sees it, especially for children. (Brant and Thomas 1996, 20)

Anthony recalls her pledge to continued activism given in a speech at a symposium on the role of first ladies in 1994,

> A hushed audience had gathered expecting to hear Hillary ooze contrition . . . but when a poised and confident Hillary began to speak, it was obvious that the first lady had no intention of offering the expected mea culpas. She would continue to be active in public life, she declared. If she did otherwise . . . "my husband and friends would probably have me committed. I, for better or worse, have spoken out on public issues for 25 years." Some kind of first lady amnesia would not have been very credible. (1999, 110)

Rodham Clinton never did back down, choosing instead to use the role of presidential spouse as a "bully pulpit," although much of what she accomplished was outside of the media spotlight. Her response to the whole health-care experience was to change tactics. Hillary was following a pattern set early on in her life, not to accept defeat, but rather to step back, devise a plan, and try again.

During an interview soon after the health care fiasco, Rodham Clinton attempted to put her actions into perspective. Speaking of the president she said,

> We have been partners for so long, we are just connected to each other in so many ways that our partnership in some respects is even stronger than it ever has been . . . although it is different, there are certain expectations that go along with the role I'm in, which I take very seriously. ("The Clintons" 1999)

During the ensuing years in the White House, Rodham Clinton went beyond traditional hostess duties, playing a significant role in many legislative and policy decisions, but she did not deliberately seek out the spotlight. Indeed, in early 1999 when many reporters and columnists were speculating whether or not she would run for the Senate, Jonathan Alter writing in *Newsweek* opined, "The real problem for Hillary is her record. She doesn't have one. With health care a failure, she has nothing to show for her years as First Lady" (1999, 32). Though many public observers during the Senate campaign echoed his words, that assessment is woefully inaccurate.

Rhetorical Roles

The roles a first lady plays are multiple: "chooser of visitors, provider of hospitality, emissary to and contact with worthy enterprises, setter of tone, selector of projects and so forth." Such are "real functions, they are also important. They are representative, political, diplomatic" (Greenfield 2000, 58). Though she came to the White House with her own career, Rodham Clinton fulfilled all of these roles expected of a first lady. In addition to being appointed chair of the President's Task Force on Health Care Reform, she also served as chair of the President's Committee on the Arts and Humanities and spearheaded the Save America's Treasures Campaign.

Rodham Clinton also worked closely with the Departments of Education, Interior, and Housing and Urban Development, forging partnerships within and outside of the government to facilitate change. Along with Attorney General Janet Reno, she helped to form the Department of Justice's Violence against Women office (Anthony 1999, 138).

With Secretary of State Madeleine Albright, Rodham Clinton formed the Vital Voices Global Democracy Initiative, the goal of which was to make women's issues a foreign policy objective. The initiative sought to provide women with access to resources such as business microloans and other paths to empowerment.

While first lady, Rodham Clinton proved a tireless advocate for a myriad of causes, most of them focusing on women and children. She kept a daunting public speaking schedule—she visited fifty-one countries sometimes delivering two or more speeches a day—and also authored, "Talking it Over," a syndicated weekly newspaper column for several years. Another pivotal role she played during her husband's administration was that of "chief defender," specializing in damage control in events such as those surrounding his impeachment.

What is noteworthy about all of this activity is that so little of it earned media attention. What did interest the mainstream media had almost nothing to do with policy. For example, soon after a speech she gave in 1998 on international violations of children's rights, an acerbic column appeared in the *New York Times* by Maureen Dowd. No mention of the speech was included in the piece; rather, the columnist centered on the fact that Rodham Clinton had attended a movie premiere with the actress Gwyneth Paltrow. "There was a time when there were large and real accomplishments that she wished to achieve. Historians will long wonder how Mrs. Clinton came in as Eleanor and left as Madonna," Dowd concluded (quoted in Anthony 1999, 113). Such criticism was commonplace throughout Rodham Clinton's tenure, but was very short-sighted.

Rhetorical Messages

Of particular interest to this chapter are the speeches and public activities of Hillary Rodham Clinton. Her official website as first lady archived a total of 284 speech texts, listed under broad subject areas: 45 percent centered on "Advancing Democracy," with fifty-nine of those texts on topics of "Human Rights" and "Women as Citizens." Other texts focused on the needs of families and children, particularly in the areas of health care and education reform. An examination of these texts clearly reveals Clinton's deep commitment to empowering women and bringing children's issues into the realm of public policy. Indeed, her political agenda is coherent and it is one she has maintained throughout her public life.

A typical speech by Rodham Clinton begins with immediate recognition of the audience and the context of the event. She consistently prefaces her remarks by recognizing (by name) others on the dais and in the immediate audience. Throughout a speech, she employs examples of particular women as evidence to support her thesis. Quite frequently, her speeches pay homage to notable women of the past, making their names and deeds accessible to modern audiences.

She is a trained public speaker, comfortable enough on the platform to include impromptu remarks. Ann Douglas notes that Rodham Clinton made "ardent fans" of the White House photographers on her Save America's Treasures Campaign because of her ability to "surprise them" by "veering off from her prepared text . . . adding new thoughts and words, responding to the particular audience she was addressing" (1998, 233). However adept she is at identifying with particular audiences, her message remains consistently authentic as she skillfully combines narrative, empirical data, and her own personal vision in each of her speeches. Karlyn Kohrs Campbell observes that her rhetorical style is characteristically masculine,

> Hillary Rodham Clinton's style of public advocacy typically omits all of the discursive markers by which women publicly enact their femininity. Her tone is usually impersonal . . . her ideas unfold deductively . . . all kinds of evidence is used . . . She is impassioned but very rarely emotional. (1998, 6)

Concluding her description of Rodham Clinton's style, Campbell asserts that Mrs. Clinton, "plays the roles for which she has been professionally trained, the roles of lawyer, advocate and expert" (1998, 6).

However, Rodham Clinton's rhetoric is not exclusively "masculine." One device she employs frequently is narrative, a technique considered "feminine" by analysts. "Traditionally, women are a family's storytellers," explains Kathleen Hall Jamieson, "In both primitive and advanced cultures, women are the repositories of parable-like dramatic vignettes, concise stories that transmit the common wisdom from woman to woman and generation to generation" (1995b, 808). Rodham Clinton explains why she thinks narratives are effective in public advocacy in a speech given on March 4, 1999, to the United Nations,

> I appreciated the Secretary General sharing some stories from his own experience. Because sometimes stories make the point much better, don't they than all the statistics and all of the talking that we can engage in at great forums. One single story can pierce through and make it clear that we are all in the same story, we all face the same challenges. (1999a)

Emphasizing the role of narrative in bridging generations, she adds: "What lessons will we bring from this 20th century into the 21st? How will we honor the past?"

A significant, but often overlooked, influence on Rodham Clinton's rhetoric is her religious faith. "Her faith is critical: Mrs. Clinton sees herself as a serious Christian," assert reporters Eleanor Clift and Howard Fineman (1996, 36.) She brings the gospel of women's empowerment and democracy wherever she goes. It is my contention that this rhetorical persona is linked to her Methodism, a denomination that embraces the credo, "Be doers of the word and not hearers only."

Rodham Clinton has been quoted as saying she derives much inspiration for her daily life from the Book of James in the New Testament (Martin 1994, 1095). James "is a known figure and possesses a standing enabling him to speak with authority" (*New American Bible* 1970, 341). The first Book of James asks, "My brothers, (sic) what good is it to profess faith without practicing it?" James asserts "without works faith is idle . . . faith without works is as dead as a body without breath" (343–44). James' admonition resonates throughout Rodham Clinton's life and rhetoric.

The basic argument Rodham Clinton makes repeatedly is, "If women are to advance, democracy must advance as well," and she uses the power of her position to spread this thesis internationally ("United Nations Speech," 1999a). No matter where the stage or what the circumstance, she urges this and other notions upon her listeners, especially the need for women to have a voice. For example, on September 5, in Beijing China, she said, "If there is one message that echoes forth from this conference, it is that human rights are women's rights and women's rights are human rights. Let us not forget that among those rights are the right to speak freely and the right to be heard" (1995).

She acknowledges the essential connection between voice and empowerment in a speech given on October 16, in Argentina,

> I would like to talk about voices, powerful voices, the voices of women in this country and my country, throughout our hemisphere and our world, and what we can do to make all of our voices heard. To have our voices heard about our shared commitment to advancing the cause of women's rights, advancing the cause of democracy, and making clear that the two are inseparable. (1997)

This theme of voice resonates throughout many of her speeches. She explains why "voice" is imperative in women's lives, when she says at Seneca Falls on July 16, "we must tell and retell, learn and relearn, these women's stories, and we must make it our personal mission, in our everyday lives, to pass these stories on to our daughters and sons" (1998b). Only those who have a voice can share their experience and pass their wisdom to their children. And only those with a voice can advocate for the well-being of others.

Rodham Clinton demonstrates her enactment of James as she pursues her agenda around the world. At the United Nations on March 4, 1999, she says, "We have learned the lessons about what importance we must place on the role of women, we know that we must continue to speak out on our own." She also offers herself as a witness to the testimony of women worldwide, "In Romania and Russia, I've heard the voices of women struggling to recreate a civil society where they had only known authoritarian rule and there had been no tradition of democracy. They are attempting to be sure that their voices are heard and their contributions recognized" (1999a). Thus, "freedom and equality for all," often repeated by Rodham Clinton, "depend first on whether or not a citizen truly has a voice" (1997).

If a particular group is silenced through custom, culture, or oppression, she offers herself as their voice to the rest of the world. She also offers other women leaders for emulation. In a July 16, 1998, speech commemorating the 150th anniversary of the first American woman's rights convention, Rodham Clinton presents suffragist Elizabeth Cady Stanton as a role model whose experiences can teach modern audiences:

> Stanton was inspired, along with the others who met, to rewrite our Declaration of Independence, and they boldly asserted, "We hold these truths to be self-evident that all men and women are created equal." "All men and all women." It was the shout heard around the world, and if we listen, we can still hear its echoes today. We can hear it in the voices of women demanding their (full) civil and political rights anywhere in the world. I've heard such voices and their echoes from women, around the world, from Belfast to Bosnia to Beijing, as they work to change the conditions for women and girls and improve their lives and the lives of their families. We can even hear those echoes today in Seneca Falls. (1998b)

In the same speech, Rodham Clinton invites her listeners to join the struggle for women's rights, and she does so artfully by using a narrative to tell the story of a glove maker, Charlotte Woodward, a young woman who attended the first convention. She begins by asking her listeners to imagine what it must have been like on the road that warm summer day so long ago; how unsure Charlotte was about the personal consequences of attending the meeting, but nonetheless still determined to go. Showing considerable rhetorical skills, Hillary uses the road as a powerful metaphor and invites her audience to join her on the journey of American women's rights. Thus, her speech positions her listeners to appreciate what their forebears have accomplished and to commit to continue this vital work.

The Seneca Falls address concludes by linking the right of American women to vote to their responsibility to participate in the democratic process. Mrs. Clinton asserts that through a long struggle, women have gained access and can make a difference through the agency of the vote. This theme resonates throughout many of her speeches.

The predictable universal routine of women's lives is also a source from which she draws inspiration and identifies with her audiences. In Northern Ireland on September 2, 1998, for example, Rodham Clinton observes,

> Wives. Mothers. Daughters. Sisters. Few were household names. But, having seen their lives and communities torn apart by violence, women came together as women have always done—around kitchen tables, at the market, in gatherings like this. It was women whose whispers of "enough" became a torrent of

voices that could no longer be ignored. If we listen carefully, their voices still echo through this room and lift ours up today. (1998a)

And in her August 27, 1996, speech in Chicago at the Democratic National Convention, she confides to her audience of millions,

> I wish we could be sitting around a kitchen table, just us, talking about our hopes and fears about our children's futures. For Bill and me, family has been the center of our lives, but we also know that our family, like your family, is part of a larger community that can help or hurt our best efforts to raise our child. (1996a)

Thus, she provides a powerful form of identification with her listeners. Though they may not share her status (or her visibility), they can relate to the images of their everyday existence as invoked by Rodham Clinton.

However, she acknowledges the risks women take when they speak out. "If we listen," she tells her audience in Northern Ireland, "we can hear the voices of women who withstood jeers and threats, prejudice and violence to make themselves heard in a political world once reserved primarily for men" (1998a). Rodham Clinton has experienced firsthand the vitriol reserved for women who speak out.

She exhorts her listeners in Seneca Falls to "help us imagine a future that keeps faith with the sentiments expressed here in 1848," and to "be on the right side of history, no matter the risk or cost" (1998b). This is a powerful testament to her own experience as a rhetor.

Referring to the women of Seneca Falls in her speech given on March 3, 1999, in New York City, Rodham Clinton advises her audience,

> They [early women's rights advocates] understood something that we also have to understand, and that is that those who advocate for progress and change will often pay a price, but if we persevere, if we see that kind of commitment through, the changes that can happen, will benefit . . . our daughters and our granddaughters. (1999b)

She is personally aware of the cost of speaking out, as she has suffered a good deal of abuse for her activism. As Karlyn Kohrs Campbell notes after describing some particularly egregious examples of this, "no prior presidential spouse has occasioned the kinds of attacks that have been directed at Hillary Rodham Clinton" (1998, 2). But again, no prior presidential spouse has challenged the status quo in the quite same way as Rodham Clinton. Undeterred, she states emphatically, "If I'm going to be criticized for doing what I believe in, I might as well just keep doing what I believe in" ("Working Women Interview").

We gain additional insight into her personal conviction from the Seneca Falls Speech, in which she speaks of Harriet Tubman's accomplishments, risking her own life countless times to bring others to freedom,

> [Tubman's] rule for all of her Underground Railroad missions was to keep going, once you started—no matter how scared you got, no matter how dangerous

it became—you were not allowed to turn back. That's a pretty good rule for life. It describes the women who gathered in Wesleyan Chapel in 1848, but it could serve as our motto for today. We, too, cannot turn back. We, too, must keep going in our commitment to the dignity of every individual—to women's rights as human rights. We are on that road of the pioneers to Seneca Falls, they started down it 150 years ago. But now, we too must keep going. (1998b)

Such willingness to take on the responsibility and the inherent risks in doing so are hallmarks of Rodham Clinton's rhetoric. She reminds her audience in Uruguay on October 2, 1998,

Today, more than at any other time in history, women have the opportunity and the responsibility not only to raise our own voices but to empower others to raise theirs as well . . . But think of the thousands and thousands and thousands of women throughout the Americas for whom no one speaks. Who believe they are not worth anything. . . . What will we do to raise our vital voices for them? (1998c)

In the aftermath of the terrorist attacks of September 11, 2001, Senator Clinton reflects on her personal experience with this "unreasoning hatred that is focused on an individual you don't know, a cause that you despise." Referring specifically to the Seattle health-care reform speech, she says, "One of the most difficult experiences that I personally had in the White House was during the health care debate, being the object of extraordinary rage. I remember being in Seattle . . . [where] radio talk show hosts had urged their listeners to come out and yell and scream and carry on and prevent people from hearing me speak" (quoted in Lemann 2001, 41). Arrests were made and weapons were found among the audience. Video footage shows Rodham Clinton facing the threats head-on, not retreating from the podium, and instead vigorously defending her plan. As a speaker and advocate, her resolve is unwavering, from the football players in the high school speech class to the hecklers in Seattle to shouldering the humiliating spectacle of her husband's infidelity, she continues her fight.

Legacy

Examination of her rhetorical record leads to the conclusion that Hillary Rodham Clinton envisioned the role of first lady as a powerful one, indeed. She imbued it with her missionary zeal to spread the gospel of democracy and women's rights, and has never backed away from the challenge of her advocacy.

During her Senate campaign, a reporter compared her role to that of a senior presidential adviser and asked whether she went "beyond the job" of first lady, "Mrs. Clinton laughed out loud and said, 'I'm not going to have it any more. And the next first lady doesn't have to do it.'"

Rodham Clinton's adult life has been a blending of the personal and political. Though many question her loyalty to Bill Clinton in light of the evidence of his infidelity, I would offer this. As first lady of the United Sates of America, Hillary Rodham Clinton was afforded an opportunity few women have ever had:

an international stage from which to espouse her personal and political views. Though the American media seemed all consumed by her hairstyle, her "failure" at health care reform, and her husband's infidelity, Rodham Clinton kept to her message and shared it at every opportunity she was given. She has said,

> As I travel around the world, I am very grateful for the opportunity that I have to meet with women and to listen to them. Their dreams, their aspirations, their hopes, their concerns. And these are the women . . . who we must do all that we can to ensure that their voices are heard, heard in city halls and board rooms, and trade union offices and political parties, in academia, in families. (1998c)

Empowered by her position, education, deep religious conviction, and feminism, hers was a "bully pulpit" which served to launch her into the next phase of her life, that of United States senator.

Rodham Clinton exemplified the feminist credo "the personal is political." As she said in her address to the 1996 Democratic National Convention, "For Bill and me, family has been the center of our lives, but we also know that our family, like your family, is part of a larger community that can help or hurt our best efforts to raise our child" (1996a). Much of her rhetoric as first lady resonated with this duality.

References

Alter, Johnathan. 1999. Paging Mrs. Roosevelt. *Newsweek*, 1 March, 32.

Anderson, Karrin Vasby. 1999. "Rhymes with Rich": "Bitch" as a Tool of Containment in Contemporary American Politics. *Rhetoric & Public Affairs*, 2, 599–623.

Anthony, Carl Sferrazza. 1999. Hillary's Hidden Power. *George*, November, 108–40.

Brant, Martha, and Evan Thomas. 1996. First Fighter. *Newsweek*, 15 January, 20–24.

Campbell, Karlyn Kohrs. 1993. Shadowboxing with Stereotypes: The Press, the Public and the Candidates' Wives. Research Paper R-9, in *The Joan Shorenstein Barone Center for the Press, Politics and Public Policy*. Cambridge, Mass.: Harvard University Press.

———. 1996. The Rhetorical Presidency: A Two-Person Career. In *Beyond the Rhetorical Presidency*, ed. Martin J. Medhurst, 178–95. College Station, Tex.: Texas A & M University Press.

———. 1998. The Discursive Performance of Femininity: Hating Hillary, *Rhetoric & Public Affairs*, 1:1, 1–19.

Clift, Eleanor, and Howard Fineman. 1996. How Hillary Keeps Going, *Newsweek*, 8 July, 36.

Clinton, Hillary Rodham. 1995. Address to the United Nations Fourth World Conference on Women. Speech given at Beijing, China, 5 September. www.whitehouse.gov/wh /eop/first_lady/html/generalspeeches, accessed 17 January, 2000.

———. 1996a. Address to the Democratic National Convention in Chicago, 27 August. www.dncc96.org/day2/speeches/, accessed 6 January 2000.

———. 1996b. *It Takes a Village: And Other Lessons Children Teach Us*. New York: Simon & Schuster.

———. 1997. Remarks by the First Lady at the United Nations. Speech given in New York City, 16 October. www.whitehouse.gov/wh/eop/first_lady/html/generalspeeches, accessed 28 January 1998.

———. 1998a. First Lady Hillary Rodham Clinton Remarks at Vital Voices Conference. Speech given in Belfast, Northern Ireland, 2 September. www.whitehouse.gov/wh /eop/first_lady/html/generalspeeches, accessed 14 September 1998.

———. 1998b. Remarks by the First Lady Hillary Rodham Clinton 150th Anniversary of the First Woman's Rights Convention. Speech given in Seneca Falls, N.Y., 16 July. www.whitehouse.gov/wh/eop/first_lady/html/generalspeeches, accessed 30 October 1999.

———. 1998c. Vital Voices of the Americas: Women in Democracy. Speech given in Montevideo, Uruguay, 2 September. www.whitehouse.gov/wh/eop/first_lady/html /generalspeeches, accessed 26 April 1999.

———. 1999a. United Nation's International Women's Day Speech on Women's Rights. Speech given in New York City, 4 March. www.whitehouse.gov/wh/eop/first_lady /html/generalspeeches, accessed 14 March 1999.

———. 1999b. Women's Leadership Forum, Speech on Women and Politics. Speech given in New York City, 3 March. www.whitehouse.gov/wh/eop/first_lady/html /generalspeeches; accessed 15 April 1999.

———. 2000. Remarks at the Democratic National Convention, Los Angeles, Calif. www.dncc96.org/day2/speeches/, accessed 6 January.

The Clintons: A Marriage of Power. 1999. Television Documentary. The Learning Channel, air date 15 February

Current Biography Illustrated. n.d. Hillary Rodham Clinton www.hwwilson.com/data bases/cbhillary.htm, accessed 13 September 2001.

Douglas, Ann. 1998. The Extraordinary Hillary Clinton. *Vogue*, December, 231–39.

Gould, Lewis L. 1996. *American First Ladies: Their Lives and Legacy.* New York: Garland.

Greenfield, Meg. 2000. First Ladyhood. In *Speaking of Hillary: A Reader's Guide to the Most Controversial Woman in America*, ed. Susan K. Flinn, 57–58. Oregon: White Cloud Press.

Hillary for U.S. Senate. n.d. www.hillary2000.org, accessed 27 February 2001.

Jamieson, Kathleen Hall. 1995a. *Beyond the Double Bind: Women and Leadership.* New York: Oxford University Press.

——— 1995b. Eloquence in an Electronic Age. In *Rhetoric: Concepts, Definitions, Boundaries*, ed. William A. Covino and David A. Jolliffe, 801–11. Needham Heights, Mass.: Allyn & Bacon.

Kennedy, Helen. 2000a. The Girl Who Became Candidate Hillary. *New York Daily News*, 6 February. www.nydailynews.com, accessed 13 September 2001.

———. 2000b. 60s Turmoil Turns Scholar Into Rebel. *New York Daily News*, 7 February. www.nydailynews.com, accessed 13 September 2001.

Lehrer Report. 2000. PBS, air date, 14 August.

Lemann, Nicholas. 2001. The Hillary Perspective. *New Yorker*, 8 October, 41.

Martin, Marty E. 1994. Methodist in Deed. *The Christian Century*, 16 November 1095.

New American Bible. 1970. Encino: Benzinger Publishing.

Osborne, Claire G., ed. 1997. *The Unique Voice of Hillary Rodham Clinton.* New York: Avon.

Schindehette, Susan. 1999. The Ties That Bind. *People*, 15 February, 78–88.

Thomas, Evan, and Debra Rosenberg. 1999. Hillary's Day in the Sun. *Newsweek.* 1 March, 25–31.

Woodward, Kenneth. 1994. Soulful Matters. *Newsweek*, 31 October, 23.

Working Women Interview. 1994. www.abcnews.com, accessed 17 June 1999.

Epilogue

Laura Bush
Using the "Magic of Words" to Educate and Advocate

Molly Meijer Wertheimer

> The power of a book lies in its power to turn a solitary act into a shared vision.... As long as we have books, we are not alone.... There is no magic like the magic of the written word.
>
> I have a lifelong passion for introducing children to the magic of words.
>
> —Laura Bush

In *A Charge to Keep*, George W. Bush made a prediction about his wife Laura's future popularity: "As America gets to know her," he wrote, "they will love her as I do" (1999, 93). According to a *USA Today/CNN*/Gallup Poll conducted December 14–16, 2001, that prediction is coming true. Mrs. Bush topped the list of the "Most Admired Women" in the United States only a year after she had received too few mentions to be ranked (McQuillan 2001, A3; Jones and Carroll 2001, 52–55).

If she seemed a reluctant first lady during her first one hundred days, consider her starting point. When Laura Lane Welch married George W. Bush, it was on condition that she would never have to become a public person—the kind who makes statements to the national press and gives speeches to a national audience. But she was marrying a man who, as journalist Frank Bruni of the *New York Times* put it, had "politics in his plasma": "Her vow of silence was doomed from the start" (2000a, A1). She gave her first political speech in Muleshoe, Texas, where she ran out of things to say and mumbled her conclusion. As her husband's political career advanced from governor of Texas to president of the United States, she could not avoid publicity. Slowly, by speaking to supportive audiences such as Republican women's groups, she gained experience and made great strides in skill and confidence as a rhetorician. Depending upon the length of time her husband remains in office and the turmoil in the Middle East, she may continue to develop her reputation as an advocate for education and for the rights of women and children all over the world. If she continues to draw upon her love of literature and uses the "magic of words" to inspire her speaking, her messages may become more memorable. She has made a small start in that direction, for example, when she borrowed a poet's phrase to call music "the speech of angels" or when she called jazz "the language of America." Her press secretary Noelia Rodriguez has aptly said: "You don't rule anything out when it comes to Laura Bush."

During spring 2001, Mrs. Bush was becoming known nationally as an advocate for education, especially early childhood cognitive development. She unveiled her "Ready to Read, Ready to Learn Initiative" and traveled around the country promoting various aspects of it. True to her husband's promise to be the "Education President," Mrs. Bush stayed on topic, though she branched out to speak about related subjects such as American libraries and librarians, authors and readers, literacy volunteers, and more. Her advocacy gained momentum gradually and would have continued to do so had it not been for the events of September 11, which thrust her into full visibility onto the nation's stage in a matter of moments. Through her actions and words, she became the nation's consoler-in-chief, helping those who heard and saw her to focus their attention on acts of kindness among strangers. Increasingly, during fall 2001 and spring 2002, she became an international advocate for the rights of women and children, especially in Afghanistan, to an education and to full participation in their societies.

Before her husband was inaugurated, journalists speculated about what kind of first lady Mrs. Bush would be. Some contrasted her sharply with activist Hillary Clinton, associating her instead with traditionalist Mamie Eisenhower known for her quip: "Ike runs the nation; I turn the lamb chops." Probably the lowest expectations of her came from Gil Troy, political scientist at McGill University, who predicted that she would "retraditionalize" the White House and have little to do with policy issues, except perhaps education, which he described as "constructive, yet benign, and suitably feminine" (Boswell 2000, B1). Sympathetic with his position was Betty Boyd Caroli who said Mrs. Bush's focus on education "is about as safe as it gets. Right up there with apple pie" (quoted in Gamerman 2001, A3). Others such as Carl S. Anthony and Lewis L. Gould stressed Mrs. Bush's complexity, warning that she should not be viewed as a one-dimensional woman (Barta 2000, A4). Because they did not know much about her, still others made her into a fashion target—her hair, dress, and shoes all became synecdoches by which to infer her character (e.g. Givhan 2000, C01).

At the time of this writing, Mrs. Bush has completed eighteen months as first lady. She has become popular with the American public and the mass media, appearing on television shows such as *Good Morning America, The Oprah Winfrey Show, The Jay Leno Show, 60 Minutes, 20/20,* MTV, and the Disney Channel; her photograph has also been on the covers of *Good Housekeeping, Ladies' Home Journal, Reader's Digest, Parade Magazine,* and *Newsweek.* She has testified before the Senate Committee on Health, Education, Labor, and Pensions and the House Committee on Education and the Workforce. She has presented speeches all over the country on behalf of early childhood education, American libraries, and other issues, and has had the distinction of being the first first lady to give an entire radio address to the nation on her own. She has made solo diplomatic trips abroad, calling the world's attention to abuses of human rights in Afghanistan and elsewhere, she has promoted education as a precondition to world peace. If she stays on her current trajectory using her white glove pulpit to do good deeds, she will exceed the low expectations some commentators have had of her. Rather than turning the lamb chops, this first lady may very well help the shepherds learn to read.

Biography

In the small West Texas oil-boom town of Midland, Laura Lane Welch was born on November 4, 1946, the only child of Harold Bruce Welch and wife, Jenna Hawkins Welch.[1] Her father was a successful contractor and her mother kept her husband's books while remaining at home. Later in life, Laura would credit her parents with instilling in her a passion for learning, a desire to do her best, and a deep faith.

Laura's childhood was filled with the girlish pleasures that come from giggling at sleepovers with friends, Brownie and Girl Scout activities, playing the piano, singing in the church choir, and playing with her pets. Reading was what she liked to do most. From the time she was a baby, Laura's mother read to her, and when she was old enough, her mother took her to the local library. Years later, Mrs. Bush would praise her mother for giving her "a most precious gift—a lifelong passion for reading." Her favorite books as a child were Laura Ingalls Wilder's *Little House on the Prairie* books, which she saved and passed on to her own daughters.

Laura attended several schools when growing up: North Elementary and James Bowie Elementary Schools, San Jacinto Junior High School, and Robert E. Lee High School. She was popular, studious, and lived a carefree life with parents who made her feel secure and loved. Probably, her only low point during these years was a car accident. She went through a stop sign, collided with another car, killing the driver—her close friend Michael Douglas. Laura was traumatized, but slowly she learned to put the accident into perspective and learn from it—how precarious life is and how much a gift.

She attended Southern Methodist University, majoring in education. From the time she was seven years old, she wanted to be a teacher. She tells how she would line up her dolls and teach them lessons. While at SMU, she took courses in Child Growth and Development, Teaching Reading in the Elementary School,

Children's Literature, the Child and the Elementary School, as well as other courses in subjects such as math, language arts, social studies, and so on (Felix 2002, 40). She graduated in 1968 with a bachelor of science degree in education.

She began her career teaching third graders at the Longfellow Elementary School in Dallas, a position she kept for a year. Next, she taught second-graders at the John F. Kennedy Elementary School in Houston—a predominantly African American school. She said, "I particularly wanted to teach in a minority school. . . . I just learned about the dignity of every human and every child . . . how important every single child is, and how important each one of their lives are" (quoted in Felix 2002, 42). She held this position until 1972. Subsequently, she moved to Austin and enrolled in a Master of Library Science Degree Program at the University of Texas. She took courses in "Children's Literature, School Libraries, Literature for Adolescents, Library Materials, Cataloguing and Classification, and Library Administration" as well as studying "about the history of libraries and information systems in various civilizations . . . [and] understanding the role of books and libraries in today's society" (Felix 2002, 43–44). Laura completed her degree in 1973, and then accepted a position as children's librarian at the McCrane-Kashmere Gardens Library in Houston. Because her position did not involve working with children, she returned to Austin in 1974, to become a librarian at the mostly Hispanic Mollie Dawson Elementary School. She remained in that position until 1977. She felt comfortable with Spanish speaking/bilingual students because she had studied that language in high school and had taken a Spanish language and cultures course in Monterrey, Mexico.

Although Laura Welch and George W. Bush attended the same junior high school in Midland, according to Barbara Bush, "they had not been aware of each other" (1994, 140–41). The two also lived in the same apartment complex—the Chateau Dijon—the two times Laura worked in Houston. Laura's official meeting with George W. was at a barbecue given by their mutual friends, Joey and Jan O'Neill. The first time they invited her over to meet him, she turned them down, saying she had little interest in politics. Eventually, she accepted the invitation.

At the time, George W. was already planning to run for a seat in the U.S. House of Representatives. He was ready to settle down, and their meeting was fateful for both of them. Laura thought George was "really cute" and a lot of fun. She told her mother: "The thing I like about him was that he made me laugh." George W. also liked her; he told his parents: "I found her to be a very thoughtful, smart, interested person—one of the great listeners. And since I am one of the great talkers, it was a great fit" (quoted in Minutaglio 1999, 184). He also wrote in his autobiography: "If it wasn't love at first sight, it happened shortly thereafter. . . . My wife is gorgeous, good-humored, quick to laugh, down-to-earth, and very smart. I recognized those attributes right away in roughly that order. . . . We both, very quickly, fell in love with one another" (G. W. Bush 1999, 79–80). They were married three months later, November 5, 1977, the first date Vice President George Bush had free and one day before Laura's thirty-first birthday. Laura left her position and moved to Midland after their short honeymoon in Mexico.

The Bushes continued to get to know each other as they campaigned all across West Texas. Although Laura had always considered herself a Democrat, she became a Republican through marriage. Before they were married, George had promised Laura that she would never have to give a political speech, especially without him being there. She was happy to help him in other ways—as a confidant, with emotional support, and so on—but she had no desire to step onto the political stage. Three months after they were married, however, George was scheduled to be in two places at one time. Laura had to act as his surrogate in Muleshoe, Texas. This was her first campaign speech, and she was not very comfortable. Although she felt confidant as a teacher in front of little children, campaigning for political office was a very different kind of speech situation. As she stood on the courthouse steps in front of a small audience, she began to utter the remarks she had prepared, but too soon she ran out of things to say, "her speech dwindling down to nothing" (Minutaglio 1999, 16–17). In an interview granted to television's Matt Lauer, she said, "I had a really great start to my speech, but I hadn't gotten far enough to have a very good ending. So I stood up and gave my few—what I thought were really pretty good—lines at the start and then I had to mumble and sit down" (quoted in Felix 2002, 77). She was embarrassed, but also angry with herself for not preparing better.

One night during that same campaign as they were driving home after George W. had delivered a campaign speech, he asked Laura whether she liked it or not. Her mother-in-law had warned her not to criticize his speeches, but Laura told him candidly that she did not think his speech was very good. He listened to her, became distracted, and then drove the car straight into the wall of their garage (G. W. Bush 1999, 83). Despite his less than perfect speech, George W. won the Republican primary in June 1978, but lost the general election to his Democratic opponent.

On November 25, 1981, Laura gave birth to twin daughters Barbara and Jenna, named after their two grandmothers. George W. was in the delivery room when they were born. Afterwards, he helped Laura take care of the children: "There was never any question that I would help take care of them," he said, "I was a modern dad" (G. W. Bush 1999, 86). For the next several years, Laura devoted herself to raising the children as her husband worked to build his energy company. They were both active members of the First United Methodist Church and were engaged in community service—Laura, the Junior League and George, the United Way. Their lives were settled—happy, peaceful.

In late 1986, Vice President George Herbert Walker Bush assembled the family at Camp David to announce his run for the U.S. presidency. To help with the campaign, George and Laura moved their family to Washington, D.C., and remained there for eighteen months. They were actively involved in campaign strategy; sometimes they traveled around the country with George Bush as he campaigned, other times they campaigned without him (Barbara Bush 1994, 242; George W. Bush 1999, 179). After he was inaugurated the forty-first president of the United States, George W. and Laura returned to Dallas, Texas. Both had learned a great deal from their experience in Campaign 1988, and from

George Bush's presidency.

Together with other investors, George W. purchased the franchise for a baseball team, the Texas Rangers, and worked as a managing partner until 1994, when he ran for governor of Texas. While he managed the team, Laura volunteered for a number of causes; she served on the board of the Friends of Dallas Public Library and Executive Committee, she was a member of the Parent Teachers Association, and library liaison at her daughters' school, the Preston Hollow Elementary School. She was involved with charity balls and fundraising activities in Dallas society. These experiences were not enough, however, to help her feel comfortable with the idea of living her life on the public stage. When her husband became interested in running for governor, she was not sure that she wanted to be "a career politician's wife." There were other reasons for her reluctance as well. George W.'s opponent would be incumbent Ann Richards, who was enormously popular in Texas, especially with women, African Americans, artists, writers, and musicians. Richards was thought to be unbeatable. She had also trashed Laura's father-in-law in a speech at the 1988 Democratic National Convention, saying that Bush senior was born "with a silver foot in his mouth." Laura was not sure her husband wanted the office for the right reasons. Was he running to achieve a kind of payback, as part of a family script, or to make Texas a better place to live? She was also afraid her husband might lose, and the Bush family had just suffered a heartbreaking defeat when Bill Clinton won the presidency in 1992 (Minutaglio 1999, 268–69).

When George W. began his campaign for governor, politically Laura was "an unproved asset." She was "still learning to tamp down the knots in her stomach when she was approached for a comment by the media or asked to speak to a civic group." When "she was pressed to give a talk, she was frequently worried about not having the speech in her hands" (Minutaglio 1999, 244). Her husband was sympathetic, and did "not push her to make speeches or public appearances." He said, "She wasn't really comfortable doing a lot of campaigning, which was fine with me" (George W. Bush 1999, 90) He treated her discomfort with humor, joking in his speeches that his wife's idea of a speech is "to put her fingers to her lips . . . [and] tell the children, 'Shhhhhhh!'" Unhappy with the comment, Laura felt it perpetuated a negative image of librarians. Laura did speak to Republican women's groups across the state, which were supportive and nonconfrontational. By the end of the race, she had traveled to 30 of Texas's 254 counties" (Minutaglio 1999, 301). On November 8, 1994, George W. Bush won the race for governor of Texas, and the Bushes moved to Austin, January 17, 1995.

First Lady of Texas

After her husband won the election, Mrs. Bush quickly realized that she could do something about the issues she cared about most such as early childhood education. Her husband said: "I don't think Laura ever anticipated her life would turn out this way. . . . Nor did she dream growing up, 'Gosh, if everything works out, I just may be the first lady of Texas.' But when she got out there, [and] started giving speeches . . . she realized people listened to her" (quoted in Romano 2000, A01). She grew increasingly confident as a public speaker. She set up an office in the Texas governor's mansion, the first first lady ever to do so (Leonard 2000a, A1), and she used the office to make a difference in people's lives.

One of the first events Mrs. Bush planned was a literary celebration. She invited seven Texas writers to read from their works as part of her husband's inaugural festivities. She was nervous about speaking at the event; according to biographer Antonio Felix, she had anxiety dreams the night before (2002, 100). Some of the authors had neither supported her husband, nor voted for him. However, their inclusion early set a bipartisan tone to her husband's administration. One writer, Sarah Bird, told her audience how impressed she was to have been invited to read because she considered herself a "raging liberal." The fact that she was invited, she said, boded well for the administration (Felix 2002, 99). It also boded well for the kind of political partnership the Bushes would develop. During her time as first lady of Texas, Mrs. Bush promoted many bipartisan initiatives to support the visual and literary arts, education, and other issues such as breast cancer awareness.

Mrs. Bush's signature issue was early childhood education and literacy, as it would continue to be when she became first lady of the United States. This was consistent with her husband's agenda, especially during his reelection campaign of 1996, when he emphasized "reading and literacy, the things his mother and wife were associated with." Politically, these were important issues that would appeal to women and minority voters (Minutaglio 1999, 313). They were also issues to which Laura Bush, as a former teacher and librarian, felt strongly committed. In the two terms she served as first lady of Texas, she either supported or launched many programs aimed at improving education in Texas schools. She worked with legislators, social service personnel, and literacy experts on an "Early Childhood Development Initiative," which consisted of four components: a Family Literacy Initiative, Reach Out and Read, Texas Ready to Read, and *Take Time for Kids* (a parenting magazine).[2]

According to Bill Minutaglio, George W.'s biographer, Laura Bush's "crowning achievement" as first lady of Texas was the Texas Book Festival (1999, 313). In 1996, Mrs. Bush joined together with the Texas Library Association, the Austin Writers League, and the Texas State Library and Archives Commission to inaugurate a celebration of writers and readers. The only one of its kind in the country, the Texas Book Festival was a combination of literary event and fund-raiser. Authors read from their works and signed books, while children listened to stories, made bookmarks, watched jugglers, and more. Money raised by the event was donated to the state's public libraries for the purchase of books. From 1996–2000, nearly 400 Texas libraries shared the nearly $1 million dollars raised. Not only did the libraries and the authors benefit, but the Bushes gained political capital because many of the authors celebrated "had once been unabashed supporters . . . and champion fundraisers for liberal causes and issues" (Minutaglio 1999, 313).

These are just some of the initiatives Mrs. Bush promoted in Texas and would continue to promote on a national scale when she became first lady of the United States. She was an active first lady of Texas, thought by some to be the best ever to serve in that role. As an advocate for literacy and breast cancer awareness, according to journalist Hillary Rose, Mrs. Bush was "perceived to be one of the most effective Governor's wives in the state's history" (2000, n.p.). On education, Frank Bruni of the *New York Times* credits her with helping to "write, lobby for, and secure passage of legislation . . . to teach preschool children in Texas to read" (2000a, A1). Mary Leonard of the *Boston Globe* writes that Laura Bush was the only first lady of Texas "to have achieved major policy success" (2000a, A1). Even Liz Carpenter, a Texas Democrat who worked for Lady Bird Johnson, comments that Mrs. Bush's projects and personality made her "beloved and appreciated" across the state (quoted in Leonard 2000a, A1). Her popularity in Texas, writes journalist Julie Bonin, was ubiquitous: "Tortilla vendors, wealthy businessmen, and even Democrats sing her praises" (2000, A18).

Campaign 2000

As an active first lady of Texas, Mrs. Bush gained considerable experience as a public speaker, and she was ready, if initially reluctant, to help her husband advance his political career. In 1998, George W. began to explore a run for the presidency; a year later, his campaign was in full swing. Once again, Mrs. Bush was hesitant about stepping into the spotlight—this time, the national spotlight of a presidential campaign. However, she had been a political apprentice for years, campaigning in state and national contests run by her husband and father-in-law. She had become part of the Bush "family business" of politics. Setting her reluctance aside, Mrs. Bush proved to be a valuable asset on the campaign trail.

Laura Bush spent about 100 days on the Campaign 2000 trail, traveling solo about 75 percent of the time and with George W. about 25 percent of the time. During the primary season, she spoke mainly to Republican women's groups and read to children in elementary schools. By the fall, after her daughters had left for college, she was by her husband's side with a microphone in hand, introducing him to audiences and even taking her own questions after their speeches. Her early speeches emphasized the difference between George W.'s character and Bill Clinton's: "Governor Bush has represented Texas with dignity and honor. . . . I'd love to see him do the same thing for our nation in our highest office" (quoted in Felix 2002, 118). She made a glaring contrast to Hillary Clinton, exhibiting no political ambition of her own, although these two women are the only first ladies who have earned advanced degrees. Mrs. Bush also focused on education in her speeches, helping to persuade voters that education would be a Bush administration priority that would get results. She appealed to women and minority voters for whom these issues were key.

Laura Bush's official debut before a national audience was her speech at the

Republican National Convention, July 31, 2000. This was not the first time she had spoken to a national audience or at a major convention. In 1996, she had addressed the GOP Convention in San Diego and earlier in 2000 (June), she had spoken before the Texas GOP Convention. This speech was especially significant, however, because it was the first major event of the convention, delivered prime time. Together with Colin Powell, who spoke immediately after her, Mrs. Bush was given the responsibility of "jump-starting" the four-day jubilee (Bruni 2000a, A1).

Newspaper articles appeared before her speech, introducing her to the public as a woman who gives her husband a steadiness, evenness, who reins him in. George W. acknowledged her positive affect on him when he said: "I feel like a better candidate when Laura is with me" (quoted in Simon 2001, 220). She also functions like a "radar detector," according to Mark McKinnon, George W.'s campaign media director. Mrs. Bush "could sense when the campaign was running off track . . . She can read him [her husband] better than anybody, so she has a good sense of when he is not being well-served or when his agenda is not being properly communicated" (quoted in Copp 2001, 17). Journalists also contrasted Mrs. Bush with Hillary Clinton, saying she is not personally ambitious, only reluctantly doing the best she can to help her husband. In an interview with Frank Bruni (2000a, A1) before her speech, she admitted to getting butterflies in her stomach just thinking about it.

Even before Mrs. Bush began to speak, she communicated her priorities to her national audience visually. Appearing on stage with her were rows of minority students from a Houston school, who were dressed in red and blue shirts and were sitting at school desks. Much as her mother-in-law, Barbara Bush, had sent a visual message about "family values" to the American public when she assembled the Bush clan on stage during her 1992 RNC speech, so Laura showed the audience where her and her husband's priorities would be—educating children.

Mrs. Bush began her speech by saying she was "a little overwhelmed" to help kick off the convention ("Education and Responsibility" 2000). She told the audience they had made an excellent choice in nominating her husband. She used humor to say that she and her husband were about to become empty nesters, and running for president seemed an extreme way to handle the situation. Laura turned her attention to her husband's record on education in Texas. To promote credibility and foster identification with teachers, she talked about her early love of teaching and her experience teaching second and third graders to read. She admitted that more needs to be done to help teachers with this difficult task. She cited a study to show that strides had been made to improve reading while George W. was governor of Texas. She pledged to continue this work on a national scale and to focus on children younger than school age. She pledged that George W. would make Head Start an early reading, early learning program. Before she ended her speech, she talked about her husband's character, comparing it to that of President Clinton's. Using a veiled attack, which was heartily received by her immediate audience, Mrs. Bush said that people often approach her husband saying: "I'm counting on you. I want my son or daughter to respect the President of the United States." She ended her speech by talking about the future, saying George W. Bush would make a great president!

After the speech, George W. said he realized "how at ease" his wife had become in her public role as he "watched her deliver flawless remarks before a national television audience" (1999, 92–93). Other commentators spoke positively about her performance: political communication specialist Rita Willock of Southern Methodist University, Laura Bush's alma mater, praised the speech saying, "it was very much in her own language. It was not a spun speech. . . . Laura's speaking effuses a sincerity that draws people to her" (quoted in Barta 2000, A4). According to *Baltimore Sun* journalists Ellen Gamerman and Gerard Shields (2000, A6), delegates interviewed at the convention said they were pleasantly surprised by her speech. They waved signs that read "Laura for First Lady," and they called her a "hidden asset" and the Republican Party's "secret weapon."

Like the wives of other politicians, Mrs. Bush played an important role in helping her husband win votes, and the pressure on her to do so increased during fall 2000. At the time of the Republican National Convention, Celinda Lake, a Democratic pollster who studies gender voting patterns, put George W. ahead of Al Gore with male voters, but in "a statistical dead heat" among female voters (Leonard 2000b, p A8). By the third week of September, Al Gore pulled ahead among female voters (Mitchell 2000, 16A), and by the middle of October, Gore's lead with women increased (Gore 46 percent to Bush's 39 percent). Polls also indicated that women made up the largest group of undecideds in the country (70 percent); they were not convinced that either candidate would represent their interests (Muir 2000, n.p.). Journalist John Lange underscored the important role Laura played during fall 2000 when he wrote, "wives on the platform can make the difference of several percentage points in an election" (2000, A8). Drafting her mother-in-law into service, as well as other well-known Republican women—Condoleezza Rice, Lynn Cheney, and in some venues, Cindy McCain—Laura Bush took to the road on a "W is for Women" campaign trip (Harnden 2000, 19). Their purpose was to convince women voters that George W. would represent women's interests well.

The races in Michigan, Pennsylvania, and Wisconsin, all rich in electoral votes, were very close. The Bush women campaigned in several venues in all three states. Barbara Bush, recovering from back surgery and still enormously popular, introduced her daughter-in-law to the audiences; Laura was the featured speaker. Both talked about what George W. was like as a son, husband, and father. They showed mutual affection and respect for each other, teasing each other playfully in front of their audiences. In many respects, Barbara Bush was passing the torch to her daughter-in-law. Laura had the last word at rallies and ran the press conferences. One of her more pointed comments to the media was when she was asked why her husband was trailing behind Al Gore with women voters. She answered the question by saying that her husband was doing well with women, but the important question was why Gore was not doing better with men (Bruni 2000b, A30).

The election between George W. Bush and Al Gore was the closest in American history. Voting day was November 7, 2000, but the outcome of the race was debated for days. The election turned on the vote in Florida, which was so close election officials called for a recount. However, the recount itself proved problematic for many reasons. Some people said the ballot was confusing, and they voted for the wrong person. Others said the polls closed too early. Lawyers for George W., Al Gore, and others debated all aspects of the case to no resolution, and then the Supreme Court made the final decision. During this time, Laura Bush said that the seven-week wait gave the Bushes time to put the election into perspective. Regardless of the outcome, she said, she knew they would be OK. On December 12, George W. Bush was announced the winner; on January 20, 2001, he was sworn in as the forty-third president of the United States. Laura Bush became the first lady.

Rhetorical Activities as First Lady

When Laura Bush became first lady, she was well positioned to play the roles expected of her. Although she admired many former first ladies, especially fellow Texan Lady Bird Johnson, she looked to her mother-in-law as a role model: "I have learned a lot . . . from watching her," she said (quoted in Romano 2000, A01). As a first lady, Barbara Bush had served as her husband's surrogate, political partner, traveling companion, and hostess. Significantly, she had also served as an advocate for literacy, actively raising public awareness of the problem by her speeches and public appearances. Through the Barbara Bush Foundation for Family Literacy and from the proceeds of *C. Fred's Story* and *Millie's Book*, she raised several million dollars to support literacy programs. Her husband acknowledged her influence on legislation when he gave her the pen he had used to sign the National Literacy Act of 1991 into law (Barbara Bush 1994, 425). Using what she learned from her mother-in-law as well as from her own experience as first lady of Texas, Laura Bush was well aware of the opportunity she would have to effect change. To show that she would use a different approach than her immediate predecessor, Hillary Clinton, she moved the first lady's office back to the East Wing. She also hired a staff and was ready to serve as an active first lady on projects she knew and cared about. "I know about education," she said, "I know about things that I've worked on. . . . Most other issues I don't know that much about. And just to put in my two cents—I don't think it is really necessary" (quoted in Bruni 2000a, A1). With some degree of trepidation natural for a woman described as "private," she was determined to make a difference. In her first week as first lady, she acknowledged: "I have a forum. . . . I won't always have it. The time is now."

Getting Started

Even before her husband was inaugurated the forty-third president of the United States, Mrs. Bush helped to set a bipartisan tone for the new administration by focusing public attention on one of her abiding interests—American authors. The first event she planned was a tribute to literature called "Laura Bush Celebrates American Authors." Using a painted library as a backdrop and standing in front of painted bookcases, Mrs. Bush told her audience: "Traditionally, inaugurations include a tribute to the first lady, but my tribute is to the thousands of people who have contributed to my life—our great American authors" (quoted in Jayson 2001, A6). She said she would use her time in the inaugural spotlight to highlight her belief that "reading is the most important skill that children learn in school." She cited books such as Thomas Paine's *Common Sense* and Harriet Beecher Stowe's *Uncle Tom's Cabin* that helped "create major changes in American Society." She mentioned other authors such as Herman Melville, Willa Cather, and Richard Wright, whom she said have helped "shape the American identity." She said, "The power of a book lies in its power to turn a solitary act into a shared vision. . . . As long as we have books, we are not alone. . . . There is no magic like the magic of the written word" (quoted in MacPherson 2001, A6). Helping children to share in that magic, one of her aids early announced, would be among the first lady's top priorities; her signature issue would be early childhood education, especially prereading skills. During the coming months, she would unveil her "Ready to Read, Ready to Learn Initiative" and travel around the United States promoting different components of it. She would also offer unmistakable support for many other priorities such as American libraries, literacy volunteers, and breast cancer research.

The Ready to Read, Ready to Learn Initiative

Mrs. Bush announced the chief area of her advocacy, early childhood education, in a speech given on February 26, 2001, at Cesar Chavez Elementary School in Hyattsville, Maryland. She began her speech by saying that her interest in education is consistent with her husband's priorities as president:

> President Bush made education his number one priority. He wants to give American teachers and schools greater flexibility, freedom and support . . . so that every child is educated and no child is left behind. . . . From the crib to the classroom children need parents, teachers, and other adults to help them prepare for success in school and in life. Some of America's schools need extra help, and President Bush has a plan to help them succeed. He wants to help you chart your own course to success through local control, high standards, accountability, and research based reading programs. This is the President's plan. And this is the President's promise. I want to help him keep that promise. ("Ready to Read" 2001a)[3]

Mrs. Bush described the component parts of her "Ready to Read, Ready to Learn" Initiative, "I want to help recruit more teachers . . . spotlight early childhood programs . . . [and] give parents, teachers, and caregivers the right kinds of information about learning and development." She discussed each component, suggesting strategies on how to achieve those goals nationally.

Mrs. Bush pledged her help in recruiting new teachers. She highlighted successful recruitment programs such as the New Teacher Project (NTP), which recruits professionals to become teachers in low-income schools; Teach for

America, which recruits college graduates to make two-year teaching commitments; and Troops to Teachers, which trains retired military personnel to teach in the classroom. As part of his education package, Mrs. Bush announced that her husband proposed to increase funding for this last program tenfold.

Mrs. Bush told her audience about successful early childhood development programs such as the LEAP curriculum (Language Enrichment Activities Program) used at a Dallas, Texas, Head Start Center. She also mentioned the Early Reading First Program, which studies the effectiveness of teaching Head Start children math and reading skills. She cited a successful Boston based program, Reach Out and Read, which gives young children and their parents valuable information on the need to read. Mrs. Bush supported this program when she was the first lady of Texas and said, during the speech, that she would like to work with leaders of the program to expand nationally.

Mrs. Bush told her audience that valuable research about early learning should be shared with parents and teachers. That research indicates how important early cognitive stimulation of the brain is as a prerequisite for later higher-level functioning. She said she would work with Dr. Paige, the new education secretary, to publicize material on their website: "How Will I Know a Good Early Reading Program When I See One?" Mrs. Bush ended her speech by reiterating her husband's ideas about accountability and not allowing children to be victimized by the "soft bigotry of low expectations."

During the spring and summer 2001, Mrs. Bush promoted different aspects of her Ready to Read, Ready to Learn Initiative. She promoted teacher recruitment in speeches given at "Teach for America" events in Los Angeles ("Occidental College" 2001d) and New York City ("Teach for America" 2001h). On both occasions, she told her audiences that she plans to help Teach for America "triple the number of program participants over the next four years." She also promoted teacher recruitment at two "Troops to Teachers" events at the San Diego Naval Base ("Troops to Teachers" 2001e) and at Fort Jackson, South Carolina, on National Teachers Day ("Troops to Teachers" 2001j). Mrs. Bush asked her audience to turn their "attention to the home front . . . to Uncle Sam's classrooms . . . where we need your service as teachers." She mentioned her husband's commitment to boost funding to the program.

In other speeches that Mrs. Bush made during spring 2001, she spotlighted successful schools, teachers, and programs. Accompanied by Vincente Fox, president of Mexico, Mrs. Bush spoke at an elementary school in California on March 22, to a largely Latino audience of 300 students, parents, and teachers ("Morningside Elementary School" 2001c). "I wish the rest of the country could see your school," she told her audience, "You care about what is going on in the classroom." Indeed, parents at this school promised to perform fifteen hours of volunteer work at the school and to read to their children twenty minutes a day; the gains the students made on standardized tests were impressive (Ritsch 2001, B1). True to her word, Mrs. Bush's appearance gave media attention to a successful educational program, one that could be a model for other schools.

Mrs. Bush spoke in Chicago at an event honoring teachers as mentors and role models. Using examples from her own life and from students' letters, she praised teachers who are influential in the lives of students ("Golden Apple Teacher Awards" 2001k). Mrs. Bush also spoke at two Reach Out and Read events, one in Chicago on May 14, and the other in Boston on June 1 ("Reach Out and Read" 2001l, 2001m). In both speeches, she praised members of her audience for showing children how valuable they are and how important reading is. She said that parents trust their pediatricians, so they take a "prescription" to read to their children seriously. She said she was proud to support the Reach Out and Read Program as it expands nationally, and in Boston, Mrs. Bush acknowledged Dr. Klass and Dr. Zuckerman, two founders of the successful program, who were in her audience.

Mrs. Bush spoke at a K–12 Education Symposium in Washington, D.C., on February 28, 2001 ("Hoover Institution" 2001b). During the summer, July 26 and 27, she cosponsored a White House Summit on Early Childhood Cognitive Development with U.S. Secretaries Rod Paige (Education) and Tommy G. Thompson (Health and Human Services). Held at Georgetown University, the rationale for the summit was to share information. Over 400 experts came from government, education, and community agencies to give presentations and to learn from others. Mrs. Bush spoke early in the summit, outlining its mission and setting its tone ("Summit on Early Childhood" 2001n). She told her audience that the summit features some of the "nation's foremost researchers, policy makers and experts" on "early childhood cognitive development and brain research" as well as those who run pediatric-based programs for language acquisition, and model preschool programs. She asked her audience to rise above partisan politics to help children learn before they reach age five.

Mrs. Bush also spoke about education at the Senate Spouses Luncheon on April 3, 2001, and at the Congressional Club on May 2, both in Washington, D.C. In both speeches, she gave members of her audience an assignment. To the senate wives (spouses) she said:

> Let me emphasize that President Bush and I firmly believe in the power of local control. You are the experts on what's best in your states. You know what your school children need; you know the programs that work; and you know what best can be done. But as a nation, we need results, and we need the evidence that shows whether our children are learning. I hope you will help us carry out a mission of better education in each of your states. ("Senate Spouses Luncheon" 2001f)

She made a similar assignment to the members of the Congressional Club, asking them to do what they can in their home districts to further the Bush's education goals ("Congressional Club" 2001i). In all of the speeches that she gave that spring, she functioned very much as her husband's political partner, helping his administration achieve their education goals.

Support for American Libraries and Librarians

Though not directly part of the Ready to Read, Ready to Learn Initiative, as a former librarian, Mrs. Bush actively promoted America's libraries. She spoke during National Library Week at the American Library Association's "@ Your

Library" event. Held at the Northeast Neighborhood Library, this event kicked off a five-year initiative to promote the use of resources in today's libraries. Speaking to an audience of twenty-five children and seventy-five adults, Mrs. Bush said: "the most valuable item in my wallet . . . [is] my library card." She praised librarians: "Our nation runs on the fuel of information and imagination that libraries provide every day, and librarians are in charge of collecting, cataloguing, and distributing it to patrons. Librarians help educate and inform the public, . . . they strengthen our great democracy." Calling libraries "community treasure chests," she said, "a wealth of information [is] available to everyone, equally . . . and the key to that treasure chest is a library card." She encouraged all Americans to sign up for cards at their local libraries and to become library volunteers ("@ Your Library" 2001g).

To further support the nation's libraries, Mrs. Bush announced the creation of the Laura Bush Foundation for American Libraries. The mission of the foundation, issued in a press release from the Office of the First Lady, is to provide grants to libraries for books:

> As school budgets have become stretched, school districts have had to apply their resources to programs and services other than libraries. It is not uncommon for libraries to receive funds for computers and related technology instead of books. As a result, some libraries lack up to date books and reference materials. . . . One of the purposes of the Laura Bush Foundation is to help libraries find a balance between technology and contemporary books by providing needed funding for book purchases. ("Laura Bush Foundation" 2001o)

For Mrs. Bush, "The new Foundation provides yet another opportunity to share with American children the magical world of books and reading."

On September 7 and 8, 2001, Mrs. Bush cosponsored a National Book Festival with James H. Billington, librarian of Congress. Held in the Library of Congress and on the east lawn of the U.S. Capitol, the festival was a consciousness raiser, not a fund-raiser. In a speech given at the festival, Mrs. Bush called the Library of Congress an "American Treasure," home of "many of our countries great written treasures." She described the purpose of the festival in an interview: "This event gives us an opportunity to inspire parents and caregivers to read to their children as early as possible and to encourage reading as a lifelong activity" (quoted in Felix 2002, 141). First Librarian Billington stated the case somewhat differently when he said, "We must all try, in every way we can, to send the message that reading is critical to our lives and to the life of our nation."

Like the Texas Book Festival, the gala atmosphere drew press attention as well as crowds. Events scheduled included author readings and book signings, panel discussions, a copyright workshop, and tours of the Library of Congress. Interested guests attended demonstrations of the new technologies and learned to do high-tech research in the National Digital Library Learning Center. Teachers learned to use the library's online collection, called American Memory. Small children met book characters such as the Cat in the Hat and Peter Rabbit, and older children met professional basketball players who promoted a "Read to

Achieve" program. Authors from other cultures and nations told stories; musicians ranged from a mariachi band to bluegrass. Unfortunately, national press coverage of this event was largely eclipsed by the terrorist attacks on the World Trade Center and the Pentagon.

September 11 and Its Aftermath

On September 11, Mrs. Bush was on her way to testify before a Senate committee when a Secret Service agent told her a plane had struck one of the World Trade Center Towers. Just before Mrs. Bush met Senator Ted Kennedy, agents told her a second plane had struck the South Tower. Immediately, she knew these were acts of terror. Mrs. Bush was taken to a secure location, but not before making a statement to the press: "Our hearts and prayers go out to the victims of terrorism, and our support goes to the rescue workers" (quoted in Fiore 2001, 1) Journalist Larry McQuillan of *USA Today* asked her: "What do you say to the children?" Mrs. Bush told reporters that parents should reassure their children. Answering that question became one of her chief priorities over the next several weeks. Through her words and actions, Mrs. Bush became what many commentators called the nation's consoler-in-chief. From the tragedy forward, according to first lady scholar Myra Gutin, "It will be much harder to take a step back to having a lower profile . . . . This is her emergence" (quoted in Fiore 2001, 5:1). Although Mrs. Bush had been an active first lady during her first eight months, she had received little national coverage prompting some to wonder what she had been doing; this situation changed overnight.

The day after the attack, Mrs. Bush wrote two letters to children—one for younger, another for older children ("Elementary School Letter" and "Middle and High School Students" 2001p), which she sent to states' top educational officials for distribution to the nation's 100,000 schools. She varied the letters slightly to adapt her message to the two different age groups. Both letters were consoling, telling children that sad things sometimes happen, but each and every one of them is important and loved. She told them they now have an opportunity to do good things for other people—to show how much others mean to them. Mrs. Bush also broadcast short messages to children on the Disney Channel, and she appeared on five networks to tell parents to turn off their television sets, to share meals with their children, to read and comfort their children. She appeared on the *Oprah Winfey Show* and relayed the same message to parents; she also talked with Leslie Stahl on *60 Minutes* about helping children cope with the images shown and shown again on television and with the horrible realities of the attacks.

Children were not the only ones Mrs. Bush consoled. In the first two days after the attacks, Mrs. Bush visited survivors of the Pentagon attack at the Walter Reed Army Medical Center and Washington Hospital. She thanked blood donors at the Eisenhower Executive Building, and helped her husband choose speakers for the National Prayer Day held on September 14. On September 17, she traveled to western Pennsylvania, Shankesville, to offer solace to the families and friends of the victims of United Airlines Flight 93. Speaking to an audience of approximately 250–300 people, she said, the "heartache and loss" they are experiencing is the kind that "none of us could have ever imagined" ("Memorial Service" 2001q). Members of her audience were overwhelmingly grateful. A week later, she made another public statement at the "Concert for America." She dedicated the concert to the victims of September 11, and to those who answered "grief and adversity with kindness and courage." She said that it was time for us to return to the good things in life, and borrowing a poet's phrase, she called music "the speech of angels" and said "it brings a special comfort to our nation" ("Kennedy Center" 2001r).

Before the end of September, Mrs. Bush traveled to New York City and met with different kinds of audiences—children, firefighters, and teachers. She visited P.S. 41, an elementary school that hosted children who had been evacuated from P.S. 234 during the attacks. She visited Battalion 9, a firehouse that had lost thirty-one men when the World Trade Center Towers collapsed. She left sunflowers tied with red, white, and blue ribbons, and left a message in their journal: "To the firefighters of Battalion 9, You showed the world that honor and bravery are alive in New York City. Thank you for being heroes. God Bless you, Laura Bush." Probably her most substantive speech was the one given at Madison Square Garden to 2000 volunteers from the "Learning Leaders," a nonprofit organization that trains volunteers to help in schools. This event had been scheduled before September 11, but she used the occasion to acknowledge members of the group as "cool-headed heroes who shepherded, sheltered, and saved" children by guiding them away from a school near the World Trade Center. She thanked teachers and school staffs for their dedication in comforting children, and called the volunteers who help them "one of the blessings that have been revealed in the aftermath ("Learning Leaders" 2001s).

During October, Mrs. Bush continued to make the aftermath of September 11 a key theme in her public appearances and speeches. In the beginning of the month, she addressed the anti-Muslim, anti-Arab feelings that were surfacing in the country by calling attention to the need for tolerance. At an event called "Close the Book on Hate," Mrs. Bush read *Amazing Grace* to two dozen children in a Washington Barnes and Noble bookstore; this is a story about an African American girl who overcomes her prejudice. She also helped address the problem of intolerance through lessons she planned as part of Teach for America Week. Her lessons developed themes related to the September 11 attacks such as understanding others, being compassionate, and embracing diversity. She combined these themes with lessons on geography, social studies, and phonics. At the end of the month, she met with recipients of Liberty Scholarships, given by the United Negro College Fund. The scholarships went to three students who had lost parents or guardians in the September 11 attacks. Mrs. Bush called the scholarships "a truly meaningful response to the tragic events of September 11" ("United Negro College Fund" 2001u). Finally, Mrs. Bush spoke at a Women's Day Awards Luncheon in New York City on October 30, 2001, to honor women who have made significant contributions in many fields. Even in this kind of speech, she connected their good deeds with the good deeds of others. So many people have acted generously, she said ("Women's Day Awards" 2001v).

When Mrs. Bush spoke at events that had little to do with September 11, she made some mention of the attacks. For example, at a three-state summit for early childhood development on October 3, she began her speech by talking about the aftermath, especially how much children need routines to feel safe ("Cognitive Development Summit" 2001t). Significantly, most of this speech detailed aspects of her Ready to Read, Ready to Learn Initiative: it was the first speech I read where, after mentioning the events of September 11, she allowed them to recede into the background.

Mrs. Bush continued to console the nation in speeches given during November. A difficult speech she gave early in the month was at a "Best Friends for Our Children" event on November 7 at the Bertie Backus Middle School in Washington, D.C. This school had lost children and teachers who were on the hijacked plane that struck the Pentagon. She presented each child in the school with a book and gave the school a collection of books for their library ("For Our Children" 2001w). Once again, she was encouraging.

Probably the most far-reaching speech she gave in November was at the National Press Club. On November 8, she spoke to nearly 200 journalists and public relations staff members for thirty minutes and accepted questions. She acknowledged the importance of Larry McQuillan's question asked on September 11: "What do you say to the children?" She said his question functioned as a "wake up call," and she quickly turned her attention to the nation's children. An underlying theme of all she said was Psalm 27: "Your face Lord do I seek . . . I believe that I shall see the goodness of the Lord in the land of the living." Throughout her speech, she cited examples of police, firefighters, teachers, and children who acted with great courage and compassion. She reminded her audience of the major role they play as journalists and publicists, and she gave them an assignment:

> You have a real opportunity to make sure that, as time passes, Americans are still informed about ways they can exercise their compassion. You have a real opportunity to highlight the needs in your communities so people know what they can specifically do to make life better where they live. ("National Press Club" 2001x)

After the speech, Mrs. Bush answered more questions than she had done in previous speeches. One journalist commented favorably on her performance, especially during the question-and-answer period when Mrs. Bush spoke without a text: "It shows when a public figure's life has been immersed in literature" (Himes 2001, A46).

Also, in November, Mrs. Bush broke with tradition to deliver, instead of her husband, a radio address in support of children and women of Afghanistan ("Radio Address" 2001y). This was the first time in U.S. history that a first lady presented an entire radio address by herself. Mrs. Bush condemned the terrorists, not only because of what they had done in our country, but also because of what they had done to their own people. She stated the point directly: "Good Morning. I am Laura Bush, and I am delivering this week's radio address to kick off a world-wide effort to focus on the brutality against women and children by the al-Qaida terrorist network and the regime it supports in Afghanistan, the Taliban." She talked about the brutal repression of women and children: "One out of every four children won't live past the age of five because health care is not available. Women have been denied access to doctors when they are sick. . . . Women cannot work outside the home or leave their homes by themselves. . . . the Taliban forbid education to women." She also encouraged Americans to continue to support the fight against terrorism.

After the speech, leaders of women's groups and women in Congress discussed the issues; Mrs. Bush met privately at the White House with women leaders from Afghanistan. She also received a great deal of media coverage probably because no one expected her to speak out so forcefully for the international rights of women and children. Melanne Verveer, one of Hillary Clinton's former staff members and head of Vital Voices, an international women's group, said about Mrs. Bush's speech: "For Mrs. Bush to be speaking out about women's rights is like Nixon going to China. . . . It's so counterintuitive and unexpected that it is having a very powerful impact and a positive value." Feminist Gloria Steinem also praised the speech: "I'm glad to hear from Mrs. Bush. Now we will find out who she is" (both quoted in Leonard 2001, A15).

During the month of December, the most significant message from Mrs. Bush to the American public was the inscription she chose for the White House Christmas card: "Thy face, Lord, do I seek: I believe that I shall see the goodness of the Lord in the land of the living" (Psalm 27: 8, 13). That was not the original Bible verse selected, but the alternative deemed more fitting after September 11. Interestingly, this is the same Bible verse the chaplain at Camp David used immediately following the terrorist attack, and it is the verse Mrs. Bush cited in her National Press Club speech. In fact, the theme runs through most of the messages she presented during fall 2001. She read the message to the American public when she showed the card to Barbara Walters during the televised tour of the White House Christmas decorations (Walters 2001). She talked about it as well on *Larry King Live*. During a discussion of how good could come from bad, Mrs. Bush said:

> The Christmas card was already well into the works by September 11. We had the artist do the artwork way last summer and it was actually at the printer. But I changed the verse to Psalm 27, the part that read, "I believe I shall see the goodness of the Lord in the land of the living." Because that's what I think happened. We saw a handful of people commit a horrible crime, but at the same time we saw hundreds and thousands of people do good things. And that's what I really think happened on September 11. (King 2001)

Resuming Advocacy: Old and New Priorities

In the first six months of 2002, Mrs. Bush continued to attend events that focused primarily on the attacks of September 11 and their aftermath. She resumed her advocacy of the Ready to Read, Ready to Learn Initiative. Significantly, she also spoke out for the international rights of women and children—to an education and to participation in public life. This was especially evident in her support of the inclusion of women in the newly forming government in Afghanistan. Both directly and indirectly, she continued to enhance her husband's political capital especially with groups who traditionally vote for Democratic candidates such as teachers, women, African Americans, and environmentalists. More so than in 2001, she began to step out solo onto the national stage to campaign for Republican candidates and onto the international stage for diplomatic missions.

Back to The Ready to Read, Ready to Learn Initiative

Like First Ladies Eleanor Roosevelt, Rosalynn Carter, and Hillary Clinton, Mrs. Bush was invited to testify before congressional committees on the need for early childhood education ("Senate Committee" 2002c). On January 24, 2002, she spoke as a mother and former teacher before the Senate Committee on Health, Education, Labor, and Pensions on the development of language in young children. She compared her own daughters' early experiences of letters, sounds, and language structures to those of the children she taught in the inner-city schools in Houston. Some of her students had not developed adequate prereading skills, and it was an uphill battle for them to learn to read. With difficulty comes frustration, she explained, then failure and the loss of self-esteem. A child may begin to hate school, may drop out, and thereafter have little chance for a college education. She recommended the inclusion of prereading activities in programs such as Head Start. Including mention of September 11 in her testimony, she said, "I have seen the faces of children who were directly affected by the attacks" and I am "doubly committed to using my voice to help give our youngest Americans a real chance to succeed in the classroom." Following her husband's lead, she called reading "the new civil right." Her testimony before the House Education and Workforce Committee on March 14, 2002, was similar, but here she stressed the need for strong teachers in our nation's schools ("House Committee" 2002h). Calling teachers "the heart and soul of our schools," she spoke of the need to recruit the brightest teachers and to train them with the best possible programs. Commenting on her Senate testimony, journalist Ann Gerhart of the *Washington Post* said that Mrs. Bush used her "signature style," a blend of "homey personal anecdotes with educational theory and current science" (2002a, C01).

Mrs. Bush engendered bipartisan support for her Ready to Read, Ready to Learn Initiative when she teamed up with Senators Hillary Clinton (D-NY) and Kay Bailey Hutchison (R-Texas) to spotlight the need for more teachers. On February 26, 2002, the trio attended a Transition to Teaching/New Teacher event at Powell Elementary School in Washington, D.C. She talked about the need to replace 2.2 million teachers who will retire in the next ten years ("Transition" 2002e). She encouraged their audience to consider teaching as an alternative occupation for midcareer professionals. Mrs. Bush told the audience that the No Child Left Behind Bill, passed by the Congress and signed into law by her husband, commits $35 million for fiscal year 2002 "to recruit, hire, and train teachers." Mrs. Bush said, "teaching is the greatest community service of all," while Mrs. Clinton said: "Uncle Sam wants you to teach." Both women supported an amendment Mrs. Clinton had introduced to an education bill, which would allow some professionals to begin teaching without completing the traditional training program (*Hillary Watch* 2002, 16).

As she had done during her first year as first lady, Mrs. Bush continued to help publicize successful educational programs and extraordinary teachers. One noteworthy example is the speech she gave at the Ebenezer Church in Atlanta to honor Doctor Martin Luther King ("Martin Luther King Jr. Day" 2002b). She praised the education he had received as a child and his life as an inspiring teacher of others. Putting him on par with Lincoln, she said, "American history is unimaginable without him." She also told her audience that she believed Doctor King would have applauded the passage of the No Child Left Behind Bill and the bipartisan support that made that possible.

The East and West Wings of the White House worked together to sponsor a conference on education, which Mrs. Bush hosted. Held on March 5, 2002, the White House Conference on Preparing Tomorrow's Teachers brought together 150 "university and business leaders, teacher education advocates, teachers' unions, public policy organizations, and foundations from across the country." The conference was part of Mrs. Bush's Ready to Read/Ready to Learn Initiative, but it was also designed to address one of the provisions of the No Child Left Behind Bill, which commits federal resources to making sure that every child in America is taught by a qualified teacher. Mrs. Bush set the agenda for the conference very directly in a speech she gave at the beginning of the meeting ("Opening Remarks" 2002f): "We all know that the most important ingredient in a child's education is a good teacher. And we all know that teachers need training, tools, and our support to help children succeed in school." She talked about her experiences as a new teacher in the inner-city schools in Houston: "Many times I didn't know enough to make the right instructional decisions." To show that the problem was not with her, the school where she had taught, or the university where she had received her degree, she added, "I took pride in my educational training, but the job was much harder than I had imagined." By recognizing the difficulties of the task instead of finding fault with the teachers, Mrs. Bush inspired a spirit of cooperation among her audience. *Washington Post* journalist Ann Gerhart credits Mrs. Bush's approach with helping her husband's administration win the support of educators, labor unions, and key politicians such as Ted Kennedy: "Her steady public respect for teachers has helped forge the administration's ability to push for improved teacher training without excoriating educators" (2002a, C01).

Resuming Support for American Libraries

During the early months of 2002, Mrs. Bush continued to support American libraries and librarians. On January 9, she spoke at the Topeka and Shawnee County Library in Kansas, telling that group that the president included in his 2003 budget a fivefold increase in funding to help libraries recruit and train professionals ("Library Gala" 2002a). She cited statistics from the *Library Journal*

Magazine and *Labor Review,* stating the high percentage of librarians and directors who will retire in the next decade. Especially targeted for recruitment are
librarians who can help parents and teachers choose material to read to preschool children and who can speak in other languages. She also sponsored a
White House Conference on American Libraries in June 2002, the purpose of
which was to bring together leaders in library research and those who run successful programs. She welcomed all of the participants in an opening address on
June 4, and then she and her mother-in-law, former first lady Barbara Bush, listened to the presentations given in the East Room of the White House. At the
close of the conference, Laura announced that the Laura Bush Foundation for
American Libraries had received pledges of $5 million dollars since its inception
in 2001, $50,000 of which was pledged by Barbara Bush ("Closing Remarks"
2002o).

Women's and Children's Rights at Home and Abroad

Probably the most significant change in Mrs. Bush's activity during her
second year as first lady was her willingness to address issues of women's and
children's rights, especially internationally. She continued to meet international
leaders in her role as presidential spouse and hostess, and to entertain them at
the White House and at her Crawford home. For example, the British prime
minister and his wife stayed with the Bushes at their ranch in early April 2002.
Comments appeared in the press about how Laura Bush and Mrs. Blair had little
in common, even though both women had spoken out six months before on behalf of the women and children of Afghanistan. However, the two women
shared an interest in promoting research for breast cancer since both knew victims. Laura's mother was a breast cancer survivor, and Mrs. Blair lost an aunt
and best friend to the disease. During that visit, the two first ladies spoke at a
Dallas Breast Cancer Fund-raiser, each in her own way. Days later, on April 9,
Mrs. Bush functioned as her husband's surrogate when she led the U.S. delegation to the funeral of the Queen Mother of England ("Presidential Delegation"
2002k). There she made a brief statement on behalf of President Bush and the
American people about "a truly remarkable woman" ("Queen Mother" 2002l).

Throughout the spring 2002, both at home and abroad, Mrs. Bush continued
to advocate for the education of women and children in Afghanistan. On January
29, she spoke at a USAID event with Hamis Karzai, at the time the interim
chairman of the Afghan Authority. She spoke about U.S. involvement in an international coalition to rebuild that country, and noted especially "our support
for the women and children." She reinforced U.S. commitment to make sure
"the women of Afghanistan again have the freedom and the resources to pursue
an education and a profession" ("USA Event" 2002d). She made a similar statement on March 8 to the UN Commission on the Status of Women in honor of
International Women's Day. She talked about the educational supplies, including 40,000 backpacks recently sent to Afghanistan for children who would
return to school later that month ("United Nations" 2002g). In commenting on
this speech, *Washington Post* journalist Lynne Duke pointed out a change in the
first lady's style of speaking: Mrs. Bush "sounded very much an advocate . . .

speaking more forcefully and in greater detail than she did . . . last fall. And in so doing, the first lady, who before September 11 seemed guarded in her speechmaking, spoke today with uncommon flourish about human rights in general" (2002, C01).

Mrs. Bush also helped raise money for school uniforms and other materials by networking behind the scenes. Sima Simar, Afghan minister for women's affairs, requested 200 manual sewing machines, 450,000 yards of fabric, buttons, thread, shoes, and socks. She wanted Afghan women, widowed by the war, to have a means to support their families. Mrs. Bush phoned Elaine Chao, U.S. labor secretary, and secured a commitment for funds to pay these women to sew uniforms (Neuffer 2002, E1). Later that month on March 20, 2002, while introducing her husband in a speech given at the Samual W. Tucker Elementary School, she thanked American corporations for their gifts of material and money ("Back-to-School" 2002i). She also thanked the children of America for raising $4 million to help the children of Afghanistan, $2500 of which had been raised by the children in her audience, many of whom were Moslem (Wax 2002, B04).

During the first six months of 2002, Mrs. Bush's foreign travel evolved from simply accompanying her husband to Asia with little substantive diplomacy of her own to her solo trip to Europe where she presented speeches at large venues, including another radio address to the people of Afghanistan. During her trip to Asia in February, her schedule was separate from her husband's, but her activities remained low-key and ceremonial, visiting with the Girl Scouts in South Korea and reading *Curious George* to children in Japan. A month later, at the end of March, Mrs. Bush accompanied her husband on a four-day trip to Latin American. Her diplomatic role during this trip was more substantial. She presented a speech in Peru on March 23 entitled: "Early Education to Eradicate Poverty and Promote Social Integration." She told her audience about initiatives used in the United States to help children learn and then mentioned new initiatives that have been proposed to help educate children in all of the Americas. She talked about "Centers for Excellence in Teacher Training" that will operate in the Andes, Central America, and the Caribbean. The purpose of the centers is teacher training, she said, especially for setting up reading programs in schools. Significantly, she pledged U.S. support for Peru's National Network for Girls Education and the Rural Girl's Education Law, both of which promote the education of girls ("Eradicate Poverty" 2002j).

From May 13 through 22, 2002, Mrs. Bush traveled to France, Hungary, and the Czech Republic. The purpose of her first solo diplomatic trip was to promote "education, social issues, and economic assistance" to the people of Afghanistan, but she did more than that. Traveling with a staff of fifteen people, including, significantly, presidential spokesperson Karen Hughes, Mrs. Bush also drew the attention of the world to the crises in the Middle East and her husband's commitment to help broker peace between Israel and Palestine.

In Paris, Mrs. Bush drew public attention to the brutality of the Taliban when she visited fragments of Buddhist art that had escaped destruction. She also presented a twenty-five-minute speech, "Education: The Door of Hope" (2002m) on May 14, to an audience of 700 people at the Organization of Economic Cooperation and Development (OECD) Forum 2002. Here she praised education as "the most important gift we can give the world's children," saying that it is the gift "most likely to lead to future peace and prosperity." Echoing a point President Bush had made in his State of the Union Address (2002), she said, "All Mothers and Fathers the world over love their children and want the very best for them." She talked about suicide bombers and said that all children should be taught "to respect human life—their own life and the life of others." In a section of the speech that she had reworked on the plane to include mention of a recent suicide bombing that took the lives of seventeen Russian children, she quoted one Russian mother as saying: "The person who did this . . . could not have been born of a mother." After her speech, reporters asked her if she felt uncomfortable commenting upon events in the Middle East, and she answered, "not really." She said she could easily identify with parents who are afraid to let their children go to the grocery store or to a bowling alley. When asked if she could identify with the Palestinians, she replied, "Can I empathize with a mother who sends her child out to kill herself and others? No." Then she added more tactfully that both sides have to come to the negotiating table (quoted in Gerhart 2002c, C01).

In Budapest, Mrs. Bush met with officials to thank them for their help in fighting against terrorism. She spoke with prominent women, telling them to "lead the way toward making women full partners in this vibrant new society (quoted in McQuillan 2002, 5A). She also met with physicians and pharmacy executives to announce a grant to help them establish a woman's health initiative. Hungary has one of the highest rates of cancer in Europe; significantly, that night Mrs. Bush met with the U.S. ambassador to Hungary, Nancy Brinker, who founded the United States Susan G. Komen Breast Cancer Foundation, which sponsors the Race for the Cure (Gerhart 2002d, C01). Years earlier, Mrs. Brinker, a friend of the Bushes from Texas, had helped Mrs. Bush become active in charity and fund raising activities before she became the first lady of Texas (Minutaglio 1999, 237).

Mrs. Bush next traveled to Prague, capital of the Czech Republic. While there, she drew public attention to the crises in the Middle East when she visited a Nazi concentration camp outside of Prague and, within that city, six synagogues where Jewish women and children had been murdered over the centuries (Gerhart 2002e, C01). She also visited Radio Free Europe/Radio Liberty, which helped her, together with Radio Free Afghanistan and Voice of America, to send a message to the people of Afghanistan on May 21. She began this speech by acknowledging all of their suffering and pledging the commitment of the American people to help them. She spoke about the efforts the United States and other countries are making in the areas of agriculture, education, and health care. Most poignant were the messages she read from American children who raised money for the children of Afghanistan. She also addressed the women of that country, encouraging them not to stand on the sidelines as new leaders of their country are selected:

> I understand the lives of women in America and the lives of women in Afghanistan are very different, and I respect our differences and your decisions.

Yet I want you to know that the isolation the Taliban regime forced on you is not normal—not by international standards, not by Islamic standards, and not by Afghanistan's own standards. Before the Taliban, women were elected representatives in Afghanistan's parliament. Women worked as teachers, doctors, and professionals. Women were educated and women were a vital part of Afghanistan's life. I hope you will be again because a society can only achieve its full potential when all of its members participate. ("Radio Address" 2002n)

Mrs. Bush concluded her speech by saying that she wished the people of Afghanistan would build their country the way Hungary and the Czech Republic have done. She reiterated the same message later that day in a statement presented during a roundtable discussion at Radio Free Europe/Radio Liberty. Again, she mentioned how difficult it must be for the women of Afghanistan to leave their isolation after so many years of being forced to remain, uneducated, in their homes. They may need help, she said, to take their places as active participants in society. Mrs. Bush ended her solo trip when she joined her husband on May 22 to continue their diplomacy in other European countries. Her time by herself, however, helped those who read about her trip shed any lingering impression of her as "a quiet first lady."

After returning from Europe, Mrs. Bush made another solo trip—to San Francisco, June 12—to speak in support of Bill Simon Jr., Republican candidate for governor of California. Although she typically travels around the country to speak about issues of concern to her—education, American libraries, literacy— she rarely goes solo to fund-raisers. This departure from the norm shows how she has grown into the role of first lady and how much Republican strategists view her as a political asset. In San Francisco, Mrs. Bush spoke to an audience of 1000 people, mostly women, as she helped raise $500,000 for Bill Simon's bid for governor. She also showed her increased media savvy in an interview with journalists from the *San Francisco Chronicle*. When asked about offshore drilling in California—an issue her husband did not condemn, as did Bill Simon, Jr.—she said that her husband "supports the moratorium here in California on offshore drilling." She added coyly, "You know, in some ways, we want to have our cake and to eat it too. . . . In America, we want to drive SUVs that use a lot of gas. Certainly, in my home state, and I think in this state, we do a lot of driving. . . . But at the same time, we don't want to drill for oil. . . . I guess we just need to figure out how to come to terms with all of everyone's interests" (quoted in Saunders 2002, A29). It is as though Mrs. Bush is assuming the role of everyone's teacher, giving her students a lesson on fair play and sharing.

Probable Legacy

Mrs. Bush is the first first lady of the twenty-first century and as such she brings to the position a unique blend of conservative and liberal tendencies. Much as her predecessors who straddled the nineteenth and twentieth centuries, Mrs. Bush continues to balance the traditional demands of the role—wife, mother, hostess—with the modern demands for a first lady to be a political partner, a savvy public relations expert, and an independent advocate for those issues in which she takes special interest. Although commentators early predicted that Mrs. Bush might be more traditional than modern, commentators today are unwilling to take a stand. The final assessment of her tenure as first lady remains very much to be written.

Before Laura Lane Welch married George W. Bush at age thirty, she had earned a bachelor's degree in education, a master's degree in library science, and she had worked for ten years as an educator and librarian teaching inner-city minority students to read. She thought of herself as a Democrat, although she was not interested in politics. After her marriage, she gave up her career and focused on raising her children, helping her husband launch a political career, and serving her community as a volunteer. When her husband became governor of Texas, she drew on her full set of experiences as a teacher and mother to help her husband focus squarely on early childhood education and what could be done to improve it. Mrs. Bush also lobbied legislators, corporations, foundations, and individuals to raise funds to initiate research based and tested educational programs.

As first lady of the United States, Mrs. Bush continues to function as her husband's political partner on education. Each brings to the partnership different kinds of experience and expertise, hers as an educator and his as a politician, though they seem to have learned a considerable amount from each other over the years. Together, they present a common desire to improve education on a national scale. Both view education as the new Civil Right, and after September 11, both have begun to present education on the international stage as a Human Right and a precondition to world stability and peace.

On the national stage, Mrs. Bush continues to function as an advocate for her Ready to Read, Ready to Learn Initiative. She travels across the country using her celebrity as a first lady to spotlight national attention on different components of it. At the time of this writing, it is difficult to predict how much long-range good she will do, but her testimony before Senate and House bipartisan committees as well as the education summits she has planned—bringing together educators, legislators, researchers, unions, foundation administrators, and so on—doubtless will have some positive effect on education in this country. Mrs. Bush has also actively promoted related initiatives such as support for American libraries, recruiting librarians, celebrating books and their authors, and honoring volunteers who serve their communities by helping people learn to read. Though she speaks for other causes such as breast cancer, the evolving pattern of her advocacy grows increasingly systematic the longer she serves as first lady, and this includes her advocacy for the education of women and children internationally. It is as though Mrs. Bush is bringing a librarian's sense of organization to the messy closet of miscellaneous educational initiatives and interests. Building on her mother-in-law's insights on literacy: "everything I worried about would be better if more people could read, write, and comprehend" (Barbara Bush 1994, 145), Laura is adding: to learn to read, children must have basic prereading experiences, which presuppose parents who can read to them and social programs to reinforce what is done (or not done) in the home.

They must have free access to libraries where families can borrow materials and to knowledgeable librarians who can recommend age appropriate material even to those who do not speak English.

Of course, Mrs. Bush has also acted as a traditional hostess. She has made sure the Bushes home in Crawford, Texas, Prairie Chapel, is a comfortable retreat for relaxing as well as for diplomacy. The Putins, Blairs, and others have been able to taste American hospitality and see American values in action in an informal situation—with a minimal of protocol. Mrs. Bush has also presented ceremonial speeches and followed in her mother-in-law's footsteps by providing a more liberal counterbalance to her husband's conservatism. She has helped him secure the support of those who typically vote Democratic such as teachers not by excoriating them but by focusing on issues of concern to them.

She has also been a steadying influence on her husband, both before and after September 11, when she became more visible and helped to steady the nation during a time of tragedy. As the "Consoler-in-Chief," Mrs. Bush comforted children and told parents how to help their children through the crises. In the aftermath, she helped the country focus on the kindness exhibited by many as the nation dug through the rubble and prepared to build a stronger, more vigilant nation. Working with advisors such as Karen Hughes, Mrs. Bush became an advocate for the rights of women and children—in Afghanistan and in other countries as well. Commenting on Mrs. Bush's performance post–September 11, Carl Anthony has said: "Her performance has been stellar. . . . It is really in moments of crises . . . that you see the true character of a first lady" (quoted in Thomma 2001, A10).

At the time of this writing, Mrs. Bush has served as first lady for eighteen months. It is not possible to say how many years she will continue to serve or how far she will take us in forging a role model for first ladies of the twenty-first century. Her greatest strength may be helping the Bush administration further its educational initiatives. If *she* had to choose what her legacy would be, she would probably say: "I would like to be known as an advocate for children" (quoted in Romano 2000, A01). In April 2001, she told journalist Tara Copp of the *Chicago Sun-Times* that she hopes "we really have recruited more teachers. . . . I hope schools around the country are making sure their children can read. Those are the issues that are most important to me" (17).

Mrs. Bush has grown tremendously as a public speaker since her first appearance as surrogate for her husband in Muleshoe, Texas. Although it is too early to write a rhetorical biography of her, this chapter has presented evidence of her development as a public speaker from the early days as she campaigned by her husband's side for U.S. representative to her solo diplomatic trips as first lady. Marveling at her accomplishments, her husband told reporters before he was elected president: "If I'd have said, 'Honey, you'll be the kickoff speaker at the Republican Convention in the year 2000,' she would have said, 'You've totally lost your mind and I'm not marrying you'" (quoted in Bruni 2000a, A1). What would she have said if her husband had told her that in 2002 she would be speaking to an international audience of 700 on a solo diplomatic trip to Europe or addressing the people of Afghanistan via Radio Free Europe?

Notes

1. I have relied on material from Felix (2002) and Stone (2001) as well as from Laura Bush's biography on the White House website to write the "biography" section. There were also many profiles of Mrs. Bush in newspapers published throughout 2000 and 2001, during Campaign 2000 and the inauguration. Material that occurs in several of the sources I have not provided citations for in the text.

2. In 1996, Laura Bush received almost $1 million from the Barbara Bush Foundation for Family Literacy to help finance her first lady's Family Literacy Initiative. She used the money to support at least fifty programs throughout Texas, including a literacy program for the deaf, programs with Head Start, and Even Start (G. W. Bush 1999, 91).

3. I have cited Mrs. Bush's speeches in the text by using an abbreviated title of each speech and the year in which it was delivered. I have made every attempt to cite the day the speech was given and the location in the text. At present, Mrs. Bush's speeches are presently on the White House website (www.whitehouse.gov/firstlady/news-speeches/). On this page, the reader can click on the date of the speech and the text will come up.

References

Barta, Carolyn. 2000. Laura Bush, an Updated Traditional First Lady. *Seattle Times*, 26 December, A4.

Bonin, Julie. 2000. Speech May Shed Light on Reticent Half of Texas' First Couple. *Atlantic Journal and Constitution*, home ed., 30 July, A18.

Boswell, Randi. 2000. First Lady Power to Take Dramatic Shift. *Ottawa Citizen*, 16 December, final ed., B1.

Bruni, Frank. 2000a. Quiet Strength: For Laura Bush, a Direction She Never Wished to Go In. *New York Times*, 31 July, final ed., A1.

———. 2000b. Barbara Bush Joins GOP Women on Stump to Try to Bridge Gender Gap. *New York Times*, final edition, 19 October, A30.

Bush, Barbara. 1994. *A Memoir.* New York: Charles Scribner's Sons.

Bush, George W. 1999. *A Charge to Keep.* New York: William Morrow and Co.

Bush, Laura. 2000, Aug. 15. Education and Responsibility. *Vital Speeches of the Day,* 66: 21, 650–51.

———. 2001a. Ready to Read, Ready to Learn. Speech delivered in Hyattsville, Md., 26 February. www.whitehouse.gov/firstlady/news-speeches/, accessed 15 October 2001.

———. 2001b. Remarks of Laura Bush to the Hoover Institution. Speech delivered in Washington, D.C., 28 February. www.whitehouse.gov/firstlady/news-speeches/, accessed 15 October 2001.

———. 2001c. Remarks of Laura Bush at Morningside Elementary School. Speech delivered in San Fernando, Calif., 22 March. www.whitehouse.gov/firstlady/news-speeches/, accessed 15 October 2001.

———. 2001d. Remarks of Laura Bush to Occidental College. Speech delivered in Los Angeles, 22 March. www.whitehouse.gov/firstlady/news-speeches/, accessed 15 October 2001.

———. 2001e. Remarks for Laura Bush at Troops to Teachers Event. Speech delivered in San Diego, 23 March. www.whitehouse.gov/firstlady/news-speeches/, accessed 15 October 2001.

———. 2001f. Remarks of Laura Bush at Senate Spouses Luncheon. Speech delivered in Washington, D.C., 3 April. www.whitehouse.gov/firstlady/news-speeches/, accessed 15 October 2001.

———. 2001g. Remarks for Laura Bush for National Library Week Celebration and American Library Associations @ Your Library Event. Speech delivered in Washington, D.C., 3 April. www.whitehouse.gov/firstlady/news-speeches/, accessed 15 October 2001.

———. 2001h. Remarks of Laura Bush at Teach for America Gala. Speech delivered in New York City, 1 May. www.whitehouse.gov/firstlady/news-speeches/, accessed 15 October 2001.

———. 2001i. Remarks of Laura Bush at the Congressional Club. Speech delivered in Washington, D.C., 2 May. www.whitehouse.gov/firstlady/news-speeches/, accessed 15 October 2001.

———. 2001j. Remarks for Laura Bush at Troops to Teachers Event. Speech delivered in Fort Jackson, S.C., 6 May. www.whitehouse.gov/firstlady/news-speeches/, accessed 15 October 2001.

———. 2001k. Remarks of Laura Bush at Golden Apple Teacher Awards. Speech delivered in Chicago, 14 May. www.whitehouse.gov/firstlady/news-speeches/, accessed 15 October 2001.

———. 2001l. Remarks of Laura Bush at Reach Out and Read Event. Speech delivered in Chicago, 14 May. www.whitehouse.gov/firstlady/news-speeches/, accessed 15 October 2001.

———. 2001m. Remarks of Laura Bush at Reach Out and Read Event. Speech delivered in Boston, Mass., 1 June. www.whitehouse.gov/firstlady/news-speeches/, accessed 15 October 2001.

———. 2001n. Remarks of Laura Bush at the White House Summit on Early Childhood Cognitive Development. Speech delivered in Washington, D.C., 26 July. www.white house.gov/firstlady/news-speeches/, accessed 28 March 2002.

———. 2001o. Mrs. Bush Announces Creation of Laura Bush Foundation for America's Libraries. Office of the First Lady Press Release, 30 July. www.whitehouse.gov/first lady/news-speeches/, accessed 15 October 2001.

———. 2001p. Elementary School Letter & Middle School Letter. 12 September. www.whitehouse.gov/firstlady/news-speeches/, accessed 15 October 2001.

———. 2001q. Remarks by Mrs. Bush at Memorial Services in Pennsylvania. Speech delivered in Shankesville, Pa., 17 September. www.whitehouse.gov/firstlady/news-speeches/, accessed 15 October 2001.

———. 2001r. Remarks by Mrs. Bush at Kennedy Center. Speech delivered in Washington, D.C., 24 September. www.whitehouse.gov/firstlady/news-speeches/, accessed 15 October 2001.

———. 2001s. Remarks by Mrs. Bush Learning Leaders. Speech delivered in New York City, 25 September. www.whitehouse.gov/firstlady/news-speeches/, accessed 15 October 2001.

———. 2001t. Remarks by Mrs. Laura Bush to Early Cognitive Development Summit. Speech delivered at Cincinnati, Ohio, 3 October. www.whitehouse.gov/firstlady/news-speeches/, accessed 15 October 2001.

———. 2001u. Laura Bush Welcomes Recipients of the United Negro College Fund Liberty Scholarship. Speech delivered in Washington, D.C., 26 October. www.white house.gov/firstlady/news-speeches/, accessed 14 March 2002.

———. 2001v. Remarks by Mrs. Bush at Women's Day Awards Luncheon. Speech given in New York City, 30 October. www.whitehouse.gov/firstlady/news-speeches/, accessed 14 March 2002.

———. 2001w. Remarks for Mrs. Bush to Best Friends "For Our Children" Event. Speech delivered in Washington, D.C., 7 November. www.whitehouse.gov/firstlady/news-speeches/, accessed 14 March 2002.

———. 2001x. Remarks by Mrs. Bush at the National Press Club. Speech delivered in Washington, D.C., 8 November. www.whitehouse.gov/firstlady/news-speeches/, accessed 14 March 2002.

———. 2001y. Radio Address by Laura Bush to the Nation. Speech delivered from Crawford, Tex., 17 November. www.whitehouse.gov/firstlady/news-speeches/, accessed 14 March 2002.

———. 2002a. Remarks for Mrs. Bush at Topeka Public Library Gala. Speech delivered in Topeka, Kans., 9 January www.whitehouse.gov/firstlady/news-speeches/, accessed 14 March 2002.

———. 2002b. Speech by the First Lady for Martin Luther King Jr. Day at Ebenezer Baptist Church. Speech given in Atlanta, Ga., 21 January. www.whitehouse.gov/firstlady/news-speeches/, accessed 14 March 2002.

———. 2002c. Mrs. Bush's Remarks before the Senate Committee on Health, Education, Labor and Pensions. Testimony delivered in Washington, D.C., 24 January. www.whitehouse.gov/firstlady/news-speeches/, accessed 14 March 2002.

———. 2002d. Remarks of Mrs. Laura Bush at USAID Event with Interim Chairman of the Afghan Authority Hamid Karzai. Speech delivered at the Ronald Reagan Building in Washington, D.C., 29 January. www.whitehouse.gov/firstlady/news-speeches/, accessed 14 March 2002.

———. 2002e. Remarks by Mrs. Bush—Transition to Teaching/New Teacher Project. Speech delivered at Powell Elementary School in Washington, D.C., 26 February. www.whitehouse.gov/firstlady/news-speeches/, accessed 3 March 2002.

———. 2002f. Opening Remarks by Mrs. Bush at White House Conference on Preparing Tomorrow's Teachers. Speech delivered at the White House in Washington, D.C., 5 March. www.whitehouse.gov/firstlady/news-speeches/, accessed 14 March 2002.

———. 2002g. Remarks by Mrs. Bush to the United Nations. Speech delivered for International Women's Day in New York City, 8 March. www.whitehouse.gov/firstlady/news-speeches/, accessed 14 March 2002.

———. 2002h. Remarks by Mrs. Bush to House Education and Workforce Committee. Testimony delivered in Washington, D.C., 14 March. www.whitehouse.gov/firstlady/news-speeches/, accessed 28 March 2002.

———. 2002i. Remarks of Mrs. Laura Bush to Back-to-School Project for Afghan Girls. Speech delivered at the Samuel W. Tucker Elementary School, 20 March. www.whitehouse.gov/firstlady/news-speeches/, accessed 28 March 2002.

———. 2002j. Remarks by Mrs. Laura Bush on Early Education to Eradicate Poverty and Promote Social Integration. Speech delivered in Peru, 23 March. www.whitehouse.gov/firstlady/news-speeches/, accessed 23 April 2002.

———. 2002k. Mrs. Laura Bush to Lead Presidential Delegation to the Ceremonial Funeral of the Queen Mother of England. Press release, Office of Mrs. Bush. 4 April. www.whitehouse.gov/firstlady/news-speeches/, accessed 23 April 2002.

———. 2002l. Statement by Mrs. Laura Bush Regarding Today's Services for the Queen Mother. Statement read in London, England, 9 April. www.whitehouse.gov/firstlady/news-speeches/, accessed 13 June 2002.

———. 2002m. Remarks by Mrs. Laura Bush at Organization for Economic Cooperation and Development (OECD) Forum Speech delivered in Paris, France, 14 May. www.whitehouse.gov/firstlady/news-speeches/, accessed 21 May 2002.

———. 2002n. Radio Address of First Lady Laura Bush to Radio Free Afghanistan. Speech delivered in Prague, Czech Republic, 21 May. www.whitehouse.gov/firstlady/news-speeches/, accessed 31 May 2002.

————. 2002o. Closing Remarks by Mrs. Bush at the White House Conference on School Libraries. Speech delivered at the White House in Washington, D.C., 4 June. www.whitehouse.gov/firstlady/news-speeches/, accessed 13 June 2002.

Copp, Tara. 2001. Laura Bush as First Lady: More Low-Key. *Chicago Sun-Times*, final ed., 21 April, 17.

Duke, Lynne. 2002. In Laura Bush, World's Women Gain Powerful Rights Advocate. *Washington Post*, final ed., 9 March, C01.

Felix, Antonia. 2002. *Laura: America's First Lady, First Mother.* Avon, Mass.: Adams Media Corporation.

Fiore, Faye. 2001. Laura Bush Has Role Changed from Seldom Heard Wife to the Nation's Comforter. *Los Angeles Times*, home ed. 10 October, part 5, 1.

Gamerman, Ellen. 2001. First Lady Makes Education "Her Issue." *Baltimore Sun*, final ed., 27 February, A3.

Gamerman, Ellen, and Gerard Shields. 2000. Laura Bush Is Hailed as Her Husband's New Secret Weapon. *Baltimore Sun*, 1 August, A6.

Gerhart, Ann. 2002a. The First Lady's Reading, Stopped by 9–11, Laura Bush Resumes Her Senate Testimony on Early Childhood Education. *Washington Post*, 25 January, C01.

————. 2002b. Laura Bush's Before-School Conference. *Washington Post*, 6 March, C01.

————. 2002c. At the Wheel, Laura Bush Shows She Can Shift Gears; First Lady Reworks Script on First Leg of Europe Trip. *Washington Post*, final ed., 15 May, C01.

————. 2002d. Laura Bush, Standing by Her Husband While Far Away. *Washington Post*, 18 May, C01.

————. 2002e. Mrs. Bush's Prague Pilgrimage; The First Lady Takes a Grand—and Sometimes Grim—Tour. *Washington Post*, final ed., 21 May, C01.

Givhan, Robin. 2000. Taking Sensible First Footsteps; Laura Bush Is Arriving Well Heeled for Washington. *Washington Post*, final ed., 29 December, C01.

Harnden, Toby. 2000. Bush Women Take to the Road to Win Over Female Vote. *Daily Telegraph* (London), 17 October, 19.

Hillary Watch. 2002. *Human Events*, 58:9, 16.

Himes, Cragg. 2001. Starring in the East Wing (and Beyond). *Houston Chronicle*, 3 star ed., 9 November, A46.

Jayson, Sharon. 2001. Laura Bush Shares Love of Books. *The Atlantic Constitution*, 20 January, A6.

Jones, Jeffrey M., and Joseph Carroll. 2001. George W. and Laura Bush Top List of Most Admired. *Gallup Poll Monthly*, December, 52–55.

King, Larry. 2001. Interview with Laura Bush. CNN, aired 18 December.

Lange, John. 2000. Expect a Lady of First Regardless of Who Wins. *Pittsburgh Post-Gazette*, two star ed., 5 March, A8.

Leavitt, Paul. 2001. Laura Bush Urges Kids to Read and Be Tolerant. *USA Today*, 12 October, A11.

Leonard, Mary. 2000a. Behind the Scenes, Mrs. Bush Has a Pivotal Role. *Boston Globe*, third edition, 31 July, A1.

————. 2000b. Campaign 2000 . . . Convention Rhetoric Targets Women. *Boston Globe*, third ed., 3 August, A8.

————. 2001. War Gives Laura Bush Her Own Cause. *Boston Globe*, 29 November, A15.

MacPherson, Karen. 2001. Laura Bush Celebrates Authors, Reading. *Pittsburgh Post-Gazette*, sooner ed., 20 January, A6.

McQuillan, Laurence. 2001. Bush Dominates Most-Admired Opinion Poll. *USA Today*, 27 December, A3.

——. 2002. First Lady Quietly Making a Statement Abroad. *USA Today*, 17 May, 5A.

Milbank, Dana. 2001. *Smashmouth: Two Years in the Gutter with Al Gore and George W. Bush—Notes from the 2000 Campaign Trail*. New York: Basic Books.

Minutaglio, Bill. 1999. *First Son: George W. Bush and the Bush Family Dynasty*. New York: Random House.

Mitchell, Alison. 2000. Reluctance Aside, Mrs. Bush Shows Savvy in Campaign, *Plain Dealer* (Cleveland), 21 September, final ed. 16A.

Muir, Kate. 2000. Stand by My Man. *Times* (London), 30 October, n.p.

Neuffer, Elizabeth. 2002. The Task: Educating a Generation of Women, and Quickly. *Boston Globe*, 17 March, E1.

Ritsch, Massie. 2001. First Lady, Mexican Leader Praise Valley School. *Los Angeles Times*, 23 March, B1.

Romano, Lois. 2000. Laura Bush: A Twist on Traditional; Reluctant Celebrity Took Unconventional Route. *Washington Post*, final ed., 14 May, A01.

Rose, Hillary. 2000. Tipper v Laura. *Times* (London), features, 24 June, n.p.

Saunders, Debra J. 2002. A Real-Life Mrs. Cleaver. *San Francisco Chronicle*, 13 June, A29.

Simon, Roger. 2001. *Divided We Stand: How Al Gore Beat George Bush and Lost the Presidency*. New York: Crown Publishers.

Smith, Lynne. 2000. The Republican Convention. *Los Angeles Times*, 31 July, 16.

Stone, Tanya Lee. 2001. *Laura Welch Bush: First Lady*. Brookfield, Conn.: Millbrook Press.

Thomma, Stephen. 2001. The First Lady Makes Her Presence Felt. *Milwaukee Journal Sentinel*, 18 September, A10.

Walters, Barbara, and Diane Sawyer. 2001. Interview with President George W. Bush and Laura Bush. *20/20* (ABC), 5 December.

Wax, Emily. 2002. VA Students Help Bush Launch Outreach to Afghan Children. *Washington Post*, 21 March, B04.

Index

About the Contributors

Karrin Vasby Anderson is assistant professor of speech communication at Colorado State University where she teaches courses in political communication, women and communication, and public speaking. Her research interests include gender and political leadership, and media coverage of political candidates. She has published articles on Hillary Rodham Clinton and Elizabeth Dole in *Rhetoric & Public Affairs* and *Women's Studies in Communication*.

Ann J. Atkinson teaches public speaking, persuasion, and the capstone course for communication majors at Keene State College in New Hampshire. Her research focuses on women in politics. She has served as chair of the Political Communication Interest Group of the Eastern Communication Association. Her essay on Frances Perkins will appear in *American Rhetoric in the New Deal Era*, Vol. 7 of *A Rhetorical History of the United States* (forthcoming).

Lisa R. Barry has taught courses on persuasion and rhetoric as well as media studies. Presently, she teaches English at Montgomery County Public Schools. She has received teaching and research awards, including top papers in Visual Communication and in the Feminist and Women's Studies Divisions of the National Communication Association. She has published her work in *Communication Teacher* and elsewhere.

Diane M. Blair is assistant professor in the Department of Communication at California State University, Fresno, where she teaches courses in rhetorical theory, rhetorical criticism, and American public address. Her research interests include political rhetoric and feminist criticism, and her scholarship has appeared in journals such as *Rhetoric and Public Affairs* and *Communication Quarterly*. She is a contributor to *The Eleanor Roosevelt Encyclopedia*.

Ann E. Burnette is associate professor of communication studies at Texas State University, San Marcos, where she teaches classes in political communication, American public address, rhetorical criticism, and persuasion. Her research interests include political discourse by and about women as well as southern political rhetoric. She has published work on contemporary and historical political discourse.

Lisa M. Burns is assistant professor of media studies at Quinnipiac University in Hamden, Connecticut, where she teaches courses including media history. She has presented papers at national conferences and participated in the 2001 National Communication Association Doctoral Honors Conference. Her research interests include political communication, feminist rhetorical criticism, and journalism history with a focus on first ladies and the media.

Diana B. Carlin is dean of the graduate school and international programs and a professor of communication studies at the University of Kansas where she teaches courses in political communication and communication and gender studies. Her research focuses on women in politics, political debates, and speech writing. She has published extensively on political communication in *Argumentation & Advocacy*, *American Behavioral Scientist*, *Political Communication*, and *Rhetoric & Public Affairs*.

M. Heather Carver is assistant professor of performance studies and theatre at the University of Missouri at Columbia. She teaches courses in the Writing for Performance Program, and has authored articles on women's representation and identity. She is coeditor of *Voices Made Flesh: Performing Women's Autobiography* and *Healthy Primates and Other One-Act Plays*. Like Bess Truman, Dr. Carver is also a proud graduate of The Barstow School in Kansas City, Missouri.

Janis L. Edwards is associate professor of communication studies at the University of Alabama where she teaches courses in rhetoric and political communication. She has published articles on visual rhetoric and the media's representation of political women in journals such as *Quarterly Journal of Speech* and *Women's Studies in Communication*. She is author of *Political Cartoons in the 1988 Presidential Campaign: Image, Metaphor and Narrative*.

Kathleen M. German is professor of communication at Miami University in Oxford, Ohio. Dr. German teaches a wide variety of courses from the basic course in public speaking to graduate seminars in rhetorical history and mass media criticism. She is coauthor with Bruce Gronbeck of a widely used textbook in the basic course as well as scholarly articles in various regional and national journals.

Nichola D. Gutgold is assistant professor of speech communication at The Pennsylvania State University, Berks-Lehigh Valley College, where she teaches courses in public speaking, speech writing, and organizational communication. She has published articles on pedagogy, organizational communication, and political rhetoric.

Catherine M. Hastings is assistant professor of communication at Susquehanna University where she also serves as director of the Film Institute and adviser to the student newspaper. She teaches courses in news and feature writing, editing, and desktop publishing, as well as communication theory, public speaking, and freshman honors English. Her research interests include environmental rhetoric, focusing especially on the Roosevelts.

Nancy L. Herron is the associate dean for academic programs for the Commonwealth College of The Pennsylvania State University and librarian with the University Libraries. She has edited reference texts for Libraries Unlimited/ Teacher Idea Press/Greenwood since 1986. Dr. Herron is a member of the honorary fraternity Beta Phi Mu, the American Association of Higher Education, and the American Library Association.

Linda B. Hobgood is the director of the Speech Center at the University of Richmond and instructor in the Department of Rhetoric and Communication Studies. She teaches a variety of courses such as the rhetoric of first ladies, political rhetoric, and speech writing. She has published articles on group communication, speaking centers, and applied theory and pedagogy.

Anne F. Mattina is an associate professor of communication as Stonehill College in Easton, Massachusetts. Her research interests include women's labor reform rhetoric and antislavery activism. Her work has appeared in such publications as *Communication Quarterly*, *The McNeese Review*, and the *Women's Studies Annual*.

Mary Mooney practices corporate communications for a Texas-based healthcare conglomerate. Ms. Mooney has taught at George Mason University, Boston College, and Emerson College. Her women's studies research includes an FDA-sponsored historical analysis of contraceptives in the American news media, an examination of women and corporate success, and related issues in gender and politics.

Janette Kenner Muir is associate dean of New Century College, an interactive and interdisciplinary program at George Mason University. Dr. Muir has taught courses in rhetorical criticism and political communication, and published research on subjects such as Clinton's presidential campaigns, Hillary Clinton, and the Hill/Thomas Hearings. She also has edited a book on how to use C-SPAN in communication classes.

Elizabeth J. Natalle is associate professor of communication and women's studies at the University of North Carolina at Greensboro. In addition to her course in gender and communication theory, she teaches a seminar on feminist rhetorical criticism. Dr. Natalle is the author of *Feminist Theatre: A Study in Persuasion* and the coauthor of *The Woman's Public Speaking Handbook.*

Shawn J. Parry-Giles is assistant professor of communication, director of the Center for Political Communication and Civic Leadership, and affiliate assistant professor of women's studies at the University of Maryland. Her courses focus on political communication, as well as rhetorical, feminist, and media criticism. Her research has appeared in the *Quarterly Journal of Speech, Political Communication, Presidential Studies Quarterly,* and *Critical Studies in Media Communication.* She is author of *The Rhetorical Presidency, Propaganda, and the Cold War, 1945–1955* and coauthor of *Constructing Clinton: Hyperreality and Presidential Image-Making in Postmodern Politics.*

Amy R. Slagell is associate professor and director of the basic course in the speech program of the Department of English at Iowa State University. Her public address research has appeared in journals such as *Rhetoric and Public Affairs* and *Communication Studies.* She is on the editorial board for *Women's Studies in Communication* and the *Basic Course Annual.*

Beth M. Waggenspack is associate professor of communication studies at Virginia Polytechnic Institute and State University. She teaches courses in rhetorical history and theory, persuasion and argumentation, and critical thinking. She has published articles and book chapters on the rhetoric of women and is the author of *The Search for Self-Sovereignty: The Oratory of Elizabeth Cady Stanton.* She is cofounder of the Eastern European Adoption Coalition (www.eeadopt.org) and has authored articles on adoption.

Molly Meijer Wertheimer is associate professor of speech communication and affiliate associate professor of women's studies at The Pennsylvania State University, Hazleton campus. She teaches courses on public speaking and on women, the humanities, and the arts. She is editor of *Listening to Their Voices: The Rhetorical Activities of Historical Women* and coauthor of *Public Speaking as a Liberal Art,* 6th ed. Her research and reviews have appeared in journals such as *Philosophy and Rhetoric,* the *Quarterly Journal of Speech,* and *Rhetorica.*

Susan Zaeske is associate professor in the Department of Communication Arts at the University of Wisconsin–Madison where she teaches courses in American women's political discourse, great speakers and speeches, rhetorical criticism, and classical rhetorical theory. Zaeske's research has been published in the *Quarterly Journal of Speech* and *Philosophy & Rhetoric.* She is the author of *Signatures of Citizenship: Petitioning, Antislavery, and Women's Political Identity.*